D1601711

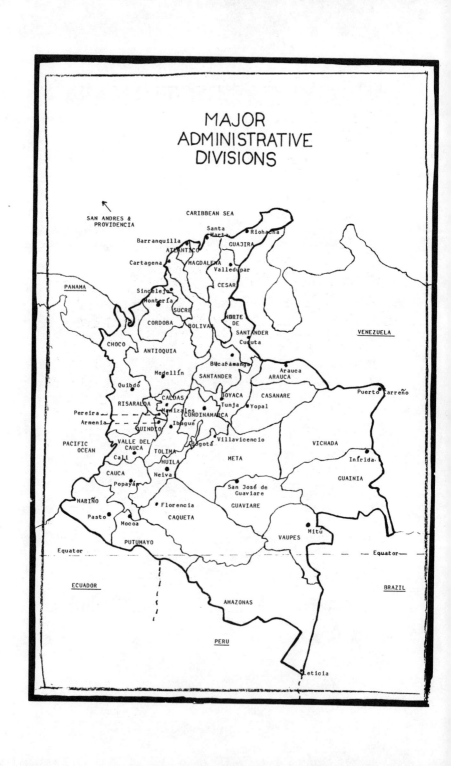

MAJOR
ADMINISTRATIVE
DIVISIONS

SAN ANDRES &
PROVIDENCIA

CARIBBEAN SEA

Santa
Marta   Riohacha
Barranquilla
ATLANTICO   GUAJIRA
Cartagena   MAGDALENA
Valledupar
CESAR
Sincelejo
Montería
SUCRE
CORDOBA   BOLIVAR
NORTE
DE
SANTANDER
Cúcuta
CHOCO   ANTIOQUIA
Bucaramanga
Medellín   Arauca
SANTANDER   ARAUCA
Quibdo
RISARALDA   CALDAS   BOYACA   CASANARE
Pereira   Manizales   Tunja   Yopal
Armenia   CUNDINAMARCA
QUINDIO   Ibague
VALLE DEL   Bogotá   Villavicencio
CAUCA
Cali   TOLIMA
HUILA   META
CAUCA   Neiva
Popayán
San José de
Guaviare
NARIÑO
Florencia   GUAVIARE
Pasto   Mocoa   CAQUETA

PUTUMAYO

VENEZUELA

PANAMA

PACIFIC
OCEAN

Puerto Carreño

VICHADA
Inírida
GUAINIA

VAUPES   Mitú

Equator   Equator

ECUADOR   BRAZIL

AMAZONAS

PERU

Leticia

HISTORICAL DICTIONARY
OF
COLOMBIA
Second Edition

by
Robert H. Davis

Latin American Historical Dictionaries, No. 23

The Scarecrow Press, Inc.
Metuchen, N.J., & London
1993

Frontispiece map and the map on page 213 reprinted by permission of Louisiana State University Press from *Rafael Nuñez and the Politics of Colombian Regionalism, 1863–1886.* Copyright © 1985 by Louisiana State University Press and with permission of the author. The map on page 241 and 435 is reprinted from David Bushnell, *The Santander Regime in Gran Colombia* (Newark, University of Delaware Press, 1954) by permission of the author, David Bushnell.

British Library Cataloguing-in-Publication data available

Library of Congress Cataloging-in-Publication Data

Davis, Robert H. (Robert Henry), 1939–
    Historical dictionary of Colombia / by Robert H. Davis—
2nd ed.
        p.   cm.—(Latin American historical dictionaries ;
no. 23)
    Includes bibliographical references (p.   ).
    ISBN 0-8108-2636-4 (alk. paper)
    1. Colombia—History—Dictionaries. I. Title.
II. Series.
F2254.D38   1993
986.1'003—dc20   93-29007

Dedicated to
Dr. J. León Helguera
with appreciation

CONTENTS

EDITOR'S FOREWORD

THE COUNTRY

Drugs, violence, and coffee are, only too often, all that the foreigner knows of Colombia. Like all stereotypes, this one does unfortunately offer a modicum of truth—but a very misunderstood one. Even the success of the Colombian drug trade is more a tribute to the entrepreneurial spirit of the *Antioqueño* than to any Colombian monopoly of "the unacceptable face of capitalism." Upholders of the dependency theory might like to note that Colombia enjoys no larger proportion of the profits of cocaine than it does of coffee—a miserable 15%, while the other 85%, in both industries, stays with the American distributors. Violence there has been aplenty, and by no means all of it drug related (although no Colombian city approaches the crime-related death rate of, say, Brazil's Belfort Rouxo). The real wonder, rather, is the extent to which so many quite wretchedly paid soldiers, policemen, lawyers, civil servants, journalists, and judges are prepared to put their lives on the line to defend democracy and the rule of law. Coffee is grown in many parts of the world outside Colombia, but in few is production so much in the hands of a myriad of small, independent growers, rather than in those of large-scale agrobusiness (as in Brazil, for instance).

And there are other, happier, aspects of this country: the secular, if quixotic, dedication to the cause of Hispanic American unity, for example, expressed in the perpetuation of the very name of the Liberator's dream: *Colombia*, "land of Columbus." Even though the country has had an unusually turbulent national development, even by Latin American standards, with oscillations between the extremes of centralism and federalism—a veritable political laboratory—this has occurred with an almost total continuity of civilian control: supposedly a reaction to domination by the Venezuelan military in the days of Bolívar's Gran Colombia. There is also a tradition of high regard for the life of the intellect, which led a 19th-century visitor to call Bogotá the "American Athens." Bolívar himself (who, if anyone, should have known) referred to New Granada (today's Colombia) as "a university," while denigrating his native Venezuela as "a barracks" and dismissing ultramontane Ecuador as "a convent."

Welcome, then, to what is in so many ways the most truly and admirably Hispanic of all Spain's successor nations in the New World—the Republic of Colombia—in Dr. Davis's broad presentation of its history and culture.

THE DICTIONARY

The new edition has been largely rewritten and substantially enlarged. A number of changes have been made at the editor's request to bring about a greater conformity among the various dictionaries in the Latin American Historical Dictionary series, particularly in the choice between Spanish and English forms of names. On the whole, English forms have been preferred for generic terms (e.g., tithes), Spanish for the names of specific institutions (e.g., Estados Unidos de Colombia). Cross references have been generously provided, in capital letters, preceded by "see" or "see also," or followed by "q.v." In addition, an asterisk has been used with the first occurrence in an entry of a word or phrase used as an entry heading elsewhere in the *Dictionary*. Thus a mention of Gabriel *García Márquez's *El *Otoño del Patriarca* would indicate the existence of entries for GARCIA MARQUEZ, Gabriel and OTOÑO DEL PATRIARCA, El. Arrangement of the entries is word-by-word according to the English alphabet. Abbreviations are filed at the head of their corresponding alphabetic sections, but acronyms (e.g., CERLAL) are filed as words. Initial articles are disregarded, with the usual exceptions of French surnames and names that have been wholly Anglicized (El Salvador, Eldorado, Los Angeles).

Laurence Hallewell
Latin American Librarian
Columbia University

INTRODUCTION

It is satisfying to an author to learn that his work, in this case the *Historical Dictionary of Colombia,* has enjoyed sufficient success in its original version to merit publication of a second. The present edition goes well beyond the original. Although the basic format— chronology, dictionary, and bibliographical essay—has been retained, the new text has been revised and expanded. Nearly all of the entries from the first edition have been retained, but many of these have been rewritten and extended. In addition there are many new entries, broadening both the range and the depth of materials covered. A comparison of the two editions would reveal greater attention to literature and the fine arts, economic history, and events of the 20th century in the expanded version.

As noted in the first edition of this book, the compilation of a short reference work is frustrating. It is difficult to strike a satisfactory balance between the desire to provide an essential survey of representative subjects and the necessity to work within the limitations of format and stylistic unity. Ultimately the selection of materials becomes somewhat arbitrary, and it is not possible to satisfy completely either the curious amateur or the enthusiastic specialist.

In the preparation of this dictionary, two criteria predominated. The first was the assumption that the work would be utilized primarily by English-language readers, and the second, that the work should emphasize those subjects that one could reasonably expect to find in the survey literature on Colombian history. Consequently, the selections included are intended neither as definitive descriptions nor, in the case of the bibliographical essay, as comprehensive listings. They are, rather, an introduction for the interested, general reader. It is assumed, however, that the work might be valuable for the beginning specialist, and perhaps even for the advanced student of Colombian history and culture.

A word is probably in order about the methodological approach for this edition. The dictionary is essentially a synthesis of existing knowledge rather than original research on most of the topics covered. Authorities do not always agree, for a number of reasons.

For example, the start of an official's term in office may be given variously as 1550, 1552, and 1556—a discrepancy that might be no more than the failure to distinguish between the dates of the royal decree authorizing the appointment, the nomination of a specific person for the office, and that person's actual arrival in Colombia. It was my intention in this edition to verify each entry from at least three different sources. For the most part this was realized in the preparation of the new text. Where there was disagreement among the authorities, I have opted to use the data given most frequently, or those for which there was a clear reason to give preference to one authority over another (for example, actual documentary evidence or more recent scholarship).

In the text, English and Spanish terms have been used interchangeably at times (for example, the *Visitador* or the Visitor; *Presidente* or President; and *La Violencia* or, the Violence). For consistency, the accent has been omitted from names commonly used in English, such as Peru, Panama, and Darien, except when these are part of the title of a work published in Spanish. Proper names, such as the Sabana de Bogotá and the Sociedad Democrática, have not been italicized. For the use of surnames, see the entry under "NAMES, Personal."

A word of appreciation should be extended to Gary Loging and Paula Anne Covington of the Vanderbilt University library and to the Joint Center for Latin America, University of Illinois, and the Latin American Studies Program, Cornell University, which gave me access to their respective university libraries. A great deal of the verification and revision of the entries in the first edition as well as significant research for additions to the new edition occurred in these collections. In Colombia, the support of Camilo Riaño, of the Colombian Academy of History, and Hector López López was especially helpful. For assistance with the bibliographical essay I am indebted to Elizabeth Kaschins, Ruth Reitan, and others of the reference staff of the Luther College Library. Dr. J. León Helguera, Vanderbilt University, provided numerous helpful comments on the text at various stages of its evolution, as did Professor René de la Pedraja Tomán, Canisius College, and Dr. Jo Ann Rayfield, Illinois State University, who each read different drafts of the text. Dr. David Bushnell, University of Florida, and Dr. James W. Park, Palomar College, graciously allowed me to reproduce maps from their previously published works. Katrinka Sieber and Margaret Baird Davis, both of Decorah, Iowa, were indispensable in the editorial preparation of the manuscript. Invaluable aid was provided by my research assistants, Deren

Kellogg (1988-1989), Kent Haugen (1989-1990), and Peter Bissinger (1990-1991), as well as the series editor, Laurence Hallewell. Final responsibility for the content rests, of course, with the author.

Robert H. Davis
Decorah, Iowa

A CHRONOLOGY OF COLOMBIAN HISTORY

B.C.

10,450   Carbon 14 dating of human artifacts at El Abra (Cundinamarca) provides earliest verified record of habitation in Colombia.

7050   Earliest dated human skeletal remains from Colombia indicate occupation at El Tequendama (Cundinamarca).

5580   Evidence of occupation at Nemocón and Sueva (Cundinamarca).

3350   Evidence of occupation at Monsú (Bolívar); ceramic remains are among oldest known in the Western Hemisphere.

3000   Evidence of occupation at Puerto Hormiga (Bolívar).

2200   Evidence of occupation at Canapoté (Bolívar).

1550   Evidence of occupation at Barlovento (Bolívar).

1200   Evidence of occupation at Malambo (Atlántico).

700   Evidence of occupation at Momil (Bolívar).

555   Evidence of occupation at San Agustín (Huila).

545   Evidence indicates beginnings of Chibcha civilization (Boyacá-Cundinamarca).

400   Evidence of occupation in the Tumaco (Nariño) region.

A.D.

610   Evidence of occupation at Tierradentro (Cauca).

860   Evidence of occupation at Miraflores (Nariño).

1000   Evidence indicates beginnings of Tairona civilization (Magdalena).

1107   Evidence of occupation at Las Cruces (Nariño).

1436   Evidence of occupation at Iles (Nariño).

1470   Zipa Saguanmachica.

1474   Accession of the Catholic Monarchs Isabella and Ferdinand
        to the Spanish thrones.

1490   Zipa Nemequene.

1493   Papal bull *Inter caetera* establishes the Line of Demarcation,
        modified in 1494 by the Treaty of Tordesillas.

1498   Columbus explores the coast of Venezuela from Trinidad to
        Margarita Island on his third voyage.

1499-1500 Alonso de Ojeda, accompanied by Amerigo Vespucci and
           Juan de la Cosa, explores the pearl coast of Venezuela
           from the Gulf of Paria to Cape Vela (Cabo de la Vela,
           off the Guajira Peninsula).

1500-1501 Rodrigo de Bastidas explores the Caribbean Coast from
           Cape Vela to Nombre de Dios, Panama.

1501-1502 Government of Coquibacoa is established.

1502   Ojeda occupies Guajira, but mutinies at Bahiahonda force
        his return to Spain.
        Columbus sails along the coast of present-day Honduras,
        Nicaragua, Costa Rica, Panama, and Colombia on his
        fourth voyage.

1503   Columbus founds Santa María de Belén in Panama.
        Cristóbal de Guerra dies exploring the coasts of Colombia.

1504-1507 Juan de la Cosa explores the area from the Gulf of Cumaná,
           Venezuela, to the Gulf of Urabá, Colombia.
           Queen Isabella dies in Spain; Ferdinand becomes Regent.

1508   Alonso de Ojeda, Governor of Nueva Andalucía.
        Diego de Nicuesa, Governor of Castilla del Oro.

1509   Ojeda's expedition suffers reverses at Cartagena Bay and is
        rescued by Nicuesa.

1510   Ojeda's expedition founds San Sebastián de Urabá, but later
        abandons it to establish Santa María de la Antigua del
        Darién.
        Martín Fernández de Enciso sails from Santo Domingo to
        Santa María, but Balboa assumes command and begins
        exploration of Panama.
        The Franciscans found their first monastery at Santa María.

1513   Balboa sights the Pacific Ocean.

1514   Zipa Tisquesusa.
        Pedrarias, Governor of Panama.
        Friar Juan de Quevedo, Bishop of Darien.

1515	Pedrarias founds Acla.
1516	Accession of Charles I as King of Spain.
1519	Pedrarias executes Balboa. He founds Panama City and makes it the seat of government.
1520	Nuevo Toledo (Cumaná), Venezuela, is founded.
1520-1521	Friar Bartolomé de las Casas attempts social experiment with Indians in Venezuela.
1522	Pascual de Andagoya explores the Pacific Coast from Panama City to the San Juan River.
1523	*Tributo* tax on the Indians is begun.
1524	The Council of the Indies is formally established.
1525	Francisco Pizarro and Diego de Almagro complete exploration of Colombia's Pacific Coast.
	Bartolomé Ruiz becomes the first Spaniard to cross the equator in the Pacific Ocean.
	Bastidas founds Santa Marta.
1526	Audiencia de Santo Domingo is established.
1527	Juan Ampués founds Coro.
1527-1532	The first Mercedarian monastery is founded at Santa Marta.
1528-1533	Ambrosius Dalfinger explores the coastal region from the Magdalena River to Lake Maracaibo.
1528-1548	The Welsers are granted land in Venezuela.
1529	García de Lerma, Governor of Santa Marta, authorizes explorations in Valledupar, the plains of La Ramada, Ciénaga, and the lower Magdalena, Cauca, and San Jorge Rivers.
	Approximately twenty Dominicans and Friar Tomás de Ortiz arrive at Santa Marta for missionary work.
1531	Friar Tomás de Ortiz, first Bishop of Santa Marta.
1532	The Panama Road is laid out.
1533	Pedro de Heredia founds Cartagena.
1534	Friar Tomás de Toro, first Bishop of Cartagena.
	Sebastián de Belalcázar founds Quito, Ecuador.
1535	Pedro Fernández de Lugo, Governor of Santa Marta, and Alonso Luis de Lugo send expeditions from Santa Marta to Guajira.
	Juan de Ampudia founds original settlement of Popayán; it was moved to its present site by Belalcázar in 1537.

Santiago de Guayaquil, Ecuador, is founded.
Sincelejo is established by 1535.

1535-1536 Heredia authorizes explorations in the vicinity of the Nechí, Cauca, and Sinú rivers and the Gulf of Urabá. Pedro de Añasco and Juan de Ampudia, agents of Sebastián de Belalcázar, explore Pasto, the Patía Valley, and the Cauca Valley with scouts as far north as Cartago.

1535-1537 Georg von Speyer explores from Coro to the Apure, Arauca, Meta, and Guaviare rivers.

1535-1539 Nicholas Federmann, at times following the route of Speyer, explores from Coro to the Sabana de Bogotá via Casanare, Meta, Tunja, Bosa, and the Mountains of Sumapaz.

1536 Juan Fernández de Angulo, Bishop of Santa Marta.
Belalcázar founds Cali.

1536-1538 Gonzalo Jiménez de Quesada leads an expedition from Santa Marta to the Sabana de Bogotá.

1536-1548 Nueva Castilla is established.

1537 Francisco César explores the territory from the Gulf of Urabá to Antioquia.
Quesada meets the Zaque at Tunja.

1538 Zipa Sagipa.
Zaque Quemunchatocha dies; Zaque Aquimin begins reign.
Quesada founds Santafé de Bogotá.
Añasco founds Timaná, first called Guaycayo, or Quarcarnallo.
Royal *audiencia* is created in Panama.

1538-1539 Juan Vadillo explores the territory from the Gulf of Urabá, through Antioquia, to Cali.

1538-1539 Belalcázar explores from Popayán to the Sabana de Bogotá via Timaná, La Plata, Guanacas, and Neiva.

1539 Gonzalo Jiménez de Quesada and Hernán Pérez de Quesada, governors of the New Kingdom of Granada.
Quesada, Federmann, and Belalcázar meet on the Sabana de Bogotá and return to Spain.
Martín Galeano founds Vélez (moved to its present site in 1540).
Lorenzo de Aldana founds San Juan de Villaviciosa, Pasto.
Gonzalo Suárez Rendón founds Tunja.
Juan de Cabrera founds Neiva.

Jorge Robledo founds Anserma (Ansermaviejo); Santa Ana de los Caballeros, now Ansermanuevo is also established.
Alonso de Heredia founds Santa Cruz de Mompós.
Pascual de Andagoya, Governor of Nueva Castilla, explores the Chocó and the Cauca Valley to Cali.

1539-1540 Jorge Robledo explores the Cauca Valley.

1539-1541 The rebellion of La Gaitana occurs around Timaná.

1540 The expedition of Jerónimo Lebrón from Santa Marta arrives at Tunja. Elvira Gutiérrez, the first Spanish woman to reach the New Kingdom of Granada, arrives.
Robledo authorizes Melchor Suer de Nava to found San Jorge de Cartago in the vicinity of present-day Pereira.
Juan Ladrillero founds Buenaventura under orders from Andagoya.

1541 Sebastián de Belalcázar, Governor of the Cauca, returns to Popayán and Cali accompanied by Mercedarian friars who found a monastery in Cali.
Robledo founds Santafé de Antioquia, moved to its present site in 1542.
Túquerres is established.

1541-1546 Philipp Hutten explores the Llanos and the Amazon Valley.

1542 Miguel López de Muñoz founds Santiago de Arma between Cartago and Antioquia.
The New Laws of the Indies are published.

1542-1543 Alonso Luis de Lugo leads an expedition from the Valledupar region to Bogotá.

1543 Alonso Luis de Lugo, Governor of the New Kingdom of Granada.
Friar Martín de Calatayud, Bishop of Santa Marta.
French corsair Robert Val attacks Santa Marta.

1544 Miguel Díaz de Armendáriz, *Visitador* to the governments of Cartagena, Santa Marta, Bogotá, and Cali, introduces the New Laws of the Indies.
Robert Val attacks Santa Marta and Cartagena.
Hernán Vanegas founds Tocaima.

1545 Riohacha is founded.
The Carare Road comes into service.
The Bishopric of Quito is created.

1546 First smallpox epidemic reported in New Granada.

1547 Pedro de Ursúa, Governor of Bogotá.
Juan del Valle, first Bishop of Popayán.

1549   Royal *audiencia* is established in Bogotá with the first officials inaugurated in 1550.

Pedro de Ursúa and Ortún Velasco found Pamplona.

Sebastián Quintero and Bartolomé Ruiz found San Sebastián de Cambis, later named San Sebastián de la Plata, which was destroyed by fire. (Present-day La Plata was founded in 1563.)

1550   The Bishop of Santa Marta is ordered to reside in Bogotá.

Dominican and Franciscan friars found their first permanent monasteries in New Granada.

Andrés López de Galarza founds San Bonifacio de Ibagué, which was moved to its present site in 1551.

Quesada returns from Spain as Marshal of the New Kingdom.

Hernando de Santana founds Valledupar.

1551   Juan de Montaño, *Visitador.*

Alonso de Fuenmayor founds San Luis de Almaguer. Hernando de Alcocer and Alonso de Olalla Herrera found San Miguel de Villeta while opening a road between Bogotá and future site of Honda.

Francisco Núñez de Pedroso founds Mariquita, which was moved to its present site in 1553.

Juan de Avellaneda founds San Juan de los Llanos, around 1551.

Pedro de Agreda founds Mocoa.

Champanes are introduced on the Magdalena River.

The Dominican Province of San Antonino is created.

1552   Friar Juan de los Barrios, Bishop of Santa Marta, resident in Bogotá.

Barquisimeto, Venezuela, is founded.

The *Mita de Boga* for Indian labor is authorized on the Magdalena River.

1553   The rebellion of Alvaro de Oyón occurs in Timaná, La Plata, Neiva, and Popayán.

La Miel is founded.

The Honda Road is constructed.

1555   Buga is founded.

1556   Accession of Philip II as King of Spain.

Bishop Barrios holds the first Diocesan Synod in New Granada.

Valencia is founded.

Trujillo is founded.

1557   Pijao Indians begin rebellion.

1558   The *audiencia* governs the New Kingdom of Granada.

1559 Luis Lanchero founds Trinidad de los Muzos.

1560 Rodrigo de Fuenmayor founds Guadalajara de Buga, which was moved to its present site in 1570.
Honda is established.

1560-1561 French pirates Jean and Martin Cote attack Cartagena.

1561 Pedro Alonso and Juan Trujillo found Alcaldes, which was moved to its present site in 1573. The name was later changed to Ocaña.
Pedro de Ursúa is murdered by Lope de Aguirre on an expedition in the Amazon Valley.
Aguirre sails to the mouth of the Amazon and later invades Venezuela before committing suicide under attack.

1562-1569 San Luis Beltán conducts missionary activity among Indians of the Atlantic Coast.

1563 The Presidency of the New Kingdom of Granada and the Archbishopric of Santafé de Bogotá are created.
The presidency and royal *audiencia* are established in Quito.
Dominicans establish the first grammar classes in Bogotá.
Pedro de Agreda founds Mocoa.

1564 Andrés Venero de Leiva, President of the New Kingdom of Granada.
Friar Juan de los Barrios, Archbishop of Bogotá.
John Hawkins forces the sale of black slaves in Riohacha.
San Pedro Hospital is established in Bogotá.
Emeralds are discovered in New Granada.
The *flota* system begins.

1565 Honda develops spontaneously as a commercial depot on the Magdalena River. It was given a formal title in 1643.

1566 Smallpox epidemic reduces population by 10%.
Fortifications are begun in Cartagena.
Spain begins collection of the *almorifazgo.*

1569 The Carmelites found their first monastery in New Granada in Bogotá.

1569-1571 Quesada explores the Llanos and founds San Fernando de Atabapo on the Orinoco River.

1571 Maracaibo, Venezuela, is founded.

1572 The cornerstone is laid for the Cathedral of Bogotá.
Sir Francis Drake attacks the Atlantic Coast.
Juan de Otálora and Francisco de Villalobos found Villa de Leiva.
Francisco Hernández de Contreras founds original settlement of Ocaña (Santa Ana de Hacarí).

1573   Friar Luis Zapata de Cárdenas, Archbisop of Bogotá.
        Franciscans found the order of Santa Clara de Tunja, the
        first feminine order in Colombia.
        Melchor Velásquez founds Toro, which was moved to its
        present site by Diego Ordóñez in 1587.

1574   Dos Ríos is created.

1575   Francisco Briceño, President of the New Kingdom of
        Granada.
        The *audiencia* governs the New Kingdom.
        The Augustinians establish their first monastery in New
        Granada in Bogotá.

1576   Santa Marta is burned by Indians.

1578   Lope Díaz Aux de Armendáriz, President of the New
        Kingdom of Granada.
        Franciscan Order of the Immaculate Conception founds its
        first convent in Pasto.

1580   Juan Bautista Monzón, *Visitador*.
        Alonso Ranjel founds Salazar de las Palmas.

1581   Gaspar de Rodas founds Zaragoza on the Nechí River.

1582   Juan Prieto de Orellana, *Visitador*.

1585   Francisco Guillén Chaparro, President of the New King-
        dom of Granada.
        Pedro Daza founds Medina de las Torres.
        San Sebastián de los Reyes is founded.

1585-1586 Drake attacks the Caribbean Coast and holds Cartagena for
        ransom.

1586   The miraculous restoration of the Virgin of Chiquinquirá
        occurs.

1587   Smallpox epidemic occurs.

1588   Pedro Daza founds Santiago de las Atalayas.

1589   The first Jesuits arrive in the New Kingdom.

1590   Antonio González, President of the New Kingdom of
        Granada.
        Gaspar Gómez founds Caguán.

1591   Royal decree authorizes private ownership of land.
        Augustinians found the Convent of Nuestra Señora de la
        Encarnación in Popayán.
        The *alcabala* is introduced in New Granada.

1592   Gonzalo de Piña founds San Juan de Pedraza.
Pedro de Cárcamo founds Nueva Córdoba and Nueva Sevilla.
Juan de Herrera founds San Juan de Isima.
Remedios is founded.

1593   Indian *resguardos* are recognized by President González.

1595-1596   Drake attacks Santa Marta and Central America.

1596   Pedro M. de Avila founds San Agustín de Avila.
Cristóbal Cordello attacks Santa Marta.
Improvements are made on the docking facilities at Honda.

1597   Francisco de Sande, President of New Granada.
Portobello is established.

1598   Accession of Philip III as King of Spain.
The *Mita de Boga* for Indian labor is abolished.

1599   Bartolomé Lobo Guerrero, Archbishop of Bogotá.

1600   The Palenque de Matuna is founded.

1602   The *audiencia* governs New Granada.

1603   Núño Núñez de Villavicencio, *Visitador*.

1604   The Jesuits found their first monasteries at Cartagena and Bogotá.

1604-1605   Colegio and Seminario de San Bartolomé are founded in Bogotá.

1605   Juan de Borja, President of New Granada.
The Tribunal de Cuentas is founded in Bogotá.

1605-1618   Borja leads campaigns against the Pijaos.

1606   Carmelites establish their first permanent convent in New Granada.

1608   Alvaro de Zambrano, *Visitador*.

1610   The Inquisition is established in Cartagena.

1610-1654   San Pedro Claver carries on missionary activities among the slaves in Cartagena.

1613   Friar Pedro Ordóñez y Flórez, Archbishop of Bogotá.

1616   Francisco Herrera Campuzano founds original settlement on the site of Medellín. Nuestra Señora de la Candelaria de Medellín is founded in 1675.
Ordinances regulating Indian working conditions are issued in New Granada.

1617-1618   Walter Raleigh attacks La Guayra and vicinity.

1618   Hernando Arias de Ugarte, Archbishop of Bogotá.

1620   A Casa de Moneda is founded in Bogotá and also in Cartagena.

1621   Accession of Philip IV as King of Spain.
       The Palenque de San Basilio is founded.

1622   Andrés de Sotomayor founds Bucaramanga.
       Antonio Jimeno de los Ríos founds San Faustino de los Ríos.
       Javeriana University is founded in Bogotá.

1625   Archbishop Arias de Ugarte holds the first Provincial Council in New Granada.

1627   Julián de Cortázar, Archbishop of Bogotá.

1628   The *audiencia* governs New Granada.

1629   Barranquilla is founded.
       English begin settlement of San Andrés y Providencia.
       English pirates attack La Guayra.

1630   Sancho Girón, President of New Granada.
       Antonio Rodríguez de San Isidro Manrique, *Visitador*.

1631   Bernardo de Almansa, Archbishop of Bogotá.
       Francisco Montilla de los Ríos founds San Juan Girón.

1632-1634   Typhus-typhoid epidemic occurs in New Granada;
       Pest of Santos Gil, 1633.

1633   Elena de la Cruz is tried for witchcraft.

1634   Rebellion of Queen Leonor occurs.

1635   Friar Cristóbal de Torres, Archbishop of Bogotá.

1635   The *Armada de Barlovento* is levied in New Granada.

1637   Martín Saavedra y Guzmán, President of New Granada.

1639   University of Santo Tomás is founded in Bogotá.
       Typhus-typhoid epidemic occurs in New Granada.
       Father Cristóbal de Acuña explores the Amazon from Quito to the Atlantic Ocean.

1640   *Papel sellado* is instituted in New Granada.

1641   Spanish expedition captures Santa Catalina, part of San Andrés y Providencia.
       Portuguese rebellion occurs in Cartagena.

1642   Asylum of Nuestra Señora de la Concepción is set up in Bogotá.

1644   Juan Fernández de Córdoba y Coalla, President of New Granada.
       Earthquake hits the Sabana de Bogotá, destroys much of Pamplona.

1646   Capuchins begin missionary work on the Caribbean Coast.

1650   The Canal del Dique is opened.

1653   The Colegio Mayor de Nuestra Señora del Rosario is founded in Bogotá.

1654   Dionisio Pérez Manrique, President of New Granada.
       Jesuit priests found Citará (Quibdó).

1655   Juan Cristóbal Cordello attacks Cartagena.

1657   San Felipe de Barajas is opened in Cartagena.

1658   Pirates under William Dawson attack Santa Marta.

1659   Juan Cornejo, *Visitador.*

1660   Dionisio Pérez Manrique, again President of New Granada.

1661   Friar Juan de Arguinao, Archbishop of Bogotá.

1662   Diego de Egües y Beaumont, President of New Granada.

1664   The *audiencia* governs New Granada.

1665   Accession of Charles II as King of Spain.

1666   Diego del Corro y Carrascal, President of New Granada.
       El Olonés attacks Maracaibo.

1668-1670   Henry Morgan and other buccaneers attack Portobello, Riohacha, Maracaibo, Chagres, and Panama City.

1671   Melchor Liñán y Cisneros, President of New Granada.
       Villa Nuestra Señora del Socorro is founded.

1674   The *audiencia* governs New Granada.

1678   Francisco Castillo de la Concha, President of New Granada.

1679-1681   Pirates attack Panama City and the Pacific Coast.

1680   The Juzgado General de Indios is established in New Granada.

1681   Antonio Sanz Lozano, Archbishop of Bogotá.
       Socorro is founded on present site.

1685   Sebastián de Velasco, President of New Granada.

1686   Gil de Cabrera y Dávalos, President of New Granada.

1687   Earthquake and "El Ruido" strike Bogotá.

1688   Copies of the *Recopilación de las Leyes de Indias*, legal code of 1680, arrive in New Granada.
Plague epidemic strikes New Granada.

1689   San Gil is founded.

1690   Friar Ignacio de Urbina, Archbishop of Bogotá.
Manuel Cañizales founds Quibdó.

1694   Pirates under Jean Baptiste Ducasse attack Cartagena.

1697   French pirates Ducasse and the Baron de Pointis attack Cartagena.

1698-1700   Scots found New Caledonia in Darien.

1700   Accession of Philip V as King of Spain.
Smallpox epidemic occurs in New Granada.

1703   Diego Córdoba de Lasso de la Vega, President of New Granada.

1706   Francisco de Cossío y Otero, Archbishop of Bogotá.

1708   English ships destroy Spanish merchant vessels off the Barú Islands near Cartagena.

1712   The *audiencia* governs New Granada.

1713   Great Britain receives the *asiento de negros* for the sale of black slaves.

1717   Nicolás Infante de Vanegas, President of New Granada.

1719   Jorge Villalonga, Viceroy of New Granada.
The Viceroyalty of the New Kingdom of Granada is established.

1723   The Viceroyalty is suppressed and the Presidency restored.

1725   Antonio Manso y Maldonado, President of New Granada.

1729   A Casa de Moneda is established in Popayán.

1731   The *audiencia* governs New Granada.
Antonio Claudio Alvarez de Quiñones, Archbishop of Bogotá.

1732   Indians rebel in Darién.

1733   Rafael de Eslava, President of New Granada.
Antonio Villamizar Pineda founds Cúcuta.

1735-1740   La Condamine leads scientific expedition to mark the equator.

1736   Earthquake damages Popayán and the Cauca Valley.

1737   The *audiencia* governs New Granada.
Fire ruins Panama City.

1738   Antonio González Manrique, President of New Granada.
Jesuits introduce the first printing press in New Granada.

1739   Francisco González Manrique, President of New Granada.
Friar Juan de Galavís, Archbishop of Bogotá.
The second Viceroyalty of the New Kingdom of Granada is
established.

1739-1742   Admiral Vernon attacks Panama and Cartagena.

1740   Sebastián de Eslava, Viceroy of New Granada.
Rebellion occurs in Vélez.

1741   Diego Fermín de Vergara, Archbishop of Bogotá.

1743   New Granada suffers drought in the interior and earthquakes from Venezuela to Popayán.

1744   The Jesuits found the University of San José in Popayán.
Juan de Torrezar Díaz Pimienta founds Montería, originally called San Jerónimo de Buenavista.

1745   Pedro Felipe de Azúa e Iturgoyen, Archbishop of Bogotá.

1746   Accession of Ferdinand VI as King of Spain.

1748   Dr. Leonardo Sudrot de la Garde initiates efforts to establish a hospital in Cali.

1749   José Alfonso Pizarro, Viceroy of New Granada.
Expeditions sent to pacify Indians on the Guajira Peninsula
and the Atlantic Coast.
Juan Manuel de Muelle and Pedro Hernández de Zurita try
to start wool manufacturing in Tunja.
State monopoly, or *estanco,* is declared on *Aguardiente.*

1750   Mail service formally organized in New Granada.

1750-1759   Baron Jacquin travels in New Granada.

1753-1759   Spanish-Portuguese Boundary Commission travels in New
Granada.

1754   Espinal is founded.

1757   Mail service is initiated between Santa Marta and Maracaibo.
The first aqueduct is inaugurated in Bogotá.

1759   Accession of Charles III as King of Spain.

1761   Pedro Messía de la Zerda, Viceroy of New Granada.

1762   José Celestino Mutis begins teaching mathematics and astronomy at the Colegio del Rosario.

1766   Earthquake damages much of Almaguer.
        Tobacco monopoly (*estanco*) is instituted in New Granada.

1767   The Jesuits are expelled from New Granada.
        A rebellion occurs in Neiva.

1770   The Convent of La Enseñanza is founded in Bogotá.

1771   Friar Agustín Manuel Camacho y Rojas, Archbishop of Bogotá.

1772   Manuel Guirior, Viceroy of New Granada.
        A map of the Viceroyalty is completed.

1774   Antonio de la Torre y Miranda founds Montería.
        Francisco Moreno y Escandón assesses educational needs in New Granada.

1774-1783 Antonio de la Torre Miranda explores and colonizes the area around Cartagena.

1775   Agustín de Alvarado y Castillo, Archbishop of Bogotá.
        El Zancudo gold and silver mining enterprise begins.

1776   Manuel Antonio Flórez, Viceroy of New Granada.
        Mail service is begun to Medellín, Remedios, Zaragoza, and Mompós.

1777   First public library is opened in Bogotá.
        The Captaincy General of Venezuela is created.

1778   Juan Francisco Gutiérrez de Piñeres, *Regente-Visitador-Intendente* of New Granada.

1779   Antonio Caballero y Góngora, Archbishop of Bogotá.

1780   Gutiérrez de Piñeres publishes new tax laws.

1780-1782 Comunero Rebellion protests tax policies.

1782   Juan de Torrezar Díaz Pimienta, Viceroy of New Granada.
        Juan Francisco Gutiérrez de Piñeres, interim regent.
        Antonio Caballero y Góngora, Archbishop, Viceroy of New Granada.
        Smallpox epidemic strikes New Granada.
        Mathematics is introduced into the curriculum at the Colegio de San Bartolomé.

1783   The Botanical Expedition is created.

1784   The Friends of the Nation Society (Amigos del País) is formed in Mompós.

1785   Earthquake ravages New Granada.
            First newspapers are published in Viceroyalty.

1785-1787   Expedition to the Isthmus of Panama pacifies most Indian groups.

1785-1789   *Visitador* Antonio Mon y Velarde tries to rejuvenate Antioquia's economy.

1785-1796   Juan José d'Elhuyar, mineralogist, tries to improve mining in New Granada.

1786   An *audiencia* is established in Caracas.

1787   Grammars of the Indian languages are requested for Catherine of Russia.

1788   Accession of Charles IV as King of Spain.

1789   Francisco Gil de Taboada y Lemos, Viceroy of New Granada.
            José de Ezpeleta, Viceroy of New Granada.
            Riohacha is made a separate province to stop contraband trade.

1789-1790   *Tertulias* are organized in Bogotá.

1790   Free navigation is permitted on the Atrato River.

1791   Baltasar Jaime Martínez de Compañón, Archbishop of Bogotá.
            The *Papel Periodico* . . . begins publication in Bogotá.
            A police force is created in Bogotá.

1792   The Coliseo Theater is opened in Bogotá.

1793   Joaquín Durán y Díaz publishes first almanac of the Viceroyalty.
            Antonio Nariño prints *The Rights of Man.*

1794   Nariño and various others are convicted of sedition.

1797   Pedro Mendinueta y Muzquiz, Viceroy of New Granada.

1799-1804   Alexander von Humboldt travels in the Viceroyalty.

1800   Friar Fernando del Portillo y Torres, Archbishop of Bogotá.

1802   Royal monopoly of platinum is instituted.

1802-1803   The National Observatory is built in Bogotá.

1803   Antonio Amar y Borbón, Viceroy of New Granada.
            The Mosquito Coast area is added to New Granada.

1804   Juan Bautista Sacristán, Archbishop of Bogotá.

1804-1805   Vaccination Expedition works in New Granada.

1805   Earthquakes strike Mariquita.

1808   March: Charles IV abdicates in favor of his son, Ferdinand
        VII, as King of Spain.
        Napoleon Bonaparte then forces the abdication of
        Ferdinand VII and installs his brother Joseph Bona-
        parte as King José I.
        May: Popular uprisings in Madrid begin civil war in Spain. A
        Junta Suprema de Gobierno in Seville establishes a
        Spanish rival to the pro-French government of José I.
        August-September: The Viceroy of New Granada and his
        administration swear allegiance to Ferdinand VII.

1809   January: The Junta Central de España calls for a Cortes to
        represent legitimate authority. It declares the Indies an
        equal part of Spain and requests representatives from
        America as delegates to the Cortes.
        August: A major rebellion occurs in Quito; a minor revolt
        takes place in Socorro.
        September: Junta of Notables meets in Bogotá to discuss
        responses to the Quito rebellion.
        November: Camilo Torres writes the *Declaration of Griev-
        ances (Memorial de agravios)*.

1810   February: The Spanish Cortes modifies its original decrees,
        increasing the number of American representatives.
        May: Public disturbances occur in Cartagena, Pamplona,
        Casanare, and Socorro. Representatives of the Cortes
        arrive in Cartagena.
        July: An incident at a Spanish merchant's shop leads to
        popular uprisings, the Act of July 20, and the formation
        of the Junta Suprema del Nuevo Reino to govern New
        Granada. Loyalty to Ferdinand VII is maintained but
        the Viceroy and the Spanish Regency are repudiated.
        José Miguel Pey, Vice President, acting President of
        the Junta Suprema of New Granada.
        August: Viceroy Amar y Borbón is expelled from New
        Granada. Mompós declares its independence from
        Spain.
        December: An unproductive congress of patriots meets in
        Bogotá.

1811   José María García de Toledo prevents Spanish counter-
        movement in Cartagena, but Colonel Tomás Acosta
        succeeds in restoring Spanish domination of Santa
        Marta.
        February: Caloto, Buga, Cartago, Anserma, Toro, and Cali
        form the Confederated Cities of the Valley. Cundi-
        namarca elects delegates to a constituent congress.

March: Battle of Bajo Palacé gives the patriots control of the Cauca Valley. Cundinamarca proclaims itself an independent state loyal to Ferdinand VII.

April-July 1812: Royalist reaction threatens patriot government in the Cauca Valley.

April-September: Jorge Tadeo Lozano, President of Cundinamarca.

May: Lozano (Cundinamarca)–Madariaga (Venezuela) Treaty forms alliance against Napoleonic Spain.

July: *La Bagatela* begins publication.

September: Lozano resigns and Antonio Nariño becomes President of Cundinamarca until 1812.

November: Cartagena proclaims itself independent of Spain. Antioquia, Cartagena, Neiva, Pamplona, and Tunja form the United Provinces of New Granada. Camilo Torres, President of United Provinces until 1814.

December: A constituent congress writes a constitution for Cundinamarca.

1812   March: Benito Pérez Brito, Viceroy of New Granada, occupies Panama.

July: Patriot forces in the Cauca Valley suffer major reversals. The head of state, Joaquín Caicedo, and commander of the army, General Alexander Macaulay, are captured and executed.

August: Manuel Benito de Castro becomes President of Cundinamarca when Nariño resigns.

September: Congress of the United Provinces convenes in Leiva and opposes the policies of Nariño and Cundinamarca.

October: Cundinamarca declares formal opposition to the United Provinces. Antonio Nariño becomes Dictator of Cundinamarca.

November: Simón Bolívar arrives at Cartagena as a refugee from the collapse of the first Venezuelan Republic.

December: Forces of the United Provinces defeat Nariño at the Battle of Ventaquemada.

1813   January: Nariño repels attempt by the United Forces to capture Bogotá. Forces from Cartagena capture large portions of Santa Marta from the royalists. Bolívar wages campaigns into February from the lower Magdalena River to Cúcuta.

May-October: Bolívar conducts the Admirable Campaign in Venezuela. He proclaims a "War to the Death" in Trujillo, June 15. On October 13 he arrives in Caracas, where he is given the title of Liberator.

July: Cundinamarca proclaims its independence from Spain.

August: Antioquia proclaims its independence from Spain. Nariño resigns and Manuel Bernardo de Alvarez becomes President of Cundinamarca.

September: Nariño begins campaign to the Cauca Valley. The Battle of Bárbula occurs.

December: Advance troops of José María Cabal and Nariño defeat the royalists at the Battle of Alto Palacé.

1814 January: The Battle of Calibío occurs.

March: Ferdinand VII, King of Spain, is restored to his throne. The Battle of San Mateo occurs.

April: Antioquia abolishes slavery.

May: Nariño at first defeats royalist forces at the Battle of Tacines but is later forced to surrender to Spanish authorities.

August: The United Provinces makes an unsuccesful attempt at reconciliation with Cundinamarca. José Fernández Madrid, José María Castillo y Rada, and Joaquín Camacho are elected as a triumvirate to govern the United Provinces.

September: Bolívar suffers reversals in Venezuela, returns to New Granada, and reports to the Congress of the United Provinces.

November-December: Bolívar campaigns against Cundinamarca. His victory at the Battle of Bogotá forces Cundinamarca to surrender to the United Provinces.

1815 January: The government of the United Provinces moves to Bogotá. Custodio García Rovira, José José Miguel Pey, and Manuel Rodríguez Torices are elected a triumvirate to govern the United Provinces. Antonio Villavicencio replaces García Rovira when he resigns.

February-May: Bolívar initiates a campaign to free Santa Marta, but a lack of supplies leads him to besiege Cartagena to force it to support him.

April: General Pablo Morillo with a Spanish army lands on the coast of Venezuela.

May: Bolívar negotiates an armistice with Cartagena and flees to Jamaica to escape capture by Morillo. A Spanish conspiracy is discovered in Bogotá.

July: Morillo arrives at Santa Marta. The Battle of the River Palo occurs.

August-December: Morillo lays siege to Cartagena, eventually forcing its surrender.

September: Bolívar issues call to arms from Jamaica.

October-March 1816: Spanish forces reconquer Antioquia.

November: Camilo Torres is elected President of the United Provinces.

1816   February-October: Patriot leaders are executed in Car-
        tagena, Bogotá, and elsewhere.
        February: General Custodio García Rovira and patriot
        forces are defeated at the Battle of Carchí.
        March: José Fernández Madrid is elected President of the
        United Provinces.
        April: Juan Francisco Montalvo is made Viceroy of New
        Granada. The Congress of the United Provinces dis-
        solves; Fernández Madrid orders a retreat to Popayán.
        General Manuel Serviez refuses to follow these orders
        and leads his army to refuge and guerrilla resistance in
        the Llanos.
        May: General Morillo recaptures Bogotá. Custodio García
        Rovira is elected President of the United Provinces,
        but Vice-President Liborio Mejía assumes command in
        his absence.
        June: Morillo begins executions, initiating the Reign of
        Terror in Bogotá. The Battle of Cuchilla del Tambo
        marks the collapse of the patriot government in the
        Cauca Valley. Bolívar fails in attempt to invade Marga-
        rita Island and Venezuela.
        July: Survivors of Cuchilla del Tambo are captured at the
        Battle of La Plata. Fernando Serrano is elected Presi-
        dent of New Granada by the patriot fugitives in
        Arauca. Francisco de Paula Santander is named com-
        mander of the army.
        September: General José Antonio Páez captures Serrano
        and is acclaimed supreme commander of the forces in
        the Llanos. Bolívar lands in the Orinoco basin.
        October: The reconquest of Antioquia is completed.
        November: Morillo leaves Bogotá; Juan Sámano is left in
        control.

1817   The first volunteer forces of the Britannic Legion are sent
        out to aid the patriots.
        April: A guerrilla movement begins in Cepitá, Santander.
        October: Policarpa Salavarrieta is executed.

1818   Juan Sámano, Viceroy of New Granada.
        January: Bolívar and Páez unite in Payara, Venezuela.

1819   February-December: Patriot congress meets at Angostura,
        Venezuela.
        May: Bolívar begins the Liberating Campaign of 1819,
        moving from the Río Apure to Guasdualito, Vene-
        zuela, and then to Arauca.
        June: Having assembled his troops in Tame, Bolívar moves
        to Pore (Casanare).

June-July: Bolívar moves from Pore, across the Páramo de Pisba, to Socha (Boyacá). The patriots fight minor engagements at Gameza and Bonza prior to the Battle of the Pantano de Vargas. Antonia Santos is executed in Socorro.

August: The Battle of Boyacá frees central New Granada. Viceroy Sámano flees the capital. Bolívar organizes a patriot administration in Bogotá. Francisco de Paula Santander, Vice President of New Granada, becomes acting chief executive.

September: Bolívar leaves Bogotá to begin campaign in Cúcuta.

December: The Congress of Angostura establishes the Republic of Gran Colombia.

1820   January: The rebellion of Colonel Rafael Riego in Spain prevents the sending of reinforcements for the Royalists in America. Patriot forces occupy the lower Magdalena River and Antioquia, January to November. The Congress of Angostura approves gradual emancipation of black slaves.

June: The Battle of Tenerife occurs.

July: Mosquera (Colombia)–Monteagudo (Peru) Treaty forms alliance.

August: Francisco Antonio Zea negotiates the loan of 1820 in England.

September: Bolívar and General Morillo negotiate a six-month armistice.

November: Bolívar and Morillo confer in Santa Ana, Venezuela.

December: Morillo leaves Venezuela and returns to Spain.

1821   February: Luis López Méndez negotiates the Mackintosh Contract in England. The Battle of Genoy occurs.

May-October: The Congress of Cúcuta writes a constitution for Colombia (July), passes laws for abolition of slavery, and elects new officials. The Lancasterian school system is introduced in Colombia.

June: The Battle of Carabobo occurs. General Mariano Montilla achieves control of Cartagena Bay for the patriots.

October: Montilla forces the Spanish to surrender the city of Cartagena. Simón Bolívar becomes President of Colombia. Francisco de Paula Santander, Vice President of Colombia, becomes acting chief executive, 1821-1827.

November: Panama joins itself to the Republic of Colombia.

December: Bolívar sets off for Popayán and campaigns in Ecuador, Peru, and Bolivia.

1822   The University of Antioquia is established.
March: The United States recognizes Colombian independence.
April: The Battle of Bomboná occurs.
May: The Battle of Pichincha occurs. Quito joins the Republic of Colombia.
June: Bolívar negotiates surrender of the Pasto area with royalist defenders and continues his movement southward toward Quito.
July: Bolívar enters Guayaquil and confers with José de San Martín, July 26-27. Colombia signs a treaty with Peru.
October: The Mosquera (Colombia)–Echeverría–Rodríguez Treaty is signed with Chile. October to June 1824: Agustín Agualongo and royalist guerrillas rebel in Pasto.
The Escuela Náutica, Colombia's first naval academy, is founded.

1823   January: General Montilla completes patriot campaigns against Santa Marta. Bolívar achieves momentary pacification of Pasto.
March: Colombia goodwill pact, the Mosquera-Rivadavia Treaty, with Argentina.
May: Bolívar agrees to lead military expeditions to Peru.
July: The Battle of Maracaibo occurs.
August: Bolívar leaves Guayaquil en route to Peru.

1824   February-January (1826): The siege of Callao occurs.
April: The Loan of 1824 is negotiated in Europe.
June: The Battle of Barbacoas occurs.
July: The Law of Ecclesiastical Patronage is adopted.
August: The Battle of Junín occurs.
October: Colombia and the United States sign their first formal agreement (the Gual-Anderson Treaty).
December: The Battle of Ayacucho occurs.

1825   The only census ever of Gran Colombia is taken.
The Gual (Colombia)–Molina (Central America) and the Gual-Torrens (Mexico) treaties are signed.
Great Britain recognizes Colombian independence by the Gual-Campbell Treaty.
The Bible Society is established in Bogotá.
The Infante Affair is concluded.
Antonio Leocadio Guzmán travels from Venezuela to Peru to persuade Bolívar to assume command of the nation.

1825-1826   Colombia and Mexico plan an expedition to Cuba.

1825-1830   El Parnasillo meets in Bogotá.

1826　March: The Plan of Studies, the first major educational program for Colombia, is adopted; the National Academy is organized.

April: General José Antonio Páez, refusing to obey orders in Venezuela, rebels against the government in Bogotá.

June-July: The Congress of Panama meets.

August-September: Movements in Guayaquil and Quito proclaim Bolívar dictator.

September-November: Bolívar journeys from Peru to Bogotá.

November: Bolívar leaves Bogotá to settle affairs in Venezuela.

1827　Fernando Caycedo y Flórez, Archbishop of Bogotá.

The University of Cartagena and the Central University of the Cauca (Popayán) are founded.

January: Bolívar and Páez meet in Venezuela; Páez is pardoned and reinstated.

April: Formal rupture occurs in relations betweeen Bolívar and Santander.

September: Bolívar returns to Bogotá and becomes President of Colombia.

1828　February: Bolívar assumes extraordinary powers.

April-June: The Congress of Ocaña meets.

June: General Pedro A. Herrán and a Junta of Notables proclaim Bolívar dictator in Bogotá.

July-March, 1829: Peru wages war against Colombia.

September: Opponents attempt to assassinate Bolívar. Numerous persons are sent into exile, and some executed, as a result.

October: Colonels José María Obando and José Hilario López begin rebellion against Bolívar's dictatorship in the Cauca.

November: The Battle of La Ladera gives Obando and López control of Popayán.

December: Bolívar leaves Bogotá to fight war with Peru in the south.

1829　January: Bolívar issues pardon for rebels in the Cauca and tries to negotiate a settlement with Obando and López and the Gual (Colombia)–Larrea (Peru) Treaty is signed.

February: The Battle of Tarqui occurs.

March: Obando and López conclude the Armistice of Juanambú with Bolívar.

September: Colombia and Peru end their war with a treaty.

In Bogotá a Junta of Notables authorizes negotiations to establish a monarchy in Colombia.

September-October: General José María Córdoba leads an abortive revolt in Antioquia.

December: Venezuelan Congress begins separatist movement.

1830   January: Bolívar returns from Ecuador and installs the Admirable Congress (Congreso Admirable). Venezuela declares its intention to become independent.

March: Bolívar resigns and plans voluntary exile. Domingo Caycedo, Vice-President of Colombia, becomes acting chief executive.

April: The Constitution of 1830 is adopted. Joaquín Mosquera becomes President of Colombia.

May: Bolívar leaves Bogotá en route to the coast following the election of Joaquín Mosquera. Ecuador establishes its independence. General Juan José Flores, in the name of Ecuador, accepts the annexation of Pasto and Buenaventura provinces, May-June.

June: General Antonio José de Sucre is assassinated. Generals Obando and López later ask to be tried for the murder and are acquitted.

August: Army units under General Rafael Urdaneta rebel. The Battle of Santuario occurs. Ecuador proclaims its own constitution. Buenaventura joins Ecuador. The Mosquera (Colombia)–Pedemonte (Peru) Treaty is signed.

September: Urdaneta proclaims a dictatorship in the name of Bolívar. The Mosquera government collapses. Venezuela proclaims its own constitution. Rafael Urdaneta becomes Dictator of Colombia.

November: In the Cauca, Generals Obando and López rebel against the dictatorship.

December: Popayán, led by Obando and López, joins Ecuador in protest against the dictatorship of Urdaneta. Bolívar dies in Santa Marta.

1831   February: Obando and López defeat the representatives of the Urdaneta regime at the Battle of Palmira. Soledad (Atlántico) and Barranquilla rebel against the dictatorship.

March: Colonel Salvador Córdoba rebels against Urdaneta. General Joaquín Posada Gutiérrez withdraws support for the dictator.

April 14: Domingo Caycedo, Vice President of Colombia, establishes a rival government in Purificación.

April: Urdaneta and Caycedo negotiate an armistice for return to legitimate authority at the Juntas de Apulo (Cundinamarca).

May: Caycedo assumes control of the government in Bogotá.

October-April 1832. A constituent congress draws up a new constitution.

November: José María Obando, Vice President of Colombia and acting chief executive, assumes office.

1832   January: The Cauca secedes from Ecuador and rejoins Colombia.

February: The Constitution of 1832 establishing the Republic of New Granada is adopted.

March: José Ignacio de Márquez, Vice President of New Granada, acting chief executive, is installed.

October: Francisco de Paula Santander, President of New Granada, takes office.

December: Obando–Posada Gutiérrez (Colombia)–Arteta (Ecuador) Treaty is signed.

1833   The National Academy is reorganized.

The Conspiracy of General José Sardá is exposed.

The Pombo-Michelena Treaties with Venezuela are signed.

1833-1834   The Barrot Affair occurs.

1834   Manuela Saénz is expelled from Bogotá.

Juan B. Elbers is given a new concession to introduce steam navigation on New Granada's rivers.

The first census of New Granada is taken.

The National Emblem is adopted.

1835   Manuel José Mosquera, Archbishop of Bogotá.

The Papacy recognizes New Granada's independence.

Charles de Thierry is granted a concession for a transisthmian canal.

1836-1837   The Russell Affair occurs.

1837   José Ignacio de Márquez, President of New Granada.

The first Papal Nuncio is received in Bogotá.

1838   Ignacio Morales forms an ultra-conservative Catholic Society to influence political action.

The *aguardiente* monopoly is abolished.

1839   An act suppressing minor convents provokes rebellion in Pasto.

The Battle of Buesaco occurs.

1840   A revolt headed by General Obando in the Cauca initiates the Guerra de los Supremos, 1840-1842.

Battles occur at La Polonia, Huilquipamba, and Buenavista.

President Márquez appeals to Ecuador for help.

Generals Herrán and Mosquera negotiate a pact of assistance with Ecuadoran President Juan José Flores.

Villavicencio is founded.

1840-1841   General Flores occupies parts of the Cauca under a pact of assistance, then announces the annexation of Pasto to Ecuador.

1841   Pedro Alcántara Herrán, President of New Granada.
Battles occur at Aratoca, Itagüi, Tescua, Riofrío, Ocaña, Salamina, and La Chanca.
General Mosquera orders executions in Cartago.

1842   Rebellion ends.
A new Plan of Studies is adopted.
Bolívar's remains are transferred to Venezuela.
The Pombo (New Granada)–Romero (Venezuela) Treaty is signed.

1843   The Constitution of 1843 is adopted.

1844   The Jesuits return to New Granada.
The Mosquera (New Granada)–Irarrazábal (Chile) Treaty is signed.

1845   Tomás C. de Mosquera, President of New Granada.
The *Recopilación Granadina* is published.

1846   The Mallarino (New Granada)–Bidlack (United States) Treaty is signed.
President Mosquera issues a plan for a national highway system.

1847   The Artisans' Society (Sociedad de Artesanos) is formed.
New Granada introduces free trade.

1849   José Hilario López, President of New Granada.
The Conservative Party is formed.
A cholera epidemic strikes New Granada.
Manizales is founded.
Democratic Societies (Sociedades Democráticas) and Popular Societies (Sociedades Populares) are created.

1850   The Jesuits are expelled.
The tobacco monopoly is abolished.
The Law of the Freedom of Studies is adopted.
The Chorographic Commission is established.
The Republican School (Escuela Republicana) and the Philotemic Society (Sociedad Filotémica) are organized.
Construction begins on the Panama Railroad.
The Clayton-Bulwer Treaty is signed.

1851   The ecclesiastical *fuero* is abolished and clerical appointments are given to local town councils.
The Rebellion of 1851-1852 begins. Battles occur at Buesaco, Gachetá, Garrapata, and Rionegro.

1852   Archbishop Mosquera is expelled from New Granada.
Slavery is abolished.
Girardot is founded.

1853   José María Obando, President of New Granada.
The Constitution of 1853 is adopted, including separation of Church and State.
Civil marriage is legalized.
Lleras (New Granada)–Lisboa (Brazil) Treaty and Lleras–Paz Soldán (Peru) Treaty are signed.
The permanent army is dissolved.

1854   The Rebellion of 1854 occurs. Major battles take place at Palmira, Pamplona, Zipaquirá, Tíquisa, Bosa Bridge, and Bogotá.
General José María Melo proclaims himself dictator of New Granada, April-December.
Tomás Herrera, acting President, and then José de Obaldía, Vice President of New Granada, acting chief executive, oppose dictatorship.

1855   The Ancízar (New Granada)–Sánchez (Peru) Treaty is signed.
Manuel Mallarino, Vice President of New Granada, is acting chief executive.
Antonio Herrán, Archbishop of Bogotá.
The Watermelon Riot occurs in Panama.

1856   The Pombo (New Granada)–Gómez de la Torre (Ecuador) Treaty is signed.
Presbyterians found the first permanent Protestant Church in New Granada.

1857   Mariano Ospina Rodríguez, President of New Granada.
The United States and New Granada negotiate a settlement (Herrán-Cass Treaty) for damages resulting from the Watermelon Riot.

1858   The Constitution of 1858 is adopted establishing the Granadine Confederation.
The Malmesbury (Great Britain)–De Francisco (New Granada) Treaty settles the Mackintosh claims.
El Mosaico begins publication.
The Pardo (New Granada)–Galvéz (Peru) Treaty is signed.

1859   The Ospina administration passes a controversial election law.
The Rebellion of 1859-1862 begins. Battles occur at La Concepción and Corozal.
Modern postal service begins.

1860   Generals Herrán and Juan José Nieto sign the Accords of 1860.

Battles occur at El Derrumbado, Manizales, Oratorio, Segovia, and Bogotá.

Generals Mosquera and Nieto sign the Pact of 1860.

1861   Bartolomé Calvo, acting President of New Granada, April–July.

Tomás C. de Mosquera, provisional President of New Granada.

Battles occur at Los Arboles, Hormezaque, Tunja, Subachoque, and Bogotá.

Mosquera orders execution of three Conservative prisoners.

The Pact of Union is signed.

The Jesuits are expelled and some religious communities closed; government permission is required for clergymen to exercise ecclesiastical functions; church property is confiscated.

Bogotá is declared a national federal district (the Distrito Especial de Bogotá), separate from the State of Cundinamarca—the Distrito Especial de Bogotá—for the first time.

Agua de Dios is formally established; soon becomes a leprosy refuge.

1862   Battles occur at San Agustín in Bogotá, Santa Bárbara de Cartago, and Tulcán.

1863   Tomás C. de Mosquera, President of the United States of Colombia.

The Convention of Rionegro adopts the Constitution of 1863 creating the United States of Colombia.

The Ecuadoran Army under General Juan José Flores invades Colombia. General Mosquera defeats the Ecuadorans at the Battle of Cuaspud. Ecuador and Colombia sign the Treaty of Pinzaquí.

The Law Concerning the Inspection of Cults is adopted.

Pereira is founded.

1864   Manuel Murillo Toro, President of Colombia.

1865   The Bank of London, Mexico, and South America opens a branch in Bogotá.

The annexation of Costa Rica is proposed by the Valenzuela-Castro Treaty.

Electric telegraph is introduced in Colombia.

1866   Tomás C. de Mosquera, President of Colombia.

The Mosquera (Colombia)–Clarendon (Great Britian) Treaty is signed, and the Mosquera-Freyre Treaty forms a secret alliance with Peru.

The first attempt to produce petroleum is made near Barranquilla.

1867   The *Rayo* Affair exposes secret diplomacy.
        The Conspiracy of May 23 deposes Mosquera.
        Santos Acosta, acting President of Colombia.
        The National University (Universidad Nacional) is established.
        Leticia is founded with the name San Antonio.

1868   Santos Gutiérrez, President of Colombia.
        Vicente Arbeláez, Archbishop of Bogotá.

1869   The Electoral League tries to influence the presidential elections.
        The Bolívar Railroad is begun.

1870   Eustorgio Salgar, President of Colombia.
        The Bank of Bogotá is founded.
        Colombia signs treaties with Peru.
        The Salgar administration begins a major program to develop public education.

1871   The Colombian Academy of Language (Academia Colombiana de la Lengua) is founded in Bogotá.
        The Colombian Society of Agriculturalists (Sociedad de Agricultores) is organized.

1872   Manuel Murillo Toro, President of Colombia.
        A contract is granted for construction of a railroad from Buenaventura to Cali.

1873   The Pérez (Colombia)–O'Leary (Great Britain) Convention is signed.
        The National Academy of Medicine is founded.
        The Correoso (Colombia)–Montúfar (Costa Rica) Treaty is signed.

1874   Santiago Pérez, President of Colombia.
        The Bank of Colombia (Banco de Colombia) is founded.
        Legislation regarding land ownership is passed.

1875   The Compañía Colombiana de Seguros is founded.
        Francisco J. Cisneros begins the Antioquia Railroad.
        Estér is performed in Bogotá.

1876   Aquileo Parra, President of Colombia.
        The Ancízar (Colombia)–Arbeláez (Papacy) Pact is signed.
        The Rebellion of 1876-1877 begins. Battles occur at Los Chancos and Garrapata.

1877   Battles occur at La Donjuana and Manizales.

1878   Julián Trujillo, President of Colombia.
        The Pacific Railroad is begun.

1879   The Compagnie Universelle, or French Panama Canal Company, is formed.

1880   Rafael Núñez, President of Colombia.
        Núñez introduces protective tariffs.
        Chile and Colombia sign goodwill treaty.
        A projected international Congress of Panama is canceled for lack of response.
        The Camargo (Colombia)–Nina (Papacy) Pact is signed.
        Costa Rica signs boundary agreement with Colombia.

1881   The National Bank (Banco Nacional) is established.
        Spain recognizes the independence of Colombia by formal treaty.
        The Arosemena (Colombia)–Guzmán (Venezuela) Treaty is signed.
        Francisco J. Cisneros begins construction of Girardot Railroad.
        The Northern Railroad is begun.

1882   Francisco Javier Zaldúa, President of Colombia.
        José Eusebio Otálora, Vice President of Colombia, acting chief executive.
        The Magdalena Railroad is begun.
        The National Academy of Music (Academia Nacional de Música) is founded.
        General Solón Wilches founds Puerto Wilches.

1883   Banana cultivation is begun around Santa Marta.

1884   Rafael Núñez, President of Colombia.
        The Camargo (Colombia)–Espinosa (Ecuador) Treaty is signed.
        Conservatives hold a strategy conference at Macaregua.
        The Rebellion of 1884-1885 begins.

1885   José Telésforo Paúl y Vergara, Archbishop of Bogotá.
        Battles occur at Barranquilla, Cartagena, Cogotes, Colón, La Humareda, Jericó, Neiva, Roldanillo, Salado, Salamina, Santa Bárbara de Cartago, and Sonso.

1885-1899   The Cerruti Affair complicates relations with Italy.

1885-1905   Colombia suffers a currency crisis resulting from an excess of paper money.

1886   The Constitution of 1886 is adopted. The Departments of Antioquia, Bolívar, Boyacá, Cauca, Cundinamarca, Magdalena, Panama, Santander, and Tolima are created.

1887   Rafael Núñez, President of Colombia.
        Eliseo Payán, Vice President of Colombia, acting chief executive.

A concordat is signed with the Papacy.
The Colombian Society of Engineers (Sociedad Colombiana de Ingenieros) is founded.

1888   The Law of the Horses is adopted.
The Cúcuta Railroad is completed.

1889   Armenia is founded.
The Panama Electric Light Company begins operation.

1889-1894   The so-called clandestine emissions of bank notes are put into circulation.
The first part of the Cundinamarca Railroad is completed.

1890   The Bogotá Electric Light Company begins operation.

1891   Bernardo Herrera Restrepo, Archbishop of Bogotá.
The Bavaria Brewing Company is founded in Bogotá.
French advisers help create a modern police force.

1892   Rafael Núñez, President of Colombia.
Miguel Antonio Caro, Vice President of Colombia, acting chief executive.
The Caro administration harasses newspaper publishers.
An additional concordat is concluded with the Papacy.
The Teatro Colón is formally inaugurated.

1894   A Congressional investigation exposes the clandestine emissions and controversial operations of the National Bank.
The Colombian Academy of Jurisprudence is founded.
The Calamar Railroad opens.

1895   The Rebellion of 1895 occurs. Battles take place at La Tribuna and Enciso.
Roldán-Passmore Renegotiation attempts foreign debt settlement.

1896   The Twenty-one publish the *Motives for Dissidence.*
The United Fruit Company begins cultivation of bananas around Santa Marta.
Energía Eléctrica de Bogotá is established.

1896-1900   Crisis in coffee market occurs.

1897   La Dorada Railroad is begun.

1898   Manuel Antonio Sanclemente, President of Colombia.
José Manuel Marroquín, Vice President of Colombia, acting chief executive.

1899   Historical Conservatives issue *Acuerdo No. 3.*
The War of the Thousand Days begins. A major battle occurs at Peralonso.

1900   The Movement of July 31 deposes President Sanclemente.
        José Manuel Marroquín, Vice President, chief executive.
        La Gruta Simbólica is formed.
        The Battle of Palonegro occurs.
        Energía Eléctrica de Bogotá begins operation.
        Antonio Acosta and others found La Dorada.

1901   The Abadía Méndez (Colombia)–Herboso (Chile) Treaty is
        signed.

1902   The Colombian Academy of History (Academia Colombi-
        ana de Historia) is formed.
        The Treaties of the *Wisconsin,* Nerlandia, and Chinácota are
        signed.

1903   The so-called law of the poor ones reestablishes the gold
        standard in an effort to end the paper money crisis,
        1885-1905.
        The Herrán (Colombia)–Hay (United States) Treaty is
        rejected by Colombia.
        Panama declares its independence.

1904   Rafael Reyes, President-Dictator of Colombia.
        The *Quinquenio* begins.
        The Department of Nariño is created.

1905   Reyes creates the National Assembly to govern in place of
        Congress.
        The law granting representation to political minorities is
        adopted.
        The Conspiracy of December 19 is exposed.
        The Holguín-Avebury Convention settles debts with Great
        Britain.
        The Germania Brewing Company is founded.
        The Barco and De Mares oil concessions are granted.
        The Departments of Atlántico, Caldas, and Huila are cre-
        ated.

1905-1909 The Banco Central regulates government finances.

1906   An attempt to assassinate General Reyes fails.

1906-1911 Treaties of 1906, 1909, and 1911 deal with the Putumayo
        dispute with Peru.

1907   Colombia attends the Second International Conference at
        The Hague.
        The Vásquez Cobo (Colombia)–Martins Treaties are con-
        cluded with Brazil.
        COLTEJER is founded.

1908   Florencia is founded by Capuchin missionaries.

1909   General Reyes resigns.
Jorge Holguín, Presidential Designate, acting chief executive.
Ramón González Valencia, Vice President, acting chief executive.
The Root (United States)–Cortés (Colombia)–Arosemena (Panama) Agreements are signed, but fail to resolve issues over Panama.

1910   Carlos Eugenio Restrepo, President of Colombia.
The National Constituent and Legislative Assembly (Asamblea Nacional Constituyente y Legislativa) restores legal government following the resignation of Reyes.
The Departments of Norte de Santander and Valle del Cauca are established.

1911   The Círculo de Obreros labor union is formed.
The Battle of La Pedrera occurs.

1912   The Intendancy of San Andrés y Providencia is created.

1913   The Uribe Cordovez (Colombia)–Dillon (Ecuador) claims settlement is signed.
The first Eucharistic Congress is held in Bogotá.

1914   José Vicente Concha, President of Colombia.

1914-1918   Colombia declares neutrality in World War I.

1914-1921   The United States recognizes Panama and, by the Urrutia-Thompson Treaty, agrees to pay Colombia for the loss of Panama.

1916   Suárez–Losada Díaz (Venezuela) and Suárez–Muñoz Vernaza (Ecuador) boundary treaties are signed.

1918   Marco Fidel Suárez, President of Colombia.
The first income tax is levied in Colombia.

1919   Colombia joins the League of Nations.
The first airmail flight is made in Colombia—Barranquilla to Puerto Colombia; SCADTA is formed.
Vicente Andamo founds socialist settlement at Lomagrande.
Law 120 asserts Colombia's subsoil rights.

1920   The National Hymn is adopted.
The first commercial airflight is made from Barranquilla to Girardot.
FABRICATO is founded.

1920-1930   The Colombian Communist Party is organized.

1921   Jorge Holguín, Presidential Designate, acting chief executive.
The Northeastern Railroad is begun.

Commercial production of oil begins at Barrancabermeja.
The Unión Sindicato Obrera is formed.

1922   Pedro Nel Ospina, President of Colombia.
Lozano (Colombia)–Salomón (Peru) Treaty resolves the Putumayo dispute.
The Fuerza Aérea (Colombian Air Force) is established.

1923   The Kemmerer mission studies Colombian economic needs.
The Bank of the Republic is founded.
The Arroyo Díez–Vincentini Incident occurs.

1924   The Caja de Crédito Agrario (Banco Agrícola Hipotecario) is established.
A treaty with Panama settles boundary problems.

1926   Miguel Abadía Méndez, President of Colombia.
Oil exports begin.
Supreme Court issues major decision on land titles.
The Revolutionary Socialist Party (Partido Socialista Revolucionario) is formed.
The Sindicato Obrero (petroleum worker's union) is established.

1927   The National Federation of Coffee Growers (Federación Nacional de Cafeteros) is organized. An emergency tariff law reduces prices on imported food.
The Caldas Railroad is completed.
Laborers strike against Tropical Oil Company.

1927-1928   The Abadía Méndez government passes stringent internal security (antisubversion) laws.

1928   Ismael Perdomo, Archbishop of Bogotá.
Brazil and Nicaragua sign treaties with Colombia concerning boundaries and possessions.
United Fruit Company strike produces violence.
Decree 150 attempts to control foreign ownership of mineral rights.

1929-1935   Colombia and others mediate the Chaco War.

1929   Public protests force resignation of high conservative officials, including the Ministers of War and Public Works.
Public radio broadcasting begins.

1930   Enrique Olaya Herrera, President of Colombia.
The Colombian Communist Party (Partido Comunista de Colombia) is formally established.

1931   The second Kemmerer mission studies Colombia.
The Commissariat of Amazonas is created.

1932   The Banco Central Hipotecario is founded.
The American Doctrine is enunciated.

1932-1934   The Leticia Dispute occurs with Peru.

1933   The Battle of Güepi occurs.
Commercial treaty with the United States is signed (but never ratified).

1934   Alfonso López Pumarejo, President of Colombia.
A treaty with Peru settles the Leticia question.
Tejicondor is founded.

1935   The Instituto Geográfico Agustín Codazzi is created.
The Employers National Economic Association (APEN) is established.
Yopal is founded.

1936   The Codification of 1936 is adopted.
Maritime facilities are completed at the Bocas de Ceniza.
The Colombian Academy of Natural Sciences (Academia Colombiana de Ciencias Exactas, Físicas, y Naturales) is founded.
Law 200 provides for an agrarian reform.
Miguel Cuervo Araoz founds Mitú.

1938   Eduardo Santos, President of Colombia.
The first national labor union, the Confederación de Trabajadores de Colombia, is organized.

1939   Colombia declares neutrality at outbreak of World War II.

1940   Colombia signs the Interamerican Coffee Agreement.
Instituto de Fomento Industrial (IFI) is created, and AVIANCA becomes the national airline.

1941   López de Mesa (Colombia)–Gil Borges (Venezuela) Treaty is signed.

1942   Alfonso López Pumarejo, President of Colombia.
A concordat with the Papacy is concluded.
The Instituto Caro y Cuervo is founded.

1943   The Mamatoco Incident occurs.
The Commissariat of Vichada is created.

1944   An attempted coup d'état in Pasto fails.
The Asociación Nacional de Industriales (ANDI) and the Compañía Nacional de Navegación (NAVENAL) are founded.

1945   Alberto Lleras Camargo, interim President.
The National Museum (Museo Nacional), the Colombian Institute of Anthropology (Instituto Colombiano de

Antropología), the Instituto de Mercado Agropecuario (IDEMA), and the Confederación de Trabajadores de Colombia Independiente are founded.

Administration of the emerald monopoly is given to the Banco de la República.

Colombia joins the United Nations.

1946   Mariano Ospina Pérez, President of Colombia.

The National Federation of Businessmen (FENALCO), the Instituto Colombiano de Seguros Sociales (I.C.S.S.), the Instituto Colombiano de Energía Eléctrica (ICEL), the Unión de Trabajadores Colombianos, and the Flota Mercante Grancolombiana are founded.

1947   Acción Cultural Popular begins in Sutatenza.

The Department of Chocó and the Commissariat of Vichada are created.

1948   Jorge E. Gaitán leads demonstration and delivers "Oration for Peace" (February 7).

The Ninth International Conference of American States meets in Bogotá.

Colombia joins the Organization of American States.

The assassination of Gaitán touches off the *Bogotazo;* some say *La Violencia* begins.

1948-1959   The so-called Protestant Persecution takes place.

1948-1966   *La Violencia* causes death and destruction in Colombia.

1949   President Ospina Pérez closes Congress to avoid impeachment.

1949-1953   Guerrilla violence is concentrated in the Llanos Orientales.

1950   Laureano Gómez, President of Colombia.

Crisanto Luque Sánchez, Archbishop of Bogotá.

The Colombian Institute for Foreign Study, ICETEX, is created.

The Banco Popular is founded.

Lauchlin Currie leads a World Bank mission to study Colombian economic problems.

1951   The Asociación Colombiana Popular de Industriales (ACOPI), the Colombian petroleum agency (ECOPETROL), and the Instituto Colombiano de Cultura Hispánica are established.

The Department of Córdoba is established.

1952   Gómez convenes the National Constituent Assembly to revise the constitution.

First Guerrilla Conference tries to articulate guerrilla demands.

Offices of *El Tiempo* and *El Espectador* are burned in Bogotá.

1953   The Echevarría Plot precipitates a coup d'état.

Gustavo Rojas Pinilla, Dictator of Colombia.

The Instituto Colombiano Agropecuario (ICA) is founded.

The Confederación Nacional de Trabajadores is formed to mobilize labor support for the government.

Archbishop Crisanto Luque Sánchez is appointed the first cardinal from Colombia.

National Revolutionary Congress at La Perdida on the River Túa in June tries to unite guerrilla movements.

General Duarte Blum receives surrender of guerrillas at Monterrey (September 15).

1953-1954   Various amnesty decrees seek to end guerrilla violence completely.

1954   SENDAS, the National Secretariat of Social Assistance, is organized.

The Banco Cafetero is established.

The modern Distrito Especial de Bogotá is established.

Center of guerrilla protests shifts to the Tolima area.

Television broadcasting begins in Colombia.

1955   Marquetalia is founded by Jacobo Prías Alape and others.

The Instituto de Investigaciones Tecnológicas is established.

The C.V.C. (Corporación Autónoma Regional del Cauca) is founded.

Steel production begins at Paz del Río.

The Intendancy of Arauca is established.

1955-1957   The Gran Central Obrera tries to organize labor support for the government.

1956   The Bullring Massacre occurs in Bogotá.

The Pact of Benidorm is signed.

1957   Military Junta governs Colombia.

The Declaration of Sitges and a national referendum lead to the formation of the National Front (Frente Nacional).

The National Service of Apprenticeship (SENA) is established.

1958   Alberto Lleras Camargo, President of Colombia.

The Atlantic Railroad is begun.

The Division of Indian Affairs (Asuntos Indígenas) is created.

Barranquilla is made a free-trade zone.

Cultivation of African palm begins at COLDESA.

Acción Comunal is founded, and Father García Herreros begins the Minute of God program.

1959 Luis Concha Córdoba, Archbishop of Bogotá.

The National Association of Sugar Growers (ASOCAÑA) is formed.

The Department of Meta is created.

1960 The Alianza Nacional Popular (ANAPO) is organized by supporters of General Gustavo Rojas Pinilla.

The Corporación Autónoma Regional de los Valles del Magdalena y del Sinú (C.V.M.) is established.

Colombia joins the Latin American Free Trade Association.

The Movimiento de Obreros, Estudiantes, y Campesinos (MOEC) is founded.

1961 The Instituto Colombiano de la Reforma Agraria (IN-CORA) and the Instituto de Recursos Naturales Renovables (INDERENA) are established.

1962 Guillermo León Valencia, President of Colombia.

Colombia joins the International Coffee Agreement.

1963 The Commissariats of Guainía and Vaupés are created.

1964 Colombia joins the Group of 77.

Marquetalia is captured by the government.

The Ejército de Liberación Nacional (E.L.N.) and the Confederación Sindical de Trabajadores de Colombia are formed.

Democracia Cristiana (the Christian Democratic Party) is established.

The Department of Guajira is established.

1964-1966 Tolima-based guerrillas form the Bloque del Sur.

1965 Father Camilo Torres tries to organize the United Front for reform.

1966 Carlos Lleras Restrepo, President of Colombia.

Camilo Torres is killed fighting with the E.L.N.

The Fuerzas Armadas Revolucionarias de Colombia (FARC) is formed.

The Asociación Colombiana de Promoción Artesanal and CAR (the Corporación Autónoma Regional de la Sabana de Bogotá) are established.

The Departments of Quindío, Risaralda, and Sucre are created.

1967 Ejército Popular de Liberación (E.P.L.) begins operations.

ACPA (Asociación Colombiana de Promoción Artesanal) is created.

1968   Pope Paul VI visits the XXXIX International Eucharistic
        Conference in Bogotá.
        The Golconda Declaration is issued.
        Labor leader José Raquel Mercado is kidnapped.
        The Instituto Colombiano de Bienestar Familiar is created.
        COLCIENCIAS (Colombian Fund for Scientific Research)
        is established.
        The Intendancy of Putumayo is created.
        The Andean Pact is signed in Bogotá.
        A trans-Andean pipeline begins moving petroleum from
        Orito (Putumayo) to Tumaco (Nariño).
        Constitutional reforms are adopted.

1970   Misael Pastrana Borrero, President of Colombia.
        ANAPO supporters claim presidential election fraud.
        An international satellite communications center is opened
        at Chocontá (Cundinamarca).

1973   A concordat is signed with the Papacy.
        The Battle of Anorí occurs.
        The M-19 (Movimiento Diecinueve de Abril) is formed.

1974   Alfonso López Michelsen, President of Colombia. Autode-
        fensa Obrera (ADO) is formed.
        M-19 steals the Liberator's Sword from the Quinta de
        Bolívar.
        María Eugenia Rojas, candidate for the Alianza Nacional
        Popular (ANAPO), becomes the first woman to run
        for the Presidency.

1975   Aníbal Muñoz Duque, Archbishop of Bogotá.
        The Intendancy of Casanare is established.
        Execution of José Rafael Mercado occurs.

1977   The General Strike (Paro Cívico) of September 17 occurs.
        The Commissariat of Guaviare is created.

1978   Gabriel Turbay Ayala, President of Colombia.
        The Security Statute is passed.
        Death of Rafael Pardo Buelvas occurs.

1978-1979 M-19 steals weapons from the Cantón del Norte arsenal.

1979   U.S.-Colombian extradition treaty for drug dealers begins.

1980   M-19 seizes the embassy of the Dominican Republic.

1981   Law 37 provides a limited amnesty for guerrillas.
        President Turbay appoints a Peace Commission.
        M-19 guerrillas attack the presidential palace, launch invasion
        of Nariño, and allegedly kidnap Chester Bitterman.
        Muerte a Secuestradores is formed by drug dealers to stop
        kidnappings.

1982   President Turbay proclaims limited amnesty, lifts state of
        siege (martial law).
        Belisario Betancur, President of Colombia.
        Law 35 (November 19) establishes amnesty for guerrillas.
        Nickel mining begins at Carromatoso.
        Jaime Bentancur is kidnapped by the E.L.N.
        The Department of Caquetá is created.
        United States–Colombia extradition agreements renewed.
        Unida Democrática de la Izquierda organized to unite
        reform groups.

1983   President Bentancur meets with guerrilla leaders in Spain.
        The Ricardo Franco Front (guerrilla group) is formed.
        Colombia joins the Non-Aligned Nations and the Conta-
        dora group.

1984   Pedro Revollo Bravo, Archbishop of Bogotá.
        M-19 launches military actions at Florencia, Corinto, Mi-
        randa, and Yumbo.
        Truce agreements signed at La Uribe between the FARC
        and the government.
        Minister of Justice Rodrigo Lara Bonilla is assassinated;
        government declares war on drug dealers.
        Authorities raid massive narcotics-processing center at Yarí
        (Caquetá).
        Drug dealers try to negotiate government amnesty.
        Coal production begins at El Cerrejón.

1985   Volcano Nevado del Ruiz erupts, destroying the city of
        Armero.
        M-19 battles army at Yarumales.
        Guerrillas issue joint declaration protesting failure to imple-
        ment reforms.
        Formation of the Unión Patriótica announced by FARC and
        other factions.
        Comando Quintín Lame begins operations.
        M-19 seizes the Palace of Justice in Bogotá.

1986   Virgilio Barco, President of Colombia.
        Pope John Paul II visits Colombia.
        M-19 signs new peace agreement.
        Guerrillas call conference to discuss social issues at Los
        Robles.
        The Central Unitaria de Trabajadores is formed.

1986-1987   Court rulings declare extradition treaty with the United
             States illegal.

1987   Coordinadora Guerrilla "Simón Bolívar" tries to unite
        guerrilla groups.

1989-1990   Luis Carlos Galán and several other presidential candidates
                    are assassinated.
             Court ruling reinstates U.S. extradition treaty.
             Drug dealers try to negotiate government amnesty.

1989   International Coffee Agreement expires.
             MORENA (Movimiento de Restauración Nacional) is or-
                    ganized.

1990   César Gaviria Trujillo, President of Colombia.
             Government tries to suppress or to negotiate surrender
                    with guerrillas and drug dealers.
             M-19 surrenders arms to political authorities; Alianza De-
                    mocrática M-19 achieves success in elections for a
                    constituent assembly.

1991   Asamblea Constituyente writes new constitution.
             Constitution of 1991 is adopted.
             Pablo Escobar and other prominent drug dealers negotiate
                    surrender with government.
             Congress is dissolved; elections are held for new legislators
                    to be inaugurated in 1992.

HISTORICAL DICTIONARY OF COLOMBIA

-A-

A.C.P., see: ACCION CULTURAL POPULAR

A.L.A.L.C., see: LATIN AMERICAN FREE TRADE ASSOCIATION

A.N.P., see: ACCION NACIONALISTA POPULAR

ABADIA MENDEZ, Miguel, 1867-1947. Born Piedras (*Tolima), June 5; died La Unión (*Cundinamarca), May 15. Lawyer, author, educator, editor/journalist, *Conservative politician, President of Colombia, 1926-1930. He received his doctorate in jurisprudence and political science from the *Colegio Mayor de Nuestra Señora del Rosario in 1888, and he practiced and taught law. He held numerous local and national political offices including Minister of Public Instruction, 1900 and 1919; Minister of Government, 1909, 1914-1918, and 1924-1925; member of the *Supreme Court; member of the *Council of State; and Extraordinary Envoy to Chile in 1902. A member of the Historical Conservatives (*Históricos), as President he tried unsuccessfully to form a bipartisan cabinet. During the so-called *dance of the millions, his administration initiated public works, and stimulated industry and transportation. His administration dealt with the *Tropical Oil Strike of 1927 and the *United Fruit Company Strike of 1928 and confronted the initial stages of the Depression of 1929. In addition, his administration encouraged missionary work among the *Indians, negotiated boundary problems with Brazil, Nicaragua, and the United States (see: BORDERS), and enacted repressive national security laws to cope with alleged threats to internal stability (see: LIBERTICIDA; ROSCA, Fall of the Conservative).

ABADIA MENDEZ–HERBOSO TREATY. Signed on September 29, 1901, by Miguel *Abadía Méndez, Colombia, and Francisco J. Herboso, Chile. It was a secret agreement whereby Chile offered to aid the incumbent Colombian administration against its opponents in the War of the *Thousand Days and to assist Colombia in detaching Ecuador from an alliance with Venezuela in exchange for Colombian support against Peru in the Tacna-Arica dispute (see: PACIFIC, War of the). By subsequent agreement, October 17, 1902, Colombia paid an indemnity of £60,000 for the destruction of the warship *Lautaro,* which had been loaned by Chile in fulfillment of the treaty terms.

ABIBE, Sierra de. A name used in the conquest period to designate the northern extremity of the *Cordillera Occidental. Named after an Indian chief, it was discovered in 1537 by Francisco *César and now forms the boundary between the Departments of *Antioquia and *Cordoba.

ABRA, El. Archeological site near *Zipaquirá (Cundinamarca) often cited as the oldest recorded location for human habitation in Colombia. By carbon 14 dating, El Abra was inhabited as early as 12,400 years ago (ca. 10,450 B.C.) though probably no earlier than 30,000 years ago. Although there were no human remains located in the excavations carried out by Gonzalo Correal and J. W. Hurt, stone implements (percussion-point cutting tools and scrapers) and climatic analysis indicate two phases of occupation: 18,000 to 10,000 years ago and 10,000 years ago to the *Chibcha era. See also: STONE AGE SETTLEMENTS

ACADEMIA COLOMBIANA DE CIENCIAS EXACTAS, FISICAS Y NATURALES. The Colombian Academy of Natural Sciences, founded by José Joaquín *Casas. It was declared an official government entity in 1936 and is located in the old National Observatory (*Observatorio Nacional).

ACADEMIA COLOMBIANA DE HISTORIA. The Colombian Academy of History, established by decree of Minister of Public Instruction José Joaqúin *Casas in 1902. It was directed in its early years by Eduardo Posada, its first president, and

Pedro María Ibañez, its first secretary. The academy has forty permanent members and numerous Colombian and foreign corresponding members. It has published the *Boletín de Historia y Antigüedades* since 1902.

ACADEMIA COLOMBIANA DE JURISPRUDENCIA. Legal academy, founded September 23, 1894, with fifty permanent members and numerous corresponding members.

ACADEMIA COLOMBIANA DE LA LENGUA. The Colombian Academy of Language, founded in 1871 by José María *Vergara y Vergara by commission from the Spanish Royal Academy of Language. The first such body established in Spanish America, it has twenty-eight official members and numerous corresponding members.

ACADEMIA NACIONAL. First established in 1826, it was a national organization designed to foster literary and scientific studies in Colombia. It was reorganized in 1833, but never fully activated.

ACADEMIA NACIONAL DE MEDICINA. National Academy of Medicine, founded January 3, 1873. It was recognized as an official consultative organ of the government in 1890.

ACADEMIA NACIONAL DE MUSICA. The National Academy of Music, founded in 1882. It became the Conservatorio Nacional de Música in 1912 and is now part of the *Universidad Nacional de Colombia.

ACADEMIE DES SCIENCES (PARIS), EXPEDITION TO SOUTH AMERICA, see: SCIENTIFIC COMMISSION OF THE ACADEMY OF SCIENCES OF PARIS

ACCION CATOLICA, see: CATHOLIC ACTION

ACCION COMUNAL. A program of self-initiated social action encouraged by the *United Nations and other agencies. It was established by law in Colombia in 1958-1959 and is administered by the Fondo de Desarrollo Comunal.

ACCION CULTURAL POPULAR. A Roman Catholic social action program, founded in 1947 in the village of Sutatenza (5° 2'N, 73° 27'W), *Boyacá, by Monsignor José Joaquín

Salcedo. Now directed by the Bishop of *Tunja, Acción
Cultural maintains adult education programs, including a network of radio transmitters, and claims significant gains in
reducing national illiteracy.

ACCION NACIONALISTA POPULAR. A splinter faction of
the *Conservative Party during the late 1930s. It was led by
Gilberto *Alzate Avendaño in opposition to Laureano
*Gómez.

ACCORDS OF 1860, see: PACTO PROVISORIO, 1860

ACERO DE LA CRUZ, Antonio, d. 1687. Painter, sculptor,
poet, born in *Bogotá. He was the son of Alonso Acero and
Jerónima Gutiérrez and a brother of Bernardo and Jerónino
Simón Acero de la Cruz, who were also painters. His commissions included works to commemorate the death of Archbishop Bernardino de Almansa (1597-1633), a copy of the
Virgin of *Chiquinquirá, and paintings for various churches.
His themes were basically religious, and his best-known pictures include Immaculate Conceptions that he painted for the
churches of San Diego, Santa Bárbara, San Francisco, and the
hospital of *San Juan de Dios, all in Bogotá.

ACEVEDO DE GOMEZ, Josefa, 1803-1861. Playwright, author;
born *Bogotá, January 23; died *hacienda* El Retiro (Pasca,
*Cundinamarca), January 19. She is considered the first Co-
lombian woman playwright. Although none of her texts survives, she is said to have written *La coqueta burlada, Mal de
novios,* and *En busca de almas.* She was also known for works
aimed at the *education of women, such as the *Tratado sobre
economía doméstica,* biographies, poetry, and *costumbrista*
narratives. Josefa was the daughter of José *Acevedo y Gómez
and the wife of Diego Fernando Gómez.

ACEVEDO Y GOMEZ, José, 1775-1817. Born Monguí
(*Boyacá); died in the Andaquí mountains (*Huila), May 2.
Known as the Tribune of the People for his defense of *creole
rights in the *Cabildo of Santafé on July 20, 1810, he drafted
the Act of Independence (*Acta del 20 de Julio) and was a
member of a Supreme *Junta, which governed in the early days
of the *independence movement. He later held other civil and
military positions and died while fleeing Spanish troops during
the *Reconquista,* 1816-1817.

ACOPI, see: ASOCIACION COLOMBIANA POPULAR DE INDUSTRIALES

ACOSTA, Joaquín, 1800-1852. Historian, scientist, military engineer, general; born *Guaduas (Cundinamarca), December 29; died Guaduas, February 21. He was Minister of Foreign Relations, 1843-1845; the author of *Compendio histórico del descubrimiento y colonización de Nueva Granada en el siglo décimo sexto* (Paris, 1848); an editor of scientific works; and the publisher of a map of *New Granada, 1847.

ACOSTA CASTILLO, Santos, 1828-1901. General, physician, legislator, *Liberal politician, acting President (May 23, 1867, to April 1, 1868). He was born in Miraflores (*Boyacá), November 1, and died in *Bogotá, January 9. General Acosta studied medicine in Bogotá, graduating in 1850, and practiced medicine, 1850-1860. Thereafter he was a military man and political leader. He was Governor of Boyacá, Minister of Government, and five times Secretary of War and the *Navy (including 1872, 1876, and 1878). He supported the Conspiracy of May 23, 1867 (see: TWENTY-THIRD OF MAY CONSPIRACY) against President *Mosquera and became acting President as a result of it. His administration repealed the 1863 Law Concerning the *Inspection of Cults, placed priests under the jurisdiction of ordinary courts, created a general accounting office, established the National University (*Universidad Nacional), negotiated a contract for the railroad between *Barranquilla and the sea, sold reserves of the *Panama Railroad, and initiated work on the Lazareto (leprosarium) de *Agua de Dios.

ACOSTA DE SAMPER, Soledad, 1833-1913. Essayist, novelist, historian, women's writer, born *Bogotá, May 5; died Bogotá, March 17. She was the daughter of historian General Joaquín *Acosta (1800-1852) and the wife of José María *Samper (1828-1888). Although a contributor to many Colombian *newspapers (including El *Mosaico) on a wide variety of subjects, she is best remembered for her works intended to educate and to improve the life of Colombian women and for her essays on Colombian history. She edited and published a periodical for women, *La mujer,* 1878-1881, and was the author of works such as *La mujer en la sociedad moderna* (1895). Although at times romanticized and novelistic, her historical works included titles such as *Biografías de hombres ilústres* . . .

del descubrimiento . . . (1883); *Los piratas en Cartagena* (1886); *Lecciones de historia de Colombia* (1908); and biographies of Joaquín Acosta (1901), Antonio *Nariño (1901), Simón *Bolívar (1909), and Antonio José de *Sucre (1909).

ACPA, see: ASOCIACION COLOMBIANA DE PROMOCION ARTESANAL

ACT OF FEDERATION, 1811, see: ACTA DE LA CONFEDERACION DE LAS PROVINCIAS UNIDAS DE LA NUEVA GRANADA

ACT OF INDEPENDENCE, see: ACTA DEL 20 DE JULIO DE 1810

ACTA DE LA CONFEDERACION DE LAS PROVINCIAS UNIDAS DE LA NUEVA GRANADA, 1811. An act of union signed November 27 by representatives of *Antioquia, *Cartagena, *Neiva, *Pamplona, and *Tunja, it created the United Provinces of New Granada, a federation of independent provinces (see: PROVINCIAS UNIDAS DE NUEVA GRANADA), with clear emphasis on providing for the common defense. It established an ill-defined executive power and a congress empowered to create judicial bodies when necessary. Although the congress assembled on October 4, 1812, in *Leiva, with deputies from Antioquia, *Casanare, Cartagena, Pamplona, *Popayán, and Tunja, conflicting political philosophies kept the delegates from establishing an effectively governed state. *Cundinamarca was conquered and forced into the union in 1814, but the United Provinces was dissolved in the Spanish Reconquest (*Reconquista*), 1816-1819.

ACTA DEL 20 DE JULIO DE 1810. The Colombian Declaration of Independence proclaimed that the *junta de gobierno* appointed by the *cabildo abierto* of *Bogotá refused to recognize any authority but that of the exiled king, Ferdinand VII, whom Napoleon had deposed two years earlier. This repudiated not only the puppet government of Joseph Bonaparte (José I), but also the Regency Council (*Consejo de Regencia) set up by the resistance forces in Spain itself. The act was largely the work of José *Acevedo y Gómez. The original document was destroyed in a fire in 1900. See also: TWENTIETH OF JULY 1810

ACUERDO NO. 3. A declaration issued August 17, 1899, by Historical Conservatives (*Históricos), *Agreement No. 3* criticized the fiscal policies of the *Caro and *Sanclemente presidencies, denounced the imposition of martial law and political manipulation of military commanders, and called for economic and political reform. Like the earlier *Motives for Dissidence* (*Motivos de disidencia), it was an expression of the division in Conservative ranks and the frustration of the Históricos with their inability to persuade the *Nationalist Conservatives to undertake reform from within the party and the government just two months before the outbreak of the War of the *Thousand Days.

ACUERDOS DE 1860, see: PACTO PROVISORIO, 1860

ACUÑA TAPIAS, Luis Alberto, 1904-. Painter, sculptor, essayist; born Suaita (*Santander), May 12. After early education in Santander and *Bogotá, he studied and traveled in France, Italy, Germany, and Spain, 1925-1929. Following his return to Colombia, he was first rector of the Center for Fine Arts in *Bucaramanga and then became professor of drawing at the *Colegio Mayor de San Bartolomé in Bogotá, where he replaced Roberto *Pizano Restrepo. He later served as professor at the School of Fine Arts in Bogotá. His works emphasized Colombian folklore and historical themes, especially the influence of Indian arts in the development of Colombia. Illustrative of the variety in his numerous works are the essay *El arte de los indios colombianos* (1936) and the statue of Gonzalo *Jiménez de Quesada in the Cathedral in Bogotá.

ADELANTADO. A title given to the leader of an expedition in the colonial period, the term implies one who is in the vanguard, in the most forward position, or on the frontier. The *adelantado,* leader of the expedition, might also be its organizer, and often held other titles, such as Governor (see: GOVERNMENT) or Captain General (see: CAPITANIA GENERAL). Perhaps the most often cited *adelantado* in Colombian colonial history was Gonzalo *Jiménez de Quesada, the founder of *Bogotá.

ADMINISTRATIVE DIVISIONS. The administrative division of the newly independent *República de Gran Colombia in 1819 was basically that of the colonial Viceroyalty of the New Kingdom of Granada (see: VIRREINATO DEL NUEVO

REINO DE GRANADA), except for the loss of Trinidad to the *United Kingdom in 1797 and the renaming of the province of *Cartagena as *Bolívar. The separation of Venezuela and Ecuador in 1831 reduced the territory of the new *República de Nueva Granada to the provinces of *Antioquia, *Bolívar, *Boyacá, *Cauca, *Cundinamarca, *Panamá, *Santa Marta (renamed *Magdalena in 1857), and *Santander. With the *Constitution of 1858 the provinces became states of the *Confederación Granadina. A new state of *Tolima was created in 1861. The unitary *Constitution of 1886 established the *República de Colombia and changed the states into *departments (*departamentos*). Their number was reduced in 1903 to eight when Panama became independent, but it has since been increased by the creation of several new departments. The present departments number 32: Antioquia, *Amazonas, *Arauca, *Atlántico, Bolívar, Boyacá, *Caldas, *Caquetá, *Casanare, Cauca, *Cesar, *Chocó, *Córdoba, Cundinamarca, *Guainía, *Guajira, *Guaviare, *Huila, Magdalena, *Meta, Nariño, *Norte de Santander, *Putumayo, *Quindío, *Risaralda, *San Andrés, Providencia y Santa Catalina, Santander, *Sucre, Tolima, *Valle del Cauca, *Vaupés, and *Vichada. These are divided into *municipalities (*municipios*). Under the *Constitution of 1886, departments were divided into *provinces (*provincias*) and then into municipal districts, but provinces were eliminated by the *Constitution of 1991. The capital of Colombia, *Bogotá, is located in the Capital District (*Distrito Capital,* see: DISTRITO ESPECIAL). See also: AUDIENCIA; CABILDO; CAPITANIA GENERAL; COMMISSARIAT; DEPARTMENT; GOVERNMENT; INTENDANCY; MUNICIPALITY; PROVINCE; STATE; TERRITORY; VICEROYALTY; and MAP: MAJOR ADMINISTRATIVE DIVISIONS

ADMIRABLE CAMPAIGN, 1813, see: CAMPAÑA ADMIRABLE

ADMIRABLE CONGRESS, 1830, see: CONGRESO ADMIRABLE

AFRICAN PALM. A source of edible oil introduced into Colombia by *Coldesa S.A. in 1958.

ADO, see: AUTODEFENSA OBRERA

AFRICAN SLAVERY. Black slavery was introduced with the earliest European penetration of *New Granada. *Nicuesa, *Bastidas, *Heredia, *Vadillo, and other conquistadors and officials had Crown permission to bring black slaves to the colony for personal use. Three periods have been distinguished within the slave trade for Spanish America. During the first, 1510-1595, slave trading was loosely regulated under an assortment of individually granted licenses. One estimate suggests that the importation of 100,000 slaves was authorized under this scheme. From 1595 to 1789, the Crown enforced the *asiento* system to conduct the slave trade, and from 1789 onward slave trading was unrestricted. The *asientos,* or contracts, were issued at times to companies, at times to foreign countries, and at times to individuals. Among the most important of the companies were the Compañía Alemana de Colonización de Venezuela (1520s), the Cacheu de Portugal, the Guinea de Francia, and the South Sea Company of England. Portugal dominated the commerce from 1595 to 1640, but the Dutch (1685), French (1702), and English (1713) were also very competitive. It is likely that more than 450,000 slaves were legally authorized under the *asiento* system. No accounting can be made for contraband importations, which were undoubtedly large. *Cartagena served as an entrepôt, and most slaves did not remain in Colombia. A conservative estimate places the total number of slaves legally imported through Cartagena before 1789 at from 130,000 to 180,000. It has also been estimated that there were about 54,000 slaves in New Granada at the end of the 18th century. It appears that slaves imported into Colombia came from all major slave regions of Africa. African slaves were most commonly used on the Atlantic and Pacific coasts and in the *Cauca Valley. Beyond mining, African slave trading may have been the single most economically productive activity in colonial Colombia. The importation of black slaves was prohibited by Cartagena in 1812, and legislation providing for the abolition of slavery in *Antioquia was passed there in 1814. *Bolívar promised to abolish slavery nationally in 1816, and the *Congress of Angostura established the principle of total, although gradual, emancipation in 1819. Nevertheless, black slavery continued to exist until it was completely abolished in 1851, effective January 1, 1852. One estimate suggests that more than 16,000 slaves were freed by the 1851 legislation. See also: BLACKS

AGRARIAN REFORM. What might be called the first agrarian reform in Colombia dates from the Royal Decree of 1591, when the Crown formally authorized private ownership of land in America. Previously the Crown had allowed the use of the land and the use of *Indians as labor, but technically actual ownership of the land remained in the hands of the monarch. Beginning in 1591, the Crown granted private ownership to individuals and corporations by means of official certification and payment of appropriate fees, thereby recognizing de jure what often had already occurred de facto. By decrees of President *González in 1593, Indian *resguardos, communal holdings, were recognized. The reform of 1591 authenticated land holdings up to 1591 and provided for future sale of public lands. It marks the beginning of legal land-owning patterns in *New Granada. Subsequent reforms that saw changes in land ownership might include the expulsion of the *Jesuits in 1767 and the *disamortization decree of 1861 (both of which resulted in government confiscation of Church-owned properties) and the *Land Laws of 1874 and 1882 (which expanded land ownership). The efforts to abolish Indian *resguardos* in the 19th century might also be cited. *Law 200 of 1936 marks the first major land reform of the 20th century. The law granted title to those who could prove actual occupation of the land and declared that property owning entailed inherent social obligations. The most ambitious program, however, was created in 1961 when *Law 135 established a national land redistribution program and created the *Instituto Colombiano de la Reforma Agraria (INCORA) to implement the reform. See also: ANTI-CLERICAL LAWS, 1861; RESGUARDOS

AGREEMENT NO. 3, see: *ACUERDO NO. 3*

AGRICULTURE. Pre-Hispanic agriculture was characterized by two distinct types of cultivation. Corn, potatoes, beans, and squash were crops dominant in the temperate and highland communities, while *yuca (manioc) was more prevalent in the tropical lowlands of the Caribbean Coast, the *Llanos, and the *Amazon region. A wide variety of plants, including sweet *potatoes, peanuts, avocados, pineapple, and other tropical fruits, were used by the *Indians. Subsistence agriculture was the most common form of farming. The remains of ridged fields have been found in the coastal lowlands, and both terracing and irrigation were used in the highlands. The Indians had access to both fresh and saltwater seafood and diets were also supplemented by small animals such as guinea pigs and wild game killed by hunters. Pastoralism was not a major occupation because the Indians lacked large domesticated mammals.

The European conquest brought with it new plants, animals, and techniques, but agriculture during the colonial period (1500-1800) remained essentially a subsistence industry. Those products that were sold commercially were consumed largely in domestic markets, and Colombia's export wealth came primarily from mineral resources such as *gold, *silver, and *emeralds. Settlements and agriculture often developed in support of mining operations. In various places, especially the highland valleys, large-scale cattle ranching (see: LIVE-STOCK) became the most lucrative commercial agricultural venture. Toward the end of the period, *tobacco became an important revenue-producing crop for the Spanish monarchy and *cotton furnished thread for an incipient textile industry in the northeast around the present-day Departments of *Santander and *Norte de Santander. *Sugarcane, *coffee, and other crops were introduced, but did not become major export products until the 19th century or later.

Although the independence movement destablized the *economy from 1810 to 1830 and recurrent *civil wars disrupted production several times thereafter, Colombia did experience a slow and irregular growth in export agriculture during the 19th century. Tobacco was the main source of wealth until the 1870s when the market for the Colombian-grown leaf collapsed. There were brief booms in *indigo, 1860s-1890s, and *cinchona bark, 1870s-1880s. But it was coffee production that became the principal source of Colombian export income in the last quarter of the century.

Domestically, subsistence agriculture remained a way of life for many Colombians. Sugarcane and cotton expanded, especially in the Cauca Valley (*Valle del Cauca). And cattle raising continued to develop in the Llanos, the highland plateaus, and the lowlands of the Caribbean Coast. Agricultural production was stimulated by the breakup of Indian *resguardos in the 1850s and the confiscation and sale of Church lands in the 1860s (see: DISAMORTIZATION DECREE). Perhaps the most significant development of previously uncultivated land resulted from the expansion of colonists south from *Antioquia.

By the end of the first century of independence, Colombia, like much of Latin America, had an economy oriented toward exporting primary products and importing finished goods. During the first quarter of the 20th century exports experienced a period of prosperity. Coffee continued to expand in the highlands. With the appearance of the *United Fruit Company, *banana cultivation and export became a major industry in the Caribbean lowlands. And *rubber gathering provided a source of wealth in the tropics of the Amazon region.

Although wide disparities in cultivation techniques continued to exist, mechanization, the use of fertilizers, irrigation, enlarged markets due to urbanization and improved *transportation, and increased acreage have contributed significantly to improved agricultural productivity in the present century. Alberto Pardo Pardo cites 1926 as the year the first tractors were imported, although wide-scale mechanization did not begin until after *World War II. *Agrarian reform and colonization projects have brought new land into cultivation. And finally, significant efforts have been made to reduce the extreme dependency on coffee revenue.

Diversification became a focus of national attention from the 1960s onward. Both cotton and sugar became important export items. New crops, such as *African palm, were introduced. And in recent times, items such as cut flowers have entered the international market. Throughout the century efforts were made to improve the breeding and raising of livestock. And, from a strictly monetary point of view, one cannot overlook the uncontrollable growth of *marijuana and *cocaine production since the 1970s. Modern Colombian agriculture now has greater diversity and productivity than at any time since the Spanish conquest. For products and quantities produced, see the listings of individual departments (Antioquia, Boyacá, etc.).

AGUA DE DIOS. A community of 9,105 people (1985 estimate) located at 4° 23'N, 74° 40'W in the Department of *Cundinamarca approximately 114 kilometers west of *Bogotá. It was founded in 1861, and a leprosarium (the Lazareto de Agua de Dios) was begun there under the administration of acting President Santos *Acosta, 1867-1868. For most of its existence Agua de Dios was governed as a national refuge for people afflicted with leprosy, but in 1963 it became the administrative center of an ordinary *municipio of the same name.

AGUADO, Pedro, b. 1513. *Franciscan, Provincial of the Monastery of San Francisco, 1573. He was the author of *Recopila-*

ción historial, a 16th-century account of *New Granada, completed about 1587 and first published in 1906.

AGUARDIENTE.   An anise-flavored alcoholic beverage made from sugarcane or honey. Similar to *chicha* in its frequent association with the lower classes, *aguardiente* was declared a royal monopoly (*estanco*) on July 17, 1749. The government monopoly was defunct by 1833, partially abandoned in 1834, and completely abolished in 1838.

AGUATERA.   *Bogotá character type: women employed in carrying water to homes in the city before the introduction of central distribution systems.

AGUIRRE, Lope de, ca. 1516-1561.   Spanish adventurer, conquistador, known variously as *el loco* ("the madman"), *el tirano* ("the tyrant"), and *el peregrino* ("the wanderer"), although the last was the only nickname he applied to himself. He first came to America in 1536 and joined several unsuccessful rebellions in Peru, including that of Gonzalo Pizarro against the Viceroy Blasco Núñez de Vela. He later joined the expedition of Pedro de *Ursúa to explore the Amazon from Peru to the Atlantic Ocean. During the course of the expedition (September 26, 1560, to July 1, 1561), he conspired to assassinate Ursúa and eventually assumed command of Ursúa's troops. After reaching the Atlantic, he seized the Island of Margarita and attacked Venezuela in an effort to return to Peru. He landed at Barburata, Venezuela, September 7, and laid siege to Valencia. He was captured and executed in Barquisimeto, October 27, after first killing his own daughter to keep her from being captured.

AIR FORCE.   The *Fuerza Aérea* was established in 1922 as the result of a French military mission, 1921-1924, but the air force became a fully independent unit only in 1943. French influence persisted as late as the 1960s when 14 Mirage jet fighters were acquired. In recent years its strength has been estimated at 4,000 men and 300 aircraft. Under the *Constitution of 1991, the air force is one of four main branches of the national *armed forces.

AIR TRANSPORT.   In a country as divided by high mountains and rugged terrain as Colombia, the advantages of air travel are obvious. *SCADTA, the precedessor of *AVIANCA, was

South America's first airline. There is now a well-developed network of domestic air services using more than 700 airfields, of which 55 have permanent hard-surfaced runways, and six have runways of 2,300 meters or more. See also: SATENA

AJIACO, see: POTATO

ALADI, see: LATIN AMERICAN INTEGRATION ASSOCIATION

ALAI, see: LATIN AMERICAN INTEGRATION ASSOCIATION

ALBATROSS GROUP, see: POST-NUEVOS GENERATION

ALCABALA. Colonial sales tax imposed on each commercial transaction. It was usually less than 5% but was cumulatively heavy and bitterly disliked. It was collected in *New Granada after 1591.

ALCALDE. Mayor (see: SPANISH EMPIRE IN AMERICA); also chief executive officer of a *municipality.

ALCAZARES, Valley of the. Valley of the castles, or fortresses. It was the name given to the plains around *Chía and *Bogotá by *Jiménez de Quesada because of the appearance of the Indian villages when he first saw them.

ALDANA, Lorenzo de, d. 1557. Conquistador who founded *Pasto in 1539. A *hidalgo* (nobleman or gentleman) from Cáceres, Aldana first appeared in Guatemala and then went to Quito with Pedro de Alvarado in 1534. Under orders from Pizarro, he assumed the government of *Popayán in *Belalcázar's absence. He commissioned exploration and settlement in the Cauca Valley (*Valle del Cauca) and then returned to Peru, where he died.

ALFINGER, Ambrosius, see: DALFINGER, Ambrosius

ALIANZA DEMOCRATICA M-19. The name given to a coalition of ex-guerrillas from the M-19 and their supporters after the M-19 surrendered in 1990 in order to run candidates in the elections later that year. The name came to be used more frequently as the designation of a political party during the

*Asamblea Constituyente y Legislativa, 1991, and subsequent elections. See also: MOVIMIENTO DIECINUEVE DE ABRIL

ALIANZA NACIONAL POPULAR. The National Popular Alliance, or ANAPO. It was founded by supporters of General *Rojas Pinilla in 1960 as a third party opposing both the *Liberals and the *Conservatives. Ideologically populist and reformist, drawing heavily on working-class support, ANAPO became a major protest force in the late 1960s and 1970s, especially in the elections of 1970, which ANAPO supporters claim General Rojas Pinilla actually won although official results fraudulently denied him the victory. In 1974, María Eugenia *Rojas de Moreno Díaz, as the ANAPO candidate, became the first woman in Colombian history to run for President. She gained about 10% of the popular vote. ANAPO officially boycotted the 1982 presidential elections. ANAPO has been described as a party advocating Christian socialism.

ALLIANCE FOR PROGRESS, see: FOREIGN AID; UNITED STATES, Relations with

ALMOJARIFAZGO. Colonial customs duty, collected after 1566. The ad valorem rate could be as high as 5% on exports and 15% on imports, but it tended to be stabilized at 6 to 7% for both after 1778.

ALTOZANEROS. *Bogotá character type: men who waited around the *altozano,* or paved terrace, at the cathedral entrance, for odd jobs or employment as day laborers.

ALVAREZ, Manuel Bernardo de, 1743-1816. Born, *Bogotá, May 21; executed by the Spanish in Bogotá, September 10. Lawyer, author, patriot martyr; Alvarez held several administrative positions in the colonial period. He signed the Act of July 20 (*Acta del 20 de Julio) and served as a member of a Supreme *Junta and as President of *Congress in 1810. He was a representative from *Cundinamarca and President-Dictator of the state, August 4, 1813, to December 12, 1814. He was ideologically a centralist (as was his nephew, Antonio *Nariño).

ALVAREZ DE QUIÑONES, Antonio Claudio, 1666-1736. Archbishop of Bogotá, 1731-1736; born Alcalá de Henares

(Spain); died *Bogotá, October 21. He was appointed Bishop of *Santo Domingo in 1712 and received his consecration in Santiago de Cuba in 1718. He was appointed Archbishop of Bogotá in 1724, but he was unable to reach the Viceroyalty of *New Granada before 1730. He assumed his duties in Bogotá in 1731. During his term in office he issued regulations regarding public behavior in church and is remembered for numerous charitable donations, including the gift of a custodial to the cathedral. He built the archbishop's palace, which stood from 1736 until it was destroyed in the *Bogotazo of 1948.

ALVAREZ GARDEAZABAL, Gustavo, 1945-. Author, journalist, critic, born Tuluá (*Valle del Cauca). He is the author of *Manual de crítica literaria,* first published in 1978, but he is best known for his novels, with their descriptions of the *Violencia and criticisms of mid-20th-century Colombian society. His novels include *La tiara del papa* (1971); *Cóndores no entierran todos los días* (1972); *El bazar de los idiotas* (1974); *El titiritero* (1977); *Los míos* (1981)—winner of the Plaza y Janés award; *Pepe Botellas* (1984); and *El Divino* (1985).

ALVAREZ LLERAS, Antonio, 1892-1956. Lawyer, playwright, diplomat, and literary critic often described as one of the most important figures in Colombian theater of the early 20th century. Born *Bogotá, July 2; died Bogotá, May 15; educated as a dentist at New York's Columbia University. His literary career was marked by an early period, 1911-1927; an absence from the theatrical world, 1927-1943; and a late period, 1943-1956. His themes consistently dealt with exposures of social injustice and the affirmation of what he considered eternal values such as loyalty, honor, filial piety, and self-sacrifice. In his early period he appeared to comprehend and speak to his time, but during the later phase he seemed out of touch with its intellectual currents, which he rejected for a return to traditional values. From 1943 to 1952 he operated the Compañía Renacimiento, a theatrical troupe in Bogotá. His theatrical works include *Víboras sociales* (1911), *Los mercenarios* (1924), and *El virrey Solís* (1947).

ALZATE AVENDAÑO, Gilberto, 1910-1960. A Conservative, from *Caldas, leader of various splinter factions within the *Conservative Party, 1930-1960. He formed the short-lived *Acción Nacionalista Popular, 1936-1939, and tended to oppose Laureano *Gómez. He was a member of the Conservative directorate, 1950, and was opposed to both the governments of General *Rojas Pinilla, 1953-1957, and the National Front (*Frente Nacional), 1958-1960.

AMADOR, Carlos Coriolano, 1835-1919. A successful *Antioqueño entrepreneur known for a variety of economic activities including mining, commerce, agriculture, public works, and urban development. He is probably best remembered as a successful manager of the El *Zancudo mines, which experienced major economic success in the 19th century, and for the urbanization of the Guayaquil section of *Medellín. The latter resulted from efforts at urban development undertaken by Carlos Coriolano on a section of his property originally known as El Pantano. The family of Carlos Coriolano and his wife, Lorenza Uribe Lema, enjoyed a lavish life-style, which led people to refer to their houses as the "palaces of the Amadors." Carlos was known as "Coro" to his friends, but dubbed the "golden burro" (el burro de oro) by his enemies.

AMAR Y BORBON, Antonio, 1742-ca. 1819. Viceroy of *New Granada, 1803-1810. He received the *Vaccination Expedition and proposed a new highway to *Zipaquirá. He was generally seen as weak—dominated by his wife—and opposed to the *creole *independence movement. Both he and his wife were expelled from *Bogotá, August 15, 1810.

AMAZON REGION. The southeastern part of Colombian territory, also referred to as Amazonia. The region includes but is not limited to the Commissariat of *Amazonas. It consists of approximately 330,000 square kilometers lying east of the *Cordillera Oriental and south of the *Llanos Orientales reaching, in its extreme point, as far as the *Amazon River. The terrain is generally lowland with tropical rain forest vegetation and a hot, humid climate. In contrast to the Llanos, the Amazon region has less seasonal variation in moisture. Major rivers in the Amazon region flow into the Amazon River, while streams from the Llanos form tributaries of the Orinoco River system. The region touches the borders of Brazil, Peru, and Ecuador.

AMAZON RIVER. The southernmost part of Colombia reaches to the Amazon River, whose left bank, opposite Peru, forms the international border for approximately 150 kilometers as far as *Leticia, which faces the Brazilian town of Benjamín Constant.

AMAZONAS, Departamento del. Located in southeastern Colombia on the borders with Peru and Brazil, Amazonas covers 109,665 square kilometers. The terrain is lowland and rain forest between latitudes 0° 20'N and 4° 12'S and longitudes 70° 31' and 74° 20'W, with tropical climate and average temperatures between 27° and 30°C. Rainy season is December to May. The department is Colombia's only direct connection to the Amazon River. *Fishing, forestry, and tourism are important commercial activities, but the predominant economic endeavor is subsistence *agriculture (*corn, rice, *yuca, and plantain). There are about 5,000 head of cattle in the department. Some 25 groups of *Indians live within the area. Estimated population in 1985 was 13,210 people with an overall population density of less than one person per square kilometer. Amazonas was created a *commissariat in 1931 and elevated to a department in 1991. *Leticia is the capital city.

AMAZONIA, see: AMAZON REGION

AMBALEMA. Village on the *Magdalena River, located at 4° 47'N, 74° 46'W in the Department of *Tolima. The river port, approximately 80 kilometers west-northwest of *Bogotá, was founded in 1776. The altitude is 241 meters, and the average temperature is 27°C. Ambalema experienced an economic boom in the 19th century when it became the center of *tobacco production, accounting for as much as half of Colombia's foreign exchange during the 1850s. It was an important commercial center for both river and *railroad traffic. Population in 1985 was 4,915 people.

AMERICAN BATTALION, see: BATALLON AMERICANO

AMERICAN DOCTRINE. A principle enunciated on August 3, 1932, by the Commission of Investigation and Conciliation appointed to deal with the *Chaco War. The declaration of principles, drafted by representatives from Colombia and the United States, said in part: "Respect for the law is a tradition among the American nations, which are opposed to the use of force and renounce it as a means of settling controversies and as an instrument of national policy in their reciprocal relations."

AMERINDIANS, see: INDIANS

AMIGOS DEL PAIS, Sociedad de.   Society of the Friends of the Nation. A voluntary association formed to stimulate internal development during the last quarter of the 18th century. The first of these societies in *New Granada was founded in *Mompós, September 12, 1784. The Patriotic Society of Friends of the Nation in *Bogotá was established November 1801. Similar societies were organized in *Cartagena in 1787 and 1811.

ANAPO, see: ALIANZA NACIONAL POPULAR

AÑASCO, Pedro de.   Captain.   Conquistador in southwestern Colombia with *Belalcázar. He was the leader of a rebellion against Spanish authorities in *Popayán during the 1530s in the region of what was to become Timaná (1° 58'N, 75° 55'W). The latter was founded December 18, 1538, by Añasco, who was killed in the uprising of La *Gaitana, which broke out one year later.

ANCIZAR, Manuel, 1811-1882.   Lawyer, diplomat, journalist, and educator, born at the *hacienda El Tintal (Fontibón, *Cundinamarca), December 25; died *Bogotá, May 21. Ancízar was a distinguished *Liberal statesman, active in a variety of fields. In 1848 he founded the printing firm and newspaper *El Neo-Granadino.* In the 1850s he was secretary of the *Chorographic Commission and author of *Peregrinación de Alpha,* a descriptive account of the social conditions he observed during his travels with the expedition. He was a member of the *House of Representatives and, in 1863, a delegate to the Convention of *Rionegro. He was Minister of Foreign Relations, 1861-1862, 1876, and 1879, and served at various times as diplomatic envoy to Venezuela, Chile, Ecuador, and Peru.

ANCIZAR-ARBELAEZ PACT OF 1876.   Signed June 1876, by Manuel *Ancízar, Minister of Foreign Relations for Colombia, and Archbishop *Arbeláez. The agreement was a détente between Church and State, allowing for religious instruction to be given in the public schools for those students whose parents requested it.

ANCIZAR-SANCHEZ TREATY. Signed in *Bogotá, June 8, 1854, by Manuel *Ancízar, for *New Granada, and J. L. Sánchez, for Peru, based on agreements signed in Lima, November 23, 1853. The treaty specified the method by which Peru would pay the debt agreed upon by the *Lleras–Paz Soldán Treaty of 1853.

ANCOM, see: ANDEAN COMMON MARKET

ANDAGOYA, Pascual de, 1495-1548. Spanish explorer. Andagoya came to America with *Pedrarias in 1514 and wrote the *Narrative of the Proceedings of Pedrarias Dávila in the Provinces of Tierra Firme or Castilla de Oro* . . . He was the first man to sail down the Pacific Coast of Colombia, 1522. Governor of San Juan (*Nueva Castilla) in 1539, he explored the *Chocó, reaching *Cali in 1540. He exceeded his authority, however, when he was recognized as Governor of *Anserma by Jorge *Robledo and, as a result, he was later arrested and sent to Spain by *Belalcázar.

ANDALUCIA, New, see: NUEVA ANDALUCIA

ANDALUCIANS. People from southern Spain. See also: CREOLES

ANDAMO, Vicente. An Italian immigrant inspired by socialist ideas who came to Colombia in 1915, Andamo organized workers' societies in *Montería and Cereté (8° 53'N, 75° 48'W, *Córdoba). In 1919 he was active in organizing several hundred *colonos,* or small farmers, to protest and to protect themselves against land seizures in the Lomagrande region of the Province of Sinú (Department of *Córdoba). Tensions were high in the Lomagrande area, 1919-1927, and several deaths resulted, including that of a police sergeant. Andamo was deported from Colombia in 1927, but Lomagrande, which came to be known as the Red Bastion (*Baluarte Roja*), continued to be the seat of fierce peasant resistance.

ANDEAN COMMON MARKET. An international development program established by the Acuerdo Subregional de Integración (also known as the Pact of Cartagena, the Andean Pact, and the Pacto Andino), signed May 26, 1969, by representatives of Colombia, Chile, Bolivia, Ecuador, and Peru. Venezuela joined the group in February 1973. It was formed to expand, specialize, and diversify industrial growth, to make maximum use of natural resources, and to establish sound, efficient economies within the signatory nations. The Pact of Cartagena led to the formation of the Andean Common Market (ANCOM), an affiliate of the *Latin American Free Trade Association (LAFTA).

ANDEAN PACT, see: ANDEAN COMMON MARKET

ANDES. A great, *earthquake-prone, mineral-rich mountain chain that dominates much of western South America. In Colombia, its major parts are three more or less parallel ranges, known as the *Cordillerra Occidental, the *Cordillera Central, and the *Cordillera Oriental, which run from southwest (Ecuador) to northeast (Venezuela).

ANDES, Universidad de los, see: UNIVERSIDAD DE LOS ANDES

ANDI, see: ASOCIACION NACIONAL DE INDUSTRIALES

ANDINA, Integración, see: ANDEAN COMMON MARKET

ANDINO. A highlander; literally "one from the Andes mountains." It is a term used to denote a regional personality type with traits of stoicism, austerity, formality, moodiness, and occasional fits of violence when provoked. In cases of race and ethnic distinctions, the term may imply an *Indian heritage (for contrast, see: COSTEÑO).

ANDRADE, Luis Ignacio. A spokesman for the right wing of the *Conservative Party, he was Minister of the Interior (*gobierno*) for the administrations of both Presidents *Ospina Pérez and *Gómez. He was responsible for the rigid government *censorship of the early 1950s.

ANGOSTURA. Pre-1849 name of present-day *Ciudad Bolívar, Venezuela.

ANGOSTURA, Congress of, see: CONGRESS OF ANGOSTURA, 1819

AÑORI, Campaign and Battle of. In the *municipio* of Añorí (7° 5'N, 75° 9'W), *Antioquia; August 7, to October 18, 1973.

Government forces pursued and finally defeated a major contingent of the *Ejército de Liberación Nacional. Much of the E.L.N.'s original leadership was killed, including two of the Vásquez Castaño brothers: Antonio (Emiliano) and Manuel (Jerónimo). The E.L.N. suffered a temporary eclipse until it was able to reorganize in the mid-1970s. See also: EJERCITO DE LIBERACION NACIONAL

ANSERMA. Municipal center located at 5° 14'N, 75° 47'W, in the Department of *Caldas about 70 kilometers northwest of *Manizales. Altitude is 1,763 meters; average temperature is 19°C; and the population in 1985 was 51,371 people. One of the earliest Spanish settlements, Anserma (Ansermaviejo) was originally founded by Jorge *Robledo in 1539, but abandoned soon afterward. Present-day Anserma was reestablished in 1870 by Matías Rivera, Tomás Arias, Crisanto Gamboa, Vicente, and Leonidas Lenis, and others. Ansermanuevo (4° 48'N, 76°W, Valle del Cauca) was established August 15, 1539, as Santa Ana de los Caballeros. The location of the settlement was subsequently changed and the name later became Ansermanuevo. The village, located in the *Cordillera Occidental near the *Cauca River, initially gave promise as a mining center, but population declined over the years, and there were only about 7,225 people in Ansermanuevo in 1985.

ANTHEM, National, see: NATIONAL ANTHEM

ANTI-CLERICAL LAWS, 1850-1853. A reference to various measures restricting ecclesiastical privileges, such as the expulsion of the *Jesuits (May 21, 1850), subjection of the clergy to civil law (May 14, 1851), civil nomination of clergymen by city councils (May 27/June 21, 1851), establishment of state supervision of the seminary (March 20, 1852), *separation of Church and State (June 15, 1853), and the legalization of civil marriage (June 20, 1853). Most of these laws were repealed or modified after 1854.

ANTI-CLERICAL LAWS, 1861. A reference to the laws of tuition (July 20), expulsion of the *Jesuits (July 26), disamortization of perpetual property (September 9; see: *Disamortization Decree), and closing of religious communities (November 5), all issued by the *Mosquera administration. The first prohibited exercise of clerical functions without government permission; the second expelled the Jesuits just as the decrees of 1767 and 1850 had done; the third authorized a compensated confiscation of designated ecclesiastical properties; and the last closed monasteries and convents that resisted any of the earlier decrees.

ANTI-CLERICAL LAWS, 1877, see: PARRA, Aquileo

ANTIOQUEÑO. A resident or native of *Antioquia. The term describes a regional personality type characterized by industriousness, thrift, and intense family and regional loyalties. There is a persistent but undocumented (most likely fallacious) legend that *antioqueños* have a Judaic (see: JEWS) heritage, which accounts for their marked economic success. For comparison, see: BOGOTANO; ANDINO; and COSTEÑO.

ANTIOQUEÑO COLONIZATION. A phrase describing the settlement of the present-day Departments of *Caldas, *Risaralda, *Quindío, northern *Valle del Cauca, and *Tolima by people from *Antioquia, especially after 1790. James Parsons and Marco Palacios have distinguished various phases of colonization. The earliest would be pre-expansion settlement in the *Medellín region before 1780. Expansion in the 19th century included settlement of the Sonsón-Abejorral region, 1780-1810; the Salamina, Neira, *Manizales phase, 1835-1850; and the *Quindío settlement, 1875-1910. Expansion southward into the Valle del Cauca, *Cauca, and Tolima regions continued into the early 20th century.

ANTIOQUIA. City; modern name for *SANTA FE DE ANTIOQUIA.

ANTIOQUIA, Departamento de. Located in northwestern Colombia on the Caribbean Coast and the Gulf of Urabá (*Golfo de Urabá) between latitudes 5° 25′ and 8° 55′N and longitudes 73° 53′ and 77° 7′W. The terrain, some 63,612 square kilometers, is mountainous, interrupted by plateaus, rolling plains, and river valleys. The climate ranges from tropical to cold. By climatic distribution, 35,622 square kilometers are tropical; 16,408, temperate; 10,899, cold; and 683, wasteland (see: CLIMATIC ZONES). Principal rivers include the *Magdalena, *Cauca, *Atrato, Medellín, and Nechi. Estimated population in 1985 was 3,720,025 people with a population density of 585 persons per square kilometer. The capital city is *Medellín. According to DANE, *Colombia estadística 86,* the principal agricultural products, with tonnage produced in 1984, include *bananas, 1,012,424 tons; plantains, 543,835; *yuca, 218,860; *potatoes, 289,500; *sugar, 185,000; *corn, 146,080; beans, 32,000; rice, 20,640; hemp, 4,800; coconuts, 4,500; sorghum, 4,210; *cacao, 3,403; and *African palm, 980. There are large cattle ranches and important minerals such as *gold, *silver, *coal, and *petroleum. *Livestock production figures for 1984 showed 547,847 head of cattle and 408,227 hogs slaughtered in the department. The department is heavily industrialized; major products include textiles, industrial chemicals, clothing, *tobacco, plastics, processed food, beverages, and transportation services. There were 523 businesses with 10 or more employees recorded in 1984. Among the provinces established in 1830, Antioquia has been an important commercial center since the 16th century. It became a sovereign state in 1856, and the Department of Antioquia was created in 1886. See also: ANTIOQUEÑO

ANTIOQUIA, University of, see: UNIVERSIDAD DE ANTIOQUIA

ANTIOQUIA RAILROAD. The Ferrocarril de Antioquia linking *Medellín with *Puerto Berrío on the *Magdalena River. The original Antioquia Railroad was begun in 1875 by Francisco J. *Cisneros under a contract concluded the preceding year. The 193-kilometer railroad between the two points was not completed, however, until 1929, when work was finished on a large tunnel. Alejandro Angel, by contract negotiated in 1907, undertook construction of the second section of the line from Medellín to the *Cauca River below Amagá (6° 3'N, 75° 42'W). The work was completed to Amagá by 1919 and to the Cauca River by 1930. The Antioquia Railroad was eventually joined to the *Pacific and *Caldas Railroads by the *Western Trunk Railroad.

ANUC, see: ASOCIACION NACIONAL DE USARIOS CAMPESINOS

APEN, see: ASOCIACION PATRONAL ECONOMICA NACIONAL

AQUIMIN. Last of the *Zaques of the *Chibchas. He ruled 1538-1541, until he was murdered by Hernán *Pérez de Quesada as part of a campaign to terrify the *Indians.

ARANA DEL AGUILA, Julio César (1864-1952). Peruvian rubber baron. In 1902 he became mayor (*alcalde*) of the key rubber trading city of Iquitos (Peru). By 1907, with the aid of 600 hired gunmen, mostly recruited in Barbados, he had won control of 30,000 square kilometers of territory, most of it in dispute between Peru and Colombia (see: PUTUMAYO DISPUTE), and had registered his Peruvian Amazon Rubber Company in London with a board of British directors as a front. When, however, *Hardenburg's revelations of his barbaric, indeed genocidal, methods aroused public opinion in Britain and the United States, this London registry, and his employment of British subjects (the Barbadians) gave the British government an excuse to investigate. The result was the collapse of Arana's empire, and the recovery of Colombian sovereignty over the Putumayo region. But many Peruvians saw Arana as a national hero who had struggled to extend his country's boundaries, and he was elected to the Peruvian Senate. As a Senator he led the opposition to ratification of the *Lozano-Salomón Treaty of 1922 between Colombia and Peru, delaying its acceptance until 1928.

ARANGO VELEZ, Carlos. A prominent *Bogotá lawyer, son of a diplomat, selected by the less radical Liberals to run for President in 1942. He lost to Alfonso *López Pumarejo, but in 1946 he was chosen *designado*.

ARATOCA, Battle of. January 9, 1841, 6° 42'N, 73° 1'W, *Santander. General T. C. de *Mosquera, for the government, defeated the rebellious forces of Colonel Manuel *González. It was a major northern victory for the government in the rebellion of 1840-1842 (see: SUPREME COMMANDERS, War of the).

ARAUCA. Capital of the Department of *Arauca, the city (located at 7° 4'N, 70° 41'W) has a population of 16,464 people (1985 estimate). It is located at an altitude of 155 meters, and the average temperature is 20°C. Modern Arauca is a border community with a bridge into Venezuela. Historically it was the headquarters for part of the patriot forces during the wars for independence, particularly during the Spanish Reconquest (*Reconquista*), 1814-1819.

ARAUCA, Departamento del. Located in eastern Colombia on the Venezuelan border, the department covers 23,490 square kilometers of predominantly tropical flatlands between 6° 2′ and 7° 6′N, and 69° 27′ and 72° 22′W. The eastern slopes of the *Cordillera Oriental rise in the west, and the region has alternating wet and dry seasons. Major rivers include the Arauca, Elo, Cravo Norte, Meta, and Casanare. The estimated population in 1973 was 46,605 people. The capital city is *Arauca. Subsistence agriculture prevails, with 23,000 hectares given to *corn, 6,500 to plantains, and 4,000 to *yuca cultivation. Approximately 6,000 hectares are devoted to commercial production of *cacao. There is extensive ranching, with some 750,000 head of cattle reported in 1984. Exploitation of forest reserves, *fishing, and *petroleum are also important. Approximately 76% of the population is concentrated in three cities: Arauca, Tame (6° 28′N, 71° 44′W), and Saravena (6° 57′N, 7° 52′W). Arauca is the site of three *Indian reservations. It was made an *intendancy in 1955 and elevated to a department in 1991.

ARAWAKS.   Linguistic-cultural group common among the *Indians of the Caribbean islands, Colombian Coast, and limited parts of the interior in 1500. The Arawaks intermingled with the *Caribs and other groups through war and commerce. It has been suggested that Arawaks in the interior of the *Llanos and *Amazon regions were responsible for the domestication of *yuca, which was then diffused down the Orinoco River system.

ARBELAEZ, Vicente, 1822-1884.   Born in El Peñón (*Antioquia), May 8; died *Bogotá, June 29. He was Archbishop of Bogotá, 1868-1884. He was ordained in 1845 and served in *Santa Marta before being appointed Archbishop of Bogotá. He opposed secular attempts to reform the Church, for which he was imprisoned and exiled, 1861-1867. He devoted great attention to the codification of regulations and to the efficient administration of the Church (for example, there were Provincial Councils in 1868 and 1874 and a Diocesan Synod in 1870). He issued numerous protests against non-Catholic *education in the public schools, secularization of cemeteries, and *Protestantism, 1868-1876. He negotiated the *Ancízar-Arbeláez Pact, 1876; approved the *Camargo-Nina Treaty, 1880; objected to the expulsion of clergymen following the *rebellion of 1876; and was often criticized by more extreme Catholics for his policy of peaceful reconciliation of Church and State.

See also: CATHOLIC CHURCH; CHURCH-STATE RELATIONS

ARBOLEDA, Julio, 1817-1862. Born Timbiquí (*Cauca), June 9; assassinated in the mountains of Berruecos (*Nariño), November 12. Poet, orator, journalist, Arboleda was a partisan *Conservative in politics. President-elect and the last defender of the Granadine Confederation (*Confederación Granadina), 1861-1862, he fought in the battle between the Confederation and Ecuador at *Tulcán (Ecuador) in 1862. He was also known as a romantic poet and his most famous poem was *Gonzalo de Oyón*, a tale of love and conquest in colonial *Popayán.

ARBOLEDA, Sergio, 1822-1888. Lawyer, educator, legislator, and author from the Department of *Cauca, born *Popayán, October 11; died Popayán, June 18. He received his law degree from the *Universidad del Cauca in 1843. A *Conservative, as was his brother, *Julio, Sergio Arboleda joined the *rebellions of 1851, 1859-1862, and 1876. He held numerous public offices, including Representative from Cauca, 1860, and Senator from *Tolima, 1872-1873 and 1876, but is most often remembered as a journalist and Conservative ideologue. He was the author of *La república en la América española* (1869) and many other political essays.

ARBOLES (Los), Battle of. July 31, 1861, *Cauca. Julio *Arboleda, defending the dying Granadine Confederation (*Confederación Granadina), defeated the forces of the *Mosquera government under General Miguel Quijano. It was a momentary and inconclusive victory.

ARCANO DE LA FILANTROPIA. A late-18th-century *tertulia.

ARCHBISHOPRIC OF BOGOTA, see: SANTA FE DE BOGOTA, Archbishopric of

ARCHDIOCESES OF COLOMBIA. The earliest dioceses of the Catholic Church in present-day Colombia were *Santa Marta, 1533; *Cartagena, 1534; *Popayán, 1546; and *Bogotá, 1552. Bogotá became the first archdiocese in 1564. In 1986, the administration of the Church in Colombia was distributed among 11 archdioceses, 33 dioceses, 1 military diocese, 2 prefectures, 8 apostolic vicariates, and 7 apostolic prefectures.

The archdioceses, the date each was first established (E), and the date it became an archdiocese (A) are Santa Fe de Bogotá, E-1552, A-1564; *Barranquilla, E-1932, A-1969; *Bucaramanga, E-1952, A-1974; *Cali, E-1910, A-1964; Cartagena, E-1534, A-1900; *Ibagué, E-1900, A-1964; *Manizales, E-1900, A-1956; *Medellín, E-1868, A-1902; Nueva Pamplona, E-1835, A-1956; Popayán, E-1546, A-1900; *Tunja, E-1880, A-1964.

ARCHEOLOGICAL SITES, see: ABRA, El; GUATAVITA, Lake; MONSU; STONE AGE SETTLEMENTS; TAIRONAS; TEQUENDAMA, El; TUNJA, Stones of

ARCHEOLOGICAL STYLES, see: CALIMA STYLE; DARIEN STYLE; MUISCA STYLE; POPAYAN STYLE; QUIMBAYA STYLE; SIERRA NEVADA DE SANTA MARTA STYLE; SINU STYLE; TOLIMA STYLE; TUMACO STYLE

ARCHEOLOGY, see: GOLD MUSEUM; GUAQUERO; INDIANS

ARCHILA INCIDENT, 1922-1925. Aristóbulo Archila, Minister of Finance for the *Conservative administration of Pedro Nel *Ospina, sent two spies to the *Liberal Party Convention in 1922 with government funds secured by falsifying records in the Ministry of War. In 1925 he was accused of misconduct in the *Senate, where the issue became a public scandal. Archila was not punished for the affair, although the evidence of irregular conduct seemed clear.

ARCHIPELAGO DE LOS MONJES, see: FRAILES, Los

ARCINIEGAS, Germán, 1900-. Lawyer, author, journalist, sociologist, historian, educator, diplomat, *Liberal politician; born *Bogotá, December 6. He served as Minister of Education, 1941-1942 and 1945-1946, was a member of the *House of Representatives, and discharged numerous diplomatic commissions. He has held university positions in both Colombia and the United States, and he also served as President of the Colombian Academy of History (*Academia Colombiana de Historia). He has a wide variety of publications (more than 40 books), including such historical works as Los comuneros (1938), The knight of El Dorado . . . (1942), Germans in the Conquest of America (1943), Amerigo and the New World . . . (1955), Latin

America: A Cultural History (1967), and *Bolívar, de Cartagena a Santa Marta* (1980). Arciniegas, one of Colombia's first authors with international influence, popularized Colombian motifs.

AREA. The present-day Republic of *Colombia (*República de Colombia) is the most northerly country in mainland South America. Its continental territory extends from 72° 30'W to 79°W, and from 12° 30'N to 4° 10'S. Its sovereignty also includes the Caribbean archipelago of *San Andrés y Providencia. The total area is 1,138,400 square kilometers (440,000 square miles), about 83,000 less than before the 1903 separation of *Panama. See also: LAW OF THE SEA

ARENAS, Jacobo, 1924-. Pseudonym or *nom de guerre* for Luis Alberto Morantes Jaime, described as chief ideologist and number-two man in the Fuerzas Armadas Revolucionarias de Colombia (FARC). From a working-class background, born January 23, in *Bucaramanga (Santander), he served a two-year period in the army with the Presidential Guard Battalion in Bogotá before entering politics after *World War II. He was subsequently president of the Liberal Youth Federation in *Santander, a member of the *Partido Comunista de Colombia, and an oil worker in *Barrancabermeja before settling in Villarica (one of the peasant communities in the Andes), 1954-1956, and later in *Marquetalia, where he joined the FARC. See also: FUERZAS ARMADAS REVOLUCIONARIAS DE COLOMBIA; MARIN, Pedro Antonio

ARENAS BETANCUR, Rodrigo, 1921-. Sculptor, born October 24 in Fredonia (*Antioquia). He studied at the Escuela de Bellas Artes in both *Medellín and *Bogotá and taught drawing at the *Universidad de Antioquia and casting at the Instituto Pascual Bravo. Arenas Betancur uses nude figures in his monumental statues, and early in his career (1944) lost his teaching job because this was so controversial. He was responsible for various public memorials in Mexico as well as Colombia, but is probably best known in his native land for a monument in the municipal plaza at *Pereira completed in 1944, now known popularly as the "Nude *Bolívar."

ARGENTINA-COLOMBIA TREATY OF 1823, see: MOSQUERA-RIVADAVIA TREATY

ARGUINAO, Juan de, 1588-1678. Dominican, Archbishop of Bogotá, 1661-1678. Born Lima (Peru), in April 1588, he was baptized there on May 8; he died in *Bogotá, October 5. He entered the *Dominican order in 1602, became a professor of theology, and was prior of monasteries in Trujillo (Peru) and Lima before being appointed the Bishop of Santa Cruz de la Sierra (Peru) in 1646. He was appointed Archbishop of Bogotá in 1659. In *New Granada, he is remembered for establishing an elaborate ceremony for the formal reception of a new archbishop, which was used in the viceroyalty from 1661 to 1728.

ARIAS DE AVILA, Pedro, see: PEDRARIAS

ARIAS DE UGARTE Y FORERO, Hernando, 1561-1638. Born *Bogotá, September 9; died in Lima (Peru), January 27. He was educated in Spain and served as a judge of *audiencias in Panama, Charcas, and Lima before his ordination in Chile around 1608. He was first Bishop of Quito, 1613-1615; then Archbishop of *Bogotá, 1618-1625; Bishop of Charcas, 1625-1628; and, finally, Archbishop of Lima, 1630-1638. He made an extensive tour of the Granadine archbishopric and became a patron of the *Indians, sometimes signing himself "Hernando, the Indian." He convoked a Provincial Council in 1625 and was later honored by Pope Urban VIII.

ARMADA, see: NAVY

ARMADA DE BARLOVENTO TAX. A tax imposed in the colonies after 1635, especially to cover the costs of a naval fleet needed to defend the Caribbean. It taxed such items as wine, honey, soap, cheese, and leather goods. The tax, which came under protest during the *COMUNEROS REVOLT, 1780-1782, was at times erroneously called the new *alcabala* and the *sisa*.

ARMED FORCES. Under the *Constitution of 1991, there are four main branches in the Colombian armed forces (*fuerzas militares*). Three deal with national defense against foreign powers: *ARMY, *NAVY, and *AIR FORCE. The National Police (Policía Nacional) maintains public order in internal affairs (see: POLICE). The armed forces are prohibited from participating in political matters, and only the armed forces may legally manufacture or possess weapons, munitions, and explosives without special permission. The cabinet post of Minister of Defense has been the senior army general since 1958. The *President of the Republic is constitutionally the commander in chief of the armed forces.

ARMENIA.   Capital of the *Quindío, located at 4° 32′N, 75° 41′W. Population is 186,604 people (1985 estimate); altitude, 1,551 meters; and average temperature, 22°C. Major industrial activities include *coffee processing, food processing, and beverage making. Founded in 1889 by José María Ocampo, Armenia is known as the "miraculous city" (a name attributed to the poet Guillermo *Valencia) for its relatively rapid growth.

ARMERO.   A small town in the Department of *Tolima located at 4° 58′N, 74° 54′W. The community and most of its population (about 4,000 people) were destroyed in the 1985 eruption of the *Nevado del Ruiz volcano.

ARMS OF THE REPUBLIC.   Adopted May 9, 1834, the national emblem remains essentially the same today. It was modified by President *Mosquera, November 26, 1861, but the original was restored after the constitutional reforms of 1886. The composition was reaffirmed by decree of May 17, 1924. Above a Swiss shield is a condor, facing front, looking to the left, with wings outstretched. In its mouth is a green laurel crown with a banner of gold and the words, *Libertad y Orden* ("Liberty and Order"). On the upper third of the shield is a field of blue with an open pomegranate, or *granada,* flanked by two cornucopias opening toward the center. The cornucopia on the left is spilling forth money and the one on the right tropical fruits. In the middle third, on a field of platinum, is a liberty cap on a staff. And in the lower third, is a representation of sailing ships on both sides of the Isthmus of *Panama. The shield is framed by four Colombian flags (two on each side) with standards pointing upward, bases crossed behind the shield, and folds gathered at the bottom behind the lower point of the shield.

ARMY.   For most of the colonial period the only regular troops were those needed at the ports for coastal defense. The permanent stationing of troops in cities in the interior began only at the end of the 18th century as a consequence of the *Comuneros Revolt. The ill-trained forces who fought for *Gran Colombia numbered about 30,000 by about 1824, but the predominance of Venezuelans among the officer corps fostered in *New Granada both resentment and anti-militarism. Once Gran Colombia had dissolved, the civilian leaders of the new *República de la Nueva Granada demanded an obedient military under congressional control. The 19th-century army was kept very limited in numbers and equipment.

Early in the 20th century, the army of Colombia, like that of many other Latin American countries, was remodeled on Prussian lines. In 1907 a military mission was welcomed from Chile's Escuela Militar, then directed by General Emil Koerner Henze. The European-type training this implanted improved the military's performance, but not sufficiently to deal effectively and decisively with the Peruvians in the *Leticia Dispute, 1932-1934. The later 1930s were marked by tension between the *Liberal President Alfonso *López Pumarejo and the largely *Conservative officer corps. *World War II brought the benefits of U.S. training missions, and Colombia was eventually the only country in South America to send troops to the *Korean War.

The army's political neutrality ended abruptly in 1953 when the commander in chief, General *Rojas Pinilla, took over the government, at least in part to prevent President Laureano *Gómez from replacing him. His military rule lasted until 1957, and a transition government returned the country to civilian rule. Since then the army has been involved in combating domestic *guerrilla movements. For this it received further U.S. training and became one of the continent's most effective counter-insurgency forces during the 1960s. The army has been unable to eliminate guerrilla movements completely, however, even though its methods have become increasingly severe. During the 1980s the army came under criticism for civil rights violations both by local groups at home and by international groups such as Amnesty International and the *Organization of American States. The internal security problems have made the ideal of a neutral civilian-controlled army increasingly difficult to maintain. The response to the 1985 attack on the *Palacio de Justicia, for instance, was regarded in some quarters as the action of a military force no longer totally amenable to civilian control. More recently the situation has been complicated by the uncontrollable illegal *drug trade, which has crossed class, ideological, and professional barriers.

In recent years the Colombian army has had a strength of nearly 60,000 men (a twentyfold increase in fifty years). Of these, 20,000 are conscripts. Under the *Constitution of 1991, the army is one of four main branches of the *armed forces.

ARMY OF NATIONAL LIBERATION, see: EJERCITO DE LIBERACION NACIONAL

AROSEMENA-GUZMAN TREATY OF 1881. Signed on September 14 by Justo Arosemena, Colombia, and Antonio Leocadio Guzmán, Venezuela. The two nations agreed to submit their boundary disputes to arbitration (see: BORDERS). On March 16, 1891, authorities in Spain rendered a decision that accepted Colombian claims in the *Guajira and *Meta regions but favored Venezuelan views on the *Arauca area.

ARROBA. A twenty-five *libra weight, equivalent since metrification to 12.5 kilograms.

ARROYO DIEZ-VICENTINI INCIDENT, 1923. A minor political scandal that occurred when the Papal Nuncio, Roberto Vicentini, refused to extend greetings to the Minister of Public Instruction, Miguel Arroyo Díez, at a gathering of civil and religious officials. Monsignor Vicentini disliked the supposedly liberal orientation of Arroyo Díez and considered education one of the fields over which the Church should have control.

ARTES Y TRADICIONES POPULARES, MUSEO DE, see: MUSEO DE ARTES Y TRADICIONES POPULARES

ARTISANS' SOCIETY, 1847, see: SOCIEDAD DE ARTESANOS

ASAMBLEA CONSTITUYENTE DE 1991. A Constituent Assembly that met in *Bogotá, February 5 to July 5, to write the *Constitution of 1991. According to one participant, there were delegates from two main blocs: the traditional Liberal-Conservative Parties and protest and guerrilla groups. They were distributed this way: *Liberal Party (27), *Conservative Party (5), *M-19 Democratic Group (19), *Movement for National Salvation (11), and *Popular Liberation Army (2). There were also two nonvoting delegates. The assembly put the new constitution into effect immediately, dissolved the then-existing *Congress, and scheduled new congressional elections for October 1991.

ASAMBLEA NACIONAL, 1905-1909. A National Assembly first convened by President Rafael *Reyes on March 15, 1905.

The body was composed of three deputies from each *department who were empowered to make constitutional revisions and to take normal legislative action. Reyes used the extralegal assembly to alter the *Constitution of 1886 and to dispense with *Congress during his dictatorship. It was disbanded after his resignation in 1909.

ASAMBLEA NACIONAL CONSTITUYENTE. The National Constituent Assembly, 1952-1957. The assembly was convoked in 1952 by acting President Roberto *Urdaneta Arbeláez to revise the constitution. It was used by General *Rojas Pinilla in 1953 to authorize his role as head of state and, from 1953 to 1957, it was a legislative force to ratify the actions of his government. It was dissolved in 1957 following the collapse of the dictatorship.

ASAMBLEA NACIONAL CONSTITUYENTE Y LEGISLATIVA, 1910. A special constituent assembly called in 1910 to revise the constitution in the wake of the *Reyes regime and to act as an interim legislature until elections could restore the normal functioning of *Congress. Generally, it reinstituted the *Constitution of 1886 and then passed a number of amendments to it, including the privilege for Congress to meet annually in its own right, rather than at the request of the executive. Other reforms included the direct election of the President for a four-year term with no immediate reelection and an absolute prohibition on the emission of paper money to cover temporary emergencies.

ASIENTO DE NEGROS, see: AFRICAN SLAVERY

ASOCAÑA, see: ASOCIACION NACIONAL DE CULTIVADORES DE CAÑA DE AZUCAR

ASOCIACION COLOMBIANA DE PROMOCION ARTESANAL (ACPA). The Colombian Association for Artisan Promotion was established in 1966 as an offshoot of an institution known as the Universidad Femenina, which closed that same year. ACPA was responsible for the creation of the *Museo de Artes y Tradiciones Populares in 1971, and has been active in collecting, storing, and maintaining examples of folk arts, crafts, and skills. It has helped to organize artisan communities, to train new artisans, and to develop educational programs both for and about local cultural groups.

ASOCIACION COLOMBIANA POPULAR DE INDUSTRIA-
LES.   ACOPI is a special-interest group founded in 1951 to
promote small and medium-sized industries in food processing, tailoring, leather goods, rubber, woodworking, chemical
derivatives, printing, metalworking, and construction. Originally founded as the Colombian Association of Small Industries, 1951-1953, ACOPI was reorganized in 1961.

ASOCIACION LATINOAMERICANA DE LIBRE COMER-
CIO, see: LATIN AMERICAN FREE TRADE ASSOCIA-
TION

ASOCIACION NACIONAL DE CULTIVADORES DE CAÑA
DE AZUCAR.   Also known as ASOCAÑA, the National
Association of *Sugarcane Growers. It was founded in 1959 by
cane producers and mill operators in the Cauca Valley (*Valle
del Cauca). The group has kept members informed about
export opportunities, represented the sugar interests in international negotiations, maintained an active economic research
department, and established a museum in *Cali.

ASOCIACION NACIONAL DE INDUSTRIALES.   ANDI, an
influential *gremio económico, or pressure group, formed September 11, 1944, in Medellín. Its purpose was to protect
business interests and to encourage industrial development.
The group excludes workers and employees from membership
and generally opposes trade and labor regulations. ANDI was
recognized as a legal entity by the Minister of Government on
October 4, 1944. Its national headquarters are still in Medellín, but regional branches have been established in *Barranquilla, *Bogotá, *Bucaramanga, *Cali, *Manizales, and
*Pereira. ANDI and FENALCO (See: FEDERACION
NACIONAL DE COMERCIANTES) have been described as
the two most important special-interest groups in Colombia.
See also: FRENTE GREMIAL

ASOCIACION NACIONAL DE USARIOS CAMPESINOS.
ANUC, the National Association of Peasant Users of State
Services, organized as a state-sponsored political-interest group
during the administration of Carlos *Lleras Restrepo, 1966-
1970. According to Paul Oquist, this group grew to more than 1
million peasant members, and during the *Pastrana Borrero
administration, became progressively radicalized. It demanded
the acceleration of *agrarian reform. The government re-

sponded by dividing the organization into the passive, official wing (*Línea Armenia*), which continued to receive state support and occupy offices and positions in the Ministry of Agriculture, and the independent wing (*Línea Sincelejo*), which was vigorously repressed.

ASOCIACION PATRONAL ECONOMICA NACIONAL. APEN, the Employers' National Economic Association formed in March 1935 under the auspices of *FEDECAFE, served as a vehicle for opposition to the programs of the *López Pumarejo administration. APEN opposed any increase in the role of the federal government in the management of economic affairs. APEN supporters often opposed state intervention in labor disputes, tax reform, and educational policies. APEN members also opposed land reform programs favored by the López government, arguing that the government sought to destroy private property. APEN viewpoints were published in two newspapers, *La razón* and *La acción,* and were influential in bringing about the Land Act (*Law 200) of 1936.

ATHENS OF SOUTH AMERICA. A reference to Colombia, and in particular to *Bogotá, attributed both to Spanish literary critic Marcelino Menéndez y Pelayo and to French traveler Elisée Reclus. It recognized the humanistic and Hispanist traditions that dominated intellectual life in Colombia at the turn of the 20th century and the number of poets, novelists, linguists, essayists, and philosophers active in Colombian cultural life. The epithet was adopted by Colombians, who used it to describe themselves; see, for example, the *Memoria* of the Minister of Education for 1929.

ATLANTIC RAILROAD. The Ferrocarril del Atlántico was a line recommended by the *Currie Mission, 1950, intended to connect all existing lines along the *Magdalena River. The first sector between La *Dorada and Puerto Berrío (6° 29'N, 74° 24'W) was opened in 1958. This was followed by *Barrancabermeja–*Puerto Wilches and Fundación-Bosconia, 1959; Bosconia-Chiriguaná, 1960; Chiriguaná-Gamarra and the remaining sections to *Santa Marta, 1961. The Atlantic Railroad was the first to connect all of Colombia's major lines, thereby forming a truly national network. See also: RAILROADS

ATLANTICO, Departamento del. Located on the Caribbean Coast along the lower *Magdalena River, the department is composed of 3,388 square kilometers of tropical lowland between latitudes 10° 16′ and 11° 6′N and longitudes 74° 42′ and 75° 15′W. Estimated population in 1985 was 1,406,545 people. Population density was estimated at 415.7 people per square kilometer. The capital city is *Barranquilla. Based on DANE, *Colombia estadística 86*, principal agricultural products, with tons produced in 1984, include *yuca*, 80,000 tons; *corn, 6,571; plantains, 6,000; *cotton, 4,060; sorghum, 3,200; and yams, 210. The department also produces *sugar, beans, rice, fruits, and wood products. In 1984, 107,042 head of cattle and 36,443 hogs were slaughtered in the department, and official records showed 447 business firms employing 10 or more workers. *Fishing is important. The area is heavily industrialized, with a large export center. Major developments within the department occurred in the late 19th and 20th centuries with the growth of Barranquilla as an industrial-commercial center. The department was established in 1905, merged with *Bolívar in 1908, and permanently reestablished in 1910. A free-trade zone was created at Barranquilla in 1958.

ATRATO RIVER. An inland waterway rising on the western slopes of the *Cordillera Occidental at 5° 41′N, 76° 23′W, in the Department of *Antioquia. It flows northward through the Departments of Antioquia and *Chocó, 750 kilometers to the Gulf of *Urabá. The Atrato was discovered by Balboa (*Nuñez de Balboa) in 1511 and explored by *Robledo in 1541. During the colonial period, navigation on the Atrato was prohibited until 1790. The river is often cited as a possible site for an *interoceanic canal.

AUDIENCIA. Literally, "Audience": a royal court with judicial, legislative, and executive functions. Composed of several *oidores*, or judges, the body was the chief vehicle for enforcing royal authority on the local level. The *audiencia* was normally headed by an appointed official known as a president, when such an officer was in residence, but the court functioned whether a president was available or not.

AUDIENCIA DE PANAMA, Real. The Royal Audiencia of Panama was a jurisdiction originally created out of the *Audiencia of Santo Domingo in 1538. From 1543 to 1564 it was dissolved and its territory incorporated into the Audiencia de los Confines, whose seat was in the Honduran city of Gracias a Dios. The Audiencia of Panama was reinstated in 1564, and for the first six years of its existence also included Costa Rica. Except for a brief interruption, 1718-1722, the new Audiencia of Panama lasted until 1751, when it was merged with the *Audiencia de Santa Fe de Bogotá. The Audiencia of Panama was part of the *Virreinato del Perú until 1739, when it passed into the jurisdiction of the newly created *Virreinato del Nuevo Reino de Granada.

AUDIENCIA DE SANTA FE DE BOGOTA, Real. The Royal Audiencia of Bogotá was authorized in 1549, and established in 1550, as the first secular governing institution founded after the conquest period. The Audiencia shared ruling authority with the President of the New Kingdom of Granada after 1564. The Audiencia's president also held, de officio, executive authority over the colony of New Granada, which was in consequence denominated the *Presidencia del Nuevo Reino de Granada. When this was replaced in 1739 with the *Virreinato del Nuevo Reino de Granada, the *viceroy presided over the Audiencia.

AUDIENCIA DE SANTO DOMINGO, Real. Established in 1526, the Audiencia on the island of Hispaniola enjoyed a brief jurisdiction over all the Spanish Caribbean and circum-Caribbean colonies. Separate jurisdictions, the *Audiencias of Panama and Santa Fe de Bogotá, were created in 1538 and 1549, respectively. Santo Domingo continued to have control over Venezuela until 1786 (except for two brief periods, 1717-1723 and 1739-1742), when government of the latter was placed under the control of the Audiencia of Santa Fe and the Viceroyalty of New Granada. See also: VENEZUELA, Relations with

AUGUSTINIANS. One of four religious orders favored for missionary work among the Indians in the 16th century. Augustinian monks appeared in *New Granada as early as the 1530s. Monasteries were established in *Bogotá, 1575; *Cartagena, 1580; *Tunja, 1582; *Cali, ca. 1582; *Pasto, 1585; and *Pamplona, 1591. The Augustinian Province of Nuestra Señora de Gracia del Nuevo Reino was founded in 1601 with jurisdiction over the monasteries then established in Bogotá, Cartagena, Pamplona, Villa de *Leiva, *Mompós, San Cristóbal, Mérida, and Gibraltar.

AUTODEFENSA OBRERA. ADO (also known as Movimiento de Autodefensa Obrera), an independent *guerrilla movement, founded in *Bogotá, some say in 1974, by Juan Manuel González Puentes (Giomar O'Beale, from Brazil). Important members of ADO have included Héctor Fabio, Edgardo and Adelaida Abadía Rey, Alfredo Camelo Franco, Armando López Suárez (Coleta), and Oscar Mateus Puerto (Julián). ADO's objectives were to understand the workers' attitudes, to raise the consciousness of the masses, and to stimulate struggle for workers' causes. ADO gained notoriety with the judgment and execution of Rafael Pardo Buelvas, former Minister of Government, in 1978. ADO signed truce agreements with the government in El Hobo (*Huila), April 23, and *Bogotá, April 24, 1984. See also: PARDO BUELVAS, Rafael

AUTOMOBILE INDUSTRY. Until the early 1960s, Colombia imported all its motor vehicles. Then two locally owned firms set up assembly plants under special contracts with the government, which included a 25% national requirement. By 1970 there were three firms producing 4,798 cars annually: Renault, Fiat, and General Motors. Twelve years later output was 35,567 vehicles (more than Peru's 21,977 and much higher than the 10,255 of Chile's declining industry). It was, however, barely a fifth of Venezuela's production figure, 155,108. The small output had cost implications, and by the middle of the decade a Colombian-assembled car cost about double that of the same model made in the manufacturer's home country. Inflation worsened the situation. Overall, the motor vehicle industry has hardly been affected by the *Andean Common Market.

AVIANCA. Aerovías Nacionales de Colombia, the Colombian national airline, was created in 1940 by a renaming of *SCADTA and its merger with SACO (*Servicio Aéreo Colombiano). The new company began with Pan American owning 80% of the stock, the Colombian government 15%, and other Colombia owners 5%. By 1975, Pan American's share of the stock had fallen to 11%. Martín del Corral was Avianca's first president. Douglas DC-3s were introduced in the early 1940s, and, in 1947, DC-4s began the first long-distance international flights with a route to Miami, Florida. Flights to Lisbon, Paris, and Rome were added in 1950. Jet service began in 1960. See also: AIR TRANSPORT

AVIATION, see: AIR FORCE; AIR TRANSPORT

AYACUCHO, Battle of. December 9, 1824. Ayacucho, Peru (13° 10'S, 63° 18'W) was the last major land battle of the wars of independence. The patriot forces under General *Sucre defeated the royalist army of Viceroy-General José de la Serna. Ayacucho was part of the Colombian contribution to the liberation of Peru. See: INDEPENDENCE MOVEMENT

AZUA E ITURGOYEN, Pedro Felipe de, 1693-1754. Archbishop of *Bogotá, 1745-1754, he was born in Santiago de Chile, where he was baptized on March 29. He died in *Cartagena, April 22. He studied law at the University of San Marcos in Lima (Peru) and became a lawyer in 1711. He was ordained in 1712. After various lesser charges, including that of schoolmaster, he was named Bishop of Botri in 1735 and Bishop of Concepción in 1742, before he was appointed Archbishop of Bogotá on December 18, 1744. In Bogotá, he issued strict regulations on the use of *chicha, 1748; ordered reform of ecclesiastical behavior, 1749-1750; and showed concern for the care and discipline of the *Indians.

AZUERO, Vicente, 1787-1844. Lawyer, patriot leader, fervent liberal ideologue, and presidential candidate; born April 27, Oiba (*Santander); died hacienda La Esperanza near La Mesa (*Cundinamarca), September 28. He was active in the *independence movement 1810-1816, a Spanish prisoner 1816-1819, and a patriot leader again after 1819. He was a delegate to the *Congress of Cúcuta (over which he presided) in 1821 and the Congress of 1823, and he was active in legal circles during the 1820s. Azuero was the author of Representación a Bolívar (1826), which objected to anti-democratic proposals then under discussion, and an ardent defender of constitutional procedures and civil liberties until he was expelled from Colombia for alleged complicity in the attempt to assassinate *Bolívar in 1828 (see: *TWENTY-FIFTH OF SEPTEMBER CONSPIRACY). He returned from exile in 1829 and was a member of the *Council of State under President Joaquín *Mosquera until the latter was overthrown by the *Urdaneta dictarorship. During the 1830s he was active in educational associations and a member of *Congress, and he was a presidential candidate in 1836 and 1840. He was imprisoned as a suspected conspirator against the state during the War of the *Supreme Commanders and retired from active politics afterward.

-B-

BACATA. A form of the name *Bogotá used by the *Chibchas.

BACHUE. Mother goddess in *Chibcha lore. She is said to have come from Lake Iguaque north of *Tunja with a three-year-old son whom she later married. From their union the human race was born. After years of teaching the new human beings arts, crafts, and moral precepts, both Bachué and her son-husband became serpents and returned to the lake. She is is also patroness of music, fertility, the night, and pleasure and is sometimes called *Chía.

BACHUES, see: POST-NUEVOS

BADILLO, Juan, see: VADILLO, Juan

BADILLO, Pedro de, d. 1528? Acting governor of *Santa Marta, 1526-1528. He was named interim governor to replace Rodrigo de *Bastidas when the latter was wounded by mutinous followers. During his short rule Badillo authorized expeditions against the Indians (*Taironas) of La Ramada and *Valledupar. He developed a reputation for cruel, avaricious behavior. In 1528, he was sent back to Spain to account for his actions, but he died en route.

BAGATELA, La. A newspaper edited by Antonio *Nariño, July 14, 1811, to April 12, 1812. There were 38 issues devoted principally to arguments in favor of centralism as opposed to federalism as a form of government for the new republics (see: CENTRALISM-FEDERALISM). The newspaper exerted a strong influence over political developments in *Cundinamarca and the United Provinces (*Provincias Unidas de Nueva Granada).

BAJO PALACE, Battle of. March 28, 1811, *Valle del Cauca. Colonel Antonio Baraya, patriot, defeated the royalist forces of Governor Miguel Tacón. It was the first major military engagement of the *independence movement.

BAL, Robert, see: VAL, Robert

BALANCE OF PAYMENTS, see: FOREIGN TRADE

BALANCE OF TRADE, see: FOREIGN TRADE

BALBOA, Vasco Nuñez de, see: NUÑEZ DE BALBOA, Vasco

BANANA ZONE STRIKE, see: UNITED FRUIT COMPANY STRIKE

BANANAS. Bananas are one of Colombia's principal export crops. According to some sources, bananas were first grown in the *Santa Marta region in 1883. Serious commercial production (particularly of the Cavendish variety) did not develop, however, until after 1899, when the *United Fruit Company began cultivation of sweet, eating bananas for export. From 1899 to 1930 commercial production was concentrated in the municipalities surrounding Santa Marta, and much of the export trade was with British markets. The United Fruit Company dominated the banana industry until after *World War II. In 1963, production of the Gros Michel variety of banana was initiated in the *Urabá region around the port of Turbo (8° 6'N, 76° 43'W, *Antioquia). Efforts to institute commercial banana production around *Tumaco (Nariño) in the 1950s proved unsuccessful. See also: UNITED FRUIT COMPANY STRIKE

BANCO AGRICOLA HIPOTECARIO, see: CAJA DE CREDITO AGRARIO, INDUSTRIAL Y MINERO

BANCO CAFETERO. Established in 1954 to aid *coffee growers, the Banco Cafetero was one of several such specialized banks. See also: BANCO POPULAR

BANCO CENTRAL. A national bank established 1905-1909 by the administration of Rafael *Reyes to create a viable national financial institution that would stabilize public revenues. It was stripped of all official status following the resignation of Reyes in 1909.

BANCO CENTRAL HIPOTECARIO. Central Mortgage Bank, established in 1932 by the administration of Enrique *Olaya Herrera. Originally funded at 20 million *pesos, the bank's purpose was to provide cheap mortgages and housing credit to low-income families.

BANCO DE BOGOTA. Founded November 15, 1870, with the first board of directors meeting on November 24, 1870, the Bank of *Bogotá is the oldest continuously functioning bank in Colombia. It was the first private bank given authority to issue government notes. Colombia's oldest banking firms also include the Banco de Colombia (founded in 1874) and the Banco del Estado (1884). A Banco Popular, founded in 1877, closed after a short time.

BANCO DE COLOMBIA. One of the country's oldest banks, founded in 1874. See: BANCO DE BOGOTA

BANCO DE LA REPUBLICA. The Bank of the Republic, founded in 1923 in accordance with recommendations of the *Kemmerer report, is the principal administrative agent for government financial matters. The bank regulates currency issues and has official control of the *emerald market. It was the originator of the *Gold Museum and has been responsible for the publication of numerous important historical and financial works. Under the *Constitution of 1991, the bank is specifically empowered to issue legal currency, to regulate international exchange and credit, to make loans to the government, and to serve as financial agent for the government. The bank is run by a board of directors (Junta Directiva) made up of the Minister of Finance (Hacienda), the Director (Gerente) of the bank, and five other directors appointed by the *President for 4-year terms.

BANCO DEL ESTADO. One of Colombia's oldest banks, founded in 1884. See: BANCO DE BOGOTA

BANCO GANADERO. Established in 1956 to aid cattle ranchers. See also: BANCO POPULAR

BANCO NACIONAL. A government-sponsored national bank, 1881-1894. It was established by the administration of Rafael *Núñez to stabilize finances and to promote internal development. Political opposition and objections to its currency manipulations forced the controversial institution into liquidation in 1894-1898.

BANCO POPULAR. One of several financial institutions established in the 1950s to promote the interests of specially designated groups. The Banco Popular (founded in 1950) was to assist people with lower incomes; the *Banco Cafetero (1954) aided *coffee producers; the Banco Ganadero (1956) benefited cattle ranchers; etc. The Banco Popular was also the name of a short-lived firm founded in 1877.

BANK OF LONDON, MEXICO, AND SOUTH AMERICA. A British-owned financial institution established in *Bogotá in 1865. It was the first foreign-owned bank in Colombia and lasted approximately one year. Suspicion and fear of foreign interference in domestic affairs caused people to take advantage of the bank and forced its closing.

BANK OF THE REPUBLIC, see: BANCO DE LA REPUBLICA

BANKS, BANKING, AND FINANCIAL INSTITUTIONS. In Colombia, as in much of Latin America, modern banking was slow to develop. As late as 1875 the country still had only two banks. A hundred years later there were twenty-four banks (seven of them foreign-owned) with a total of 1,900 branches and agencies. In the late 1870s the banking sector began to grow quickly, and by 1881 there were a total of forty-two banks. But the withdrawal of the right of note emission from all but the *Banco Nacional in 1887 reduced profits so drastically that five years later all but fourteen of these early banks had closed. The Banco Nacional was itself liquidated in 1894, leaving the nation without a central bank until 1905 when the *Banco Central was established. The latter lost its central status in 1909. Colombia's present central bank, the *Banco de la República, came about as a result of the *Kemmerer report in 1923. Despite its official role, the Banco de la República was privately owned until the government took it over in April 1973. Until the mid-20th century, banks provided only short-term credit. Economic growth depended on entrepreneurs' own savings and reinvestment of profits. *Bogotá and *Medellín have stock exchanges, but these supply only limited capital equity. Shares do not attract the Colombian investor, who seeks a high current return rather than capital appreciation. During the Depression of the 1930s, government investment became significant. In the 1940s and 1950s, the government encouraged new financial institutions willing to undertake long-term loans. The first of these was the government's own *Instituto de Fomento Industrial.

BARBA JACOB, Porfirio, see: OSORIO BENITEZ, Miguel Angel

BARBACOAS, Battle of. June 1, 1824, 1° 41'N, 78° 8'W, *Nariño. Patriot victory in which the then Lieutenant Colonel Tomás C. de *Mosquera was wounded while defeating the guerrilla leader Agustín Agualongo. Barbacoas was an example of the rather frequent guerrilla warfare characteristic of the Nariño area in the 19th century.

BARBULA, Battle of. September 30, 1813, Venezuela. Patriot forces under *Bolívar disrupted the movement of royalist General Domingo Monteverde. The patriot victory is remembered for the heroic action and death of Colonel Atanasio *Girardot.

BARCO CONCESSION. The oldest petroleum concession in Colombia. A contract signed with Colonel Virgilio Barco, October 16, 1905, granted the right to exploit oil deposits (originally discovered by Ramón Leandro Peñado) in the *Catatumbo region (*Norte de Santander). The privilege was revoked for noncompliance in 1926 and 1928, but the Folson-Chaux contract approved by *Congress on June 20, 1931, reauthorized it for another 50 years. Control of the concession passed first to the Colombian Petroleum Company formed in 1918 by Barco and representatives of the Carib Syndicate Carl McFadden, W. E. Griffiths, and George Du Bois, and then to South American Gulf Oil. Development of the concession was eventually effected by the construction of a pipeline from Petrolea (Norte de Santander) to Coveñas (*Sucre).

BARCO VARGAS, Virgilio, 1921-. Economist, civil engineer, legislator, *Liberal politician, President of Colombia, 1986-1990. Born in *Cúcuta, Barco received his degree in civil engineering from the *Universidad Nacional in *Bogotá and his master's degree in economics from Massachusetts Institute of Technology. He was Minister of Communications, 1945-1946; Minister of Public Works, 1958-1961; Minister of Agriculture, 1963-1964; and Mayor of *Bogotá, 1966-1969. He has served in both houses of *Congress and as Ambassador to the *United Kingdom, 1961-1962, and to the United States, 1977-1980. He has also been Executive Director of the World Bank, 1969-1974. Virgilio Barco won the 1986 presidential election with 4,123,176 votes (58.2% of those cast). He formed a partisan (Liberal) cabinet, thereby becoming the first president since the formation of the *Frente Nacional not to choose bipartisan ministers. His administration was able to conclude a peace settlement with the *Movimiento Diecinueve de Abril, but it was marked by intense conflict with dealers in the illegal *drug trade and a drop in coffee revenue when the *International Coffee Agreement collapsed (1989).

BARRANCABERMEJA.   Commercial center located at 7° 4'N, 73° 52'W, on the *Magdalena River in the Department of *Santander. Altitude is 75 meters; the average temperature, 28°C; and population 139,708 people (1985 estimate). Barrancabermeja has become an important agricultural, commercial, transportation, and *petroleum production center. It is about 163 kilometers from *Bucaramanga, served by air, highway, rail, and river traffic, and is connected to Puerto Salgar (5° 30'N, 74° 39'W, *Cundinamarca) by means of an oil pipeline. Established on the site of an Indian village called La Tora discovered by *Jiménez de Quesada in 1536, the settlement was first called Barrancas Coloradas by the early colonists and then eventually Barrancabermeja.

BARRANQUILLA.   Capital of *Atlántico situated at 11° N, 74° 48'W, at an altitude of 4 meters with an average temperature of 28°C. The fourth largest city in Colombia, Barranquilla's greater metropolitan area has a population of 1,120,975 people (1985 estimate). It is a commercial-industrial center with more than 70 shipping firms. It was declared a free-trade zone in 1958. The city was founded in 1629 by cattle ranchers from nearby Galapa (10° 54'N, 74° 53'W). It became the capital of Barlovento in the Province of *Cartagena, April 7, 1813. Barranquilla was the departure point for the first Colombian airmail flight—Barranquilla to Puerto Colombia (11° 8'N, 75° 9'W)—on June 18, 1919, and the first commercial flight—Barranquilla to Girardot (4° 18'N, 74° 48'W)—on October 20, 1920. Barranquilla is well known for its annual carnival celebrations. See also: BOCAS DE CENIZA

BARRANQUILLA, Battle of.   February 11, 1885. *Atlántico. *Liberal Generals Ricardo Gaitán Obeso, Ramón Collante, Nicolás Jimeno, and José F. Acevedo, commanders of rebel forces, successfully withstood the siege of Barranquilla by *Conservative General Carlos V. Urueta, for the government.

BARRANQUILLA GROUP.   The Grupo de Barranquilla, a literary group composed of Germán Vargas (1919-), Alvaro

Cepeda Samudio (1926-1972), Alonso Fuenmayor (1927-), and Gabriel *García Márquez (1927-), important in regional cultural events and national literature since the 1960s. The work of this regional cultural group was disseminated, in particular, by Germán Vargas and his columns in El *Heraldo, a major Barranquilla newspaper. For the group's most widely known figure, see also: GARCIA MARQUEZ, Gabriel.

BARRIOS Y TOLEDO, Juan de los, ca. 1496-1569. Franciscan. Bishop of *Santa Marta, 1552-1563, and first Archbishop of Bogotá, 1564-1569. He was born in the Villa de Pedroche (Extremadura, Spain); died *Bogotá, February 12. After serving as a missionary in Peru, he was named Bishop of Asunción (Paraguay) in 1547, but he was never able to reach Asunción. While still Bishop of Santa Marta, he was ordered to reside in Bogotá. As Bishop, and then later the first Archbishop of Bogotá, he was remembered for his organizational ability; his efforts to build a permanent cathedral; the founding of *San Pedro Hospital, 1564; convocation of the first Diocesan Synod in New Granada, 1566; and numerous pastoral visits to churches outside of Bogotá.

BARROT AFFAIR. A diplomatic dispute arising from the arrest of French Consul Adolphe Barrot in *Cartagena, September 3, 1833. French warships threatened to bombard the port, 1833-1834. *New Granada eventually paid damages in a negotiated settlement, which indicated the weakness of the new republic. See also: RUSSELL AFFAIR

BASQUES. A people from northeastern Spain. See also: CREOLES, Origins of

BASTIDAS, Rodrigo de, 1460-1526. Conquistador, born in Seville (Spain). Bastidas first reached Colombia, 1500-1501, when he sailed along most of the Caribbean Coast, naming the *Magdalena River in the process. Arrested by *Pedrarias for allegedly exceeding his authority, Bastidas was forced to return to Spain to stand trial in 1503, but he was acquitted and given permission to establish a colony in 1521. He founded *Santa Marta in 1525 but ran into conflicts with his men over their treatment of the *Indians. He died in Cuba in 1526, the victim of a stabbing by one of his rebellious followers.

BASUCO. Also spelled "bazuco"; a partially refined *coca paste or powder intended for smoking. Basuco is not so purified as cocaine and can be even more dangerous because it often retains processing residues. See: COCAINE

BATALLON AMERICANO. The American Battalion was an international *guerrilla group announced January 1986 by Carlos *Pizarro Leongómez, then military commander of the *Movimiento Diecinueve de Abril. The intent was to unite guerrilla fighters from several nations, especially Colombia, Ecuador, and Peru. While some members of the *Coordinadora Guerrillera "Simon Bolívar" joined the proposed group, and the American Battalion claimed responsibility for seizing two towns in the Department of *Cauca (Belalcázar on August 7, and Inzá on September 7), the battalion was short-lived and never fully developed.

BATEMAN CAYON, Jaime, ca. 1938-1983. *Guerrilla leader, born in *Santa Marta to a father of United States descent. He joined the *Juventud Comunista as a student and later the *Partido Comunista de Chile, which sent him to the Soviet Union for training in the Consomol (Komsomol). On his return in 1966, he joined FARC (the *Fuerzas Armadas Revolucionarias de Colombia) where he served as a secretary to "Tiro Fijo" (Pedro Antonio *Marín). Expelled from the Communists and FARC in 1972, he became a founding father of the M-19 (*Movimiento Diecinueve de Abril). On April 28, 1983, he was killed when a small plane in which he was traveling with a *cocaine smuggler, Antonio Escobar Bravo, crashed en route to Panama. Bateman was known in M-19 as Pablo Pueblo, Pablo García, and El Flaco. He was succeeded by his second in command, Iván Marino *Ospina.

BATTLES, see: ANORI; ARBOLES, Los; AYACUCHO; BAJO PALACE; BARBACOAS; BARRANQUILLA; BOGOTA; BOMBONA, BOSA BRIDGE; BOYACA; BUENAVISTA; BUESACO; CALIBIO; CARABOBO; CHANCA, La; CHANCOS, Los; COLON; CONCEPCION; COROZAL; CUASPUD; CUCHILLA DEL TAMBO; DERRUMBADO, El; DON JUANA, La; ENCISO; GACHETA; GARRA-PATA; GUEPI; HORMAZEQUE; HUMAREDA; ITAGUI; JUNIN; MANIZALES; MARACAIBO; NEIVA; OCAÑA; ORATORIO; PALACIO DE JUSTICIA; PALMIRA; PALO RIVER; PALONEGRO; PAMPLONA; PANTANO DE

VARGAS; PEDRERA, La; POLONIA, La; RIOFRIO; RI-
ONEGRO; ROLDANILLO; SALADO; SALAMINA; SAN
AGUSTIN; SAN MATEO; SANTA BARBARA DE CAR-
TAGO; SANTUARIO; SEGOVIA; SONSO; SUB-
ACHOQUE; TARQUI; TENERIFE; TESCUA; TISQUISA;
TRIBUNAL, La; TULCAN; ZIPAQUIRA. See also: RIOTS

BAZUCO, see: BASUCO

BEAUTEMPS, Jean de. Known by the Spanish as "Don Juan," he
was a 16th-century pirate and ally of Martin *Cote. See:
PIRACY

BELALCAZAR (also, Benalcázar), Sebastián de, 1495-1551.
Born in Belalcázar (Spain), he first came to America with the
expedition of Pedro Arias de Avila (*Pedrarias) and later
joined the expedition of Francisco *Pizarro to Peru. Acting on
authority from Pizarro, Belalcázar became the explorer and
conqueror of southern Colombia and the Cauca Valley (*Valle
del Cauca), 1535-1539. The founder of *Cali and *Popayán, he
was named governor of the latter in 1540 and remained active
in the development of southern Colombia until his death.
Accused of irregularities in the arrest of Pascual de *Andagoya
and the execution of Jorge *Robledo, he died in *Cartagena en
route to Spain to defend himself against the charges.

BELTRAN, Luis, 1526-1581. Saint; born January 1, he was a
Dominican missionary who visited Colombia from 1562 to
1569, working with the Indians around Santa Marta. Later
canonized, San Luis Beltrán was named Principal Patron of the
*Nuevo Reino de Granada by Pope Alexander VIII in 1690.

BELTRAN, Manuela. A member of the artisan class, she is
frequently cited as the instigator of the *Comunero Revolt in
*Socorro, March 16, 1781, because she touched off the vio-
lence by tearing up a royal tax edict while shouting, "Long live
the King! Down with bad government!" Little else is known
about her.

BENALCAZAR, Sebastián de, see: BELALCAZAR, Sebastián de

BENIDORM, Pact of. An agreement concluded July 18-23,
1956, in Benidorm, Spain, between Alberto *Lleras Camargo
for the *Liberal Party and Laureano *Gómez for the *Conser-

vatives. The pact laid the foundation for cooperation between the two parties and eventually led to the formation of the National Front (*Frente Nacional). It was followed by a joint declaration of the parties, March 20, 1957; the *Sitges Accord, July 1957; and a national referendum, December 1957.

BENTHAMISM.   A reference to the philosophy of utilitarianism and the influence of Jeremy Bentham (1748-1832). Together with the concepts of Antoine Louis Claude Destutt de Tracy (1754-1836), Benthamism strongly influenced the national *education programs from 1826 to 1842. The ideology was advocated by progressive liberals but opposed by conservatives and more orthodox Catholics.

BERBEO, Juan Francisco, 1729-1795.   General Commander of the *Comunero Revolt, 1781; baptized *Socorro, June 17; died Socorro, June 28. A businessman of reasonably well-to-do fortune in Socorro, he accepted the command of the Comunero Revolt somewhat reluctantly and led the movement until June 4-8, when he negotiated a truce with the royal authorities. He is said to have been responsible for keeping the movement from becoming more violent and destructive than it was. As a result of this and his peaceful negotiation of a truce, he was given a royal appointment following the settlement. This was later withdrawn, however, and he died in relative obscurity.

BERRIO MUÑOZ, Gustavo.   *Rojas Pinilla's Minister of War.

BERRUECOS, Crime of.   The assassination, June 4, 1830, of General Antonio José de *Sucre at Berruecos Mountain, *Nariño. The crime has never been satisfactorily explained, but accusations naming General José María *Obando as the principal instigator contributed to political tensions in *New Granada until 1849. Berruecos was also the scene of the death of Julio *Arboleda in 1862.

BETANCOURT DE LISA, Regina.   Presidential candidate in the May 1986 elections, who represented the Movimiento Megapolítico Unitario. She received less than 1% of the popular vote.

BETANCUR, Kidnapping of Jaime.   On November 22, 1983, members of the *Ejército de Liberación Nacional (E.L.N.) kidnapped Jaime Betancur, the brother of President Belisario

*Betancur and a member of the *Council of State, in *Bogotá. E.L.N. ransom demands included a rise in the national minimum wage, freezing of prices, firing of managers of public services, demilitarization of peasant zones, and the arrest of all leaders of the Death to Kidnappers (*Muerte a Secuestradores) group. None of the demands was met, and Fidel Castro appealed to the E.L.N. to free the President's brother. Betancur was released in December.

BETANCUR CUARTAS, Belisario, 1923-. Lawyer, author, *Conservative politician, President of Colombia, 1982-1986. Born Amagá (*Antioquia), February 4. He received his law degree from the Universidad Católica Bolivariana in *Medellín in 1947. He was Dean of the Law Faculty at the National University (*Universidad Nacional) in *Bogotá; Deputy to the Assembly of Antioquia, 1945-1947; various times Representative or Senator in the national *Congress; Minister of Education, 1960; Minister of Labor, 1963; and Ambassador to Spain. He was director of the newspapers La Defensa, *El Siglo, Semana, Promete, and La Unidad, as well as the author of numerous works, including Sí se puede (1982). His presidency was most notable for a "declaration of peace" and his efforts to negotiate settlements with *guerrilla factions in Colombia. In foreign affairs Betancur pursued the *Contadora initiative in Central America and received Pope *John Paul II when he visited Colombia in 1986. The ill-fated siege of the Palace of Justice (*Palacio de Justicia) in 1985 was probably the most unfortunate and controversial incident of his term in office.

BIBLE SOCIETY, see: SOCIEDAD BIBLICA

BIBLIOTECA LUIS ANGEL ARANGO. Located in *Bogotá, the library was inspired by a former director of the *Banco de la República, for whom it was named. It was founded in 1958 under the auspices of the bank and is one of the largest modern technical libraries in Colombia.

BIBLIOTECA NACIONAL. The National Library of Colombia, located in *Bogotá. Originally, it was the Royal Library, proposed by Antonio *Moreno y Escandón in 1774. Authorized in 1775, it was opened February 2, 1777, by Viceroy Manuel Antonio *Flórez with a collection of books based on the works confiscated from the *Jesuits in 1767. The most famous director of the colonial period was Manuel del Socorro

*Rodríguez. The library has been in more or less continuous service since 1777 and is now a responsibility of the Ministry of National Education. It has suffered, however, from chronic underfunding, and its entitlement by legal deposit to a copy of each work published in the nation has never been adequately enforced. The staff often is insufficient and has relatively few trained librarians. The total collection is estimated at 300,000 volumes (compared to the national libraries of Mexico, Chile, and Brazil, which have 1 million, 2 million, and 4 million, respectively). The national bibliography (the *Anuario Bibliográfico Colombiano*) is compiled by the *Instituto Caro y Cuervo rather than the National Library.

BI-FRONT GENERATION, see: SOCIALISTIC GENERATION

BIOHO, Domingo. A black leader, originally brought to *New Granada in 1596 as a slave named Benkos-Bioho. Rechristened Domingo Bioho, he escaped from his master in 1596 and became king of the *Palenque of *Matuna, which developed near *Cartagena, 1600-1621. This *cimarrón* (*maroon) community organized its own government and flourished until 1621, having negotiated a truce with Spanish officials in 1605. The community disbanded in 1621 after Bioho was captured and executed. See also: SAN BASILIO, Palenque de

BISHOPRICS, see: ARCHDIOCESES OF COLOMBIA

BITTERMAN, Chester, 1952-1981. Missionary-translator, born November 30, Lancaster, Pennsylvania (U.S.A.), Bitterman was working for the Summer Institute of Linguistics when he was kidnapped in *Bogotá in January 1981. He was supposedly abducted by members of the M-19 (*Movimiento Diecinueve de Abril), who accused him of working for the C.I.A. and foreign businesses. The kidnappers demanded that the Summer Institute leave Colombia. It refused, and Bitterman was found shot in a bus in March. One year later, March 1982, an M-19 guerrilla, Hugo Osvaldo Chávez Urrutia, arrested in Bogotá, was said to have confessed to the murder.

BLACKS. A history of *African slavery has given Colombia a large population of African origin, the bulk of it still in the former plantation and mining areas along the Atlantic and Pacific Coasts. Such a large proportion of the population of

*Chocó is of African descent that the term *chocoano* is used elsewhere in Colombia as a popular word for a black. Some communities on the site of former *palenques,* *maroon villages, are wholly black. Estimates of the number of Colombia's blacks range from 2% to 8% of the nation. More precise figures are precluded by the omission of racial categories in the *census since 1918.

BOCAS DE CENIZA. The area at the mouth of the *Magdalena River (11° 6'N, 74° 51'W). More specifically, a land bar that impeded direct entry from the Caribbean Sea to the river. Various projects were considered for removing or restructuring the bar between 1876 and 1925. Beginning in 1925 and concluding in 1936, an entry canal was built through the Bocas de Ceniza, and maritime facilities were provided to allow ocean vessels access to *Barranquilla. The works have been renovated several times since then.

BOCHICA. Also *Nemquetaba or Zue, a beneficent deity of the *Chibchas, sometimes identified with the sun. He was patron of weaving. His legends are frequently intermingled or confused with those of Garachacha, the civilizer. According to legend, Bochica was the creator of the *Tequendama Falls. He also punished his fellow deity, Chibchacum, for abusive treatment of the Chibcha *Indians by making him carry the world on his shoulders. See also: CHIBCHACUM

BOGOTA. Capital of *Cundinamarca and, as the Distrito Especial de Bogotá, capital of Colombia. Estimated population in 1985 was 3,967,318 people (with a density of approximately 2,500 people per square kilometer). Bogotá is located at 4° 35'N, 74° 4'W, at the foot of two mountains known as Guadaloupe and Monserrate. The altitude is 2,600 meters, and the average temperature, 14°C. Bogotá was formally established August 6, 1538, by *Jiménez de Quesada, with the name Santa Fe. Its first *cabildo met April 29, 1539. The settlement was elevated to the rank of city with a coat of arms in 1548, and the Real *Audiencia de Santa Fe de Bogotá was established there in 1549. The largest city in Colombia, Bogotá is an important industrial and cultural center, for more than 400 years the seat of civil and ecclesiastical administrative institutions. The development of the metropolitan area of Bogotá can be seen in these representative census figures 1673 (3,000 people); 1780 (18,000); 1807 (22,870); 1851 (29,649); 1881

(84,723); 1893 (135,000); 1905 (140,000); 1928 (235,421); 1948 (552,877); and 1957 (1,000,000). See also: DISTRITO ESPECIAL DE BOGOTA; SANTA FE DE BOGOTA

BOGOTA, ARCHBISHOPRIC OF, see: SANTA FE DE BOGOTA, Archbishopric of

BOGOTA, "Battle of." March 7, 1861. A descriptive reference to the excessive violence used by forces of the Granadine Confederation (*Confederación Granadina) in foiling the attempted escape of political prisoners. Numerous deaths prompted Archbishop Antonio *Herrán to intervene on behalf of the prisoners.

BOGOTA, Battle of, 1854. December 4; *Cundinamarca. Government forces under General Pedro A. *Herrán defeated the troops of General José M. *Melo, ending his dictatorship.

BOGOTA, Battle of, 1861. July 18 (see: BOGOTA, Capture of).

BOGOTA, Battles of, 1813-1814. January 9, 1813, the federalist army of the United Provinces (*Provincias Unidas de Nueva Granada) under Colonel Antonio Baraya failed in its efforts to capture the centralist capital of *Cundinamarca. However, on December 9-12, 1814, the centralist forces under General José Ramón de Leyva were defeated by the federalists under *Bolívar. See also: CENTRALISM-FEDERALISM

BOGOTA, Capture of. July 18, 1861, *Cundinamarca. General T. C. de *Mosquera, rebel, defeated General Ramón Espina, overthrowing the acting President, Bartolomé *Calvo, and the *Confederación Granadina.

BOGOTA, Defense of, 1840, see: GRAN SEMANA, La

BOGOTA, Distrito Especial de, see: DISTRITO ESPECIAL DE BOGOTA

BOGOTA ELECTRIC LIGHT COMPANY. The first major electricity-producing firm organized in *Bogotá and present-day Colombia. (The *Panama Electric Light Company began operation in *Panama in 1889.) It was formed on the basis of a government contract dated August 4, 1886, with the firm of Ospina Brothers of *Medellín for the purpose of providing street lighting for the city of Bogotá. The English name was used after July 6, 1891. Operating on capital provided by the Ospina family, the *Banco de Bogotá, the Carrizoza family, and others, the company began distributing electrical service on January 1, 1890, in the districts of La Catedral and Parque de Santander. From public street lighting, the company expanded its clientele to include industrial and private electrical service. The company, which based its production on coal-generated electricity, was inoperative by 1898, and the machinery was purchased by the national government in 1905.

BOGOTANO. A resident of *Bogotá. Also a descriptive term denoting a character of austerity and excessive formality. Among the upper classes, the term may imply sophistication, superficial cleverness, and wit. See also: ANDINO; REINOSO; TINTERILLO

BOGOTAZO. Popular name for the riots touched off on April 9, 1948, by the assassination of Jorge Eliécer *Gaitán in *Bogotá; also known as the Nueve de Abril. Although the major outbursts were subdued by April 11, the *Bogotazo* might be cited as the beginning of "the Violence" (see: VIOLENCIA, La), which lasted for years in various parts of Colombia. Portions of the central city were destroyed during these riots in Bogotá.

BOLIVAR, Departamento de. Located on the Caribbean Coast paralleling the lower *Magdalena River, Bolívar covers an area of 25,978 square kilometers between latitudes 7° 2' and 10° 48'N, and longitudes 73° 45' and 75° 43'W. The terrain is lowland with rolling hills; 24,126 square kilometers with tropical climate and 1,852 in more temperate zones. Average temperatures are 26°-30°C. The population in 1985 was 1,199,437 people, with an estimated density of 46.2 people per square kilometer. Principal rivers include the Magdalena, *Cauca, and Brazo de Loba. The jurisdiction of Bolívar includes the offshore Archipelago of Rosario and the islands of Barú and Tierrabomba. *Cartagena is the capital city. Based on DANE, *Colombia estadística 86,* principal crops, with tonnage produced in 1984, were plantains, 98,000 tons; *yuca, 96,000; rice, 30,610; *corn, 30,368; sorghum, 15,080; yams, 15,000; *cotton, 10,440; *sugar, 4,800; *tobacco, 3,600; beans, 800; sesame, 50; and *cacao, 25. *Fishing, *petroleum processing, and *livestock are important industries. Livestock figures show 123,812 head of cattle and 19,389 hogs were slaughtered in

1984. Cartagena is heavily industrialized and is a major import-export center. There were 1,983 businesses employing 10 or more people in 1983. The department was established in 1886, but reduced in size in 1910, 1951, and 1966 to allow formation of the Departments of *Atlántico, *Córdoba, and *Sucre. Its name derives from the renaming of the then-province of Cartagena in honor of Simón *Bolívar in the early years of Colombian independence.

BOLIVAR, Simón, 1783-1830. Born Caracas (Venezuela), July 24; died at the estate of San Pedro Alejandrino (near *Santa Marta), December 17. Bolívar received part of his education from his private tutor, Simón Rodríguez, and entered military service as a sublieutenant in the Sixth Company of the Batallion of White Militia in the Valley of Aragua in 1798. He completed his education traveling in Europe and the United States, 1799-1802 and 1803-1807. He joined the patriot movement in Venezuela in 1810 and tried to negotiate aid for the *independence movement in England. After the collapse of the first Venezuelan Republic, 1811-1812, he joined the independence movement in *Cartagena and the United Provinces (*Provincias Unidas de Nueva Granada) in present-day Colombia, 1812-1813. In 1813-1814, he led the Admirable Campaign (*Campaña Admirable) to free Venezuela, and in December 1814 forced *Cundinamarca to join the United Provinces. However, in 1815, Bolívar was forced to flee Colombia when General Pablo *Morillo launched the Spanish Reconquest (*Reconquista). He spent 1815-1816 in Jamaica and Haiti organizing expeditions to invade the mainland. After an unsuccessful invasion of the Venezuelan coast in 1816, he settled in the *Llanos where he organized a new patriot army 1816-1819. In 1819, he conducted the Liberating Campaign (*Campaña Libertadora), which culminated in the Battle of *Boyacá and the collapse of royal government in *New Granada. In 1820-1821, he fought the Spanish in Venezuela, and he conducted campaigns to free Ecuador, Peru, and Bolivia, 1821-1826. Named the *Liberator as a result of campaigns in Venezuela, Bolívar was President of *Gran Colombia, 1819-1828, and dictator, 1828-1830. He was also the author of the *Bolivian Constitution, or the Constitution of 1826, and the initiator of the *Congress of Panama, 1826. See also: TWENTY-FIFTH OF SEPTEMBER CONSPIRACY

BOLIVAR RAILROAD.   The second railway built in Colombia, it connected *Barranquilla to the Atlantic Ocean at Puerto Salgar (5° 30'N 74° 39'W). It was authorized in 1850, but actual construction was undertaken 1869-1871 by the German firm of Hoenigsberg, Wessel and Co. The railroad effectively linked Barranquilla to the sea until the *Bocas de Ceniza, north of the city, began to receive oceangoing vessels. Service on the line was discontinued after 1940. See also: RAILROADS

BOLIVAR'S SWORD, Theft of.   On January 17, 1974, members of the newly formed *Movimiento Diecinueve de Abril (M-19) stole the Liberator's sword from the *Quinta de Bolívar in *Bogotá. The gesture was designed to announce the creation of the M-19 and to identify the legacy of *Bolívar with the social protests of the mid-20th century. Return of the sword was promised when significant social reforms had been implemented. The sword was moved many times but remained hidden over the following seventeen years. Carlos *Pizarro Leongómez claimed that it was safe but in another Latin American country when much of the M-19 surrendered in 1990. It was finally returned to authorities at the Quinta on January 31, 1991, by Antonio *Navarro Wolff after members of the M-19 had ceased fighting and participated in elections leading to a constituent assembly in February 1991.

BOLIVIAN CONSTITUTION.   The Constitution of Bolivia, adopted in 1825, written by Simón *Bolívar; also known in Colombia as the Constitution of 1826. It provided for a lifetime executive, appointment of some legislators, and censors to maintain public morality. Although he achieved its adoption in Bolivia and, briefly, in Peru, the Liberator was not successful in his attempts to extend it to Colombia. His supporters failed most conspicuously at the *Congress of Ocaña, where they were unable to secure its adoption in 1828.

BOLIVIANOS.   Supporters of *Bolívar, 1820s-1840s. The term implied either support for the actions of Bolívar as a person or a belief in his political ideas. Bolivianos tended to be authoritarian and centralistic. They were quite willing to suspend civil liberties when they deemed it desirable, and they tended to encourage the military as an active instrument of national policy.

BOMBONA, Battle of.   April 7, 1822, *Nariño. Royalist forces under Colonel Basilio García impeded the progress of *Bolívar's expedition to Ecuador and Peru. The patriots suffered a temporary setback.

BONPLAND, Aimé, 1773-1858. French botanist who accompanied Alexander von *Humboldt on his 1799-1804 travels in the Americas.

BOOKS, see: PUBLISHING

BORDERS. *Colombia is the only South American country with substantial coastlines on both the Atlantic (1,600 kilometers) and the Pacific (1,300 kilometers) oceans. The longest land frontier is that with Venezuela (2,219 kilometers). This has been the subject of several treaties (*Pombo-Michelena, 1833; *Pombo-Romero, 1842; *Arosemena-Guzmán, 1881; *Suárez-Losada 1916; and the *López de Mesa–Borges, 1941), but it is still disputed in the *Guajira Peninsula region. The extreme Venezuelan nationalist might even dispute Colombian possession of *Vichada and *Guainía. The Brazilian border is 1,645 kilometers long. It was first surveyed in 1753-1759 as a result of the 1750 Treaty of Madrid between Spain and Portugal. But the work of the *Boundary Commission was inadequate because of Portuguese procrastination, and when newly independent *Gran Colombia first proposed a treaty of limits, Brazil declined because the whole area was so unknown. In 1853, when an attempt to define the border was at last made by the *Lleras-Lisboa Treaty, it was rejected by Colombia. Agreement was eventually reached by the *Vasquez Cobo–Martins Treaty of 1907, and later clarified by the *García Ortiz–Mangabeira Treaty of 1928. The present 1,626 kilometers of the border with Peru date from 1941, when the Treaty of *Rio de Janeiro confirmed Peruvian occupation of most of Ecuadoran Amazonia. Colombia fought a border war with Peru from August 1828 to July 1829, which was eventually settled by the *Gual-Larrea Treaty of 1829. The two nations disputed the *Putumayo River boundary, which they resolved in the *Lozano-Salomón Treaty of 1922, and engaged in a brief war over occupation of *Leticia from 1932 to 1934. The border with Ecuador, now 586 kilometers, was disputed, 1830-1832, when Ecuador occupied the *Cauca, and was settled only in 1936 by the *Suárez-Muñoz Treaty. Until 1903, Colombia had a border with Costa Rica (see: COSTA RICA, Relations with). This ended in 1903 with the independence of *Panama. Since then, Colombia and Panama share a densely forested border of some 266 kilometers. The Caribbean islands of *San Andrés y Providencia lie within the maritime boundaries claimed by Nicaragua, and a few small keys within the archipelago are disputed by Honduras. The mostly rural and underdeveloped nature of Colombia's long borders make smuggling and illegal migration (principally into Venezuela) longstanding problems. See also: AREA; LAW OF THE SEA

BORJA, Juan de, 1564-1628. President of the *Nuevo Reino de Granada, 1605-1628. Best known for his successful conduct of the war against the *Pijaos, 1605-1618, his administration also saw the creation of the *Tribunal de Contadores de Cuentas, 1605, and the establishment of the *Inquisition, 1610. Borja supervised the fortification of *Cartagena; approved ordinances for protection of the *Indians, 1612 and 1616; encouraged mining and other economic activities; and founded the *Casa de Moneda, 1620.

BOSA BRIDGE, Battle of. November 22, 1854, at approximately 4° 37'N, 74° 11'W, *Cundinamarca. General José Hilario *López, for the legitimate government, defeated the forces of the dictator, General José M. *Melo.

BOTANICAL EXPEDITION. Famous scientific commission that collected, identified, and painted pictures of plants in the Viceroyalty of *New Granada, 1783-1816. Authorized by Viceroy *Caballero y Góngora, November 1, 1783, it was first directed by José Celestino *Mutis, 1783-1808, and then by Sinforoso Mutis. Its collection was transferred to Spain in 1817.

BOTERO, Fernando, 1932-. Painter, sculptor, known for his stylistic use of what have been called gorditos, or little fat people. He was born in *Medellín, and his first formal public exhibition was held in *Bogotá in 1951. He studied art in Colombia, in Spain, and in Italy, 1952-1955, and is said to have been influenced by Colombia's colonial and *Indian arts, the Mexican muralists, and his European teachers. He has lived and worked in New York, 1961-1973, and Paris, 1975-1977. During his stay in Paris, he became a sculptor as well as a painter. He has been called the *García Márquez of Colombian painting and described as a satirist known for his use of exaggerated human forms and his copies of old masters.

BOUNDARIES, National, see: BORDERS

BOUNDARY COMMISSION, Spanish-Portuguese. Headed by José de Carvajal, Spain, and Tomás de Silva y Telles, Portugal, the commission was sent to establish the geographic limits between Spanish and Portuguese possessions, following the boundary treaty between the two powers in 1750. It traveled through the viceroyalty, 1753-1759, but accomplished little. See also: BORDERS

BOURBON REFORMS, see: SPANISH EMPIRE IN AMERICA, Administration of the

BOUSSINGAULT, Jean Baptiste, 1802-1887. French naturalist who came to Colombia as part of an unsuccessful effort to found a major national museum in the 1820s. He traveled in Venezuela, Ecuador, and Colombia, 1822-1832, and later published a description of his observations in the region.

BOYACA, Battle of. August 7, 1819. The battle was the turning point in Colombia's *independence movement. Generals Simón *Bolívar, Francisco de Paula *Santander, José Antonio Anzoátegui, and others defeated the royalist army of Colonels José María Barreiro and Francisco Jiménez. Patriot forces were estimated at 2,850 troops; Spanish forces had approximately 2,760. The victory caused Viceroy Juan *Sámano to abandon the capital, leaving central Colombia to the patriots. August 7 is now a national holiday and the day on which each new President formally assumes office.

BOYACA, Cruz de. The "Cross of Boyacá," a civil and military order for distinguished services to the nation. It was created by decree in 1919 to commemorate the centenary of the Battle of Boyacá (see: BOYACA, Battle of). The original order was exclusively military, but its range was broadened first in 1922 and again definitively in 1930. The medal of Boyacá, a pendant cross on a green ribbon, was created by a *cabildo abierto in *Bogotá, September 9, 1819.

BOYACA, Departamento de. Located in eastern Colombia, Boyacá has a total of 23,189 square kilometers of mountainous terrain broken by numerous valleys and plateaus lying between latitudes 4° 50' and 7° 8'N and longitudes 67° 50' and 74° 48'W. By climatic distribution 4,648 square kilometers are tropical; 3,933, temperate; 8,415, cold; and 6,193, wasteland. Major rivers include the *Magdalena, Guaguaquí, Suárez, Chicamocha, and Garagoa. The Sierra Nevada del Cocuy has peaks reaching 5,495 meters in altitude. Estimated population of the department in 1985 was 1,085,387 people, with population density at 47 people per square kilometer. *Tunja is the capital city. According to DANE, *Colombia estadística 86,* principal agricultural products, with tonnage produced in 1984, include *potatoes, 750,000 tons; *sugar, 54,000; *corn, 51,740; plantains, 49,000; *yuca, 29,200; wheat, 15,320; barley, 5,400; beans, 4,140; *tobacco 4,000; hemp, 2,200; rice, 2,155; sorghum, 694; *cacao, 410; and soybeans, 100. *Livestock statistics show 104,750 head of cattle and 25,169 hogs slaughtered in 1984. The department also has textile, beverage, transportation equipment, and food-processing industries, as well as cement, *iron, *coal, *copper, *petroleum, and *emerald production. In 1983 the department had 39 businesses employing 10 or more workers. Boyacá is the site of important pre-Hispanic Indian settlements, especially those of the *Chibchas, and a famous patriot victory during the wars of independence. The department was first established by the *Constitution of 1821. It was modified numerous times until it was permanently established by the *Constitution of 1886. The department was reduced in size in 1911 and 1973 to allow for the formation of the Intendancies of *Arauca and *Casanare.

BRAZIL, Relations with.   Although Simón *Bolívar sent diplomatic agents to Mexico, Peru, Chile, and Buenos Aires to negotiate bilateral treaties of alliance with newly independent *Gran Colombia, none was sent to Brazil because the territory was still a Portuguese colony. Even when Dom Pedro I proclaimed Brazil's independence in 1822, Colombia was unsympathetic to an American country with a monarchical form of government. When, however, Portugal and the *United Kingdom recognized Brazilian independence in 1825, *Bolívar invited the new nation to send a representative to the *Congress of Panama, and he began negotiations to establish formal diplomatic relations. In 1827, Gran Colombia became the first Latin American country to have a permanent legation in Rio de Janeiro. In 1826, Pedro *Gual had officially rejoiced at the victories of Oriental (Uruguayan) patriots over the Brazilian army of occupation in Uruguay, but the 1828-1829 war with *Peru led Colombia to look to Brazil as a potential ally against Peru and its supporter, Argentina. The breakup of Gran Colombia ended dreams of a continental foreign policy, and Colombia and Brazil closed their respective legations in Rio and *Bogotá in 1831-1832. Since then the greatest single factor in relations between the two countries has been their shared economic dependence on *coffee. For many years Colombian coffee producers benefited from a world price kept artifically high by the Brazilian valorization program paid for by the Brazilian taxpayer. When Colombia tried to increase her share of a world market diminished by the Great Depression of the 1930s, Brazil—the world's leading coffee producer—threatened to depress prices by releasing her accumulated stocks. Only in 1940 did the two countries admit their mutual interest in stabilizing output and prices by signing the Inter-American Coffee Agreement. Disputes over their common frontier (see: BORDERS) have not been significant, although this might change with the recent rapid development of the *Amazon region and the increase in the cross-border *drug trade.

BRAZIL-COLOMBIA TREATY OF 1907, see: VASQUEZ COBO–MARTINS TREATY

BRAZIL-COLOMBIA TREATY OF 1928, see: GARCIA ORTIZ–MANGABEIRA TREATY

BRAZIL–NEW GRANADA TREATIES OF 1853, see: LLERAS-LISBOA TREATIES

BRITAIN, see: UNITED KINGDOM

BRITANNIC LEGION, see: LEGION BRITANICA

BRITISH INFLUENCE, see: UNITED KINGDOM, Relations with

BRITISH LEGION.   A term, which in the context of Colombian history, refers to a group of foreigners (See: LEGION BRITANICA) in the war for independence from Spain. Confusion should be avoided with a veteran's association, similar to the American Legion, in the *United Kingdom.

BRITISH LOANS, see: LONDON LOANS

BROADCASTING, see: RADIO BROADCASTING; TELEVISION

BUCARAMANGA. Capital of *Santander, located at 7° 8'N, 73° 8'W; population, 592,412 (1985 estimate for the greater metropolitan area); altitude, 1,018 meters; average temperature, 24°C. Bucaramanga, the fifth largest city in Colombia, is a modern university and industrial city, sometimes called the "city of parks." Textiles, farm machinery, and food processing are among the more important *manufacturing industries. The city was founded December 22, 1622, by Andrés Páez de Sotomayor and Miguel Trujillo. It became the capital of Santander between 1857 and 1862, was temporarily replaced by *Socorro from 1862 to 1886, but was restored again after 1886.

BUEN GUSTO, Tertulia de. A literary society founded around 1801, in *Bogotá. Manuela Sanz de Santamaría de Manrique presided over the group whose members were said to include Camilio *Torres, Francisco Ulloa, José Montalvo, Frutos and José María Gutiérrez, José *Fernández Madrid, José María Salazar and Custodio *García Rovira. See: TERTULIA

BUENAVENTURA. Colombia's only important port on the Pacific Ocean since the loss of *Panama. Founded in 1540, it did not become important until after it was moved to its present site on the Island of Cascajal (3° 54'N, 77° 5'W). The *Pacific Railroad from the port to *Cali (150 kilometers away) via a mountain pass through the *Cordillera Occidental was one of the nation's first railways. Expansion of the port in the 1950s directly contributed to the rapid growth of Cali since then. Buenaventura had an estimated population of 122,500 people in 1986.

BUENAVISTA, Battle of. October 28, 1840, *Cundinamarca. The joint actions at the *hacienda* Buenavista and Culebrera lane between Funza (4° 43'N, 74° 13'W) and Chia (4° 52'N, 74° 4'W) saw Colonel Juan José *Neira and General Francisco de Paula Vélez, for the government, defeat the rebel forces of Colonel Manuel *González. The battles saved *Bogotá from capture by the rebels.

BUESACO, First Battle of, 1839. August 31, at 1° 24'N, 77° 9'W, *Nariño. General Pedro A. *Herrán, for the government, defeated the rebels who opposed the closing of minor convents in *Pasto. See: MINOR CONVENTS, Rebellion of the

BUESACO, Second Battle of, 1851.   July 10, at 1° 24'N, 77° 9'W, *Nariño. General Manuel María Franco, for the government, defeated the rebel forces of Julio *Arboleda. Arboleda was forced into exile following the loss.

BUGA.   Urban center located at 3° 54'N, 76° 18'W in the eastern foothills of the *Cordillera Central in the Department of *Valle del Cauca about 78 kilometers northeast of *Cali. Altitude is 969 meters; average temperature is 23°C; and population in 1985 was 82,766 people. Also the see of a bishophric, Buga was first established in 1555 and then moved to its present location on March 4, 1560.

BUITRAGO, Fanny, 1945-.   Journalist, novelist, playwright, born in *Barranquilla, October 26. She grew up in *Cali and later moved to *Bogotá. She was associated with the *nadaísta* movement of the 1960s (see: NADAISMO). Her works include plays such as *El hombre de paja* (1964), which won the National Theater Prize; short stories, such as the anthologies *La otra gente* (1974) and *Bahía sonora* (1976); and novels: *El hostigante verano de los dioses* (1963), *Cola de zorro* (1970), and *Los Pañamanes* (1979).

BULLFIGHTING.   This Spanish tradition remains as important in modern Colombia as it does in Spain, although it fails to rival the popularity of soccer.

BULLRING MASSACRE.   Sunday, February 5, 1956, *Bogotá. During the bullfight on January 29, 1956, María Eugenia *Rojas de Moreno Díaz, daughter of then-dictator General *Rojas Pinilla, was insulted by the crowd, who then applauded opposition leader Alberto *Lleras Camargo. The following week, on February 5, supporters of General Rojas Pinilla rioted during the bullfight, killing at least eight people and injuring many others who would not join in demonstrations of loyalty to the dictator. Harsh public criticism of the government followed the massacre.

BULWER-CLAYTON TREATY, see: CLAYTON-BULWER TREATY

BURITICA. A governmental seat for the *municipio* of the same name at 6° 43'N, 75° 55'W in the Department of *Antioquia. The community is located about 148 kilometers northwest of *Medellín at an altitude of 1,643 meters, with an average temperature of 19°C. In 1985, estimated population for the community was 1,214 people and for the whole *municipio,* 8,397. The area surrounding Buriticá has a long history as a center for *gold mining. Sites near the river Turibí were worked by *Indians before the conquest. Visited by Juan *Vadillo in 1538, the area became a major mining center for *New Granada during the colonial period. Indians were working in mines at San Antonio de Buriticá in 1615, and the date of the founding of the community of Buriticá is said to be either 1616 or 1625.

-C-

C.G.S.B., see: COORDINADORA GUERRILLERA "SIMON BOLIVAR"

C.G.T., see: CONFEDERACION GENERAL DEL TRABAJO

C.N.G., see: COORDINADORA GUERRILLERA "SIMON BOLIVAR"

C.N.S., see: CONSEJO NACIONAL SINDICAL

C.N.T., see: CONFEDERACION NACIONAL DE TRABAJADORES

C.S.T.C., see: CONFEDERACION SINDICAL DE TRABAJADORES DE COLOMBIA

C.T.C., see: CONFEDERACION DE TRABAJADORES DE COLOMBIA

C.T.C.I., see: CONFEDERACION DE TRABAJADORES DE COLOMBIA INDEPENDIENTE

C.V.C., see: CORPORACION AUTONOMA REGIONAL DEL CAUCA

C.V.M., see: CORPORACION AUTONOMA REGIONAL DE
LOS VALLES DEL MAGADALENA Y DEL SINU

CABALLERO CALDERON, Eduardo, 1910-. Author, journal-
ist, diplomat, born *Bogotá, March 6. A *Liberal politician,
Caballero Calderón served as a deputy to various provincial
legislatures and held diplomatic posts in various European and
Latin American countries. He enjoyed a longtime affiliation
with *El *Tiempo,* one of Bogotá's leading newspapers.
His works, which include *Caminos subterráneos* . . . (1936),
Suramérica, tierra del hombre (1944), and *Latinoamérica, un
mundo por hacer* (1944), are said to display a strong Latin
American nationalism. He is the author of several novels,
including *El Cristo de espaldas* (1952), *La penúltima hora* (1955),
Siervo sin tierra (1960), and *El buen salvaje* (1966). Caballero
Calderón is also the author of several historical and descriptive
works, among which are *Historia privade de los colombianos*
(1960), *Memorias infantiles, 1916-1924* (1964), and *Yo el
alcalde . . . Tipacoque, 1969-1971* (1971).

CABALLERO Y GONGORA, Antonio, 1723-1796. Archbishop
of *Bogotá, 1779-1788; Viceroy of *New Granada, 1782-
1789. He concluded the *Comuneros Revolt, 1782; improved
medical treatment for smallpox and leprosy; opened a school
for girls, 1783; created the *Botanical Expedition; tried to
stimulate development in *Antioquia with the missions of
*Mon y Velarde and *D'Elhuyar; founded chairs of natural
sciences, physics, and chemistry; sought to establish a national
university; and ordered the *census of 1788-1789.

CABILDO. In colonial Spanish America, the *cabildo,* was an
institution analogous to a town council. An ordinary *cabildo*
meeting was open only to designated members. A *cabildo
abierto* was a special meeting open to anyone.

CACAO. The tree from whose nuts cocoa powder and chocolate
are obtained. A native of the lowlands of tropical Central and
South America, it was an important export crop by the end of
the colonial era in Venezuela and Ecuador, but not in *New
Granada. As a crop that deteriorated rapidly after harvesting,
it was less attractive in a country with poor transportation
facilities than *coffee, which can be stored for longer periods
of time. After independence its cultivation was discouraged
because it was among products subject to a 10% ad valorem

export duty (from which coffee and *cotton were exempt). For many years production was not enough even to meet domestic consumption. Since *World War II, however, it has attained moderate importance in the Colombian economy, though still behind coffee, *bananas, and *sugar. Total output has grown from 21,200 metric tons in 1975 to 33,300 in 1979; exports increased from 4,757 tons in 1980 to 17,921 in 1984.

CACHACO. A term derived from *casacas,* "dress coats," implying an aristocratic figure, often with intellectual pretensions, as opposed to the *ruanas,* or those who wore lower-class clothing. It was particularly significant in *Bogotá in the 1850s when the terms implied class conflict.

CACIQUE. A *Carib word for an *Indian chieftain that has come to mean a local political boss or "big shot," but one with less influence than a *caudillo.*

CAICEDO ROJAS, José María, 1816-1897. Romantic poet, author. His works extolled the themes of nature, domestic life, and faith. His principal poems were "La fuente de Torca" and "El primer baño de Eva." He wrote numerous essays on diverse subjects, and his *Apuntes de ranchería* were autobiographical memoirs.

CAJA DE CREDITO AGRARIO, INDUSTRIAL Y MINERO. Founded in 1924, as the Banco Agrícola Hipotecario, the institution was intended to grant long-term loans to small farmers. It soon began buying land for resale as well. Following the Depression of 1929, the bank was reorganized in 1931 as the Caja de Crédito Agrario, with authority to foment economic development in general. The bank was awarded the Cruz de Boyacá (see: BOYACA, Cruz de) in 1969 for its services to the nation.

CALAMAR RAILROAD. The Ferrocarril de Calamar, a line connecting *Cartagena with the *Magdalena River at Calamar (10° 15'N, 74° 55'W, *Bolívar). It was first proposed in 1865 as, among other things, a substitute for the *Dique Canal. It was built between 1889 and 1894, and began public service in the latter year. The railroad was closed in 1951 after the government decided to do major repair and dredging on the Dique Canal.

CALARCA, d. 1607.   A chieftain among the *Pijao and Quindío *Indians, he was the major war leader with whom Juan de *Borja was forced to contend during the Pijao War, 1605-1618. Calarcá was killed during one of the battles of the war.

CALDAS, Departamento de.   Located in central Colombia, touching both the *Magdalena and *Cauca Rivers and parts of the *Crodilleras Occidental and Central, the department covers 7,888 square kilometers lying between latitudes 4° 48' and 5° 47'N and longitudes 74° 37' and 75° 58'W. The terrain is mountainous, interrupted by river valleys, with climates from tropical to perpetual snow distributed thus: tropical, 2,246 square kilometers; temperate, 2,770; cold, 1,902; and wasteland, 970. Major rivers include the Magdalena, Cauca, Guarinó, Samaná, and La Miel. The snow-covered *Nevado del Ruiz rises to an altitude of 5,300 meters. Population in 1985 was estimated at 789,730 people, with an overall density of 351 people per square kilometer. The capital city is *Manizles. Based on DANE, *Colombia estadística 86,* principal agricultural products, with tonnage produced in 1984, include plantains, 145,700 tons; *sugar, 45,000; *potatoes, 38,300; coconuts, 18,706; *yuca, 15,000; *corn, 8,173; sorghum, 3,255; *cacao, 1,770; soybeans, 1,480; beans, 1,020; rice, 555; *cotton, 360; and peanuts, 105. Within the department, 105,747 head of cattle and 59,753 hogs were slaughtered in 1983. Industries include mining, cement processing, textiles, and other types of light *manufacturing. In 1983 there were 115 businesses employing 10 or more people. Caldas is also a hydroelectric center (see: HYDROELECTRICITY). The department was created in 1905 from territory that previously belonged to *Antioquia. It was reduced in size in 1966 to allow establishment of the Departments of *Risaralda and *Quindío.

CALDAS, Francisco José de, 1771-1816.   Scientist, lawyer, engineer, patriot, martyr; born *Popayán, November 17; executed by the Spanish in *Bogotá, October 29. Caldas received his law degree from the *Colegio Mayor de Nuestra Señora del Rosario in Bogotá in 1791, but devoted his life to scientific studies of *New Granada's natural resources. As a scientist he was the inventor of the hypsometer, a member of the *Botanical Expedition, and director of the *Observatorio nacional. He accompanied Alexander von *Humboldt on his travels in Ecuador and New Granada, 1801. He joined the patriot cause in the *independence movement as a military engineer, especially in *Antioquia, and was executed during the Spanish *Reconquista.*

CALDAS RAILROAD. Authorized in 1911, the Caldas Railroad was meant to link *Manizales with a major port on the *Cauca River. The line from Manizales to *Cartago via *Pereira was completed in 1927. It joins the *Pacific Railroad and the *Western Trunk at Cartago. Service was interrupted between Pereira and Manizales in 1959 when citizens of the former destroyed the tracks between the two cities. See also RAIL-ROADS

CALEDONIA, Nueva, see: DARIEN, Scottish colony of

CALI. Capital of *Valle del Cauca located at 3° 27'N, 76° 32'W. Altitude is 987 meters; average temperature, 25°C; and population, 1,389,276 people (1985 estimate for the greater metropolitan area). An industrial and university center, Cali is the third largest city in Colombia. It was founded July 25, 1536, by Sebastián de *Belalcázar and moved to its present location by Miguel López Muñoz in December of that same year. Cali has been a strategic administrative and transportation site for four and a half centuries.

CALI CARTEL. A reference to the group of drug dealers headed by the families and associates of Gilberto Rodríguez Orjuela and José Santa Cruz Londoño operating from Cali. Members of the Cali Cartel are said to control much of the international trade with New York and parts of the West Coast in the United States. In the late 1980s, the Cali Cartel was at war with the *Medellín Cartel. Reasons advanced for the conflict include the arrest of Jorge Luis *Ochoa Vásquez in November 1987, which Cali may have facilitated; the January 1988 bombing of a building belonging to Pablo *Escobar Gaviria, which Rodríguez Orjuela may have arranged; and Medellín's attempt to move into Cali's trade with New York. Of the two, the Cali Cartel is said to have the more sophisticated business techniques. In the 1990-1991 period, the Cali group was said to have surpassed the Medellín Cartel in the *cocaine trade and to have begun a serious effort to grow poppies and to market *heroin. See also: DRUG TRADE; MEDELLIN CARTEL

CALIBIO, Battle of. January 15, 1814. *Cauca. General Antonio *Nariño, patriot commander, defeated the royalist forces of

Colonel Juan *Sámano. Calibío was a major patriot victory in the period 1813-1816, although not a conclusive one.

CALIMA STYLE. An archeological term used to describe types of pre-conquest Indian *goldwork and pottery found in the Departments of *Cauca and *Valley del Cauca, which may or may not have been produced by the *Indians referred to as the *Calimas at the time of the Spanish conquest. In modern archeological usage, Calima designates a type of goldwork characterized by a mixture of techniques, including casting through the lost-wax process, hammering, repoussé, and mounting on packed clay or wooden cores. Lamination, large pieces, and dangling pendant decoration are prominent. Typical pieces in this style are diadems, nosepieces, earrings, breastplates, bracelets, batons, and throwing pieces. The conch shell and zoomorphic figures are common. Works in the Calima style resemble motifs found in the *San Agustín, *Tierradentro, and Pacific Coast cultures of Central America and Peru. Calima Style is less well defined when applied to pottery, but recent classification attempts have suggested three major subdivisions labeled Yotoco, Sonso, and Moralba for ceramics of the same area.

CALIMAS. A term applied vaguely or imprecisely to groups of Indians living largely in the Department of *Valle del Cauca, and parts of *Cauca, at the time of the Spanish conquest. Major subgroups included in the generic term "Calimas" were the Liles (near present-day *Cali), the Jamundíes (near Jamundí, 3° 16'N, 76° 32'W), the Gorrones (from the *Cordillera Occidental north of Cali), the Aguales (along the *Cauca River), and the Bugas (from the *Cordillera Occidental). They were loosely organized into small chiefdoms with economies based on fishing, hunting, and *agriculture (*corn, *yuca, and beans), supplemented by commerce in *gold, *salt, textiles, agricultural products, *emeralds, and slaves.

CALLAO, El. Port of Lima, the capital of Peru. By February 5, 1824, it had become Spain's last stronghold on the Pacific Coast. It was besieged by the patriot forces of *Gran Colombia under Generals Simón *Bolívar and Bartolomé *Salóm, February 5, 1824, to January 22, 1826. The fall of the Real Felipe fortress on this latter date completed both the liberation of Peru and the struggle for South American independence (see: *INDEPENDENCE MOVEMENT).

CALVO, Bartolomé, 1815-1889. Lawyer, journalist, diplomat, born *Cartagena, August 24; died Quito (Ecuador), January 2. Onetime governor of *Panama, Calvo was attorney general for the *Confederación Granadina, 1858-1861, and acting President of the Confederation, April 1 to July 18, 1861. He was overthrown as a result of the Battle of *Subachoque, briefly imprisoned, and exiled thereafter. He settled in Ecuador and was later Colombian Minister to Ecuador. Although a candidate for various offices after 1861, Calvo never returned to accept any of them. He was a contributor to the *newspaper *Los Andes*.

CALVO OCAMPO, Jairo de Jesús.   An alias for Ernesto *Rojas.

CAMARA DE REPRESENTANTES.   House of Representatives (see: CONGRESS).

CAMARGO-ESPINOSA TREATY, 1884.   Signed Quito, June 28, by Sergio Camargo, Colombia, and José Modesto Espinosa, Ecuador, the treaty stipulated that all Colombian claims then existing against Ecuador would be settled by arbitration. In 1887, the settlement awarded 80,000 *pesos to Columbia.

CAMARGO-NINA PACT, 1880.   Signed June 21, in Rome, by Sergio Camargo, Colombia, and Cardinal Lorenzo Nina, *Papacy. Both sides agreed to negotiate points of contention that had arisen, 1850-1880. Diplomatic contact was to be maintained in *Bogotá and Rome in the meantime, and the Church accepted as a *Fait accompli* the *disamortization law of 1861.

CAMELLON.   A duty on goods entering *Bogotá imposed by Viceroy José Alonso *Pizarro (1749-1753), also used by later viceroys to finance *highway construction.

CAMINO REAL.   Literally, the "Royal Road," also known as the Royal Road of Peru and the Royal Road of the Incas. It was the principal *highway of the Viceroyalty of *New Granada, linking Lima (Peru) with Caracas (Venezuela). The highway, parts of which predated the European conquest, ran from Lima to Quito and then to *Pasto and *Popayán. North of Popayán, it split into two sections, with the eastern route reaching *Bogotá via La Plata (2° 23'N, 75° 56'W) and *Neiva (Huila), and *Tacaima (Cundinamarca), while the western route connected Popayán to *Cali, *Buga, and *Cartago (all in Valle del

Cauca), *Ibagué and *Honda (Tolima), and then Bogotá (see also: HONDA ROAD). North of Bogotá, the road extended to Caracas, passing through *Tunja (Boyacá), and *Pamplona and *Cúcuta (Norte de Santander). Subsidiary roads ran from Cartago to *Anserma (Caldas), from Pamplona to Puerto Río de Oro (8° 18'N, 73° 23'W, *Cesar), and from Cali to *Buenaventura (Valle del Cauca). The road was also connected to a route from Chita (6° 11'N, 72° 29'W, Boyacá) to Guayana by means of the Casanare, Meta, and Orinoco Rivers.

CAMISAS NEGRAS. Literally, "black shirts," a popular name for members of the *Falange Colombiana.

CAMPAÑA ADMIRABLE. The Admirable Campaign, May 15 to October 13, 1813. Patriot forces under *Bolívar marched from *Mompós to Caracas (Venezuela), occupying formerly royalist positions along the way. It was a tremendous boost to patriot morale, even though Bolívar withdrew from Venezuela in 1814.

CAMPAÑA LIBERTADORA DE 1819. The Liberating Campaign conducted by Simón *Bolívar and the patriot forces, May-August 1819. Beginning in the *Llanos of Venezuela, Bolívar moved his forces through the present Intendancies of *Arauca and *Casanare and then from the Llanos of Casanare across the *Cordillera Oriental at the *Páramo de Pisba to the Department of *Boyacá. The campaign culminated with the battles of the *Pantano de Vargas and *Boyacá, followed by Bolívar's occupation of *Bogotá.

CANAL COMPANY, French, see: COMPAGNIE UNIVERSELLE DU CANAL INTER-OCEANIQUE DE PANAMA

CANO ISAZA, Guillermo. Editor of El *Espectador, assassinated December 17, 1986, presumably on orders from agents of illegal *drug traders. El Espectador had supported the *extradition treaty with the United States aimed at suppressing the commerce in narcotics. When judge Consuelo Sánchez ordered the arrest of *cocaine trafficker Pablo *Escobar in connection with Cano Isaza's death, he received a death threat.

CANO MARQUEZ, María de los Angeles, 1887-1967. Labor leader, socialist, orator, known as the National Flower of

Labor. Born *Medellín, April 26. In 1925 she was named the Flower of Labor in Medellín, and in 1926 she was given the title of National Flower of Labor by the Third National Congress of Workers in *Bogotá. Between 1926 and 1928 she made seven tours through various parts of Colombia to encourage the development of labor organizations and the Socialist Party (*Partido Socialista Revolucionario). She supported the strikes against *Tropical Oil Company (1927) and was accused of fomenting armed rebellion with a Central Committee for Conspiracy in 1929. Although she remained a supporter of labor causes, her public career was less dramatic after 1935.

CANTON DEL NORTE ROBBERY.   *Bogotá, December 31, 1978, to January 1, 1979. Members of the *Movimiento Diecinueve de Abril succeeded in carrying off an estimated 5,000 weapons from a military arsenal late New Year's Eve and early New Year's Day. The robbery was achieved by means of a tunnel running under the street from a house facing the arsenal. The fact that the tunnel had taken some time to prepare and the number of weapons stolen were extremely embarrassing and alarming to the government. The bulk of the weapons was recovered within a relatively short period of time.

CAPITAL, The.   The capital city and administrative center of what is now the *República de Colombia has been, since the earliest days of Spanish rule, the city of *Bogotá, formerly called *Santa Fe de Bogotá, and since 1991, again so called officially. The city and the immediately adjacent area has enjoyed a special legal status since 1861. (See: DISTRITO ESPECIAL DE BOGOTA.) In 1991, Distrito Capital was declared as the formal name of the seat of the national government. See also: CAPITOLIO NACIONAL

CAPITAL PUNISHMENT.   A penal sanction abolished by the *Constitution of 1863 and again by the *Constitution of 1991.

CAPITANIA GENERAL.   Captaincy General, an administrative division with military-defensive functions. The chief executive, the *capitán general*, enjoyed a large degree of autonomy. Colonial Venezuela held the status of a captaincy general after 1777.

CAPITANIA GENERAL DEL NUEVO REINO DE GRANADA.   The name given to *New Granada by the

Cortes of Cadiz after it had abolished the *Virreinato del Nuevo Reino de Granada. It was never an effectively functioning governmental unit because of the beginning of the *independence movement.

CAPITOLIO NACIONAL. The seat of Colombia's *Congress, located on the Plaza Bolívar in *Bogotá. Originally intended to house all major branches of the national government, the building project was begun under the auspices of President T. C. de *Mosquera. The chief architect was Thomas Reed, a Danish engineer brought to Colombia especially to design the building. He drew up the first set of plans for the structure in 1847, and work was begun almost immediately. Construction was interrupted on numerous occasions because of insufficient funds, political problems, and revisions in the plans. It was not formally declared finished until 1926, by which time the government had become much too large to be housed in one building, and the Capitolio Nacional became essentially a congressional building. See also: CAPITAL, The; DISTRITO ESPECIAL DE BOGOTA

CAPITULACION. A formal contract or agreement between the Spanish Crown and one or more of its subjects, which authorized the discovery, exploration, and/or exploitation of lands or resources held by the Crown. It specified the territory or resource to be developed, the conditions under which the development would occur, and the division of wealth and honors to be made as a result of the development.

CAPUCHINS. Order of religious men, established in *New Granada in 1646 as an independent order of the *Franciscans. Devoted to missionary work among the *Indians, the order developed a network of mission stations along the present Colombian-Venezuelan border from *Arauca to the Atlantic Ocean and all along the coast and the Isthmus of *Panama.

CAQUETA, Departamento de. Located in south central Colombia, roughly between latitudes 2° 45'N and 0° 30'S and longitudes 72° 25' and 76° 18'W, the department covers some 88,965 square kilometers of varied terrain—plains, mountains, and tropical rain forest. The climate is predominantly tropical with temperatures averaging between 27 and 29°C. The major rivers include the Caquetá, Caguán, Orteguaza, Anaporí, Yarí, and Sunciva. In 1985 estimated population was 177,259 people, with a population density of 2 people per square kilometer. The capital city is *Florencia. According to DANE, *Colombia estadística 86*, principal agricultural products, with tonnage produced in 1984, included plantains, 64,500 tons; *yuca, 56,000; *corn, 49,500; *sugar, 27,000; *African palm, 383; *cacao, 160; beans, 140; sorghum, 112; and peanuts, 20. *Livestock slaughtered in the department in 1983 included 33,451 head of cattle and 14,874 hogs. Caquetá has forest reserves. Although the department appears in royal documents as early as 1549, effective settlement did not begin until 1860. In the late 19th century the Gutiérrez family (Francisco, Eloy, Urbano, Venancio, and Roberto) began exploitation of *quinine reserves, and, after 1894, the Gutiérrez family joined with Pedro Antonio Pizarro, Juan Urbano, Cenón Mavesoy, and Juan Ventura Cuéllar to exploit *rubber in the region. In 1902, Doroteo de Pupiales, a *Capuchin missionary, explored the area between Puerto Limón and present-day Florencia. The capital city was founded December 25, 1902, and the Intendancy of the Caquetá was established in 1950. The Department of Caquetá was authorized in 1981 and formally established in 1982.

CAR, see: CORPORACION AUTONOMA REGIONAL DE LA SABANA DE BOGOTA Y DE LOS VALLES DE UBATE Y CHIQUINQUIRA

CARABOBO, Battle of.   June 24, 1821, near Valencia, Venezuela. *Bolívar defeated royalist forces under Field Marshal Miguel de La Torre. The battle broke major Spanish efforts in Venezuela, although it did not eliminate royalist resistance completely.

CARARE ROAD.   A road from the port of Carare (6° 46'N, 73° 52'W, *Santander) on the *Magdalena River to *Vélez (Santander), which allowed access to the northeastern interior of *New Granada. First opened around 1545, it was maintained intermittently thereafter but was always subject to strong opposition from the port of *Honda and the *Honda Road. The Carare Road was especially important in the period 1574-1600. Later documentation shows that it was reopened in 1754 and again in 1802. A modern highway, the Carretera del Carare, runs from Barbosa (5° 56'N, 73° 37'W, Santander) on the Río Suárez to Puerto Berrío (6° 29'N, 74°

24'W, *Antioquia) via Vélez and Cimitarra (6° 19'N, 73° 57'W).

CARDENAS, Antonio, 1797-1854.   A distinguished soldier from *Leiva (Department of Boyacá) who fought in the struggle for *independence and was military chief of *Pasto from June 20 to October 31, 1840, during the War of the *Supreme Commanders.

CARDINALS OF COLOMBIA.   From 1953 to 1985, four Colombian prelates were elevated to the position of Cardinal. In 1953, the *Papacy named Archbishop Crisanto *Luque Sánchez the first Apostolic Cardinal of *Bogotá. Cardinal Luque Sánchez was succeeded by Archbishop Luis *Concha Córdoba in 1959, and he in turn was replaced by Archbishop Aníbal *Muñoz Duque in 1973. The Archbishop of Medellín, Alfonso (López Trujillo, was named the first Apostolic Cardinal of Medellín in 1983.

CARDONA LONDOÑO, Carmenze, d. 1981.   A member of the *Movimiento Diecinueve de Abril (M-19), she served as the organization's negotiator during its occupation of the (Dominican Embassy. The Colombian press dubbed her "La Chiqui." She was killed in combat with the *army in April 1981.

CARIBS.   A linguistic-cultural group (also known as Caribe, Carib, or Karib) prevailing in 1500 among *Indians along the Caribbean Coast, the *Magadalena and *Cauca Rivers, and some parts of the interior. During the conquest, the term often meant any Indian who practiced cannibalism.

CARMELITE MONASTERY, 1569-1573.   A monastery founded in *Bogotá in 1569 by Friar Gonzalo Ramírez. It was closed in 1573 by Archbishop Luis *Zapata de Cárdenas. It was the first attempt to establish the Carmelite order in *New Granada, and it failed partially because of personal conflicts with Ramírez, but, more importantly, because the Crown ordered that no monasteries be established except those of the *Dominicans, *Franciscans, *Augustinians, and, later, the *Jesuits. Subsequently, Carmelite nuns established themselves in New Granada in 1606.

CARO, José Eusebio, 1817-1853.   Poet, journalist, *Conservative ideologue, accountant, born Ocaña (*Norte de Santander),

March 5; died *Santa Marta, January 28. He was a member of the *House of Representatives during the *Herrán presidency and Secretary of Finance under the first *Mosquera administration in the 1840s, and also edited and published at least two *newspapers, *El Granadino* (1840-1845), by himself, and *La Civilización* (1849-1851), jointly with Mariano *Ospina Rodríguez. Caro and Ospina Rodríguez were also responsible for the first *Conservative Party platform in 1849. Beyond the realm of politics, Caro is considered by some to be the finest of Colombia's romantic poets. He emphasized the themes of love, nature, and family life. See, for example, "El bautismo," "Una lágrima de felicidad," "El Vals," "Estar contigo," "A mi primogénito," and "La hamaca del destierro."

CARO, Miguel Antonio, 1843-1909.   Author, poet, linguist, legislator; the son of José Eusebio *Caro, born *Bogotá, November 3; died Bogotá, August 5. A *Nationalist Conservative, Caro was a member of the National Council of Delegates in 1886 and was largely responsible for drafting the *Constitution of 1886, which it adopted. He was acting President 1892-1898. His administration signed a convention with the *Papacy in 1892, but it is most often remembered for its persecution of political opponents and suppression of the *rebellion of 1895. With Rufino José *Cuervo, Caro was the author of *Gramática de la lengua latina para el uso de los que hablan castellano* (1867) as well as numerous articles in periodicals, such as *La Fe, La Nación,* and *El Tradicionista.* He was a distinguished orator and philosopher known for his strong defense of the Hispanic tradition in America.

CARRASQUILLA, Rafael María, 1857-1930   Priest, noted religious orator, author, and educator; Minister of Public Instruction, 1893; and Rector of the *Colegio Mayor de Nuestra Señora del Rosario, 1890-1930. Born *Bogotá, December 18; died Bogotá, March 18. He was ordained in 1883, appointed a Canon of the Cathedral of Bogotá in 1899, and awarded the title of Doctor of Sacred Theology by Pope Pius X in 1904. Monsignor Carrasquilla was a member of the *Academia Colombiana de la Lengua and an honorary member of the *Academia Colombiana de Historia. He was the author of numerous literary, historical, and religious works, including *Apuntes sobre literatura* (1894), *Lo nuevo y lo viejo en la enseñanza* (1909), and *Sermones y discursos escogidos* (1913).

CARRASQUILLA, Tomás, 1858-1940. Novelist, essayist, poet, and critic, born Santo Domingo (*Antioquia), January 19; died *Medellín, December 19. During his lifetime, Carrasquilla was employed in a number of bureaucratic positions, as a tailor, and in the mines of Antioquia until his health began to fail in 1926. He is best remembered as a *costumbrista* author from Antioquia through works such as *Frutos de mi tierra* (1895), *La Marquesa de Yolombó* (1928), and *Hace tiempos* (1935-1936). Carrasquilla has been called the first authentic nationalist writer in Colombia, and his work has been described as simultaneously *Antioqueño,* Colombian, and Latin American. See also: COSTUMBRISMO

CARTAGENA. Capital of *Bolívar, located at 10° 26'N, 75° 33'W; altitude, 3 meters; average temperature, 28°C. Cartagena is the sixth largest city in Colombia, with a population of 529,622 people (1985 estimate). Founded January 20, 1533, by Pedro de *Heredia, Cartagena was a center for treasure collection in the Spanish empire. Frequently attacked by pirates (see: PIRACY), the city was protected by massive fortifications, especially the castle of San Felipe de Barajas. It was the capital of the independent Republic of Cartagena, 1810-1815, and the birthplace of Rafael *Núñez, whose home, "El Cabrero," may still be seen there.

CARTAGENA, Acuerdo de, see: ANDEAN COMMON MARKET

CARTAGENA, Colonization Plan of 1774. A reference to the efforts of Captain Antonio de la Torre Miranda, who was authorized by Governor Juan Pimienta to explore and colonize the area around Cartagena in 1774. Torre Miranda spent nine years fulfilling this commission. He was responsible for the founding of approximately forty-three villages, as well as the construction of roads linking some of them. *Montería and modern *Sincelejo are perhaps the most important of those that have survived.

CARTAGENA, Provincia de. Founded November 11, 1811, when Cartagena declared itself independent. It is also known as the Republic of Cartagena and is commonly said to have been the first Colombian territory to make a complete break with Spain, although Orlando Fals Borda insists that *Mompós declared independence on August 6, 1810. Cartagena joined the *Provincias Unidas de Nueva Granada shortly after proclaiming independence.

CARTAGENA, Siege of 1740-1742. Admiral Edward *VERNON with an English fleet tried unsuccessfully to capture Cartagena, which was defended by the Spanish General of the Navy, Blas de *LEZO.

CARTAGENA, Siege of 1815. First, from March 23 to May 8, General Simón *Bolívar made an unsuccessful attempt to capture the city, but he withdrew after a negotiated truce. Then, from August 18 to December 6, General Pablo *Morillo conducted the worst siege in the history of the port. Disease, lack of supplies, and starvation finally forced surrender of the city.

CARTAGENA, Siege of 1820-1821. July 10, 1820, to October 10, 1821; Colonel Mariano Montilla, patriot, forced royalist Governor Gabriel de Torres to surrender the city.

CARTAGENA, Siege of 1885. Following a siege of 20 days, government forces under Generals Santodomingo Vila and Francisco de Palacios, with José Manuel Goenaga, successfully withstood attacks by rebel forces under Generals Siervo Sarmiento, Manuel Cabeza, and Ricardo Gaitán Obeso, May 7-8.

CARTAGENA DE (LAS) INDIAS. The colonial name for Cartagena to distinguish it from its namesake in Spain.

CARTAGENA FORTIFICATIONS. Built between 1566 and 1778, these are massive bulwarks with bastions enclosing a major part of colonial Cartagena. The dominant structure is the Castle of San Felipe de Barajas, opened in 1657. In the 18th century, a breakwater closed the major entrance to the bay (Boca Grande) and Fort San Fernando and the Battery of San Luis guarded the only other entrance (Boca Chica). Along with Veracruz, Mexico, and Havana, Cuba, Cartagena was one of three heavily fortified ports on the Caribbean designated as centers for the assembling of the annual treasure fleets. See: FLOTA SYSTEM

CARTAGENA PACT. The *Acuerdo de Cartagena* of 1969 established the *ANDEAN COMMON MARKET.

CARTAGENA RAILWAY COMPANY. The British-owned corporation that built the *CALAMAR RAILROAD. In 1913 it was merged with the *Colombian Navigation Company to form the *Colombian Railway and Navigation Company.

CARTAGENA UNIVERSITY, see: UNIVERSIDAD DE CARTAGENA

CARTAGENA WITCHES. A reference to an alleged epidemic of witchcraft reported in the Province of Cartagena in 1633. Elena de la *Cruz of Tolú (9° 32'N, 75° 35'W, *Sucre), and Paula de Eguiluz and Elena Victoria, both of *Cartagena, were accused of heading covens of witches. Membership in a society of witches is said to have provided economic advantage, secret weapons (poisons), entertainment, and sexual license. Numerous persons of both sexes and all social classes were implicated in the cases and tried before the *Inquisition. The coven of Paula de Eguiluz was said to have been aristocratic in nature, with admission dependent upon racial and social qualifications.

CARTAGO. City of 92,231 people (1985 estimate) situated at 4° 45'N, 75° 35'W, in the Department of *Valle del Cauca. Altitude is 917 meters; average temperature, 23°C. San Jorge de Cartago was originally founded by Jorge *Robledo on August 9, 1540, on the banks of the Otún River. It was moved to its present location on the Vieja River with access to the *Cordillera del Quindío on April 21, 1691, by Father Manuel de Castro y Mendoza. Cartago has always been a strategic point linking east-west traffic across the *Cordillera Central and north-south communications throughout the *Cauca Valley with the *San Juan and *Atrato Rivers.

CARTAGO, Escaño de. Literally, the "Bench of Cartago"; see: CARTAGO EXECUTIONS.

CARTAGO EXECUTIONS. Reference to the controversial executions of Colonel Salvador *Córdoba and six other prisoners of war in *Cartago, July 8, 1841, by General T. C. de *Mosquera, during the War of the *Supreme Commanders, 1840-1842. All seven were sent before the firing squad at one time, five seated on a bench, the *escaño de Cartago,* with one person standing at each end of it.

CARTEL. In the Colombian context, "cartel" is a term used to describe coalitions of *narcotraficantes* (drug dealers) or crime families who control the narcotics trade. Individual families or gangs are sometimes referred to as syndicates. The two most commonly mentioned are in *Medellín and *Cali, which are said to control as much as 60 to 70% of the cocaine exported from Colombia. See also: CALI CARTEL; DRUG TRADE; MEDELLIN CARTEL

CASA DE CONTRATACION. The House of Trade, or Contracts, established in Seville by the Spanish Crown in 1503. It had charge of shipping, trade, and migration to the New World, as well as collection of customs duties. After 1524 it was subordinated to the *Council of the Indies. During the 18th century its monopoly was gradually eroded and finally abolished in 1790.

CASA DE MONEDA. A government mint. The first in New *Granada was founded in *Bogotá in 1620, and put into continuous service after 1627. It was run by private contractors until 1756, then by royal officials until 1819, and, finally, by republican governments thereafter. Mints were also established in *Cartago, 1541-1629; *Cartagena, 1620; and *Popayán, 1729.

CASA DE MONEDA DE POPAYAN. A royal mint, it was founded in 1729. The mint in Popayán functioned throughout most of the colonial period, although it was closed for a time after 1762.

CASACAS. A sociopolitical term of the 1850s referring to a 19th-century frock or dress coat and, thus, to a member of the upper class. See also: CACHACO; RUANA

CASANARE, Departamento del. Casanare is located in the *Llanos, bounded in the west by the Department of *Boyacá and the *Cordillera Oriental, in the north by the Casanare River and the Department of *Arauca, in the south and east by the Meta River, the Department of *Vichada, and the Department of *Meta. The department covers 44,640 square kilometers and is predominantly rolling flatland, between approximately 5° 17' and 6° 20' N latitude and 69° 50' and 73° 5' W longitude. The climate is tropical with alternating wet and dry seasons and average temperatures between 24° and 30°C. The population is 24,443 people (1985 estimate). *Yopal is the capital. Cattle raising is a major activity; there were 1,800,000 head of cattle in the intendancy in 1985. *Agriculture is largely subsistence, with 11,540 hectares planted in rice; 4,300 in *corn; 3,700 in plantains; 1,300 in *sugar; and 800 in *African palm. Some *coffee, *cotton, and *cacao are also grown, and forestry reserves are exploited. There are five Indian reservations in the department. Casanare was an independent province during the wars of independence and a separate national territory in the late 19th century. Until 1975, it was a part of the Department of Boyacá. It was the *Intendancy of Casanare, 1975-1991, and became a department under the *Constitution of 1991.

CASAS, Bartolomé de las, 1474-1566.   Well-known *Dominican, "Protector of the *Indians." He accompanied the expedition of Alonso de *Ojeda and unsuccessfully attempted a social experiment with Indian communities in Venezuela, 1520-1521. However, most of his work was carried out in places other than in the Viceroyalty of *New Granada.

CASAS, Domingo de las, 1507-1544.   *Dominican; a cousin of Bartolomé de las *Casas. He accompanied the expedition of *Jiménez de Quesada, 1536-1539, during which he ministered to and encouraged the troops, objected to the treatment given the last *Zipa, and assisted in negotiations between Jiménez de Quesada, *Federmann, and *Belalcázar. He was the first clergyman to serve in *Bogotá. He returned to Spain in 1539.

CASAS, José Joaquin, 1865-1951   Poet, lawyer, orator, diplomat, journalist; born *Chiquinquirá (Boyacá), February 24; died *Bogotá, October 8. He was on different occasions Minister of War, Public Instruction, and Foreign Relations. He was a devout Catholic, and his poetry, such as *Crónicas de aldea,* described the Colombian countryside and regional life. See also: ACADEMIA COLOMBIANA DE HISTORIA; ACADEMIA COLOMBIANA DE CIENCIAS EXACTAS, FISICAS Y NATURALES

CASEMENT, (Sir) Roger David (1864-1916).   A Protestant Irishman in the British foreign service who exposed *Arana del Aguila's reign of terror in the Putumayo region (see: RUBBER TRADE). In 1910, as British consul in Rio de Janeiro, he was appointed to investigate Walter *Hardenburg's allegations against Arana's Peruvian Amazon Rubber Company. His devastating report brought about the downfall of Arana's empire and won Casement his knighthood. In 1916, however, he was hanged for treason for having tried to enlist German support for the cause of Irish independence.

CASS-HERRAN TREATY, see: HERRAN-CASS TREATY OF 1857

CASSANI, José, 1673-1750. *Jesuit missionary. He was the author of *Historia de . . . misiones en el reino, llanos, Meta y Río Orinoco . . .*, published in Madrid in 1741.

CASSAVA, see: YUCA

CASTELLANOS, Juan de, 1522-1607. Conquistador, 1530s-1554; later a priest at *Tunja, 1568. He was the author of *Elegías de varones ilustres de indias,* a poetic account of the discovery of the Antilles and the conquest of *New Granada. The *Elegías* . . . , with 113,609 verses, is said to be the longest epic poem of the Western world. The first of its four parts was published in 1589; the projected fifth part was never completed. The work has been published in its entirety only twice, first in 1930-1932 and again in 1955.

CASTILLA DEL ORO. A name applied to a grant of land running from the Gulf of (*Golfo de) Urabá to Cape Gracias a Dios in *Panama. It was given to Diego de *Nicuesa in 1508. The Government of Castilla de Oro was established July 27, 1513, and Pedro Arias de Avila (*Pedrarias) was its first governor. *Santa María la Antigua del Darién was its capital city until the government moved to *Panama City in 1519. The name was later used to designate much of present-day Panama where *gold mines were developed and worked with African slaves (see: AFRICAN SLAVERY).

CASTILLO Y GUEVARA, Francisca Josefa de, 1671-1742. Madre Castillo, a nun of the Convent of Santa Clara in *Tunja, was a noted mystic and devotional writer, born in Tunja, October 6; died, Tunja, February 22. Her best-known works are *La vida,* an autobiography, and *Afectos espirituales,* a collection of aesthetic and mystical pieces that draw heavily on biblical passages. Her complete works were published by the *Banco de la República in 1968.

CATALANS.   People from Catalonia in eastern Spain; See: CRE-
OLES

CATATUMBO.   A region of dense, tropical vegetation in northeastern Colombia (*Norte de Santander), extending into Venezuela. The Catatumbo River rises at 7° 64'N, 73° 12'W, and
empties into Lake Maracaibo. It became important in the 1920s
and 1930s through the exploitation of *petroleum deposits
located there. The so-called Catatumbo Lights is an unexplained
luminous phenomenon visible for great distances at night.

CATHEDRAL OF SALT.   Name given to the church built by the
*Banco de la República inside the salt mine at *Zipaquirá
(Cundinamarca). Miners built the first altar in the salt mine to
honor the Virgin of the Rosary known as the Morenita de
Guazá, whose intercession they sought for protection against
the dangers of working in the mine. In 1950, the Bank of the
Republic undertook the excavation and construction of a
public church within the mine. Monsignor Antonio Samoré,
Papal Nuncio for Pope Pius XII, gave official blessing to the
sanctuary on October 7, 1950, and the church was opened on
August 15, 1954. José María González Concha was chief
architect of the church, whose style was chosen to accentuate
the natural environment in which it was built. Official capacity
for the Cathedral of Salt, which has become a well-known
tourist attraction, is 8,000 people.

CATHOLIC ACTION.   Acción Católica is the name of a number
of national Catholic organizations of socially concerned laymen,
originating in Western Europe in the 1920s. The Colombian
body, calling itself Acción Católica Social, was not formed until
1944. *Acción Cultural Popular is an offshoot.

CATHOLIC CHURCH, see: ARCHDIOCESES; AUGUSTINI-
ANS; CAPUCHINS; CARDINALS OF THE CHURCH;
CATHOLIC ACTION; CHURCH-STATE RELATIONS;
CIRCULO DE OBREROS; CONSEJO EPISCOPAL
LATINOAMERICANO; DISAMORTIZATION DECREE;
DOMINICANS; EUCHARISTIC CONGRESS; FRANCIS-
CANS; INQUISITION; JESUITS; MERCEDARIANS;
PAPACY; RELIGIOUS ORDERS

CATHOLIC SOCIETY, see: SOCIEDAD CATOLICA

CATTLE, see: LIVESTOCK

CAUCA, Departamento de. Located in southwestern Colombia, on the Pacific Coast, near the source of the *Cauca River, the department covers 29,308 square kilometers of undulating to mountainous terrain between 0° 57' and 3° 20'N and 75° 4' and 77° 57'W. The department is distributed in climatic zones from tropical to cold, with 9,906 square kilometers tropical; 10,023 temperate; 6,184 cold; and 3,195 wasteland. Major rivers include the Cauca, Caquetá, Patía, Guapi, Maya, Micay, Mayo, and Timbiquí. High points in the department include the volcanos Puracé and Sotará and the Nevado del Huila (5,750 meters). Population was estimated in 1985 at 674,824 people, with a population density of 23 people per square kilometer. *Popayán is the capital city. Based on DANE, *Colombia estadística 86,* principal agricultural products, with tonnage produced in 1984, include *sugar, 2,212,000 tons; *potatoes, 23,500; *yuca, 23,400; *corn, 23,295; rice, 14,835; sorghum, 6,440; soybeans, 2,816; beans, 1,240; *cacao, 470; and *cotton, 400. *Livestock slaughtered in 1984 included 67,954 head of cattle and 16,645 hogs. *Fishing is important on the Pacific Coast, and *coal, *platinum, sulfur, *copper, *lead, *zinc, *tin, and other *minerals are mined within the department. In 1983 there were 23 businesses employing 10 or more workers. The Cauca has been an important political and cultural region since the 1530s. The modern department was established in 1886 and subsequently reduced in size by creation of the Departments of *Valle del Cauca and *Nariño.

CAUCA, Ecuadoran Annexation of. Annexation of the Cauca by Ecuador was attempted May 13, 1830, to December 8, 1832. General Juan José *Flores declared the independence of Ecuador and incorporated the provinces of *Pasto, *Popayán, *Buenaventura, and *Chocó into the new state. At times aided, but finally opposed, by Generals José María *Obando and José Hilario *López, the Ecuadorans were forced to repudiate the annexations and withdraw from the Cauca. See: OBANDO–POSADA GUTIERREZ–ARTETA TREATY

CAUCA RAILROAD, see: PACIFIC RAILROAD

CAUCA RIVER. Historically, Colombia's second major waterway. It rises in the *Andes Mountains in what is known as the Macizo Colombiano (see: CORDILLERA CENTRAL), at 2°N, 76° 34'W in the Department of *Cauca. It flows in a northerly direction approximately 1,350 kilometers between the

*Cordillera Occidental and the *Cordillera Central before joining the Brazo de Loba of the *Magdalena River at 8° 55'N, 74° 29'W opposite the *municipio* of Pinillos (8° 55'N, 74° 28'W) in the Department of Bolívar. In addition to Cauca and Bolívar, it passes through parts of the Departments of *Valle del Cauca, *Risaralda, *Caldas, and *Antioquia. The upper Cauca is navigable by light craft until La Virginia (4° 54'N, 75° 53'W, Risaralda), and the lower Cauca is usable from Puerto Valdivia (Antioquia) to the Magdalena River. Navigation is difficult or impossible between La Virginia and Puerto Valdivia.

CAUCA STYLE, see: POPAYAN STYLE

CAUCA UNIVERSITY, see: UNIVERSIDAD DEL CAUCA

CAUCA VALLEY, see: VALLE DEL CAUCA

CAUCA VALLEY AUTHORITY, see: CORPORACION AU-TONOMA REGIONAL DEL CAUCA

CAUDILLO.   A political or regional boss often with charismatic, financial, or military attributes. A *caudillo* has a wider scope of influence than a *cacique,* which is most often used with reference to Indian matters.

CAYCEDO.   Also written "Caicedo." For General and acting President, see: CAYCEDO y SANTAMARIA, Domingo.

CAYCEDO, María Clemencia de, 1707-1779.   A wealthy widow who endowed the Convent of La Enseñanza for the education of women. Founded in 1770, but not opened until 1783, it was among the first such schools in Spanish America.

CAYCEDO Y FLOREZ, Fernando, 1756-1832.   Born Suaita (*Santander), July 15; died *Bogotá, February 17; he was the first Archbishop of Bogotá (1827-1832) after the independence period. He defended ecclesiastical immunity before the *Junta Suprema de Gobierno in 1811. He was a member of the *Colegio Electoral declaring absolute independence for *Cundinamarca in 1813 and was later imprisoned by *Morillo, 1816-1821. He served as Provisor and Capitular Vicar (acting archbishop), 1823-1826, during which time he was especially concerned with seminary training for new priests, 1823; the adoption of the Law of Ecclesiastical Patronage (see: PATRONATO REAL) by *Congress, 1824; and the publication of the national *education program, 1826. In 1830, he issued a decree intended to correct abuses among the clergy.

CAYCEDO Y SANTAMARIA, Domingo, 1783-1843. General, lawyer, and political leader, Caycedo was acting President of Colombia (*New Granada) in 1830, 1840, and 1841. Born *Bogotá, August 4; died at the *hacienda* Puente Aranda near Bogotá, July 1. He held numerous public offices in the colonial period and after. He supported *Nariño, 1813-1814, and was a legislator, 1820s-1840s. In addition, he was Minister of Interior and Foreign Relations, 1829-1830; Secretary of Finance, 1823; and Vice President, 1839-1843.

CELAM, see: CONSEJO EPISCOPAL LATINOAMERICANO

CENSORSHIP. Although freedom of the press was enacted by the *Congress of Cúcuta, the *Constitution of 1886 guaranteed it only in peacetime, and even then the press is held responsible for any attack on public tranquillity, the social order, or the honor of any individual. The President is empowered to enforce these limitations by imposing conditions that can be tantamount to censorship. This was one of the abuses cited in the *Motivos de disidencia* of 1896. The majority of *newspapers have always been avowedly partisan and have seldom sought editorial objectivity. In such circumstances, Colombian presidents have all too often yielded to the temptation to muzzle the opposition press. Although this may be said of Presidents *Nuñez, *López Pumarejo, *Ospina Pérez, and *Gómez, it was *Rojas Pinilla who earned the most foreign criticism for this. *Turbay Ayala lifted all such restrictions, including the requirement that the texts of *television news broadcasts be submitted for government approval 30 minutes before being put on the air. In 1979, the Turbay Ayala administration also ended the self-censorship that had been imposed on radio stations by the threat of canceling their licenses to operate. But even this liberalization did not prevent the government from imposing an effective news blackout during the 1980 seizure of the *Dominican Republic's embassy. There also continues to be a general caution in all the Colombian media about matters affecting the *armed forces or the *Catholic Church. The 1975 law enjoining licensing of journalists is perhaps a potential means of indirect censorship, but this has not proven to be the case. The 1980s added the unofficial but more sinister form of censorship through terror from people engaged in the *drug trade. See also: LIBERTI-CIDA

CENSUSES. There was a viceregal census in 1770, and *New Granada took part in an ambitious attempt at a census of all Spanish America in 1778. After independence, censuses were taken in 1825, 1835, 1845 (a gross underestimate), and 1851. A law of 1858 specified that a *population census be taken every eight years. One was taken in 1864, but thereafter the law became a dead letter. After 1871, there were various partial censuses but no further attempt at a national census until 1912. The 1912 effort was the best yet made, but it was not acceptable to *Congress. Another enumeration was taken in 1918 by the Dirección General de Estadística. Decennial censuses followed in 1928 and 1938, this latter including the first data on housing. After World War II census taking became the responsibility of the new *Departamento Administrativo Nacional de Estadística. The May 9, 1951, census (which also included housing) failed to cover some 1.7% of the population. The July 15, 1964, census (population only) was the first to cover the remoter parts of the country instead of just estimating their populations. Compilation of the October 24, 1973, population and housing census was very slow, with the final results not being published until 1980. The latest census dates from October 15, 1985. See also: POPULATION

CENTENARY GENERATION.The *generación del centenario,* a group of intellectuals and political leaders who developed or were prominent between 1905 and 1920, taking its name from the centennial of the *independence movement from Spain (1810-1820). The generation has been described as one of classicists, academicians, and advocates of bipartisan cooperation. One list of representative figures included Luis Cano, Eduardo *Santos, Armando Solano (journalists); Guillermo *Uribe Holguín (musician); Agustín Nieto Caballero (educator); Laureano *Gómez, Alfonso *López Pumarejo, Enrique *Olaya Herrera (politicians); Carlos Echeverry (diplomat); Coroliano Leudo (painter); Luis Carlos López, Porfirio *Barba Jacob, Miguel Rasch Isla, Eduardo Castillo, José Eustacio *Rivera (literary figures); Luis *López de Mesa (essayist); and Antonio *Alvarez Lleras (dramatist). For another definition, see: MODERNIST GENERATION.

CENTRAL AMERICA, Relations with.   Shortly after New Spain became independent as the Mexican Empire in 1821, the territories that had formed the *Audiencia of Guatemala broke away. From 1825 to 1838, Colombia's northern neighbor was the Federation of Central America. Costa Rica then left the federation, which was dissolved in 1844, although intermittent attempts have been made to revive it ever since. See also: COSTA RICA, Relations with

CENTRAL AMERICA–COLOMBIA TREATY OF 1825, see: GUAL-MOLINA TREATY

CENTRAL CORDILLERA OF THE ANDES, see: CORDILLERA CENTRAL

CENTRAL UNITARIA DE TRABAJADORES.   CUT, or the Unified Workers' Central, is a national confederation of laborers formed November 15-17, 1986, under the sponsorship of the *Confederación Sindical de Trabajadores de Colombia. The Central attracted a large number of independent labor unions, and it claimed to represent over 1,000 groups by early 1987. CUT was accorded legal recognition by President *Barco in April 1987. By midyear it claimed to represent as much as 80% of organized labor, but this figure was disputed. CUT is allegedly supported by the *Partido Comunista de Colombia, but the relationship is not clear. See also: TRADE UNIONS

CENTRALISM-FEDERALISM.   The argument over the organization of government and the distribution of power between the national authority and local institutions was a constant rival of *CHURCH-STATE RELATIONS for the distinction of being the most consistent and troublesome domestic problem of the 19th and early 20th centuries. Those who rejected the colonial heritage of Colombia and who considered themselves progressive and liberal favored a federalist (decentralized) form of government. They looked to the United States for a model, especially prior to the U.S. Civil War. Those who favored a stronger state, reminiscent of the Spanish monarchy, advocated a centralized government. Allowing for numerous exceptions, generalizations would identify the *Liberal Party with federalism and the *Conservative Party with centralism. The *Constitutions of 1842 and 1886 are normally described as centralistic, while those of 1858 and 1863 are the most federalistic.

CERREJON, El.   The name given to a coal mining project located in the *Guajira Peninsula. The coal fields at El Cerrejón began production in 1984 in what has been termed the largest mining project in Colombian history. The Cerrejón coal reserves have been estimated at 3,600,000,000 metric tons. Production was undertaken by means of contracts between CARBOCOL, an agency of the Colombian government, and a consortium of Colombian and Spanish firms, on the one hand, and CARBOCOL and INTERCOR (a subsidiary of Exxon) on the other. See also: CERROMATOSO NICKEL MINING PROJECT

CERROMATOSO NICKEL MINING PROJECT.   Production began at the nickel deposits at Cerromatoso (*Córdoba) in 1982, under contracts with the Instituto de Fomento Industrial (IFI), for the government, and Hanna Chevron, a foreign corporation. The mining venture is now run jointly by IFI and Biliton, a Shell subsidary. Initial production efforts were marked by repeated breakdowns and cost overruns, but by the end of the decade, Colombian production was accounting for about 12% of world nickel sales. The Cerramatosa deposits yield about 800,000 metric tons of ore per year. Most ore is shipped abroad from the port of *Cartagena, about 167 miles from the mining field. Earnings in 1988 totaled US$160,500,000. The Cerromatoso contract, together with the El Cerrejón coal concessions, produced a heated debate over the role of foreign investment in Colombian resources. See also: CERREJON, El; NICKEL

CERRUTI, Ernesto Buenaventura Giacomo María, 1844-1915.   An Italian immigrant who is reputed to have become the richest man in the *Cauca Valley during his stay in Colombia and who was certainly the person responsible for one of the most scandalous diplomatic affairs in 19th-century Colombian history (see: CERRUTI AFFAIR). Born September 14 in Turin, Italy; died, February 11 in Perugia, Italy. Cerruti left a military career in 1869, and after brief stays in *Panama and *Buenaventura, he settled in *Cali in 1872. He made his fortune primarily, though not exclusively, in the export-import business using personal relationships, government connections, and companies known variously as Ernesto Cerruti, Ernesto Cerruti & Cía., and E. Cerruti & Cía. He never became a Colombian citizen and from 1870 to 1882 was the Italian consul in the Cauca Valley. As a foreigner with some diplomatic status he was supposed to avoid intervention in domestic politics, but Cerruti supported the *Radical faction of the *Liberals. He was accused of taking part in the *rebellion of 1885, and much of his personal assets were confiscated by the government. Claiming his Italian citizenship Cerruti returned to Europe in 1886, and from there he waged a fierce diplomatic attack on Colombia and successfully recovered damages for part of his losses.

CERRUTI AFFAIR. A reference to the arrest of Ernesto *Cerruti in *Cali and the confiscation of his property during the *rebellion of 1885. Cerruti's claims and his appeals to the Italian government led to a long bitter diplomatic dispute during which Italian warships threatened Colombian ports in 1885 and 1898. President Grover Cleveland of the United States acted as arbitrator in 1897, and the Colombian government was forced to pay 2,430,000 *pesos in damages in 1899. As a diplomatic cause célèbre, the incident was comparable only to the *Mackintosh Contract and the Watermelon Riot (see: PANAMA RIOT, 1856).

CESAR, Departamento de. Located in northeastern Colombia on the Venezuelan border, Cesar covers 22,905 square kilometers of widely varied terrain between 7° 41' and 10° 52'N latitude and 72° 53' and 74° 8'W longitude. Climatic distribution shows 19,528 square kilometers in tropical climates; 2,198 in temperate; 849 in cold; and 330 in wastelands. Major rivers include the *Magdalena, César, Lebrija, Ariguaní, Badillo, and Guatapurí. Highest points include the *Sierra Nevada de Santa Marta with the peaks of Bolívar (5,775 meters) and Colón (5,770 meters), the highest points in Colombia. Population in 1985 was estimated at 584,152 people, with a population density of 25.5 people per square kilometer. The capital city is *Valledupar. According to DANE, *Colombia estadística 86,* principal agricultural products, with tonnage produced in 1984, include rice, 228,883 tons; plantains, 77,000; *yuca,* 54,000; *cotton, 54,000; *African palm, 50,830; *corn, 47,830; sorghum, 46,000; *sugar, 35,800; beans 2,050; *tobacco, 290; sesame, 245; yams, 180; and soybeans, 36. Cattle ranching is a major industry, with 75,897 head of cattle and 10,722 hogs slaughtered in 1983. In 1984 there were 18 businesses employing ten or more people.

The department was created on December 21, 1967, from territory previously included in the Department of *Magdalena.

CESAR, Francisco, d. 1538. Conquistador, popular leader. He accompanied Pedro de *Heredia to *Cartagena in 1532. In 1537, with permission to hunt the treasure of Dabaibe, he led an expedition from the *Golfo de Urabá, along the Sierra de *Abibe, into the valley of the *Cauca River, where he fought the *Indians under Chief Nutibara, and then returned. He died during Juan *Vadillo's expedition in 1538.

CHACO WAR. An armed conflict between Bolivia and Paraguay, 1928-1935. Along with the United States, Mexico, Uruguay, Cuba, Bolivia, and Paraguay, Colombia was appointed to a Commission of Investigation and Conciliation established in 1929 to resolve the conflict by negotiation. Efforts to achieve a settlement of the conflict were finally successful in 1935, and a formal treaty was signed in 1938. See also: AMERICAN DOCTRINE

CHACON DE LUNA, Alvaro, see: VELEZ REBELLION

CHAGRES. Once important Caribbean port on the Isthmus of *Panama at the mouth of the Chagres River about 25 kilometers north of present-day *Colón. Chagres (located at approximately 9° 20'N, 79° 54'W) was valuable during the colonial period for its access to a transisthmian transportation route. The city was guarded by the fortress San Lorenzo until the latter was allowed to decay late in the 18th century. Both river and port derived their names from an Indian chief known as Chagre at the time of the European conquest. Chagres was replaced by Colón in the mid-19th century, and much of the surrounding area was flooded by the creation of Lake Gatun in the 20th century.

CHAMPAN. A large, flat-bottomed riverboat with enclosed, arch-shaped sides open at the ends. It was approximately 13 meters long, 2 meters wide, and 1 meter tall. The *champán* had a capacity of approximately 20 to 25 tons. It had a crew of anywhere from 12 to 21 *bogas,* or boatmen, and could travel about 20 kilometers per day against the current or 40 kilometers per day with it. It was used for freight and passengers, especially on the *Magdalena River, from the colonial period (1551) through the 19th century. In the 16th century, the crews were composed principally of *Indians, but after 1598 they were predominately made up of *blacks.

CHANCA (La), Battle of. July 11, 1841; *Valle del Cauca. Colonel Joaquín Barriga, for the government, defeated rebel forces under General José María *Obando. La Chanca was a major southern victory in the rebellion of 1840-1842 (see: the War of the *Supreme Commanders).

CHANCOS (Los), Battle of. August 31, 1876, *Valle del Cauca. General Julián *Trujillo, for the government, defeated the rebel forces of General Joaquín M. Córdoba in the Los Chancos Valley between Tuluá (4° 5' N, 76° 12' W) and *Buga. It was a decisive victory in the *rebellion of 1876-1877.

CHAPETON. A pejorative term for *Peninsular Spaniards (see also: CREOLE) in the late colonial period and the wars for independence. *Gachupín* and *Godo* were similar terms. After independence was achieved, *godo* was used to mean ultraconservative, authoritarian, or aristocratic.

CHARRO NEGRO. A nickname for Jacobo *PRIAS ALAPE.

CHARRY RINCON, Fermín. Alias of Jacobo *PRIAS ALAPE. See also: MARQUETALIA

CHASQUI. From the 18th century, a mail carrier; the term was borrowed from Peruvian usage.

CHAUX, Francisco José, b. 1889. *Quibdó-born lawyer-politician who lived most of his life in *Popayán. A diplomat, senator, and Minister of Industry under Presidents *Abadía Méndez and *Olaya Herrera. He supported *Arango Vélez in 1942, but then became a *gaitanista*. After *Gaitán's assassination he was seen for a while as his possible successor.

CHIA. The *Indian goddess *Bachué, especially in her identification with lunar cults, and also a place (today a town) near *Bogotá with important ceremonial links to the household of the *Zipa.

CHIBCHA. A linguistic stock that probably originated in Central America and diffused throughout much of Colombia. The name was commonly used to designate the Muisca, a Chibcha-speaking people, who dominated the central highlands of Colombia at the time of the conquest. The Chibcha, or Muisca, territory ran from the River Sogamoso (*Boyacá) south to the mountains of Sumapaz (*Cundinamarca) and from the *Cordillera Oriental to the *Magdalena River. Chibcha settlement, by carbon 14 dating, began at least as early as 545 B.C. The Chibchas formed sedentary village confederations ruled by the *Zipa at *Bogotá and the *Zaque, whose seat of government was Hunza (*Tunja). The Zipa was supposedly descended from the moon and the Zaque from the sun. Government was inherited by the ruler's nephew, his sister's son. The *economy was based on the cultivation of *corn, *potatoes, and beans by means of terracing and irrigation/drainage systems. In addition, the Chibcha maintained a complex trading system with fixed markets at different sites every eight days. They produced goldwork (see: MUISCA STYLE), *salt, pottery, *emeralds, and *cotton textiles, which they exchanged with other societies. There were important ceremonial centers at *Sogamoso, *Facatativá, and Lake *Guatavita. For Chibcha mythology see: BACHUE; BOCHICA; CHIBCHACUM; CHIMINIGAGUA; ELDORADO; GUATAVITA; NEMQUETABA.

CHIBCHACUM.   Patron deity of the *Chibchas. According to Chibcha lore, he was capricious, often hostile, and once flooded the plains of *Bogotá in a fit of anger. However, the Indians were saved by *Bochica, who made the *Tequendama Falls to drain off the waters. As punishment for abusing the Chibchas, Bochica condemned Chibchacum to carry the world on his shoulders, and he supposedly caused *earthquakes shifting the weight from side to side. Chibchacum was also the patron of merchants, goldsmiths, and farmers.

CHICHA.   A local, beerlike beverage made of *corn fermented with saliva. It was comparable to *aquardiente in use. Repeated efforts were made to ban or regulate its consumption during the colonial period. It has been replaced in the 20th century by beer and wine and the development of the modern brewing industry.

CHILE, Relations with.   Colombia and Chile first came into contact when the armies of both participated in the liberation of Peru. The *Mosquera-Echeverría-Rodríguez Treaty of 1822 and the *Abadía Méndez–Herboso Treaty of 1901 were both alliances promising help against respective enemies, but Colombia's neutrality during the War of the *Pacific strained relationships. The *Chile-Colombia Treaty of 1880 was partially aimed at reassuring Chile during its war with Peru and Bolivia. Admiration for Chile's military led to, imitation by Colombia at the turn of the century. The *Mosquera-Irarrazábal Treaty of 1844 was an effort to regulate trade in the 19th century, and both nations initially joined the *Andean Common Market in this century. Relations have not been exceptionally cordial, however. In the early years of the Andean Common Market, Colombia was opposed to Chilean demands for restrictions on *foreign investments, and the change of government in 1973 brought about such a complete reversal in Chile's policies that it withdrew from the market in December 1976. At the same time, relations also deteriorated as many Chilean exiles sought asylum in Colombia, and there were allegations of illegal harassment on Colombian soil by agents of DINA, the Chilean secret service.

CHILE-COLOMBIA TREATY OF 1822, see: MOSQUERA-ECHEVERRIA-RODRIGUEZ TREATY

CHILE-COLOMBIA TREATY OF 1880.   Signed on September 3, as an effort to reassure Chile of Colombian goodwill during the War of the *Pacific. The treaty provided that all disputes between the two countries would be settled by arbitration if it proved impossible to do so by negotiation. Although it was never ratified by Colombia, it stimulated the effort to hold an international congress in Panama that year (see: CONGRESS OF PANAMA, 1880).

CHILE-COLOMBIA TREATY OF 1901, see: ABADIA MENDEZ–HERBOSO TREATY

CHILE–NEW GRANADA TREATY OF 1844, see: MOSQUERA-IRARRAZABAL TREATY

CHIMINIGAGUA.   God of creation in *Chibcha lore. In primordial time, the world was in darkness and Chiminigagua sent two large black birds to fly about the earth spreading light. He then created the sun and the rest of the universe.

CHINACOTA TREATY, see: WISCONSIN TREATY

CHINCHONA, see: CINCHONA

CHIQUINQUIRA. A city on the plateau of the same name at 50° 37'N, 73° 49'W, in the Departamento de *Boyacá, 130 kilometers due north of *Bogotá. The population was 17,965 in 1985.

CHIQINQUIRA, Virgin Mary of the Rosary of. A sacred picture of the Virgin Mary with St. Anthony of Padua and St. Andrew, painted on cotton cloth around 1555 for *encomendero Antonio de Santana in the territory of Sutamarchán. It was later damaged and discarded until December 26, 1586, when it was miraculously restored at *Chiquinquirá in the presence of María Ramos and an Indian woman. The Virgin was taken from Chiquinquirá in 1587, 1633, 1816, and 1841 for intercession against disease and the menaces of war. Authorization for coronation of the image was granted by the Pope in 1910, and the image was crowned the Queen of Colombia on July 9, 1919. The sanctuary of the sacred image was visited by Pope *John Paul II on July 3, 1986.

CHOCO, Departamento de. Located in northwestern Colombia on the border with *Panama, the Chocó has coastlines on both the Atlantic and the Pacific Oceans. It covers 46,530 square kilometers, distributed by climatic zones in this manner: 42,985 square kilometers are tropical; 2,315, temperate; 1,114, cold; and 116, wasteland. The terrain is tropical lowland rain forest situated between latitudes 4° 2' and 8° 41'N and longitudes 76° and 77° 54'W. Major rivers include the *Atrato, *San Juan, Andágueda, Truandó, Baudó, and Bojayá. Rainfall in the Chocó is among the highest in the Western Hemisphere. In 1985 the estimated population was 68,506 people, and population density was 1.5 persons per square kilometer. The capital city is *Quibdó. Based on DANE, *Colombia estadística 86*, principal agricultural products, with tonnage produced in 1984, included plantains, 25,105 tons; *corn, 16,680; *yuca, 7,500; *sugar, 6,900; coconuts, 5,040; *cacao, 2,200; and beans, 50. *Livestock records show 5,942 head of cattle and 6,999 hogs slaughtered in the department in 1984. The Chocó is a former slaveholding area, historically important for *gold mining. Gold, *silver, and *platinum are still mined in the department. Other industry is in an incipient stage of development, with some production of beverages. The department was created November 3, 1947. See also: INTEROCEANIC CANAL

CHOCOANO. An inhabitant of the *Chocó. The word is also used popularly, though inaccurately, for anyone of African descent. See: BLACKS

CHOROGRAPHIC COMMISSION. A scientific commission authorized in 1839, established in 1850, to explore and chart *New Granada's national territory and to survey natural resources. Directed first by Colonel Agustín *Codazzi and later by Manuel Ponce de León and Manuel María Paz, the commission produced various maps, paintings, and written descriptions.

CHRISTIAN DEMOCRATS, see: DEMOCRACIA CRISTIANA

CHULAVITAS. A name given to conservatively oriented policemen, or strongmen, during the *Violencia. The name is derived from *Chulavo, a municipio, or county, in *Boyacá. Chulavita is also the name of a small town. The region was known locally as a *Conservative Party bastion. Although originally applied to policemen recruited from the area, the term came to mean any conservatively oriented officials or individuals who were sent to persecute *Liberals or other alleged subversives. See also: PAJAROS

CHURCH-STATE RELATIONS, see: ANCIZAR-ARBELAEZ PACT; ANTI-CLERICAL LAWS; CODIFICATION OF 1936; CONCORDAT OF 1887; CONCORDAT OF 1942; CONCORDAT OF 1973; INSPECTION OF CULTS, Law Concerning; PAPACY; PATRONATO; SEPARATION OF CHURCH AND STATE

CHURCHES, see: CATHEDRAL OF SALT; CATHOLIC CHURCH; PRESBYTERIAN CHURCH; PROTESTANTISM

CIEN AÑOS DE SOLEDAD, see: ONE HUNDRED YEARS OF SOLITUDE

CIEZA DE LEON, Pedro de, 1518-1560. Conquistador, author. He participated in numerous expeditions into the countries of the Pacific Coast. His Crónicas del Perú includes descriptions of the conquest of the *Cauca Valley and the explorations of Juan *Vadillo and Jorge de *Robledo.

CIMARRONES, see: MAROONS

CINCHONA. A native shrub of the valleys of the tropical Andes whose bark is the source of *QUININE. Also called chinchona, it was named for the Marchioness of Chincón, Vicereine of Peru, after the use of it alleviated her malaria.

CIRCULO DE OBREROS (CO). The Workers' Circle, or CO, was founded January 1, 1911, in *Bogotá, by the *Jesuit Father José María Campoamor. The first successful labor organization under the patronage of the *Catholic Church, the CO functioned more as a mutual aid society than as a defender of workers' rights or an organizer of *strikes. CO members included skilled and unskilled workers and small businessmen. The Workers' Circle was eclipsed by the rise of the more militant *Confederación de Trabajadores de Colombia, but many CO members eventually joined the *Unión de Trabajadores de Colombia after 1946.

CISNEROS, Francisco Javier, 1836-1898. Cuban-born, naturalized U.S. engineer and financier, active in railroad development in Colombia, 1874-1898. He undertook the construction of parts of the *Antioquia, *Pacific, *Girardot, and La *Dorada railways, as well as colonization of the areas served by them. He also contributed to the development of commerce on the *Magdalena River.

CITARA. The early colonial name of *QUIBDO.

CIUDAD BOLIVAR. The name of two Venezuelan cities, the larger and more easterly of which (on the Orinoco River at 8° 9'N, 63° 36'W) was the site of the *CONGRESS OF ANGOSTURA.

CIUDAD PERDIDA. An archeological site, which, together with Taironaca and Pueblito (Chairama), is the best-known city of the *Tairona Indian civilization. Literally, the "lost city," Ciudad Perdida was essentially unknown from the early 17th century until 1976, when the Colombian Institute of Anthropology (*Instituto Colombiano de Antropología) authorized restorations at the site. The remains of Ciudad Perdida (located at altitudes between 800 and 1,300 meters on the Buritaca River in the *Sierra Nevada de Santa Marta) include a central arterial road with a network of interconnected secondary roads. Structural ruins include a well-preserved collection of terraces, retaining walls, aqueducts, building sites, and an amphitheater. Buildings were normally round with dwellings up to 10 meters in diameter, although some houses at other sites reached as much as 24 meters in diameter. Since the superstructures were of wood, only the stone foundations remain. Many of the Tairona ruins are now protected in a government archeological park.

CIUDADES CONFEDERADAS DEL VALLE. The Confederated Cities of the Valley was a union of the cities of Caloto (3° 1'N, 76° 25'W) *Buga, *Cartago, *Anserma, Toro, and *Cali, formed February 1, 1811. The first republican government in the *Cauca Valley, it moved to *Popayán after the Battle of *Bajo Palacé, March 28, 1811, and was extinguished after the Battle of *Cuchilla del Tambo, June 29, 1816.

CIVIC FRONT. A term sometimes used to translate the *FRENTE NACIONAL.

CIVIL CODE, see: LAW

CIVIL WARS, see: COMUNEROS REVOLT; GUERRILLA MOVEMENTS; MINOR CONVENTS, Rebellion of; PORTUGUESE REBELLION; REBELLION OF NEIVA; REBELLION OF 1830-1831; REBELLION OF 1851-1852; REBELLION OF 1854; REBELLION OF 1859-1862; REBELLION OF 1876-1877; REBELLION OF 1884-1885; SUPREME COMMANDERS, War of the; THOUSAND DAYS, War of the; VIOLENCIA, La

CIVILIAN GENERATION, see: FOUNDING GENERATION

CLANDESTINE EMISSIONS. A reference to the secret issuance of national bank notes from 1889 to 1894 by Carlos Martínez Silva and others of the treasury department. Although a maximum of 12 million *pesos had been established by law in 1887, treasury officials decided to issue a larger amount, using the excess notes to exchange for other currency, which would then be retired from service to achieve the legal maximum. The intent was to bring some uniformity to a system in which there were more than 20 kinds of notes in circulation and to cancel old government debts without paying interest on them. The emissions, exposed in 1894, became the object of a major political controversy.

CLARIBALTE, Libro del muy esforzado y invencible cavallero. The first novel written in the Western Hemisphere; see: FERNANDEZ DE OVIEDO Y VALDES, Gonzalo

CLASSIC GENERATION. The group of cultural leaders who, in the terms of Abel Naranjo Villegas, developed or were prominent from 1880 to 1905. Naranjo Villegas characterizes the period as one marked by authoritarianism, dogmatic and ideologically oriented thinking, a sentimental attachment to Spanish culture, and an individualistic, egocentric approach to life. Ernesto Cortés Ahumada calls this the Humanist Generation (key date, 1885). Representative figures include Manuel Briceño, Clímaco Calderón, Miguel Antonio *Caro, Rafael María *Carrasquilla, Tomás *Carrasquilla, Carlos Cuervo Márquez, Ramón *González Valencia, Benjamín Herrera, Jorge *Holguín, Pedro María Ibañez, Jorge *Isaacs, Luis Martínez Silva, Pedro Nel *Ospina, Eduardo Posada, Rafael *Reyes, Manuel María *Sanclemente, Baldomero *Sanín Cano, Marco Fidel *Suárez, Juan de Díos Uribe (El Indio), Rafael *Uribe Uribe, and José María *Vargas Vila. See also: GENERATIONS

CLAVER, Pedro, 1580-1654. Saint; *Jesuit missionary, known as the "apostle of the Negroes," born in Verdú (Spain). He took holy orders in 1602 and arrived in *Cartagena in 1610. He finished his religious studies in *Tunja and was ordained in 1616. For the rest of his life, he worked with the slaves around Cartagena. San Pedro Claver died in Cartagena on September 8, 1654, and was canonized on January 8, 1888, by Pope Leo XIII.

CLAYTON-BULWER TREATY OF 1850. Signed on April 19 by John Clayton for the United States and Henry L. Bulwer for Great Britain. The treaty established the neutrality of the *Isthmus of Panama and provided that neither nation would build or maintain exclusive control of a canal in the territory. Great Britain specified the boundaries of Belize (British Honduras) and renounced its protectorate over the *Mosquito Coast.

CLIMATIC ZONES. Although the equator passes through southern Colombia, local climates are determined as much by the altitude as by the latitude. Temperatures and rainfall decline as the elevation rises. Standard conventions for designating climatic zones in Colombia and elsewhere in the *Andes are *tierra caliente* (0-1,000 meters above sea level); *tierra templada* (1,000-2,000 meters); *tierra fría* (2,000-3,000 meters); *páramo* (3,000-4,800 meters); and *nieve* or *tierra nevada* (above 4,800 meters). *Tierra caliente*, literally "hot land," is tropical, with temperatures above 24°C, and accounts for about 83% of the national territory and about 40% of the population. Examples of *tierra caliente* are the coastal lowlands, the eastern *Llanos, the *Amazon basin, and river valleys such as the *Cauca and *Magdalena. *Tierra templada*, or "temperate land," has temperatures between 17.5°C and 24°C. It covers about 9% of the land with 37% of the population. Lower mountain slopes, highland river valleys, and cities such as *Medellín are typical of temperate zones. *Tierra fría*, or "cold land," has temperatures between 12°C and 17.5°C, extending over 6% of the land, providing homes for about 22% of the population. *Tierra fría* is found on upper mountain slopes and highland plateaus such as the *Sabana de Bogotá. *Páramo*, or "wasteland," has temperatures from 0°C to 12°C, accounting for about 15% of the land but less than 1% of the population. *Nieve*, or *tierra nevada*, the perpetual snow region, has temperatures below 0°C. In Colombia, *Nieve* accounts for less than 1% of the land mass and has no permanent population. Elsewhere in this work, the terms "hot" or "tropical" are used to designate *tierra caliente;* "temperate" to describe *tierra templada;* "cold" to describe *tierra fría;* and "wasteland" to include *páramo* and *nieve*.

CO, see: CIRCULO DE OBREROS

COAL PRODUCTION.   Colombia claims as much as 64% of the known coal deposits in Latin America, ranking twelfth with regard to world coal reserves. Major deposits have been identified around *Bogotá, *Medellín, *Cali, Carare (*Santander), El *Cerrejón (Guajira), and La Jagua (*Cesar). Production of coal in Colombia was not of major importance until the mid-1960s. Since then, efforts have been made to develop coal as a major export. In 1989, the Colombian Information Service listed current production at 19 million metric tons per year. See also: CERREJON, El

COAT OF ARMS OF THE REPUBLIC, see: ARMS OF THE REPUBLIC

COCA.   A name for the shrub from whose leaves *COCAINE is
derived. The coca bush is difficult to destroy and originally
grew wild in the foothills of the Peruvian and Bolivian *Andes.
As many as 250 wild species are known, but there are only four
major varieties of coca cultivated in Latin America today.
These are *Erythroxylum coca* (most commonly grown in the
Andes mountains of Peru and Bolivia and often referred to as
Huánuco or Bolivian coca); *Erythroxylum coca ipadu* (Amazonian coca, found in the lowlands of southeastern Colombia
and the Amazon region of Brazil); *Erythroxylum novogranatense*
(cultivated in the highlands of Colombia and commonly called
Colombian coca); and *Erythroxylum novogranatense truxillense*
(Trujillo coca, grown in Peru). The name "coca" comes from
the Spanish *coca* (Quechua *cuca*) and is Aymaran in origin. Since
pre-Columbian times, various Indian groups have chewed the
coca leaves, releasing their narcotic affect by mixing the leaf,
lime, and saliva. Coca use was widespread in the Incan empire,
and continues today as an analgesic against hunger and extreme
physical exertion among many *Indians in the high Andes.
Some coca is grown in Colombia, mainly in the *Meta,
*Guaviare, *Vaupés, *Caquetá, and *Putumayo regions and
the *Sierra Nevada de Santa Marta. But Colombian coca is
inferior to that grown in Peru and Bolivia, with only ⅓ to ½
as much alkaloid content, and most leaves for the Colombian
*drug trade (perhaps as much as 80% of those processed) are
imported.

COCAINE.   *Cocaina,* or cocaine, is the narcotic benzoylmethyl
ecgonine, the most important of the 13 active alkaloids in the
leaves of the *coca plant. It constitutes about 1% of the leaf
and has been known as a drug since its isolation in 1855. It
gained rapid acceptance as a wonder drug (even making up part
of the original Coca-Cola formula) until the dangers of addic-
tion became recognized about 90 years ago. Its use was
outlawed in the United States in 1914.
    Modern cocaine is produced in a two-stage process often
referred to as "cooking." According to Charles Nicholl, *The
Fruit Palace,* the leaves are "cooked" until a paste (*pasta*) is
achieved by a combination of salting (*la salada*), soaking (*la
mojadura*), pressing (*la prensa*), processing (*la guapería*), and
drying (*la secadería*). The *pasta* or *pasta lavada* can then be
refined into cocaine (*perica*) immediately or easily transported
for refinement at another location. *Basuco,* a brown powder
made from the coca paste in the penultimate stage of refining,

is the form of cocaine most often consumed in Latin America. It is smoked, rather than inhaled or injected. "Crack" is a concentrate of refined cocaine more commonly used in the United States. Much of the cocaine processing has been concentrated in *Antioquia and the middle *Magdalena River valley between Puerto Triunfo and *Puerto Berrío.

It is estimated that Colombia processes 70% to 90% of the cocaine entering the United States, but primarily from leaves imported from Peru and Bolivia rather than locally grown ones. In December 1978, Roberto Junguito and Carlos Caballero Argáez estimated Colombia's total cocaine exports at 10 to 18 metric *tons a year, worth about US$154 million gross. This was equivalent to 9% of Colombia's national gross domestic product after production costs were discounted (*Coyuntura económica*, 8[4]: 103-139). Estimates in 1988-1989 placed the sales of Colombian cocaine in the United States at US$180 million and the European market was rapidly approaching the same magnitude. See also: DRUG TRADE; MEDELLIN CARTEL; MULE

COCOA. A chocolate powder produced from the nut of the *CACAO tree. It has no relationship to and should not be confused with *COCA.

CODAZZI, Agustín, 1793-1859. Italian-born colonel, engineer, head of the *Chorographic Commission, 1849-1859, he entered military service in Italy in 1809 and joined patriot forces in *New Granada, 1817-1819. After a time in the United States and Europe, he returned to Colombia in 1826, settling in Venezuela shortly thereafter. In 1830, the administration of General José Antonio Páez commissioned him to prepare a cartographical survey of the new Republic of Venezuela. The results of his work were the *Atlas físico y político de la República de Venezuela* and the *Resumen de la geografía de Venezuela,* published in Paris in 1841. On December 20, 1849, he was appointed the head of the Chorographic Commission designed to produce similar work for New Granada. Although incomplete at the time of his death, Codazzi's *Atlas geográfico e histórico de la República de Colombia* (edited by Manuel María Paz and Felipe Pérez) was published in Paris in 1889. See also: INSTITUTO GEOGRAFICO AGUSTIN CODAZZI

CODES, Legal, see: LAW

CODIFICATION OF 1936. A revision of the *Constitution of 1886 adopted by the *Liberal administration of President Alfonso *López Pumarejo, some of its most outstanding features included the declarations that labor enjoyed the protection of the state (Article 17) and was entitled to the right to strike (Article 18); that public assistance was a function of the state (Article 19); that the possession of property carried social obligations (Article 20); and that the state might intervene in the conduct of private and public businesses where the general social welfare was concerned (Article 32). Several provisions restricted the role of the Church in public affairs (see: CHURCH-STATE RELATIONS), but many of these were revised within a short time.

COFFEE. Coffee is Colombia's major income-producing export. Coffee cultivation seems to have been introduced into the Western Hemisphere through the French West Indies. Coffee growing is said to have appeared in Colombia in the middle of the 18th century. Some authorities credit Father José *Gumilla, a *Jesuit missionary who worked in Colombia 1715-1738, with the introduction of coffee into the Apure and Guarico River region of the *Llanos. However, cultivation in this area deteriorated with the explusion of the Jesuits in 1767. Sustained coffee husbandry probably spread overland from Venezuela, which in turn had received it through Dutch influence via Suriname and the Guianas. Coffee was first grown in the present-day Departments of *Norte de Santander and *Santander, fanning out from *Cúcuta. An early 19th-century stimulus is attributed to a Father Romero, who systematically assigned his parishioners the planting of coffee trees as penances. It later spread to the *Cundinamarca-*Tolima region, *Antioquia, and the *Cauca Valley (the northern part of which is sometimes called the MAM—*Medellín, *Armenia, *Manizales—axis).

Andrés Uribe Campuzano has identified three basic varieties of early coffee stock: Coffee Canephora (*coffea canephora*), which was tested in the *Sierra Nevada de Santa Marta; Coffee Liberica (*coffea liberica*), or *robusta*, which grew in *tierra caliente*, or the lowlands; and various varieties of Coffee Arabica, or *abrigo*, which was grown in *tierra templada*, or mountain elevations. This *abrigo*, also known as *café suave*, is the premium-flavored mountain-grown coffee for which Colombia is internationally famous.

Café suave flourishes in the temperate climates (17°-24°C) at altitudes between 1,200 and 1,800 meters. Early coffee cultivation, especially in warmer regions, alternated rows of coffee trees between rows of plantains, or other larger plants, which provided protective shade. Coffee cultivation in Colombia is often carried on by small producers (perhaps epitomized by Juan *VALDEZ), especially in the Santander and Medellín-Manizales regions. The first "coffee census," taken in 1932, recorded 150,000 coffee farms, most of which were under 10 hectares (about 25 acres). Coffee production requires an initial investment—trees must be five to six years old before the first crop can be harvested—and is labor intensive at specified times in the growth cycle, but it lends itself to small and medium-sized family-farm cultivation. Plantation or large estate production was historically dominant in Cundinamarca and parts of Antioquia.

Statistics regarding the exportation of coffee are available from as early as 1835, but major sales abroad date from about 1874. Coffee exports rose rapidly 1887-1896. Declining prices led to a *coffee crisis 1896-1900, but export revenue rose again after that. One estimate says that coffee accounted for 82.6% of all Colombian exports and 21% of total world production by 1953. However, Marco Palacio, *Coffee in Colombia, 1850-1970,* says the proportion of world production in 1953 was only 19%. His figures for exports (annual average in 60-kilo bags for three-year cycles, 1853-1907) are as follows: 1853-1855 (1,186 bags), 1865-1867 (36,553 bags), 1877-1879 (100,744 bags), 1887-1888 (127,000 bags), 1895-1897 (266,000 bags), and 1907-1909 (400,000 bags). Partial 20th-century figures show 1930 (3,118,000 bags), 1940 (4,457,000 bags), 1950 (4,472,000 bags), 1960 (5,938,000 bags), and 1970 (6,509,000 bags). Under the International Coffee Agreement, Colombia's projected exports for 1988-1989 were 10,890,049 bags. As a percentage of total exports, coffee reached its peak in the 1960s. Since then coffee exports remain high, but production in the economy as a whole has diversified, and the overall percentage of exports has shown a relative decline. In 1987-1988 some 720,000 tons of coffee were exported, accounting for 16% of the world total and $2,400 million, or 62% of Colombia's total legal exports.

The National Federation of Coffee Growers was established in 1927, and a national Center for Coffee Research (Centro Nacional de Investigaciones de Café) was established at Chinchiná (4° 59'N, 75° 36'W, *Caldas) near Manizales in 1932. Colombia joined the Inter-American Coffee Agreement, November 28, 1940, and the International Coffee Agreement in

1962. In 1979 the principal customers for Colombian coffee were the United States (44% of the total) and the German Federal Republic (17%). See: FEDERACION NACIONAL DE CAFETEROS; INTERNATIONAL COFFEE AGREEMENT

COFFEE CRISIS OF 1896-1900. After several years of expansion and high profits, coffee prices fell markedly during the period 1896-1900, causing a major economic crisis within Colombia. Many coffee producers were hurt, and government revenues fell causing a shortage of funds for sustaining normal government operations. The crisis has been cited as a contributing factor in the outbreak of the War of the *Thousand Days in October 1899. The Department of *Santander, where the war began, was one of the areas most adversely affected by the severe drop in coffee prices. From the standpoint of domestic coffee producers, the crisis in the international coffee trade was intensified by an export tax President *Caro imposed by means of Decree No. 75, March 22, 1895. Intended to increase government revenue, the tax was not repealed until 1898, although collection of the tax was temporarily suspended by Decree No. 301, July 13, 1897.

COGOTES, Battle of. March 2, 1885, *Tolima. Generals Manuel Casabianca and Juan N. Matéus defeated the rebellious forces of *Liberal General Francisco Losada, Germán Rojas, David Tovar, and Patrocinio Falla.

COINAGE. *New Granada's original coinage was that of Castile, but Spanish coins began to be minted locally from 1620 (see: CASA DE MONEDA). The government of independent *Gran Colombia decided on a total recoinage, and its first *pesos, called *colombianos, were minted in 1823. However, lack of confidence in the new regime limited their acceptability. In April 1847, the *granadino (worth ten reales intead of eight, or about one French gold franc) was introduced. This became the new unit on the 1853 decimalization and was renamed the peso the following year. The old peso sencillo was declared worth eighty centavos, the peseta worth twenty centavos, and the *real (called officially a décimo) worth ten centavos. Quarters (cuartillos) circulated from 1861 to 1920, but since then only the more truly decimal fraction of 20 centavos has been minted.

*Gold was coined (in pieces of one *peso* and above) until 1932, but the amount issued declined drastically after the *rebellion of 1851-1852, and none was minted from 1877 to 1884. *Silver coins have ranged from 10 *centavos* to a *peso*. None was minted between 1889 and 1906, or after 1946, although silver alloy was used until 1956. Baser coin metals have included *copper (from 1823), *nickel (from 1852), copper-nickel to replace silver (from 1942), bronze (two-*centavo* coins, 1952-1965), and nickel-plated steel (one-*centavo* coins, 1952-1957). See also: CURRENCY

COLCIENCIAS. The Colombian Fund for Scientific Research (Fondo Colombiana para Investigaciones Científicas), which is responsible for implementing policies formulated by CONI-CYPT (the Consejo Nacional de Investigaciones Científicas y Tecnológicas). CONICYPT was established in 1968 for research and development of scientific and technological programs. Both COLCIENCIAS and CONICYPT are directly subordinate to the President and are responsible for coordinating government-supported research programs, locally and internationally, on such things as metallurgy, nutrition, energy resources, conservation, housing, and health.

COLDESA S.A. A business firm and plantation located near the port of Turbo (8° 6'N, 76° 43'W, *Antioquia), it was the scene of the first commercial cultivation of *African palm in Colombia. Operations began at COLDESA in 1958, when this edible oilseed plant was imported from Africa. Production of oil from the African palm began in 1966. Cultivation of the plant has since spread to other parts of the country.

COLEGIO CONSTITUYENTE DE SANTA FE DE BOGOTA, 1811. A legislative body that met February 28 to March 30 in *Bogotá, it proclaimed the independence of the State of *Cundinamarca, effective April 4, under the monarchy of Ferdinand VII, and convoked a national congress to govern the new nation.

COLEGIO ELECTORAL. Literally, the "Electoral College" (or Academy); a legislative body for the state of *Cundinamarca that was responsible for declaring complete independence from Spain. On July 16, 1813, it repudiated loyalty to Ferdinand VII or any other representative of the Spanish monarchy and asserted its right to independent government. From 1811 to 1813, Cundinamarca had supported the *Junta Suprema de Gobierno and the *Junta Central of Spain, which remained loyal to Ferdinand VII (see: COLEGIO CONSTITUYENTE DE SANTA FE DE BOGOTA). Although one of the earliest acts to declare complete independence, Cundinamarca's move was preceded by a proclamation from *Cartagena on November 11, 1811, and by that of *Mompós, August 6, 1810.

COLEGIO MAYOR DE NUESTRA SEÑORA DEL ROSARIO. Educational institution founded in *Bogotá in 1653 by Archbishop Cristóbal de *Torres. It was run by the *Dominicans. Its functions varied but, at times, it included both secondary and higher educational programs. The institution has functioned more or less continuously since 1653. See also: COLEGIO MAYOR DE SAN BARTOLOME

COLEGIO MAYOR DE SAN BARTOLOME. Also known as the Seminario y Colegio Mayor de San Bartolomé, it was an educational institution in *Bogotá organized in 1604 by Archbishop *Lobo Guerrero, who entrusted it to the *Jesuits. Aside from clerical training, the school had, at various times, secondary and higher educational functions. It was incorporated into the *Universidad Nacional in 1867. The *Colegio Mayor de Nuestra Señora del Rosario and the Colegio San Bartolomé were the two principal secondary schools in *Bogotá and much of Colombia until well into the 19th century.

COLISEO RAMIREZ. Also known simply as El Coliseo, the Coliseo Ramírez, the first theater built in *Bogotá, was constructed 1791-1792 by José Tomás Ramírez on the site of the present-day *Teatro Colón. Ramírez directed the theater 1792-1795, during which time some 39 works were presented. Although Ramírez died in *Tocaima (Cundinamarca) in 1805, the Coliseo retained his name until 1840, when it was purchased by Bruno and Domingo Maldonado, who rechristened it the Teatro Maldonado. In 1885 it was demolished to make way for the present Teatro Colón, which opened in 1892.

COLOMBIA. Homage to the accomplishments of Christopher *Columbus, the Genoese-born early explorer of the New World, frequently appears in the use of the terms "Colombia" and "Colón" (Spanish) and "Columbia" (English). Although a European mapmaker seems largely responsible for inadvertently giving the name America (América), after the Florentine navigator Amerigo *Vespucci, to most of the Western Hemisphere, commemorative uses of names derived from Columbus are far more numerous. A few examples serve to make the point: República de Colombia, Teatro Colón, British Columbia, the District of Columbia, and Columbia University. Historically, portions of the present Republic of Colombia have been known as the *Nuevo Reino de Granada (1538-1563), the *Presidencia del Nuevo Reino de Granada (1563-1719 and 1723-1739), the *Virreinato del Nuevo Reino de Granada (1719-1723 and 1739-1810/19), the *Provincias Unidas de Nueva Granada (1811-1816), the *República de Gran Colombia (1819-1832), the *República de Nueva Granada (1832-1858), the *Confederación Granadina (1858-1861), the *Estados Unidos de Nueva Granada (1861-1863), the *Estados Unidos de Colombia (1863-1886), and the *Republica de Colombia, (1886-). The name appears officially in Colombian history when the *Congress of Angostura established the República de Gran Colombia. The Liberator, Simón *Bolívar, may well have hoped to see all the former Spanish colonies in a single Colombian union. The name reappeared in the United States of Colombia in 1863, and permanently in the Republic of Colombia in 1886. See also the successive state titles, and: ADMINISTRATIVE DIVISIONS; AREA; BORDERS; CLIMATIC ZONES; ECONOMY, The; GEOGRAPHY; HOLIDAYS; POPULATION; PRESIDENTS OF COLOMBIA; TIME

COLOMBIA, Republic of, see: REPUBLICA DE COLOMBIA; REPUBLICA DE GRAN COLOMBIA

COLOMBIA, United States of, see: ESTADOS UNIDOS DE COLOMBIA

COLOMBIA NAVIGATION COMPANY. British-owned corporation operating steamships on the *Magdalena River. In 1913 it merged with the *Cartagena Railway Company to form the *Colombian Railway and Navigation Company.

COLOMBIA RAILWAY AND NAVIGATION COMPANY. British-owned corporation, formed in 1913, with capital of £875,000, to operate the *CALAMAR RAILROAD together with a river steamboat service on the *Magdalena River and the dock at *Cartagena.

COLOMBIAN ACADEMY OF HISTORY, see: ACADEMIA COLOMBIANA DE HISTORIA

COLOMBIAN ACADEMY OF JURISPRUDENCE, see: ACADEMIA COLOMBIANA DE JURISPRUDENCIA

COLOMBIAN ACADEMY OF LANGUAGE, see: ACADEMIA COLOMBIANA DE LA LENGUA

COLOMBIAN ACADEMY OF NATURAL SCIENCES, see: ACADEMIA COLOMBIANA DE CIENCIAS EXACTAS, FISICAS Y NATURALES

COLOMBIAN INSTITUTE OF AGRARIAN REFORM, see: INSTITUTO COLOMBIANO DE LA REFORMA AGRARIA

COLOMBIAN NATIONAL RAILROADS, see: FERROCAR-RILES NACIONALES DE COLOMBIA

COLOMBIAN NATIONAL RAILWAY. A private corporation that built and operated the *GIRARDOT RAILROAD.

COLOMBIAN NORTHERN RAILWAY. A British-owned corporation that built and operated the *Bogotá-Nemocón-*Chiquinquirá section of the *NORTHERN RAILWAY.

COLOMBIAN SOUTHERN RAILWAY. A British-owned corporation that built and operated the *SOUTHERN RAIL-ROAD. The company was bought out by the Colombian government in 1914.

COLOMBIANO. The gold one-*peso* coin introduced in 1823 by the newly independent *Gran Colombia.

COLOMBIANO, El. A Conservative daily *newspaper of *Medellín established February 6, 1912, by Francisco de Paula Pérez and Juan B. Londoño. The name was taken from a *Bogotá newspaper directed by General Daniel de Angulo in 1900. Its current circulation is around 120,000.

COLON. City in *Panama at 9° 21'N, 79° 54'W, built as the Caribbean terminus of the *Panama Railroad. Originally known as Aspinwall, the settlement was begun in 1850 on

Manzanilla Island on the eastern shore of Navy Bay (Bay of Limón), about four miles northeast of the mouth of the Chagres River. It displaced the city of *Chagres (which had itself replaced *Portobello only thirty years before) as the main entrepôt on the north coast of the isthmus.

COLON, Battle of. March 31, 1885, *Panama. Colonel Ramón Ulloa and General Carlos Gónima, for the government, captured Colón from General Rafael Aizpurú and Pedro Prestán. Order was restored to a large part of the isthmus, but Colón itself was badly damaged by fire.

COLON, Cristóbal, see: COLUMBUS, Christopher

COLON THEATER, see: TEATRO COLON

COLONIAL ADMINISTRATION, see: SPANISH EMPIRE IN AMERICA, Administration of the

COLTEJER, see: COMPAÑIA COLOMBIANA DE TEJIDOS

COLUMBUS, Christopher (Cristóbal Colón, in Spanish), 1451-1506. Explorer of America, he sailed along the coast of Venezuela on his third voyage (1498) and along the coast of Central America from Honduras to the Gulf of *Darien on his fourth voyage (1502-1503). See also: COLOMBIA

COLUMNA ANTONIO NARIÑO. A force of 90 members of the *Movimiento Diecinueve de Abril (M-19) that assembled in Cuba and then disembarked on the Pacific shore of southern Colombia, marching inland to occupy the town of *Mocoa. See: NARIÑO, Invasion of

COMANDO QUINTIN LAME. A *guerrilla self-defense group formed in March 1985 by the Páez (*Paeces) and Guambiano Indians, who felt themselves caught in a power struggle between local non-Indian landlords, members of the *Fuerzas Armadas Revolucionarias de Colombia (FARC), and government troops. Although originally seen as protectors against the landlords who wanted to seize control of Indian *resguardos, FARC guerrillas began to extort protection money from landowners, and the Indians found themselves opposing both forces. The Páez and Guambiano Indians publicly announced their defense group, the Comando Quintín Lame (named after

Manuel *Quintín Lame) on April 1, 1985, at a press conference held for reporters they had kidnapped from *Popayán. The Quintín Lame Brigade, as it is sometimes called, participated in joint actions with the *Ricardo Franco Front and the *Movimiento Diecinueve de Abril, and it became a supporter of the *Coordinadora Guerrillera "Simón Bolívar."

COMMISSARIAT. A *comisaría*, also known as a commissary and sometimes a commissaryship, was an administrative division of the Republic of Colombia under the *Constitution of 1886. It was the smallest unit, with fewer people than a *department or an *intendancy. *Amazonas was created a commissariat in 1931, *Vichada in 1943, *Guainía and *Vaupés both in 1963, and *Guaviare in 1977. Each consisted of a single *municipio* (*municipality). The *Constitution of 1991 did not provide for commissariats. The existing units became departments.

COMMONERS' REVOLT, see: COMUNEROS REVOLT

COMMUNIST PARTY, see: PARTIDO COMUNISTA DE COLOMBIA

COMMUNIST YOUTH, see: JUVENTUD COMUNISTA

COMPAGNIE UNIVERSELLE DU CANAL INTER-OCEANIQUE DE PANAMA. A French canal company, founded in 1879, as a result of a canal concession granted to Lucien Napoleon Bonaparte Wyse in 1878. It was headed by the French engineer Ferdinand de *Lesseps, and initiated work in 1883. It was declared bankrupt in 1888 because of scandals concerning its management. The firm was reorganized in 1890 and later granted an extension until 1910, but the company was never able to complete construction as planned. Much of its assets were sold to the United States after 1903. See also: FRANCE, Relations with

COMPAÑIA COLOMBIANA DE SEGUROS. The oldest and one of the largest Colombian insurance firms, it was founded October 28, 1875, in *Bogotá to provide coverage for the transportation industry. In 1904 it absorbed the Sociedad Nacional de Seguros de Vida, a life insurance firm, and in 1920 it incorporated the Compañía General de Seguros, a general agency. The company was an important influence in the development of Colombian economic history during the early 20th century.

COMPAÑIA COLOMBIANA DE TEJIDOS. More commonly known as COLTEJER, Colombia's oldest continually functioning and most important textile firm. It was founded in *Medellín on October 22, 1907, by Alejandro Echavarría (1859-1928) and his sons, Gabriel and Guillermo Echavarría. General Rafael *Reyes, then chief executive of Colombia, inaugurated the company by remote control from *Bogotá.

COMPAÑIA DE JESUS, see: JESUITS

COMPAÑIA ELECTRICA DE BUCARAMANGA. The second major electrical company formed in present-day Colombia (preceded by the less important *Panama Electric Light Company and the *Bogotá Electric Light Company), it introduced the incandescent light to Colombia and established the nation's first hydroelectric (see: HYDROELECTRICITY) plant at Chitota on the Suratá River. It was formed by Julio Jones Benítez and his cousin, Reinaldo Goekel Jones, on the basis of a contract with the municipal government of *Bucaramanga, May 10, 1890. In 1893 it formally became the Compañía Anónima Eléctrica de Bucaramanga and later simply the Compañía Eléctrica de Bucaramanga. Service was begun on August 30, 1891, but it was quickly interrupted by an accident. Only on November 20, 1891, was service securely reestablished.

COMPAÑIA NACIONAL DE ELECTRICIDAD. Formed in April 1920 by José D. Dávila Pumarejo and the Dávila family of *Bogotá, the company began electrical service to the public at the end of 1924. However, it functioned only three years before it was merged with the *Empresas Unidas de Energía Eléctrica in 1927.

COMPAÑIA NACIONAL DE NAVEGACION S.A. (NAVENAL). A government corporation created by law in 1944 to supervise and develop inland waterways. Political pressures forced it into ocean navigation, which contributed to its bankruptcy. The company was inoperative after 1983.

COMPANY OF SCOTLAND TRADING TO AFRICA AND THE INDIES. Scottish trading company whose first and only venture was the ill-fated attempt to set up a *tobacco-growing colony called New Caledonia in *Panama. See: DAR-IEN, Scottish colony of

COMUNEROS REVOLT. The Commoners' Rebellion occurred 1780-1782 in *Santander, *Norte de Santander, *Nariño, *Antioquia, *Casanare, and elsewhere. Housewives and workingmen rebelled against the tax policies of Intendant Juan Francisco *Gutiérrez de Piñeres. The movement was led first in 1781 by Manuela *Beltrán, Ambrosio *Pisco, and Juan Francisco *Berbeo, the general commander who concluded a truce with royal officials and Archbishop Antonio *Caballero y Góngora on June 4-8, 1781. The rebellion was continued by José Antonio *Galán and others, June-October 1781, especially when Gutiérrez de Piñeres repudiated the truce terms. It was terminated by the arrest and execution of various leaders, including Galán, and by a pardon issued by Viceroy Caballero y Góngora in 1782.

CONCENTRACION NACIONAL. A loose political grouping of Liberals and Conservatives who supported the administration of President Enrique *Olaya Herrera, 1930-1934. The coalition was reminiscent of the Republican Union (*Unión Republicana), which Olaya Herrera had helped to organize in 1909-1910.

CONCEPCION (La), Battle of. August 29, 1859, approximately 6° 46'N, 72° 42'W in *Santander. Colonel Santos Gutiérrez, for the *Liberal government of *Santander, defeated the *Conservative forces of Colonels Juan José Márquez and Melchor Corena.

CONCEPTIONISTS. The *Franciscan Order of the Immaculate Conception, or the Conceptionists, is the second oldest order of religious women in Colombia. Its first convents were founded in *Pasto (1578), *Bogotá (1595), and *Tunja (1600).

CONCHA, José Vicente, 1867-1929. Lawyer, legislator, diplomat, President of Colombia (1914-1918); born *Bogotá, April 21; died Rome (Italy), December 8. He received his doctorate in law and political science from the *Universidad Nacional in *Bogotá and served as secretary to President *Caro, Governor of Cundinamarca, and Minister of War. He was elected President by the so-called Bloc of *Liberals (led by General Rafael *Uribe Uribe) and *Conservatives. His administration confronted an economic crisis and retrenchment in public works projects. It undertook financial reorganization of the state and declared Colombia neutral during *World War I. Concha held diplomatic posts in the United States, France, Germany, and Belgium, and he died in Rome while serving as Minister to the *Vatican.

CONCHA CORDOBA, Luis, 1891-1975. Born *Bogotá, November 7, he was the son of former President José Vicente *Concha. He was ordained a priest on October 28, 1916, and subsequently served as Bishop of *Manizales (1935), the director of *Acción Católica Colombiana (1944), and the first Archbishop of Manizales (1954). He served as Archbishop of *Bogotá, 1959-1975, and was made a *Cardinal of the Church, January 16, 1961.

CONCORDAT OF 1887. Signed December 31 by General Joaquín F. Vélez, Colombia, and Cardinal Mariano Rampolla del Tindaro, *Papacy, it established the principles of Church-State relations following the *Constitution of 1886 and was considered a model agreement by the Papacy. The terms specified that Roman Catholicism was indispensable to the social order. The Church was given complete autonomy as a legal corporation, as well as the right to supervise public *education with regard to morals and doctrines contrary to Catholicism. Indemnification payments were negotiated in agreements signed September 24, 1888; August 4, 1898; August 4, 1908; and January 1, 1919. Laws or agreements regarding cemeteries, the ecclesiastical *fuero, civil registry, marriages, and divorces were signed July 20, 1892; December 5, 1924; and July 12, 1973. Missions were established or regulated in agreements of December 27, 1902; March 30, 1905; May 5, 1928; and January 29, 1953. See also: CONCORDAT OF 1942, CONCORDAT OF 1973

CONCORDAT OF 1942. An agreement with the *Papacy, signed April 22 in Vatican City, by Darío *Echandía, Colombia, and Cardinal Luigi Maglione, Secretary of State for the *Papacy, regulating clerical activities in Colombia. Following the lines of the *Codification of 1936, the Church's control over public *education was limited, bishops and archbishops were forced to swear allegiance to the government of Colombia, and the Papacy agreed that only Colombian nationals would be appointed to ecclesiastical posts in Colombia.

CONCORDAT OF 1973. An agreement with the *Papacy, signed in *Bogotá, July 12, by Alfredo Vásquez Carrizosa, for Colombia, and the Papal Nuncio, Angelo Palmas. It was a general agreement with clauses concerning separation of Church and State, *Indian missions, marriage, divorce, cemeteries, *education, ecclesiastical appointments, court proceedings, clerical property, and religious art.

CONDAMINE, Charles-Marie de la, see: LA CONDAMINE, Charles Marie de

CONFEDERACION DE TRABAJADORES DE COLOMBIA (C.T.C.). The first modern labor union to attempt national integration. It evolved from the Confederación Sindical de Colombia (founded 1934), but changed its name in 1938 (following the *Codificatión of 1936), according to René de la Pedraja Tomán, at the suggestion of Mexican labor leader Vicente Lombardo Toledano. Originally said to have represented some 900 local unions and approximately 100,000 workers, it had significant communist influence in its early years and was beset by ideological disputes between the pro-communist and pro–*Liberal Party factions. The C.T.C. reached a low point in membership and effectiveness between 1946 and 1959 because of its identification with the *Liberal Party and the establishment of the rival *Unión de Trabajadores Colombianos. The C.T.C. remained closely identified with the Liberal Party under the presidencies of labor leaders Gustavo Serpa and José Rafael *Mercado. In recent years, however, Manuel Felipe Hurtado led the C.T.C. with a more independent-to-*Conservative orientation.

CONFEDERACION DE TRABAJADORES DE COLOMBIA INDEPENDIENTE (C.T.C.I.). A national labor organization founded in 1950 by communist-based opposition to the *Confederación de Trabajadores de Colombia and other labor groups.

CONFEDERACION GENERAL DEL TRABAJO (C.G.T.). A national labor union founded in April 1971. Originally based on an *Antioqueño labor association, the C.G.T. has been unsuccessful in attracting widespread national support. It received a significant boost in its estimated 10,000 members in 1981 when rivalry within the *Unión de Trabajadores Colombianos between its president, Tulio Cuevas, and Alvaro Ramírez brought much of the Ramírez faction (an estimated 100,000 people) into the C.G.T. Ramírez was elected president of the C.G.T. in May 1981. However, membership has not grown noticeably since then. The C.G.T., or General Confederation of Labor, supported the National Unionist Council (*Consejo Nacional Sindical) in organizing the general strike of 1977 (see: PARO CIVICO DE 1977).

CONFEDERACION GRANADINA. The Granadine Confederation, a union of semi-sovereign states that existed briefly from 1858 to 1861. Mariano *Ospina Rodríguez was its only elected President, although Bartolomé *Calvo ruled as acting President in 1861 before being deposed by the victorious civil war leader, General T. C. de *Mosquera. The Confederation came into being with the *Constitution of 1858 and ceased to exist with the *Pacto de Unión, 1861.

CONFEDERACION NACIONAL DE TRABAJADORES (C.N.T.). A Peronist-inspired labor federation, active 1953-1955, it was sponsored and patronized by General *Rojas Pinilla. The organization tried to use third-party tactics in politics (Movimiento de Acción Nacional) and eventually gave way to the *Gran Central Obrera organized by the Rojas Pinilla administration.

CONFEDERACION OBRERA NACIONAL, see: SOCIALISM

CONFEDERACION SINDICAL DE COLOMBIA, see: CONFEDERACION DE TRABAJADORES DE COLOMBIA

CONFEDERACION SINDICAL DE TRABAJADORES DE COLOMBIA (C.S.T.C.). A communist-backed national labor union, founded in 1964, at least in part by workers expelled from the *Unión de Trabajadores Colombianos in 1960. The founding of the C.S.T.C. marked the end of the traditional communist-*Liberal alliance in the *Confederación de Trabajadores de Colombia. Although limited in size during the 1960s, the C.S.T.C. grew in strength during the 1970s and 1980s. In 1984 it was estimated to have about 200,000 members. J. Pastor Pérez Martínez was president of the union until 1984, and the C.S.T.C. formed part of the National Unionist Council (*Consejo Nacional Sindical) created in

1977. The C.S.T.C. sponsors a series of essays on social problems, the *Estudios Marxistas.*

CONFEDERATED CITIES OF THE VALLEY, see: CIUDADES CONFEDERADAS DEL VALLE

CONFEDERATION OF COLOMBIAN WORKERS, see: CONFEDERACION DE TRABAJADORES COLOMBIANOS

CONGRESO ADMIRABLE. The so-called Admirable Congress of 1830 met from January 20 to May 10, during which time it promulgated the *Constitution of 1830, received the resignation of President-Dictator Simón *Bolívar, and elected Joaquín *Mosquera and Domingo *Caycedo as President and Vice President, respectively. The Constitution of 1830 was short-lived, functioning only a few months before the dictatorship of General Rafael *Urdaneta supplanted it.

CONGRESS. The major lawmaking branch of the national government under the *Constitution of 1991, Congress is a bicameral legislature composed of a Senate (Senado de la República) and a House of Representatives (Cámara de Representantes). Among other things, Congress is authorized to pass laws, to approve the *National Development Plan, to establish or modify territorial boundaries, to grant extraordinary powers to the *President, to levy taxes and to make public expenditures, to approve or reject treaties and government contracts, and to establish and regulate the national currency. The House of Representatives is charged specifically with electing a public defender, examining records of public expenditures, presenting impeachment charges against the *President to the Senate, and hearing complaints against other public officials. The Senate has the power to approve military promotions, to grant the President temporary permission to leave his official position or the country, to declare war, to permit foreign troops to cross national territory, to elect supreme court justices, and to try impeachment charges against the President. Legislators from both houses are elected for 4-year terms. To be elected Senator a person must be a native-born Colombian citizen in good standing at least 30 years old, and a Representative must be at least 25 years old and a Colombian citizen in good standing. The Constitution provides for 100 ordinary Senators and two Senators from Indian communities. Each national territory has a minimum of two Representatives and additional legislators for every 250,000 people. Congress meets annually in sessions divided into two legislative periods. All of Colombia's previous constitutions had provided for a similar bicameral legislature composed of a Senate and a House of Representatives.

CONGRESS OF ANGOSTURA, 1819. Patriot assembly of varying membership, February-December, held at Angostura (now *Ciudad Bolívar) on the Orinoco River in Venezuela. This congress authorized *Bolívar's campaign to liberate *New Granada (June-August) and established the *República de Gran Colombia, December 17, 1819. The latter action united portions of Venezuela, Colombia, Ecuador, and Panama into a single state and provided for a constitutional convention to be held at *Cúcuta in 1821.

CONGRESS OF CUCUTA, 1821. A legislative assembly convened at Villa Rosario de *Cúcuta (*Norte de Santander), May 6 to October 21, 1821, as a result of the action of the *Congress of Angostura in 1819. Ninety-five delegates were elected to the Congress, which promulgated the *Constitution of 1821 giving legal form to the *Repúblic de Gran Colombia. It passed laws dealing with the abolition of the slave trade, free birth for the children of slaves born in Colombia (see: AFRICAN SLAVERY), suppression of Indian tribute (see: TRIBUTO), distribution of Indian lands (see: RESGUARDOS), *education, freedom of the press, and abolition of the *Inquisition. It began organization of the department of public finance, and it elected Simón *Bolívar as President of the new state and Francisco de Paula *Santander, Vice President.

CONGRESS OF LEIVA. The Congreso de Leiva was the name given to an assembly of delegates from the provinces of *Antioquia, *Cartagena, *Casanare, *Cundinamarca, *Pamplona, *Popayán, and *Tunja, convened in Villa de *Leiva (Tunja), October 4, 1812, during the *Patria Boba period of the *independence movement. Although technically a congress of the *Provincias Unidas de Nueva Granada, the assembly's purpose was to end civil war between the federally oriented United Provinces (who elected Camilo *Torres as their President) and the centralistic state of Cundinamarca, headed by Antonio *Nariño. The attempt at conciliation was unsuccessful.

CONGRESS OF OCAÑA, 1828. Called to revise the *Constitution of 1821, the Congress met April 9 to June 10, 1828, but accomplished little. Supporters of Vice President *Santander and advocates of more decentralized government (see: CENTRALISM-FEDERALISM) dominated the Congress. Partisans of President *Bolívar, unable to secure adoption of the highly centralistic *Bolivian Constitution, walked out in protest, disrupting the proceedings. Failure of the Congress of Ocaña precipitated the establishment of a dictatorship by Bolívar.

CONGRESS OF PANAMA, 1826. June 22 to July 15. Instigated by *Bolívar, it was attended by representatives from Colombia, Central America, Peru, Mexico, Great Britain, the Netherlands, and, belatedly, from the United States. The Congress was intended to promote unity among the new American nations, with British patronage as an international support. Little of permanent significance was accomplished, although the Congress is frequently cited as the beginning of the Pan-American movement (see also: INTERNATIONAL CONFERENCE OF AMERICAN STATES).

CONGRESS OF PANAMA, 1880. An abortive attempt to hold a Pan-American convention in *Panama. The *Núñez administration, by declaration October 11, 1880, invited all the American nations to sign arbitration treaties similar to the one it had just concluded with Chile (see: CHILE-COLOMBIA TREATY OF 1880). The congress was canceled because of inadequate response.

CONSEJO DE DELEGATORIOS, see: CONSEJO NACIONAL DE DELEGATORIOS

CONSEJO DE ESTADO, see: COUNCIL OF STATE

CONSEJO DE GUERRA PERMANENTE. The Permanent Council of War, a Spanish military administration in *Bogotá during the *REIGN OF TERROR.

CONSEJO DE LAS INDIAS, see: COUNCIL OF THE INDIES

CONSEJO DE PURIFICACION. A Spanish tribunal to try cases of treason in *Bogotá during the *REIGN OF TERROR.

CONSEJO DE REGENCIA. The Council of Regency, or Regency Council, also called the Consejo de Regencia de España e Indias, established in 1810. It was the successor of the *Junta Suprema de Gobierno (1808) and the *Junta Central (1809) formed by Spanish loyalists to defend the rights of Ferdinand VII against the Bonaparte attempt to establish a rival monarchy in Spain. It attempted to gain Spanish American support for a government that included representatives from the colonies, but *creole spokesmen from *New Granada found the number of deputies accorded the colonies (12 out of 48) to be inadequate (see: MEMORIAL DE AGRAVIOS). The Consejo de Regencia was responsible for sending Antonio *Villavicencio to *New Granada to attempt conciliation with the colonies, but it could not prevent the beginning of the *independence movement. The Regency Council ceded its authority to the *Cortes of Cadiz a short time later.

CONSEJO EPISCOPAL LATINOAMERICANO (CELAM). The Council of Latin American Bishops, established in 1966, has its headquarters in *Bogotá. Its policies, particularly in the social field, have been markedly more reformist than those taken by much of the Church hierarchy in Colombia.

CONSEJO NACIONAL DE DELEGATORIOS. The body responsible for drawing up the unitary *CONSTITUTION OF 1886. *Panama's representation in this assembly was entrusted to *Bogotanos in the belief that any Panameño would be committed to *federalism. This nonrepresentation was later used to justify in part the *PANAMANIAN REVOLUTION of 1903.

CONSEJO NACIONAL DE PLANEACION, see: PLAN NACIONAL DE DESARROLLO

CONSEJO NACIONAL SINDICAL. The National Unionist Council, a body formed in August 1977 to mobilize support for the general strike of that year (see: PARO CIVICO DE 1977). It was composed of four centralized labor unions, or centrals as they are called: the *Confederación de Trabajadores de Colombia (C.T.C.), the *Unión de Trabajadores Colombianos (U.T.C.), the *Confederación General del Trabajo (C.G.T.), and the *Confederación Sindical de Trabajadores de Colombia (C.S.T.C.). The council was formally adopted by these groups in 1980, but it did not become a sustained political force.

CONSEJO REGIONAL PARA EL LIBRO EN AMERICA LATINA Y EL CARIBE (CERLAL). The Regional Council for the Book in Latin America and the Caribbean, headquartered in *Bogotá, is a UNESCO agency for promoting reading and the book trade in Latin America.

CONSERVATIVE. An adjective or noun that, when capitalized (Conservative), is used to describe the ideology, political program, and members of the *CONSERVATIVE PARTY.

CONSERVATIVE PARTY. Originally the Partido Conservador Colombiano, but now the Partido Conservador Social. Founded in 1849, with a statement of principles written by Mariano *Ospina Rodríguez and José Eusebio *Caro, the Partido Conservador tends to support close cooperation with the *Catholic Church, strong central government, and maintenance of class privileges. It is frequently but erroneously said to have been founded by *Bolívar. Its emblematic color is blue, and it is traditionally one of Colombia's two predominant parties (See also: LIBERAL PARTY). The party has frequently divided into factions, most notably in the late 19th century when the groups were the *Nationalists and the Historicals (*Históricos). In the mid-20th century, major divisions were between the *Unionists and the *Independents, and more recently between the supporters of Alvaro *Gómez Hurtado (Alvaristas), Misael *Pastrana Borero (Pastranistas), and Gustavo Rodríguez Vargas (Gustavistas).

CONSPIRACIES, see: PLOTS AND CONSPIRACIES

CONSTITUENT ASSEMBLY OF 1821, see: CONGRESS OF CUCUTA

CONSTITUENT ASSEMBLY OF 1828, see: CONGRESS OF OCAÑA

CONSTITUENT ASSEMBLY OF 1830, see: CONGRESO ADMIRABLE

CONSTITUENT ASSEMBLY OF 1863, see: RIONEGRO, Convention of

CONSTITUENT ASSEMBLY OF 1886, see: CONSEJO NACIONAL DE DELEGATORIOS

CONSTITUENT ASSEMBLY OF 1905, see: ASAMBLEA NACIONAL

CONSTITUENT ASSEMBLY OF 1910, see: ASAMBLEA NACIONAL CONSTITUYENTE Y LEGISLATIVA

CONSTITUENT ASSEMBLY OF 1952, see: ASAMBLEA NACIONAL CONSTITUYENTE

CONSTITUENT ASSEMBLY OF 1991, see: ASAMBLEA CONSTITUYENTE DE 1991

CONSTITUTION OF CUCUTA, see: CONSTITUTION OF 1821

CONSTITUTION OF 1811, see: ACTA DE LA CONFEDERA-CION DE LAS PROVINCIAS DE LA NUEVA GRANADA

CONSTITUTION OF 1812, see: CORTES

CONSTITUTION OF 1821. Also known as the Constitution of *Cúcuta, it established the *República de Gran Colombia as a limited federal state and divided the national territory into *departments, *provinces, cantons, and parishes governed by a bicameral legislature (*Congress) and an executive (*President) on the national level, with appointed officials (*Intendants) on the departmental level. Elections were largely indirect, and judges were appointed by the executive and legislative branches. The Constitution also provided for a *Council of State, which the President was required to consult on important matters. The Constitution was replaced in 1830, but it had been abrogated in reality by *Bolívar's dictatorship as early as 1828. It was considered too centralistic by the more doctrinaire federalists (see: CENTRALISM-FEDERALISM).

CONSTITUTION OF 1826, see: BOLIVIAN CONSTITUTION

CONSTITUTION OF 1830. Promulgated by the *Congreso Admirable, the Constitution of 1830 retained much of the *Constitution of 1821, including the name *República de Colombia. Some significant modifications were introduced: the office of Attorney General was created; terms for the President and Vice President did not coincide; the chief executive was not permitted to assume extraordinary powers; departmental assemblies were created; and some changes were made in the selection of judges. The Constitution made limited concessions to the demand for decentralization of authority.

CONSTITUTION OF 1832. The most federalistic or decentralized of the national constitutions before 1853, the Constitution of 1832 established the *República de Nueva Granada (Republic of New Granada) with a bicameral legislature elected by the *provinces on a population basis. The President was allowed to assume extraordinary powers, but his appointive authority was limited. Provincial legislatures were created and empowered to make appointments, levy taxes, and supervise fiscal accounts.

CONSTITUTION OF 1843. Considered highly centralistic, the Constitution of 1843 provided a strong executive authority with unrestricted appointive power and ministers who could both initiate and debate legislation in *Congress. Provincial assemblies were made subordinate to Congress and their appointive power was reduced. Essentially a reaction to the *Constitution of 1832 and the rebellion of 1840-1842 (War of the *Supreme Commanders), the Constitution introduced little change in the functional administrative organization of the government while centralizing political power.

CONSTITUTION OF 1853. Initiating a decentralizing trend that culminated in 1863, the Constitution of 1853 embodied numerous liberal reforms. *African slavery was abolished, trial by jury extended, freedom of the press proclaimed, male suffrage broadened, formal separation of Church and State was declared; officials were popularly elected; and the role of the provincial legislatures was strengthened, thereby reducing the dominance of the central government. The name, *República de Nueva Granada, was retained.

CONSTITUTION OF 1858. The Constitution of 1858 continued the decentralizing trend begun in 1853 by creating the *Confederación Granadina composed of the sovereign states of *Antioquia, *Bolívar, *Boyacá, *Cauca, *Cundinamarca, *Magdalena, *Panama, and *Santander. Residual powers remained with the states; only specified powers were granted to the national government. The President was enpowered to maintain peace within the nation, and the *Supreme Court was allowed to decide disputes between the states. Religious toleration and freedom of the press were reaffirmed.

CONSTITUTION OF 1861, see: PACTO DE UNION, 1861

CONSTITUTION OF 1863. Adopted May 8, 1863, by the Convention of *Rionegro and lasting until 1886, this was the most federalistic (see: CENTRALISM-FEDERALISM) of all Colombian constitutions. Extreme localism predominated. The sovereign states of *Antioquia, *Bolívar, *Boyacá, *Cauca, *Cundinamarca, *Magdalena, *Panama, *Santander, and *Tolima joined in the formation of the United States of Colombia (*Estados Unidos de Colombia). The central government was deliberately weakened to prevent its interfering in the governmental affairs of individual states or in disputes between states. The term of the President was set at two years with no immediate reelection. Religious toleration was emphasized, and capital punishment abolished. See also: MAP: UNITED STATES OF COLOMBIA, 1863-1885

CONSTITUTION OF 1886. Adopted August 4 in Bogotá, this document established the unitary República de Colombia. As revised in 1936, 1945, 1957, and 1968, it provided for legislative, executive, and judicial branches of government. A bicameral legislature, Congress, was composed of a House of Representatives and a Senate, whose members were elected for four-year terms. The chief executive, or *President, was also elected for four years, and judges were elected or appointed by the legislative and executive branches. Provisions were made for ministers, a Council of State, and a *designado* who acted for the President when necessary, but there was no *Vice President. For administrative purposes, the nation was divided into *departments, provinces, and *municipal districts, all subordinate to the national government. The *Catholic Church enjoyed preferential status, although Church and State were separated.

CONSTITUTION OF 1991. Adopted in Bogotá in July 1991, by a special constituent assembly, the constitution has 380 articles, a fact that has led some commentators to describe it as the longest constitution in the world. It is certainly the most comprehensive ever written for Colombia. The constitution establishes a democratic republic that is both unitary and decentralized into autonomous territories. The official language is Spanish but bilingualism is permitted for ethnic groups who choose to speak a second language. All people are equal under the law, and persons living in Colombia enjoy freedom of thought in all matters religious or secular as well as freedom of speech. No mention is made of the *Catholic Church. Capital punishment, exile, imprisonment for life, and extradition (especially for drug related offenses) are all prohibited. There are numerous provisions relating to the sanctity of the family and social security, including the right to minimal standards of housing, education, work, wages, and recreation. The national government is divided into executive, legislative, and judicial branches headed by a *President, *Congress, and *Supreme Court, respectively. Major territorial divisions include *departments, municipal districts (*municipalities), and the Capital District (formerly the *Distrito Especial). See also: ADMINISTRATIVE DIVISIONS; MAP: MAJOR ADMINISTRATIVE DIVISIONS

CONSTITUTION OF THE UNITED STATES OF COLOMBIA, see: CONSTITUTION OF 1863

CONSTITUTION OF THE UNITED STATES OF NEW GRANADA, see: PACTO DE UNION, 1861

CONSTITUTIONAL COURT, see: SUPREME COURT

CONSTITUTIONAL REFORM OF 1968.   The modifications of 1968 anticipated the end of the *Frente Nacional in stages, 1974-1978; they have been nicknamed the *desmonte* ("dismantling" process). A two-thirds majority requirement for approval of acts of *Congress was ended, and, relatively speaking, the power of the executive was increased. Initiation of economic measures was reserved for the executive branch, and the president was given the right to limit the time that the legislature can debate a proposed law. Under Article 120, however, sharing of political offices was to continue in such a way that equitable representation was assured the two major political parties, although no fixed ratio was established for achieving this goal.

CONTADORA.   The name given to a group of nations (Colombia, Mexico, Panama, and Venezuela) whose foreign ministers met formally for the first time January 8-9, 1983, on the Island of Contadora (Republic of Panama). The group's efforts were directed to achieving a peaceful, negotiated settlement for international problems in Central America. A document of objectives was adopted by the foreign ministers on September 9, 1983, after three days of meetings in *Panama City, and the group submitted an Act for Peace and Cooperation in Central America to the five Central American heads of state on June 9, 1984 (revised text dated September 7, 1984). In general, if adopted, the signatories of the act would have agreed to avoid interference, in any way, in each other's internal affairs and to settle any disputes that might arise between nations by peaceful means. The draft treaty also contained sections on human rights, democratic government, armaments, military advisers, irregular forces, direct communications systems, refugees, and socioeconomic issues. Negotiations toward the adoption of a treaty based on the act remained inconclusive 1984-1987, but contributed to a separate peace treaty signed in 1987.

CONTROLARIA GENERAL DE LA REPUBLICA. The General Comptrollership, or Accounting Office, was created to supervise the fiscal management of government. It was an autonomous agency established as a result of the recommendations of the Edwin W. *Kemmerer commission of the early 1920s. Under the *Constitution of 1991, the head of this branch of government is the General Comptroller, or General Accountant, who is elected by *Congress for the same term as the *President of the Republic. The Comptroller must be a native-born Colombian in good standing, thirty-five years old, with a university degree and/or other professional qualifications. The Controlaría is charged with keeping records, promoting government efficiency, and calling to account those guilty of misconduct with public resources.

CONVENTION OF 1892. An amendment to the *CONCORDAT OF 1887.

CONVENTION OF RIONEGRO, see: RIONEGRO, Convention of

CONVENTO DE LA ENSEÑANZA, see: CAYCEDO, María Clemencia de

CONVENTO DE NUESTRA SEÑORA DE LA ENCARNACION. The Convent of Our Lady of the Incarnation, founded in *Popayán in 1591 by the *Augustinians. Preceded by the Convents of *Santa Clara and the *Conceptionists, this was the third religious institution for women founded in Colombia.

CONVENTOS, Guerra de los, see: MINOR CONVENTS, Rebellion of the

CONVIVENCIA. "Conviviality"; the politics of civility, or living together; a term used to describe the ruling elite's concept of public life and politics, 1930-1949. It was the raison d'être of a governing class that separated itself from the masses it governed and maintained a distinction between public life and private life. It saw government as the noble calling of highly educated, dedicated leaders whose benevolent policies served to preserve public order while slowly educating and uplifting the general population. According to Herbert Braun, it produced an era of coexistence and limited cooperation between members of opposing parties, 1930-1938. However, the idea of *convivencia* began to disintegrate 1938-1944, and it fell apart completely 1945-1949.

COORDINADORA GUERRILLERA "SIMON BOLIVAR." The C.G.S.B., also known as the Coordinadora Nacional Guerrillera, was an alleged merger of most of Colombia's *guerrilla movements, formed in June and announced on October 2, 1985. It included the parts of the *Ejército Popular de Liberación, the *Ejército de Liberación Nacional, the *Fuerzas Armadas Revolucionarias de Colombia, the *Movimiento Diecinueve de Abril, the Partido Revolucionario de los Trabajadores, Patria Libre, the *Ricardo Franco Front, and the Comando *Quintín Lame, all of which had refused to sign the armistice offered by the *Betancur administration, or those who had decided that it was not working. The purpose of the C.G.S.B. was to coordinate all actions against the armed forces or the government. Coordinadora Guerrillera actions were centered along the upper *Cauca River and the Department of *Antioquia. Parts of the Coordinadora continued to wage war throughout much of 1991 although the Partido Revolucionario de los Trabajadores surrendered to the government in January in exchange for one seat in the *Asamblea Constituyente later that year.

COORDINADORA NACIONAL GUERRILLERA, see: COORDINADORA GUERRILLERA "SIMON BOLIVAR"

COPPER. Alexander Walker's *Colombia* of 1822 mentions copper as an important *mineral, and three years later two British firms invested £116,500 in Colombian copper mining. The metal is currently mined in *Boyacá, *Cauca, *Cundinamarca, *Huila, *Nariño, *Norte de Santander, *Quindío, and *Putumayo. Although total production has increased from 100 metric tons in 1975 to 800 tons in 1985, this is still less than 0.1% of that annually produced by Chile.

COQUIBACOA, Gobierno de. Also spelled "Coquivacoa," it was the first administrative subdivision established on continental America. Coquibacoa existed from 1501 to 1502 on what is now the *Guajira Peninsula. Alonso de *Ojeda was its only governor. Three fortresses were built in the territory, but the settlement collapsed when Ojeda was overthrown by his subordinates, Juan de Vergara and García del Campo.

COQUIVACOA, see: COQUIBACOA

CORDERO, Juan José, 1783-1825. Soldier who fought in the struggle for *independence after 1810. He fought the Spanish *Reconquista and from 1816 to 1819 was forced to take refuge in the mountains. He returned after the triumph of Simón *Bolívar.

CORDILLERA CENTRAL. Also known historically as the Cordillera del *Quindío and the Sierra de los *Pijaos, it is the highest of Colombia's three principal branches of the *Andes Mountains. The central mountain range runs from *Pasto in the south to *Medellín in the north. After separating from the main Andean range at the *Nudo de los Pastos, the Cordillera Central (or Macizo Colombiano) bifurcates in the departments of *Cauca and *Huila to form the *Cordilleras Central and Oriental. Average altitude in the mountain range is above 3,000 meters. The Nevado del Huila (5,750 meters) is the highest point in the Cordillera. Other major peaks in the Cordillera Central are the *Nevado del Ruiz (5,400 meters), Tolima (5,215 meters), Quindío (5,150 meters), Santa Isabel (5,100 meters), Pan de Azúcar (4,670 meters), Puracé (4,646 meters), Sotará (4,580 meters), Barragán (4,500 meters), and Galeras (4,276 meters).

CORDILLERA DEL QUINDIO, see: CORDILLERA CENTRAL

CORDILLERA OCCIDENTAL. Known historically in its north-ernmost regions as the Sierra de *Abibe, it is the principal western mountain range in Colombia and lies roughly parallel to the Pacific Coast. The Cordillera Occidental enters Colombia in the south as part of the main Andean range and separates from the *Cordilleras Central and Oriental at the Nudo de los Pastos. It is drained by the *San Juan and *Atrato Rivers to the north and west and by the *Cauca River on the east. Average altitude in the range, the lowest of Colombia's three main Cordilleras, is 2,000 meters. The highest elevation is the Farallones de Cali (4,280 meters), not counting *Cumbal (4,764 meters) and *Chiles (4,748 meters) in the Nudo de los Pastos in the extreme south. Other major elevations include Tamaná (4,200 meters), Frontino (4,080 meters), Azufral (4,070 meters), Gualcalá (3,950 meters), Tatamá (3,950 meters), Caramanta (3,900 meters), and Torrá (3,670 meters).

CORDILLERA ORIENTAL. Most eastern of Colombia's three principal mountain ranges, running southwest to northeast from *Caquetá to the Venezuelan border and the *Guajira Peninsula. It branches off from the *Cordillera Central, or the Macizo Colombiano, in the departments of *Cauca and *Huila, and runs between the *Magdalena River and the *Llanos, forming the eastern boundary of the *Sabana de Bogotá. The range is dotted with numerous intermontane valleys suitable for cultivation and grazing. Average altitude is above 3,000 meters in the central part of the range, tapering to an average of 1,500 to 2,000 in the northern part. Ritacuva del Cocuy (5,493 meters) is the highest point in the range. Other major peaks include Rechíniga (4,650 meters), El Nevado de Sumapaz (4,560 meters), La Rusia (4,320 meters), Saboyá (4,300 meters), and Jurisdicciones (3,850 meters).

CORDOBA, Departamento de. Located on the Caribbean Coast, including the valleys of the *Sinú, San Jorge, and Canalete Rivers, the Department of Córdoba is undulating lowland situated between latitudes 7° 11′ and 9° 26′N and longitudes 74° 52′ and 76° 32′W, with a predominantly tropical climate. The population is 878,738 people (estimated 1985), with a density of 35.1 people per square kilometer. *Montería is the capital city. According to DANE, *Colombia estadística 86*, principal agricultural products, with tonnage produced in 1984, include plantains, 116,200 tons; *yuca, 110,000; *corn, 88,740; rice, 51,616; sorghum, 41,650; yams, 39,900; coconuts, 28,150; *cotton, 20,260; *sugar, 800; sesame, 500; *cacao, 300; and beans, 270. *Livestock raising is important; 37,953 head of cattle and 69,953 hogs were slaughtered in the department in 1984. *Gold and *silver are mined, and there were 32 businesses employing ten or more people in 1983. Córdoba was historically important as the site of the *Sinú Indian burial grounds. The coast was visited by *Bastidas in 1501 and later by *Ojeda, *Pizarro, and *Fernández de Enciso, but settlement was slow until after the colonization efforts of Antonio de la Torre y Miranda in the 18th century. The department, formerly part of *Bolívar, was created December 18, 1951.

CORDOBA, José María, 1799-1829.   General and a military leader of the wars for independence; born Concepción (*Antioquia), September 8. Córdoba joined the patriot cause as a youth and served in various campaigns 1815-1819. He fought in the major battles at *Boyacá (Colombia), *Pichincha (Ecuador), and *Ayacucho (Peru). He served as Minister of War, 1828-1829. Although initially a collaborator of President *Bolívar, Córdoba rebelled against the dictatorship in 1829 and was killed by Rupert Hand and other Bolivarian supporters on October 17 at Santuario (Antioquia). General José María Córdoba was a brother of Colonel Salvador *Córdoba.

CORDOBA, Salvador, 1801-1841.   Colonel, distinguished soldier of the *independence movement; born Concepción (*Antioquia); died *Cartago, July 7. He joined the patriot cause in 1819 and participated in campaigns in Antioquia, the *Magdalena River valley, the south of Colombia, Ecuador, and Peru (including the Battles of *Junín and *Ayacucho). Córdoba opposed the dictatorships of *Bolívar and *Urdaneta 1828-1830, but rebelled against the government of President *Márquez in the War of the *Supreme Commanders. Following his capture in 1841, he was one of those executed at what became known as the bench (escaño) of Cartago (see: CARTAGO EXECUTIONS). Although Colonel Salvador Córdoba was a brother of General José María *Córdoba, his surname is often written "Córdova."

CORDOBA Y COALLA, Juan Francisco.   President of the *Nuevo Reino de Granada, 1644-1654. During his administration, the *Dique Canal opened near *Cartagena, 1650, and, in

*Bogotá, the Tribunal de Tributos y Azogues (tribute and mining) was established, 1653.

CORDOVA. Alternative spelling of *CORDOBA.

CORDOVES MOURE, José María, 1835-1918. Civil servant in the finance and interior ministries who was author of a six-volume classic, *Reminiscencias de Santa Fé y Bogotá*.

CORN. Often referred to as maize (*maís*), corn is a food crop native to the Western Hemisphere. It is probably the crop most widely used as a staple of daily diets throughout Latin America, although *potatoes and *yuca* are close rivals in some areas. Domestication of corn has been traced to *Indians in central Mexico before the coming of European influence. Because of its importance in the human diet, corn has been studied carefully by agricultural specialists in Colombia. In the early 1950s, researchers introduced a variety of corn known as Eto (after the Estación Tulio Ospina where it was developed). Eto was especially useful because it was high yielding, disease resistant, and easily usable in peasant households. Work in Colombia also resulted in the introduction of more-nutritious plant varieties known as high-lysine corn.

COROZAL, Battle of. October 31 to November 4, 1859, 9° 19'N, 75° 18'W, *Sucre. General Joaquín *Posada Gutiérrez, for the State of *Bolívar, was defeated by the rebel forces of Manuel Pereira de Plata.

CORPORACION AUTONOMA REGIONAL DE LA SABANA DE BOGOTA Y DE LOS VALLES DE UBATE Y CHIQ-UINQUIRA. CAR, an autonomous regional development corporation, analogous to the Tennessee Valley Authority in the United States. Established in 1961, CAR was authorized to undertake the production of *hydroelectric power, rural electrification, flood control, land reclamation, and reforestation in the areas of its jurisdiction (parts of *Cundinamarca and *Boyacá).

CORPORACION AUTONOMA REGIONAL DE LOS VALLES DEL MAGDALENA Y DEL SINU. C.V.M., an autonomous regional development corporation, analogous to the Tennessee Valley Authority in the United States. It was established in 1960 to foster the development of forest reserves, to promote the fishing industry, to supervise the national parks, and to encourage conservation and land reclamation in the lower *Magdalena and Sinú River valleys.

CORPORACION AUTONOMA REGIONAL DEL CAUCA. The Cauca Valley Authority, or C.V.C., an autonomous regional development corporation intended to promote flood control and production of hydroelectric power in the *Cauca Valley. Analogous to the Tennessee Valley Authority in the United States, the C.V.C. began operation in 1955. It was proposed in 1945 and officially created in 1954 with advice from the Development and Resources Corporation of New York and David Lilienthal, former director of the T.V.A.

CORRAL, Juan del, 1778-1814. Patriot dictator of *Antioquia, July 31, 1813, until his death April 7, 1814. Born *Mompós (Bolívar), June 23; died *Rionegro (Antioquia). He was responsible for declaring the independence of Antioquia, and his government initiated numerous administrative and military reforms to strengthen the new state. He was also responsible for one of the first laws abolishing *African slavery in Colombia.

CORRAL, Manuel del, 1811-1870. Son of Juan del *Corral. He fought in the struggle for independence, distinguishing himself at Chorros Blancos and at the siege of *Cartagena.

CORREOS, see: POSTAL SERVICE

CORREOSO-MONTUFAR TREATY. Treaty of limits between Colombia and Costa Rica, negotiated by Costa Rican foreign minister Lorenzo Montúfar and Colombia's General Buenaventura Correoso in 1873. It was never ratified. See: COSTA RICA, Relations with

CORTE CONSTITUCIONAL, see: SUPREME COURT

CORTE SUPREMA DE JUSTICA, see: SUPREME COURT

CORTES. The Spanish parliament. Of particular importance in the transition to independence was the Cortes of Cadiz, to which the *Regency Council (acting for the captive Ferdinand VII during the French invasion of Spain) devolved its power in September 1810. A token proportion of the 107 seats were reserved for representatives from the Americas. These included Domingo *Caycedo, deputy from *Bogotá. A new and very liberal constitution was enacted by the Cortes in 1812, but never applied in *New Granada, which had already declared its independence. By the time Spanish rule was restored in the *Reconquista, the new constitution was largely a dead letter, having been annulled by Ferdinand VII upon his restoration in 1814.

COSA, Juan de la, d. 1510. Spanish navigator and cartographer. He made voyages to various parts of the Colombian coast, including two with *Columbus, 1492-1494; two with *Ojeda, 1499-1500 and 1509-1510; one with *Bastidas, 1501; and one by himself, 1504-1507. As a member of Ojeda's expedition, he died fighting *Indians in the *Golfo de Urabá.

COSTA. "Coast." When used as a generic term it often means the Atlantic (Caribbean) Coast and the adjacent territory. See also: COSTEÑO

COSTA RICA, Proposed Annexation of. Annexation of Costa Rica as a sovereign state under the *Constitution of 1863 was proposed by the *Murillo Toro administration in 1865. As an initial step, the government concluded a treaty, signed *Bogotá, March 28, 1865, by Teodoro Valenzuela, Colombia, and José María Castro, Costa Rica. The treaty ceded some thirty leagues of disputed territory to Costa Rica in exchange for the latter's recognition of the Constitution of 1863. The union was never culminated because of bitter opposition in Colombia, where the treaty was rejected by *Congress.

COSTA RICA, Relations with. The boundary between Costa Rica and the Real *Audiencia de Santa Fe de Bogotá was first fixed in 1560. It ran along the Rio de Culebra, some 10 kilometers on the Panamanian side of Costa Rica's present frontier, including the site of the town of Almirante. In 1803 the entire eastern coast of Central America as far as Cape Gracias a Dios in present-day Honduras was transferred from the Captaincy General of Nicaragua to the Santa Fe Audiencia. The *Gual-Molina Treaty of 1825 between the newly independent Central American Federation and the *República de Gran Colombia accepted the de facto situation as a basis for negotiation, but this was complicated by *United Kingdom claims to the entire *Mosquito Coast. British claims to the southern part of the coast were surrendered in the *Clayton-Bulwer Treaty of 1850. Six years later the *HERRAN-CALVO TREATY with Costa Rica—separated from the Central American Federation since 1838—would have meant returning to the 1560 boundary, but it was never ratified. Negotiations in 1864-1865 combined a return to the 1560 boundaries with Costa Rica's becoming a member of the *Estados Unidos de Colombia, but this Valenzuela-Castro Treaty was also never ratified (see: COSTA RICA, Proposed Annexation of). Nor was the *COR-REOSO-MONTUFAR TREATY of 1873. In the QUIJANO OTERO–CASTRO TREATY of 1880 the two countries agreed to arbitration over the Almirante region on the Atlantic Coast and the Coto region on the Pacific. A convention of 1886 chose King Alfonso XII of Spain as arbitrator, but he died that same year, and President Emile Loubet of France was eventually chosen instead. His decision of September 11, 1900, favored Colombia, but Costa Rica refused to accept it. The *Panamanian Revolution of 1903 removed Colombian interest in further negotiation, but it had the satisfaction of knowing that Loubet's award confirmed her possession of *San Andrés y Providencia. Colombia has the odd distinction of being the first country to which Costa Rican coffee was exported, in 1821. At the present time, the Costa Rican market has moderate importance for Colombian *exports. Some $5.5 million worth of goods were sold there in 1980 and $8.6 million in 1986. *Imports from Costa Rica are minimal (US$900,000 in 1986).

COSTA RICA–COLOMBIA TREATIES, see: COSTA RICA, Relations with

COSTEÑO. A resident of the Atlantic Coast (*costa). A regional personality type showing openness, generosity, sensuality, and playfulness. With racial and ethnic connotations, the term frequently suggests an Afro-American heritage. For contrast, see: ANDINO; BOGOTANO

COSTUMBRISMO. From *cuadros de costumbres,* sketches of daily life or customs; the work of *costumbrista* authors. It was a type of literature prominent in Colombia during the last half of the 19th century. It was characterized by minute attention to detail and local color. These works, most often in prose, were at the same time artistic expressions and accurate descriptions of segments of Colombian society. Probably the best-known *costumbrista* novels by Colombian authors are **Manuela* by Eugenio *Díaz and *El alférez real* by Eustaquio Palacios. Other prominent writers who used this style were José María *Caicedo Rojas, José María *Samper, and Luis Segundo de Silvestre. See also: MOSAICO, EL

COSTUMBRISTA GENERATION. The group of cultural leaders who, in the terminology of Abel Naranjo Villegas, developed or were prominent from 1860 to 1880. He describes the *Costumbrista* Generation as one inspired by ingenuity and originality with a magical or supernatural sense of existence. Ernesto Cortés Ahumada subdivides the period into the *Costumbrista* Generation (key date, 1855) and the Ideological Generation (key date, 1870). Representative figures of the *Costumbrista* Generation were Santos *Acosta, Julio *Arboleda, Sergio *Arboleda, Salvador Camacho Roldán, Leonardo Canal, Aníbal Galindo, José David Guarín, Santos *Gutiérrez, Carlos *Holguín, José Manuel *Marroquín, Rafael *Nuñez, Aquileo *Parra, Próspero Pereira Gamba, Felipe Pérez, Santiago Pérez, Juan de Dios Restrepo, José María *Samper, José María Torres Caicedo, Julián *Trujillo, Marcelino Vélez, and José María *Vergara y Vergara. Important figures of the Ideological Generation would include Pablo Arosemena, Miguel Antonio *Caro, Rufino José *Cuervo, Nicolás Esguerra, Diego Fallón, Carlos Martínez Silva, Santiago Pérez Triana, Rafael *Pombo, José María Quijano Otero, José María Quijano Wallis, and Ezequiel *Uricoechea. See also: GENERATIONS

COTE, Martin. Buccaneer who, along with Jean de *Beautemps (known as Don Juan), sacked but did not completely capture *Cartagena in 1559 (see: PIRACY).

COTTON. Some cotton was grown in the *Barranquilla region in the early 19th century. World shortages caused by the United States Civil War led to a boom in cotton production in Colombia as elsewhere. By 1867 cotton was providing 10.3% of Colombia's exports, but recovery in the United States led to a decline in exports (to a mere .02% by 1881). Even though clothing and textiles spearheaded the development of the *manufacturing industry, cotton growing did not even keep pace with domestic demand until the 20th century. *Coffee was a more profitable crop. After *World War II, however, perennial cotton began to replace *bananas in the coastal areas affected by Sigatoka disease. There followed in the 1950s a rapid expansion of the higher-yielding annual cotton in *Tolima and *Valle del Cauca, both of which were closer to the textile factories of *Medellín and *Bogotá. By the late 1960s, production was not only meeting internal demand, but was making cotton one of Colombia's most important nontraditional exports. Total output of cottonseed has grown from 6,474 metric *tons in 1951 to 68,732 tons in 1960; 276,400 in 1970; and 353,200 in 1980.

COUNCIL OF REGENCY, see: CONSEJO DE REGENCIA

COUNCIL OF STATE. Established by the *Constitution of 1886, the Council of State (*Consejo de Estado*) was created as a supreme court in matters of administrative law and disputes within the government. It was also charged with preparing legislation to be presented to *Congress, and it was given the power to commute the death penalty. The actions of the Council, however, were considered binding only in the latter case. The Constitution provided for a Council of six members with the option for Ministers of State to participate as nonvoting members. In 1987, the Council had grown to 20 members, known as Counselors of State, and its duties included approving proposals to create new departments (*departamentos*), offering the government legal opinions on issues of public disorders and the movement of foreign troops within national territory, recommending legal reforms, and authorizing extraordinary expenses in the absence of Congress. Under the *Constitution of 1991 the Council of State forms part of the judiciary branch of government. It is an advisory body to the national government and a supreme tribunal in government administrative disputes, and it has the authority to rule on the constitutionality of government actions where jurisdiction has not been assigned specifically to the Constitutional Court (see: SUPREME COURT).

COUNCIL OF THE INDIES. The highest administrative body in the Spanish American empire. A *Junta de Indias* was set up by the Spanish Crown in 1519 to control all government functions in the Americas. In 1524 it was replaced by the more grandiloquently named Real y Supremo Consejo de las Indias, which has traditionally been shortened simply to the Consejo de Indias, or Council of the Indies in English usage. In 1714, with the accession of the Bourbons, the Council became subordinate to the newly created Secretariat of the Indies. In 1770 its powers were further reduced, making it little more than an advisory body. It was abolished by the *Cortes of Cadiz in 1812, revived by Ferdinand VII in 1814, and definitively abolished in 1834, long after *Colombia had obtained its independence (see also: SPANISH EMPIRE IN AMERICA, Administration of the).

CREOLE. The Spanish term *criollo,* in its general sense, may mean anything or anyone (not indigenous) born, created, bred, or developed in areas of European settlement; hence, creole cuisine, creole cattle (descendants of the original Spanish longhorns), creole dialects, or creole slaves (those born in the colonies, as opposed to those transported from Africa).

The word was particularly used in the Spanish colonies to denote a locally born white, as opposed to someone born in Spain, who was known as a *peninsular.* Under Spanish rule the distinction carried important social connotations. Not only did the European-born consider themselves superior, but they enjoyed some specific legal advantages over creole whites, beyond the privileges both groups enjoyed compared to persons of nonwhite ancestry. Such discrimination against the creoles is one of the major inequities cited in the *Memorial de agravios* by Camilo Torres in 1809. See also: MESTIZO; PENINSULAR

CREOLES, Origins of.   Since Seville, and later Cadiz, were Spain's only ports legally permitted to trade with the *Indies, Andalucians formed the largest single group among Spanish settlers. They were certainly the most ubiquitous, and their descendants can be found in all parts of modern Colombia. Castilians seem to have been attracted most to the administrative center of *Santa Fe de Bogotá and Catalans to the trading port of *Cartagena. Basques were attracted to *Antioquia, and have sometimes been given credit popularly, though without conclusive evidence, for the economic success of *Medellín and the *Antioqueño* region. All of these groups probably included small numbers of *conversos,* Sephardic *Jews who had at least nominally accepted Christianity to escape the 1492 mass expulsion from Spain. Although emigration did not mean total escape from the *Inquisition, it did mean much less rigorous supervision.

CRIOLLO, see: CREOLE

CRUZ, Elena de la, d. 1634. A Spanish-born resident of Tolú (9° 32'N, 75° 35'W, *Sucre), accused of witchcraft in 1633. She was arrested on May 10, confined for eight months, and then released under penalty of silence and four years exile from Tolú. She was rearrested, after insisting upon her innocence, and died in prison (see: CARTAGENA, Witches of).

CRUZ DE BOYACA, see: BOYACA, Cruz de

CRUZ ROJA COLOMBIANA, see: RED CROSS

CUASPUD, Battle of. December 6, 1863, Ecuador. General *Mosquera defeated the Ecuadoran army under General *Flores. The victory led to the Treaty of *Pinzaquí.

CUBA, Relations with. The continuance of Spanish rule in Cuba after all mainland Spanish America had achieved independence was anathema to many in the *República de Gran Colombia. This led to the projected *CUBAN AND PUERTO RICAN EXPEDITION in 1825-1826. In the 1870s there was strong disagreement between *Liberals and *Conservatives over the fund-raising visit to Colombia of Cuban freedom fighter General Manuel Quesada. Members of the *Conservative Party feared that a Cuba freed from Spain might simply be absorbed by the United States. In December 1960 relations with Cuba were broken, and Colombia accepted the 1964 sanctions against Fidel Castro's government imposed by the *Organization of American States. Factors influencing the decision were gratitude for United States support of the *Frente Nacional and Cuban aid to *guerrilla movements in Colombia. President *López Michelsen renewed relations with Cuba in 1975, and, impressed by an increase in Colombian exports to Cuba, sent a trade mission to the island in 1976. López Michelsen also refused a United States request to condemn Cuban involvement in Angola. Relations between the two nations were temporarily disrupted once again, however, in 1981 when the *Columna Antonio Nariño invaded the southern part of Colombia (see: NARIÑO, Invasion of) after having been trained in Cuba.

CUBAN AND PUERTO RICAN EXPEDITION. A projected but unrealized expedition to free Cuba and Puerto Rico from Spanish rule in 1825-1826. A joint Colombian-Mexican venture, it died from lack of sustained support and because of opposition from the United States and Great Britain.

CUCHILLA DEL TAMBO, Battle of. June 29, 1816, *Cauca. Colonel Liborio *Mejía and patriot forces were decisively defeated by Brigadier General Juan *Sámano. It resulted in the collapse of patriot efforts and facilitated the Spanish *Reconquista* of the *Cauca Valley.

CUCUTA. Capital of *Norte de Santander, located at 7° 54'N, 72° 30'W, with an altitude of 215 meters and an average temperature of 29°C. Cúcuta is the seventh largest city in Colombia, with a population of 440,823 people (1985 estimate). The city, which derives its name from a powerful Indian chieftain of the region at the time of the Spanish conquest, is the site of an international bridge between Venezuela and Colombia. A Captain Juan de San Martín is said to have led the first Spanish into the vicinity in 1623, but the city itself was not founded until 1733 by Antonio Villamizar Pineda. Formally named San José de Cúcuta, it is located about 10 kilometers from the Villa Rosario de Cúcuta, site of *Santander's birthplace and the *Congress of Cúcuta in 1821. The settlement was destroyed by an earthquake in 1875 and again by conflict during the War of the *Thousand Days in 1900.

CUCUTA, Congress of, see: CONGRESS OF CUCUTA

CUCUTA CONSTITUTION, see: CONSTITUTION OF 1821

CUCUTA RAILROAD. After those of *Panama and *Bolívar, the Cúcuta Railroad (*Norte de Santander) was the third put into service in Colombia (see: RAILROADS). The line running from *Cúcuta to Puerto Villamizar was built 1880-1888 on the basis of a contract negotiated in 1876. Cúcuta was connected to the Táchira River by rails laid 1893-1897 and then to Puerto Santander on the Venezuelan border in 1926. Until it was closed in 1958, this border company enjoyed the distinction of being the only Colombian railway with international connections. The Táchira and Villamizar lines were joined in Cúcuta by a trolley service in 1926. A branch later extended the railroad to Petrolea in the *Catatumbo oil fields, and an unfinished branch intended to connect Cúcuta and *Pamplona was under construction 1923-1933.

CUERVO, Rufino José, 1844-1911. Linguist, classicist, lexicographer, and author; born *Bogotá, September 19; died Paris (France), July 11. Cuervo was a student of many languages, including those of some *Indians. He was noted for his studies of Spanish and its colloquial usage in Colombia. He was the author of a book on Latin for Spanish-speaking people (see: CARO, Miguel Antonio); *Apuntaciones críticas sobre la lengua bogotana;* a dictionary of the Spanish language that remained incomplete at the time of his death; and other philological studies. Although politically a member of the *Conservative Party, Cuervo chose to live in France after 1882. The Caro y Cuervo Institute (*Instituto Caro y Cuervo) founded in Bogotá in 1942 and named after Cuervo and Miguel Antonio Caro, carries on the tradition of linguistic studies in Colombia.

CULEBRERA (La) Battle of, see: BUENAVISTA, Battle of

CUNDINAMARCA, Departamento de. Located in the highlands of the *Cordillera Oriental, covering some 24,210 square kilometers, Cundinamarca includes terrain varying from tropical river valleys to highland plateaus and mountains between latitudes 3° 42' and 5° 51'N and longitudes 73° 3' and 74° 54'W. By *climatic zones, 6,246 square kilometers are tropical; 5,277, temperate; 9,055, cold; and 2,377, wasteland. Major rivers include the *Magdalena, Guavío, Sumapaz, Bogotá, Humea, and the Negro. The capital city, *Bogotá, is located on a highland pleateau known as the *Sabana de Bogotá. Estimated population in 1985 was 1,358,978 people, not counting the *Distrito Especial de Bogotá. Population density in the department is 60 people per square kilometer. DANE, *Colombia estadística 86* lists the principal agricultural products, with tonnage produced in 1984, as *potatoes, 876,250 tons; plantains, 189,000; *sugar, 96,800; *corn, 93,750; *yuca, 90,000; rice, 19,035; *cotton, 19,200; sorghum, 15,500; barley, 11,430; wheat, 11,010; beans, 7,700; *cacao, 1,650; peanuts, 275; and sesame, 75. In 1984, some 211,317 head of cattle and 68,008 hogs were slaughtered in the department. Cundinamarca is an important mining center, with *coal, *salt, lime, *iron, sulfur, quartz, *lead, *copper, *zinc, marble, gypsum, and *emeralds mined within its borders. The salt mines at *Zipaquirá and the emerald mines at Muzo and elsewhere have been important since pre-Hispanic times. Cundinamarca is highly industrialized, accounting for as much as one-third of all national industry. There were 2,377 businesses employing ten or more people in 1983. In pre-Hispanic times Cundinamarca and *Boyacá were the locale of the *Chibcha Indian civilization. Lake *Guatavita in Cundinamarca was the site of the ceremony of *Eldorado. During the *independence movement, the State of Cundinamarca existed as a separate government from April 4, 1811, until it was forced into the *Provincias Unidas in 1814. The region has been an important administrative center since the 16th century, but the modern department was established in 1886.

CUNDINAMARCA RAILROAD, see: SABANA RAILWAY

CURRENCY.   Colonial currency was originally that of Spain. Local minting of coins began in the 1620s (see: CASA DE MONEDA; COINAGE), but all of the American colonies suffered a chronic shortage. It became necessary to use unminted bars of precious metal, the origin of the *peso, which later became a coin, and the *macuquina. By the time of independence the currency unit was the silver peso, divisible into eight reales, but a wide variety of national monies were in circulation. The currency was decimalized in 1857, at the same time *weights and measures were converted to the metric system. The traditional bimetalism was replaced by the *GOLD STANDARD in 1871, but financial difficulties led to a flood of *PAPER MONEY a few years later. Due to inflation (see: EXCHANGE RATE), the one-centavo coin no longer circulates.

CURRIE, Laughlin Bernard, 1902-.   Canadian-born and U.S.-educated economist. After a distinguished career in the United States, Currie was appointed the director of an economic mission sent by the International Bank for Reconstruction and Development (now the World Bank) to study the problems of Colombia in 1950. See The Basis of a Development Program for Colombia . . . (Washington, D.C., 1950).

CUT, see: CENTRAL UNITARIA DE TRABAJADORES

-D-

D.C., see: DEMOCRACIA CRISTIANA

D.L.N., see: DIRECTORIO LIBERAL NACIONAL

D.N.C., see: DIRECTORIO NACIONAL CONSERVADOR

DAIRY FARMING, see: LIVESTOCK

DALFINGER, Ambrosius, d. 1533. German explorer, representative of the *Welsers, who is known as the "cruelest of the cruel" for his treatment of the *Indians. He led three expeditions from Coro (Venezuela), 1528-1533, exploring as far east as Maracaibo and west into present-day Colombia as far as the *Magdalena River and the Valley of Chinácota (7° 37'N, 72° 36'W, *Norte de Santander) until he was killed by the Indians. The name is also written "Alfinger," "Micer Ambrosius Dalfinger," and "Ambrosius Ehinger."

DANCE OF THE MILLIONS. The *danza de los millones,* a term applied to the decade of the 1920s to describe the impact of large amounts of foreign capital, which entered Colombia during the period. Estimates suggest that some US$200-$300 million came from abroad, much of it from New York banks and the U.S.-Colombian settlement of the *Panamanian Revolution problem. The rapid influx of funds created a brief economic boom and a wave of financial speculation. The specific phrase—"dance of the millions"—was used by Vernon Fluharty as the title of his account of Colombian politics from 1930 through the early *Rojas Pinilla years. The phrase is also used to describe the 1920s in Cuba.

DANE, see: DEPARTAMENTO ADMINISTRATIVO NACIONAL DE ESTADISTICA

DARIEN. Darién (in Spanish) is the Panamanian province immediately adjacent to the frontier with Colombia, bordered on the east by the Golfo del Darien (9° 36'N, 77° 54'W) and on the west by the Golfo de Panama (7° 45'N, 79° 20'W). It remains largely a roadless wilderness of rain forest and swamp. The *Pan American Highway is still incomplete here. Darién is also the name of the mountains separating Panama from Colombia, of the province's main river (alias the Tuira), and of the large estuary at the river's mouth. Major high points in the Darién Mountains include Tacaruña (1,910 meters) and Anachucuna (1,340 meters).

DARIEN, Scottish colony of. New Caledonia in *Darién (*Panama) and Nova Scotia (Canada) were two attempts by Scotland to plant colonies overseas (before the union with England). The Company of Scotland Trading to Africa and the Indies established the settlement of New Caledonia, under the leadership of William *Paterson, on the Darien section of the Isthmus of Panama in 1698. They began growing *tobacco, and jealous London merchants soon protested to King William III. In the difficult position of being the king of both a country at peace with Spain (England) and one occupying Spanish territory (Scotland), King William withdrew his approval and support from the Scottish colony. The enterprise (already beset with disease and other problems resulting from the climate) collapsed and the survivors withdrew in 1700. Many were escorted to Jamaica by Spanish forces under the command of Juan Díaz Pimienta. This unhappy outcome revived support in Scotland for political union with England, which was achieved with the creation of Great Britain in May 1707. See also: UNITED KINGDOM, Relations with

DARIEN STYLE.   A type of pre-conquest *Indian *goldwork characterized by casting through the lost-wax process or by hammering with soldered details. Decoration is sparse, although some cast wire ornamentation is evident. Anthropomorphic figures are common, as is the use of a stylized head with a large, protruding snout, possibly a crocodile. The style, closely related to the *Sinú, is not well differentiated from it.

DAYS OF MAY, 1957.   The period of student demonstrations, strikes, and riots in early May that preceded the fall of *Rojas Pinilla.

DE FRANCISCO MARTIN–MALMESBURY TREATY OF 1858.   Signed in London on June 11 by Juan de Francisco Martín, New Granada, and Lord Malmesbury, Great Britain. *New Granada accepted and paid claims arising from the *Mackintosh Contract of 1821.

DE MARES CONCESSION.   The second oldest *PETROLEUM concession in Colombia. By authorization of the Minister of Public Works, Modesto Garcés, on November 28, 1905, and then by a contract of March 7, 1906, Roberto de Mares was given the right to develop oil in the Infantas region near *Barrancabermeja (Santander) for a thirty-year period. Although the concession was declared void on October 22, 1909, for failure to comply with the terms of development, work was begun at the site on October 13, 1915. Claim to the concession was reasserted by the Act of San Vicente de Chucurí in 1916. The first well came into production on November 11, 1918; refining began in Barrancabermeja on January 22, 1922; and a pipeline between Barrancabermeja and *Cartagena was completed in 1926. De Mares sold major interests in the concession to the Tropical Oil Company (a firm registered in the state of Delaware, U.S.A.) headed by Milo C. Treet, Michael Benedum, and George W. Crawford in 1919. Controlling interests passed to the International Petroleum Company, Limited, of Canada (a subsidiary of Standard Oil of New Jersey) in 1920. In 1919, the Andean National Corporation (with James Flanagan as manager) was formed to develop pipeline operations, and in 1924, it was also revealed as a dependency of Standard Oil of New Jersey. The concession finally reverted to the government in 1951. See also: BARCO CONCESSION; TROPICAL OIL STRIKES

DE NICOLO, JAVIER.   Salesian priest, responsible for programs aimed at reforming *gamines in Bogotá. In the early 1970s, Father De Nicolo began Operation Friendship, whereby he established contact with the street urchins in their own environment. He opened a day shelter in downtown Bogotá, El Patio de la Once, which provided lunch, medical care, and a social environment for its clients. His program, eventually endorsed by some clergy, government officials, and lay people, developed a five-point rehabilitation program for educating and training the street children for gainful employment.

DEATH PENALTY, see: CAPITAL PUNISHMENT

DEATH SQUADS.   A name given to right-wing guerrilla, or perhaps more accurately anti-guerrilla, groups who persecute and often execute alleged terrorists, radicals, or communist supporters. There appeared to be numerous, uncoordinated groups operating in the 1980s. By one report, death squads were responsible for killing 560 people in the Department of *Risaralda between January and August of 1980. *Muerte a Secuestradores (Death to Kidnappers), or MAS, founded in 1981, and the Legión Blanca (White Legion), founded in 1984, were two of these extra-legal associations. See also: EXTRADITABLES, Los

DECADENTISM. A literary movement, also known as Symbolism, that flourished in Colombia between 1895 and 1925. It was characterized by anarchy in form and content and was profoundly negative and destructive in tone. Perhaps the most well-known decadentists were members of the Symbolic Grotto, or *Gruta Simbólica.

DECLARATION OF GRIEVANCES, see: *MEMORIAL DE AGRAVIOS*

DECLARATION OF INDEPENDENCE, see: ACTA DEL 20 DE JULIO DE 1810

DECLARATION OF SITGES, see: SITGES ACCORDS

DECREE 150 OF JANUARY 28, 1928. Decree 150 was part of the effort by the administration of President *Abadía Méndez and his Minister of Industries, José Antonio Montalvo, to assert Colombia's national rights to control its own *mineral resources. Acting under emergency powers (Law 84 of November 17, 1927), the administration issued Decree 150, which required companies holding lands to submit documentary proof of ownership within thirty days and provided for royalty payments of 10 to 20% on lands owned before 1873. Authority to rule on the validity of land titles was vested in the Ministry of Industries. The law was rendered useless when the emergency powers act was ruled unconstitutional in 1929. See also: DECREE 1225 BIS; LAW 120

DECREE 1225 BIS, 1919. This was a controversial and short-lived measure promulgated by President Marco Fidel *Suárez on June 20, 1919. Intended to regulate *petroleum production, the decree reaffirmed and expanded an 1829 act of *Bolívar that claimed for the nation the right to all kinds of mines and subsoil *mineral deposits. The 1919 decree also required government authorization before any exploration and a report of the findings. The decree was reminiscent of provisions in the 1917 constitution adopted by Mexico, and engendered sharp protests from oil interests in the United States. The United States Senate refused to ratify the *Urrutia-Thomson Treaty over *Panama claims unless the decree was rescinded. In November, the Colombian *Supreme Court ruled much of the decree unconstitutional, and President Suárez yielded to commercial and political pressure by revoking the entire decree. See: DECREE 150; LAW 120; SUB-SOIL MINERAL RIGHTS

D'ELHUYAR, Juan José, 1754-1796.   Spanish mineralogist and metallurgist sent to *New Granada by the Crown in 1784. He settled in *Mariquita and devoted his attention to improving *mining techniques, 1785-1796. He is particularly important for introducing the process of refining *silver by amalgamation with *mercury. Juan José was the brother of Fausto de Elhuyar, 1755-1843, who carried out a similar mission in Mexico. The spelling of the surname varies.

DEMOCRACIA CRISTIANA (D.C.).   The Christian Democrats, a political party founded in August 1964. The D.C. followed a middle-of-the-road program calling for social justice and effective democracy. Its own candidates have run with scant success, and the D.C. has, at times, supported the nominees of other parties. In the mid-1980s, José Agustín Linares was president of the party.

DEMOCRATIC ALLIANCE M-19, see: ALIANZA DE-MOCRATICA M-19; MOVIMIENTO DIECINUEVE DE ABRIL

DEMOCRATIC SOCIETY, see: SOCIEDAD DEMOCRATICA

DEMOCRATIC UNITY OF THE LEFT, see: UNIDAD DE-MOCRATICA DE LA IZQUIERDA

DEPARTAMENTO ADMINISTRATIVO NACIONAL DE ES-TADISTICA.   Commonly referred to simply as DANE, Colombia's national statistical agency was formed in 1952 from the Dirección Nacional de Estadística (whose origins go back to the 1875 Oficina de Estadística Nacional) and the Dirección General de los Censos. DANE was one of the first such institutions in Latin America to computerize its data gathering, and now many of its data are no longer available in traditional form. DANE is responsible for numerous publications, such as the annual volumes of *Colombia estadística*.

DEPARTMENT.   A *departamento* is the largest administrative division established by the *Constitution of 1991. It is analagous to a state in the United States. Each department has subdivisions known as *municipios* (see: MUNICIPALITIES).

The nine original departments of 1886 correspond to the states of the *Estados Unidos de Colombia: *Antioquia, *Bolívar, *Boyacá, *Cauca, *Cundinamarca, *Magdalena, *Panama, *Santander, and *Tolima. Panama became an independent republic in 1903. New departments and territories of lesser rank (*intendancies and *commissariats) have been formed by division of preexisting units in 1905, 1910, 1912, 1913, 1943, 1947, 1950, 1954, 1955, 1959, 1961, 1963, 1964, 1966, 1967, 1968, 1974, and 1977. The newer departments are *Atlántico, *Caldas, *Cesar, *Córdoba, *Chocó, *Huila, La *Guajira, *Meta, *Nariño, *Norte de Santander, *Quindío, *Risaralda, *Sucre, and *Valle del Cauca. Most recently, the Constitution of 1991 elevated the intendancies of Arauca, Casanare, Putumayo, and the Archipelago of San Andrés, Providencia, and Santa Catalina, along with the commissariats of Amazonas, Guaviare, Guainía, Vaupés, and Vichada to departmental status (see also: ADMINISTRATIVE DIVISIONS; MAP: MAJOR ADMINISTRATIVE DIVISIONS). Under the Constitution of 1991, departments are governed by a legislative body known as a Departmental Assembly (Asamblea Departamental) and a governor (Gobernador). The governor is responsible to the *President. The Governor and deputies to the Asamblea Departamental are elected for three years. Deputies must be citizens in good standing and at least 21 years of age.

DERRUMBADO (El), Battle of.   February 22, 1860, *Valle del Cauca. Generals T. C. de *Mosquera and José María *Obando, for the state of *Cauca, defeated General Pedro P. Prías and forces of the *Confederación Granadina.

DESAMORTIZACION DE LOS MANOS MUERTOS, see: DISAMORTIZATION DECREE

DESIGNADO.   The Colombian equivalent of a Vice President under the *Constitution of 1886 from 1910 to 1991. The Designado was elected for a two-year term by a joint session of *Congress. He assumed the office of the President when either the President or Congress issued written authorization for him to do so. The office of Designado replaced that of Vice President in 1910, but the vice presidency was restored under the *Constitution of 1991.

DIARIO DE LA COSTA.   Daily newspaper of *Cartagena, founded December 1, 1916, by Gabriel Eduardo O'Byrne.

Five years later the paper was sold to Carlos Escallón Miranda, who directed the newspaper from 1921 until his death in 1945. He was succeeded by his son, Rafael Escallón Vila. The paper has appeared continuously since 1916 except for two weeks following the events of the *Nueve de Abril (Bogotazo)* in 1948. It uses the subtitle of "Dean of the Coastal Press" (*Decano de la prensa costeña*).

DIARIO DEL CARIBE. *Barranquilla daily newspaper, established September 10, 1956, by Luis Paccini Santodomingo. Early publication was coordinated by Alberto Acosta with an editorial staff that included Alberto Giraldo, José Yepes Lema, Mario Acosta, Hernando Sánchez, Carlos Sanín V., Arturo Sánchez, Arnoldo Valencia Conto, and Alfonso Pérez.

DIAZ, Eugenio, 1804-1865. Agriculturalist and *costumbrista* novelist. He was one of the founders of El *Mosaico* and the author of a number of works, including the novel *Manuela.* The latter, set in a small village on the *Sabana de Bogotá, details the trials and mistreatment of Manuela, the laundress, by Tadeo Forero, boss of the village. The work contains excellent descriptions of provincial life in the 19th century.

DIAZ DE ARMENDARIZ, Miguel, d. ca. 1550. He was the first judge sent out to conduct *Visitas* and *Residencias* for *Cartagena, *Santa Marta, *Santa Fe de Bogotá, and *Cali, 1544-1550. He indicted Pedro de *Heredia for misconduct in Cartagena, 1544; named Pedro de *Ursúa Governor of *Bogotá, 1545; and authorized various expeditions for exploration and colonization. He promulgated the *New Laws of the Indies after 1544 and secured the erection of an *Audiencia in Bogotá in 1550. See: RESIDENCIA; VISITADOR

DIAZ DIAZ, Oswaldo, 1910-1967. Educator, historian, playwright; born Gachetá (*Cundinamarca), September 19; died *Bogotá, December 15. Although he studied law at the *Universidad Nacional, he never practiced, becoming instead an educator of university and secondary school students. As an author he was known for his historical works, plays, radio scripts, and juvenile literature. A bibliography of his published works appeared in the *Boletín de Historia y Antigüedades* (55:639-641 [Jan.-Mar. 1968], 12-19). He has been called a literary historian for his combination of historical and literary themes. His play, *Sueño de una noche de septiembre* (1966), for example, combined the *Twenty-fifth of September conspiracy to assassinate *Bolívar with an attempt to portray the *Liberator as an ordinary man rather than an idealized hero. Díaz Díaz has been called a transitional figure in Colombian theater because of his ability to transfer traditional stage plays to radio broadcasts.

DIEZ DE ARMENDARIZ, Miguel, see: DIAZ DE ARMENDARIZ, Miguel

DIEZMOS, see: TITHES

DIOCESES, see: ARCHDIOCESES OF COLOMBIA

DIQUE CANAL.   An artificial channel connecting the lower *Magdalena River (10° 16'N, 74° 55'W) and the Caribbean Sea (10° 18'N, 75° 13'W) near *Cartagena. It was first opened in 1650 when Pedro Zapata was Governor of Cartagena. The Dique has been repaired numerous times since then.

DIRECTORIO LIBERAL NACIONAL.   Four-man top executive committee of the *LIBERAL PARTY.

DIRECTORIO NACIONAL CONSERVADOR.   Executive committee of the *CONSERVATIVE PARTY.

DISAMORTIZATION DECREE.   Decree issued September 9, 1861, abolishing mortmain (inalienable tenure of property by institutions, chiefly the Catholic Church)—*manos muertas* in Spanish. The law is considered a major contribution to the economic development of Colombia (see: ANTI-CLERICAL LAWS, 1861).

DISESTABLISHMENT, see: SEPARATION OF CHURCH AND STATE

DISTRITO CAPITAL, see: DISTRITO ESPECIAL DE BOGOTA

DISTRITO ESPECIAL DE BOGOTA.   Also, *Bogotá, D.E. The Special District of *Bogotá, an administrative subdivision analogous to Washington, D.C., situated between latitudes 3° 42' and 4° 5'N and longitudes 73° 59' and 74° 31'W. Bogotá was designated the capital of the *República de Gran Colombia by the *Congress of Angostura in 1819. The Federal District of

Bogotá was created in 1861 and formally incorporated into Article 7 of the *Constitution of 1863. Thereafter it was suppressed in 1886, reestablished in 1905, suppressed in 1910, and revived or reformed numerous times until 1954. By legislative Decree 3640 of December 1954, Bogotá and six adjacent boroughs (Bosa, Engativá, Fontibón, Suba, Usaquén, and Usme) were designated as an autonomous entity governed by a mayor appointed by the *President. All public services, administration, and planning activities were entrusted to the mayor and a publicly elected council. By Act No. 16, December 9, 1972, amended by Act No. 7, December 4, 1974, the Distrito was divided into 18 *alcaldías menores* (Antonio Nariño, Barrios Unidos, Bosa, Ciudad Kennedy, Chapinero, Engativá, Fontibón, La Candelaria, Mártires, Puente Aranda, Rafael Uribe Uribe, San Cristóbal, Santa Fe, Suba, Teusaquillo, Tunjuelito, Usaquén, and Usme) for more administrative efficiency. The Distrito Especial covers 1,487 square kilometers. Most points range between 2,500 and 2,700 meters in altitude, but some peaks reach as high as 4,560 meters. Major rivers in the Special District include the Bogotá, Tunjuelito, Pilar, Sumapaz, San Juan, Santa Rosa, and Tabaco. In 1984, the district recorded 1,978 businesses employing ten or more people. Under the *Constitution of 1991, the name of the Distrito Especial was changed to the Distrito Capital. The Distrito Capital is governed by a council (Consejo Distrital), composed of council members (consejales) elected on the basis of one councilman for every 150,000 inhabitants. The chief executive is an *alcalde elected for three years. See also: CAPITOLIO NACIONAL

DIVISION DE ASUNTOS INDIGENAS. The Division of Indian Affairs, an administrative agency under the Minister of Government, created in 1958. The first national agency charged with the management of Indian affairs, the division undertakes statistical and social analyses of problems and attempts to implement programs to resolve them. A census the division took in 1964 reported 170,159 *Indians in Colombia, but the data are considered incomplete, and some estimated that the figure was as high as 500,000.

DOGMA OF THE 12 MILLION, see: PAPER MONEY CRISIS OF 1885-1905

DOMINGUEZ CAMARGO, Hernando, 1606-1659. Colonial poet. Born in *Bogotá, educated by the *Jesuits in Quito, Domínguez Camargo himself became a Jesuit but left the order in 1636. He served as a priest in Gachetá (4° 49'N, 73° 38'W *Cundinamarca) and elsewhere and composed the *Poema heróico de San Ignacio de Loyola* (Madrid, Spain, 1666), a five-volume account, in poetry (1,200 octaves), of the life of the founder of the Jesuit order. The *Elegías* . . . of Juan de *Castellanos, and the *Poema heróico* . . . might be considered the most ambitious and sophisticated poems of the colonial period in Colombian history. Domínguez Camargo has been called the Góngora of America, after the style of writing derived from the Spanish author Luis de Góngora y Argote (1571-1627).

DOMINICAN EMBASSY, Seizure of. February-April 1980. Members of the M-19 (*Movimiento Diecinueve de Abril), led by Rosemberg *Pabón Pabón, seized the embassy of the *Dominican Republic in *Bogotá during a public reception on February 27, taking hostage diplomatic representatives from eleven countries, including the United States. M-19 demanded release of about 300 political prisoners, publication of a manifesto, and $1 million in ransom in exchange for the hostages held in the embassy. The crisis was resolved in April when the government of Cuba was persuaded to provide an airplane on which the guerrillas and the hostages flew to Cuba, where the hostages were released. Although the M-19 did not secure its original demands in full, the episode was considered a success because of the international publicity it received. See also: CARDONA LONDOÑO, Carmenza

DOMINICAN REPUBLIC, Relations with. The Dominican Republic obtained its independence in 1844. Until then the Spanish-speaking part of the island of Hispaniola had been known as *SANTO DOMINGO. When the state of Dominican affairs caused a U.S. intervention in 1965, Colombia was included in the *Organization of American States peace mission of May 1, and the Colombians voted for the May 22 resolution to send an OAS peacekeeping force to replace the United States Marines who had been sent there. The Colombian government did not contribute troops to the force, however.

DOMINICANS. One of four religious orders favored for missionary work among the *Indians in the 16th century. The first

Dominicans probably arrived in *Santa Marta around 1529, in *Cartagena about 1535, and in *Bogotá around 1540. The Dominican Province of San Antonino of the *Nuevo Reino de Granada, with jurisdiction over the New Kingdom, *Popayán, Cartagena, Santa Marta, and Venezuela, was created in 1551. Monasteries were founded in Cartagena in 1539; Bogotá, 1550; *Tunja, 1551; *Pamplona, 1563; *Mariquita and *Ibagué, 1565; *Tocaima, around 1566; *Valledupar, Trinidad de los Muzos, and Tolú (9° 32'N, 75° 35'W), around 1567; *Buga and *Cali, 1575; Santa Marta, 1578; and Popayán, around 1584.

DONJUANA (La), Battle of. January 27, 1877, *Norte de Santander. General Sergio Camargo, for the government, defeated the rebellious forces of General Alejandro Posada and others.

DORADA, La. A municipal seat located at 5° 27'N, 74° 40'W, on the west bank of the *Magdalena River in the Department of *Caldas. The city has an altitude of 178 meters, an average temperature of 27°C, and a population of 43,053 people (1985 estimate). It is an important regional agricultural, commercial, transportation, and *petroleum-processing center. The city is said to have been founded by Antonio Acosta and others in 1900.

DORADA RAILWAY, La. The Ferrocarril de la Dorada, a line connecting the *Magdalena River ports of La *Dorada (Caldas) and *Honda (Tolima), later extended to *Ambalema (Tolima). The railroad was proposed as early as 1872 but was not begun until Francisco J. *Cisneros undertook construction in 1881. It was completed to Honda in 1897, and the extension from Honda to Ambalema was built 1905-1907.

DORADO, El, see: ELDORADO

DOS RIOS, Gobierno de. A governmental area established in 1574 between the *Cauca and *Magdalena Rivers in parts of present-day *Antioquia and *Bolívar. The principal governor was Gaspar de *Rodas. The area was incorporated into the Province of Antioquia in 1579.

DRACONIANOS. Literally, "Draconians." It is a term used to describe the more moderate or less doctrinaire *Liberals,

1849-1854, and occasionally thereafter, distinguishing them from the radical *Gólgotas. Draconians were more closely aligned to the Artisans' Society (*Sociedad de Artesanos) and the Democratic Society (*Sociedad Democrática), while the Gólgothas favored the Republican School (*Escuela Republicana). They were also less hostile to the military than were the *Radicals.

DRAKE, (Sir) Francis, ca. 1543-1596. English navigator and buccaneer who raided Spanish ports after 1567. His expedition of 1572-1573 attacked *Santa Marta, *Cartagena, Nombre de Dios (9° 34'N, 70° 28'W), and *Portobello. He sailed around the world attacking Spanish America on the Atlantic and Pacific Coasts, 1577-1580, and was knighted by Elizabeth I in 1581. He attacked Santo Domingo, *Cartagena, and Florida (U.S.A.), 1585-1586; raided the Spanish fleet off Cadiz in 1587; fought the Spanish Armada, 1588; and led an expedition against Santa Marta and Central America, 1595-1596. Known as "El Draque," the gentleman pirate, he died off the coast of Portobello. See also: PIRACY

DRAMA, see: LITERATURE

DRUG TRADE. The production and exportation of illicit narcotics became a major socioeconomic and political problem in Colombia during the late 1970s. What has become known as the "other" (or "unofficial") economy was estimated at US$3.2 billion in 1979, with 81% of this coming from narcotics. A 1985 estimate put income from the drug trade at US$5 billion. The official gross national product was approximately US$26 billion in 1979 and US$32 billion in 1985, respectively.

Although *marijuana and *coca were grown at locations throughout the nation, production and smuggling of *marijuana—known variously as baretta, marimba, or mota—were concentrated along the Caribbean Coast in the Departments of *Magdalena, *Cesar, and *Guajira, including the *Sierra Nevada de Santa Marta. Control and administration of the drug trade, however, was most often reputed to be in *Medellín (see: MEDELLIN CARTEL). Many sources credit Pablo *Escobar Gaviria and Fabio Ochoa with the first systematic organization of the narcotics traffic, which eventually came to be controlled by a group of bosses—capos—known collectively as the mafia. In addition to a center for local production, Colombia also became a site for processing and transshipment of *cocaine—cousin Charlie, *perica,* etc.—moving northward from Peru, Bolivia, and other points to the south.

The drug industry employed people from all social classes. Presidential administrations of the early 1980s denounced the drug trade and officially initiated policies to suppress it. The *Betancur administration cooperated with the United States to prosecute drug dealers by means of an extradition treaty and launched a series of raids on known drug centers after the assassination of Minister of Justice Rodrigo *Lara Bonilla. A similar crackdown occurred during the *Barco presidency following the murder of Luis Carlos *Galán. During late 1989 and 1990 open warfare existed between the government and the drug dealers, and the nation experienced several months of unpredictable and uncontrolled public violence. Accusations of corruption in major governmental agencies have been widespread, and the large influx of money has created economic problems, but efforts to terminate the drug trade have been only partially successful. See also: COCA; COCAINE; EXTRADITION TREATIES; HEROIN; LEHDER RIVAS, Carlos; MEDELLIN CARTEL; MULE

DUCASSE, Jean Baptiste, 1640-1715. French buccaneer. He carried slaves to Santo Domingo in 1686 and attacked *Cartagena in 1695. He attacked Cartagena again with Baron de *Pointis in 1697, at which time they carried off valuable religious objects that were eventually returned to Spain by Louis XIV. See also: PIRACY

DUQUESNE DE LA MADRID, José Domingo, 1748-1822. Priest in the parish of Gachancipá (5°N, 72° 52'W *Cundinamarca). He was the author of a dissertation on the calendar of the Muiscas, first published by Joaquín *Acosta in 1848.

DURAN Y DIAZ, Joaquín. Spanish captain. Author of the first descriptive and statistical almanac of Colombia, *Guía de forasteros del Nuevo Reino de Granada . . .* , published in *Bogotá in 1793. A second version, much enlarged, appeared in 1794.

-E-

E.L.N., see: EJERCITO DE LIBERATION NACIONAL

E.P.L., see: EJERCITO POPULAR DE LIBERACION

EARTHQUAKES.   Colombia suffers from frequent earthquakes, although not so much as some other Andean countries. Noteworthy quakes in the colonial period occurred in 1595 (*Mariquita), 1643 (*Popayán), 1644 (*Pamplona), 1687 (Mariquita, noteworthy for El *Ruido), 1765 (Popayán and *Cali), 1778 (*Tumaco, Nariño), 1785 (Popayán), 1797 (central Colombia), and 1805 (Mariquita). The early years of independence saw quakes in 1834 (*Pasto), 1835 (Pasto and Tumaco), and 1868 (central Colombia). The tremor of 1875 affected large areas of Colombia and Venezuela, with some 16,000 deaths. In Colombia, *Cúcuta was the town worst hit. Other quakes followed in 1878 (*Manizales), 1885 (Popayán), January 31, 1906 (Tumaco and central Colombia), August 31, 1917 (*Bogotá), and December 12 and 22 (on the Ecuadoran border and Bogotá). Bogotá had another more violent earthquake on June 6, 1925. There were a number of quakes in 1935-1936: Pasto was shaken (eight dead) on August 9, 1935, severely damaged on October 29-30, and damaged again on July 18, 1936. Fifty people were killed on the west coast on August 9, 1935; *Antioquia and *Caldas were hit on September 19, 1935. Hundreds were killed in southern Colombia, January 11, 1936, and a series of quakes July 18-21 that same year damaged Pasto and destroyed much of *Túquerres (Nariño), 25 miles to the southwest. Bogotá was hit on May 14, 1941. Three died and many were hurt at Lorica (9° 14'N, 75° 49'W, *Bolívar), December 26, 1942. Quakes on July 8-11, 1950, killed 139 in *Norte de Santander. In 1962, forty were killed in Bogotá on February 19. Fatalities reached eighty-seven and 200 were injured at Manizales, *Pereira, and on the west coast between July 31 and August 4 of the same year. One hundred were killed and more than 400 hurt on February 6, 1967, when an earthquake struck the upper Magdalena Valley with its epicenter at *Neiva. On July 29, 1967, ten died and 100 were hurt in *Santander and *Boyacá. A little more than two years later, November 23, 1979, saw an earthquake that registered 6.5 on the Richter scale. Its epicenter was in the Pacific Ocean, 240 kilometers southwest of Bogotá. Sixty were killed; 600 were injured; and 1,000 buildings were destroyed with damages estimated at US$20 million. On March 31, 1983, a Richter scale quake of 5.5 killed 250 people, wounded 2,000 more, and destroyed or damaged 3,000 buildings.

ECCLESIASTICAL PATRONAGE, Law of, see: PATRONATO

ECCLESIASTICAL PROPERTY CONFISCATION, see: DIS-AMORTIZATION DECREE

ECHANDIA OLAYA, Darío, 1897-1989. Distinguished lawyer, diplomat, and *Liberal Party leader; born Chaparral (*Tolima), October 13; died *Ibagué, May 7. Echandía received his doctorate of law from the *Colegio Mayor de Nuestra Señora del Rosario in 1917. He taught law on several occasions and was a justice of the *Supreme Court. From 1934 to 1935 he was Minister of Foreign Relations, and he also held diplomatic appointments to the *United Kingdom, the *Papacy, and the *United Nations. He was Minister of Education and Minister of Government in the first administration of Alfonso *López Pumarejo, where he was active in securing passage of the *Codification of 1936. He was acting President, 1943-1944, 1960, and 1967. A reformist *Liberal, Echandía assumed control of the party after the death of Jorge Eliécer *Gaitán in 1948. He was temporarily Minister of Government in the coalition cabinet of Mariano *Ospina Pérez following the *Bogotazo. An unsuccessful candidate for the presidency in 1950, he formed part of the opposition under both the presidency of Laureano *Gómez and the dictatorship of General *Rojas Pinilla.

ECHAVARRIA CONSPIRACY. Named after Felipe Echavarría Olózaga, a *Conservative *Medellín industrialist who allegedly plotted to assassinate General *Rojas Pinilla in 1953. The plot implicated the government and supporters of President Laureano *Gómez. Handling of the affair created serious tensions within the administration and precipitated the coup d'état carried out by General Rojas Pinilla on June 13, 1953. Felipe Echavarría later published his own account of the events (*Historia de una monstruosa farsa* . . . ; 3rd ed., Rome/Madrid, 1964), according to which he was arrested on June 5 and imprisoned without charges until August 14. He was tortured and then eventually set free by court order on November 3. A year later, November 19, 1954, the government issued a pardon to Echavarría, Humberto Pérez Restrepo, Luis Eduardo Nieto Caballero, Carmenza J. Martínez, Cecilia López, and Roberto Pelufo R. However, Echavarría denied his complicity in the affair and refused the amnesty.

ECONOMY, The. Pre-Columbian Indian societies in present-day Colombia had well-developed *mining and metallurgic techniques and active trade networks, in addition to subsistence agriculture based on *corn, *yuca, *potatoes, and seafood. Perhaps the most notable long-range products were *gold and *salt. Gold mining seems to have been concentrated along the Caribbean and Pacific coasts and in the region of *Antioquia. The most noteworthy salt deposits were in the *Boyacá-*Cundinamarca region, especially those in *Zipaquirá. Various items passed along the trade networks; for example, the *Chibchas apparently traded salt for gold. Diverse styles of goldwork, however, indicate that metalworking was practiced by widely dispersed groups, including those who did not actually mine the gold. The *Indians also produced *tobacco and *coca leaves, largely for their own consumption.

During the colonial period, economic development in Colombia (*New Granada) was systematically limited by an official colonial policy aimed at maintaining the economic dependency of the colony. Mining (gold, *silver, and *emeralds) formed the principal source of export wealth. Gold production in the 17th century approached 40% of the world's total output. The Isthmus of *Panama and the fortress city of *Cartagena served as major commercial entrepôts and military outposts for defense. Internally European settlements engaged in subsistence *agriculture and *livestock husbandry, with limited *sugar, *tobacco, and munitions production. In addition the colonists developed various artisan handicrafts and small industries, such as weaving, hemp (fique) products, and hat making (jipas, or Panama hats) for local consumption. Both relatively and literally speaking, however, colonial New Granada remained a poor region.

Economic wealth in the 19th century was generated largely from export agriculture, especially tobacco, *indigo, and *coffee. Tobacco enjoyed a prominence between 1850 (after the abolition of the *estanco, or state monopoly) and 1875, and indigo experienced a shorter boom as tobacco declined. Both tobacco and indigo were eclipsed by the rise of coffee after 1875. Products of lesser commercial importance included sugar, Panama hats, *quinine, and tagua (an ivorylike vegetable product).

On the industrial front, Enrique Caballero has argued that only small-scale *ironworks enjoyed any sustained growth during the 1800s. Although there were attempts at various kinds of factories (paper, matches, cigarettes, china, cloth, breweries, tiles, etc.), industrial development was impeded by repeated warfare (first the *independence movement and then numerous *civil wars), free-trade policies introduced in the 1840s and 1850s, and lack of banking facilities (see: BANKS). In addition, Frank Safford stresses the lack of good transportation systems, even though *railroad construction began in the 1850s.

Modern industrial expansion (see: MANUFACTURING INDUSTRY) dates from the early 20th century. Within the first twenty-five years a number of factors coalesced. Peace was restored in the wake of the War of the *Thousand Days, and a spirit of nationalism developed in the aftermath of the separation of *Panama. New wealth was generated by coffee exportation and the growth of the *banana trade. Capital was generated from abroad through *foreign investment and indemnification resulting from the *Urrutia-Thomson Treaty, which settled claims growing out of the *Panamanian Revolution. The *Reyes administration introduced a *currency stabilization program, and the Bank of the Republic (*Banco de la República) was established in 1923. Founding of the Bavaria company by Leo S. Kopp in 1891 marked the beginning of a modern brewing industry, and the turn of the century also saw significant growth of textile manufacturing in *Antioquia. The first electrical companies created a relatively cheap source of energy; construction was stimulated when the Samper family founded the first cement company in 1906, and the first concessions for *petroleum production were granted in 1905. Railway mileage was expanded, and in 1919, *air transport was introduced. At the end of the period, in 1928, the Colombian stock market was established.

*World War I and the Great Depression of 1929 created temporary difficulties for the Colombian economy, but Enrique Caballero has argued that the nation recovered quickly and the years 1931-1938 saw the greatest annual growth rates in Colombian history. *World War II contributed to further internal growth by forcing import substitution policies. However, the postwar adjustments contributed to the socioeconomic tensions that have been characteristic of Colombia since 1948.

Colombia took a major step toward economic self-sufficiency with the establishment of the *Paz del Río ironworks in 1955. The nation began to stress economic diversification and lessened dependency on coffee monoculture in 1962, and sugar exports expanded greatly in the 1960s. Colombia has participated in various international marketing programs, such as the *Latin American Common Market and the *Andean Pact.

Economic growth was threatened by the world energy crisis of the 1970s, and the *Betancur administration found it necessary to restrict imports for a while in the early 1980s. The 1970s and 1980s also saw the rise of the "unofficial" economy in illegal narcotics (see: DRUG TRADE). The latter created inflationary problems as well as international complications. Colombia's *foreign debt is relatively low, and economic potential remains high, but current problems necessitate careful management.

According to the Colombian Information Service, in 1988, manufacturing and agriculture accounted for 21.5% and 21.3%, respectively, of the nation's gross domestic product. Other sectors and their contributions were trade, 12%; transport, 9.1%; government services, 7.9%; construction, 4%; mining, 3.6%; and all other activities, 20.6%. In agriculture coffee continues to be the country's chief legal export, followed by *cotton, bananas, sugar, tobacco, cacao, cut flowers, and citrus fruit. Some production figures for 1985 (in metric tons) were: sugar, 25,000,000; *yuca*, 1,720,000; bananas, 1,200,000; corn, 882,000; coffee, 642,000; cacao, 43,000; and tobacco, 42,000. There are 22 million head of cattle, a record in South America surpassed only by Brazil and Argentina.

Economically important minerals include petroleum, *coal, iron ore, emeralds (50% of the world's supply in recent years), gold, *platinum (the worlds largest reserves), silver (output up from 2.8 metric tons in 1977 to 6.2 metric tons in 1985), and *nickel. There is also mining of *copper and *zinc, and production of *natural gas. Partial industrial figures for 1988 included crude petroleum, 136,422,797 barrels; Portland cement, 6,367,000 metric tons (estimated); crude steel ingots, 725,000 metric tons (estimated); caustic soda, 21,318 metric tons; and soda ash, 114,087 metric tons. The per capita gross domestic product in 1988 was US$1,684. See also: EXPORTS; IMPORTS

ECOPETROL, see: EMPRESA COLOMBIANA DE PETROLEOS

ECUADOR, Intervention in New Granada, 1840-1841, see: ECUADOR–NEW GRANADA TREATIES OF 1840-1841

ECUADOR, Relations with. In colonial times, *Cauca had been administratively part of the *Nuevo Reino de Granada but judicially within the jurisdiction of the *Audiencia of Quito. The region, and particularly its capital, *Popayán, was very traditional and deeply Catholic. Throughout the 19th century, many of the people of Cauca tended to look sympathetically toward Ecuador, a circumstance that gave the area a very volatile political life. In 1830, when *Gran Colombia split up, factions in the provinces of the Cauca actively sought annexation to Ecuador (see: CAUCA, Ecuadoran Annexation of). Ecuadoran General Juan José *Flores moved quickly to occupy *Pasto and *Buenaventura, but Generals José María *Obando and José Hilario *López eventually forced him to withdraw. The *OBANDO–POSADA GUTIERREZ–ARTETA TREATY of 1832 restored the previous boundary along the Tulcán River. Eight years later, Ecuador intervened in *New Granada's domestic affairs on behalf of the government during the rebellion known as the War of the *SUPREME COMMANDERS. Ecuadoran leaders hoped to reannex part of the Cauca, but they ultimately secured little that the New Granadan *Congress would approve after the civil war was over (see: ECUADOR–NEW GRANADA TREATIES OF 1840-1841). Disputes over the Cauca were finally settled in the *POMBO–GOMEZ DE LA TORRE TREATY Of 1856 and the TREATY OF *PINZAQUI in 1863. During the *rebellion of 1859-1862, some of the supporters of General *Mosquera used Ecuador as a refuge. Some New Granadan *Conservative forces followed them across the frontier in hot pursuit in 1862, and a brief war resulted. Julio *Arboleda, representing the government of the dying *Confederación Granadina defeated Ecuador at the Battle of *Tulcán on July 11, 1862, but released the Ecuadoran president, his war minister, and other prisoners in exchange for recognition of Arboleda and the Confederación Granadina, a supply of arms, and 20,000 *pesos. Arboleda was on the point of invading Ecuador for failing to fulfill the treaty when he was assassinated. In August 1863, the now-victorious Mosquera issued a proclamation at Popayán calling upon Ecuadoran Liberals to rise against the Conservative government in Ecuador and help restore Gran Colombia. The brief war that resulted, from November 1863 to February 1864, ended in a spectacular victory over Flores and the Ecuadoran forces at *Cuaspud on December 4, 1863. The TREATY OF *PINZAQUI restored conditions existing before the war. But sympathy with Ecuador remained strong in the Cauca, and the failure of the Conservative *rebellion of 1876 drove many to take refuge in the neighboring country. Then Liberal Ignacio de Veintemilla seized power in Ecuador, September 8, 1876, and requested Colombian help in suppressing a Conservative counterrevolt in October. Colombia sent 3,000 men who arrived after the rebellion was over but stayed until Ecuador paid 10,000 pesos for the cost of the expedition. In 1884 the *CAMARGO-ESPINOSA TREATY accepted arbitration of Colombian claims against Ecuador, and a Tripartite Arbitration Convention was agreed to by Colombia, Ecuador, and Peru on December 15, 1894. In 1885 when the future Ecuadoran president, José Eloy Alfaro, was a refugee in Panama, the Colombian government acceded to Ecuadoran demands that he be expelled. When, ten years later, Alfaro seized power, Colombian President Miguel Antonio *Caro declared neutrality with regard to Ecuador's internal affairs.

The extension of the *Amazon *rubber trade upstream beyond Brazilian jurisdiction led to Peruvian concern for its authority in the region. This caused border problems with Ecuador, and Colombia was drawn into the conflict when it signed the first of a series of *PUTUMAYO TREATIES (the Tanco Argáez–Prado Ugarteche–Velarde Treaty) with Peru in 1906. By implication the treaty suggested a common border between the two nations, thereby ignoring Ecuador's claims. The treaty was never ratified, but it did contribute to further disputes between Colombia and Ecuador. Boundary questions between these two were resolved by the *SUAREZ–MUÑOZ VERNAZA TREATY OF 1916. Existing claims between the two had been settled previously by agreement in 1913 (*URIBE CORDOVEZ–DILLON TREATY). In more recent years, relations have generally been friendly, and the two countries have been able to cooperate in such ventures as the *FLOTA MERCANTE GRANCOLOMBIANA of 1964 and the *ANDEAN COMMON MARKET of 1968. Colombia's success against the *M-19's invasion of *Nariño in 1981 was aided by the fact that all those of the *Columna Antonio Nariño who sought refuge in Colombia's southern neighbor were returned by Ecuador.

ECUADOR-COLOMBIA TREATY OF 1863, see: PINZAQUI, Treaty of

ECUADOR-COLOMBIA TREATY OF 1884, see: CAMARGO-ESPINOSA TREATY

ECUADOR-COLOMBIA TREATY OF 1913, see: URIBE CORDOVEZ–DILLON TREATY

ECUADOR-COLOMBIA TREATY OF 1916, see: SUAREZ–MUÑOZ VERNAZA TREATY

ECUADOR–NEW GRANADA TREATIES OF 1840-1841. By agreement between Generals Pedro A. *Herrán and T. C. de *Mosquera, for *New Granada, and Generals Juan José *Flores and Leonardo Stagg, for Ecuador, signed at *Túquerres, September 23, 1840, Ecuador provided military aid against rebellions in New Granada in exchange for consideration of advantageous boundary changes. Ecuadoran troops began occupation of parts of New Granada on September 17, 1840, and attempts were made to annex *Pasto in May 1841. The troops were withdrawn following an agreement signed in Túquerres, November 3, 1841, by Generals Joaquín *Posada Gutiérrez, New Granada, and Bernardo Daste, Ecuador. The treaty ceded Túquerres and the Island of *Tumaco to Ecuador but was never ratified by New Granada.

ECUADOR–NEW GRANADA TREATY OF 1832, see: OBANDO–POSADA GUTIERREZ–ARTETA TREATY

ECUADOR–NEW GRANADA TREATY OF 1856, see: POMBO–GOMEZ DE LA TORRE TREATY

EDUCATION. Medieval government looked upon education as a responsibility of the family, aided by the Church, and anything beyond the elementary level was considered unnecessary for anyone but clergymen or members of the upper class. This attitude persisted in colonial Hispanic America at least until the end of the 18th century. *New Granada's first secondary and higher educational institutions were provided by religious orders, principally the *Jesuits from the early 17th century onward. The expulsion of the Jesuits in 1767 led the government of Viceroy *Flórez to encourage the *cabildos to provide public schools, and in 1770 María Clemencia de *Caycedo founded a pioneer girls' school. In 1820 the government of independent *Gran Colombia under Vice President *Santander made the local provision of schools obligatory. This was followed by the Plan general de estudios superiores of 1826 (see: PLAN DE ESTUDIOS, 1826). Over the next decade, three national *UNIVERSITIES were established, as were secondary schools in *Tunja, *Ibagué, *Medellín, *Cali, *Pamplona, *Santa Marta, San Gil, and *Cartagena. *Lancasterian schools were introduced at the primary level 1821-

1835. *Conservative victory in the War of the *Supreme Commanders led to a new curriculum, the *PLAN DE ESTUDIOS, 1842. Despite its generally reactionary intent, especially in its emphasis on religious instruction, the plan (authored by Mariano *Ospina Rodríguez) saw the first serious provisions for female education. The public schools in 1844 had 19,161 male students and 7,762 female students. The first modern private schools for women also date from 1844. Much more far-reaching was the Organic Law of Public Elementary Education (*Decreto orgánico de la instrucción pública*) of 1870, which created a Dirección General de la Instrucción Pública within the Ministry of the Interior. The director was a presidential appointee with cabinet rank. The costs of complying with the very detailed Organic Law were divided among the federal government, the states, and the municipalities. An Escuela Normal (Normal School, or teacher training school) was set up and staffed by teachers recruited in Germany (see: GERMANY, Relations with). The conservative unitary *Constitution of 1886 restored a strong Church influence on education. A new organic law established the principle that public education should be free in 1903, and a law of 1927 made it obligatory at the elementary level, at least in theory. A *Liberal administration adopted a measure to outlaw racial and religious discrimination in education in 1936. The post–*World War II period saw an enormous expansion in the Colombian educational system. Enrollment grew between 1945 and 1970 from 678,386 students to 3,286,052 at the elementary level and from 67,877 to 750,055 at the secondary. Five new state universities opened in the 1940s, three in the 1950s, six in the 1960s, and six in the 1970s. In spite of the unitary nature of the constitution, however, decentralization has been a limiting factor in development. Implementation of the Ministry of Education directives depend on departmental secretaries of education who are political appointees of the government of each department. A reform was launched in 1968 in an effort to create a more effective, centralized control called the Regional Educational Funds Program (Fondos educativos regionales). Unfortunately, it has had only limited success. For further information, consult Mark Hanson, *Educational Reform and Administrative Development: The Cases of Colombia and Venezuela* (Stanford, 1986). In 1986, Colombia had 292,741 children in nursery (preschool) education; 3,740,379 elementary pupils; 1,648,731 high school students; and 417,786 students in higher education.

EGUILUZ, Paula de, see: CARTAGENA WITCHES

EHINGER, Ambrosius, see: DALFINGER, Ambrosius

EHINGER, Heinrich. Agent for the *Welsers in Venezuela who has sometimes been confused with Ambrosius *Dalfinger.

EJERCITO DE LIBERACION NACIONAL (E.L.N.). Guerrilla movement begun in the Department of *Santander, July 4, 1964, by a number of people influenced by the Cuban revolution. Led by Fabio Vásquez Castaño, the movement included his brothers, Manuel (Jerónimo) and Antonio, Víctor Medina Morón, Ricardo Larra Parada, Carlos Puyana, Pedrito Solano (Yirapavas), Marco Palacios Rozo, Juan de Dios Aguilera, Alonso Ojeda Awad, and Jaime Arenas Reyes. Many early members of the E.L.N. came from the short-lived José Antonio Galán Brigade (Brigada Pro Liberación Nacional de Colombia José Antonio *Galán), organized in Cuba in 1963, or from the Revolutionary Liberal Youth Movement (J.M.R.L.). Beginning with the seizure of Simacota (6° 27'N, 73° 20'W), forces of the E.L.N. operated out of the Department of *Santander from bases at Simacota, San Vicente de Chucurí, El Toboso, La Rochela, and elsewhere, including parts of the Departments of *Antioquia, *Atlántico, *Bolívar, and *Norte de Santander, the Intendancy of *Arauca, and an area known as the *bota caucana* in southeastern *Cauca, *Huila, and *Caquetá. It achieved prominence in 1965-1966 as the group with which Father Camilo *Torres fought and died. Although there were internal disagreements that resulted in the deaths of members such as Víctor Medina Morón and Jaime Arenas Reyes, the E.L.N. flourished from 1966-1973, until the disastrous campaign and defeat at the Battle of *Anorí (Antioquia) in 1973. Anorí brought the deaths of Manuel and Antonio Vásquez Castaño and the exile of their brother, Fabio. After a brief hiatus, the group renewed activities in 1975 with a change in tactics and ideology that some have called the *Replantamiento,* and Manuel Pérez Martínez (Poliarco) and Nicolás Rodríguez Bautista (Gabino) emerged as the new leaders. The E.L.N. described itself as a Marxist-Leninist movement adapted to Colombian realities. The E.L.N. was responsible for the kidnapping of Jaime *Betancur (November 1983), and it helped to form the *Coordinadora Guerrillera "Simón Bolívar." Although some individuals accepted the amnesty of 1984, the E.L.N. as an organization never officially adhered to the truce agreements, and E.L.N. guerrillas continued to fight through-out the decade. They were responsible for disrupting petro-leum exploration and production in *Arauca and the kidnap-ping of fourteen people in April 1988, and portions of the E.L.N. remained active thoughout 1991. See also: GUER-RILLA MOVEMENTS

EJERCITO NACIONAL, see: ARMY

EJERCITO POPULAR DE LIBERACION (E.P.L.). Guerrilla movement founded on December 17, 1967, with Pedro Vásquez Rendón and Pedro León Arboleda (d. 1975) as its first political leaders, and Francisco Caraballo and Ernesto *Rojas (Jairo de Jesús Calvo Ocampo, d. February 1987) as its first military leaders. Other founding members included Bernardo Fulvio Ferreira, Libardo Mora Toro, Gonzalo González Mantilla, and Oscar William Calvo Ocampo (twin brother of Jairo de Jesús). Its early base of operations included parts of the Departments of *Antioquia and *Córdoba, espe-cially the Sinú, San Jorge, and *Cauca Rivers, the *Urabá region, and the so-called Zone X on the border of the Departments of *Santander and *Bolívar. The E.P.L., originally influenced by the success of the Cuban revolution and Maoist ideology, was reorganized in April 1980, and again in 1983. In the mid-1980s, Oscar William Calvo Ocampo headed the organization until he was shot in Bogotá, November 30, 1985. The E.P.L. signed a truce with the government in *Medellín, April 24, 1984, but much of the agreement appeared to be ineffective by mid-1985. E.P.L. members announced their return to active struggle fol-lowing Oscar William's assassination, and they joined the *Coor-dinadora Guerrillera "Simón Bolívar." The Pedro León Ar-boleda Brigade was a splinter group of the E.P.L., active in the area around Medellín. Francisco Caraballo became the leader of the E.P.L. after the death of Jairo de Jesús Calvo Ocampo. Much of the E.P.L. formally surrendered again on March 1, 1991. See also: GUERRILLA MOVEMENTS

ELBERS, Juan Bernardo, 1776-1853. Prussian-born businessman who emigrated to Colombia. He was active in financing and supplying patriot causes, 1818-1823, but is most often remem-bered for his efforts to establish steam navigation on the *Magdalena River, 1823-1838. Acting on a contract with the state in 1823, Elbers was able to introduce steam vessels on the

Magdalena as early as 1825, but he was never able to sustain service for more than short periods at a time.

ELDORADO. Also *El Dorado,* literally the "gilded one" or "golden man." It was originally a reference to the periodic ritual in which a chieftain covered his body with gold and ceremoniously entered Lake *Guatavita. Long held to be legendary, the rite was given greater credence in the 20th century after the discovery near Pasca (*Cundinamarca) of a piece of goldwork depicting the ritual. This artifact is now housed in the *Gold Museum in *Bogotá. The term *Eldorado* came to mean any legendary treasure.

ELECTORAL COLLEGE, see: COLEGIO ELECTORAL

ELECTORAL LEAGUE, see: LIGA ELECTORAL

ELECTRICITY, see: ENERGY AND POWER; HYDROELECTRICITY

ELHUYAR, Juan José, see: D'ELHUYAR, Juan José

EMERALDS. Colombia is the world's largest producer of emeralds, having accounted at times for as much as 95% of total output. These precious stones were first reported in 1564. The first commercial company, based on labor from an Indian *encomienda,* was organized by Captain Benito de Póveda, 1567, and the first Crown administrator, Captain Alvaro Cepeda de Ayala was appointed in 1572. The mines were inactive from around 1800 until 1828, when they were reopened as a government monopoly until 1870. Exploitation was decentralized from 1870 to 1886 and then reestablished as a government prerogative. By Law 32 of 1903, revenue from emerald production was designated to amortize paper money then in circulation. On February 27, 1904, the Syndicate of Muzo was set up to administer the program with Laureano García Ortiz as its director. The sale of emeralds was temporarily suspended in 1907 because of an economic crisis. On December 23, 1908, the Colombian Emerald Company was established to control the emerald market and to administer the mines. After the fall of the *Reyes government, the company's contract was terminated. At other times in the 20th century, the mines were under direct government control and at times closed. The *Banco de la República operated them from 1954-1969, and the Colombian Mining Enterprise (ECOMINAS) has managed them under differing arrangements since then. The most well known and the largest mines are the Muzo (5° 32'N, 74° 7'W), Chivor, and Coscuez, but other sites have also been exploited in Somondoco (4° 59'N, 73° 26'W), Coper, Gachalá, and Ubalá (4° 43'N, 73° 32'W), all in *Boyacá or *Cundinamarca. Colombia currently produces about 50% of the world's supply, followed by Zambia (20%), and Brazil (15%). Zimbabwe, Pakistan, the states of the former Soviet Union, and other smaller producers account for the remaining 15%.

EMPLOYERS' NATIONAL ECONOMIC ASSOCIATION, see: ASOCIACION PATRONAL ECONOMICA NACIONAL

EMPRESA COLOMBIANA DE PETROLEOS.   ECOPETROL, a government *petroleum corporation authorized by law in 1948, founded in 1951, and reorganized from 1956-1958. The *De Mares Concession with Tropical Oil, 1951, and the El Carare Concession with Cities Service, 1955, were two of its earliest developments.

EMPRESAS UNIDAS DE ENERGIA ELECTRICA.   An electrical company formed in February 1927, to purchase and unite the facilities of the company *Energía Eléctrica de Bogotá and the Compañía Nacional de Electricidad into a single municipally owned public utility. The newly formed corporation began service to *Bogotá on September 1, 1927. See also: BOGOTA ELECTRIC LIGHT COMPANY; COMPAÑIA NACIONAL DE ELECTRICIDAD; ENERGIA ELECTRICA DE BOGOTA

ENCISO, Battle of.   March 15, 1895, 6° 8'N, 73° 7'W, *Santander. General Rafael *Reyes, for the government, defeated the rebel forces of General José María Ruiz. The encounter was a decisive loss for the *Liberal rebellion.

ENCISO, Martín Fernández de, see: FERNANDEZ DE ENCISO, Martín

ENCOMENDERO.   A person who was entrusted with the management of an *ENCOMIENDA.

ENCOMIENDA.   Royal institution prevalent in *New Granada during the colonial period, especially in the 16th century. It was an agreement whereby the *Indians were "commended" to the care of designated Spaniards. In exchange for providing religious instruction and livelihood for the Indians, the Spanish were allowed to use them as a labor force. Often abused in practice, the *encomienda* amounted to virtual enslavement. The *New Laws of the Indies of 1542 tried to limit the establishment of new *encomiendas* and to prevent the continuation of existing ones, but protests from colonists caused modification of the laws. The *encomienda* declined in usage generally after 1592, when the Crown legalized the sale of land to private owners. The *mita or *repartimiento* then served as a substitute. Although some *encomiendas* contained as many as 2,000 to 3,000 Indians, the average size has been estimated at about 300 Indians.

ENERGIA ELECTRICA DE BOGOTA.   The second major electrical company in *Bogotá, Energía Eléctrica de Bogotá was established August 13, 1896, by the firm of Samper Brush and Company as a rival to the *Bogotá Electric Light Company. The Samper brothers began to form the company in 1892, and the Energía Eléctrica name was used after 1894. The company built the second important hydroelectric plant in Colombia at El Charquito on the Bogotá River and began public service on August 6, 1900. Production facilities were enlarged in 1904, 1908, 1920-1923, and 1924, and a dam was built at Alicachín, 1906-1911, to provide water reserves in dry seasons. The company was merged into the Empresas Unidas de Energía Eléctrica in 1927. See also: COMPAÑIA ELECTRICA DE BUCARAMANGA; EMPRESAS UNIDAS DE ENERGIA ELECTRICA

ENERGY AND POWER.   Colombia has been self-sufficient in *petroleum and *natural gas much of the time since the 1930s; these make up about half the current national consumption of energy. The country has been self-sufficient in *coal only since the 1960s, but this now provides 12% of the nation's energy, a proportion that is expected to increase. The first electric power station, that of the *Panama Electric Light Company, began functioning in 1889, followed within a year by that of the *Bogotá Electric Light Company: both were coal fired. The Bogotá company was merged with the *Compañía Nacional de Electricidad in 1927, to form the *Empresas Unidas de Energía Eléctrica. Provision of *hydroelectricity began with the *Compañía Eléctrica de Bucaramanga in 1891, and this is now the dominant form of electric power in Colombia. It accounted for 10% of the nation's total energy consumption in 1980.

ENGANCHAMIENTO. Literally, a "hooking," or perhaps "to be hooked," this is a term associated with a system of contract labor to supply workers for *coffee plantations. Workers were lured, sometimes forced, into new coffee-producing regions by various wage agreements, some of which might include land that workers could pay for by labor or produce in kind. The *enganchador,* or recruiter, was especially important for ensuring a supply of seasonal workers for peak labor periods. Various kinds of *enganchamientos* were instrumental in stimulating the expansion of the coffee industry.

ENSEÑANZA, Convento de la, see: CAYCEDO, María Clemencia de

EPIDEMICS, 1546-1881. Among the recorded epidemics in Colombia were: smallpox in 1546, 1566, 1587, 1700, 1782, 1815, 1840, 1857, 1869, and 1881; typhoid, typhus, and other fevers in 1632-1634, 1639, and 1831; plague, 1688; whooping cough, 1814; measles, 1820; goiter and syphilis, 1822; cholera morbus, 1849; jaundice, 1869; and gangrenous angina, 1873.

EPONYMOUS GENERATION, see: HEROIC GENERATION

ESCAÑO DE CARTAGO. Literally, the "bench of *Cartago," on which the *CARTAGO EXECUTIONS were carried out in 1841.

ESCOBAR GAVIRIA, Pablo Emilio, 1950-. Billionaire *narcotraficante* and reputed head of the Medellín Cartel. A native of *Rionegro (Antioquia), Pablo Escobar entered the *drug trade in the early 1970s and rose rapidly within it. He is known to have numerous business interests in Medellín and elsewhere including his estate, "Nápoles" (Antioquia), and he has cultivated a popular following through philanthropic works. He is supported by *Medellín Cívico,* a newspaper founded by his uncle, Hernán Gaviria Berrío, and, in 1984, was elected an alternate representative (*suplente*) to *Congress from the *Liberal Party in the Department of *Antioquia. In 1984 and again in 1989-1990 he was part of a group of drug dealers who attempted unsuccessfully to negotiate an amnesty settlement with the Colombian government. He is said to have been one of the owners of the *Yarí complex raided in 1984 and one of the founders of *Muerte a Secuestradores (although he has denied the latter). In 1988-1990 he was included in *Forbes* magazine's list of the world's billionaires (as were fellow drug dealers Jorge Luis *Ochoa and Gonzalo Rodríguez Gacha) (see also: MEDELLIN CARTEL). Escobar was wanted for extradition to the United States, but in exchange for guarantees that he would not be extradited, he surrendered to Colombian authorities on June 20, 1991, and was confined to house arrest in the *Medellín suburb of Envigado.

ESCOBAR SOTO, Nicolás. Head of Texaco's Colombian subsidiary who was kidnapped by the *Movimiento Diecinueve de Abril and died when the hideout where he was being held was found and attacked by the *army on January 4, 1979. M-19 was said to have killed him to prevent his being freed in the attack.

ESCUELA NAVAL DE CADETES. Naval School, located in *Cartagena, founded in 1935. There have been three naval schools in Colombia's history: the Escuela Naútica, 1822-1823; the Escuela Naval Nacional, 1907-1910; and the Escuela Naval de Cadetes.

ESCUELA REPUBLICANA. The Republican School, founded September 25, 1850. It was a political pressure group whose membership came largely from young, upper-class intellectuals and university students with tendencies toward doctrinaire liberalism and romantic socialism. See the related terms GOLGOTAS and SOCIEDAD DEMOCRATICA; for contrast, see SOCIEDAD FILOTEMICA and SOCIEDAD POPULAR.

ESGUERRA–BARCENAS MENESES TREATY OF 1928. Signed March 24 by Manuel Esguerra, Colombia, and José Bárcenas Meneses, Nicaragua. The treaty settled a dispute that had arisen when Nicaragua tried to cede part of the Archipelago of *San Andrés y Providencia to the United States. Nicaragua recognized Colombia's claims to the islands, and Colombia relinquished all claims to the *Mosquito Coast and the adjacent offshore islands Mangle Grande and Mangle Chico. The Mangle islands had previously been claimed by Colombia as part of the Archipelago of San Andrés y Providencia, but they had been occupied by Nicaragua since 1890.

ESLAVA, Sebastián de, 1685-1759. Second Viceroy of *New Granada, 1739-1749; a brother of former President Rafael de Eslava, 1733. His administration dealt with the attacks of Admiral *Vernon, 1740-1742, and the *Vélez Rebellion, 1740.

ESPACIO, El. Liberal daily afternoon *newspaper established in *Bogotá on June 21, 1965, with Jaime Ardila Casamitjana as its proprietor-director. Current circulation is about 25,000.

ESPECTADOR, El. Colombia's oldest daily newspaper, founded in *Medellín, March 22, 1887, by Fidel Cano (1854-1919). Publication of *El Espectador* was temporarily suspended under political pressure from the government several times from 1887-1904 and completely from 1904-1913. It reappeared in 1913 under the direction of Fidel and Gabriel Cano (d. 1981). Publication of the newspaper in Bogotá was initiated in 1915 by Fidel and Luis Cano (d. 1950), and the Medellín press was closed in 1923. Still operated by the Cano family, the newspaper has remained loyal to the *Liberal Party and its ideas; as a result it was suspended at times during the *1950s. Its support for extradiction of Colombian *drug traders led to the 1986 murder of its editor, Guillermo *Cano Isaza. Issued nowadays in three regional editions, it has a circulation of 220,000, slightly ahead of its closest rival, El *Tiempo.

ESPINAL. Commercial and transportation center located at 4° 8'N, 74° 53'W, about 51 kilometers southeast of *Ibagué in the Department of *Tolima. Altitude is 323 meters; average temperature, 26°C; and population in 1985 was 34,980 people. The rolling plain around Espinal is good for *agriculture and *livestock. It is the site of important *railroad workshops, has some reputation as a tourist center, and serves as a major distribution point for the Departments of Huila and Tolima. The settlement of Espinal, originally founded about 1754 on the *hacienda* Llano Grande de Espinal owned by Antonio Vásquez Forero and Manuel Moya Guzmán, was moved to its present site in 1783.

ESTADO. "State," in all senses. This was the title of the constituent elements (the largest administrative subdivisions) of each of the mid-19th-century Colombian federal republics: the *Confederación Granadina, 1858-1861, the *Estados Unidos de Nueva Granada, 1861-1863, and the *Estados Unidos de Colombia, 1863-1885.

ESTADOS UNIDOS DE COLOMBIA. The United States of
Colombia, a federation of sovereign states established by the
*Constitution of 1863, which lasted until 1885. The period of
the United States of Colombia is generally referred to as the
"Liberal Ascendancy" because of the predominance of the
*Liberal Party. See: CONSTITUTION OF 1863; RIONE-
GRO, Convention of; MAP: UNITED STATES OF COLOM-
BIA, 1863-1885

UNITED STATES OF COLOMBIA, 1863–1885

ESTADOS UNIDOS DE NUEVA GRANADA. A federal republic created by the *Pact of Union, 1861, the United States
of *New Granada was an interim government between the
collapse of the *Confederación Granadina, 1861, and the
establishment of the United States of Colombia (*Estados

Unidos de Colombia), 1863. General *Mosquera was the predominant executive.

ESTANCO. A state monopoly in manufacture and retailing of luxuries, such as playing cards, liquor, and *tobacco. Introduced in the mid-18th century, the tobacco *estanco* became an important source of government revenue. In colonial times all tobacco for the *estanco* was imported by the *Casa de Contratación, and none was legally permitted to be grown in *New Granada. After independence, abolition of the tobacco *estanco* was delayed because of its revenue importance and was secured only in May 1850. The *aguardiente estanco* lasted from 1749 to 1838. See also: TAXATION

ESTATUTO DE SEGURIDAD, 1978. A law sanctioned by the administration of President *Turbay Ayala in September 1978, it was intended to control public disorders. The law, according to administration defenders, did little more than codify numerous regulations that had been issued previously as separate laws. Administration critics, however, claimed that the law went much further than any previous ones. The Security Statute prohibited the broadcasting of any kind of material that might incite public disorder. It provided harsh sentences for persons convicted of political crimes and assigned trials for political crimes to military courts. Arrests were frequent under the statute, and so were allegations of torture and police brutality.

ESTER. Opera, written by Rafael *Pombo (libretto) and José María Ponce de León (music). Fernando González Cajiao, *Historia del teatro en Colombia,* designates *Estér* and *Florinda* (by the same authors) as the first operas known to have been composed and written by Colombians. *Estér* was first performed by a group of Italian singers, the Forellini Company, in Bogotá in 1875. Soprano Emilia Benic sang the first performance of *Florinda* in *Bogotá in 1876.

EUCHARISTIC CONGRESS. The first Colombian eucharistic conference was held in *Bogotá in 1913. The XXXIX International Congress, also held in Bogotá, August 18-25, 1968, was visited by Pope *Paul VI, August 22-24.

EUTROPELICA, Tertulia. A literary society of the 1790s, headed by Manuel del Socorro *Rodríguez whose activities included publication of the *Papel periódico . . . ,* Colombia's first important *newspaper. Members of the society, which met in the national library (*Biblioteca Nacional), included Francisco Antonio Rodríguez, José María Valdés, and José María Grueso. See also: TERTULIA

EXCHANGE RATE. The Spanish colonial *peso was the origin of the U.S. dollar, and as long as later *coinages minted silver coins of the same weight, the U.S. and Colombian monetary units remained roughly at par. Colonial *currency was effectively bimetallic, and a bimetallic standard was officially adopted in 1857. But this was followed in 1861 by the issuing of paper money in such quantities as to cause a crisis by 1867. In 1871 a *gold standard was introduced, but excessive paper issues began again in 1885 (see: CLANDESTINE EMISSIONS; PAPER MONEY CRISIS OF 1885-1905). By 1898 the paper peso was down to 2.17 to the dollar. The War of the *Thousand Days (1899-1903) soon reduced it to 18.90 to the dollar, and by the end of the war it was worth barely a U.S. cent. In 1907 the gold standard was reestablished, at 5 pesos to the pound sterling (more or less its traditional value of parity with the dollar). This sterling link was maintained until the *United Kingdom itself was forced off gold: Colombia quickly followed, on September 25, 1931. Like all countries whose economies were based on the export of raw materials and agricultural products, Colombia was unable to maintain the value of her currency in the Great Depression of the 1930s. By 1935 the peso stood at 8.71 to the pound sterling (or 1.765 to the U.S. dollar). In common with many other Third World countries, Colombia adopted a system of multiple exchange rates (varying according to the purpose for which the currency was being bought or sold). And naturally, a parallel black market inevitably sprang up, making yet other rates available in illegal exchange dealings. The following data are therefore only approximate. A floating exchange rate was introduced in 1967.

Colombian pesos to the U.S. dollar	
1937	1.76
1939-1947	1.74
1948-1950	1.95
1951-1956	2.50
1957	4.28
1958	4.84
1959	6.40
1960-1961	6.70

1962-1964	9.00
1965-1966	13.50
1967	15.82
1968	16.95
1969	17.93
1970	19.17
1971	21.00
1972	22.88
1973	24.89
1974	25.76
1975	30.93
1976	34.70
1977	36.78
1978	39.10
1979	44.80
1980	50.92
1981	59.07
1982	70.29
1983	88.77
1984	113.84
1985	172.20
1986	216.00
1987	262.00
1988	332.00
1989	405.44
1990	500.00+

EXECUTIONS OF CARTAGO, see: CARTAGO EXECUTIONS

EXECUTIONS OF 1861.   *Conservative leaders Andrés Aguilar, Plácido Morales, and Ambrosio Hernández were executed on July 19. Their death was a vindictive action ordered by General T. C. de *Mosquera, following the Battle of *Subachoque.

EXPORTS.   *Gold was almost the only important export from colonial New Granada. During the 19th century there was some export of other *minerals, such as *emeralds, and an export agriculture developed. *Coffee became the leading export crop in the last quarter of the century, although *bananas also became important at the turn of the century. *Tobacco, *cacao, *indigo, and *quinine were also sent abroad. *Petroleum exporting began in the 1920s, and the *livestock industry expanded enough to have sufficient surplus to enter the international meat market. After *World War II, a number of nontraditional exports became significant, including *cotton, textiles, clothing, *sugar, cut flowers, and books (see:

PUBLISHING). Illegal drugs, at first *marijuana, later *cocaine, reached significant amounts in the 1970s. The era of coffee as the predominant export peaked in 1955, when it produced 82% of legal export earnings. By 1974 its share had fallen to 43%. But improvement in the world price enabled it to regain 59% in 1980. Petroleum declined from 17.5% in 1949 to 3.5% in 1972, recovering to 4% in 1986. Colombia's total exports have risen from US$260 million in 1928, to US$843 million in 1970, US$4,786 million in 1986, and US$6,545 million in 1988, to which anything from US$200 to US$900 million for illegal narcotic exports should be added. The *United States has long been Colombia's main trading partner, although Colombia has tried to reduce such close dependency. Germany, Sweden, and the Netherlands have always been good customers for Colombian coffee. In the mid-1930s, European countries bought a quarter of Colombia's exports (24% in 1936), but this fell to 1% by the second year of World War II. In 1986, the geographical distribution of exports was as follows:

United States	US$1,853,700,000
EEC countries	1,803,900,000
German Federal Republic	905,100,000
Netherlands	213,700,000
France	149,500,000
Spain	137,500,000
United Kingdom	126,000,000
Latin America except Cuba	596,100,000
*Andean Common Market	175,000,000
Japan	246,300,000
Sweden	156,800,000
COMECON countries	56,300,000

The Colombian Information Service listed major exports in 1988 as follows:

Coffee	US$1,604,000,000
Crude petroleum	726,000,000
Coal	425,000,000
Textiles and garments	357,000,000
Fuel and refined products	300,000,000
Bananas	300,000,000
Flowers	206,000,000
Ferronickel	179,000,000
Plastics	138,000,000
Chemicals	123,000,000

Printed materials	107,000,000
Emeralds	90,000,000
Cotton fiber	73,000,000
Crustacea and fish	63,000,000
Sugar (raw)	55,000,000
Footwear	42,000,000
Other products	1,017,000,000
TOTAL	5,805,000,000

See also: ECONOMY, The

EXPROPRIATION OF PROPERTIES IN MORTMAIN, see: DISAMORTIZATION DECREE

EXTRADITABLES, Los.   A name used by a paramilitary group of drug dealers. The term is a defiant allusion to the U.S.-Colombian *Extradition Treaties regarding trade in illegal narcotics, and the group's actions are intended to protest the extradition arrangement. In January 1988, Los Extraditables declared total war against "traitors" who supported the U.S.-Colombian agreement. They were responsible for the death of Carlos *Maura Hoyos and the kidnapping and later release of Andrés Pastrana (*Conservative candidate for Mayor of Bogotá) in order to attract attention. Government resistance and efforts to suppress the *drug trade remained firm, however, and Los Extraditables declared a unilateral truce on July 27, 1990, in an effort to promote negotiations with the government. Nevertheless, they were responsible for a wave of kidnappings from August 1990 to May 1991. Journalists Diana Turbay, daughter of ex-President *Turbay Ayala, and Marina Montoya were murdered by drug traffickers, and Francisco Santos, an editor of El *Tiempo, and Maruja Pachón, director of the Cinematographic Development Institute, were among those kidnapped and released while the *Asamblea Constituyente de 1991 was negating the extradition treaties.

EXTRADITION TREATIES.   Agreements were concluded between Colombia and the United States in 1979 and March 1982 for the prosecution of dealers in the illegal *drug trade. Those accused of criminal activities in narcotics cases could be extradited from Colombia to stand trial in the United States under the laws and legal system of the U.S. The intent was to counteract the assassination threats and other forms of intimidation that had made prosecution difficult in Colombia. The first person so extradited was Hernán Botero Moreno in 1984. His name was promptly adopted by one of the drug-supporting *death squads, who redoubled their efforts. In December 1986 the Colombian *Supreme Court declared the treaty unconstitutional because it had been signed by Interior Minister Germán Zea Hernández as acting President, and not by the President himself as Colombian law required. President Virgilio *Barco, availing himself of his executive authority under the *state of siege then in force, reinstated the treaty by presidential decree, December 15, 1986. This enabled leading drug dealer Carlos *Lehder Rivas to be extradited in February 1987, and he was convicted and sentenced in Miami in May 1988. Sixteen extraditions had been carried out when further extraditions were blocked by the Supreme Court, on June 25, 1987, when it overturned the presidential decree. When, however, the assassination of presidential candidate Luis Carlos *Galán was attributed to the drug dealers, President Barco took advantage of the national public reaction to decree the reinstatement of the treaty (August 18, 1989). On October 4, the Colombian Supreme Court reversed its earlier extradition ruling and upheld the decree. There were nevertheless strong feelings in many quarters, voiced by Gabriel *García Márquez among others, that the treaty was demeaning to a sovereign state. By late 1989 the United States had requested the extradition of Pablo Emilio *Escobar Gaviria, Gonzalo Rodríguez Gacha (d. December 15, 1989), the Ochoa Vásquez brothers (Jorge, Fabio, and Juan David) and the Rodríguez Orjuela brothers. A total of 27 extraditions had been carried out when the process was declared illegal by the *Constitution of 1991.

EZPELETA GALDEANO, José de, 1742-1823. Viceroy of *New Granada, 1789-1797. He organized a police force in *Bogotá, 1791; finished the Puente Común over the River Funza, 1792; opened the first theater in Bogotá, 1792; and arrested and tried *Nariño for publishing *The *Rights of Man*, 1793-1794.

-F-

F.N.C., see: FERROCARRILES NACIONALES DE COLOMBIA

FABRICA DE HILADOS Y TEJIDOS DEL HATO. More commonly known as FABRICATO, a commercial establishment that, after COLTEJER (the *Compañía Colombiana de Tejidos), is perhaps Colombia's most important textile firm. The company is said to have been founded in 1920 by Carlos Mejía Restrepo in collaboration with Lázaro Mejía S. & Co., Ramón Echavarría & Co., and Miguel Navarro & Co. Production facilities were formally opened in *Medellín on August 7, 1923, according to José Solís Moncado, *Almanaque histórico de Antioquia*. Ramón Echavarría and Enrique Echavarría were early administrators of the company. President Pedro Nel *Ospina is said to have attended the opening ceremony.

FACATATIVA. Agricultural, livestock-raising, commercial, and industrial center on the *Sabana de Bogotá (4° 49'N, 74° 21'W), 42 kilometers northwest of *Bogotá in the Department of *Cundinamarca. Situated at an altitude of 2,586 meters, its average temperature is 14°C, and population in 1985 was 43,765 people. The name "Facatativá" is said to be derived from an Indian expression meaning a strong wall or garden at the end of the plain (*cercado fuerte al fin de la llanura*), and the city is located near the Stones of *Tunja and the *cercado de los Zipas*. It was the place where *Tisquesusa was killed by Alonso Dominguez, one of *Jiménez de Quesada's men, during the Spanish conquest. The city was founded from 1561-1564 by Alonso de Olalla and Hernando de Alcócer. Since 1909 Facatativá has been a *railroad junction for the *Girardot and *Sabana lines.

FAJARDO RUBIO, Julio, 1910-. Painter, sculptor, ceramist, born in *Honda. He studied painting in the Escuela de Bellas Artes in *Bogotá and in Chile and Argentina. In 1938 he established himself in *Ibagué. His works have been described as *costumbrismo* in subject and tone, and his paintings use oil and fresco techniques. In 1956 he studied ceramics in Italy. His sculptural pieces include an elaborate commemorative monument to Alfonso *Lopez Pumarejo.

FALANGE. Literally, a "phalanx"; the name was used by a radical conservative, ultranationalist Catholic youth movement founded in Spain in 1933 by the son of deposed dictator Primo de Rivera. It advocated a corporatist society reminiscent of Salazar's Portugal or Benito Mussolini's Italy. Imitative groups followed in Hispanic America (in Chile, for example), often as offshoots of a Conservative Party. Laureano *Gómez was supposed to have organized a group like this, the *Camisas negras* ("Black shirts") within the Colombian *Conservative Party.

FANAL, see: FEDERACION AGRARIA NACIONAL

FARC, see: FUERZAS ARMADAS REVOLUCIONARIAS DE COLOMBIA

FAYAD DELGADO, Alvaro. Psychologist, known as El Turco, leader of the *Movimiento Diecinueve de April *guerrilla group. He was killed by police in *Bogotá, March 12, 1986, and was succeded by Carlos *Pizarro Leongómez.

FEDECAFE, see: FEDERACION NACIONAL DE CAFETEROS

FEDERACION AGRARIA NACIONAL. A Church-organized National Land Federation (FANAL) formed in 1946; it took part in some of the land invasions of the 1960s.

FEDERACION NACIONAL DE CAFETEROS. Abbreviated FEDECAFE, or FEDERACAFE, it is a private corporation created in Medellín in June 1927 at the close of the Second National Congress of Colombian Coffee Growers. It was designed to represent *coffee producers, many of them small farmers, and to protect them from the economic power of the few large buyers who dominated the industry. Its eleven-member board has six representatives of the growers, one from the *Caja de Crédito Agrario, Industrial y Minero, and one member each from the ministries of foreign affairs, finance, development, and agriculture. FEDECAFE finances the purchase and storage of 60 to 75% of the coffee crop, which enables it to guarantee a support price and also to supply the domestic market at prices below costs. This latter stimulates a contraband export trade. FEDECAFE conducts a forceful promotion campaign in consumer countries, with the character Juan *VALDEZ as its archetypal Colombian small farmer. The association also has numerous social and economic programs to promote the sale of coffee and to raise the standard of living for coffee producers. It carries out research and provides rural areas with roads, water resources, schools, and health care. By encouraging the replacement of Colombia's traditional mild arabic coffee with the higher-yielding casturra variety, it helped increase the annual harvest from 8 million 60-kilogram bags in 1974-1975 to 12.5 million bags in 1979-1980.

FEDERACION NACIONAL DE COMERCIANTES. A special-interest group, or *gremio económico, FENALCO, was organized in Bogotá in May 1945 to protect merchants and commercial interests. FENALCO was organized in reponse to trade policies of the *López Pumarejo administration, which sought to end alleged price abuses that had developed during *World War II. FENALCO members found the government measures excessive. Originally workers and employees were excluded from membership, and the association opposed trade and labor regulations. It evolved into what has been described as a decentralized, service-oriented federation with numerous regional offices. See also: ASOCIACION NACIONAL DE INDUSTRIALES

FEDERAL WAR, see: REBELLION OF 1859-1862

FEDERALISM-CENTRALISM, see: CENTRALISM-FEDERALISM

FEDERMANN, Nicholas, 1506-1541. A German-speaking conquistador named to succeed Ambrosius *Dalfinger in 1533. He led a joint expedition with Georg von *Speyer in 1535, first eastward to Coro and Cape Vela, then back to Barquisimeto, following Speyer to *Casanare and *Meta. He arrived at the *Sabana de Bogotá in 1538, where he met *Belalcázar and *Jiménez de Quesada and returned with them to Spain in 1539. He was the author of *Indianische Historia,* or *Historia indiana,* published in 1557. The name is also written "Nicholaus Federmann of Ulm."

FENALCO, see: FEDERACION NACIONAL DE COMERCIANTES

FERNANDEZ DE ENCISO, Martín, 1469-1530. Cartographer. He sailed from Santo Domingo to *Cartagena and along the coast from the latter to *San Sebastián de Urabá. He abandoned San Sebastián and founded *Santa María la Antigua del Darién in 1510, but he was later deposed by *Nuñez de Balboa. He is the author of *Suma de geografía* (Seville, 1519), which describes the Colombian coastline.

FERNANDEZ DE LUGO, Pedro (d. 1536). Conquistador who became Governor of *Santa Marta in 1536. His expedition brought with it a number of important explorers, including Gonzalo *Suárez Rendón and Gonzalo *Jiménez de Quesada. He attempted to expand the territory controlled by the Spanish, but little was accomplished during his short term in office. His son, Alonso Luis de *Lugo, abandoned his father's command and sought his own commission from Spain, and Pedro died a few months after arriving in Santa Marta.

FERNANDEZ DE OVIEDO Y VALDES, Gonzalo, 1478-1557. Also known as *Sobrepeña,* he was born in Madrid and first came to America with the expedition of *Pedrarias in 1514. Fernández de Oviedo was in *Santa María la Antigua del Darien, 1514-1515, and in Santa María and elsewhere on the coasts of Colombia, 1520-1523 and 1526-1527. He was in Central America 1527-1530, and settled in Santo Domingo, 1530-1537. In 1532 he was appointed General Chronicler of the Indies and is best known for his *Historia general y natural de las indias, islas y tierra firme del mar océano,* the first portion of which was published in Toledo, 1526. He was also the author of *El sumario de la historia natural de las Indias* (1526) and, among other things, a novel entitled *Claribalte, Libro del muy esforzado e invencible cavallero* (1519). The last was written while Fernández de Oviedo was in Santa Marta, which leads Héctor Orjuela to call it the first novel written in the New World, although not the first to deal with Latin American themes.

FERNANDEZ DE PIEDRAHITA, Lucas, 1624-1688. A native of *Bogotá, he entered the Church and became the curate at Fusagasugá (4° 21'N, 74° 22'W, *Cundinamarca), a canon of the cathedral in *Bogotá, and Bishop of *Santa Marta after 1669. He was captured by pirates, 1677, but released by Henry *Morgan. He was the author of *Historia general de las conquistas del Nuevo Reino de Granada,* first published in Antwerp, 1688.

FERNANDEZ DE SOLIS Y VALENZUELA, Fernando, 1616-1677. Colombian author of *LA LAUREA CRITICA.* He was the brother of Pedro de *Solís y Valenzuela. Fernando is also known as Bruno de Valenzuela, the name he used after entering the *Carthusians in Segovia (Spain) after 1633.

FERNANDEZ MADRID, José, 1789-1830. Physician, legislator, poet, journalist; born *Cartagena, February 9; died Barnes (England), June 28. He joined the patriot cause in Cartagena, 1810, and attended the Congress of the *Provincias Unidas de Nueva Granada, 1812-1814. He was a member of the governing triumvirate of the United Provinces, 1814, and President of the United Provinces, 1816. After a period of exile in Cuba, 1816-1825, he was appointed Colombia's diplomatic representative to France and England, 1825-1830. He was, at times, editor of *El Argos,* a poet, and author of two plays, *Atala* and *Guatimoc, o Guatimozín.*

FERROCARRIL DE ANTIOQUIA, see: ANTIOQUIA RAILROAD

FERROCARRIL DE BOLIVAR, see: BOLIVAR RAILROAD

FERROCARRIL DE GIRARDOT, see: GIRARDOT RAILROAD

FERROCARRIL DE LA DORADA, see: DORADA RAILWAY

FERROCARRIL DE LA SABANA, see: SABANA RAILWAY

FERROCARRIL DE SANTA MARTA, see: SANTA MARTA RAILWAY

FERROCARRIL DE TOLIMA, see: TOLIMA RAILROAD

FERROCARRIL DEL ATLANTICO, see: ATLANTIC RAILROAD

FERROCARRIL DEL NORTE, see: NORTHERN RAILROAD

FERROCARRIL DEL PACIFICO, see: PACIFIC RAILROAD

FERROCARRIL DEL SUR, see: SOUTHERN RAILROAD

FERROCARRILES NACIONALES DE COLOMBIA. The Colombian National Railways (F.N.C.), a state enterprise formed in 1954, that monopolizes railroad operation in Colombia. Although part of the rail network was taken over by the government before *World War I, most remained in private ownership. The F.N.C. was formed to take over and coordinate the operation of the various existing lines, most of which were unconnected. These lines became operating divisions of the new system. Since then, some of the lines have been linked up, although the new routes created were often very circuitous (see: RAILROADS). Until the 1970s, the National Railways deteriorated from inadequate maintenance and investment.

Passenger traffic declined by 78% in the 1960s. Since then, however, World Bank loans have begun to permit some rehabilitation and modernization. Because of rail's advantage for long-distance transport of bulk cargo, the National Railways were still carrying 18% of the nation's freight traffic in 1975.

FICTION, see: LITERATURE

FIGUEROA, Baltasar de Vargas, d. 1667. Painter, born in *Bogotá, the son of Gaspar de Figueroa (d. 1658), and grandson of Baltasar Figueroa the Elder, both of whom were also painters. His father, Gaspar, organized a well-known art school in Bogotá, where his son was trained to continue the tradition established by his grandfather. Baltasar's works were essentially on religious themes, and one of his best-known works is a portrait of the Archbishop Fray Juan de *Arguinao. He is also said to have been the teacher of Gregorio *Vásquez Arce y Ceballos.

FISHING. Spain's contribution to the defeat of the Turks at Lepanto in 1571 was rewarded by a papal dispensation from meatless Fridays. Fish ceased thereafter to be an essential part of Hispanic diets, and the fishing industry declined. For much of Colombia's history its fishing was of little economic importance. What existed was riverine or inshore. A lack of good sailors was a major factor in the failure of Vice President *Santander's ambitious plans for a Colombian *navy in the 1820s. Since *World War II there has been some development of fisheries, in part to provide a nontraditional export. The 1986 catch was 80,400 metric tons. The bulk of this was freshwater fish, particularly from the *Magdalena River. Only 25.6% were caught at sea: 15.2% in the Pacific Ocean and 10.4% in the Caribbean.

FLAG, National. The Colombian national flag is an unadorned tricolor of horizontal stripes. The uppermost band is yellow and twice as thick as the blue and red bands (equal in size) below it. This banner was adopted November 26, 1861, and evolved from flags whose origins go back at least to 1806 when the Venezuelan patriot Francisco de *Miranda took the red and gold of Spain and separated them by a strip of blue, symbolizing the ocean dividing the soon-to-be insurgent Hispanic Americas from the mother country. Miranda's tricolor became the basis for the flag used by the first Venezuelan Republic, 1810-1811. In 1815, the *Provincias Unidas de la Nueva Granada also adopted a tricolor, but one of yellow, green, and red, with the green symbolic of the mountain landscape. The *Congress of Cúcuta, on July 12, 1821, maintained the tricolor pattern for the Republic of *Gran Colombia, but opted for Miranda's blue band rather than the green of the United Provinces. When Gran Colombia dissolved, the *República de Nueva Granada adopted a tricolor banner with the same colors on May 8, 1834, but one with vertical instead of horizontal stripes. This was replaced with the present flag in 1861. Rules regulating the use of the flag were approved on November 9, 1949. Although the national flag is unadorned, the merchant marine jack bears a single white star in a red-bordered blue ellipse in the center of the flag. The naval ensign, which is also the presidential standard, has the *ARMS OF THE REPUBLIC in a red-bordered white circle.

FLORENCIA.   Capital of *Caquetá, located at 1° 36′N, 75° 31′W, with a population of 77,598 people (1985 estimate); an altitude of 450 meters; and an average temperature of 26°C. The city, in the eastern foothills of the *Cordillera Oriental, about 572 kilometers from Bogotá, was founded December 25, 1908, by *Capuchin missionaries, and serves as a commercial and agricultural entry to the *Amazon region.

FLORES, Juan José, 1800-1864.   General, Venezuelan-born veteran of the wars of independence; President of Ecuador, 1830-1835 and 1839-1845. Flores was involved in attempts to annex *Pasto and parts of the *Cauca Valley to Ecuador in 1830 and 1840. He was a nearly continual threat 1845-1855 because of projected expeditions involving *New Granada and other nations. He was the Ecuadoran commander in the war with New Granada, 1863.

FLOREZ, Manuel Antonio, ca. 1723-1799 Viceroy of *New Granada, 1776-1782. He implemented various educational proposals made by Manuel Guirior and Francisco Antonio *Moreno y Escandón. He brought the first secular printer, Antonio Espinosa de los Monteros, to New Granada, 1777, and converted the abandoned *Jesuit press to public use, 1779 (see: PRINTING, Introduction of). The Crown transferred his authority over treasury matters to the Regent-Visitor-Intendant Juan Francisco *Gutiérrez de Piñeres, whose methods provoked the *Comuneros Revolt, 1780-1782. When Flórez's repeated warnings about the impending revolt went unheeded, he shrewdly moved to *Cartagena to take command of military operations against the British, leaving Gutiérrez de Piñeres to bear full blame for inciting the Comuneros Revolt.

FLOREZ DE OCARIZ, Juan, 1612-1692. Royal accountant. He arrived in *New Granada in 1626, and he is best known as the author of the extensive genealogical-historical compilation *Genealogías del Nuevo Reino de Granada,* the first part of which was published in Madrid, 1674.

FLOTA MERCANTE GRANCOLOMBIANA. An international shipping fleet established in 1946 with funding from Colombia, 45%; Venezuela, 45%; and Ecuador, 10%. A major impetus in Colombia came from the national *coffee producers. Venezuela withdrew in 1953, leaving the fleet 80% Colombian and 20% Ecuadoran.

FLOTA SYSTEM. The *flota,* or fleet, was the name applied to a system of armed convoys designed to protect Spanish shipping from hostile attack. Normally, the isthmus fleet, or *galeón,* left San Lúcar, Spain, in August, sailing first to *Panama and then to *Cartagena. It left *New Granada in January, joined the *flota* from New Spain at Havana, Cuba, in March, and sailed for Spain in early summer. Formally instituted around 1564, the fleet system was used intermittently until 1789, although voyages to Cartagena were suspended after 1740. See: CARTAGENA; GALLEON

FOOD PROCESSING, see: MANUFACTURING INDUSTRY

FOREIGN AID. Since *World War II, Colombia has been one of Latin America's major recipients of foreign loans and assistance. As one of the first to adopt the policy of comprehensive government-directed economic planning, it became the leading beneficiary of the United States Alliance for Progress. Between 1961 and 1972 Columbia's educational system alone received US$107.2 million worth of aid from the United States. On Colombian initiative, the International Consultative Group (I.C.G.) was set up in 1962 to coordinate external assistance in economic infrastructure, housing, *education, and the development of such basic industry as steel production.

The members of the I.C.G. include the Inter-American Development Bank, the World Bank, and the governments of thirteen developed nations (the U.S., Canada, Japan, and ten in Europe). More than $800 million was received in grants and loans from this and other sources in just four years, 1961-1964. Military assistance, mainly from the U.S., has also been significant. By 1975, when the U.S. ended nonmilitary assistance, US$101.8 million in military aid (mostly loans) had been received. This had begun with the first U.S. military mission in 1939, but most of it was subsequent to a bilateral Mutual Assistance Treaty of 1952, and it included training Colombian officers for counterinsurgency methods at the Escuela de las Américas (more than 5,500 by 1973).

Between 1946 and 1984 Colombia received a total amount in international aid of US$6.601 billion. Of this, the U.S. had provided $988.8 million in loans and $382 million in grants.

FOREIGN DEBT.   Unrealistic expectations of *Gran Colombia's economic prospects held by British investors in the early 1820s led the new country to take on far too much indebtedness. The nation defaulted on its foreign debt in September 1826, and payment was not resumed until the 1860s. Colombia's poor credit record practically closed the London money market to it by the 1880s (see: LONDON LOANS), and the *Nuñez government turned to New York. The *Roldán-Passmore renegotiation of 1896 was rendered inoperative by the War of the *Thousand Days, and the *Holguín-Avebury Convention of 1906 replaced it. This and the return to the *gold standard the following year restored the country's credit. No immediate advantage was taken of this, however, and in 1923 the foreign debt stood at only US$24.1 million. As elsewhere in Latin America the later 1920s were an era of heavy borrowing, mainly for infrastructure development. By 1932 when the Depression forced a partial suspension of payments, the debt had reached US$236 million. Colombia defaulted in 1935 and renegotiated in 1940, 1942, 1944, and 1949. By 1945 the debt had fallen to US$135 million. Although borrowing was then resumed, it was restrained by Latin American standards. It reached US$642 million by 1956, and US$3.82 billion (250% of annual export earnings) in 1974. As a percentage of export earnings, it then steadily declined, and Colombia enjoyed the best record of foreign debt management of all Latin America. By late 1980 the debt was only US$800 million, or 21% of export earnings. The expansionist policies of the *Turbay Ayala administration, however, changed the situation somewhat. Colombia began to borrow at a rapid rate. By 1982 there was a deficit on current account of US$2.9 billion and the foreign debt rose to US$12.525 billion by 1984 and US$15.685 billion (70% of its public debt) by mid-1987. In spite of this, Colombia still enjoys a favorable reputation and a comfortable foreign debt burden, relatively speaking.

FOREIGN INVESTMENT. Pre–*World War I foreign investment was mostly in *mining and *railroads, and mostly British. Eleven of the country's fourteen railways were British owned, representing by 1913 an investment of £6,139,000. Even non-British investments were channeled through London, as with the French-owned but U.K.-registered New Emeralds Co., Ltd., of Colombia, established in 1892. After *World War I, the United States replaced the *United Kingdom as Colombia's main source for foreign investment. Outside the *petroleum sector, little of this went into industry, which remained largely Colombian financed and owned (except in the sense that many Colombian entrepreneurs of the early 20th century were naturalized immigrants). After *World War II, however, foreign investment widened its range. Recent estimates show that foreign investment accounts for 45% of Colombia's chemical industry, 63% of the paper industry, 70% of rubber, 10% of food processing, and 7% of the textiles. Foreign ownership is also substantial in electrical machinery and equipment and in timber and wood products. Entry into the *Andean Common Market required Colombia to place restrictions on new foreign investment, including a total ban on public services, telecommunications, advertising, transportation, insurance, and banking. It was estimated that by 1970 about 15% of the industrial labor force was working for foreign-controlled companies.

FOREIGN LOANS, see: FOREIGN AID; FOREIGN DEBT; LONDON LOANS; NEW YORK LOANS

FOREIGN TRADE. Except for *gold mining, Colombia was of little economic importance in the colonial period. Independence brought aggressive selling by British merchants with overoptimistic visions of wealth in the Indies. During the 1820s and 1830s, Colombia ran large balance-of-payments deficits. From the mid-19th century until the Depression of 1929, economic development, principally in *coffee, permitted a small but steady and more firmly based growth of overseas trade. The 1930s saw a fiscal, trade, and monetary crisis. In Colombia, as in many countries, exchange controls, a more protective tariff, and devaluation followed, encouraging import substitution. *World War II created a shortage of foreign goods to buy and a buildup of foreign exchange reserves. When these were depleted in the brief postwar consumer boom, a balance-of-payments crisis followed in 1951. This was solved by a devaluation and then a boom in trade until coffee prices fell in 1957. This led to a relatively successful government effort to stimulate nontraditional exports. The result was a generally favorable foreign trade position until the *petroleum crisis of 1973. The commercial balance since then has fluctuated as follows (in thousands of U.S. dollars): 1973 (+115,821), 1974 (−180,324), 1975 (−29,607), 1976 (+37,033), 1977 (+415,914), 1978 (+532,000), 1979 (+606,000), 1980 (−482,000), 1981 (−1,725,000), 1982 (−1,933,000), 1983 (−1,397,000), 1984 (−246,000), 1985 (−23,000), and 1986 (+1,890,000). These figures should be adjusted to include the large net inflows from the *drug trade—perhaps as much as US$300 million in 1971 and US$850 million in 1977. See also: ECONOMY, The; EXPORTS; IMPORTS

FOUNDING GENERATION. The group of cultural leaders who, in the terms of Abel Naranjo Villegas, developed or were prominent from 1830 to 1860. Dominant strains of the era were a militant defense of personal rights, democratic egalitarianism, the rise of local bosses, or *caudillos, and a romantic or theatrical sense of life. Ernesto Cortés Ahumada subdivides the period into the Civilian (Civilista) Generation (key date, 1825) and the Founding Generation (key date, 1840). Representative figures of the Civilian Generation included Joaquín *Acosta, Juan de Dios Aranzazu, José María *Córdoba, Salvador *Córdoba, Rufino Cuervo, José Manuel Groot, Pedro Alcántara *Herrán, José Hilario *López, José Ignacio de *Márquez, Manuel María Mosquera, Tomás Cipriano de *Mosquera, ManuelJosé *Mosquera, José María *Obando, Lino de Pombo, Joaquín *Posada Gutiérrez, Francisco de Paula *Santander, and Luis *Vargas Tejada. Important figures of the Founding Generation might include Manuel *Ancízar, José Eusebio *Caro, Eugenio *Díaz, Florentino *González, Ignacio Gutiérrez Vergara, Lorenzo María Lleras, Manuel María Madiedo, Manuel María *Mallarino, Manuel *Murillo Toro, Mariano *Ospina Rodríguez, José María Plata, and Francisco Javier *Zaldúa. See also: GENERATIONS

FRAILES, Los. A group of uninhabited islands (also known as the Archipelago de los Monjes) at the entrance of the Golfo de Maracaibo, long a bone of contention between Colombia and Venezuela. They have some economic value for their guano deposits. The seven islands to the northeast of Margarita were described by Columbus, who called them Los Guardas. Colombia conceded sovereignty over them to Venezuela in 1952.

FRANCE, Relations with. Under the Hapsburgs, hostilities between Spain and France were endemic. *New Granada suffered from attacks by French pirates and privateers beginning with those of Jean and Martin *Cote, 1555-1560. This changed in 1700 with the accession to the throne of Spain of a branch of the French royal house. This led to a political alliance—the family compact (*Pacto de familia*)—and to the introduction of French administrative methods—the so-called Bourbon reforms of the later 18th century. The ideas of the French Enlightenment and the French Revolution of 1789 profoundly affected the attitudes toward life and government of *creoles in the Spanish colonies. Among the most famous of these might be the *Botanical Expedition of 1783-1816 and Antonio *Nariño's translation of The *Rights of Man in 1793. The French Revolution of 1848 inspired the *Liberals with ideas of social equality, democracy, the elimination of capital punishment, and anti-clericalism. It influenced Colombia's abolition of *African slavery in 1851. As in much of Latin America in the 19th century, French culture affected literary tastes and social customs, stimulating the import of luxury goods. French loans and investments, which flowed readily into Mexico, Argentina, Brazil, and Peru, tended to pass Colombia by, with the one exception of the 20 million francs (US$400 million) of the Panama Canal Company (see: COMPAGNIE UNIVERSELLE DU CANAL INTER-OCEANIQUE DE PANAMA). French military influence replaced that of Germany after the latter's defeat in *World War I. It had the most impact on the development of the Colombian *air force, where its influence has survived the country's post-1939 links with the United States. Colombian *law has been strongly influenced by the Napoleonic Code. There is also a heritage of French influence in the national *police force, which was originally organized and trained by a specially recruited French police commissioner in 1891. Formal relationships between France and Colombia have been relatively cordial after an initial diplomatic conflict, the *Barrot Affair, in 1833.

FRANCISCANS. One of four religious orders favored for missionary work among the *Indians in the 16th century. The first Franciscans arrived at least as early as 1509, and the first monastery was established at *Santa María la Antigua del Darién. Other monasteries were founded in *Bogotá, *Tunja, and probably *Pasto, 1550; *Vélez, 1551; Tolú (9° 32'N, 75° 35'W), around 1559; Trinidad de los Muzos and La Palma (5° 22'N, 74° 24'W), 1566; *Cartagena, 1567; *Popayán, 1570; *Anserma, 1572; *Cartago, 1578; *Mompós, 1580; *Ocaña, 1584; *Mariquita, 1585; and *Pamplona, 1590. The Franciscan Province of Santa Fe del Nuevo Reino de Granada was established in 1565.

FREEDOM OF STUDIES LAW. The phrase most often used to refer to the Law of Public Instruction (*Ley sobre Instrucción Pública*), adopted May 15, 1850. It was an ill-concieved attempt to eliminate class distinctions. The law declared that instruction in all fields of science, letters, and arts was unregulated (*libre*), and it abolished all degrees except the doctorates of law, medicine, and theology. This made it possible to practice many professions without a formal degree.

FREEDOM OF THE PRESS, see: CENSORSHIP

FREILE, Juan Rodríguez, see: RODRIGUEZ FREILE, Juan

FRENTE GREMIAL. A union of special-interest groups formed February 20, 1981, by the *Asociación Nacional de Industriales, the Asociaión Nacional de Instituciones Financieras, the Cámara Nacional de la Construcción, the Federación Colombiana de Industrias Metalurgicas, and the *Federación Nacional de Comerciantes. The Frente tried to influence government economic policies, especially those of President *Turbay Ayala, who had previously refused to discuss national economic problems. The President initially ignored the Frente, but eventually sought its cooperation in avoiding a general strike. See also: GREMIOS ECONOMICOS

FRENTE NACIONAL. The National Front, a name given to the union of the *Liberal and *Conservative Parties in 1958. The union, originally projected for twelve years, provided parity between the parties in national appointments and for alternation of the presidency. The Front developed in opposition to the government of General *Rojas Pinilla. In practice, it seemed to work to the benefit of the Conservative Party more than the Liberal, and it provoked unforeseen opposition from those groups not included in the agreement. The arrangement worked for sixteen years, ending in 1974.

FRENTE UNIDO DE ACCION REVOLUCIONARIA. FUAR, as it is commonly known, was a *guerrilla movement established in 1962 by Jorge Eliécer *Gaitán's daughter and son-in-law (Gloria *Gaitán de Valenzuela and Luis Emiro Valenzuela) and Antonio García.

FRENTE UNIDO DEL PUEBLO. The United Front (as it is generally known in English) was a movement led by the priest Camilo *Torres Restrepo. Based on a program he outlined in *Medellín, March 17, 1962, it sought to unite all reform opposition movements into a single alliance to work for social changes within the legal system. Frustrated in its attempt, however, the movement turned to violence, embarking on a policy of armed conflict in January 1966. It disintegrated soon after Torres was killed in February of the same year.

FRESLE, Juan Rodríguez, see: RODRIGUEZ FREILE, Juan

FREYLE, Juan Rodríguez, see: RODRIGUEZ FREILE, Juan

FRIENDS OF THE NATION, Society of, see: AMIGOS DEL PAIS, Sociedad de

FRONTIER DISPUTES, see: BORDERS

FUAR, see: FRENTE UNIDO DE ACCION REVOLUCIONARIA

FUERO. A royal charter bestowing special legal privileges on a corporation or private individual. Fueros granted to the *army and the *Church gave soldiers and clergy the right to trial in military or ecclesiastical courts, circumventing normal legal procedure. Abolition of such special privileges, particularly the eccesiastical fuero, was a controversial issue throughout most of the 19th century. See: SEPARATION OF CHURCH AND STATE

FUERZAS ARMADAS REVOLUCIONARIAS DE COLOMBIA. (FARC). Probably the oldest and largest of Colombia's guerrilla movements, formed on July 20, 1964, by various factions including refugees from *Marquetalia and the Bloque del Sur (which existed from 1964 to 1966). FARC (also known as the FARC-EP: Fuerzas Armadas Revolucionarias de Colombia–Ejército del Pueblo) was headed from 1964-1984 by Pedro Antonio *Marín, better known as Manuel Marulanda Vélez, or Tirofijo. Other important members included Jacobo Arenas (alias Luis Alberto Morantes), Jaime Guaracas, Rigoberto Lozada (Joselo), Miguel Pascuas, Jaime Bustos, Raúl Reyes, Timoleón Jiménez, Isauro Yosa (Major Lister), Alfonso Cano, and Commander Olimpo. FARC was identified with the central committee of the Communist Party (*Partido Comunista de Colombia), and its ideology has been described as "orthodox communism." Its program stressed defense of peasant land claims and a willingness to work within the normal legal system while maintaining independent military action to defend itself. FARC was estimated to have about 5,000 active members in 1983, working from sixteen to twenty different *frentes,* or fronts. After nearly twenty years of guerrilla activity, FARC representatives signed a truce agreement with the government at *La Uribe (*Meta) on May 24, 1984, and FARC members subsequently joined in the formation of the *Unión Patriótica, or Patriotic Union, a political party, to pursue its program within the constitutional political system. FARC did not disband completely, however, and by one estimate, in 1987 there were still armed forces in the Departments of *Meta (five groups), *Caquetá (four groups), *Guaviare (one group), *Cauca (three groups), and *Antioquia (four groups). Elements of the FARC remained active throughout much of 1991. The *Ricardo Franco Front and the Ricardo Franco Comando–Southern Front, splinter groups from the FARC, refused to support the 1984 truce agreements and continued activity independent of the main organization. See: GUERRILLA MOVEMENTS

-G-

GACHETA, Battle of. July 29, 1851 (4° 49'N, 73° 38'W) in *Cundinamarca. Rebel leader Pastor Ospina was captured by

Colonel Evaristo de la Torre, for the government, during the *rebellion of 1851-1852.

GAITAN, Jorge Eliécer, 1898-1948. Lawyer, orator, Liberal reformer; born *Bogotá, January 26; assassinated Bogotá, April 9. In addition to serving in the national legislature, Gaitán was Minister of Education, Minister of Labor, and Mayor of Bogotá. He was the author of *Socialist Ideas in Colombia,* 1924; investigator of the Banana Zone strike (see: UNITED FRUIT COMPANY STRIKE), 1929; founder of a short-lived movement known as the National Leftist Revolutionary Union (*UNION NACIONAL IZQUIERDISTA REVOLUCIONARIA, or UNIR); a presidential candidate in 1946; and leader of the *Liberal Party, 1946-1948. His death in 1948 touched off the riots that became known as the Nueve de Abril, or the *Bogotazo.*

GAITAN DE VALENZUELA, Gloria. Daughter of Jorge Eliécer *Gaitán. In January of 1960, she and her husband, Luis Emiro Valenzuela, a socialist, denounced the *Liberal Party for deserting its principles and proclaimed their intention to revive *gaitanismo.* They formed the Movimiento Popular Revolucionario (M.P.R.), which was not connected to and should not be confused with *López Michelsen's *Movimiento Revolucionario Liberal (M.R.L.). In 1962 she and her husband opted for a more violent course, forming the *Frente Unido de Acción Revolucionaria (see: GUERRILLA MOVEMENTS).

GAITANA, La. A Yalcón *Indian, the mother of a chieftain named Yalcón. Aided by another chieftain, Pigoanza, she led a rebellion to avenge her son's death at the hands of Pedro *Añasco, whom she captured and killed. Her *rebellion, 1539-1541, damaged settlements around Timaná (1° 58'N, 75° 55'W) but was finally subdued.

GALAN, José Antonio, 1749-1782. A military leader of the *Comuneros Revolt, May-October 1781, he was a native of Mongui de Charalá (*Santander). He was of humble background, reared by parents who were modest *tobacco farmers and cloth weavers, and appears to have been only minimally educated. He lived for a short while in *Socorro and served a period in the Fixed Regiment in *Cartagena. His death sentence noted several previous encounters with the law. During the Comuneros Revolt, from May to June 7, 1781, Galán led a successful military campaign in the upper *Magdalena Valley, cutting off links between *Bogotá and *Cartagena just before Juan Francisco *Berbeo entered into negotiations to end the rebellion in *Zipaquirá. In the Department of *Cundinamara, he occupied Las Cuevas (*Facatativá), May 27; *Guaduas, June 4; and *Ambalema, June 25. These victories were influential in the truce negotiations, June 4-8. Galán then returned to Santander, August-October, but renewed hostilities with the Bogotá authorities in September. He led the second campaign more or less independently, partially because he disagreed with the enforcement of the June truce and partially because the royal authorities had issued orders for his arrest in mid-July. He was apprehended in Onzaga (6° 21'N, 72° 49'W), Santander, on October 13, later tried, and executed February 1, 1782. Galán became a symbol of peasant martyrdom and social protest.

GALAN, Luis Carlos, 1943-1989.   Statesman, journalist, orator, and *Liberal politician. Galán studied law at the *Universidad Javeriana, where he began his role as a Liberal journalist by collaborating on a student newspaper called *El Vértice*. He subsequently wrote for *El *Tiempo* and the *Nueva Frontera*, both Liberal publications. He served as Minister of Education in the administration of President *Pastrana Borrero. He had also served as a Senator (1978), Ambassador to Rome, and a member of the municipal government of *Bogotá. He was active in the Liberal reform group known as *Nuevo Liberalismo and received an estimated 800,000 votes as its candidate for President in 1982. He left the Nuevo Liberalismo movement and returned to the main branch of the *Liberal Party at the party convention in *Cartagena in 1988. Galán had called for a moral regeneration in Colombian society and was known for his stand against the *drug trade. He was shot to death while campaigning for the Liberal Party's nomination for president.

GALEANO, Martín, ca. 1500-ca. 1554.   Conquistador, born in Valencia, Spain. He arrived in the West Indies in 1535. He founded *Vélez and served as its *alcalde* (mayor).

GALLEON.   Or *galeón* in Spanish; the name of a sailing vessel and a term used to denote the Spanish treasure fleet during the colonial period. A galleon was a type of large oceangoing ship during the period from 1550-1700, and the mainstay of the *flota* system of convoys by which Spain's links with her American possessions were maintained. The galleon largely replaced both the tiny lateen-rigged caravel and the ungainly carrack, whose overhanging forecastle had made sailing to windward almost impossible. With its narrower, more streamlined hull, lower sterncastle, much reduced and pointed forecastle, and combination of square-rigged fore- and mainmasts and lateen-rigged mizzen, the galleon revolutionized naval warfare. Instead of having to sail close and take an opponent by boarding, the galleon could hold its position to windward and sink the enemy with broadside cannonades. It reminded many contemporaries of the Mediterranean oared galley, from which its name derives. More specifically, the name applied to the isthmus fleet component of the *FLOTA SYSTEM.

GAMINES. Street children; homeless children who have been abandoned or orphaned, or who have run away from their families. They live in makeshift housing and raise money by begging, stealing, or short-term employment. Gangs of *gamines* are known as *pandillas* or *galladas.* There are no accurate records of the number of *gamines,* but estimates of them in Colombia have often run into the thousands in major urban centers. The figure of 20 million has been used for all of Latin America.

GARCIA MARQUEZ, Gabriel, 1927-. Novelist, journalist; born March 27. His best-known work is the novel *Cien años de soledad* (*One Hundred Years of Solitude*), a surrealistic portrait of a Colombian family through several generations. García Márquez was awarded the Neustadt International Prize for Literature in 1972 and the Nobel Prize for Literature in 1982. His work is often described as belonging to the style known as *MAGICAL REALISM, and is part of what has been called the boom in Latin American writing of the 1960s and 1970s. Other major novels include *El otoño del patriarca* (The *Autumn of the Patriarch*), 1975; *El amor en los tiempos del cólera* (*Love in the Time of Cholera*), 1985; and *El general en su labrinto* (*The General in his Labyrinth*), 1989.

GARCIA MORENO, Gabriel, 1821-1875. Conservative President of Ecuador, 1861-1875, known for his extreme identification with Catholicism and the *Papacy. He was responsible for wars with Colombia in July 1862 (when he was taken prisoner on the field of *Tulcán), and in 1863-1864. In 1870 he unsuccessfully sought Colombian backing for his government's protest to Italy for its annexation of the papal province of Latium (Lazzio).

GARCIA ORTIZ–MANGABEIRA TREATY, 1928. Signed November 15, 1928, by Octavio Mangabeira, Brazil, and Laureano García Ortiz, Colombia. The treaty established the Brazilian-Colombian boundary between the Apaporis River and the *Amazon River, clarifying a Treaty of 1907. It also provided for the free navigation of the Amazon, Putumayo, and other rivers. See also: BORDERS

GARCIA ROVIRA, Custodio, 1780-1816. General, patriot, martyr. He was President of *Socorro, 1812-1813; a member of the triumvirate of the *Provincias Unidas de Nueva Granada, 1814-1815; and the last President of the United Provinces, 1816.

GARRAPATA, First Battle of, 1851. August 7, on the Garrapata Plain in the Department of *Tolima. General Rafael Mendoza, for the government, defeated rebel forces under *Conservative Colonel Francisco de Paula Diago during the *rebellion of 1851-1852.

GARRAPATA, Second Battle of, 1876. November 20-22, *Tolima. *Liberal Generals Santos *Acosta and Sergio Camargo, for the government, defeated rebel forces under General Marcelino Vélez during the *rebellion of 1876-1877. The engagement ended with a negotiated settlement.

GAS, Nautral, see: NATURAL GAS

GAVIRIA TRUJILLO, César, 1947-. Economist, *Liberal, elected as President of Colombia for the period 1990-1994. Born in *Pereira, Risaralda, Gaviria graduated from the *Universidad de los Andes (*Bogotá), served as mayor of his native city, and was director of planning for Risaralda. He was elected to the *House of Representatives and had been Vice-Minister of Development before being named Minister of Finance by President *Barco. In 1989, he left the cabinet to become campaign manager for presidential candidate Luis Carlos *Galán, and then he became the candidate first for *Nuevo Liberalismo and then for the Liberal Party when Galán was assassinated. His campaign stressed a tough anti-drug program, and he won 47.5% of the popular vote, thereby becoming the youngest man to be elected President of Colombia in the 20th century. During his term in office Gaviria sought to reach settlements with active *guerrilla groups, tried to bring the illegal *drug trade under control, cooperated with the *Asamblea Constituyente of 1991 and its implementation of a new constitution, and worked to form free-trade agreements in the Western Hemisphere.

GENERAL CONFEDERATION OF LABOR, see: CONFEDERACION GENERAL DEL TRABAJO

GENERAL STRIKE OF 1977, see: PARO CIVICO DE 1977

GENERATIONS. Abel Naranjo Villegas, *Morfología de la nación colombiana* (1965), proposed a scheme for understanding the evolution of Colombian history by dividing the 19th and 20th centuries into different generations. In this context, a generation is understood as a group of people who worked more or less simultaneously within the same social, cultural, and political context, even though their approaches to the phenomena of the time might have been quite different. In some cases it is possible to generalize about the characteristics of a generation; in other cases the extremes of thought and action make this less feasible. In the terminology of Naranjo Villegas, Colombian history has evolved through at least seven generations: I. The *Heroic Generation, 1800-1830; II. The *Founding Generation, 1830-1860; III. The *Costumbrista* Generation, 1860-1880; IV. The *Classic Generation, 1880-1905; V. The *Republican Generation, 1905-1920; VI. The *Modernist Generation, 1920-1950; and VII. The *Socialistic (*Socializadora*) Generation, 1950-1980. Ernesto Cortés Ahumada, *Las generaciones colombianas* (1968), proposed a somewhat overlapping scheme based on fifteen-year cycles. His generational classification includes: I. The *Eponymous, 1795; II. The *Heroic, 1810; III. The *Civilian (*Civilista*), 1825; IV. The *Founding, 1840; V. The *Costumbrista, 1855; VI. The Ideological, 1870; VII. The Humanist, 1885; VIII. The *Republican, 1900; IX. The *Centenary, 1915; X. The Modernist Political, 1930; XI. The Bi-Front (*Bifronte*), 1945; and XII. The Urban-Social, 1960. The Naranjo Villegas terms have a strong literary orientation. Cortés Ahumada and others have added terms such as "Pre-Centenary" and "Centenary," which are more political in nature. Some of these can be correlated, more or less, with the Naranjo Villegas classification. Still others have used designations such as Los *Nuevos, *Post-Nuevos, Nameless Generation, State of Siege, Mid-Century, Cuadernícola, *Piedra y Cielo, Nadaísta (*NADAISMO), Cántico, Violencia, and Canapé to describe groups of the 20th century.

GENOY, Battle of.   February 2, 1821, *Nariño. General Manuel Valdés and patriot forces were defeated by royalists under Colonel Basilio García.

GEOGRAPHY.   Colombia's *area of 1,138,400 square kilometers (440,000 square miles) makes it the fourth largest nation of South America and fifth largest in Latin America (smaller only than Brazil, 8,511,965 square kilometers; Argentina, 2,766,889 square kilometers; Peru, 1,285,216 square kilometers; and Mexico, 1,972,547 square kilometers). Its topography is dominated by three parallel ranges of the *ANDES, running roughly from southwest to northeast across the nation. The *population, now more urban than rural, is mostly in the plateaus, savannahs (see: SABANA), and basins, among these cordilleras and in the valleys of the two major rivers, the *Magdalena and the *Cauca, which flow between them. The lowlands along the western (Pacific) shore and the vast area east of the Andes (the *LLANOS ORIENTALES) and southeast toward the *Amazon region are still only sparsely populated, although they account for more than half of the national territory. Overall the terrain makes communication difficult. *Railroads and *highways require circuitous routes that have made them expensive to build and maintain. The resulting isolation of different parts of the country has produced a strong sense of regionalism, which has contributed a great deal to the tumultuous history of the nation. Although the Andes are prone to *earthquakes, they are also rich in *minerals, and their rivers provide an easy source of *energy and power. See also: ADMINISTRATIVE UNITS; AGRICULTURE; AIR TRANSPORT; AREA; BORDERS; ECONOMY, The; MAP: GEOGRAPHICAL FEATURES

GERMANY, Relations with.   During the reign of the Holy Roman Emperor Charles V (Carlos I of Spain) a number of Germans took part in the exploration and development of the New World, including the *Welsers in Venezuela. But his less cosmopolitan son, Philip II, preferred to reserve these new lands for the Castilian Spanish. There were no further significant contacts with Germany (unless one counts the exploratory

COLOMBIA
GEOGRAPHICAL FEATURES

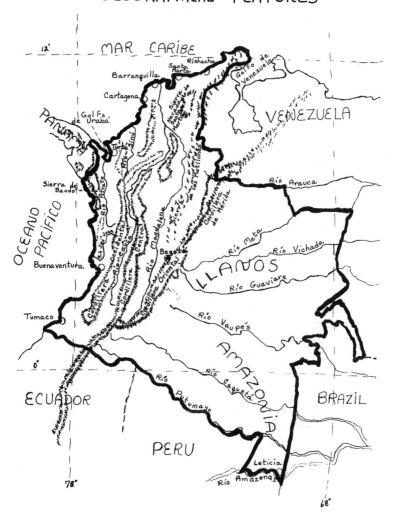

visit of Alexander von *Humboldt, 1799-1804) until the mid-19th century, when Bremen became the chief European market for Colombian *tobacco. Later in the century, Germany also became one of the major buyers of Colombian *coffee. Germany's victory over France in the War of 1870-1871 had a tremendous impact on the elite in Colombia as in other Latin American countries. In early 1872, an educational mission of nine German teachers was brought to Colombia to create normal schools (the *escuelas normales*—teacher-training institutions) needed to implement the *education reforms of 1870. In 1907, a Chilean military mission arrived to reform the Colombian *army along German lines. German pre–*World War I investment and banking in Latin America favored the ABC countries—Argentina, Brazil, and Chile—but Germans pioneered Colombian *air transportation in the years immediately following the war. The *Antioquia Railroad was also built with German capital. Such ties with Germany (which included a limited but influential immigration) helped account for Colombia's neutrality in World War I. In contrast, during *World War II, the pro-U.S. policy of President Eduardo *Santos led to a diplomatic break, and in November 1943, under his successor, Alfonso *López Pumarejo, Colombia declared war on Germany. German properties in Colombia, including the airlines, were expropriated, and immigrants who had kept their German nationality were expelled or interned. Since the war, Colombian relations with the new Federal Republic have been friendly. West Germany became the country's second largest trading partner (after the U.S.), both as a market for Colombian goods, particularly coffee (see: EXPORTS) and as a source of *imports. Militarily, West German influence has been strong in the Colombian *navy.

GIL DE TABOADA Y LEMOS, Francisco, 1733-1810. Viceroy of *New Granada, 1789. He tried to suppress contraband on the Atlantic Coast and to reduce expenses in administration. He established free navigation on the *Atrato River.

GILIJ, Felipe Salvador, 1721-1789. *Jesuit missionary. He enrolled at the *Universidad Javeriana, *Bogotá, in 1743, and was ordained in 1748. He served 18 years, 1749-1767, as a missionary to the *Indians in the Orinoco River basin until he was forced to leave *New Granada with the other members of his order. Father Gilij was the author of *Ensayo de historia americana, o sea historia natural, civil y sacra de los reinos, y de las* *provincias de tierra firme en la América meridional,* published in Spanish in *Bogotá, 1955, but originally published in Italian in Rome, 1780-1784.

GIRARDOT. Important transportation and tourist center located at 4° 18′N, 74° 48′W, in the Department of *Cundinamarca. Altitude is 289 meters; average temperature, 27°C; and population 65,281 people (1985 estimate). The *municipio* and city, named for Atanasio *Girardot, were officially established October 9, 1852, although small informal settlements had existed before.

GIRARDOT, Atanasio, 1791-1813. Colonel; born in *Medellín, May 8; died in Venezuela, September 30. He was among the patriots at *Bajo Palacé, 1811; with the armies of the Provincias Unidas, 1812-1813; and part of the Admirable Campaign (*Campaña Admirable), 1813. He is remembered as a heroic martyr for his action in the Battle of *Bárbula.

GIRARDOT RAILROAD. A line linking *Girardot (Cundinamarca) and the *Magdalena River, with connections to nearby *Bogotá. It was authorized by the government in 1880, and construction was undertaken by Francisco J. *Cisneros in 1881. Cisneros completed the work as far as *Tocaima by 1885, but service with Bogotá was not inaugurated until 1909, after the Girardot Railroad joined the *Sabana Railway line at *Facatativá. See also: RAILROADS

GIRON CONVENTION. An agreement on March 1, 1829, that temporarily ended war with Peru. It provided for a limited truce and for further negotiations toward a boundary settlement.

GOBIERNO, see: GOVERNMENT

GODO. Literally, a "Goth." In Hispanic America it was used in the late colonial and early republican periods as a pejorative term for a *Peninsular Spaniard or a conservative who held a Spanish-like political philosophy. See also: CHAPETON

GOD'S MINUTE, see: MINUTO DE DIOS

GOLCONDA MOVEMENT. A reform movement initiated by a group of approximately 50 Catholic priests in 1968. Meeting in

July at an estate named Golconda (near Viotá, *Cundinamarca) and again in December at *Buenaventura (Valle del Cauca), the group issued what became known as the Golconda Declaration. Inspired by Pope Paul VI's encyclical *Populorum progessio* (1967), the conclusions of the Latin American Bishops Conference (*Consejo Episcopal Latinoamericana—CELAM) in Medellín (1968), the career of Father Camilo *Torres (1929-1966), and the patronage of the Bishop of Buenaventura, Gerardo Valencia Cano (1917-1971), the statement repudiated the *Liberal and *Conservative Parties and the traditional oligarchy. It called for an end to foreign influences in national economic development and encouraged militant social revolution. The Golconda Movement was important in 1969 and 1970, although the disparate elements that composed it were not able to agree on a concerted program of action.

GOLD. Gold *mining in Colombia dates from pre-Columbian times. *Indians mined and/or traded gold throughout Colombia, but deposits were especially rich in the *Antioquia and *Chocó regions. Gold was produced through excavation (shaft mining) and placer mining. Based on the classification developed by Robert West, major gold mining regions in colonial Colombia included the *Cauca Valley, with major sites at *Anserma, *Cartago, *Popayán, and Almaguer (1° 55'N, 76° 50'W); the Pacific lowlands, including the *Chocó and Barbacoas (1° 41'N, 78° 8'W); *Antioquia, especially *Buriticá, *Santa Fe de Antioquia, Cáceres (7° 35'N, 75° 31'W), and Zaragoza (7° 30'N, 74° 52'W); the *Magdalena Valley, with locations at *Mariquita, *Ibagué, Remedios (7° 2'N, 72° 42'W), *Neiva, San Lucas, and San Francisco; and the *Cordillera Oriental in the *Bucarramanga-*Pamplona region. Germán Colmenares has distinguished three distinct periods of gold mining in the colonial period. Peak production cycles 1550-1640 and 1680-1800 were interrupted by a period of stagnation, 1640-1680. The first production cycle seems to have flourished in the highlands, based largely on Indian labor, while the second was more concentrated in the Chocó and much more dependent on *African slavery. Mining, principally gold, provided the major source of wealth from Colombia throughout the colonial period. During the 17th century, gold from Colombia (*New Granada) is said to have reached as much as 39.1% of total world production. As late as the 1830s, Colombia still accounted for 16.15% of the world's production, but the percentage declined rapidly after the 1840s, accounting for less than 1% of total world production in 1926. The largest part of the gold mined in Colombia was exported, leaving the gold-producing regions relatively poor and under-developed in spite of the wealth produced. Nevertheless, there has been considerable growth in recent years. Eight tons were mined in 1977, 14 tons in 1983, 36 tons in 1985, and 42 tons in 1986. Colombia has now overtaken Chile (which mines about 20 tons a year) and is second in Latin America only to Brazil, where output has been expanding very fast in the last few decades and is now estimated at 80 tons a year. See also: BURITICA; PLATINUM; ZANCUDO, El

GOLD MUSEUM. The Museo del Oro, or the Gold Museum, in *Bogotá is owner of the largest collection of pre-Hispanic *Indian goldwork in the world. It was organized in 1939 when Julio Caro and Luis Angel *Arango, director and assistant director of the *Banco de la República, were authorized to buy examples of pre-conquest goldwork. Among the major styles distinguishable in the present collection are the *Calima, *Darien, *Muisca, *Quimbaya, *Sinú, *Sierra Nevada de Santa Marta, and *Tolima.

GOLD STANDARD. The *patrón de oro,* or gold standard, in Colombia has varied since independence. Bimetallism—having a currency based on the values of both *gold and *silver—is inherently unstable because of the fluctuations of the relative values of these two metals. The Bank of England's 1815 monetary reform introduced a pure gold standard: silver coins continued to circulate but with a purely nominal value. Due to the *United Kingdom's world financial hegemony, orthodox financial wisdom by the late 19th century required every nation to go on gold with a fixed *exchange rate for its *currency in terms of gold, which meant in effect in terms of the English gold pound, or sovereign. The need for financial respectability to reassure foreign lenders and investors obli-gated most Latin American countries to conform, usually at considerable economic cost. Chile adopted the gold rate in 1895, Costa Rica in 1896, and so on. A gold standard for the Colombian *peso was first adopted in 1871, but could not be sustained. Not until the country became stabilized politically after the War of the *Thousand Days could another attempt be made. The gold standard was reestablished in 1907 at five *pesos* to the pound sterling. Responding to recommendations of the fiscally orthodox *Kemmerer mission of 1923, Colombia maintained this sterling link, with some difficulty, until the Bank of England itself was forced off gold by the Great Depression in September 1931. After World War II, the United States took over Britain's former role as the world's banker, and Colombia, like other Latin American countries, tied her currency to the dollar. There were repeated devaluations, until a floating *exchange rate was adopted in 1967.

GOLFO DE URABA. The Gulf of Urabá is located on the Caribbean Coast of Colombia between 7° 55' and 8° 40'N latitude and 76° 44' and 77° 20'W longitude. It forms the international boundary between *Colombia and *Panama and is bordered internally by the Departments of *Chocó and *Antioquia. It was the scene of settlements early in the conquest period, *San Sebastián de Urabá and *Santa María la Antigua del Darien in 1510, but neither endured very long, and the area has never been highly developed. Perhaps the most important modern settlement is Turbo (8° 2'N, 76° 43'W), an entrepôt in the Department of Antioquia. The name is said to be derived from Arién, a chieftain at the time of European exploration and conquest.

GOLGOTAS. "Golgothas," i.e., radical, doctrinaire *Liberals, 1849-1854. The derisive term compared the extreme measures favored by these reformers to the ultimate Passion of Christ on Golgotha. See the related terms: DRACONIANOS; ESCUELA REPUBLICANA; SOCIEDAD DEMOCRATICA

GOMEZ. For President, see: GOMEZ, Laureano; for presidential candidate, see: GOMEZ HURTADO, Alvaro.

GOMEZ, Laureano, 1889-1965. Engineer, journalist, legislator, *Conservative leader, President of Colombia, 1950-1953. Born in *Bogotá, February 20; died, Bogotá, July 31; he received his engineering degree from the *Universidad Nacional in 1909. He was a congressional leader and cofounder of El *Siglo (1936). He served as Minister of Foreign Relations and presided over the Ninth *International Conference of American States in Bogotá in 1948. He was also Minister to Argentina, 1923-1925, and Minister to Germany, 1931-1932. Ideologically a Hispanist, a Falangist (see: FALANGE), and a partisan President, Gómez was overthrown by a coup d'état in 1953. He later acted as opposition leader from abroad. He agreed to the Pact of *Benidorm and the *Sitges

Accord, and supported the *FRENTE NACIONAL in 1958. He was director of La *Unidad, the Revista Colombiana, and El Siglo. The first portion of his collected works, Obras completas, was published in 1984.

GOMEZ AGUDELO, Pedro Nel, b. 1899. Muralist, painter, architect, engineer; born *Anorí (Antioquia), July 4. After early studies in *Medellín and *Bogotá, his first individual show was held in Bogotá in 1925. He traveled and studied in Italy, 1925-1930, and directed the Institute of Fine Arts in Medellín, 1930-1932. He was responsible for numerous murals in public buildings in Medellín and the capital city, including one in the principal hall of the *Banco de la República in Bogotá (1956).

GOMEZ HURTADO, Alvaro, 1919-. Lawyer, journalist, diplomat; *Conservative Party leader; born *Bogotá, May 8. Gómez Hurtado received his law degree from the *Universidad Javeriana (Bogotá) and was a *Conservative congressional leader, 1940s-1980s. He was a supporter of President *Gómez (his father), 1950-1953, and a leader of the *Independent Conservatives after 1950. He was a candidate for the presidency in 1974, 1986, and 1990, and Presidential *Designado, 1982-1984. He has held diplomatic posts in Europe and the United States and participated in various international conferences. He was director of the Revista Colombiana and El *Siglo; founder of Síntesis económica, a weekly economics review; and author of various works including La Revolución en América (1960), Una política conservadora para Colombia (1969), and La calidad de la vida (1981).

GONGORA, Lionel or Leonel, 1932-. Artist, painter, art teacher; born in *Cartago (Valle del Cauca). He studied art in both the Escuela de Bellas Artes in *Bogotá and the school of fine arts at Washington University, and he taught art at the University of Massachusetts. His drawings and paintings are said to be inspired by the works of Goya, whom he considered the fundamental source of modern expressionism. Major themes include women, human relationships, and the paranoia of modern society. He is known for his sensual line drawings. His works have been exhibited in Europe, the United States, and Mexico, as well as Colombia.

GONZALEZ. For Presidents of colonial New Granada, see: GONZALEZ, Antonio and GONZALEZ MANRIQUE, Francisco; for President of Colombia, 1909-1910, see: GONZALEZ VALENCIA, Ramón; and for Liberal ideologue, see: GONZALEZ, Florentino

GONZALEZ, Antonio, d. 1601. President of the *Nuevo Reino de Granada, 1590-1597. He established private property from Crown estates; began collection of the *alcabala; improved operation of the Las Lajas, La Manga, and Santa Ana *silver mines near *Mariquita; and tried to regulate the currency in circulation.

GONZALEZ, Florentino, 1805-1874. Professor of law, essayist, journalist, legislator, diplomat; born Cincelada (*Santander), July 30; died Buenos Aires (Argentina), January 31. He was Minister of Finance, Justice of the *Supreme Court, Attorney General, and a prominent *Liberal ideologue, 1828-1858. He collaborated with President *Santander, 1832-1840, and was responsible for the introduction of free trade in 1847. He was an expatriate after 1859.

GONZALEZ, Manuel, 1797-1841. Colonel, born San Gil (*Santander); died *Ocaña (Norte de Santander), March 21, 1841. He was a patriot soldier in the independence movement, and his military engagements included the siege of *Callao. In 1840, he was the governor of *Socorro, but he rebelled against the government during the War of the *Supreme Commanders, and proclaimed himself Jefe Superior of the State of Socorro on September 21. He and his supporters were victorious against government forces at the Battle of La *Polonia (September 29). They occupied *Zipaquirá (October 27 and November 25) and attempted to take *Bogotá, but failed at the Battles of *Buenavista and Culebrera (see: *GRAN SEMANA, La). He was decisively defeated at the Battle of *Aratoca (January 9, 1841) and died in *Ocaña before the war was completely ended.

GONZALEZ MANRIQUE, Francisco, ca. 1699-1747. Last President of the *Nuevo Reino de Granada, 1739-1740, and a brother of Antonio González Manrique, President, 1738. He prepared *Cartagena to resist attacks by the English navy.

GONZALEZ VALENCIA, Ramón, 1854-1928. General, agriculturalist, legislator, President of Colombia, August 3, 1909, to August 7, 1910. Born on the *hacienda Chitigá (*Norte de Santander), May 24; died *Pamplona (Norte de Santander), October 4. González Valencia spent his early life as an agriculturalist on various haciendas and then entered military service. During the War of the *Thousand Days he fought in the Battles of *Peralonso and *Palonegro. He was then Minister of War, 1901; Commander of the National *Army; and one of the signers of the treaty that ended the war in *Santander. He was Vice President, 1904-1905, until removed by General *Reyes, and then President, 1909-1910, after the fall of Reyes. He called the convention (*Asamblea Nacional Constituyente y Legislativa) that made the constitutional reforms of 1910, and he presided over the celebrations commemorating the centennial of the declaration of independence (*Acta del 20 de Julio de 1810). In addition to being Governor of *Cundinamarca and Governor of Santander, he was Minister to Venezuela in 1911.

GORANCHACHA. Great civilizer of the *Chibchas. Prophet, demigod, mythical bringer of civilization. He was worshiped at the Temple of Suamo, *Sogamoso. Legends of him frequently were intermingled or confused with those of *Bochica.

GOVERNMENT. 1. From the Spanish gobierno, an administrative subdivision of the colonial period. In *New Granada *Coquibacoa and *Dos Rios were gobiernos.
2. The Ministerio de Gobierno is the interior ministry.

GRAMALOTE. The original name for *VILLAVICENCIO.

GRAN CENTRAL OBRERA. 1955-1957. A short-lived, Peronist-inspired labor association instituted by the government of General *Rojas Pinilla in an attempt to mobilize organized labor in support of the administration.

GRAN COLOMBIA. "Great" (or "Greater") "Colombia" is the English translation of the name commonly given to the union of Venezuela, *New Granada (present-day Colombia, including *Panama), and Ecuador. In general usage, however, the name is almost never translated, and the term "Gran Colombia" is used instead (see: REPUBLICA DE GRAN COLOMBIA). Although the Republic of Gran Colombia ceased to exist in the 1830s, the term is still used to refer to the three countries collectively, as in *Flota Mercante Grancolombiana, their jointly owned merchant marine.

GRAN PAUSA. Literally, the "Great Pause." A phrase used to describe the administration of *Eduardo Santos, whose approach to social reform was much more conservative than that of his predecessor, Alfonso *López Pumarejo. Santos described his policies as those "without pause or haste." However, since López Pumarejo was President before (1934-1938) and after (1942-1945) Santos (1938-1942), the Santos presidency seemed a "great pause," or interlude, between the two more militantly reformist presidencies of López Pumarejo.

GRAN SEMANA, La. The "Great" (or "Grand") "Week," November 22-29, 1840. Local residents of all social classes united to defend *Bogotá against threatened attacks by Colonel Manuel *González during the War of the *Supreme Commanders, 1840-1842. González's attack was turned back by the Battles of *Buenavista and Culebrera.

GRANADINE CONFEDERATION, see: CONFEDERACION GRANADINA

GRANADINO. An adjective used to designate a citizen of *New Granada; also, the name given to the new *peso de diez *reales following the decimalization of the *coinage in 1853.

GRAU, Enrique, 1920-. Painter, draftsman, printmaker; born December 18, in La Manga, *Cartagena. Largely self-taught, Grau grew up in Cartagena, where he began his artistic production at the same time that he performed with a local theatrical group. He exhibited his first paintings in 1940 in the Primer Salón de Artistas Colombianos, where he won honorable mention for a painting entitled *La mulata*. He studied in New York, 1940-1943, and traveled in the U.S. and Europe, 1956-1957. His work is multifaceted in subjects, motifs, and functions, including theatrical sets and book illustrations. He is known for his appealing, often sensuous, character studies. Carmen Ortega Ricaurte has described him as a "figurative expressionist."

GREAT BRITAIN, see: UNITED KINGDOM

GREAT COLOMBIA, see: GRAN COLOMBIA

GREAT NORTHERN CENTRAL RAILWAY. The company responsible for building the Puerto Wilches Railroad, the first section of the *GREAT NORTHERN RAILROAD.

GREAT PAUSE, see: GRAN PAUSA

GREIFF, León de, 1895-1967. Poet, engineer, railroad administrator, banker, born *Medellín; died Caracas, Venezuela. He has been called one of the most intense and original of Colombia's 20th-century poets. He used inventive language, and his major themes were nature, love, the demonic, and music. León de Greiff used many pseudonyms. He was a contributor to the *tertulia* of Los *Nuevos, the founder of a periodical called *Panida,* and director of the *Revista de las Indias.* Among his works were *Tergiversaciones de Leo Legris* (1925), *Libro de los signos* (1930), *Variaciones alrededor de nada* (1936), and *Nova et vetera* (1974). A three-volume edition of his collected works was published in 1975.

GREMIOS ECONOMICOS. Special-interest groups formed to promote the economic, social, and political welfare of their membership. The *Sociedad de Agricultores de Colombia (SAC), formed in 1871, is the oldest major interest group in Colombia, and the *Asociación Nacional de Industriales (ANDI), 1944, is probably the most influential. Other important groups, with the year each was established, include the *Federación Nacional de Cafeteros (FEDECAFE), 1927; Asociación Bancaria de Colombia (ASOBANCARIA), 1936; *Federación Nacional de Comerciantes (FENALCO), 1945; *Asociación Colombiana Popular de Industriales (ACOPI), 1951; Federación Colombiana de Industrias Metalurgicas (FEDEMETAL), 1955; Cámara Colombiana de la Construcción (CAMACOL), 1957; *Asociación Nacional de Cultivadores de Caña de Azúcar (ASOCA°A), 1959; Federación Colombiana de Ganaderos (FEDEGAN), 1963; and Asociación Nacional de Instituciones Finiancieras (ANIF), 1974. See also: FRENTE GREMIAL

GROUP OF 77. An international organization formed by the Joint Declaration of 77 Nations of the Third World adopted in Geneva, Switzerland, June 15-16, 1964, at the close of the first session of the United Nations Conference on Trade and Development (UNCTAD). The Group of 77 was intended to promote rapid economic growth among developing or underdeveloped nations, and it was instrumental in securing adoption of the Declaration and Programme of Action for a New International Economic Order by the United Nations General Asssembly in 1974-1975. Membership in the group had grown to 126 nations in 1984. Colombia has been affiliated with the Group of 77 since its inception.

GRUESO, José María, 1779-1835. Romantic poet, one of the first in Colombia. His major themes were the emotions and lost love. Among his better-known works are the poems "Las Noches de Zacarías Geussor" (ca. 1804) and "Lamentación de Pubén" (ca. 1820).

GRUTA SIMBOLICA, La. Literally, "The Symbolic Grotto"; a literary society, or *tertulia*. It was founded one evening in 1900 by Rafael Espinosa Guzmán (known as "Reg"), Carlos Tamayo, Julio de Francisco, Luis Galán Gómez, Pedro Ignacio Escobar, Julio Flórez, Luis María Mora, Ignacio Posse Amaya, Miguel A. Peñarredonda, and Rudesindo Gómez as they improvised satires on current politics, unable to go home because of a military curfew. Subsequent gatherings of the group attracted large numbers of poets, authors, and curiosity seekers with widely differing styles and opinions. In 1904, Manuel Castello founded a theatrical company affiliated with the Grotto, and the house where it met (Carrera Quinta, No. 203, between Calles 14 and 15) became a small theater.

GUADUAS. Rural governmental seat of a *municipio* of the same name, situated at 5° 4'N, 74° 36'W, about 126 kilometers from *Bogotá in the Department of *Cundinamarca. Guaduas is well known historically as a pleasant rest stop and tourist center on the main route from the *Magdalena River at *Honda to Bogotá. Located on the slopes of the *Cordillera Oriental at an altitude of 992 meters, it has an average temperature of 23°C. Population in 1985 was 6,317 people for the community and 22,397 for the *municipio* as a whole. Guaduas was founded in 1551 by Alonso de Olalla and Hernando de Alcocer.

GUAINIA, Departamento del. Located in southeastern Colombia on the borders with Venezuela and Brazil, Guainía covers 72,238 square kilometers of tropical lowland, with the southern part extending into the *Amazon region. Most of the department lies between 1° 10' and 4°N latitude and 66° 50' and 71° 5'W longitude. The climate varies with alternating wet and dry seasons, with an average temperature of 27°C. Major rivers include the Guaviare, Inírida, Guainía, and Isana. The population, mostly *Indians, is 3,311 (1985 figures) or less than one person per square kilometer. The capital city is Puerto *Inírida. Principal economic activities include *fishing, subsistence *agriculture, and cattle ranching (see: LIVE-STOCK). The last is especially important around Barranco Minas. There is some commercial production of chiquichiqui palm, chicle, and wood products. The Commissariat of Guainía was legally established July 13, 1963, and elevated to a department in 1991.

GUAJIRA, Departamento de la. A territory of some 20,848 square kilometers, consisting of the *Guajira Peninsula and part of the *Sierra Nevada de Santa Marta. The Department of the Guajira is bordered on the north and part of the east by the Caribbean Sea, on much of the east and south by Venezuela, and on the west by the Departments of Cesar and Magdalena. Latitude is between 10° 23' and 12° 28'N, and longitude between 71° 6' and 73° 39'W. A lowland, rising toward the south, the department's climate is arid in the north to humid in the south, with 19,526 square kilometers in tropical altitudes; 672, temperate; 444, cold; and 207, wasteland. Major rivers include the Ranchería, Ancho, Camarones, Cañas, Garavito, and Lucici. The population is 245,284 people (1985 estimate); population density is about twelve people per square kilometer. The capital city is *Riohacha. The Alta Guajira (north) is arid, with small *livestock production, *salt and talc mining, and shrimp fishing. The Baja Guajira (south) is humid, with *livestock, *agriculture, and cement and *coal production. According to DANE, *Colombia estadística 86,* major agricultural products, with tonnage produced in 1984, include *yuca, 33,000 tons; rice, 16,695; *cotton, 8,400; sorghum, 7,200; plantains, 7,000; *corn, 5,650; coconuts, 1,690; *tobacco, 800; beans, 320; and sesame, 50. Livestock slaughtered in the department included 18,511 head of cattle and 5,607 hogs. The department has potential wealth from mineral, coal, and *natural gas deposits. The Guajira is the traditional home of the Guajiro, Motilón, and other *Indian groups. Alonso de *Ojeda is often said to have been the first European to visit the Guajira Peninsula on his voyage in 1499, although some say a contraband dealer named Juan Ojeda was there in 1498. The department was under the jurisdiction of *Magdalena until 1871.

254 / Guajira Peninsula

Thereafter it was a national territory, 1871-1898; an *intendancy, 1898-1911; a special *commissariat, 1911-1954; and again an intendancy, 1954-1964. The department was created November 10, 1964. Its isolation made it an early center of illegal *marijuana cultivation.

GUAJIRA PENINSULA.   A neck of land in the extreme north of Colombia bordering on the Caribbean Sea and Venezuela. In colonial times it was under the *Audiencia de Santa Fe in judicial matters, but fiscally subject to Maracaibo. This made the area a bone of contention between Colombia and Venezuela after the breakup of *Gran Colombia. Even after Colombian rights to the mainland were accepted, the dispute was prolonged over surrounding waters and the *Frailes Islands. The peninsula is now part of the Departamento de la *Guajira.

GUAL, Pedro, 1794-1862.   Patriot leader; Colombia's first Minister of Foreign Relations, sometimes referred to as the "First Diplomat of the New World." He was born in Caracas (Venezuela), January 31, and died in Guayaquil (Ecuador), May 6. Gual was a secretary to Francisco *Miranda in Venezuela, 1811-1812; active in *Cartagena's independence movement, 1813-1815; and a representative from Cartagena at the *Congress of Cúcuta, 1821. He was Gran Colombia's Minister of Foreign Relations, 1821-1825, and a delegate to the *Congress of Panama, 1826. A newspaper that he edited in Cartagena, *El Observador Colombiano* (1813), is said to have been one of the first to advocate a unified republic for the territories formally in the *Virreinato del Nuevo Reino de Granada.

GUAL-ANDERSON TREATY OF 1824.   Signed October 3, by Pedro Gual, Colombia, and Richard C. Anderson, for the United States. It was the first formal treaty between the United States and Colombia. The agreement established terms of friendship and commerce on the basis of most-favored-nation status, and it guaranteed freedom of religion. With somewhat modified and extended terms, the treaty lasted 12 years.

GUAL-CAMPBELL TREATY OF 1825.   Signed in *Bogotá on April 18 by Pedro Gual, Colombia, and Patrick Campbell, Great Britain. It recognized the independence of Colombia, granted commercial reciprocity, and provided for cooperation to abolish the international slave trade. See also: UNITED KINGDOM, Relations with

GUAL-LARREA TREATY OF 1829. Signed in Guayaquil (2° 16'S, 79° 53'W, Ecuador), September 22, by Pedro Gual, Colombia, and José Larrea y Laredo, Peru. The agreement accepted the principle that the boundaries should be those of the old Viceroyalties of Peru and *New Granada (see: VIRREINATO DEL NUEVO REINO DE GRANADA; VIRREINATO DEL PERU), but it failed to specify them in geographical terms. The treaty was disliked by many Colombians.

GUAL-MOLINA TREATY OF 1825. Signed in *Bogotá, March 5, by Pedro Gual, Colombia, and Pedro Molina, Central America, it was a treaty of friendship and alliance that accepted the principle of *uti possidetis* of 1810 for boundary settlements. The two governments agreed to negotiate disputed areas, particularly the *Mosquito Coast.

GUAL-TORRENS TREATY OF 1825. Signed in *Bogotá on August 19, by Pedro Gual, Colombia, and Colonel José Anastasio Torrens, Mexico. It was a treaty of friendship and alliance that led to plans for an abortive expedition to Cuba and Puerto Rico (see: CUBAN AND PUERTO RICAN EXPEDITION).

GUAQUERO. A grave finder or grave robber; one who finds and enters *las guacas,* *Indian graves. According to some authorities, the term dates from the 16th century, when *Heredia and *Vadillo discovered the burial grounds of the *Sinú. It may be derived from the Peruvian word *huaca,* a kind of spirit. *Guaquería* is a term that applies to the general action of discovering and opening Indian tombs.

GUATAVITA, Lake. Mountain lake in the *Cordillera Oriental, located at an altitude of 3,100 meters in the *municipio* of Sesquilé (5° 3'N, 73° 48'W) in the Department of *Cundinamarca. It was the scene of the ceremony of *Eldorado* and the legend of the *cacique* of Guatavita. The latter recounts the story of a chieftain who neglected his beautiful young wife until she committed an indiscretion with a visiting warrior. When the affair was discovered, the warrior was tortured and killed. The princess took her young daughter and both disappeared into the lake. The grieving and repentant *cacique* honored their memory by periodic offerings to the body of water. Because of reputed treasure, attempts have been made to drain the lake. The first of these was by Lázaro Fonte. After that, an attempt was made by Antonio de Sepúlveda in 1580; by José Ignacio París in 1822; and, most recently, by a British firm, Contractors, Ltd, at the end of the 19th century. See also: ELDORADO

GUAVIARE, Departamento del. Located in south central Colombia, the Department of Guaviare covers 42,327 square kilometers of tropical lowland, largely between 0° 50' and 2° 50'N latitude and 70° 40' and 73° 30'W longitude. Average temperatures range from 27° to 30°C. The dry season is December to March, with consistent rain April to November. About 8,200 hectares of land are cultivated (*corn, plantains, rice, *cacao, and *sugar). Thirty thousand head of cattle have been reported in the department, and chicle is produced for commercial sale. Major rivers include the Guaviare (which joins the Orinoco River) and the Unilla-Vaupés, Mecoya, and Apaporis (tributaries of the *Amazon). The population is largely *Indian. There are 12,351 people in the department (1985 figures), with a density of less than one person per square kilometer. *San José de Guaviare is the capital city. Guaviare was a *commissariat 1977-1991 and became a department under the *Constitution of 1991.

GUAYAQUIL, Treaty of, see: GUAL-LARREA TREATY

GUAYAQUIL CONFERENCE. July 26-27, 1822, in the (now Ecuadoran) port of Guayaquil (2° 16'S, 79° 53'W). This controversial meeting occurred between General Simón *Bolívar, liberator of northern South America, and José de San Martín, liberator of southern South America. Its secret sessions became the center of a bitter international dispute because San Martín later claimed that Bolívar had refused help for the liberation of Peru, while Bolívar insisted that San Martín had never requested any aid.

GÜEPI, Battle of. March 27, 1933, Peru. Colombian forces successfully fought a nine-hour engagement, occupying a 15-kilometer stretch of territory to keep Peruvian troops from obstructing traffic on the Putumayo River during the *Leticia dispute.

GUERRA DE LOS CONVENTOS, see: MINOR CONVENTS, Rebellion of the

GUERRA DE LOS MIL DIAS, see: THOUSAND DAYS, War of the

GUERRA DE LOS SUPREMOS, see: SUPREME COMMAND-ERS, War of the

GUERRA DEL PACIFICO, see: PACIFIC, War of the

GUERRILLA MOVEMENTS. Colombian politics saw the formation of a number of guerrilla organizations in the 1960s. The most important of these were the *Movimiento de Obreros, Estudiantes y Campesinos (MOEC); the *Movimiento Obrero Independiente Revolucionario (MOIR); the *Frente Unido de Acción Revolucionaria (FUAR); the *Ejército de Liberación Nacional (E.L.N.); the *Fuerzas Armadas Revolucionarias de Colombia (FARC); and the *Ejército Popular de Liberación (E.P.L.). MOEC, the Movement of Workers, Students, and Peasants, was founded in January 1959, by a student leader, Antonio Larrota (d. 1961), and was later led by Federico Arango. MOEC held its first formal congress in *Cali, July 20, 1960. The organization fell apart after its second congress in 1965 because of methodological disputes. FUAR, the United Front for Revolutionary Action, was established in 1962 by Gloria *Gaitán, daughter of Jorge Eliécer *Gaitán, her husband, Luis Emiro Valenzuela, and Antonio García. MOIR, the Independent Worker Movement, was established 1965-1969 by militant pro-Chinese sympathizers. E.L.N., the National Liberation Army, was formed July 4, 1964, under the leadership of Fabio Vásquez Castaño, with activities focusing on the Department of *Santander. (Its first formal proclamation was dated Simacota, January 7, 1965.) FARC, the Revolutionary Armed Forces of Colombia, was organized in 1966, directed by Pedro Antonio *Marín (alias Manuel *Marulanda Vélez and "Tiro Fijo") with a pro-Soviet orientation. E.P.L., the Popular Army of Liberation, formed in January 1968, operated out of the Department of *Córdoba. It had a pro-Maoist ideological emphasis. See also: COMMANDO QUINTIN LAME; COORDINADORA GUERRILLERA "SIMON BOLIVAR"; FRENTE UNIDO DEL PUEBLO; RICARDO FRANCO FRONT

GUIRIOR, Manuel, 1708-1788. *Viceroy of *New Granada, 1773-1776. He campaigned against the *Indians, recommended free trade for the viceroyalty; commissioned an educational survey; and established the Public Library of *Bogotá.

GUMILLA, José, 1686-1750. *Jesuit missionary in *New Granada, 1715-1738. He arrived in 1705 and studied in *Bogotá, 1705-1715. He was the author of *El Orinoco Ilustrado* ..., describing the land and people of the Orinoco River basin. It was first published in Madrid, 1741.

GUSTAVISTA. Supporter of Gustavo *Rodríguez Vargas. See also: UNIONIST CONSERVATIVES

GUTIERREZ, Santos, 1820-1872. General, lawyer, *Liberal legislator, diplomat, President of Colombia, 1868-1870. Born El Cocuy (*Boyacá), October 24; died *Bogotá, February 6. He received his law degree from the *Colegio Mayor de San Bartolomé in 1847 and served in both houses of *Congress. He was a delegate to the conventions that wrote the *Constitutions of 1858 and 1863 and was President of Boyacá (1863) and *Cundinamarca (1864), as well as a supporter of the Liberal *rebellion of 1859-1861. As President he stifled a threatened revolt by the Governor of Cundinamarca, Ignacio Gutiérrez Vergara, in October 1868, and made unsuccessful efforts to stimulate construction of a transisthmian canal. He encouraged restoration of the Colegio de San Bartolomé and the *Colegio Mayor de Nuestra Señora del Rosario and founded the Lazareto de *Agua de Dios. In addition, he was Minister to France.

GUTIERREZ DE PINÈRES, Juan Francisco, b. ca. 1732. Regent-*Visitor-*Intendant of *New Granada, 1778-1784. He was charged with collecting taxes to cover the expenses of the Spanish-English war, 1779-1783, but his arbitrary methods provoked public protests. Especially disliked was his decree regarding the *alcabala* and the *Armada de Barlovento* taxes, dated October 12, 1780. It provoked the *Comuneros Revolt, 1780-1782. Gutiérrez de Piñeres refused to negotiate with the Comuneros and opposed Viceroy Manuel Antonio *Flórez when he issued pardons.

GUTIERREZ GONZALEZ, Gregorio, 1826-1872. Romantic poet, lawyer, judge, agriculturalist, and miner; born in La Ceja del Tambo (*Antioquia), May 9; died *Medellín, July 6. Although educated in *Bogotá, he returned to spend most of his life in his native province. The major themes of his poetry were nature, folklore, and love. He is remembered for his *Memoria científica sobre el cultivo del maíz* . . . (1866), a poetic essay on the cultivation of *corn in Antioquia, and other poems, such as "Mi muerte," "A Julia" (1850), and "A Medellín, desde el alto de Santa-Helena" (1850). His poem "A Julia" has been termed the best love poem of the romantic period in Colombian history.

-H-

HACIENDA. 1. A form of latifundio, or large estate, which tended to be self-sufficient, especially in the colonial and early republican periods. Based on *agriculture and cattle raising (see: LIVESTOCK), *haciendas* frequently included mining, handicrafts, and small industries as well. *Haciendas* were autocratic and hierarchical in social structure, controlled by the owner and his family through a secondary class of foremen and overseers, who were in turn in charge of paid labor, peons, slaves, and *Indians who worked on the estates. *Haciendas* have been described as subsistence (those whose production was largely for internal consumption), commercial (those whose products were sold outside the estate), and idle (those held largely for social prestige with little effective economic production). *Hacienda* owners, or *hacendados*, made up a major part of the ruling class. *Haciendas* might be controlled by religious or other corporations as well as by private individuals. Among the more famous *haciendas* in Colombian history might be Hato Grande (*Cundinamarca), which belonged to General *Santander; El Salitre (Paipa, *Boyacá) of the Liberator Simón *Bolívar; and Yerbabuena (*Cundinamarca), which belonged to the *Marroquín family and is now the site of the *Instituto Caro y Cuervo.

2. The *Ministerio de Hacienda* is the finance ministry.

HAGUE CONFERENCE, 1907, see: INTERNATIONAL CONFERENCE AT THE HAGUE (SECOND), 1907

HARDENBURG, Walter Ernest (1886-1942). U.S. citzen, born in Galena, Illinois, who exposed the horrors of the *rubber trade along the Putumayo River. He emigrated to Colombia in 1904 to work on the *Pacific Railroad. After fifteen months he started for Brazil to work on a railway then being constructed from the Bolivian frontier at Marmoré to the Madeira River. He traveled over the *Andes and down the Putumayo, only to blunder into the territory controlled by Julio César *Arana del Aguila's Peruvian Amazon Rubber Company. Appalled at what he witnessed and narrowly escaping execution as an unwanted interloper, he went to London to awaken world opinion to the situation. The result was an official investigation by Roger *Casement, British consul in Rio de Janeiro, the collapse of Arana's rubber empire, and the restoration of effective Colombian sovereignty along the north bank of the Putumayo (see also: PUTUMAYO DISPUTE; RUBBER TRADE).

HAWKINS, (Sir) John, 1532-1595. English buccaneer. He brought slaves to *New Granada and threatened violence if he was not allowed to sell them in *Riohacha, 1564-1565 and again 1567-1569. He fought the Spanish Armada, 1588, and sailed with Sir Francis *Drake, 1595. He died at sea.

HAY-HERRAN TREATY, see: HERRAN-HAY TREATY

HEALTH, see: EPIDEMICS; PUBLIC HEALTH

HERALDO, El. Daily newspaper of *Barranquilla, founded March 14, 1933, under the direction of Enrique de la Rosa and Julio Montes. Shortly after its establishment, El Heraldo was purchased by *Liberal leaders Juan B. Fernández Ortega, Luis Eduardo Manotas Wilches, and Alberto Pumarejo. Fernández Ortega served as the leading editorial figure for the next fifty years and was eventually succeeded by his heir, Juan B. Fernández Renowitzky. The paper was closed temporarily in 1934-1935, for a short time following the assassination of *Gaitán in 1948, under the *Gómez presidency in 1951, and during the government of *Rojas Pinilla. The paper is well known as a vehicle for members of the *Barranquilla Group. Its circulation is about 65,100 copies daily. El Heraldo was also the name of a semiofficial *Medellín newspaper of the latter 19th century.

HEREDIA, Alonso de. Conquistador, explorer in the *Cauca region. He was the elder brother of Pedro de *Heredia, though less well known.

HEREDIA, Pedro de, 1500-1554. Conquistador, explorer, born in Madrid. He set up a sugar mill in *Santo Domingo after fleeing legal difficulties in Spain. Then, returning to his native land, he secured the *government (*gobierno*) of *Nueva Andalucía. He left Cadiz in November 1532, reached the Bay of Cartagena and founded the city of *Cartagena, January 14, 1533. From there he authorized exploring forays, 1533-1537 and after 1540. Perhaps his most famous expedition was that which discovered the *Sinú burial grounds. He was an important figure in the early history of Cartagena. The Crown sent at least three Visitors (*visitadores*)—Juan (some say Pedro) de Badillo, Miguel Díaz de Armendáriz, and Juan de Maldonado—to investigate his government. Heredia was returning to Spain to answer charges raised against him when he drowned, January 27, 1554.

HEROIC GENERATION. The group of cultural leaders who, in the terms of Abel Naranjo Villegas, developed or were prominent from 1800 to 1830. He characterizes the period as one largely preoccupied with the struggle for political independence. Ernesto Cortés Ahumada subdivides this period into the Eponymous Generation (key date, 1795) and the Heroic Generation (key date, 1810). Representative figures from the Eponymous Generation include Antonio *Nariño, Francisco José de *Caldas, José Félix Restrepo, Camilo *Torres, and Francisco Antonio *Zea. The Heroic Generation would include such men as José *Acevedo y Gómez, Simón *Bolívar, Domingo *Caycedo, José María Castillo y Rada, Custodio *García Rovira, Joaquín *Mosquera, and José Manuel *Restrepo. See also: GENERATIONS

HEROIN. An addictive narcotic produced from the opium poppy. The opium poppy is said to be well suited to the climate of southern Colombia, but until very recent times, the illicit *drug trade was dominated by *marijuana and *cocaine. Attempts were made to produce heroin in the *Antioquia region in the 1980s, but they did not prove commercially successful. According to accounts published in 1991, however, it appears that the *Cali Cartel was making a serious effort to grow poppies and to market heroin in addition to, or as a replacement for, cocaine. Heroin refining is easier and cheaper then cocaine processing, and given equal quantities, heroin is the more profitable of the two. The Cali Cartel has long cooperated with heroin dealers in the United States.

HERRAN. For the President and General see: HERRAN Y ZALDUA, Pedro Alcántara; for the Archbishop see: HERRAN Y ZALDUA, Antonio

HERRAN-CALVO TREATY OF 1856. An agreement signed by General P. A. *Herrán, for *New Granada, and J. B. Calvo Rosales, for Costa Rica. It would have canceled most of Costa Rica's claims to the Almirante region, but it was never ratified.

HERRAN-CASS TREATY OF 1857. An agreement signed September 10 by General P. A. *Herrán for Colombia and Secretary of State Lewis Cass for the United States. Colombia assumed responsibility for the *Panama Riot of 1856 and agreed to settle all claims registered prior to September 1, 1859. By supplemental treaty in 1864, Colombia eventually paid more than $400,000 in damages.

HERRAN-HAY TREATY OF 1903. Negotiated by Tomás Herrán for Colombia and John Hay for the United States, the treaty granted the United States an exclusive concession to canal rights in the Isthmus of *Panama for 99 years, with renewal options, in exchange for a cash payment and an annual rent. The treaty was accepted by the United States but rejected by the Colombian *Congress.

HERRAN Y ZALDUA, Antonio, 1797-1868. Archbishop of Bogotá, 1855-1868. He sponsored the founding of a local Sisters of Charity organization in *Bogotá in 1855 and patronized the Society of St. Vincent de Paul, established by prominent citizens of Bogotá in 1858. He supervised development of a seminary, 1855-1868; recalled the *Jesuits to Colombia, 1858; and resisted the *anti-clerical laws of 1861. Archbishop Herrán was confined and then exiled from Bogotá, 1861-1864, but he later encouraged reconciliation and acceptance of the religious provisions of the *Constitution of 1863.

HERRAN Y ZALDUA, Pedro Alcántara, 1800-1872. General, legislator, diplomat, President of *New Granada, 1841-1845. Born *Bogotá, October 19; died Bogotá, April 26. He joined the patriot military forces, 1814-1816 and 1820-1826. He served as Minister of War, 1830; Minister of the Interior and Foreign Relations, 1838-1839; and Minister to the United States. He supported the government in the rebellion of the *MINOR CONVENTS, 1839; the War of the *SUPREME

COMMANDERS, 1840-1842; the revolt of José María *Melo, 1854; and the *rebellion of 1859-1862; and he was several times commander of the *army. His presidential administration concluded the rebellion of 1840-1842; attempted reconciliation of disparate political elements; tried to reestablish the national treasury; reorganized public *education; sponsored the *Constitution of 1843; and recalled the *Jesuits to New Granada, 1842. He was a brother of Archbishop *Herrán and the son-in-law of General *Mosquera. General Herrán was out of Colombia, 1849-1854 and 1861-1867. In the latter case, his absence was partially a result of political differences with Mosquera, who overthrew the government of the *Confederación Granadina in 1861.

HERRERA, Tomás, 1800-1854. Panamanian, general, legislator, acting President of *New Granada, April 21 to August 5, 1854. Born Panama City, December 21; died *Bogotá, December 5, as a result of wounds suffered in the *Battle of Bogotá the day before. He joined the patriot forces in 1820 and served the cause of independence in *Panama and *Peru. He was exiled in 1828 and again in 1841-1845, as a result of rebellions in *Cartagena and *Panama, respectively, but he fought against the *Urdaneta dictatorship in 1830. He was Governor of Panama, 1832; a member of *Congress in 1837 and after. As President of the *Senate, he signed the *Constitution of 1853. Herrera served as Minister of War, 1849-1850, and then, both as acting President of New Granada and military commander, he fought the *Melo dictatorship in 1854.

HERRERA RESTREPO, Bernardo, 1844-1928. Archbishop of Bogotá, 1891-1928; born *Bogotá, September 11; died Bogotá, January 2. He was ordained in 1869 and directed the seminary in Bogotá before becoming Bishop of *Medellín, 1885-1891. As Archbishop of Bogotá, he presided over the Latin American Plenary Council in Rome, 1899; held the first Eucharistic Congress in Colombia, 1913; and brought more than a dozen religious orders to Colombia, 1893-1928. He was named Primate of Colombia, 1902, and was authorized to proclaim the Cathedral of Bogotá a minor basilica in 1907.

HERRERA Y TORDESILLAS, Antonio, 1549-1625. A historian commissioned by Philip II. He was the author of *Historia general de los hechos de los Castellanos en las islas y tierra firme del mar océano,* first published in Madrid, 1601-1615. The title varies, and the work is also known as *Las décadas.*

HIGHWAYS. Transportation in colonial *New Granada was largely by water. Such roads as existed (the partly pre-conquest *CAMINO REAL, the *CARARE ROAD of 1545, the *HONDA ROAD of 1553, and the *Cali-*Buenaventura road of the 1560s) were little more than trails for pack mules. Mid-18th-century viceroys like José Antonio *Flórez endeavored to improve the road network, particularly around *Bogotá, but they were limited by scarce resources and the reluctance of the population to accept any increase in *taxation. The early 1850s saw Colombia's first macadamized road, the 45 kilometers from Bogotá to *Facatativá. By 1865 there were some 150 kilometers of these roads in the vicinity of the capital. The construction of automobile highways began in the 1920s. By early 1929 the country had 1,000 kilometers of motor roads for its 15,350 automobiles. Progress was slowed by the Depression of the 1930s, but another spurt of construction followed *World War II. During the 1970s, the total network grew from 40,000 to 76,000 kilometers for 500,000 vehicles. Of this network, 12% of the roads were paved. The national roads (those built and maintained by the Ministry of Public Works and Transportation) consist of an uncoordinated system of three main sections totaling about 12,000 kilometers: the Western Trunk Highway (Colombia's portion of the *Pan American Highway), which runs from the Caribbean Coast through *Medellín to the Ecuadoran border; the parallel Central Trunk Highway, from the Caribbean to Ecuador via *Bucaramanga and Bogotá; and the Caribbean Trunk Highway, from *Barranquilla along the North Coast into Venezuela. Although maintenance is a chronic problem, the highways have attracted the lion's share of shipping away from the even worse-maintained *railroads and now carry nearly 80% of freight movements. See also: SIMON BOLIVAR HIGHWAY

HIMNO NACIONAL, see: NATIONAL ANTHEM

HISTORICOS. The Historical *Conservatives; that faction of the party sometimes labeled doctrinaire. The Históricos were those who did not support the *Núñez-*Caro *Nationalists during the 1880s and 1890s, including partisans of General

Marcelino Vélez in the elections of 1892 and the Twenty-one who issued the *Motivos de disidencia* in 1896.

HOLGUIN, Carlos, 1832-1894. Lawyer, legislator, diplomat, journalist, acting President of Colombia, 1887-1892. Born Nóvita (*Chocó), July 11; died *Bogotá, October 19. Holguín received his law degree from the *Universidad del Cauca in 1854. In addition to serving in both houses of *Congress, he was a judge of the *Supreme Court and Minister to Great Britain, 1880-1886, and Spain, 1883-1887. He was a delegate to the Constituent Congress in 1858, and Minister of Government in 1888. His presidential administration defended the *Constitution of 1886 and the controversial Law of the Horses (*Ley de los caballos), 1888. It encouraged numerous internal improvements, such as the construction of a road between *Cundinamarca and *Boyacá and one connecting the southern *Cauca with the Pacific Ocean. It established steam navigation on the lower *Cauca and Nechí Rivers, cleaned the *Dique Canal in *Bolívar, and contributed to completion of numerous public buildings in Bogotá.

HOLGUIN, Jorge, 1848-1928. General, diplomat, author, financier, acting President in 1909 and again in 1921-1922. Born *Cali, October 30; died *Bogotá, March 2. He was a member of the *Consejo Nacional de Delegatorios, which revised the constitution and, as acting President, advocated ratification of the treaty pending between the United States and Colombia. He also served as Minister of the Treasury, 1885, Minister of War, Minister of Foreign Relations, 1897-1898, and Governor of *Cundinamarca.

HOLGUIN-AVEBURY CONVENTION. Signed by General Jorge *Holguín, Colombia, and Lord Avebury, Great Britain, in 1905. It was an agreement that settled the question of claims against Colombia for disputes of the 19th century. Most of the claims were accepted and settled before 1930. See: UNITED KINGDOM, Relations with

HOLIDAYS, Public. Colombia recognizes six national holidays. In chronological order during the year these are: January 1, New Year's Day; May 1, International Labor Day; July 20, Independence Day; August 7, Battle of *Boyacá Day; October 12, *Columbus Day (Día de la Raza); and November 11, *Cartagena's Independence Day (1811). The *Catholic Church in Colombia recognizes two official holidays: December 8, dedicated to the Immaculate Conception of the Virgin Mary, and December 25, the birth of Christ.

HOLY OFFICE, see: INQUISITION, Holy

HONDA. Historically important commercial center in the Department of *Tolima, situated at 5° 12'N, 74° 44'W, 97 kilometers northwest of *Bogotá. Founded on August 24, 1560, where navigation on the *Magdalena River is obstructed by the rapids (*Salto de Honda*), the river port became one of the principal shipping centers connecting Bogotá and other inland points with the Caribbean Sea via the Magdalena (see also: HONDA ROAD). The town was damaged by an *earthquake in 1805. It has been served by the *Sabana Railway since 1884 and by the *Dorada Railway since 1897.

HONDA ROAD. The Camino de Honda, the principal road that connected *Bogotá with the *Magdalena River and the Caribbean Sea. It ran approximately 141 kilometers from the port of *Honda (Tolima) to Bogotá via *Guaduas, Villeta de San Miguel (5° 1'N, 74° 28'W), and *Facatativá. The road was built in 1553 by the partnership of Hernando Alcócer and Alonso de Olalla Herrera, who founded the city of Villeta (October 20, 1551), as headquarters for their construction crews. The section from Bogotá to Facatativá was macadamized in the late 1840s, the first road to be so paved in Colombia. See also: HIGHWAYS

HORMEZAQUE, Battle of. February 14, 1861, *Boyacá. Colonel Santos *Gutiérrez, rebel, defeated the forces of the *Confederación Granadina. He was able to occupy Boyacá following the flight of Confederation officials during the *rebellion of 1859-1862.

HORSES, Law of the, see: LEY DE LOS CABALLOS

HOUSE OF REPRESENTATIVES, see: CONGRESS

HUERTA DE JAIME. Formerly a well-known recreational site in *Bogotá, now called Plaza of the Martyrs (Municipal Ordinance No. 112 of 1850), in commemoration of the large number of patriots executed there by General Pablo *Morillo in 1816. It is also the site of the execution of three *Conservative leaders by General T. C. de *Mosquera, July 19, 1861.

HUILA, Departamento de.   Located in south central Colombia, between 1° 30' and 3° 48'N latitude and 74° 28' and 76° 37'W longitude, Huila covers 19,890 square kilometers. Of these 5,528 are in tropical climate; 7,713 are temperate; 5,290, cold; and 1,359, wasteland. Within the department the *Cordillera Oriental separates from the *Cordillera Central, and the terrain is mountainous, cut by river valleys. Both the *Magdalena River and the *Cauca River originate within the mountains of Huila. Other major rivers include the Cabrera, Iquira, Ceibas, Aipe, Bache, and La Plata. High points in the department include the Nevado del Huila (5,750 meters), and the region is also known for the cave of Los Guácharos. Population is 636,642 people (1985 estimate), with a population density of about thirty-two people per square kilometer. *Neiva is the capital city. According to DANE, *Colombia estadística 86,* principal agricultural products, with tonnage produced in 1984, include rice, 196,200 tons; plantains, 83,000; *yuca, 60,000; sorghum, 46,550; *sugar, 33,600; *potatoes, 12,900; beans, 12,205; *cotton, 8,600; *corn, 8,275; *cacao, 3,800; *tobacco, 2,900; soybeans, 1,668; sesame, 53; peanuts, 15. *Livestock slaughtered in 1984 included 82,557 head of cattle and 26,483 hogs. There is incipient industrialization, with 27 businesses employing ten or more workers recorded in 1983. Mining of *iron, *copper, *lead, mica, marble, quartz, and calcite is important. Huila was the pre-conquest home of various Indian groups including the *Pijaos, *Paeces, and the Yalcones. Early exploration was carried out by Sebestián de *Belalcázar, Juan de Ampudia, and Pedro de *Añasco, with the latter founding Timaná (1° 58'N, 75° 55'W) in 1538. The Department of Huila was created April 29, 1905, from territory that formerly belonged to *Tolima. Huila is the site of *San Agustín, perhaps the most widely known of Colombia's archeological remains.

HUILQUIPAMBA, Battle of.   On September 30, 1840, in *Nariño, Generals P. A. *Herrán and T. C. de *Mosquera, for the government, defeated the rebellious forces of General José María *Obando during what became the War of the *Supreme Commanders, 1840-1842. Obando was presumed dead, incorrectly, for some time after the battle.

HUMANIST GENERATION, see: CLASSIC GENERATION

HUMAREDA, Battle of. June 17, 1885, La Humareda and El Hobo in the Department of *Bolívar, on the *Magdalena River. Rebel forces under the *Liberal General Sergio Camargo achieved a victory over government forces under General Guillermo Quintero Calderón, only to suffer a crippling loss of ammunition in a fire aboard the gunboat *María Emma*. Gunshots from another Liberal vessel, the *Confianza*, killed its own troops during the battle. The encounter was a demoralizing loss, which led to the collapse of the *rebellion of 1884-1885.

HUMBOLDT, Alexander von, 1769-1859. Prussian naturalist, who, accompanied by French botanist Aimé *Bonpland (1773-1858), traveled through Central and South America, 1799-1804. Humboldt collected specimens and conferred with scientists of the *Botanical Expedition in *New Granada and later published accounts of his experience. Humboldt Bay (6° 56'N, 77° 40'W) and the Humboldt Current, both in the Pacific Ocean, were named for him.

HUTTEN, Philip von, 1511-1545. German-speaking explorer, a representative of the *Welsers in Venezuela. He led an expedition from Coro into the *Llanos of Colombia and Venezuela, exploring the Caquetá and Amazon River valleys, 1541-1545. He was executed by Juan Carvajal in a jurisdictional dispute upon returning to Coro in 1545.

HYDROELECTRICITY. High mountains and steep, narrow river valleys in an area of abundant rainfall give *Colombia a vast hydroelectric potential, of which barely 5% has so far been tapped. The first hydroelectric station was built by the *Compañía Eléctrica de Bucaramanga, and began functioning in August 1891. Expansion was gradual, and largely confined to urban areas until the post–*World War II years. By 1949 the supply was growing at more than 10% a year. In 1955 the C.V.C. (*Corporación Autónoma Regional del Cauca) was created in imitation of the Tennessee Valley Authority. Its success led to a number of similar public bodies on other rivers: CAR is the *Corporación Autónoma Regional de la Sabana de Bogotá y de los Valles de Ubaté y Chiquinquirá; the C.V.M. is the *Corporación Autónoma Regional de los Valles del Magdalena y del Sinú. To unite the output of these and other suppliers into a national grid, the *Sociedad de Interconexión Eléctrica S.A.

was set up in 1967, and made subordinate the following year to the new *Instituto Colombiano de Energía Eléctrica (ICEL). At present hydroelectricity supplies a tenth of the country's *energy and power. This proportion could double by the end of the century.

-I-

I.C.S.S., see: INSTITUTO COLOMBIANO DE SEGUROS SOCIALES

IBAGUE. The capital of *Tolima, with a population of 285,409 people (1985 estimate), Ibagué is the tenth largest city of Colombia. Located on the Combeima River at 4° 27'N, 75° 15'W, with an altitude of 1,256 meters and an average temperature of 21°C, Ibagué is sometimes called the musical city of Colombia and is well known for tourism and the national folklore festival. It is also a regional agricultural-industrial center. The city was founded by Captain Antonio López de Galarza on October 14, 1550, with the name San Bonifacio de Ibagué. It was moved to its present site in 1551, and has long been a strategic location on transportation routes.

ICA, see: INSTITUTO COLOMBIANO AGROPECUARIO; INTERNATIONAL COFFEE AGREEMENT

ICEL, see: INSTITUTO COLOMBIANO DE ENERGIA ELECTRICA

ICETEX, see: INSTITUTO COLOMBIANO DE CREDITO EDUCATIVO DE ESTUDIOS TECNICOS EN EL EXTERIOR

IDEMA, see: INSTITUTO DE MERCADEO AGROPECUARIO

IFI, see: INSTITUTO DE FOMENTO INDUSTRIAL

IMA, see: INSTITUTO DE MERCADEO AGROPECUARIO

IMMIGRATION. In contrast to Argentina, Brazil, Chile, and even Peru, Colombia has had no intensive immigration since the early Spanish conquest and settlement (see: CREOLES). Other parts of America were more attractive economically, had systematic policies of encouraging immigration, and generally escaped the deterrent of as much internal conflict (see: CIVIL WARS). Protestant immigrants in particular were not encouraged to settle in Colombia. Measures were planned in the early post–*World War II period to admit refugees and attract skilled technicians, but they were never fully implemented. In recent years, emigration has exceeded immigration. Nevertheless, a number of immigrant groups have made their presence felt, often having influence in commerce and industry out of proportion to their actual numbers. Many clergy have come from Spain. Germans have been prominent in the *coffee trade and pioneered *air transport. There are many Italians and Lebanese and some Jews in the commerce of the coastal cities. The United States has contributed businessmen and Protestant missionaries (see: PROTESTANTISM).

IMPORTS. The *United Kingdom was already an important supplier of contraband goods in the colonial period. In the first decades after independence it became Colombia's chief source of imports, followed by France as the chief source of luxury goods. Toward the end of the 19th century, the *United States became important and by the 1930s was Colombia's largest supplier, a position it still retains. Germany achieved second place soon after *World War II, but is now challenged by Japan, whose exports zoomed from 4.6 billion yen in 1965 to 101 billion yen (US$397,638,000) in 1985. The total value of Colombian imports in 1987 was US$4,228,000,000 and US$5,005,000,000 in 1988.
These were distributed (in 1981) thus:

United States and Canada	US$1,689,200,000
European Economic Community	940,000,000
*ALADI countries except the Andean Common Market	424,400,000
East Asia except mainland China	420,100,000
*Andean Common Market	227,800,000
European Free Trade Area (EFTA)	211,900,000
COMECON	49,800,000

This represented a substantial decrease since 1982 when Colombia imported US$5,477,700,000 worth of products, but the decline has affected different countries differently. Imports from the U.S. fell from US$1,895,600,000 in 1982 to US$1,514,7000,000 in 1987. Those from the German Federal Republic dropped from $334,000,000 in 1981 to $307,100,000 in 1986, but recovered to $383,560,000 in 1987. Japanese imports into Colombia reached $673,000,000 in 1981 and then decreased to $428,300,000 in 1986 and $362,500,000 in 1987. Imports from Britain were $145,800,000 in 1981 and $93,500,000 in 1986. Among Latin American countries, Brazil supplied Colombia with only $150,500,000 worth of goods in 1987, compared with $286,300,000 worth in 1982. In contrast, imports from Mexico went from $61,700,000 in 1980 to $149,300,000 in 1985 and fell only slightly (to $148,600,000) in 1987. According to the Colombian Information Service, major imports in 1988 were represented as follows:

Animal products	US$28,000,000
Vegetable products	304,000,000
Edible fats and oils	62,000,000
Manufactured foodstuffs	100,000,000
Motor gasoline	174,000,000
Chemicals	1,175,000,000
Rubber	93,000,000
Plastics	266,000,000
Pulp and paper	204,000,000
Textiles and garments	129,000,000
Iron and steel products	454,000,000
Other metal products	207,000,000
Transport equipment	666,000,000
Machinery and other equipment	1,601,000,000
Other imports	383,000,000
TOTAL IMPORTS	US$5,866,000,000

INA, see: INSTITUTO NACIONAL DE ABASTECIMIENTOS

INCARNATION, Convent of Our Lady of the, see: CONVENTO DE NUESTRA SEÑORA DE LA ENCARNACION

INCOME TAX. Income taxes were first introduced in Colombia in 1918. Law 56 of that year decreed taxes on income in three categories: income from capital only, to be taxed at a rate of 3%; income from a combination of capital and labor, to be taxed at 2%; and income from labor only, to be taxed at a rate

of 1%. There were certain specified exemptions. The method
of taxation has been revised since 1918, but the principle of the
income tax has persisted.

INCORA, see: INSTITUTO COLOMBIANO DE LA REFORMA
AGRARIA

INDEPENDENCE MOVEMENT. Napoleon I's detention of
Charles IV of Spain and his son, the Prince of Asturias (the
future Ferdinand VII of Spain), in order to place his brother,
Joseph Bonaparte, on the Spanish throne in 1808 led to a
widespread rebellion in Spain. A *junta central {de España},
which attempted to coordinate the revolt, constituted itself as
a regency council (*consejo de regencia) in the name of Ferdinand
VII, and convoked a *Cortes. The initial reaction in much of
Hispanic America was to see this as an opportunity to seek
reforms, as, for example *Cundinamarca's *Memorial de agravios. When little was achieved this way, *cabildos in the
colonies established *juntas to rule locally in Ferdinand VII's
name. In *Bogotá, this took the form of the *ACTA DEL 20
DE JULIO DE 1810. Many patriots attempted to achieve unity
over a larger area, while others argued for local autonomy. In
*New Granada this basic disagreement characterized the years
1810-1816, the so-called *PATRIA BOBA period. Those
favoring a more decentralized governing authority achieved
the Act of Federation, creating the *Provincias Unidas de la
Nueva Granada (see: ACTA DE LA CONFEDERACION DE
LAS PROVINCIAS UNIDAS DE LA NUEVA
GRANADA), while those supporting a more centralized gov-
ernment controlled Cundinamarca and its capital, Bogotá.
Venezuelan-born Simón *Bolívar sought the unity of *Gran
Colombia (the former *Virreinato del Nuevo Reino de
Granada, or present-day Venezuela, Colombia, Panama, and
Ecuador). His Admirable Campaign (see: CAMPAÑA ADMI-
RABLE) of May-October 1813, did much to bring this about.
By the end of the Napoleonic wars, the consequent accession
of Ferdinand VII produced a reaction in Spain and freed it to
attempt the restoration of Spanish authority in the Americas.
An expeditionary force under General Pablo *MORILLO
secured a temporary reconquest of the viceroyalty, 1816-1819
(see: RECONQUISTA). Such factors as the revulsion caused
by Spanish terrorism (see: REIGN OF TERROR) and the aid
of Peninsular War veterans from the *Legión Británica enabled
Bolívar and the patriot forces to make a comeback in 1817. His

freedom march (see: CAMPAÑA LIBERTADORA) of 1819 culminated in victory at the Battle of *BOYACA on August 7. A constituent *Congress of Angostura established the *República de Gran Colombia on December 19, 1819, leaving for the *Congress of Cúcuta in 1821 the actual formal organization of the nation. A Liberal revolt in Spain (the Riego Revolt) in 1820 prevented any further Spanish initiatives at reconquest, and enabled Bolívar, *Sucre, José María *Córdoba, and others to move southward for the liberation of Quito (Ecuador), Lower Peru (Peru), and Upper Peru (Bolivia). The decisive victory of *Ayacucho in 1822 and the surrender of the last royalist stronghold, the port of El *Callao, in 1826 brought the major military campaigns to a close.

INDEPENDENT CONSERVATIVES. A faction of the *Conservative Party, important after 1950. It was also called Laureanist after its founder, Laureano *Gómez. Later led by his son, Alvaro *Gómez Hurtado, Independent Conservatism was highly nationalistic, anti-communistic, and heavily influenced by Franco's Spain. The Independents gave official but erratic support to the National Front (*Frente Nacional). See also: UNIONIST CONSERVATIVES

INDEPENDENT LIBERALS. A term applied to moderate *Liberals, as opposed to the *Radicals, from the mid-1870s to the late 1890s. Many collaborated with the *Nationalist Conservatives in support of the *Regeneration. For example, Liberals such as Eustorgio *Salgar, Carlos Martín, Teodoro Valenzuela, Salvador Camacho Roldán, Pablo Arosemena, Antonio Ferro, Ramón Santodomingo Vila, and Francisco Javier *Zaldúa refused to support *Aquileo Parra, the official candidate, in the elections of 1876, inclining instead toward the candidacy of Rafael *Nuñez.

INDERENA, see: INSTITUTO DE RECURSOS NATURALES RENOVABLES

INDIAN AFFAIRS, Division of, see: DIVISION DE ASUNTOS INDIGENAS

INDIAN AFFAIRS, General Court of, see: JUZGADO GENERAL DE INDIOS

INDIAN RESERVATIONS, see: RESGUARDOS

INDIAN SLAVERY. Authorization to capture and sell *Indians who were cannibals or who refused to accept Christianity was given to *Columbus in 1503 and also to *Pedrarias in 1513. The Crown attempted to restrict actual enslavement in 1526 and 1530 and abolished it altogether in the *New Laws of the Indies, 1542. Nevertheless, the *encomienda, established in the Antilles by 1503, the *mita, and the *repartimiento frequently amounted to virtual enslavement for the *Indians throughout the colonial period.

INDIANS. Based on the figures of Angel Rosenblat, the pre-conquest population of Colombia was approximately 850,000, distributed more or less in this manner: Cunas (*Panama), 8,000; Chocoes (*Chocó), 6,400; Calimas (*Valle del Cauca and *Tolima), 8,000; Guambianos, *Paeces, Quillancingas, Pastos, and Cuaiqueres (*Cauca, *Nariño, and *Huila), 136,000; Chaimes, *Quimbayas, *Pijaos (*Caldas, *Risaralda, *Quindío, and Tolima), 100,000; *Taironas (*Magdalena, *Cesar) 28,800; Chimilas (Magdalena, Cesar), 19,200; Caribes (along the *Magdalena River from the *Cauca to *Puerto Berrío, 66,400; *Motilones (*Cesar, *Guajira), 23,200; Muzos (*Boyacá, *Santander, *Cundinamarca), 20,000; *Chibchas, Sutagos, Tunebos, and Guanes (*Cundinamarca, *Boyacá, *Santander, *Norte de Santander, and *Arauca), 56,400; and other small groups, 16,000. In 1978, there were an estimated 547,000 Indians in Colombia. See also: ARAWAKS; CARIBS; CHIBCHAS; MESTIZOS; MISKITOS; MOTILONES; NARIÑO STYLE; PIJAOS; SINU; TAIRONAS; TUMACO

INDIES. Or, Indias, the colonial term for the Americas. The Indies are often referred to as the West Indies to distinguish them from the East Indies, territories near the subcontinent of India. The West Indies were governed by the *Council of the Indies and the *Laws of the Indies. The inhabitants were termed Indios, or *Indians.

INDIGO. Colombia enjoyed a boom in indigo production between 1860 and 1890. Cultivation tended to be concentrated in areas previously devoted to *tobacco growing. The peak year for indigo production was perhaps 1870-1871, when about 182,197 kilograms were produced. Production declined after 1890 because of poor farming methods and the development of a chemical substitute, although exportation of indigo from Colombia continued as late as 1918.

INFANTE AFFAIR. A reference to the murder trial and execution of Venezuelan-born Colonel Leonardo Infante (1795-1825). It was a cause célèbre in 1824-1825 because Judge Miguel Peña, also a Venezuelan, would not sign the court sentence. The affair contributed to Venezuelan-New Granadan tensions, leading to the dissolution of *Gran Colombia.

INGERMINA, O LA HIJA DE CALAMAR. A novel by Juan José *Nieto, accorded the distinction of being the first novel published by a Colombian author. The story of an *Indian princess who fell in love with Pedro de *Heredia, it was published in Kingston, Jamaica, in 1844.

INIRIDA. Also known as Puerto Inírida, San Felipe (Obando), and simply Obando, the capital of *Guainía is located on the Inírida River at 3° 49'N, 67° 52'W where it joins the Guaviare River near the Venezuelan border. The altitude is 100 meters, and the average temperature 29°C. Estimated population in 1985 was 3,311 people.

INQUISITION, Holy. The Tribunal del Santo Oficio, most often known simply as the Inquisition, established a court in *Cartagena, 1610, for the Bishoprics of Cartagena, *Santa Marta, Caracas, *Popayán, *Panama, Puerto Rico, *Santo Domingo, and Cuba. During its lifetime, there were an estimated 767 convictions, with 12 public and 33 private autos-da-fé. Abolished during the *Patria Boba, it was reestablished from 1816 to 1819 and then permanently closed after 1821.

INRAVISION. A television agency operated by the government under the Ministry of Communications. See also: TELEVISION

INSPECTION OF CULTS, Law Concerning the. Law 11, April 23, 1863. It forbade any minister of whatever religious sect to exercise his functions without first swearing allegiance to Colombia and to the *Constitution of 1863 before the civil authorities in the place of his calling. It also forbade the establishment of any *religious order in Colombia. The law was not enforced vigorously after 1867. See also: PROTESTANTISM; SEPARATION OF CHURCH AND STATE

INSTITUTO CARO Y CUERVO. National linguistic and literary institute near *Bogotá, founded in 1942. It was named after the distinguished Colombian linguists Miguel Antonio *Caro and José Rufino *Cuervo. The institute patronizes numerous studies in language and literature.

INSTITUTO COLOMBIANO AGROPECUARIO. ICA is an organization created in collaboration with the Rockefeller Foundation in 1963 to compile and disseminate the results of technical experiments of importance to agriculture and livestock production. ICA is also supported by the Kellogg Foundation. It maintains eleven experimental stations.

INSTITUTO COLOMBIANO DE ANTROPOLOGIA. The Colombian Institute of Anthropology, created in 1952 by the fusion of the Archeological Service (established in 1938) and the National Ethnological Institute (established in 1941). A government-supported agency devoted to archeological and anthropological research, it has published or sponsored the *Revista Colombiana de Folclor* (1952-), the *Revista Colombiana de Antropología* (1953-), and other works.

INSTITUTO COLOMBIANO DE BIENESTAR FAMILIAR. Institute of Family Welfare, created in 1968. It gives particular attention to the protection and welfare of children through *education, nutrition, day care, and so on.

INSTITUTO COLOMBIANO DE CREDITO EDUCATIVO DE ESTUDIOS TECNICOS EN EL EXTERIOR. ICETEX was authorized in 1950 and established in 1952. This national institution provides financial assistance to university students for technical studies in Colombia and abroad.

INSTITUTO COLOMBIANO DE CULTURA HISPANICA. Colombian Institute of Hispanic Culture, founded in 1951 to strengthen cultural ties between Spain and countries of Spanish America; part of the *Hispanidad* movement current in the 1950s.

INSTITUTO COLOMBIANO DE ENERGIA ELECTRICA. ICEL is a government agency formed in 1968 to stimulate the production and distribution of electric power through the facilities of fifteen affiliated companies. Originally formed in 1946 as the Instituto de Aprovechamiento de Aguas y Fomento Eléctrico, ICEL was estabished by Decree No. 3175 of 1968, which reorganized the earlier institute. According to official estimates, ICEL was largely responsible for the fact that electrical power produced by the various regional plants doubled between 1966 and 1970. ICEL was also a major sponsor of ISA (the Society for Electrical Interconnection) and its efforts to form a nationally integrated electrical network in Colombia. See also: ENERGY AND POWER

INSTITUTO COLOMBIANO DE LA REFORMA AGRARIA. INCORA, the Colombian Institute of *Agrarian Reform, was created in 1961 to undertake agricultural reform in Colombia. It has programs of education, land redistribution, resettlement, conservation, and so on. By 1970, the institute claimed to have acquired 3,867,800 hectares (1974) or 7.2 million acres (1975) and to have redistributed 135,000 land titles by 1975.

INSTITUTO COLOMBIANO DE SEGUROS SOCIALES. I.C.S.S. is the national social security agency, created by law in 1946. It began functioning in 1949 and was charged with providing benefits for designated illnesses, maternity cases, on-the-job accidents, disability, old age, and death.

INSTITUTO DE APROVECHAMIENTO DE AGUAS Y FOMENTO ELECTRICO. A government agency for generating *hydroelectricity formed in 1946 and reorganized in 1968 as the INSTITUTO COLOMBIANO DE ENERGIA ELECTRICA.

INSTITUTO DE FOMENTO INDUSTRIAL. IFI is a government organization created in 1940 to promote industries considered essential to the national welfare that had not attracted sufficient attention from private enterprise. In 1963, it was given the right to make public loans to encourage hydroelectric development, irrigation projects, airports, and drainage systems. IFI was extremely important in the development of the steel processing facilities at *Paz del Río.

INSTITUTO DE INVESTIGACIONES TECNOLOGICAS. Founded in 1955, the Institute of Technological Investigations was organized by the Armour Research Foundation and patronized by the *Banco de la República, the *Federación Nacional de Cafeteros, and *ECOPETROL, the national *petroleum corporation. It collaborates with the *United Nations. The institute emphasizes research in agricultural problems.

INSTITUTO DE MERCADEO AGROPECUARIO. IDEMA is an organization charged with regulating the flow of designated goods to markets in order to maintain even supplies and regular prices. It may buy, sell, and make loans to affect conditions on foreign and domestic markets. IDEMA was known as the *Instituto Nacional de Abastecimientos, or INA, from 1945 to 1968.

INSTITUTO DE RECURSOS NATURALES RENOVABLES. INDERENA is an institute authorized in 1960 and established in 1961 to survey and regulate the use of national water resources, soils, marine life, wildlife, forests, and national parks. In 1968, INDERENA was specifically charged with preserving and renewing all forest resources. Colombia's forest reserves are frequently cited as the second largest in the world.

INSTITUTO GEOGRAFICO AGUSTIN CODAZZI. Founded in 1935, it is charged with geographical, geophysical, climatological, and cartographical studies of Colombia. It is a successor to and is named after *Codazzi, the first director of the *Chorographic Commission of the 19th century.

INSTITUTO NACIONAL DE ABASTECIMIENTOS. The early name of the *INSTITUTO DE MERCADEO AGROPECUARIO.

INSURANCE, see: COMPAÑIA COLOMBIANA DE SEGUROS

INTEGRACION ANDINA, see: ANDEAN COMMON MARKET

INTENDANCY. The *intendencia* was an administrative subdivision of the Spanish empire, headed by an official known as an Intendant. The intendancy system was designed to make law enforcement, the administration of justice and defense, and the regulation of public finances more effective. Established first in Havana, Cuba, around 1765, the system was extended throughout Spanish America in the latter half of the 18th century. Nevertheless, it was not well developed in the Viceroyalty of *New Granada. Intendancies were established in Caracas (Venezuela) in 1776, Quito (Ecuador) in 1783, and Cuenca (Ecuador) in 1786, but plans for similar units administered from *Bogotá, *Popayán, *Honda, *Panama, and *Cartagena were never fully implemented as a result of the *Comuneros Revolt of 1781. Juan Francisco *Gutiérrez de Piñeres was probably the most significant Intendant in central New Granada, and his actions were in large part responsible for provoking the Comuneros Revolt. As used in more modern times under the *Constitution of 1886, an *intendencia* was the name of a governing unit smaller than a *department or a *province. The *Constitution of 1991 did not provide for intendancies, and the then-existing units—*Arauca, *Casanare, *Putumayo, and *San Andres, Providencia (y Santa Catalina)—became departments. See also: ADMINISTRATIVE DIVISIONS

INTENDANT. The *Intendente*: the official in charge of an *INTENDANCY.

INTER-AMERICAN COFFEE AGREEMENT, see: BRAZIL, Relations with

INTER-AMERICAN CONFERENCES, see: INTERNATIONAL CONFERENCE OF AMERICAN STATES

INTERMEDIO, EL. The name used by EL *TIEMPO, 1956-1957.

INTERNATIONAL COFFEE AGREEMENT (ICA). An arrangement for producing and marketing coffee reached in 1962, ICA lasted for twenty-seven years, with revisions in 1968, 1976, and 1983. Including at times as many as seventy-four nations, the agreement sought to provide economic stability with a steady flow of coffee and fair prices, and an International Coffee Organization (with headquarters in London) was created to supervise the arrangement. Export quotas were established for member nations annually on the basis of the kind of coffee produced (milds, arabicas, and robustas). In the 1985-1989 period Brazil was the largest producer, with 33.2% of the world quota; Colombia was second, with 19.9%. Other large producers were Indonesia, 6.8%; Mexico, 5.8%; and Ivory Coast, 4.9%. The agreement expired in September 1989, and efforts to renew it immediately were not successful.

INTERNATIONAL CONFERENCE AT THE HAGUE (SECOND), 1907. Colombia was represented by Jorge *Holguín,

Marcelino Vargas, and Santiago Pérez Triana. The delegation supported efforts to have the Drago Doctrine, which repudiated the use of force for collecting foreign debts, accepted as a general principle of international law.

INTERNATIONAL CONFERENCE OF AMERICAN STATES, I-VIII. From 1889 to 1948 there were nine meetings of representatives from Western Hemisphere nations. The first of these was held in Washington, D.C., in 1889, and Colombia was represented at the conference by José Marcelino Hurtado, Clímaco Calderón, and Carlos *Martínez Silva. Subsequent meetings were convened in Mexico City, 1901-1902, with Carlos Martínez Silva and Rafael *Reyes as representatives; Rio de Janeiro, 1906, Rafael *Uribe Uribe and Guillermo *Valencia, representatives; Buenos Aires, 1910, with Roberto Ancízar as representative; Santiago, Chile, 1923, Guillermo Valencia, Laureano *Gómez, and Carlos Uribe Echeverri, representatives; Havana, Cuba, 1928, with Enrique *Olaya Herrera, Roberto *Urdaneta Arbeláez, and Jesús Yepes, representatives; and Montevideo, 1933, with Alfonso *López Pumarejo, José Camacho Carreño, and Raimundo Rivas as representatives. The eighth Inter-American Conference was held in Lima in 1938, and the ninth in *Bogotá (see: INTERNATIONAL CONFERENCE OF AMERICAN STATES, IX, 1948). The most persistent problems discussed by the various conferences concerned arbitration or other means of achieving peaceful settlements of disputes. The Pan American Union grew out of the first conference, and the *Organization of American States was established at the ninth.

INTERNATIONAL CONFERENCE OF AMERICAN STATES, IX, 1948. Held in April in *Bogotá, the conference was presided over in part by Laureano *Gómez, then Colombia's Foreign Minister. Its chief concerns were with hemispheric defense. Although the meetings were interrupted by the *Bogotazo on April 9 (el Nueve de Abril), the conference completed its scheduled agenda. The *Organization of American States was established as a result of the conference.

INTERNATIONAL EUCHARISTIC CONGRESS (XXXIXth), 1968. An ecclesiastical conference held in *Bogotá, August 18-25, visited by Pope *Paul VI, August 22-24.

INTEROCEANIC CANAL. Historically, Colombia possessed two areas considered potentially useful as locations for interoceanic canals. These were the Isthmus of *Panama, where the only existing canal was built between 1904 and 1914, and the Department of *Chocó. At least four separate routes have been proposed for a canal joining the Atlantic and Pacific Oceans through the Chocó in the 20th century. The most often cited interconnection would link the *Atrato and the *San Juan rivers by the formation of two large lakes between them. A second alternative would run from the *Golfo de Urabá on the Atlantic to Humboldt Bay (6° 56′N, 77° 40′W) on the Pacific, via the Atrato and Truando Rivers. A third route would utilize the Atrato and the Napipí Rivers, with the latter emptying into the Pacific at Cupica Bay. The final possibility would connect the Atrato River with the Turia River (*Panama), which empties into the Gulf of San Miguel. Some authorities credit Captain John Illingworth (or Ilngrot)—later an important figure in Guayaquil, Ecuador—with having made the first interoceanic journey by means of the Napipí and Atrato Rivers in 1820.

INTER-OCEANIC CANAL COMPANY, see: COMPAGNIE UNIVERSELLE DU CANAL INTER-OCEANIQUE DE PANAMA

IRACA. The high priest of the *Chibchas in charge of the Temple of Suamo at *Sogamoso; also the name of the valley in which the Temple of Suamo was located. By some accounts, the last Iraca, Sugamuxi, was converted to Christianity and given a Christian burial when he died in 1560.

IRON AND STEEL. The most important iron ore deposits are in the Department of *Boyacá, but there are others in *Cundinamarca, *Huila, *Norte de Santander, *Tolima, *Valle del Cauca, and *Nariño. Small iron foundries were in existence in the 19th century and earlier. Important present-day steel mills are in *Medellín (Empresa Siderúgica), *Cali (Siderúgica del Pacífico), and *Bogotá (Siderúgica del Muna), but the most important steel complex is at *PAZ DEL RIO. Total national production in the late 1960s amounted to 200,000 metric *tons of pig iron, 252,000 tons of crude steel, and 240,000 tons of finished steel, about half the national consumption. In recent years Colombia has been self-sufficient in its iron requirements and is expected to stay that way for several decades. Existing iron ore reserves are estimated at about 100 million metric tons. See also: STEEL PRODUCTION

ISA, see: SOCIEDAD DE INTERCONEXION ELECTRICA S.A.

ISAACS, Jorge, 1837-1895. Poet, novelist, essayist, soldier, and Indianist. Born *Cali, April 1; died *Ibagué, April 17. He was educated in *Bogotá and published his early poetry in El *Mosaico. He supported the government in the *rebellions of 1854 and 1859-1862. Politically he was affiliated with the *Conservative Party until about 1870, after which he joined the *Liberals. He was active in politics in *Antioquia and helped to suppress a rebellion against the state in 1880. Isáacs was at times a landowner, a businessman, a bureaucrat, and a manager of *coal mines, but he is most often remembered as the author of *María, a romantic novel of unfulfilled love, set in the *Cauca Valley, first published in 1867. He was also the author of Estudio sobre las tribus indígenas del Estado del Magdalena, antes provincia de Santa Marta (1887).

ISTHMUS OF PANAMA, see: PANAMA

ITAGÜI, Battle of. February 2, 1841, at 6° 11'N, 75° 36'W, in the Department of *Antioquia, during the War of the *Supreme Commanders. It was an inconclusive encounter between General Eusebio Borrero, for the government, and Colonel Salvador *Córdoba, rebel, which resulted in a negotiated truce favorable to Córdoba.

-J-

JACQUIN, Nicholas Joseph, Baron de, 1727-1817. Botanist-physician; born Leiden (Netherlands); died Vienna (Austria). He studied and worked most of his life in Vienna. From 1755 to 1759 he traveled in *New Granada and elsewhere in the Western Hemisphere collecting information, and he later published Selectarum stirpium americanarum historia (Vienna, 1763).

JARAMILLO GIRALDO, Alipio, 1913-. Mural painter whose works were heavily influenced by Mexican artists Diego Rivera and David Alfaro Siqueiros. He was born in *Manizales, studied art at the Escuela de Bellas Artes in *Bogotá, and traveled in much of South America. His works express Indian or peasant themes, often with a strong social-protest emphasis.

JAVERIANA UNIVERSITY, see: UNIVERSIDAD JAVERIANA

JERICO, Battle of. March 6, 1885, 5° 48'N, 75° 47'W, in the Department of *Antioquia. General Marcelino Vélez, for the government, defeated the rebellious forces of *Liberal General Cándido Tolosa during the *rebellion of 1884-1885.

"JERUSALEM, To pass by." Historically, to engage in the contraband trade in Jamaica.

JESUITS. Members of the Society of Jesus (the Compañía de Jesús), an order of religious men, founded by the Basque Ignatius Loyola in 1540. The first Jesuits entered *New Granada in 1589, but they were not authorized to establish their houses until 1602. The Jesuit Province of the New Kingdom and Quito was created from 1605-1607, and within their first forty years the Jesuits had founded houses, missions, or schools in *Cartagena and *Bogotá, 1604; *Tunja, 1611; *Honda, 1622; the *Llanos, 1625; Mérida, 1629; *Popayán, 1640; *Mompós, 1643; *Pasto, 1644; and *Panama City, 1651. In 1738 they were responsible for bringing the colony its first *printing press. By 1767, they had 13 schools in New Granada, including one of the degree-granting *universities, the *Universidad Javeriana. A decree expelling the order from all Spanish dominions was issued in April 1767 because the Crown feared its political power, many people coveted the wealth the Jesuits had amassed, and the order's ultramontanism was seen as an obstacle to reform. Its concern to protect the *Indians was also an acknowledged factor. Pope Pius VII reestablished the Society in 1814, and it was permitted to return to Colombia in 1844, at least in part because officially it was expected to be useful in acculturating Indians in the border regions. In 1850, however, the *Liberal government expelled the order again by simply declaring that the decree of Charles III was still in effect. A *Conservative administration invited it back again in 1858, but the return of the Liberals led to their expulsion a third time in 1861. They were permitted to return permanently under the government of Rafael *Núñez in 1885.

JEWS. Many of Spain's Sephardic Jews accepted, or feigned, conversion to Roman Catholicism to avoid being expelled from Spain in the 1490s. Known as *conversos,* or New Christians, they suffered from the attentions of the *Inquisition, which suspected them of apostasy and coveted their wealth. Many were attracted to the New World, where the Inquisition was less effective due to the size of the territory. Since independence, and mainly in the 20th century, there has been some immigration into Colombia of Ashkenazim from eastern and central Europe. They and their descendants probably number no more than 10,000 to 20,000.

JIMENEZ DE QUESADA, Gonzalo, 1499(1509?)-1579. Conquistador, lawyer, author, born in Granada (Spain) of a *converso* (see: JEWS) family; died *Mariquita (Tolima), February 15. He arrived at *Santa Marta in 1535 and was given permission to explore by Pedro *Fernández de Lugo in 1536. His expedition from Santa Marta to the *Sabana de Bogotá, 1536-1539, initiated with 670 men traveling by land and 200 by river, was responsible for the founding of *Bogotá in 1538. Jiménez de Quesada went to Spain with *Belalcázar and *Federmann in 1539. He returned in 1550 as Marshal (*Adelantado*) of the *Nuevo Reino de Granada. He served as a military officer and explorer in the *Llanos of New Granada, 1567-1579. He was the author of *Ratos de Suesca,* which appears to have been lost; *El antijovio* (Bogotá, 1952); and other works. The name is also written as "Ximénez de Quesada" and often shortened simply to Quesada.

JOHN PAUL II, Pope. Juan Pablo II (Karol Wojtyla) was in Colombia July 1-7, 1986, when he visited *Bogotá, *Chiquinquirá, *Armero, and *Barranquilla. He had visited Latin Amercia seven years before, in 1979, when he attended the *Consejo Episcopal Latinoamericano in Puebla, Mexico. See also: PAPAL VISITS

JUAN, Jorge, see: JUAN AND ULLOA, Expedition of

JUAN AND ULLOA, Expedition of. Jorge Juan y Santacilia (1713-1773) and Antonio de Ulloa (1716-1795), royal commissioners, visited America, including parts of *New Granada, 1735-1740, recording socioeconomic data for the Crown. Portions of their reports were published at various times, including 1749, 1772, and 1826. In the last case, the *Noticias* *secretas de América* . . . was published in London as anti-Spanish propaganda.

JUCO, see: JUVENTUD COMUNISTA

JULIAN, Antonio, 1722-1790.   *Jesuit missionary who worked in the vicinity of *Santa Marta, 1749-1767. Father Julián was the author of *La perla de la América, provincia de Santa Marta,* a personal analysis of the natural resources and the *Indian communities he had observed. It was first published in Madrid in 1787.

JUNIN, Battle of.   August 6, 1824, Peru. Patriot forces of Simón *Bolívar won a major victory over royalist troops under General José de Canterac. The battle was part of Colombia's contribution to the liberation of Peru (see: INDEPENDENCE MOVEMENT).

JUNTA.   A committee or board, but particularly a *junta de gobierno,* an ad hoc group, often relatively small, that assumes governing authority in a time of political emergency. The idea first became familiar on both sides of the Atlantic during the French attempt to create a puppet regime in Madrid under Napoleon's brother, Joseph Bonaparte, 1808-1814. Various juntas were formed in 1808 to support Ferdinand VII against the Bonaparte regime. The most prominent of these was that of Seville, which called itself the *JUNTA SUPREMA DE GOBIERNO. In *New Granada, a *JUNTA OF NOTABLES (Junta de Notables), or group of important citizens, was called in September 1809, to discuss a response to the *Quito Rebellion, and a *JUNTA SUPREMA DEL NUEVO REINO was formed in 1810.

JUNTA CENTRAL (DE ESPAÑA).   A governing body formed in 1808 by the *Junta Suprema de España e Indias and other groups who supported Ferdinand VII against Joseph Bonaparte. On January 22, 1809, it issued a call for representatives to form a congress to govern all Spanish territories. The Junta Central's action was revolutionary in that it specifically invited the Spanish American colonies to become a part of the new government. Many American colonists initially allied themselves to the Junta Central but eventually opted for complete independence (see also: COLEGIO ELECTORAL). One of the most famous responses to the Junta's call for delegates to a congress was the *Memorial de agravios* by Camilo *Torres, which declared that the number of representatives allocated to the American colonies (twelve out of forty-eight) was inadequate and unfair. When the Junta Central was forced into exile on Isla de León in 1810, government was left in the hands of a five-member *CONSEJO DE REGENCIA.

JUNTA DE SECUESTROS. The Board of Confiscations that formed part of the Spanish *REIGN OF TERROR in *Bogotá in 1816.

JUNTA OF NOTABLES, 1809. A term that could be applied to the group of royal officials, *audiencia* judges (*oidores*), religious leaders, landowners, and other prominent residents convoked in *Bogotá by Viceroy *Amar y Borbón, as a *cabildo abierto,* in 1809 to discuss an appropriate response to the *Quito Rebellion. The Junta of Notables convened on September 6 and met several times over the next three months. It eventually produced the *Memorial de agravios* intended for the *Junta Central (de España), in Spain, but little effective action to deal directly with events in Quito. Many of those engaged in the deliberations were in sympathy with the Quito movement and more interested in discussing affairs in central *New Granada than in reasserting royal control in Ecuador.

JUNTA SUPREMA DE ESPAÑA E INDIAS, see: JUNTA SUPREMA DE GOBIERNO (DE SEVILLA)

JUNTA SUPREMA DE GOBIERNO (DE SEVILLA). A ruling council formed in the wake of Napoleon Bonaparte's attempt to place his brother, Joseph (José I), on the throne of Spain in 1808. The Supreme Junta proclaimed its loyalty to Ferdinand VII of Spain and sought to rule on his behalf until normal order could be restored. The junta of Seville, which called itself the Junta Suprema de España e Indias, joined with representatives from other provincial *juntas to form a unified authority (*JUNTA CENTRAL) that would govern all pro-Ferdinand forces.

JUNTA SUPREMA DEL NUEVO REINO, 1810-1811. Also known as the Junta Suprema del Reino, the Junta Suprema de Santa Fe, or simply as the Junta Suprema (Supreme Junta). It was formed in Bogotá, July 20-21, 1810, following the *Acta del 20 de Julio. It was charged with organizing a government loyal to Ferdinand VII but independent of the *Regency Council of Spain. The Supreme Junta issued a call for delegates to assemble in Bogotá to form a legislature for the whole of *New Granada. Several of the provinces were offended that the Supreme Junta of Santa Fe should assume automatically that it had the right to act for the whole kingdom and responded with their own individual proclamations, thus beginning the *Patria Boba period. The Junta Suprema de Santa Fe was replaced by the *Colegio Constituyente de Santa Fe de Bogotá and the State of *Cundinamarca.

JUNTAS DE APULO, Agreements of. Signed April 18, 1831, Juntas de Apulo, *Cundinamarca, by Dictator Rafael *Urdaneta and acting President Domingo *Caycedo. After conferences April 26-28, the two agreed to work for reunion of all factions under one government, to issue a general pardon for all people implicated in the *rebellion of 1830-1831, to recognize military promotions made by Urdaneta, to retain the armies of both sides temporarily at their existing levels, and to abolish distinctions between *Granadinos and Venezuelans. The agreement brought an end to the Urdaneta dictatorship and reestablished legitimate authority in Colombia.

JURO. Income paying treasury obligations. Imposed in *New Granada by President Saavedra y Guzmán in 1639.

JUVENTUD COMUNISTA. Youth wing of the *Partido Comunista de Colombia.

JUZGADO GENERAL DE INDIOS. A General Court of *Indian Affairs established in *New Granada in 1680, its purpose was to hear cases arising from disputes within Indian communities as well as between Indian and non-Indian groups. It functioned in conjunction with the Royal *Audiencia.

-K-

KELLOGG-BRIAND PACT. Also known as the Pact of Paris; multilateral international antiwar treaty signed August 27, 1928. Colombia adhered to the treaty by legislative act in 1930.

KEMMERER, Edwin Walter, 1875-1945. Princeton University economist who was head of an economic mission asked by the administration of President Pedro Nel *Ospina to study Colombian financial and administrative needs in 1923. His recommendations resulted in the creation of a national bank (the *Banco de la República), a consolidated budget, a comptroller general's office (see: *Controlaría General de la República), an agricultural credit and mortgage bank, and a pipeline from the *Magdalena River to *Barrancabermeja (Santander). A second mission in 1931 produced further reforms, including laws concerning *railroads, *banana exportation, customs administration, and *income tax.

KOREAN WAR, 1950-1953. Colombia contributed a frigate, the *Almirante Padilla,* and a battalion of approximately 1,000 men as part of a *United Nations peace force. The Colombian Battalion served from 1951-1954 with a United States contingent, principally the 7th Infantry Division. Colonels Jaime Puyo, Alberto Ruiz Novoa, and Carlos Ortiz Torres were the principal commanders of the Colombian forces in Korea. Many veterans of the Korean conflict later served as part of the United Nations mission to Egypt during the Suez Canal crisis, 1956-1958.

-L-

LA CONDAMINE, Charles Marie de, 1701-1774. French naturalist and mathematician. See also: SCIENTIFIC COMMISSION OF THE ACADEMY OF SCIENCES OF PARIS

LA DORADA RAILROAD, see: DORADA RAILWAY, La

LABOR LEGISLATION OF THE 1920s. Several laws to protect workers and improve working conditions were passed in 1923, in what might be called one of the early waves of labor reform. These included laws regarding contracts, rest days on Sunday, the eight-hour workday, profit sharing, a commission on social affairs, a federation of workers, protection of women workers, an office of labor affairs, and a program of general social benefits. In addition, paid holidays were the subject of legislation in 1921 and 1926, and laws regarding the right to strike and workers' insurance were passed in 1919 and 1921, respectively.

LABOR UNIONS, see: TRADE UNIONS

LAFTA, see: LATIN AMERICAN FREE TRADE ASSOCIATION

LAIA, see: LATIN AMERICAN INTEGRATION ASSOCIATION

LAIN, Domingo, d. 1974. A Spanish-born priest who left the *Golconda movement to become a guerrilla in the *Ejército de Liberación Nacional.

LANCASTERIAN SCHOOLS. Schools using the method of instruction popularized by English educator Joseph Lancaster (1778-1838), which used advanced students to teach beginning students. The method was useful for reaching large numbers with limited resources. Following legislation in 1821, Lancaster himself came to *Bogotá in 1822 to establish his system in Colombia, especially in normal schools. The Lancasterian method was influential in Colombian educational history, 1821-1835. See also: EDUCATION

LAND LAW OF 1936, see: LAW 200 OF 1936

LAND LAWS OF 1874 and 1882. Law 61 of 1874 and Law 48 of 1882 established policies dealing with colonization of public lands. The laws exemplified a "land to the tiller" philosophy, saying that public lands could be claimed only by those who actively exploited them. Persons bringing land into cultivation could claim it and an adjacent parcel. The intention was to encourage both large-scale entrepreneurs and small farmers to increase overall national production. Squatters on public lands who had made good-faith improvements could claim the land as theirs, but the law encouraged them to file for formal titles to avoid future problems. Many of these principles were reinforced by Law 48 of 1882, which also limited the maximum size of a grant to 5,000 hectares.

LAND REFORM, see: AGRARIAN REFORM

LAND TITLES DECISION OF 1926. In addressing the problem of public lands, private lands, and land ownership, the Colombian *Supreme Court declared in 1926 that, in the case of land disputes, land should be considered to be public, state-owned land unless proven otherwise. Proof of ownership could be established by producing the original grant by which the state had ceded ownership from the public domain to a private individual or group. Wills, bills of sale, or previous court decisions were no longer sufficient to prove ownership. The court's pronouncement created widespread confusion since few owners could supply the documentary proof demanded. The government attempted to recover some disputed acreage beginning in 1927, and land disputes continued to increase until *Congress passed the Land Act (*LAW 200) of 1936, which clarified private and public land titles in a much more definitive fashion.

LARA, Patricia, 1953-. *Newspaperwoman who, as an alumna of Columbia University Graduate School of Journalism, was invited to an awards ceremony there. She was detained arbitrarily by U.S. officials at Kennedy Airport for five days and then deported October 17, 1986. The widely publicized event derived, most believed, from her best-selling account of the *Movimiento Diecinueve de Abril, *Siembras vientos y recogerás tempestades* (Sow the winds and reap the whirlwinds), which had made her persona non grata to the United States government.

LARA BONILLA, Rodrigo, d. 1984. Minister of Justice for the *Betancur administration, assassinated April 30, 1984, in *Bogotá. As Minister of Justice Lara Bonilla had been active in attempting to suppress the illegal *drug trade. The Betancur administration, convinced that the assassins had been hired by the drug bosses, retaliated with a mass of raids on suspected narcotics dealers—one source claiming as many as 80 raids in the city of *Medellín alone. He was succeeded by Enrique *Parejo González. An agreement among *Andean Common Market countries for joint action against the drug trade, signed April 30, 1986, was named the Acuerdo Lara Bonilla in his memory.

LATIFUNDIOS. Literally, "wide" or "large fields"; a term used to describe large landholdings, such as plantations (the Caribbean region), *estancias* (Argentina), *fazendas* (Brazil), *fundos* (Chile), and *haciendas* (Mexico, Colombia, and elsewhere). Historically, latifundios, and the owners of latifundios (*latifundistas*), have created the dominant social structure and lifestyle of Latin American society. See also: HACIENDA; MINIFUNDIOS

LATIN AMERICA (*América Latina*). The appelation "Latin" to distinguish the *Roman Catholic, Spanish-speaking countries of America from the Protestant, English-speaking ones, was coined in the mid-1830s by the French minister in Washington, Maxime Chevalier. It was intended to promote the idea that the Spanish-speaking peoples should look to his country (another Romance-, or Latin-, language nation) rather than to the United States or the United Kingdom for political support and cultural leadership. The term was seized upon by many Colombian exiles in Paris, notably José María Torres Caicedo, to avoid the more offensive term "Spanish." It was further encouraged during the Mexican adventure of Maximilian, which was sponsored from France by Napoleon III during the 1860s. It seems not to have found its way into general English-language usage until the early years of the 20th century. As often employed in the United States by the State Department and others, it has acquired a sociopolitical definition as a generalized term for all developing countries in the Western Hemisphere south of the Rio Grande, regardless of their cultural heritage.

LATIN AMERICAN FREE TRADE ASSOCIATION. Also known as LAFTA and the Latin American Common Market, an international trade association created by the Treaty of Montevideo in 1960. Argentina, Bolivia, Brazil, Chile, Colombia, Ecuador, Mexico, Paraguay, Peru, Uruguay, and Venezuela adhered to the agreement, which was designed to promote economic integration among the member nations, to achieve a favorable trading position vis-à-vis nonmember nations, and to encourage efficient use of available resources. The *Andean Common Market (ANCOM), to which Colombia also belongs, is a regional affiliate of LAFTA, which has now become the *LATIN AMERICAN INTEGRATION ASSOCIATION.

LATIN AMERICAN INTEGRATION ASSOCIATION. LAIA (ALADI or ALAI after its Spanish name, Alianza Latinoamericana de Integración) was created June 1980 as a successor organization to the *LATIN AMERICAN FREE TRADE ASSOCIATION. It is a less formal, less ambitious group operating on the principle of bilateral tariff reductions between any two members with the option of other members joining the agreement if they wish.

LAUREA CRITICA, La. A play written in 1629 by Fernando *Fernández de Solís y Valenzuela (1616-1677), said to be the first theatrical piece known to have been written by a Colombian author. Fernández de Solís y Valenzuela is also known as Bruno de Valenzuela, the name he used after entering the Carthusian order in Segovia (Spain) after 1633. He was a brother of Pedro de *Solís y Valenzuela.

LAUREANISTAS, see: INDEPENDENT CONSERVATIVES

LAW. The European conquest of Spanish America brought with it basically Roman legal traditions that were made more rigid by the bureaucratic formalism of Philip II. The early years of the colonies were a combination of Castilian law and the Laws of Burgos (1512-1513), the first effort at a set of regulations specifically for the new lands. The peculiar circumstances of the Indies eventually produced the *NEW LAWS OF THE INDIES (1542) and a second codification known as the *Recopilación de todas las leyes de las Indias* in 1681 (see: LAWS OF THE INDIES). Independent Colombia embarked on a new codification in which the French Napoleonic Code was a new external influence. The Penal Code was promulgated in 1837 and rewritten in 1858 and 1873. Following the *Constitution of 1886, the 1858 Penal Code (with some amendments) was restored until the present code of 1936 came into effect in 1938. The 1873 Civil Code is still operative, although the matrimonial provisions were substantially modernized in 1932. During the period of decentralization (1860-1886), each state adopted its own commercial code. The unitary Constitution of 1886 selected the 1869 Panama code (itself largely taken from the Chilean commercial code of 1865) as the model for the new national commercial code. This was substantially modified in the 1920s and 1930s as a result of the *Kemmerer Mission. In 1935 an entirely new commercial code was embarked upon. The commission charged with its preparation took twenty years to report. *Labor legislation was systematized in an all-embracing Labor Code in 1950, the *Código Substantivo de Trabajo.* See also: *RECOPILACION GRANADINA*

LAW OF THE HORSES, see: LEY DE LOS CABALLOS

LAW OF THE SEA. Like many other nations since *World War II, Colombia has extended its territorial waters from the traditional 3-mile limit to one of 12 miles out from the shore. More recently, following the lead of its Pacific Coast neighbors (Ecuador, Peru, and Chile), it has joined the worldwide movement claiming the right to exclusive economic exploitation within a range of 200 miles.

LAW 120 OF 30 DECEMBER 1919.   Passed by *Congress after the *Supreme Court nullified measures by the *Suárez administration to assert control of Colombia's subsoil mineral rights. Law 120 provided that the subsoil rights belonged to the party who controlled the surface, specifically in the case of all lands gained before October 28, 1873. On public lands, or lands acquired after 1873, however, subsoil rights were retained by the nation, although the law did recognize the public benefit to be derived from developing these resources. The law was part of an ongoing struggle by Colombian governments to cope with *foreign investments and to protect national interests in the early 20th century. See also: DECREE 150; DECREE 1225 BIS; SUBSOIL MINERAL RIGHTS

LAW 135 OF 1961.   An *agrarian reform act intended to increase rural production and to address land imbalances by redistribution programs. The law established the *Instituto Colombiano de la Reforma Agraria (INCORA) and authorized the government to purchase and to redistribute land to peasants or small farmers who would actually undertake cultivation of it. Areas singled out for specific attention were Sumapaz (*Cundinamarca), Cunday, Iconosco, and Villarica in *Tolima, and the coastal *banana zone. INCORA was able to stimulate redistribution of some lands and colonization of new lands, but opposition to its programs and prolonged legal disputes kept the institute from achieving the wide-scale success its founders had hoped for.

LAW 200 OF 1936.   Widely regarded as the first modern Colombian *agrarian reform act, the bill was presented to *Congress by the *López Pumarejo administration, July 22, 1935, and eventually adopted in 1936. It sought to deal with existing land disputes, to avoid future conflicts, and to stimulate national productivity. On lands where there were squatter disputes, ownership had to be established by an original title or deed dating from the colonial period. If documentation could not be found, the lands were considered *baldíos,* or public lands, and colonists on the land could apply to the government for free land grants. If titles could be established by owners, then colonists had to be compensated for improvements before eviction. This addressed the land invasion, a squatters' rights issue. The law further provided that where no disputes existed, traditional documentation, such as wills and deeds of thirty years' duration, was accepted as proof of ownership. This clarified ambiguities of ownership in large numbers of cases, formally creating a recognizable juridical distinction between public and private lands. Finally, Law 200 established the concept of the social function of property and provided that private land that had not been productively exploited for ten years could be expropriated by the state, reverting to public land under state ownership.

LAWS OF THE INDIES.   The mass of legislation promulgated by the Spanish Crown to promote the good governance of its new American possessions evolved in stages, the three most prominent of which were the Laws of Burgos (1512-1513), the *NEW LAWS OF THE INDIES (1542), and the *Recopilación . . . (1681). The Laws of Burgos, although concerned with regulating the colonists' relations with the *Indian population, have been described as little more than a formal enunciation of current practice in the Indies. The laws gave validity to the existence of *encomiendas and tried to establish limits to the demands colonists could make of Indian laborers as well as the benefits workers could expect from the Spanish-Indian relationship. Partly in response to the criticisms and revelations of abuses made by Bartolomé de las *Casas and others, an attempt was made to improve living and working conditions for the Indians in the New Laws of the Indies (1542), introduced into *New Granada in 1544. Public protests against the New Laws began among the European colonists almost immediately, and the Crown softened the laws restricting Spanish treatment of the Indians in the 1550s. Many provisions were simply never put into effect. Continual issuance of laws on various subjects led to a major codification effort in the late 1600s. An enormous nine-volume *Recopilación de leyes de los reynos de las Indias* was issued in Spain in 1681, but continued changes in administration and commercial regulations required a three-volume supplement in 1791. A completely new compilation, the *Novísima recopilación de las leyes de Indias,* began to appear in 1805, but the twelve-volume work was still incomplete when the Spanish American empire began to dissolve a few years later.

LEAD. A little lead is mined in *Cundinamarca, *Huila, *Risaralda, *Cauca, and *Tolima. In 1980 production was 300 metric *tons, and in 1985 there were 100 tons (or about 1% of Peru's 200,000 tons per year).

LEAGUE OF COMMERCE, see: LIGA DE COMERCIO

LEAGUE OF NATIONS. An organization for international cooperation formed at the close of *World War I by the Treaty of Versailles, 1919. Colombia joined the league by legislative action in 1919 and was a consistent supporter of the association, to which it submitted the *Leticia dispute with Peru for adjudication in 1933.

LEBRON, Jerónimo. Governor of *Santa Marta in 1540. He sought to take control of *Bogotá from Hernán *Pérez de Quesada. When the latter resisted, Lebrón negotiated a cash settlement and returned to Santa Marta. His expedition is credited with having brought the first Spanish women to Bogotá.

LEGION BLANCA. Name given to one of the more notorious *DEATH SQUADS.

LEGION BRITANICA. Reference to groups of British-led soldiers recruited for the wars of independence, 1817-1824. Major expeditions were sent from Great Britain under Colonel George Hippisley in 1817, and Colonel James English, Captain George Elsom, General John D'Evereux, and General Gregor MacGregor, all in 1819. See also: INDEPENDENCE MOVEMENT; BRITISH LEGION

LEHDER RIVAS, Carlos. Drug dealer found guilty on May 18, 1988, of trying to smuggle 3.3 tons of *cocaine into the United States. His seven-month trial, held in Jacksonville, Florida, resulted in a sentence of life plus 135 years in prison. Lehder Rivas was a major drug lord who operated out of *Medellín, the Department of *Quindío, and Norman's Key in the Bahama Islands. He formed his own political party (the *MOVIMIENTO LATINO NACIONAL) and newspaper (*Quindío Libre*), constructed a hotel complex (Posada Alemana) in *Armenia, and developed a large following in Colombia for his strong nationalistic, anti-imperialist stance and for numerous philanthropical works. He was the first major drug dealer extradited and convicted under the U.S.-Colombian *Extradition Treaties.

LEIVA (LEYVA). Municipal center located at 5° 38'N, 73° 32'W, in the Department of *Boyacá. Altitude is 2,145 meters, average temperature 17°C, and the population 2,561 (1985 estimate). Villa de Leyva, as the city is also known, was founded June 12, 1572, and became a tourist center for the aristocracy during the colonial period. It is remembered as the birthplace of Antonio *Ricuarte, the place where Antonio *Nariño died, and the site of the *Congress of Leiva. Several examples of colonial architecture have been preserved in the city, and the locale has been used as a setting for a number of motion pictures.

LEIVA, Congress of, see: CONGRESS OF LEIVA

LEON GOMEZ, Adolfo, 1858-1927. Lawyer, poet, playwright, journalist, historian; born at the *hacienda* El Retiro near Pasca (*Cundinamarca), September 19; died *Agua de Dios (Cundinamarca), June 27. Professionally a lawyer and jurist and a member of the *Liberal Party, León Gómez was better known for his crusading journalism (defense of the rights of the downtrodden, anti-imperialism, pro-Hispanic unity, and so on), especially the *newspaper *Sur América,* which he edited from 1903-1918. He was a political prisoner during the War of the *Thousand Days and later published *Secretos del panóptico* (1905), which described local prison life. He was a founding member of the *Academia Colombiana de Historia and the author of *El Tribuno de 1810* (1910), which focused on his great-grandfather, José *Acevedo y Gómez. From July 1, 1919, until his death, he was a resident of the leprosarium at *Agua de Dios, which he described in his book *La ciudad de dolor* (1923). He was the grandson of Josefa *Acevedo de Gómez and the great-grandfather of Carlos *PIZARRO LEONGOMEZ.

LEONOR, THE BLACK QUEEN. Titular head of a short-lived union of black slaves and *cimarrones* (*maroons) in 1634. Ex-slaves from the *palenques* of Limón, Poloni, and Sanaguare, in the vicinity of *Cartagena, rebelled, proclaiming themselves independent under Queen Leonor. Slave owners feared massive rebellion, and Governor Francisco de Murga attacked and destroyed the *palenques,* capturing at least thirty-three of the rebels, who were forced to stand trial. Little is known specifically about Leonor herself.

LEOPARDOS, Los. A name given to a group of political figures in the 1920s who were influenced by and supporters of European fascism. Members of Los Leopardos included José Camacho Carreño (diplomat), Augusto Ramírez Moreno (orator); Eliseo Arango (Minister of Education); and Silvio Villegas (director of *El Debate*). According to Herbert Braun, they were motivated by a Christian concern over the growth of materialism, and they became acerbic critics of the *Liberals after 1930.

LESSEPS, Ferdinand de, 1805-1894.   French diplomat, born November 14, at Versailles; died, December 7, at Le Chenaie. Lesseps (or De Lesseps) was responsible for the building of the Suez Canal, April-November 1859. His success in Egypt led him to attempt construction of a canal across the *Isthmus of Panama after the International Congress of Geographical Sciences had endorsed the idea of such a project in 1879. Unfortunately, the size of the undertaking, errors in judgment, and Lesseps' own personal temperament led to the project's failure in 1889. The French government investigated and prosecuted the officials of the canal construction company (the *COMPAGNIE UNIVERSELLE DU CANAL INTER-OCEANIQUE DE PANAMA) for improper management, 1892-1893. Lesseps was sentenced to prison but never actually forced to spend time in jail.

LETICIA.   Capital of the Commissariat of *Amazonas, located at 4° 12'N, 69° 56'W. The altitude is 96 meters; the average temperature, 29°C; and the estimated population in 1985 was 13,210 people. Colombia's principal port on the *Amazon River, Leticia is a center for tourism, hunting, *fishing, and native handicrafts. The settlement was originally established on April 25, 1867, with the name San Antonio. It passed to Colombian jurisdiction in 1930 as a result of the *Lozano-Salomón Treaty, and was the center of the *Leticia dispute with Peru, 1932-1934. In more recent times it has been a major point for the transfer of illegal narcotics.

LETICIA DISPUTE, 1932-1934.   A group of Peruvians, repudiating the *Lozano-Salomón Treaty of 1922, forcibly occupied *Leticia on September 1, 1932. Unable to secure the Peruvian government's aid in evacuating the port, Colombia submitted the dispute to the *League of Nations in January 1933. By peace agreement signed May 25, 1933, the League took over the area from Peru and, after a year's occupation, returned Leticia to Colombia on June 19, 1934.

LEY DE LOS CABALLOS. "Law of the Horses," a name given to Law No. 61 of 1888, which granted the President of Colombia extraordinary powers to control internal disorder. These included the power to imprison, exile, or deprive suspects of civil rights and permission to prohibit the meeting of any group. The controversial law was not revoked until 1898. The name is derived from an incident in which the slaughter of several horses in the *Cauca was reported as an indication that a rebellion was planned against the government.

LEYES DE LAS INDIAS, see: LAWS OF THE INDIES

LEYVA, see: LEIVA

LEZO, Blas de, 1689-1741. Heroic naval commander, born Guipúzcoa (Spain), March 13; died *Cartagena, September 11. Blas de Lezo entered the navy as a young man. In 1723 he was made Chief of the Squadron of the Sea (Jefe de la Escuadra del Mar), and in 1732, Lieutenant General of the Armada. He suffered the loss of his left leg and left eye and the use of his right arm in various European battles before coming to *New Granada. Although fatally wounded in the siege of Cartagena, he defended the city successfully against the attack of Admiral *Vernon and the British fleet in 1741.

LIBERAL. An adjective or noun that, when capitalized ("Liberal"), is used to refer to the ideology, political program, and members of the *LIBERAL PARTY.

LIBERAL PARTY. The Partido Liberal, one of Colombia's two major traditional political parties. It developed in the mid-19th century during the presidencies of Generals José Hilario *López and José María *Obando. It is sometimes said to have been founded or inspired by Francisco de Paula *Santander. The party tends to support religious toleration, decentralized administration, and more representative government. Mildly reformist, its emblematic color is red. A member of the National Front (*Frente Nacional), 1958-1974, the party has been split by factionalism since the 1960s, with the main branch of the Liberals known at times as "Turbayistas" after Julio César *Turbay Ayala, and supporters of Alfonso *López Michelsen ("Lopistas") and the *Movimiento Revolucionario Liberal. In the 1980s, New Liberalism (Nuevo Liberalismo) became a third major splinter group. The Turbayistas have tended to be tougher in antiguerrilla tactics and approaches toward Cuba and Nicaragua. In contrast, the Lopistas were more flexible and open to negotiations with dissident groups. See also: NUEVO LIBERALISMO

LIBERAL REVOLUTIONARY MOVEMENT, see: MOVIMIENTO REVOLUCIONARIO LIBERAL

LIBERATING CAMPAIGN OF 1819, see: CAMPAÑA LIBERTADORA

LIBERTADOR, El. "The Liberator," an honorary title bestowed on Simón *BOLIVAR, October 14, 1813, by a *cabildo* in Caracas (Venezuela). As a result of the *Campaña Admirable, Bolívar entered Caracas on October 13 as a victorious leader, and a special *cabildo* was convened to celebrate the patriots' defeat of the royalist forces. On the following day, Bolívar was recognized as Captain General of the army and given the special title of Liberator. As either *el Libertador, El Libertador,* or simply *Libertador,* the title became a synonym or sobriquet frequently used in place of his actual name.

LIBERTICIDA. Literally, the "murder of personal liberty"; a name coined by journalists to describe the effect of the government security laws passed 1927-1928 to allow national police forces greater latitude in suppressing alleged threats to the state. The law of 1927 allowed search of private homes on the simple suspicion that something might be amiss. In 1928 the government proposed to arrest anyone who attacked established concepts of the family, the sacred right to property, or the idea of the state as it then existed.

LIBRA. A pound, either the weight or the currency unit. In weight, twenty-five *libra* make an *arroba,* and four *arrobas* equal a *quintal.* The pre-1857 *libra* equaled 461.92 grams, making the *arroba* 11.548 and the *quintal* 46.192 kilograms, respectively. It is now interpreted as 500 grams, making the *arroba* 12.5 kilograms and the *quintal* 50. (Elsewhere in Latin America, the *quintal métrico* is 100 kilograms.) Two thousand *libras* make the metric ton (*tonelada métrica*) or "tonne" of 1,000 kilograms, which is 1.11002 short (U.S.) tons or 0.9842 long tons.

LIEVANO AGUIRRE, Indalecio 1917-1982. Historian, Liberal legislator, diplomat, Presidential *Designado, 1975. Born *Bogotá, July 24; died Bogotá. He received his degree in law, social sciences, and economics from the *Universidad Javeriana in 1944 and subsequently taught at both the Javeriana and the *Universidad de los Andes. His public appointments included terms in both houses of the national *Congress; secretary to the Presidency, 1943; diplomatic posts in Cuba, 1953, the *Organization of American States, 1954, and the *United Nations, 1976-1978; and Minister of Foreign Relations, 1974. He was also a well-known historian. *Los grandes conflictos sociales y económicos de nuestra historia,* first published as a series of newspaper articles, is his most often cited work.

LIGA DE COMERCIO. The League of Commerce, a political pressure group, was formed as a result of a meeting in *Bogotá, May 28, 1899. It was composed of *Liberals who opposed rebellion, Historical Conservatives (*Históricos), and leading merchants, and its aim was to persuade the government to stabilize currency and to address economic and political reforms in order to avoid civil war. The administration of President *Sanclemente initially yielded to the league's requests, promising government economy and limitations on new paper money issues as well as redemption of paper money then in circulation. Neither the league's influence nor limited government action, however, prevented the outbreak of the War of the *Thousand Days in October of the same year.

LIGA ELECTORAL. The Electoral League, an association formed by an agreement signed April 5, 1869, by José M. Rojas Garrido, Ramón Mercado, and Angel María Céspedes, *Liberals, and Recaredo de Villa, Luis Segundo Silvestre, and Leonardo Canal, *Conservatives. It founded an unsuccessful alliance of Conservatives and authoritarian Liberals (*Draconianos) who aimed to prevent the election of radical Liberal Santiago Pérez, by uniting behind the ex-President, General T. C. de *Mosquera. Mosquera, however, refused the candidacy.

LITERATURE. Virtually nothing of pre-conquest Indian literature from present-day Colombia has survived, due at least in part to the fact that writing was in an incipient stage of development among the *Indians in the 16th century. *El *Yurupary*, an oral epic collected from Indians of the *Vaupés region (first published in 1890) can be taken as an example of a literary tradition that may have existed prior to the coming of the Europeans.

During the colonial period (1492-1810), Colombian literature was heavily influenced by models from peninsular Spain, Spanish control of intellectual life, and the isolation of Colombian writers. Literature was produced by a political-military-ecclesiastical elite and was intended largely for local consumption by a privileged upper-class minority. The conquest itself, local society, and religious themes dominate the work of colonial authors.

The work *Claribalte, libro del muy forzado e invencible cavallero* (1519) by Gonzalo *Fernández de Oviedo (1478-1557) has been called the first novel written in the New World, although this is largely a coincidence of history since neither the author nor the subject of the work can be identified as essentially Hispanic American. Gonzalo *Jiménez de Quesada (1499-1579), *El antijovio;* Juan de *Castellanos (1522-1607), *Elegías de varones ilustres . . . ;* and Juan *Rodríguez Freile (1566-1642), *El carnero,* are among the most distinguished accounts from the conquest and colonial society. Quesada and Castellanos were both conquerors. Quesada's work, a defense of Spain and Spanish actions, may be the earliest known text by a Colombian writer available in published form; Castellanos's account of the conquest, in verse, has been called one of the longest poems ever written. Rodníguez Freile's *El carnero* is a narrative description of life and events in Bogotá from about 1539 to 1636.

Noteworthy examples of the religious influence on authors can be seen in the works of a nun, Francisca Josefa del *Castillo y Guevara (1671-1742). Mother Castillo's *Afectos espirituales* and *Su vida* exemplify Hispanic mysticism. Hernando *Domínguez Camargo (ca. 1606-1659) reflects the domination of European/Spanish and religious motifs in his *Poema heróico de San Ignacio de Loyola.* Fernando *Fernández de Solís y Valenzuela (1616-1677) has been credited with the first dramatic work written in Colombia, *La *laurea crítica;* and *El desierto prodigioso y pródigo de desierto* by Pedro de *Solís y Valenzuela (1624-1711) may be the first novel by a native writer on a Latin American theme.

The influence of the Enlightenment can be seen in the late 18th century with the founding of the first *newspapers (see: *Papel periódico . . .), Antonio *Nariño's publication of *The*

Rights of Man (1793), and the turn-of-the-century scientific works of José Celestino *Mutis (1732-1808) and Francisco José de *Caldas (1771-1816).

Colombian independence may be dated from 1832, and at least one author has suggested that post-independence (or 19th-century) writing followed a pattern that began with political essays and creative literature based on neoclassical forms. There followed two generations dominated by *romanticism, *costumbrismo,* and realism, and the end of the century saw the rise of *modernism.

In the case of the novel, the noteworthy authors included Juan José *Nieto (1804-1866), whose work *Ingermina, o la hija de Calamar,* published in Jamaica in 1844, is often cited as the first novel by a Colombian (rather than a member of Spanish colonial society) on a Colombian theme. *Costumbrismo,* the use of detailed descriptions of local regions and customs, influenced many of Colombia's 19th-century authors. *El *Mosaico,* a newspaper published 1858-1872, included numerous *costumbrista* pieces. *Manuela* (1858) by Eugenio *Díaz (1804-1865) is one of the most often cited *costumbrismo* novels. *María* by Jorge *Isaacs (1837-1895) is a combination of romanticism and *costumbrista* influences, first published in 1867. *María* remains one of the most widely read novels ever written by a Latin American. Spanning the latter part of 19th and early 20th centuries, the works of Tomás *Carrasquilla (1858-1940), such as *Frutos de mi tierra* and *La Marquesa de Yolombó,* combined realism, *costumbrista,* and regional—*Antioqueño*—influences.

Poetry bore a marked influence of romanticism for much of the period. José Eusebio *Caro (1817-1853) is often cited as one of the best early romantics. Rafael *Pombo (1833-1912), however, was a much more widely read author in the latter part of the century, and José Asunción *Silva (1865-1896) is said to have been the precursor of modernism in Colombia. The works of Miguel Antonio *Caro (1843-1909) were rooted in traditional Spanish, humanistic models and motifs.

Writing for the theater, or drama, was not widely practiced by Colombians in the 19th century, although a few works were created, such as the lost plays of Josefa *Acevedo de Gómez; *Un alcalde a la antigua y dos primos a la moderna* by José María *Samper (1828-1888); and the opera liberettos of Rafael Pombo. The linguistic studies of Miguel Antonio Caro and Rufino José *Cuervo (1844-1911) should be noted also before leaving the 19th century.

The early part of the 20th century was dominated by modernism, which has been described both as an emphasis on the esthetic and as aristocratic escapism. In poetry, the most widely known figure was Guillermo *Valencia (1873-1943), and the 1897 novel, El moro, the autobiography of a horse, by José Manuel *Marroquín (1827-1908) is often cited as an example of the conservative *oligarchy's nostalgic defense of an idealized rural society against the incipient modernization, urbanization, and democratization of Colombian society.

In addition to Valencia, major poets of the early part of the century include Porfirio Barba Jacob (Miguel Angel *Osorio, 1883-1942) and León de *Greiff (1895-1967). Both were influenced by modernism, but Barba Jacob's poetry emphasized death, desolation, and the funereal, while León de Greiff represented the avant-garde and contributed to the renovation of Colombian verse in the 1930s.

In contrast to the oligarchic escapism of many writers, especially the modernist poets of the time, novelists José María *Vargas Vila (1860-1933) and José Antonio *Osorio Lizarazo (1900-1964) were writing iconoclastic, protest-oriented works. Vargas Vila wrote more than thirty novels filled with grammatical experimentation, strong anti-clericalism, and opposition to the conservative ruling elite. Osorio Lizarazo's themes dealt with the lives of urban, working-class people and efforts to cope with modern, technical, and industrialized society. The works of the best-known dramatists of the time, Antonio *Alvarez Lleras (1892-1956) and Luis Enrique *Osorio (1896-1966), encompass many similar social and intellectual themes. Perhaps the successful fusion of the socially conscious and the traditional aesthetic concern can be seen in *La vorágine, published in 1924 by José Eustacio *Rivera (1888-1928). This well-known work is an account of the futile struggle for survival by rubber workers in the *Amazon region and at the same time a conscious attempt to probe the intellectual's role in society.

From the 1920s onward, Colombian literature has been marked by a diversity too broad to follow closely in a short summary. Repeatedly, names such as Los *Nuevos, *Mito, *Piedra y Cielo, and the *Barranquilla Group have signaled the appearance of new literary associations, each with its own innovating thrust. The development of a movement or style known as *magical realism, La *Violencia, and rejection of traditional elitism have served as the most important stimuli or motivation for 20th-century writers.

Associated with the Barranquilla group, Gabriel *García Márquez (1927-) eventually became the most well known of the authors whose style falls under the category of magical realism. After a number of short stories and novels in the 1950s and 1960s, his 1967 masterpiece, *One Hundred Years of Solitude*, is a superb example of magical realism, combining history and fantasy, philosophy and social criticism, the ideal and the absurd as it chronicles the life of the Buendía family. Magical realism uses the exaggerated and the fantastic, to describe, to commemorate, and to criticize the reality of life, often in a humorous way.

La Violencia and its aftermath in Colombian society affected not only García Márquez, whose novels abound with criticisms of sociopolitical violence, but numerous other authors as well. Seldom humorous, a representative sampling of these works from the 1950s to the 1970s might include *El cristo de espaldas* (1952) by Eduardo *Caballero Calderón (1910-), *El día señalado* (1964) by Manuel Mejía *Vallejo (1923-), and *Condores no entierran todos los días* (1972) by Gustavo Alvarez *Gardeazábal (1945-). Whether based on factual situations (*Condores . . .*) or fictional ones (*El día . . .*), these works convey the arbitrariness and the terror of social conflict in Colombia.

The Violence left its mark even on poetry. The anti-elitism and concern for the effects of the Violence were illustrated in the *nadaísta* movement of the 1960s (see: NADAISMO). The *nadaísta* poets rejected what they called "establishment writers," defended their right to be concerned with violence in literature, and often adopted extreme and avant-garde themes and techniques.

Contemporary Colombian literature exhibits a vitality and diversity that augurs well, although the precise direction its development will take by the end of 20th century remains an open question. See also: GENERATIONS; PUBLISHING

LITHIC SETTLEMENTS, see: STONE AGE SETTLEMENTS

LIVESTOCK. The introduction of Andalusian-style cattle ranching was one of Spain's major contributions to the Americas, and some 20% of Colombian cattle are still the original *creole longhorns. Before 1870, the combination of these creole cattle and native grasses limited the size of herds, so that at the beginning of this century the primary economic importance of cattle remained their hides, although there was some export of live animals, chiefly to Cuba. Since then the introduction of new grasses from Africa and Brazil, the importation of Brahman (cebú) bulls from Europe and elsewhere, and barbed wire have changed the emphasis to beef production. Herds have grown as much as tenfold, from 3,120,000 head in 1912 to 20 million in the 1970s and 30 million in the 1980s. The extensive pastures of the Atlantic lowlands in the Departments of *Atlántico, *Bolívar, *Córdoba, and *Magdalena contain 40% of Colombia's cattle; the *Llanos of *Arauca, *Boyacá, and *Meta account for another 15%. The hinterland of *Cúcuta is also important, not least as the source of extensive smuggling of rustled cattle into Venezuela. The *Cauca Valley is declining in importance as cattle country, although *Medellín continues to hold an important cattle fair. The central highlands have most of the dairy farms, but these amount to only 3% of the national herd. Much Colombian milk is obtained from cows kept primarily for slaughter. Nationally, a milk shortage is chronic. Current production of 2,800,000 metric tons may be compared with Argentina's 5,600,000 tons for almost the same size population.

While cattle herds have grown tenfold over 75 years, sheep flocks (concentrated in *Santander, *Boyacá, *Cundinamarca, *Caldas, and *Nariño) barely doubled, growing from 1,200,000 to 2,700,000. Hispanic taste and cuisine favor beef, and Colombian sheep are kept primarily for their wool. The latter tends to be of poor quality, however, acceptable only to cottage industry. The textile mills rely on imported wools.

In the same period, the number of swine has hardly grown at all. There were 2,200,000 in 1912, and 2,400,000 in 1986— fewer even than in Ecuador or Cuba. Horses, mules, and asses are naturally less important in the mechanical age than previously, and their numbers show only a small increase since before *World War I, growing from 1,100,000 to 1,900,000. The number of poultry, on the other hand, has gone up considerably since factory farming came to Colombia in the 1970s.

LLANOS ORIENTALES. The eastern plains covering an estimated 328,000 square kilometers, the Llanos (as they are most often called) extend from the *Cordillera Oriental east to the borders of Venezuela and south to the *Amazon region. They are drained largely by tributaries of the Orinoco River system. The climate is hot, with alternating wet and dry seasons. Historically, the area was wild, semiwasteland, but more recently it has been the scene of some modern colonization efforts. The major economic activity is *livestock raising, especially cattle ranching.

LLANOS ORIENTALES, Violence in the, 1949-1953. Modern guerrilla violence, dating from the 1940s, might be said to have begun in the *Llanos on November 27, 1949, when Captain Alfredo Silva, a commander at Apiay air base, and Hernán Dussán, *Liberal Directorate representative, launched an abortive coup d'état by seizing *Villavicencio. When the coup failed, many of the participants fled to Puerto López (4° 5'N, 72° 58'W, *Meta), which had been taken over by Eliseo Vásquez, a local *caudillo. Thereafter, various *guerrilla movements developed, 1949-1953, led by people such as Vásquez, Guadalupe Salcedo, the Bautista brothers—Pacho, Manuel, and Tulio—and Alvear Restrepo. Efforts were made to unite the related but uncoordinated movements, 1952-1953, but the majority of guerrilla activities came to an end in 1953 when General Duarte Blum, acting for the *Rojas Pinilla government, negotiated truce arrangements, and the guerrilla forces surrendered in public ceremonies at Monterrey on September 15. After 1953, the focus of guerrilla activity shifted to other parts of the nation. See also: VIOLENCIA, La

LLERAS CAMARGO, Alberto, 1906-1990. *Liberal legislator, diplomat, interim President, 1945-1946; President, 1958-1962. Born *Bogotá, July 3; died Bogotá, January 4; he was three-time Minister of Government and Minister of Foreign Relations in 1945. He was ambassador to the United States, Secretary General of the *Organization of American States (eight years), and a delegate to other international conferences. In addition, he was correspondent for El Mundo in Spain, director of the magazines Semana and Visión, and contributor to various *newspapers including El Liberal, El *Tiempo, El *Espectador, and La Tarde. He organized the National Union in 1946, a coalition that elected Mariano *Ospina Pérez President. He opposed General *Rojas Pinilla's dictatorship and figured as opposition leader in the events leading to the *bullring massacre January 29, 1956. He negotiated the Pact of *Benidorm and the *Sitges Accord, forming the *Frente Nacional, 1956-1958. His administration tried to cope with *guerrilla violence and to restore domestic tranquillity, 1958-1962. It was responsible for *Law 135 of 1961, which enacted *agrarian reform and established INCORA (*Instituto Colombiano de la Reforma Agraria) to implement the program.

LLERAS-LISBOA TREATIES, 1853. *New Granada–Brazilian agreements signed June 1853, in *Bogotá by New Granada's Minister of Foreign Relations, Lorenzo María Lleras, and Manuel María Lisboa, Barón de Yaputá, for Brazil. They were early but unsuccessful attempts to settle boundaries, river navigation, and extradition problems. New Granada rejected the boundary settlement because it departed from the formula *uti possidetis* of 1810 (see: BORDERS). Brazil refused to ratify the agreement on the free navigation of rivers, preferring a doctrine that gave control to governments adjacent to the *waterways. The extradition treaty was simply suspended indefinitely.

LLERAS–PAZ SOLDAN TREATY, 1853. Signed in *Bogotá, June 25, by Minister of Foreign Relations, Lorenzo María Lleras, *New Granada, and José Gregorio Paz Soldán, Peruvian representative. Peru agreed to pay New Granada the sum of 2 million Peruvian pesos at 4.5% interest to settle the debt arising from the *Mosquera-Monteagudo Treaty of 1820.

LLERAS RESTREPO, Carlos, 1908-. *Liberal, economist, educator, diplomat, President 1966-1970. Born *Bogotá, April 12, he completed his studies in law and political science at the *Universidad Nacional in 1930. He served as deputy to the *Cundinamarca Assembly in 1930 and was Secretary of the Government of Bogotá in 1932. He was Comptroller General for Colombia, 1936-1937, Minister of Finance, 1938 and 1943, and Vice President (*Designado) of Colombia in 1960. An active Liberal leader, he was head of his party in 1941, 1948, and 1961, as well as many times a member of its national directorate. In addition to serving as managing editor of the newspaper *El *Tiempo* and the magazine *La nueva frontera,* he was for many years a professor of public finance at the National University and elsewhere. He was a delegate to various international conferences and Colombian representative to the *United Nations. A member of both *House and *Senate, Lleras Restrepo was known for his support of reformist legislation. His presidency was responsible for instituting a population control policy (1966), Decree No. 444 (1967), which encouraged export diversification, a new *agrarian reform law (1968), the *constitutional reforms of 1968, and formation of the *Andean Common Market (1969).

LOAN OF 1820. On August 1, 1820, Francisco Antonio *Zea negotiated the *Loan of 1820 with British financiers Charles

Herring, John Powles, and William Graham for an 80% loan of £2 million at 6%. The actual contract was repudiated by the Colombian *Congress in 1823 but the £1,600,000 already advanced was accepted as part of the legitimate national debt. See also: LONDON LOANS

LOAN OF 1824.   Negotiated April 24, 1824, by Manuel Antonio Arrubla and Francisco *Montoya with the British firm of B. A. Goldschmidt and Co. The 88.5% loan of £4,750,000 at 6% was approved by *Congress in 1825. Together with the obligations accepted from the *Loan of 1820, the Loan of 1824 was the first major *foreign debt contracted by Colombia. See also: LONDON LOANS

LOBO GUERRERO, Bartolomé, ca. 1546-1622   Archbishop of *Bogotá, 1599-1609. He presided over the creation of the seminary and school of San Bartolomé, 1604-1605 (see: COLEGIO MAYOR DE SAN BARTOLOME); held a second Diocesan Synod and established the *Carmelite Order in *New Granada, 1606; and carried out significant physical improvements in the cathedral.

LOMAGRANDE.   A socialist settlement led by Vicente *Andamo.

LONDON LOANS.   The London money market was Colombia's chief source of public external borrowing until the 1920s, and for many years its almost exclusive source. The first foreign debt negotiated by the newly independent *República de Gran Colombia was the *Mackintosh Contract of 1819, signed in 1821, for £150,000 at 12%. In August 1820, Francisco Antonio *Zea negotiated a loan of £2 million with financiers Charles Herring, John Powles, and William Graham (see: LOAN OF 1820). And on April 24, 1824, Manuel Antonio Arrubla and Francisco *Montoya negotiated a loan of £4,750,000 with the London house of B. A. Goldschmidt and Co. (see: LOAN OF 1824). By 1826 all of these loans were in default. With the breakup of Gran Colombia, the national debt was apportioned between the new republics of Ecuador, *New Granada, and Venezuela. This was arranged in 1835 when President Francisco de Paula *Santander generously accepted one-half ($12,663,009) as *New Granada's share. Two loans of £3,312,975, each at varying interest rates, were negotiated in 1845, and almost the whole sum was used to refinance the

accumulated existing debt. In 1863, Tomás Cipriano de
*Mosquera raised an 86% loan of £200,000 ($1 million) at 6%
to build a highway from the *Cauca River to the port of
*Buenaventura. The project was hopelessly mismanaged and
the money ran out after a mere eight miles had been completed. The world crisis of 1873 led to a £2 million refinancing
loan to avoid default. After that Colombia's poor credit (see:
PAPER MONEY CRISIS OF 1885-1905) made it very difficult to raise further loans in London, and the next big loan was
obtained in New York in December 1880.

LOPEZ.   For the Presidents, see: LOPEZ, José Hilario; LOPEZ
MICHELSEN, Alfonso; and LOPEZ PUMAREJO, Alfonso.

LOPEZ, José Hilario, 1798-1869.   General, legislator, President
of *New Granada, 1849-1853. Born *Popayán, February 18;
died Campoalegre (*Huila), November 27. López was a patriot military officer, 1812-1830. He was Minister of War,
1832, and Minister of Foreign Relations, 1863, as well as a
delegate to both the *Congress of Ocaña in 1828 and the
Convention of *Rionegro in 1863. He was President of
*Tolima, representative to the *Vatican, and at various times
a member of the *Senate. His presidential administration was
militantly reformist, responsible for the abolition of *African
slavery, freedom of the press (see: CENSORSHIP), expulsion
of the *Jesuits, suppression of the ecclesiastical *fuero, legalization of divorce, expulsion of Archibshop *Mosquera from
New Granada, and creation of the *Chorographic Commission.

LOPEZ DE MESA, Luis, 1884-1967.   Doctor, educator, sociologist, essayist, and legislator, born, Don Matías (*Antioquia),
October 12; died *Medellín, October 18. He was a member of
the legislature for the Department of *Cundinamarca, representative to the national *Congress, Minister of Education
1934-1935, and rector of the *Universidad Nacional. His
numerous works include *El libro de los apólogos* (1918); *La
civilización contemporánea* (1928); *Introducción a la historia de la
cultura en Colombia* (1930); *Cómo se ha formado la nación
colombiana* (1934); and *Escrutinio sociológico de la historia
colombiana* (1955). His analysis of Colombian history was one
of the earliest attempts to stress the evolution of secular social
institutions rather than individual or religious forces in the
determination of events.

LOPEZ DE MESA–GIL BORGES TREATY OF 1941. Signed on April 5 at *Cúcuta by delegations from Colombia (Luis *López de Mesa and Alberto Pumarejo) and Venezuela (E. Gil Borges and José Santiago Rodríguez). The treaty specified the method by which any remaining territorial questions would be resolved and declared that the boundaries between the two nations had been completely delineated by law (see: BORDERS). A clause providing for the free navigation of jointly held rivers was included in the treaty.

LOPEZ MICHELSEN, Alfonso 1913-. Lawyer, educator, legislator, President of Colombia, 1974-1978. Born *Bogotá, June 30, he received his law degree from the *Colegio Mayor de Nuestra Señora del Rosario and then took postgraduate work in Chile and the United States. He has taught law at the Universidad Libre, the *Universidad Nacional, and the *Colegio Mayor de Nuestra Señora del Rosario. During the 1950s, he lived in Mexico, where he published the novel *Los elegidos.* He has been a member of both houses of *Congress; Governor of *Cesar, 1967-1968; and Minister of Foreign Relations, 1968-1970. He founded and led the *Movimiento Liberal Revolucionario (M.L.R.), 1958-1967, and edited *El Liberal.* López Michelsen is the son of ex-President Alfonso *López Pumarejo and the author of various works, including *Introducción al estudio de la constitución de Colombia* (1943). His presidential administration was responsible for a tax reform (1974) and programs aimed at inflation control. The latter was especially difficult because Colombia passed from a *petroleum exporter to a petroleum importer, there was a boom in *coffee revenues because of crop failures in other countries, and income from the international *drug trade began to circulate in the economy. His administration also negotiated contracts for the development of *coal reserves in the *Guajira Peninsula (see: CERREJON, EL). López Michelsen was an unsuccessful candidate for reelection in the presidential campaign of 1982.

LOPEZ PUMAREJO, Alfonso, 1886-1959. *Liberal legislator, banker, diplomat, reformist President, 1934-1938 and 1942-1945. Born *Honda (Tolima), January 13; died London (England), November 20; López Pumarejo was the editor of various newspapers including *El Diario Nacional, La *República,* and *El Liberal,* the last of which he founded in 1938. He was representative to the *United Nations, 1958, and ambassador to the *United Kingdom, 1958-1959. His first presidency instituted tax reforms, labor laws, Church restrictions, constitutional amendments, and land partitioning. Its program became known as "the Forward-Moving Revolution" (la Revolución en marcha). His second presidency supported the Allied Powers in *World War II, 1942-1945, but was marred by an obstructive opposition, accusations of corruption, and an attempted coup d'état in Pasto, July 10, 1944. He resigned in August 1945. Alfonso López Pumarejo was a grandson of Ambrosio López, founder of the *Sociedad de Artesanos in 1847, and father of Alfonso *López Michelsen.

LOPISTA. Supporter of Alfonso *López Michelsen.

LOZANO-MADARIAGA TREATY OF 1811. Signed May 28, by Jorge Tadeo Lozano, for the State of *Cundinamarca, and José Cortés Madariaga, Venezuela. A treaty of friendship and alliance pledging mutual support for the wars of independence, it was probably the first treaty signed after the beginning of the *independence movement.

LOZANO-SALOMON TREATY OF 1922. Signed March 24, by Fabio Lozano Torrijos, Colombia, and Alberto Salomón, Peru. The treaty resolved territorial disputes in the *Putumayo region and established Colombia's boundary on the *Amazon River. It also provided for free navigation of the rivers. Ratification of the treaty was delayed until 1928 because of objections by some Peruvians and Brazil. See also: ARANA DEL AGUILA, Julio César; BORDERS; LETICIA

LUGO, Alonso Luis de. Conquistador who arrived in Santa Marta in 1536 with his father, Pedro *Fernández de Lugo, the newly appointed governor. He stole part of his father's resources and fled, seeking his own independent commission from the Crown. In 1542 he returned to *New Granada with supplies to reinforce the existing settlements and an expedition of 300 men. After raiding the royal treasury at Cape Vela, he led an expedition from *Valledupar to *Vélez, 1542-1543, and was received as governor in *Bogotá, 1543-1544. He is said to have brought the first cattle to the capital, and he was known as a greedy, heavy-handed ruler. He eventually returned to Spain and was subsequently appointed to serve with Spanish forces in Italy.

LUGO, Bernardo de.   A native of *Bogotá, an early grammarian. He compiled the *Gramática de la lengua general del Nuevo Reino de Granada, llamada mosca* (Madrid, 1619), one of the few attempts made to preserve the language of the *Chibchas.

LUQUE SANCHEZ, Crisanto, 1889-1959.   Bishop of *Tunja, 1931-1950; Archbishop of *Bogotá, 1950-1959; first Colombian *Cardinal, 1953. He was primate of Colombia during *La *Violencia,* the presidency of Laureano *Gómez, the dictatorship of *Rojas Pinilla, and the Protestant persecutions of the 1950s (see: PROTESTANTISM). He was considered an inflexible *Conservative partisan by many, although his pastorals called for restoration of peace and enjoined the clergy against taking political actions.

-M-

M-19, see: MOVIMIENTO DIECINUEVE DE ABRIL

M.L.N., see: MOVIMIENTO LATINO NACIONAL

M.N.P., see: MOVIMIENTO NACIONAL POPULAR

M.P.R., see: MOVIMIENTO POPULAR REVOLUCIONARIO

M.R.L., see: MOVIMIENTO REVOLUCIONARIO LIBERAL

M.R.N., see: MOVIMIENTO DE RENOVACION NACIONAL

MACAREGUA CONFERENCE.   September 1884, at an estate near San Gil (6° 33'N, 73° 6'W), *Santander. *Conservative leaders Luis Martínez Silva, Tobías Valenzuela, and others agreed to encourage *Radical rebellion in Santander as a strategy to achieve political gains with the *Núñez administration.

MACKINTOSH CONTRACT.   An agreement signed February 27, 1821, by Luis López Méndez, Colombia, and James Mackintosh, British merchant, whereby the latter undertook to arm, equip, and transport to Colombia some 10,000 troops in exchange for £150,000 at 12% interest per annum. Although never ratified by *Congress, the contract remained the source of diplomatic dispute until claims were settled in 1858. It was considered one of the most persistently troublesome and financially disadvantageous problems in Colombian diplomacy, 1821-1858. See also: LONDON LOANS; UNITED KINGDOM, Relations with

MACUQUINA. A form of stamped *silver *currency whose value was difficult to control. It was withdrawn from circulation in the late 1840s.

MADRE CASTILLO, see: CASTILLO Y GUEVARA, Francisca Josefa de

MADRE LAURA, see: MONTOYA UPEGUI, Laura

MAFIA. A term sometimes used to describe members of the illegal *DRUG TRADE. Drug dealers who are leaders of families or groups engaged in the trade are often referred to as "capos" (see also: CALI CARTEL; MEDELLIN CARTEL).

MAGDALENA, Departamento de. Located on the Caribbean Coast on the lower *Magdalena River, the department is composed of 23,188 square kilometers of coastal lowland lying between 8° 58' and 11° 21'N latitude and 73° 33' and 74° 57'W longitude. The area is dotted with swamps and the climate is predominantly tropical (19,800 square kilometers), with only a small portion of the territory at cooler altitudes: 1,757 square kilometers temperate; 790 cold; and 841 wasteland. Major rivers include the Ariguaní, Magdalena, Aracataca, Don Diego, Frío, Fundación, and Sevilla. The department includes the *Sierra Nevada de Santa Marta with Mt. Simón Bolívar (5,775 meters) and Mt. Cristóbal Colón (5,770 meters), the highest in Colombia. Population is 760,611 people (1985 estimate), with a population density of thirty-three people per square kilometer. The capital city is *Santa Marta. Based on DANE, *Colombia estadística 86,* principal agricultural products, with tonnage produced in 1984, include *bananas, 93,729 tons; *yuca, 56,800; rice, 54,310; plantains, 38,000; *corn, 30,299; sorghum, 13,200; *African palm, 12,800; *tobacco, 7,200; *cotton, 5,400; coconuts, 3,460; *cacao, 1,080; sesame, 600; beans, 62; and *potatoes (1,800 in 1983). *Livestock marketed in 1984 included 66,661 head of cattle and 12,386 hogs. There is also some *fishing, a brewing and bottling industry, and tourism. In 1983 there were seventeen businesses employing ten or more people. In pre-Hispanic times the *Tairona Indians flourished there. Alonso de *Ojeda is credited with being the first of the Spanish explorers to visit the coast (1499), and Rodrigo de *Bastidas founded Santa Marta on July 29, 1525. During the colonial period, the region was known as the province of Santa Marta, and the city of Santa Marta is the site of San Pedro Alejandrino, the estate where *Bolívar died. In 1857 it became the State of Magdalena, composed of the Departments of El Banco, Padilla, Santa Marta, Tenerife, and Valledupar, and in 1886 the State of Magdalena became the Department of Magdalena. It was subsequently reduced in size when the Departments of *Guajira and *Cesar were established.

MAGDALENA RAILROAD, see: SANTA MARTA RAILWAY

MAGDALENA RIVER. The principal river system, known historically as the lifeline of Colombia. It originates in the *Andes Mountains in what is called the Macizo Colombiana at the juncture of the *Cordilleras Oriental and Central in lake (lagoon) La Magdalena (1° 56′N, 76° 35′W). Beginning at an altitude of 3,685 meters, the river flows northeast some 1,538 kilometers to the *Bocas de Ceniza (11° 6′N, 74° 51′W) on the Caribbean Sea. It is navigable as far inland as the Salto de Honda (rapids or waterfall) at *Honda, approximately 1,317 kilometers. The river was explored by Rodrigo de *Bastidas, starting on April 1, 1501, and the first commercial fleet on the river was established by Alonso de Olalla and Hernando de Alcocer in 1550. Steam navigation of the river was introduced by Juan Bernardo *Elbers in 1824. The *Cauca River is its largest tributary.

MAGICAL REALISM. The name given to a literary style associated with what has been called the boom in Latin American *literature in the 1960s and 1970s. The seemingly contradictory effect achieved by combining supernatural (magic) and natural (realistic) elements suggests the complexity of both the works written in this style and of life itself. Reality is described by exaggeration or fantasy, which illustrates the essence of truth through absurd or unbelievable events. Probably one of the best-known works in this genre is the novel *One Hundred Years of Solitude by Gabriel *García Márquez. In this story characters with excessive virility or beauty, or lives of self-denial or meaningless repetition, are accepted as normal, while events based on the *United Fruit Company Strike of 1928 are erased from history by a conspiracy of denial because the horror of their reality is too much to believe.

MAHECHA, Raúl Eduardo. A communist leader of the 1920s and 1930s, Mahecha was an early ideologue and leader of the Socialist Revolutionary Party (*Partido Socialista Revolucionario) and other pro-labor groups. He opposed the influence of foreign businesses (mainly U.S. companies) in Colombia and tried to organize workers along the *Magdalena River. He published *Vanguardia obrera* in *Barrancabermeja and supported the strikes against the *Tropical Oil Company in 1924 and 1927 and against the *United Fruit Company in 1928.

MAIZE, see: CORN

MALLARINO, Manuel María, 1808-1872. Judge, legislator, diplomat, acting President, 1855-1857. Born *Cali, June 18; died *Bogotá, March 6; Mallarino received his law degree from the *Universidad del Cauca (*Popayán) in 1831 and taught there as well as in Cali (at Santa Librada) and in Bogotá. He was a member of both the *House and the *Senate; twice Minister of Foreign Relations; and director of primary *education under the *Salgar presidency. He founded *La escuela normal,* an educational journal, in 1871. His bipartisan interim presidency in the wake of the *Melo rebellion of 1854 was largely devoted to reestablishing efficient administration and sound economic policies.

MALLARINO-BIDLACK TREATY OF 1846. A treaty, negotiated by Manuel María *Mallarino of *New Granada and Benjamin Allen Bidlack of the United States, signed December 12. New Granada secured a guarantee of the sovereignty and property of the Isthmus of *Panama from the United States in exchange for a grant of free transit across the isthmus and the abolition of discriminatory tariffs. Under the provisions of the treaty, the United States intervened in Panama in 1856, 1860, 1862, 1865, 1873, 1885, 1901, and 1903. See also: UNITED STATES, Relations with

MAMATOCO INCIDENT. A scandal in 1943 resulting from accusations of official corruption following the assassination of a prizefighter known as Mamatoco, who was the publisher of a newspaper, *Voz del Pueblo.* The implication of some public officials and the national police in his death proved embarrassing to the *López Pumarejo administration.

MAN. Acronym of *MOVIMIENTO DE ACCION NACIONAL.

MANIFESTATION OF SILENCE, see: ORACION DE LA PAZ

MANIOC, see: YUCA

MANIZALES. Capital of the Department of *Caldas, situated at 5° 14'N, 75° 31'W, at an altitude of 2,216 meters, in the *Cordillera Central about 187 kilometers from Bogotá. The average temperature is 17°C, and the estimated population in 1985 was 327,806 people. The ninth largest city in Colombia, Manizales is a commercial, industrial, and university center founded in 1849 by colonists from *Antioquia, including José M. Osorio, Joaquín Arango, Antonio Arango, Vicente Gil, Manuel Grisales, Antonio Ceballos, Victoriano Arango, Eduardo Hoyos, Marcelino Palacio, and Gabriel Arango. The city was badly damaged by fire in 1922 and again in 1924. The city is located in a picturesque but not easily accessible mountain setting, chosen for its easy defensibility on a crossroads of transportation routes. It is connected to *Mariquita by an aerial cable car. Manizales is well known as a tourist center and for its annual festival, the *fería de Manizales.*

MANIZALES, First Battle of. August 28, 1860, *Caldas. An inconclusive engagement between General T. C. de *Mosquera, President of *Cauca, rebel, and General Joaquín *Posada Gutiérrez, for the *Confederacion Granadina, during the *rebellion of 1859-1862. See also: MANIZALES AGREEMENTS

MANIZALES, Second Battle of. April 3-5, 1877, *Caldas. General Julián *Trujillo, *Liberal leader for the government, defeated the rebellious forces of *Conservative leader General Marcelino Vélez. Surrender was negotiated on April 6, marking the end of the *rebellion of 1876-1877.

MANIZALES AGREEMENTS. August 29, 1860. Following the First Battle of *Manizales, August 28, generals T. C. de *Mosquera and Joaquín *Posada Gutiérrez agreed to mutual cessation of hostilities and a general amnesty, pending government action to deal with Mosquera's grievances during the *rebellion of 1859-1862. The agreements were rejected by President Mariano *Ospina Rodríguez, and the war continued.

MANOS MUERTAS, see: MORTMAIN

MANUELA. One of Colombia's best-known *costumbrista* novels (see: COSTUMBRISMO). The work of Eugenio *Díaz, it is set in a small village on the *Sabana de Bogotá and details the trials and mistreatment of Manuela, a laundress, at the hands of Tadeo Forero, boss of the village. It contains excellent descriptions of 19th-century provincial life.

MANUFACTURING INDUSTRY. Colombian industrialization began early in the 20th century—mainly in *Medellín—stimulated by capital made available by rising incomes from *coffee production. As in the closely parallel situation in São Paulo, Brazil, this movement began in textiles and food processing where consumer demand was greatest. The number of industrial plants employing more than 50 workers grew from under 20 in 1900 to about 60 by 1925, 150 in the early 1930s and 425 by 1945. Already by 1928 the manufacturing sector was large enough to justify the creation of the Bogotá *Bolsa de Valores* (stock exchange). The country's oldest textile firms still existing are the *Compañía Colombiana de Tejidos of 1907 and the *Fábrica de Hilados y Tejidos del Hato of 1920. The decline in Colombia's foreign earnings caused by the Great Depression of the 1930s fostered import substitution on a much wider scale, including products using paper, *rubber, chemicals, metals, and minerals, although food processing and textiles remained the dominant sectors. Even in the 1980s, these two industries, together with petrochemicals, constituted nearly two-thirds of Colombian industrial production.

When the external situation changed following the end of *World War II, industrial interests were already strong enough to secure a protective tariff policy (introduced in 1950). To provide the necessary energy, the development of *hydroelectric power proceeded apace, increasing in the 1950s at nearly 12% a year. In 1953 the government ignored the World Bank's discouragement and went ahead with the *Paz del Río steel complex. By the 1960s the Colombian manufacturing sector was large and prosperous enough to stimulate the interest of multinationals. One result was the building of the first *automobile assembly plants. Their production peaked at 48,677 units in 1979, but has since declined to 42,154 (35,526 passenger cars, 6,628 commercial vehicles) in 1985, and within the *Andean Pact countries the Colombian motor vehicle industry remains a very poor second to the Venezuelan.

As it has grown, the Colombian manufacturing industry has ceased to be centered in Medellín. Other important centers include *Bogotá, *Cali, *Cartagena, *Bucaramanga, *Barrancabermeja, *Manizales and *Palmira. The period of rapid industrial growth now seems to be coming to an end, in part because the most clear-cut opportunities for import substitution have already been seized. By the 1970s revenue from the illegal *drug trade was becoming significant. The foreign exchange surplus this created reduced the price incentive to export manufactures, but for a while there was ample compensation in the boost given to internal consumer demand. More recently drug trade profits have begun to be invested abroad, adding capital flight to the other deleterious effects of the trade.

An important role in industrial development has been played by the official *Instituto de Fomento Industrial, founded in 1948. Important private organizations are the *Asociación Nacional de Industriales and the *Asociación Colombiana Popular de Industriales.

MANZUR LONDOÑO, David, 1929-. Muralist, painter, born in *Neiva. He studied art in the Canary Islands, New York, Mexico, and the Escuela de Bellas Artes in *Bogotá. "Elements for an Angel" is a well-known set of paintings. In addition to his abstract paintings, which are described as modern art, he has worked with theatrical set design and taught drawing and fresco painting at the *Universidad de los Andes.

MARACAIBO, Battle of. July 24, 1823, Venezuela. A land and naval battle in which General José *Padilla, naval commander, and General Manuel Manrique, land commander, led patriot forces to victory over Admiral Angel Laborde and General Francisco Tomás Morales. The battle forced the Spanish to relinquish their last stronghold on the Caribbean Coast.

MARES, Roberto de, see: DE MARES CONCESSION

MARIA. The best-remembered work of Jorge *ISAACS, a romantic novel of unfulfilled love, set in *Valle del Cauca. It is basically a love story, but it has *costumbrista qualities, describing life in the region. It was first published in 1867 and has been called the most widely read novel written by a Latin American.

MARICHUELAS, Las. A reference to María Magdalena de San José Galaéz and her daughters, Petronila de Ospina y Galaéz and María Lugarda de Ospina. An affair between the latter and the Viceroy *Solís Folch de Cardona created a scandal in *Bogotá. María Lugarda de Ospina entered Santa Clara convent in 1758 to escape gossip, but she later left it and was exiled from Bogotá by Viceroy *Messía de la Zerda.

MARIJUANA. Often translated from the Spanish colloquially as "Mary Jane," marijuana is also, though infrequently, spelled "marihuana." It was the first important crop of the Colombian *DRUG TRADE and was already being grown extensively in the 1950s, mostly in the region between the *Sierra Nevada de Santa Marta and the *Guajira Peninsula. Although it has since been eclipsed in the newspaper headlines by *cocaine, it remains of great economic importance. In December 1978, authors Roberto Bonnet and Carlos Caballero Argáez (in "La otra economía," *Coyuntura económica* 8[4]: 103-139) estimated that revenue from marijuana exports to the United States were about $500 million gross and $130 million net, or 2.7% of Colombia's gross domestic product, or three times the contribution from cocaine at that time.

MARIN, Pedro Antonio, 1928-. A *campesino,* or peasant, better known by the aliases of Manuel Marulanda Vélez and Tiro Fijo. Born May 12, in the present-day Department of *Quindío, he was active as a guerrilla with forces of the *Liberal Party and the *Partido Comunista de Colombia in the 1940s and 1950s. He succeeded Jacobo *Prías Alape as head of the settlement of *Marquetalia, and then became leader of the *Fuerzas Armadas Revolucionarias de Colombia (FARC) from 1964 to 1984.

MARINERO Y TRUCCO, Juan Bautista, 1831-1918. An Italian immigrant who became a major entrepreneur in the development of the *Chocó, *Antioquia, *Bolívar, and *Cundinamarca. Born in Pietra Ligure, Italy, he immigrated to Colombia as a result of political events in Italy in 1848. He was influential in mining in the Chocó and the Zaragoza region of Antioquia, eventually becoming the second largest investor (after Carlos Coriolano *AMADOR) in El *Zancudo, a *gold and *silver mine that became the largest Colombian economic enterprise of the 19th century. He was active in the early cattle industry in Bolívar and in numerous real estate and business ventures in *Cartagena, where he founded the Banco de Cartagena in 1880. He maintained close contacts with Italy and made numerous journeys to his homeland; he also served as the Italian consul in Cartagena from 1898 to 1918. He was essentially neutral in Colombian politics, but he did come to the aid of the nation in the case of the *Cerruti Affair by helping to moderate potential Italian attacks on Cartagena and by offering to help the government meet damages it was forced to pay.

MARIQUITA. Agricultural, commercial, industrial, and mining community located at 5° 13'N, 74° 52'W, in the Department of *Tolima. Mariquita is an important transportation center, located on the *railroad 16 kilometers west of *Honda and 125 kilometers north of *Ibagué. Average temperature is 26°C; the altitude, 495 meters; and population in 1985 was 15,754 people (estimate). It is the eastern terminus of the *Manizales-Mariquita aerial cable car. Mariquita was founded on August 8, 1551, after Francisco Nuñez Pedrozo was commissioned to establish a settlement October 29, 1549. Important as a gold and silver mining region through much of its lifetime, the city is also remembered as the place where Gonzalo *Jiménez de Quesada died and for its role as the capital of a province of the same name, 1815-1816. The city was moved to its present location on January 8, 1853.

MAROON. A runaway slave or *cimarrón*; literally, "he who takes to the high peaks" (*cimas*). Many maroons (as the term is often Anglicized from the Spanish) were mulattoes or *mestizos with some African ancestry. Among colonial *New Granada's most well known maroons was *Leonor, the Black Queen, but the most famous was probably Domingo *BIOHO. Maroon settlements in *Colombia were known as *palenques* (see: PALENQUE).

MARQUETALIA. A settlement founded in the region known as El Támara (*Tolima) in 1955 by Jacobo *Prías Alape (Fermín Charry Rincón/Charro Negro) with inhabitants from various places including Gaitanía. Marquetalia, led by Pedro Antonio *Marín (Manuel Marulanda Vélez) after the assassination of Charro Negro, was one of an estimated seventeen so-called independent republics that flourished during the 1950s and 1960s. The phrase "independent republics" is attributed to a speech by Alvaro *Gómez Hurtado. These settlements, including

Riochiquito (Cauca), El Pato (Caquetá), Guayabero and Villarica, enforced their own civil law and military defense, often as a result of La *Violencia*, which had partially paralyzed operations of the national government. These settlements, composed largely of peasants, were inspired by various reform ideologies and fought to defend land claims. They were essentially eliminated by government amnesty programs or military action in the mid-1960s. Marquetalia was captured in a campaign begun May 18, 1964. The final assault, led by General José Joaquín Matallana, June 14-15, revealed that the inhabitants had already abandoned the settlement. Refugees from Marquetalia joined together to form the *Fuerzas Armadas Revolucionarias de Colombia (FARC) in 1964. An unrelated settlement named Marquetalia (formerly called Núñez) was founded at 5° 18'N, 75° 3'W in the Department of *Caldas in 1924. See also: GUERRILLA MOVEMENTS

MARQUEZ BARRETO, José Ignacio de, 1793-1880. Lawyer, justice, legislator, Vice President and acting President, 1832; President, 1837-1841. Born Ramiriquí (*Boyacá), September 8; died *Bogotá, March 21. He received his law degree from the *Colegio Mayor de San Bartolomé. He was a delegate to the *Congress of Cúcuta (1821), the *Congress of Ocaña (1828), the *Congreso Admirable (1830), and the Congress of 1832, as well as the legislative congresses of *New Granada in the 1830s. As acting President in 1832 he did much to organize public administration in New Granada. He was inaugurated President in 1837 after a controversial election. His administration ratified the *Pombo-Michelena Treaty, 1837; sanctioned a new penal code, 1838; refused to repeal the *Benthamistic educational program then in force; suppressed minor convents and dealt with the resulting Rebellion of the *Minor Convents, 1839; and tried to suppress the War of the *Supreme Commanders, 1840-1842.

MARROQUIN, José Manuel, 1827-1908. Author, poet, linguist, Vice President of Colombia, 1898-1904; acting President, 1898 and 1900-1904. Born in *Bogotá, August 6; died in Bogotá, September 19. He studied law at the *Colegio Mayor de San Bartolomé, but he is more widely known as a figure of literary-linguistic studies. He was the author of several novels including *Blas Gil* (1896), *Entre primos* (1897), *El Moro* (1897), and *Amores y leyes* (1898). *El Moro*, the imaginary autobiography of a horse, is probably the best known. Marroquín was director of the Universidad Católica, rector of the *Colegio Mayor de Nuestra Señora del Rosario (1887-1890), and director of the Instituto de la Yerbabuena, as well as a founding member of the *Academia Colombiana de la Lengua. As acting President, he initially proposed bipartisan, conciliatory policies but was stopped by President Manuel Antonio *Sanclemente, 1898-1900. Restored to the presidency by the Movement of July 31, 1900, he then followed a partisan policy that extended rather than shortened the War of the *Thousand Days. His administration failed to suppress the *Panamanian Revolution of 1903 or to prevent the loss of Panama.

MARULANDA VELEZ, Manuel. Pseudonym of Pedro Antonio *MARIN. See also: GUERRILLA MOVEMENTS; MARQUETALIA

MAS, see: MUERTE A SECUESTRADORES

MATUNA. A *palenque (a *maroon community) near *Cartagena that flourished in the early 1600s under Domingo *BIOHO. It disbanded after Bioho was captured and executed in 1621, and survivors of the community set up the longer-lasting *palenque* of *San Basilio.

MAURO HOYOS, Carlos. Attorney General of *Colombia who was kidnapped and shot dead near *Medellín by sympathizers with the *drug trade leaders known as "Los *Extraditables" on January 25, 1988. His successor, Alfredo Gutiérrez, was led to suggest that, if fighting the *drug trade was a failure, it should be legalized.

MEDELLIN. Capital of *Antioquia, known as the city of eternal spring, located at 6° 16'N, 75° 34'W. The population of the greater metropolitan area is 2,068,892 people (1985 estimate); the altitude, 1,487 meters; and the average temperature, 20°C. The city (approximately 473 kilometers from *Bogotá) is heavily industrialized, particularly in the textile industry. It is a university center and a site known for orchid cultivation, and, in very recent times, as a center for the illegal *drug trade. The second largest city in Colombia, Medellín is located in the Valley of Aburrá, first discovered August 24, 1541, by Jerónimo Luis Tejelo, a subordinate of Jorge *Robledo. Much of the region was under the jurisdiction of Gaspar de *Rodas, 1579-1607. What was to become Medellín was originally established by Francisco de Herrera Campuzano on March 2, 1616, with the name San Lorenzo de Aburrá. The location of the settlement was changed in 1646, and a *cabildo* was formally installed and the name changed to Nuestra Señora de la Candelaria de Medellín on November 2, 1675. Medellín replaced *Santa Fe de Antioquia as the capital of the Department of Antioquia on April 17, 1826. The modern city is known for its festival of flowers (*fería de flores*) and cattle fair (*fería de ganado*).

MEDELLIN CARTEL.   The name given to a group of illegal *drug dealers (*narcotraficantes*) operating out of Medellín. Together with a rival group, the *CALI CARTEL, the Medellín Cartel is said to have processed and distributed as much as 60 to 70% of the *cocaine exported to the U.S. during the 1980s. Although strictly speaking not a cartel, this union of drug lords controls many aspects of the Colombian narcotics trade. It has been headed by Pablo Escobar Gaviria, Jorge Luis *Ochoa Vásquez (and brothers Fabio and Juan David), Gustavo de Jesús Gaviria Rivero (d. August 11, 1990), José Antonio Ocampo Obando, and José Gonzalo Rodríguez Gacha—*el Mejicano* (d. December 15, 1989). See also: COCA; COCAINE; DRUG TRADE; ESCOBAR GAVIRIA, Pablo

MEJIA, Liborio, 1792-1816.   Colonel, educator, patriot martyr, Vice President of the *Provincias Unidas. Born *Rionegro, July 23; executed in *Bogotá, September 16. He was a lawyer and educator in Antioquia, where he joined the patriot forces and later participated in the campaigns in southern Colombia in 1814. He was commander of the patriot forces at the Battle of *Cuchilla del Tambo in 1816 and participated in the Battle of La *Plata. Mejía was executed by Spanish forces during the *Reconquista.

MEJIA VALLEJO, Manuel, 1923-.   Author, journalist, educator, born Jericó (*Antioquia), April 23. He has served as director of the Taller de Escritores of the *Universidad de Antioquia. His novels include *La tierra éramos nosotros* (1945), *Al pie de la ciudad* (1958), *El día señalado* (1963), *Aire de tango* (1973), *Las muertas ajenas* (1979), *Tarde de verano* (1980), and *Y el mundo sigue andando* (1984). Mejía Vallejo was awarded the Nadal Prize for Literature for *El día señalado* in 1963 and the Premio Nacional de Novela Vivencias for *Aire de tango* in 1973.

MELO, José María, 1800-1860. General, born Chaparral (*Tolima), October 9; executed June 1 on the *hacienda* Juncaná (Chiapas, Mexico) as a result of an armed rebellion. He was a patriot military officer, 1819-1830. Active in Venezuela during the 1830s, he was again in military service in *New Granada in 1846. He displaced the *Obando presidency in the *rebellion of 1854 and proclaimed a dictatorship, April 17, 1854. His brief administration was defeated at the Battle of *Bogotá, December 4, 1854, and he was exiled thereafter in Central America and Mexico.

MEMORIAL DE AGRAVIOS. Declaration of Grievances, November 20, 1809. Written largely by Camilo *Torres, this petition was directed to the Central Junta of Spain (*Junta Central [de España]), asking consideration of stated colonial problems. The declaration noted that the American colonies had more wealth and a larger population than Spain. It stressed the equality of *creole and *peninsular Spaniards, attributed any momentary lack of development to repressive colonial policies, and demanded increased representation (more than twelve delegates out of forty-eight) in the Spanish legislative assembly, the *Cortes. It was suppressed by the colonial administration in *New Granada. See also: JUNTA OF NOTABLES

MENDINUETA Y MUZQUIZ, Pedro, 1736-1825. Viceroy of *New Granada, 1797-1803. He aided the expedition of *Humboldt and *Bonpland; decreed a monopoly on *platinum, 1802; established the *Observatorio Nacional, 1803; commissioned a *census and map of *Bogotá; and dealt with *Nariño's return to New Granada.

MERCADO, José Rafael, d. 1976. The kidnapping, trial, and execution of Mercado, February-April 1976, was one of the actions for which the *Movimiento Diecinueve de Abril (M-19) claimed responsibility. M-19 kidnapped Mercado, a labor leader and president of the *Confederación de Trabajadores de Colombia, and accused him of fraud and misconduct in office. M-19 appealed to Colombian workers to indicate whether Mercado was guilty or not guilty by writing their "vote" on walls in public places. The kidnappers then pronounced Mercado guilty of betraying the trust workers had placed in him. His body was discovered in *Bogotá on April 20, 1976.

MERCEDARIANS. One of four orders favored for missionary work among the *Indians in the 16th century, although not so highly favored as the *Dominicans, *Franciscans, and *Augustinians. Never a large group in *New Granada, they were one of the earliest. The first Mercedarians arrived at *Santa Marta in 1527 and established a monastery prior to 1532. Monasteries were also established in *Cali, around 1538; *Anserma, 1539; and *Pasto, 1561.

MERCHANT MARINE. Colombia has three shipping lines, with a total of some twenty-five vessels. Of these, seventeen belong to the *FLOTA MERCANTE GRANCOLOMBIANA. See also: COMPAÑIA NACIONAL DE NAVEGACION S.A.

MERCURY. Mercury is mentioned as an economic asset in Alexander Walker's *Colombia* of 1822. Current output is small, all from *Tolima.

MESSIA DE LA ZERDA, Pedro, 1700-1783. Viceroy of *New Granada, 1761-1772. He authorized *Mutis to introduce the study of mathematics, astronomy, and physics, 1762; founded a gunpowder factory in *Bogotá; established the *tobacco monopoly (*estanco) in New Granada, 1766; dealt with the expulsion of the *Jesuits and a rebellion in *Neiva, 1767; commissioned a map of the viceroyalty, completed in 1772; and exiled María Lugarda de Ospina from Bogotá (see: MARIACHUELAS, Las).

MESTIZO. In modern usage, "mestizo" means simply a person of mixed ancestry. In the colonial period, however, it referred specifically to a person of European and *Indian ancestry. The position of mestizos in society varied, but often carried with it a social stigma or formal discrimination because of the Spanish and upper-class prejudice for racial and religious purity, *limpieza de sangre,* especially in the 16th and 17th centuries. Families, including a few wealthy black families, would establish their "purity of lineage" through the process known as *gracias al sacar,* by which they acquired official recognition of their genealogies. Within the Spanish colonies, degrees of racial mixing were well defined. By one scheme of classification common in Colombia, a person born in America of European parents on both sides was a *creole (*criollo*); creole with creole produced another creole; European or creole with Indian produced a mestizo; European or creole with Negro produced mulatto; Negro and Indian produced *zambo;* mestizo and Indian produced *cholo;* mestizo and European or creole produced *castizo;* mulatto and European or creole produced *morisco;* European/creole and *morisco* produced *albino;* and Negro and *zambo* produced *zambo prieto.* Terms such as *galfarro, salto atrás, calpán mulata, chino, tente en el aire, lobo, jíbaro, barcino, cambujo, coyote, ochavón,* and *cuarterón* indicated further possible combinations in colonial Spanish America. See also: CREOLE; PENINSULAR

META, Departamento de. Located in southeastern Colombia, the department covers 85,635 square kilometers of mostly tropical plains and *Llanos lying between 1° 39' and 4° 53'N latitude and 71° 5' and 75° 2'W longitude. Of the total area, 76,215 square kilometers are tropical; 4,281 temperate; 3,854 cold; and 1,285 wasteland. Major rivers are the Meta, Ariari, and Manacacías. The department is bordered in the west by the eastern slopes of the *Andes Mountains. In the Llanos, the climate is marked by distinct wet (May-November) and dry (December-April) seasons, with an average temperature of 29°C. Elsewhere in the department temperatures average 25° to 27°C, and there are alternating wet (March-May and September-December) and dry (June-August and January-February) periods. The population in 1985 was 321,563 people (estimate), with a population density of four people per square kilometer. *Villavicencio is the capital city. There is limited industry, and settlement is sparse. Based on DANE, *Colombia estadística 86,* principal agricultural products, with tonnage produced in 1984, include rice, 276,480 tons; *yuca,* 67,500; plantains, 54,600; sorghum, 34,000; *corn, 33,310; *African palm, 18,200; *cotton, 8,700; *cacao, 2,820; *tobacco, 150; beans, 57; and soybeans, 45. *Livestock slaughtered in 1984 included 77,430 head of cattle and 18,261 hogs. In 1983 there were twenty-three businesses employing ten or more people. The region was part of *Cundinamarca until 1868. It was the Territory of San Martín, 1868-1906, the Territory of Meta, 1906-1909, and the Intendancy of Meta, 1909-1959. The Department of Meta was created December 16, 1959.

METRIC SYSTEM, see: WEIGHTS AND MEASURES

MEXICO, Relations with. Miguel Santamaría (1789-1837) secretary of the *Congress of Cúcuta in 1821 was a Mexican from

Veracruz, and relations between the two countries were very close at the time of independence. The *Gual-Torrens Treaty of 1825 established friendly relations between them and led to plans for a cooperative Mexican-Colombian expedition to *Cuba and Puerto Rico in 1825. In more recent times, both countries have been concerned about the peace and tranquillity of Central America; both belonged to the *Contadora Group. Mexico has also provided a neutral ground for negotiations between the Colombian authorities and the *Movimiento Diecinueve de Abril, such as the 1983 meeting between Communications Minister Bernardo Ramírez and Alvaro *Fayad Delgado. Colombians who have settled in Mexico include the writer and biographer of General José de San Martín, Juan García del Río (1794-1856), and the poet Miguel Angel *Osorio Benítez, both of whom died there. Mexico became one of Colombia's chief trading partners within the *Latin American Free Trade Association. In 1987, imports from Mexico amounted to US$148,600,000 (almost as much as those from Brazil), although Colombia's exports to Mexico were only US$8,200,000. This was due in part to the cheaper Mexican peso; imports from Mexico in 1980 had been US$61,600,000.

MEXICO-COLOMBIA TREATY OF 1825, see: GUAL-TORRENS TREATY

MINERALS. Colombia has been important for its minerals from pre-Columbian times. Those currently produced include *iron, *gold, *silver, *platinum, *zinc, *nickel, *mercury, *copper, *lead, and *tin. Colombia also produces precious stones— *emeralds in particular; *petroleum and *natural gas; and many other things, including asbestos, talc, calcite, mica, sulfur, granite, marble, quartz, lime, *salt, and *coal. See also: SUBSOIL MINERAL RIGHTS

MINIFUNDIOS. Literally, "small" or "tiny fields." In contrast to *latifundios, minifundios are very small landholdings, often less than one hectare (or 2.47 acres). The majority of Latin American landholdings are minifundios, often not large enough to sustain a family and frequently ineffectively farmed due to lack of capital and technological skills on the part of the owners.

MINING, see: MINERALS

MINISTERIALES. A political faction; pro-administration supporters during the *Herrán administration and the first presidency of General T. C. de *Mosquera.

MINISTRIES. Prior to the *Constitution of 1886, the major departments of state were called *secretarías:* "secretariats," "secretaryships," or simply the "office of the secretary." *Gran Colombia had five: *hacienda* (finance), *interior* (internal affairs), *relaciones exteriores (sic:* foreign relations), *guerra* (war), and *marina* (the navy and shipping), although the same person held the last two portfolios, and in 1827 they were formally combined. In 1831, *New Granada decided to combine *interior* and *relaciones exteriores,* but these were separated again in 1843. Two years later, in 1845, the name *interior* was changed to *gobierno,* and this, from 1858 and 1861, was joined with war and navy as *gobierno i guerra.* Foreign relations became briefly *estado i relaciones exteriories,* 1861-1863, and from 1863 to 1905 there was a new secretariat, *tesoro i crédito nacional.* Also in 1863, *hacienda* became *hacienda i fomento* (finance and development), but these became separate departments in 1880 when *education was given its own *secretaría de instrucción pública.* Law 7 of August 25, 1886, provided for seven *ministerios,* or ministeries: *fomento, gobierno, guerra, hacienda, instrucción pública, relaciones exteriores,* and *tesoro.* A *ministerio de justicia* was added in 1890, only to be abolished in 1894, along with the *ministerio de fomento. Fomento* was reestablished in 1905 as *obras públicas* (public works). *Tesoro* separated from *hacienda* in 1909 but was merged again as *hacienda y crédito público* in 1923. An *agriculture and trade ministry (*agricultura y comercio*) was established in August 1914, and an industry ministry (*ministerio de industria)* was added in July 1923. These two were briefly merged from 1927-1931 and again after 1938, in this latter case as the *ministerio de economía nacional.* Labor (*trabajo*) was added to the title of the industry ministry in 1934 and then made a separate agency in 1938. Health (*salubridad pública*) joined the title of the education ministry in 1923, but in 1938 was transferred to the new labor ministry as *higiene y provisión social.* It then became an independent *ministerio de higiene* in 1946. The justice ministry was reestablished in 1947, and a ministry of mail and telegraphs (*correos y telégrafos*) was created in 1923. During the *Betancur presidency, 1982-1986, there were thirteen ministries: *gobierno, relaciones exteriores, justicia, hacienda y crédito público, defensa nacional, agricultura, trabajo y seguridad social, salud pública, minas y energía, desar-

rollo económico, educación nacional, comunicaciones, and *obras públicas y transportes.*

MINOR CONVENTS, Rebellion of the.   Also called the rebellion of 1839, it took place in *Pasto, July-August. The movement was led by Father Francisco Solano de la Villota in opposition to the closing of minor convents. The most important military engagement of the rebellion was the first Battle of *Buesaco, but numerous guerrilla skirmishes followed in the period from September to December.

MINORITIES REPRESENTATION LAW.   Law No. 8, April 13, 1905, legalized representation of political minorities in *Congress. It heralded a significant change from the practices of 1886-1904, which had virtually excluded *Liberals and other minority parties from public office.

MINT, see: CASA DE LA MONEDA

MINUTO DE DIOS.   "Minute of God," or "God's Minute," a social reform program aimed at providing low-cost housing for the urban poor. Begun in 1958 by Father Rafael García Herreros, the Minute of God is financed by widely publicized fund-raising dinners known as "banquets of the million." The program attempts to establish self-directing communities with Christian values in working-class neighborhoods.

MIRANDA, Francisco José, 1750-1816.   Independence leader, much more closely associated with Venezuela than Colombia, whose design for a national *flag was one of those influencing the banner *Gran Colombia adopted.

MISKITO INDIANS.   Modern form of the name of the indigenous inhabitants of the *MOSQUITO COAST of Central America.

MISSIONARY ORDERS, Colonial.   A reference to the fact that the Spanish monarchy favored four *religious orders for missionary work among the *Indians in the 16th century: *Dominicans, *Franciscans, *Augustinians, and *Mercedarians. The last were eventually eliminated. Although there were other orders at work with the Indians occasionally, preference for these four forced closing of a *Carmelite monastery in *Bogotá in 1573 and prevented the *Jesuits from establishing themselves until the 17th century.

MITA.   A forced-work levy introduced by the Spanish to manipu-
late Indian laborers, the *mita* required the members of a group,
clan, or tribe of *Indians to perform designated tasks for a
fixed period of time in exchange for predetermined payment.
There were various kinds of *mitas,* including those for *agriculture (*agraria*), *mining (*minería*), textile production (*obrajes*),
transportation of goods (*transporte, acarreo,* and *de boga*), domestic service, and public works. In general, Indian laborers
worked a minimum of 1.5 months annually fulfilling *mita*
obligations. The agriculture *mita* was normally three to four
months, but the mining *mitas* were often ten months at a time.
In some cases, such as transportation of goods, *mita* terms
might be stated as number of loads or quantities of goods
required. For example, wood carriers (*leñateros*) were required
to move twenty-four loads a month. Javier Ocampo López has
suggested that some forms of the agricultural *mita* (the *concierto
agrario*) lasted as late as the 20th century in parts of *Santander
and *Boyacá. See also: REPARTIMIENTO

MITA DE BOGA.   A work levy regulating the use of *Indians for
the transportation of freight and passengers on the *Magdalena
River. First authorized by royal *cédula,* August 11, 1552, it was
abolished in 1598, after which time *blacks were substituted
for the Indians.

MITO.   A literary review published from April 1955 to June 1962,
Mito has been described as a publication that marked the
opening of the modern era, in which the Colombian intellectual
life of the first half of the century yielded to that of the second
half. Founded by Pedro Gómez Valderrama, Jorge Gaitán
Durán, and Hernando Valencia Goelkel, *Mito* published opposing political and aesthetic philosophies and became a sounding
board for new ideas and forms of addressing Colombia's social
and intellectual crises of the mid-20th century.

MITU.   Capital of the Department of *Vaupés, located at 1° 8'N,
70° 3'W, Mitú is a port city on the Vaupés River. It is situated
660 kilometers from *Bogotá, at an altitude of 180 meters,
with an average temperature of 27°C. Estimated population in
1985 was 3,414 people. Mitú was founded in 1936 by Miguel
Cuervo Araoz.

MOCOA.   Capital of the Department of *Putumayo, located at 1°
8'N, 76° 38'W, in the foothills of the Andes on the Mocoa

River, approximately 995 kilometers southwest of Bogotá and 70 kilometers east of *Pasto. Altitude is 595 meters and the average temperature is 25°C. The population has grown from 1,500 people in 1950 to 6,221 in 1974, and approximately 28,000 people in 1985. Founded in 1551 by Pedro de Agreda, Mocoa is an agricultural, cattle-raising, commercial, hunting, and fishing center in one of Colombia's southernmost territories.

MODERNISM. A 20th-century literary movement in poetry. It encompassed a number of forms and styles, all sharing a common emphasis on aesthetics, the artistic use of language, and sophisticated conceptualization. Modernism tended to be restrained, anti-romantic, and highly nationalistic. It has been described as a rejection of localized and immediate experience in search of a universal, timeless reality, but it has also been criticized as aristocratic, intellectual escapism that allowed its devotees to avoid active engagement with the socioeconomic conditions in which they lived. Probably the best-known Colombian modernist in the first half of the century was Guillermo *Valencia (1873-1943). José Asunción *Silva (1865-1895) is often called the precursor of modernism in Colombia.

MODERNIST GENERATION. The group of cultural leaders who, in the terms of Abel Naranjo Villegas, developed or were prominent from 1920 to 1950. Naranjo Villegas describes the generation as one characterized by nonconformist ideas, incongruity between the public and private lives of its leaders, and tendencies that led to violence in the next generation. Ernesto Cortés Ahumada subdivides the period into the *Centenary Generation (key date, 1915) and the Modernist Political Generation (key date, 1930). Representative figures of the Centenary Generation include Antonio *Alvarez Lleras, Gustavo Arboleda, José María Arboleda Llorente, Porfirio *Barba Jacob, Luis Cano, Roberto Cortázar, Carlos Cortés Vargas, Laureano *Gómez, Alfonso *López Pumarejo, Luis *López de Mesa, Luis Eduardo Nieto Caballero, Enrique *Olaya Herrera, Mariano *Ospina Pérez, Raimundo Rivas, José Eustacio *Rivera, Tomás Rueda Vargas, Eduardo *Santos, Enrique Santos, and Roberto *Urdaneta Arbeláez. Important figures of the Modernist Political Generation might include Luis Alberto *Acuña, Germán *Arciniegas, Abel Cruz Santos, Luis Cuervo Márquez, Oswaldo *Díaz Díaz, Darío *Echandía, Jorge Eliécer *Gaitán, León de *Greiff, Guillermo Hernández de Alba, Alberto *Lleras Camargo, Luis Martínez Delgado, Alejandro Gómez, Rafael Maya, Plinio Mendoza Neira, Gerardo Molina, José Antonio *Osorio Lizarazo, Luis Ospina Vásquez, Roberto *Pizano Restrepo, Milton Puentes, Gustavo *Rojas Pinilla, Joaquín Tamayo, Gabriel *Turbay, Luis Vidales, Silvio Villegas, and Jorge *Zalamea. See also: GENERATIONS

MOEC, see: MOVIMIENTO DE OBREROS, ESTUDIANTES Y CAMPESINOS

MOIR, see: MOVIMIENTO OBRERO INDEPENDIENTE REVOLUCIONARIO

MOMPOS.   Port city in the Department of *Bolívar, located on Margarita Island on the Brazo de Mompós branch of the *Magdalena River, at 9° 14'N, 74° 26'W. Altitude is 32 meters above sea level; the average temperature, 28°C; and the population, 16,708 people (1985 estimate). Formally established as Santa Cruz de Mompós in 1539 by Alonso de *Heredia, the city is situated approximately 248 kilometers from *Cartagena and has a long history as a commercial entrepôt, although its importance declined as alternatives to river traffic developed. Mompós declared its absolute independence from Spain on August 6, 1810, and earned the title of *Ciudad Valerosa* (Valorous City) for its actions during the *independence movement, especially in battles that occurred January 21, 1811, and October 19, 1812. Mompós is also spelled Mompox, and the name is said to have been taken from an Indian chieftain named Mampo or Mampoo.

MON Y VELARDE, Juan Antonio, 1747-ca. 1791.   He was a member of the *Audiencia of Bogotá, 1781-1785; Visitor (*Visitador*) of *Antioquia, 1785-1788; and President of the Audiencia of Quito, 1790-1791. He was called the "regenerator of Antioquia" for an ambitious reform program instituted during his term as Visitor.

MONARCHY, Project for a.   A reference to the negotiations undertaken, 1829-1830, to establish a monarchy in Colombia as a means of stabilizing domestic affairs. The negotiations were authorized by a *Junta of Notables, including members of the *Council of State, in 1829. They were unsuccessful although supported by elements in France, England, and Spain.

MONEDA, Casa de, see: CASA DE MONEDA

MONEY, see: BANKS, BANKING AND FINANCIAL INSTITUTIONS; COINAGE; CURRENCY; EXCHANGE RATE; PESO

MONGES, Archipelago de, see: FRAILES, Los

MONSU. Archeological site in the Department of *Bolívar near the village of Turbana (10° 17'N, 75°27'W). Located near the Caribbean Coast, Monsú has yielded carbon 14 dates as early as 3350 B.C. Gerardo Reichel-Dolmatoff has established five phases of occupation at the site: I. Turbana (undated); II. Monzú (3350 B.C.); III. Pangola (2250 B.C.); IV. Macaví (1940 B.C.); and V. Barlovento (1560 B.C.-1030 B.C.). An intrusive burial is dated 800 B.C. Ceramics from the Turbana and Monsú phases are the oldest known in the Western Hemisphere. They appear more technologically advanced than those of *PUERTO HORMIGA.

MONTERIA. The capital of the Department of *Córdoba, located on the banks of the Sinú River at 8° 45'N, 75° 53'W. Altitude is 18 meters; average temperature, 28°C; and the estimated population in 1985 was 158,064. Montería serves principally as a commercial center for cattle ranching and agriculture, but it also has some light industry and potential importance for mineral production (*petroleum, *coal, *gold, and *platinum). First called San Jerónimo de Buenavista, the city was founded by Juan de Torrezar Díaz Pimienta in 1744. After the original settlement was destroyed by *Indians, the city was reestablished on its present site (approximately 902 kilometers from Bogotá) by Antonio de la Torre Miranda in 1774 and the name was changed to San Jerónimo de Montería. The name "Montería" is said to be derived from the fact that it was an early place where hunting parties (*monteros*) gathered. It became the capital of Córdoba when the department was created in 1951.

MONTOYA UPEGUI, Laura, 1878-1949. Madre Laura, founder of the Congregation of Missionary Sisters of María Inmaculada and Santa Catalina de Sena. Madre Laura was first an educator and then a nun devoted to training missionaries. She directed numerous teaching activities from her convent in *Medellín. She was also the author of many devotional works. A movement to canonize her, begun soon after her death, is still pending.

MONTOYA ZAPATA, Francisco, 1789-1862. Businessman, financier; born *Rionegro (Antioquia), December 22; died *Bogotá, July 25. During the wars for independence he supported the patriot cause, fighting in campaigns in the *Cauca region, including the battles at El *Palo and *Cuchilla del Tambo. He left the country during the *Reconquista, returning after independence to become a prominent merchant-industrialist. He was involved in negotiating the controversial foreign *loan of 1824. He promoted the introduction of steam navigation on the *Magdalena River, and he was an important merchant in the *tobacco trade and other commercial ventures until the collapse of his business interests in 1857.

MORA, Luis María, 1869-1936. Educator, author, born in *Bogotá, March 28. He was for many years professor of humanities in the *Colegio Mayor del Nuestra Señora del Rosario and author of numerous articles and books on literature, history, education, and politics. He was the author of Los contertulios de la Gruta Simbólica, an account of the *tertulia to which he belonged. His works include Apuntes sobre Balmes (1897), El alma nacional (1922), and Croniquillas de mi ciudad (1936). Mora has been described as the epitome of the upper-class man of letters and one of the last representatives of conservative (aristocratic) humanism in Colombian *literature.

MORENA, see: MOVIMIENTO DE RESTAURACION NACIONAL

MORENO Y ESCANDON, Francisco Antonio, 1736-1792. Lawyer, administrator, born *Mariquita (Tolima). An aide to Viceroy *Messía de la Zerda, educated at the University of Valladolid (Spain), he carried out the order to expel the *Jesuits in 1767. Commissioned to study educational needs in 1774, he recommended the creation of a system of primary schools, the establishment of a secular university, and the creation of a national library (see: BIBLIOTECA NACIONAL). He also encouraged the establishment of royal asylums. All of his recommendations were implemented in part or in whole, except the secular university, which the clergy opposed. He was later appointed a Regent of Chile, where he died. Moreno y Escandón was one of the highest *creole appointees in the royal administrative service during the colonial period in Latin America. See also: EDUCATION

MORGAN, (Sir) Henry, 1635-1688. Welsh buccaneer in the Caribbean after 1665. He raided *Portobello, 1668; Maracaibo, 1669; and *Chagres and *Panama City, 1671. He was knighted by King Charles II of England in 1674 and later was appointed Lieutenant Governor of Jamaica.

MORILLO, Pablo, 1778-1837. Spanish general, the "Pacifier." He was the commander in charge of the *Reconquista, 1816-1819, and was bitterly resented for his ruthlessness in reestablishing Spanish authority. He was responsible for numerous executions during the so-called *reign of terror. Militarily stalemated, he negotiated a settlement with *Bolívar on December 17, 1820, and then returned to Spain.

MORTMAIN. A reference to the practice of perpetual holding of land. The traditional view of the *Catholic Church in Latin America was that ecclesiastically owned property was inalienable. Manos muertas, as it is known in Spanish, allowed the Church to acquire land by purchase or donation but not to sell it or give it away once acquired. The practice was legally abolished in Colombia by the *DISAMORTIZATION DECREE of 1861.

MOSAICO, El. A literary society, or *tertulia, that flourished in the 1860s; also a newspaper published between 1858 and 1872 by members of the society. A literary journal with a great deal of *costumbrista work, El Mosaico was directed largely by Eugenio *Díaz, José María *Vergara y Vergara, José Joaquín Borda, José Manuel *Marroquín, and Ricardo Carrasquilla. Among others who frequented the society were José María *Samper, Diego Fallon, Ezequiel *Uricoechea, Aníbal Galindo, Próspero Pereira Gamba, and José María Quijano Otero.

MOSQUERA. For the President of Gran Colombia, see: MOSQUERA Y ARBOLEDA, Joaquín; for the General and President, see: MOSQUERA Y ARBOLEDA, Tomás Cipriano de; for the Archbishop, see: MOSQUERA Y ARBOLEDA, Manuel José.

MOSQUERA-CLARENDON TREATY OF 1866. Signed in London on February 16 by General T. C. de *Mosquera,

Colombia, and Lord Clarendon, Great Britain. The treaty was a reasonably definitive agreement between the two nations regulating commerce, navigation, and especially consular responsibilities.

MOSQUERA-ECHEVERRIA-RODRIGUEZ TREATY OF 1822. Signed in Santiago, Chile, on October 21, by Joaquín *Mosquera, Colombia, and Joaquín Echeverría and José Antonio Rodríguez, Chile. It was a treaty of union and alliance against Spain and other foreign enemies.

MOSQUERA-FREYRE TREATY OF 1866. A secret agreement signed in *Bogotá on August 28 by Rudesindo López and Froilán Largacha, for Colombian President T. C. de *Mosquera, and Colonel Manuel Freyre, for Peru. It was a treaty of alliance whereby Peru entrusted designated warships to Colombian care, while Colombia agreed to disguise the ownership in exchange for 500,000 pesos to renovate the fortresses of *Cartagena if Colombia joined an anti-Spanish coalition composed of Chile, Bolivia, Ecuador, and Peru. The treaty led to the *Rayo Affair and serious difficulties for President Mosquera.

MOSQUERA-IRARRAZABAL TREATY OF 1844. Signed in Santiago, Chile, on February 16 by General T. C. de *Mosquera, *New Granada, and Ramón Luis de Irarrazábal, Chile. A treaty of friendship, commerce, and navigation, with a most-favored-nation clause, it was supplemented by an agreement of October 8, 1844, concerning extradition, contraband, and diplomatic immunity.

MOSQUERA MISSION OF 1842-1845. A diplomatic mission to Peru, Bolivia, and Chile. Tomás Cipriano de *Mosquera's commission officially dealt with boundary problems, debt settlements, and international cooperation, but his actions seemed more ostensibly a personal vendetta against General José María *Obando, whose extradition he sought as a consequence of the War of the *Supreme Commanders, 1840-1842. The mission did achieve a treaty of friendship, commerce, and navigation with Chile on February 16, 1844.

MOSQUERA-MONTEAGUDO TREATY OF 1820. Signed Lima, July 6, by Joaquín *Mosquera, Colombia, and Bernardo Monteagudo, Peru. A treaty of alliance by which Colombia pledged military assistance to free Peru from Spain, and Peru agreed to bear expenses for the aid. Boundary settlements were to be negotiated at a later time.

MOSQUERA-PEDEMONTE TREATY OF 1830. Signed in Lima, August 11, by General T. C. de *Mosquera, Colombia, and Carlos Pedemonte, Peru. Major provisions dealt with a boundary settlement considered favorable to Colombia. The treaty was never ratified or acknowledged by Peru.

MOSQUERA-RIVADAVIA TREATY, 1823. Signed in Buenos Aires on March 8 by Joaquín *Mosquera, Colombia, and Bernardo Rivadavia, Argentina. It was a treaty of friendship and good will, exchanging legal recognition but stopping short of a formal league of alliance.

MOSQUERA Y ARBOLEDA, Joaquín, 1787-1878. Lawyer, educator, legislator, President of Colombia, June 13 to September 4, 1830. Born *Popayán, December 14; died Popayán, April 4. After receiving his doctorate of law from the *Colegio Mayor de Nuestra Señora del Rosario in 1805, he was first a member of the patriot junta in Popayán, 1812, and then diplomatic agent to Peru, Chile, and Buenos Aires, 1821-1824. After attending the *Congress of Panama in 1826, he was the last President of *Gran Colombia (overthrown by General Rafael *Urdaneta in 1830). He was Vice President of *New Granada, 1833-1835, various times a member of *Congress, and rector of the *Universidad del Cauca. He was the brother of General T. C. de *Mosquera and the twins Archbishop Manuel José *Mosquera and diplomat Manuel María Mosquera.

MOSQUERA Y ARBOLEDA, Manuel José, 1800-1853. Archbishop of *Bogotá, 1835-1853. Born *Popayán, April 11; died in exile in Marseilles (France), December 10. A brother of Joaquín *Mosquera and Tomás Cipriano de *Mosquera and twin brother of Manuel María Mosquera (1800-1882), he was educated at the Universidad Tomística in Quito and ordained a priest in 1823. He served as rector of the *Universidad del Cauca in Popayán before being named Archbishop of Bogotá. As Archbishop, he received the first Papal Nuncio in 1837 and devoted great attention to canonical studies, 1837, and seminary operation, 1840-1851. He opposed the Bible Society (*Sociedad Bíblica) and the Catholic Society (*Sociedad Católica), 1838; patronized the religious newspaper *El Catoli-*

cismo, 1849-1852; and resisted the *anti-clerical laws of 1850-1853. He was exiled from *New Granada, 1852-1853.

MOSQUERA Y ARBOLEDA, Tomás Cipriano de, 1798-1878. General, President of *New Granada 1845-1849 and 1861-1863 and of Colombia, 1863-1864 and 1866-1867. Born *Popayán, September 26; died on the *hacienda* Coconuco near Popayán, October 7. He was a patriot military officer 1815-1816 and 1820-1825, nicknamed "Mascachochas" because his jaw was permanently injured in the Battle of *Barbacoas in 1824. As a military officer Mosquera successfully defended the national government against the War of the *Supreme Commanders, 1840-1842, and the *Melo revolt, 1854, as well as against the Ecuadorans in 1863. However, he overthrew the *Confederación Granadina in 1861, thereby becoming the only leader to succeed at armed rebellion against the state in the 19th century. He was a diplomatic agent to Peru 1829-1830, and to Chile and Peru 1842-1845. He was Minister of Foreign Relations, 1839, and at least twice Governor of *Cauca. As President he was responsible for the introduction of free trade, 1847; strong anti-clerical measures, 1861-1864 (see: ANTI-CLERICAL LAWS, 1861; DISAMORTIZATION DECREE); and abuse of authority for which he was removed from office in 1867. General Mosquera was a brother of President Joaquín *Mosquera and the twins Archbishop Manuel José *Mosquera and Manuel María Mosquera.

MOSQUITO COAST. The region inhabited by the Mosquito, or Miskito, *Indians; an imprecise term applied at times to portions of the Caribbean Coasts of Honduras, Nicaragua, Costa Rica, and *Panama. The Mosquito Gulf lies off the coast of Panama. By royal decree, dated San Lorenzo, November 30, 1803, the coastal territory between the Chagres River (Panama) and Cape Gracias a Dios (Nicaraguan-Honduran border) was separated from the Captaincy General of Guatemala and annexed to the Viceroyalty of *New Granada. Colombia, by virtue of the decree of 1803 and the doctrine of *uti possidetis*, 1810, asserted claims to this part of the Mosquito Coast in the *Gual-Molina Treaty with the Central American Confederation in 1825. Following the collapse of the Confederation in 1838, Colombia pressed her claims with the newly emergent nations of Costa Rica and Nicaragua, while simultaneously protesting movements to secure control over the area by interests from the United States and Great Britain. The British had proclaimed a protectorate over parts of the Mosquito Coast. Tensions with these latter powers lessened after the signing of the *Clayton-Bulwer Treaty in 1850, but disputes were not settled with Costa Rica until 1903 and not with Nicaragua until 1928. The Mosquito Coast claimed by Colombia was contiguous with the bulk of the national territory until the creation of the Republic of *Panama in 1903. Colombian interests in the region were largely defensive (to prevent hostile forces from seizing control of the land) and economic (to enhance Colombia's role in the development of transisthmian commerce).

MOTILONES. A group of *Indians inhabiting the *Guajira–*Sierra Nevada de Santa Marta area. Housed in sedentary villages based on agriculture (*corn) and hunting, the Motilones were historically considered dangerous and inhospitable. They were considered particularly troublesome to workers of the Colombian Petroleum Company after it began *petroleum development in the 1930s. Members of the *Capuchin order were active in attempting to found missions with the Motilones, 1691-1813 and again after 1888. In 1974 the Colombian government established a Motilón forest reservation. The Indians seem to have responded well to programs of the Division of Indian Affairs (*División de Asuntos Indígenas), which estimated their population at 2,538 in 1978.

MOTIVES FOR DISSIDENCE, see: *MOTIVOS DE DISIDENCIA*

MOTIVOS DE DISIDENCIA. Also called the "Petition of the Twenty-one," a declaration published in 1896 by Historical Conservatives (*Históricos) listing the abuses of the governing party (*Nationalist Conservatives) since 1886, but especially after 1892. The Twenty-one acknowledged that the nation had made gains in national unity and religious harmony, but these were outweighed by a virtual executive dictatorship, a systematic exclusion of the opposition, a chronic abuse of civil rights by means of "extraordinary powers," persecution of the press, poor administration of government revenues, a *currency crisis, and lack of concern for public *education. The statement does much to explain the political causes of the War of the *Thousand Days.

MOVIMIENTO DE ACCION NACIONAL (MAN). The name adopted for a short-lived attempt to found a party supportive of the government of General *Rojas Pinilla, December 1954 to February 1955. Although it hoped to attract support from all segments of society, its most prominent endorsement (aside from the Rojas Pinilla administration) came from the *Confederación Nacional de Trabajadores. MAN was an unsuccessful forerunner of the *ALIANZA NACIONAL POPULAR.

MOVIMIENTO DE OBREROS, ESTUDIANTES Y CAMPESINOS (MOEC). The *guerrilla movement of Workers, Students and Peasants was founded in January 1959 by student leader Antonio Larrota (d. 1961) and was later led by Federico Arango. Its first formal congress was held in *Cali, July 20, 1960. The organization fell apart after its second congress in 1965 because of methodological disputes. See also: GUERRILLA MOVEMENTS

MOVIMIENTO DE RENOVACION NACIONAL (M.R.N.). A short-lived political party formed in late 1977. It described itself as democratic and conservative, stressing moral issues. General Alvaro Valencia Tovar was its candidate in the 1978 presidential elections.

MOVIMIENTO DE RESTAURACION NACIONAL (MORENA). Literally, the "Movement of National Restoration," but also translated into English as the "Movement of National Renewal" and the "Movement of National Reconstruction," MORENA is an extreme right-wing political party formed in August 1989, based in Puerto Boyacá (5° 58'N, 74° 36'W) and the *Magdalena valley. Pro-capitalist, virulently anti-communist and ostensibly Catholic, it has been linked allegedly with latifundista cattle-ranching interests, anti-guerrilla self-defense organizations, and the so-called barons of the *drug trade.

MOVIMIENTO DE SALVACION NACIONAL (M.S.N.). A splinter faction of the *Conservative Party, formalized as a separate group in 1990. The Movement of National Salvation, headed by Alvaro *Gómez Hurtado, is reminiscent of the *Históricos of the late 19th century and has in recent times been known as the Alvarista branch of the party. The main faction of the Conservatives, now known as the Social Conservative Party, traces its lineage back to the *Nationalists, and has more recently been known as the Ospinista-Pastranista following, after former Presidents Mariano *Ospina Pérez and

Misael *Pastrana Borrero. The M.S.N. did surprisingly well in the congressional elections for the *Asamblea Constituyente in 1990, and Gómez Hurtado became one of the presiding officers of the assembly.

MOVIMIENTO DIECINUEVE DE ABRIL. The Movement of April 19 (M-19), a *guerrilla association, was formed in late 1973 by Jaime *Bateman Cayón (Pablo), Iván Marino *Ospina (Felipe González), Alvaro *Fayad (El Turco), Carlos *Pizarro Leongómez—all of whom served successively as its leaders—and Israel Santamaría, Gustavo Arias Londoño, and others. Many early members were also members of *ANAPO, and the name M-19 (Movement of April 19) referred to the date of the presidential elections of April 19, 1970, which many ANAPO members claimed had been stolen from their candidate. M-19's program has been described as the achievement of a democratic socialist society by political means. It has described itself as nonaligned, although some of its founders studied in the Soviet Union. M-19 began its operations in January 1974 with a newspaper advertising campaign, "Watch Out for M-19," appearing to announce a new medicine for internal parasites. Its first public act was the theft of *BOLIVAR'S SWORD that same month, and it has claimed responsiblity for the kidnapping and death of José Rafael *MERCADO (1976), the theft of some 5,000 weapons from a military arsenal in the *CANTON DEL NORTE (1978-1979), occupation of the *DOMINICAN EMBASSY in Bogotá (1980), and the seizure of the *PALACIO DE JUSTICIA (1985). Representatives of M-19 signed truce agreements with the government in *Medellín, April 24, 1984 (see: URIBE [La], Agreements of) but later became disillusioned over what they saw as the government's failure to implement promised reforms. From May 29 to July 20, 1988, they kidnapped and held prisoner Alvaro *Gomez Hurtado as a means of publicizing their demands for renewed dialogue with the government. New negotiations between the *Barco government and M-19 representatives, conducted from January-September 1989, culminated in a peace settlement late in the year. In February 1990, President Barco pardoned a number of those involved in the Palacio de Justicia attack, and from March 8 to 10, members of M-19 officially surrendered their weapons to the government. As ex-guerrillas-turned-politicians within the legal system, members of the M-19 formed a political group sometimes referred to as the Democratic Alliance M-19 (Alianza Democrática, or

M-19AD). They achieved surprising successes in the elections of 1990-1991. See also: ESCOBAR SOTO, Nicolás; GUERRILLA MOVEMENTS; NARIÑO, Invasion of; NAVARRO WOLFF, Antonio

MOVIMIENTO LATINO NACIONAL. A political party founded in the Department of *Quindío by Carlos *Lehder Rivas in 1983, the M.L.N. stressed a form of nationalism specifically opposed to imperialism, neo-colonialism, communism, and Zionism. It called for nationalization of banks, transport, and the assets of multinational businesses; abrogation of the *Extradition Treaties for cases dealing with the *drug trade; legalization of *marijuana for personal use; an end to foreign interference in Colombian life; and the formation of a united Latin American army to prevent intervention in Latin American affairs. The party also supported various measures to protect the environment and natural resources, and its party flag was symbolically green. The M.L.N. published a newspaper, *Quindío Libre,* and was surprisingly successful in the 1984 elections in the Department of Quindío. It lost importance, however, as the career of Lehder Rivas declined.

MOVIMIENTO NACIONAL. A name used by Belisario *Betancur and his supporters in the elections of 1978 and 1982 to distinguish themselves from the traditional *Conservative and *Liberal parties. It was a loose coalition of independents, Conservatives, dissident Liberals, Christian Democrats (*Democracia Cristiana), and old *ANAPO supporters. It called for a new national unity, attacked clientelism and corruption, and stressed social issues, such as housing and education.

MOVIMIENTO NACIONAL POPULAR. A Castroite party founded in 1964 by dissidents from the *Movimiento Revolucionario Liberal.

MOVIMIENTO OBRERO INDEPENDIENTE REVOLUCIONARIO (MOIR). Guerrilla movement and political party, founded in 1965, by militant factions of the MOEC (*Movimiento de Obreros, Estudiantes y Campesinos), the P.C.C. (*Partido Comunista de Colombia), and others. MOIR formally proclaimed its existence on September 14, 1969, in *Medellín. It had a strong Maoist orientation. The movement has often been split by intense ideological disputes.

MOVIMIENTO POPULAR REVOLUCIONARIO (M.P.R.). Forerunner of the *FRENTE UNIDO DE ACCION REVO-LUCIONARIA.

MOVIMIENTO REVOLUCIONARIO LIBERAL. The M.R.L. was the Liberal Revolutionary Movement, a splinter faction of the *Liberal Party, 1958-1967. It refused to support the *Frente Nacional and demanded a policy of *agrarian and urban reform. Its principal leader was Alfonso *López Michelsen.

MUERTE A SECUESTRADORES. "Death to kidnappers," or MAS, as it is commonly known, is a clandestine extralegal organization formed in 1981 by leaders of the *drug trade as a response to the kidnapping of Marta Nieves Ochoa Vásquez, the sister of drug dealer Jorge Luis *Ochoa Vásquez, on November 12. According to public statements, 223 drug leaders (which may have included Pablo *Escobar Gaviria and Manuel Antonio Garcés) met in Cali on December 1, 1981 (others say at the Hotel Intercontinental in Medellín) and formed MAS to retaliate against kidnappers. The *Movimiento Diecinueve de Abril was believed responsible for the kidnapping, and MAS has been right wing in its political views, opposed to reformers such as unionists, intellectuals, and students, as well as guerrillas and kidnappers. MAS is allegedly supported by members of the military with strong anti-communist views. Its actions have included the August 1984 assassination of Carlos *Toledo Plata, which was an apparent attempt to wreck negotiations for a truce between government authorities and the *M-19 guerrillas. See also: DEATH SQUADS

MUISCA STYLE. A type of pre-conquest Indian goldwork found in the eastern highlands of Colombia. It is characterized by the use of *gold and *copper alloy in a mixture of techniques, including casting, lamination, repoussé, and the lost-wax process. Frequent decoration with cast wires is common. Peculiar to the Muisca Style are the *tunjos,* anthropomorphic figures with cast wire decoration depicting a great variety of scenes from daily life. Other items include large rectangular nose pieces, collars, bells, and such zoomorphic figures as serpents and mythological dragons.

MUISCAS, see: CHIBCHAS

MULE. A 20th-century term associated with the *drug trade, a mule is a person who smuggles narcotics by hiding the illicit drug in one or more body cavities. For example, cocaine sealed in a rubber glove can be swallowed, carried through customs in the stomach of the "mule," and then recovered after a bowel movement. The process can prove fatal, however, if the protective covering ruptures while in the body cavity. In less precise usage, a mule may be anyone who transports illegal narcotics. See also: DRUG TRADE

MUNICIPALITY. The usual English translation for *municipio*. Because the jurisdiction of each *municipio* has traditionally included a town and the surrounding rural area, it may better be compared to an Anglo-American county than to a simple town or urban area. Under the *Constitution of 1886 it was the third ranking-unit: *department, *province, and municipality. Provinces were abolished by the *Constitution of 1991. In 1979 there were 967 *municipios,* ranging from 120 in *Boyacá to one in each of the *comissariats and in the *Intendancy of *San Andrés y Providencia. The municipality is governed by a Municipal Council (Concejo Municipal) composed of 7 to 21 officials known as *Consejales* and an *alcalde,* all democratically elected for 3-year terms. Municipalities have jurisdiction over local economic life, taxes, public expenditures, land use, and ecological polices.

MUÑOZ DUQUE, Aníbal, 1908-. Archbishop of Bogotá, 1975-1984. Born October 3, Santa Rosa de Osos (*Antioquia), he was ordained November 19, 1933, and consecrated in 1951. Prior to his appointment to the episcopate, he was rector of a seminary at Yarumal (6° 57'N, 75° 24'W, Antioquia). In 1984 he was appointed a *Cardinal of the Church.

MURILLO TORO, Manuel, 1816-1880. Lawyer, journalist, *Radical Liberal, President of Colombia 1864-1866 and 1872-1874. Born Chaparral (*Tolima), January 1; died *Bogotá, December 26. He received his doctorate in law from the *Colegio Mayor de Nuestra Señora del Rosario in 1836. He rebelled against the *Márquez administration in 1840. In addition to serving in both houses of *Congress, he was a diplomatic representative to the United States, France, and Venezuela, and was at various times Secretary of Foreign Relations and Justice of the *Supreme Court. He was Minister of Finance in the *López administration and President of

*Santander, 1857, before becoming President of Colombia in 1864. He was noted for strict adherence to established legal procedures and the defense of civil rights. His first administration ordered printing of the maps from the *Chorographic Commission; introduced the telegraph, 1865; enlarged the Convent of Santo Domingo for use as government offices; and regularly published treasury reports. His second administration concluded a beneficial reorganization of both the foreign and domestic debts and presided over lavish commemorative services for the 50th anniversary of the end of the wars of independence, 1872.

MURRAY CONTRACT INCIDENT. A reference to the *petroleum concession negotiated by Lord Murray of Elibank for the British firm of S. Pearson and Son and the diplomatic embroilment that resulted when the United States objected to it. After preliminary negotiations, President Carlos *Restrepo and his Council of Ministers approved the so-called Murray Contract between Colombia and the Pearson firm on April 24, 1913. The proposed contract granted the British company exploitation rights to petroleum and hydrocarbons in a 3,800-square-mile territory, as well as permission to construct *railroads, pipelines, and canals necessary to carry out the concession. In October, the United States began to pressure the Colombian government to reject final ratification of the contract because it objected to European penetration of Latin American strategic resources and to monopolistic concessions in general and, specifically, to the possibility of another canal to rival the soon-to-be-completed Panama Canal. The efforts of the U.S. were successful, and Lord Murray withdrew the contract proposal from consideration on November 24, 1913.

MUSEO DE ARTES Y TRADICIONES POPULARES. The Museum of Popular Arts and Traditions was founded in *Bogotá in 1971 by the *Asociación Colombiana de Promoción Artesanal (ACPA) in a restored 18th-century convent. The museum collects artifacts illustrative of folk arts, both historical and contemporary, and it seeks to preserve various arts and crafts by encouraging local artisans and helping them to develop markets for their products.

MUSEO DEL ARTE COLONIAL. The Museum of Colonial Art, *Bogotá, opened in 1942. It is housed in a 17th-century cloister adjoining the Church of San Ignacio. The building was designed by Juan Bautista Coluchini, and the principal masons in charge of its construction were Martín de la Cruz, Felipe de Santiago, and Juan de León. The museum houses the largest known collection of paintings by Gregorio *Vásquez Arce y Ceballos; works by Gaspar and Baltasar *Figueroa, with whom Vásquez studied; and numerous other pieces by colonial artists and sculptors.

MUSEO DEL ORO, see: GOLD MUSEUM

MUSEO NACIONAL. The National Museum in *Bogotá developed from an act of *Congress (1931) which resulted in the founding of the National Service of Archeology in 1938 and the National Institute of Ethnology in 1941. The two were reorganized into the National Museum of Archeology and Ethnology in 1945 and transferred to the present building, a former penitentiary, in 1946. Antecedents of the modern museum would include the Royal *Botanical Expedition of the 18th century; the *Academia Nacional founded in 1826 and renewed in 1833; the National Lyceum of 1857; the National Institute of Sciences and Arts, 1865; the *Universidad Nacional, 1867; the Permanent Scientific Commission, 1881; the *Academia Colombiana de Historia, 1902; the national organization of museums undertaken in 1903; and the first law regarding preservation of historical sites in 1918.

MUSEUM OF POPULAR ARTS AND TRADITIONS, see: MUSEO DE ARTES Y TRADICIONES POPULARES

MUTIS, José Celestino, 1732-1808. Naturalist, physician to Viceroy *Messía de la Zerda;, born Cadiz (Spain), April 6; died *Bogotá, September 12. He received his medical degree in Madrid and then studied in Bologna, Leiden, London, and Paris before accompanying Viceroy *Messía de la Zerda to *New Granada in 1760. He was an innovator in *education, instructor of mathematics at the *Colegio Mayor de Nuestra Señora del Rosario after 1762, and he was ordained a priest in 1772. Mutis is most often remembered for his work as Director of the *Botanical Expedition, 1783-1808.

MUZO MINES, see: EMERALDS

-N-

NADAISMO.   The term used to describe the work of the *nadaísta* movement in *literature, 1959-1966. The term is attributed to Gonzalo Arango, who in an interview in 1950, defended the right of young writers to be concerned with violence and *La *Violencia* in literature even though it might accomplish nothing (*nada*). The movement originated in *Medellín as a protest against what were considered the archaic standards of establishment writers. It climaxed with public protests against the awarding of the Esso Prize for Literature in 1965 and 1966 and the short-lived creation of a rival *nadaísta* prize. It has been characterized by terms such as "avant-garde," "extremist," "iconoclastic," and "black humor." Names associated with the movement, in addition to Gonzalo Arango, include Amílcar Osorio (Amilkar U.), Elmo Valencia, Jaime Jaramillo (X-504), Pilarica Alvear Sanín, Fanny Buitrago (who denies the association), J. Mario (Jotamario), Bor Torre, J. Eutiquio Leal, Diego León Giraldo, Eduardo Escobar, and Humberto Navarro.

NAMES, Personal.   Colombians have one or more given names (*nombres*). These are frequently taken from saints of the *Catholic Church and their attributes (José, María, Piedad, and so on.) or from classical antiquity, such as Julio César. The full surname has two elements, which may themselves occasionally be compounded. The first element is the paternal family name. This is usually followed by the maternal family name frequently introduced by *y*. For example, the name Joaquín *Mosquera y Arboleda illustrates the usual form of combination. On marriage, a woman normally replaces the maternal surname with her husband's name, almost always introduced by *de*: Gloria *Gaitán de Valenzuela. More often than not, however, the full legal name is restricted to very formal situations. Normally it is the second surname (or *apellido*) that is dropped in everyday use: Camilo *Torres Restrepo becomes simply Camilo Torres. Less common, but also possible would be Camilo Torres R. Sometimes, however, individuals will drop their first *apellido* instead, usually because the second one is more distinctive or more famous. Thus, the explorer Vasco *Núñez de Balboa becomes Balboa in normal usage.

   This dictionary usually enters persons by their full legal name at biographical entries. This extended form is also used less frequently at times on the occasion of the first mention of a person in entries elsewhere in the dictionary and to facilitate cross-referencing where similar names might be confusing. This is done for the reader's convenience and should not be taken as necessarily indicating the usual way the person is referred to. In most cases references other than the formal biographical entries are given as they are commonly found and explanatory notes have been inserted where there are several figures with similar names. See, for example, HERRAN and LOPEZ. Where context or time period make the identification obvious, no explanation is supplied. The convention in most Colombian reference works is to enter persons under the full family name, but ignore the second *apellido* in alphabetizing, so that, for instance, "Herrera y Tordesillas, Antonio," will file before "Herrera Restrepo, Bernardo." Entries in this work, however, follow normal English alphabetization.

NARCOTICS TRAFFIC, see: DRUG TRADE

NARCOTRAFICANTE.   The Colombian term for dealers in the illegal *DRUG TRADE. Although the term "drug dealer" often has a negative connotation, *narcotraficante* is preferred by some members of the narcotics trade because it suggests that they are practitioners of a defensible business rather than professional criminals and it distinguishes them from political guerrilla groups.

NARIÑO, Antonio, 1765-1823.   Administrator, journalist, known as the "Precursor" for his role in the *independence movement. Born *Bogotá, April 9; died Villa de *Leiva (Boyacá), December 13. Nariño held various colonial offices including treasurer of the *diezmos* (*tithes). He published a Spanish version of *The *Rights of Man* in 1793, for which he was imprisoned in 1794. He escaped captivity in Spain and returned to *New Granada in 1797. He joined the patriot forces in 1810 and published a centralist (see: CENTRALISM-FEDERALISM) newspaper, *La *Bagatela,* 1811-1812. He was President of *Cundinamarca, 1812-1813, and leader of a military campaign in the south, 1813. After being once again a prisoner of the Spanish, 1813-1819, he returned to Colombia and attended the *Congress of Cúcuta in 1821 and the national *Congress in 1823.

NARIÑO, Departamento de.   Located in the extreme southwest of Colombia on the border with Ecuador, the department covers 35,268 square kilometers lying between 0° 21' and 2°

40'N latitude and 76° 50' and 79° 2'W longitude. Within the department the *Andes Mountains form the *Nudo de los Pastos near the southern border, branching out into the *Cordillera Occidental and the *Cordillera Central to the north. The terrain is varied but mostly mountainous: 18,661 square kilometers have a tropical climate; 5,731 temperate; 6,026 cold; and 2,850 are wasteland. Major rivers include Patía, Iscuandé, Mira, Guáitara, Juanambú, and Mataje, which flow to the Pacific Ocean, and Guamés, Nambué, and Bobo, which drain eastward. Volcanic peaks in the department include the Cumbal (4,764 meters), Chiles (4,748 meters), Galeras (4,276), Doña Juana (4,250 meters), and Azufral (4,070 meters. Nariño, with 20 recorded volcanos, is one of the most geologically volatile areas of Colombia. Population is 848,618 people (1985 estimate), with a population density of 25.5 people per square kilometer. *Pasto is the capital city. According to DANE, *Colombia estadística 86,* principal agricultural products, with tonnage produced in 1984, include *potatoes 265,200 tons; *sugar, 74,200; *corn, 30,290; plantains, 26,800; wheat, 23,385; coconuts, 16,820; *yuca,* 11,700; barley, 10,423; *African palm, 10,150; beans, 7,500; hemp, 4,500; *cacao, 2,320; and peanuts, 78. *Livestock slaughtered in 1984 included 34,361 head of cattle and 19,832 hogs. Sheep ranching is also important. In 1984, *gold, *silver, *nickel, *iron, *copper, marble, and gypsum were mined in the department. There is limited industrialization. *Tumaco is its port on the Pacific Ocean. The region was invaded by Sebastián de *Belalcázar in 1535 after exploratory incursions by his subordinates, Pedro de Tapias (*Túquerres), Pedro de *Añasco, and Juan de Ampudia. Historically significant because of its proximity to the Ecuadoran border, Nariño was part of the Province or Government of *Cauca, 1821-1861, the State of Cauca, 1861-1886, and then the Department of Cauca, 1886-1904. The present Department of Nariño was separated from the Department of Cauca in 1904.

NARIÑO, Invasion of. A Colombian-recruited, but Cuban-trained, guerrilla force of the *Movimiento Diecinueve de Abril, transported in vessels from *Panama, landed on the Pacific Coast near *Tumaco in 1981. Shortly after invading the region, the guerrillas met government military forces on the river Mira, where they suffered a decisive defeat. The army claimed to have captured seventy-five guerrillas, killed sixteen others, and seized a major deposit of weapons and munitions. Colombia temporarily broke diplomatic relations with Cuba as a result of the affair.

NARIÑO RAILROAD. The "Ferrocarril de Nariño" was a term first applied to a plan intended to link the American nations, 1890-1892. This scheme projected a railroad from the *Atrato River up the *Cauca Valley to *Popayán, *Pasto, and Tulcán (Ecuador). Alternative plans connecting Pasto to the Pacific and then to the Putumayo region were devised between 1905 and 1912, but what actually became the Nariño railroad was approved in 1922, when authorization was given for a line from the port of *Tumaco to Popayán via Ipiales (0° 52'N, 77° 38'W) and Pasto. The first phase of construction, 1925-1932, failed to connect Tumaco and Pasto. Work between 1937 and 1944 completed approximately 11 kilometers of track, from the Island of Tumaco to the mainland, but it reached no farther than 111 kilometers in all. The line was closed and replaced by a *highway, following the recommendation of the *Currie mission in 1950.

NARIÑO STYLE. An archeological term applied to the cultures of pre-conquest Indian groups in the present-day Department of *Nariño, especially the Pasto, Quillacinga, and *Tumaco *Indians (see also: TUMACO STYLE). The Pasto and Quillacinga groups occupied the *Andes Mountains and the eastern Amazonian plains. Of the two, the Pasto Indians seem to have been the oldest. Carbon 14 dates show occupation at Miraflores (5° 12'N, 73° 9'W) from A.D. 860 to A.D. 1140, at Las Cruces in 1107, and in Iles in 1436. The Quillacinga were the more warlike of the two Indian groups and may have practiced cannibalism. Small chiefdoms were the predominant political unit. The economies were based on *agriculture (*corn and tuber cultivation) and hunting. Pottery styles have been classified in phases labeled Capulí, Piartal, and Tuza. Lithic statuary and *goldwork were also common.

NATIONAL ACADEMY, see: ACADEMIA NACIONAL

NATIONAL ACADEMY OF MEDICINE, see: ACADEMIA NACIONAL DE MEDICINA

NATIONAL ANTHEM. The *Himno Nacional* ["Oh, gloria inmarcesible!"], with words by President Rafael *Núñez and music composed by Orestes Sindici, was first performed in 1887 and officially adopted as the national anthem on October

28, 1920. The hymn, which consists of eleven verses and a chorus, is a poetic recollection of the wars for independence from Spain. This is the chorus and first verse, with an English translation by the present author:

Coro:
¡Oh, gloria inmarcesible!
¡Oh, júbilo inmortal!
en surcos de dolores
el bien germina ya.

Chorus:
Oh, glory ever-gleaming!
Oh, never-ending joy!
In furrows sown with sorrow
Our prosperity will grow.

Estrofa:
Cesó la horrible noche
la libertad sublime
derrama las auroras
de su invencible luz.
La humanidad entera,
que entre cadenas gime,
comprende las palabras
del que murió en la cruz.

Verse I:
The horrible night has ended;
Our liberty sublime
Spreads forth a new day dawning
With its invincible light.
And every human being,
Who writhes within his chains,
Understands the words
of He who died upon the cross.

NATIONAL ASSEMBLY, see: ASAMBLEA NACIONAL

NATIONAL ASSOCIATION OF PEASANT USERS OF GOVERNMENT SERVICES, see: ASOCIACION NACIONAL DE USUARIOS CAMPESINOS

NATIONAL CONCENTRATION, see: CONCENTRACION NACIONAL

NATIONAL CONSTITUENT AND LEGISLATIVE ASSEMBLY, see: ASAMBLEA NACIONAL CONSTITUYENTE Y LEGISLATIVA

NATIONAL CONSTITUENT ASSEMBLY, see: ASAMBLEA NACIONAL CONSTITUYENTE

NATIONAL DEVELOPMENT PLAN, see: PLAN NACIONAL DE DESARROLLO

NATIONAL EMBLEM, see: ARMS OF THE REPUBLIC

NATIONAL FEDERATION OF COFFEE GROWERS, see: FEDERACION NACIONAL DE CAFETEROS

NATIONAL FLAG, see: FLAG, National

NATIONAL FRONT, see: FRENTE NACIONAL

NATIONAL HOLIDAYS, see: HOLIDAYS, Public

NATIONAL LIBRARY, see: BIBLIOTECA NACIONAL

NATIONAL MUSEUM, see: MUSEO NACIONAL

NATIONAL OBSERVATORY, see: OBSERVATORIO NACIONAL

NATIONAL PARTY, see: PARTIDO NACIONAL

NATIONAL POPULAR ALLIANCE, see: ALIANZA NACIONAL POPULAR

NATIONAL SECRETARIAT OF SOCIAL ASSISTANCE, see: SECRETARIADO NACIONAL DE ASISTENCIA SOCIAL

NATIONAL UNION, see: UNION NACIONAL

NATIONAL UNIONIST COUNCIL, see: CONSEJO NACIONAL SINDICAL

NATIONAL UNIVERSITY, see: UNIVERSIDAD NACIONAL DE COLOMBIA

NATIONALISTS. *Conservatives, that faction of the party led first by Rafael *Núñez and then by Miguel Antonio *Caro. Originally a more moderate group responsible for the *Regeneration and the *Constitution of 1886, the Nationalists became increasingly partisan and authoritarian after 1892. The faction disappeared altogether after 1900. See also: PARTIDO NACIONAL

NATURAL GAS. Colombia's natural gas reserves are estimated at 4 trillion cubic feet and predicted to last about twenty-two years. The bulk of these reserves are located around the *Guajira Peninsula. Natural gas production is used exclusively for domestic consumption. One estimate for the mid-1970s indicated 53% was used to generate electricity, 39% for industrial purposes, and the other 8% for residential consumption. Recent theories have projected natural gas for a motor vehicle fuel as a substitute for gasoline and diesel fuel. Natural gas has been called a more economical and ecologically safe alternative to expanded use of petroleum-based fuels. During the 1980s, a network of major service and fueling stations was authorized along the Atlantic Coast, and the first two were begun in *Barranquilla and *Cartagena.

NAU, Jean David, 1630-1671.   Buccaneer known as El Olonés, or L'Olonnais, after his birthplace, Les Sables-d'Olonne, France. He raided the Caribbean Sea after 1653, attacking Maracaibo and San Antonio de Gibraltar in present-day Venezuela in 1666. He was later killed by *Indians from the Barú Islands in the Gulf of *Darien. See: PIRACY

NAVARRO WOLFF (or WOLF), Antonio.   Second-in-command of the *Movimiento Diecinueve de Abril under Carlos *Pizarro Leongómez, 1976-1990. He became the presidential candidate for the *Unión Patriótica after the death of Pizarro Leongómez in 1990, winning 12.5% of the vote, and he was named Minister of Health by the newly inaugurated President, César *Gaviria, in August 1990. The forty-three-year-old ex-guerrilla was one of three officials presiding over the *Asamblea Constituyente de 1991. The son of a Colombian father and an English mother, he was educated at the London School of Economics and is an engineer by profession. He was seriously wounded in an explosion in 1985 and went to Cuba to recuperate. Following the M-19's negotiated truce with the government, his own strong showing in the elections of 1990, and his role in the drafting of the *Constitution of 1991, Navarro Wolff was projected by many as a strong presidential possibility in the elections of 1994.

NAVENAL, see: COMPAÑIA NACIONAL DE NAVEGACION S.A.

NAVY.   Colombia's navy has always been far less important than the *army. In recent years its vessels—three destroyers, five frigates, two submarines, and two midget submarines—have been manned by 5,200 sailors and 2,800 marines. Much of its equipment is West German. The principal naval bases are *Buenaventura on the Pacific and *Barranquilla and *Cartagena on the Caribbean. Under the *Constitution of 1991, the navy is one of four main branches of the national *armed forces.

NEGRET, Edgar, 1920-. Internationally recognized sculptor whose major theme is life in the modern industrial age. His works combine various kinds of metal objects, such as nuts, bolts, and crowbars, to form what are called magic machines. His works have been exhibited in numerous places in Europe and the Western Hemisphere.

NEIRA, Juan José, 1793-1841. Colonel. A landlord and patriot military officer, 1812-1821, he opposed the *Urdaneta dictatorship, 1830-1831. He was the hero of *Buenavista and La Culebrera, 1840. Unfortunately, Neira was wounded in these engagements and died in January 1841.

NEIVA. Capital of the Department of *Huila, located on the *Magdalena River at 2° 56'N, 75° 18'W, approximately 312 kilometers from Bogotá. Altitude is 442 meters; average temperature, 27°C; population, 193,101 people (1985 estimate). Neiva functions as an agricultural and cattle-raising center with important highway and railroad connections linking central and southern Colombia. It is also the gateway to recent colonization areas in the Department of Caquetá. First founded in 1539 as Villa de la Limpia Concepción del Valle de Neiva by Captain Juan de Cabrera at a site known as Las Tapias about 30 kilometers from the present city, the settlement was destroyed by *Indians. Reestablished at Aposentos de Villavieja by Juan Alonso in 1551, it was destroyed in 1569. The present city was founded May 24, 1612, by Diego Ospina y Medinilla. Neiva was the scene of the execution of a group of patriot leaders on September 26, 1816. During the 19th century, it was the capital first of a province of the same name and then of the Departmento del Sur of the Estado Soberano del Tolima. It became capital of the Department of Huila in 1907. Modern Neiva is a popular tourist center and host city for the annual folk dance celebration, the Festival del Bambuco.

NEIVA, Battle of. July 16, 1885, *Huila. Nicolás Faya and Guillermo Perafán, rebel commanders, attempted unsuccessfully to capture Neiva during the *rebellion of 1884-1885.

NEIVA REBELLION, 1767, see: REBELLION OF NEIVA

NEMEQUENE.   *Zipa of the *Chibchas, 1490-1514. A nephew
of *Saguamachica, succeeded by *Tisquesusa, he was known
for his successful military campaigns and imperialistic expansion against rival *Indian groups. He died in battle against the
*Zaque at Chocontá (5° 9'N, 73° 42'W, Cundinamarca).

NEMQUETABA.   Venerable sage of the *Chibchas, whose legends bear resemblance to that of Quetzalcoatl in Mexico.
Distinguished by a long, flowing beard, he arrived riding a
strange animal, and eventually left, possibly in disgrace, with a
promise to return in the future. He taught the Chibcha the arts
of *agriculture, weaving, pottery, and metallurgy, as well as the
difference between good and evil and the cult of sun worship.
After his departure he was known as Sugamuxi, *el despreciado*
("the scorned one"). See also: BOCHICA

NERLANDIA TREATY, see: *WISCONSIN* TREATY

NEVADO DEL RUIZ.   Volcano, 5,210 meters high, in the
Department of *Tolima. The volcano erupted November 13,
1985, killing an estimated 23,800 people and injuring 4,470
more. The eruption completely destroyed the city of *Armero
(founded 1906), which had been known as the White City for
the *cotton fields in the surrounding area. The last previously
known eruption of the Nevado del Ruiz was March 12, 1595,
as recorded by Friar Pedro *Simón. The volcano is still active.

NEW ANDALUCIA, see: NUEVA ANDALUCIA

NEW CALEDONIA.   Name meaning New Scotland, given to the
Scottish settlement at Darien. See also: DARIEN, Scottish
colony of

NEW CASTILE, see: NUEVA CASTILLA

NEW GRANADA.   Nueva Granada, the name of what is now
*Colombia for most of the time before 1863. Gonzalo *Ji-
ménez de Quesada, the founder of *Santa Fe de Bogotá,
named the territory he conquered the New Kingdom of
Granada (*Nuevo Reino de Granada) because it reminded him
of his native Spanish province of Granada. From 1563 to 1719
and 1723 to 1739, New Granada was the *Presidencia del
Nuevo Reino de Granada under the *Virreinato (Viceroyalty)
del Peru. A new viceroyalty (the *Virreinato del Nuevo Reino

de Granada), encompassing much of present-day Colombia, Venezuela, and Ecuador, was established first, 1719-1723, and then permanently in 1739. During the *Patria Boba, the first period of independence from Spain, the rebel provinces attempted to federate as the United Provinces of New Granada (*Provincias Unidas de Nueva Granada), 1811-1816. When independence was restored after the Spanish *Reconquista of 1815-1819, the new state styled itself the *República de Gran Colombia, but the old name was restored in the *República de Nueva Granada (1832-1858) and its federal successors, the *Confederación Granadina (Granadine Confederation) of 1858-1861 and *Estados Unidos de Nueva Granada (United States of New Granada), 1861-1863. The name *Colombia was revived in the *Estados Unidos de Colombia of 1863-1886 and has been used ever since. The inhabitants of the New Kingdom were knowns as *Granadinos and *Reinosos.

NEW GRANADA, REPUBLIC OF, see: REPUBLICA DE NUEVA GRANADA

NEW GRANADA, UNITED PROVINCES OF, see: ACTA DE LA CONFEDERACION DE LAS PROVINCIAS UNIDAS DE NUEVA GRANADA, 1811

NEW GRANADA, UNITED STATES OF, see: ESTADOS UNIDOS DE NUEVA GRANADA

NEW KINGDOM OF GRANADA, see: NUEVO REINO DE GRANADA

NEW LAWS OF THE INDIES, 1542. The commonly used English short form of the formal codification called *Las leyes nuevas de 1542-1543: ordenanzas para la gobernación de las Indias y buen tratamiento y conservación de los indios,* a legal code for the Spanish colonies, promulgated by the Spanish Crown. The laws abolished *Indian slavery, tried to improve Indian living conditions, and restricted the inheritance of *encomiendas. The laws were introduced in *New Granada by Miguel *Díaz de Armendáriz in 1544. They caused public protests and were eventually modified by the Crown in 1552, especially with respect to the inheritance of *encomiendas.* See also: LAWS OF THE INDIES

NEW LIBERALISM, see: NUEVO LIBERALISMO

NEW YORK LOANS. Practically all of the early *foreign debt of independent Colombia was contracted in Britain (see: LONDON LOANS), but the country's repayment record was poor and raising capital on the London market became increasingly difficult. When President Rafael *Núñez needed money to create a central bank (the *Banco Nacional), he turned instead to New York, where in December of 1888 he obtained a US$3 million loan on the security of the government's revenue from the *Panama Railroad. From then on, the New York money market became Colombia's chief source of public foreign loans. During the 1920s more than US$150 million was raised there, mainly to finance economic development, particularly railroad construction. Since *World War II, such other sources as the World Bank have become important, but U.S. banks remain among the country's chief lenders. See also: FOREIGN AID

NEWSPAPERS, 1785-1809. The first newspapers printed in New Granada were *Aviso del Terremoto* (3 numbers) and *Gaceta de Santafé de Bogotá* (3 numbers), 1785. The first major newspaper was the *Papel Periódico de la Ciudad de Santafé de Bogotá* (approximately 170 numbers), 1791-1797. It was followed by *Correo Curioso, Erudito, Económico y Mercantil de la Ciudad de Santafé de Bogotá* (46 numbers), 1801; *El Redactor Americano* (71 numbers), 1806-1809; and *El Alternativo del Redactor . . .* (47 numbers), 1807-1808. The last newspaper of the colonial period was *El Semanario del Nuevo Reino de Granada*, edited by *Caldas, 1808-1811.

NEWSPAPERS, 1810-. The press in independent Colombia developed separately in each of the main urban centers. By the mid-1960s the nation had some forty-four daily newspapers. The total has since been contracting: There were only thirty-one in 1987, six of them published in the capital. The reduction is due in part to the major papers achieving a readership beyond their home city. *El *Espectador* of *Bogotá is now produced in three regional editions. There is a tradition of family ownership and of definite party political allegiance; often the two are closely connected. *Conservative leader Laureano *Gómez with *El *Siglo,* and *Liberal Eduardo *Santos with *El *Tiempo* are representative examples. Other papers include *Medellín's *El Colombiano,* a respected Conservative daily, and Consuelo de Montejo's popular and populist afternoon tabloid *El Bogotano.* Total newspaper circulation in Colombia is about 1,500,000.

NICARAGUA, Relations with.   The 1803 changes in the boundary between the *Audiencia de Santa Fe and that of Nicaragua
(see: COSTA RICA, Relations with) led to uncertainty about
jurisdiction over the Archipelago of *San Andrés y Providencia. This was apparently settled by the *Esguerra–Bárcenas
Meneses Treaty of 1928, which was abrogated by the Sandinista government of Nicaragua in 1980, when Nicaraguan
claims to the islands were revived. Colombia was also concerned by the Nicaraguan government's dispute with the
United States over the former's alleged assistance to insur-
gents in El Salvador and the latter's support of the so-called
Contras fighting the Nicaraguan government. The desire to
develop a Latin American–inspired restoration of peace as a
counter to solutions from outside the region led Colombia to
join the *Contadora peace movement.

NICARAGUA-COLOMBIA TREATY OF 1928, see:
ESGUERRA–BARCENAS MENESES TREATY

NICKEL.   Colombia has produced ferronickel for export since
1982. Commercial quantities of nickel have been found in the
Departments of *Nariño and *Cordoba. The latter includes the
*CERROMATOSO NICKEL MINING PROJECT, whose
estimated 21,000 short-ton projected annual output may be
compared with Cuba's actual 35,370 short-tons. Colombia's
nickel reserves are estimated to be at least 17 million metric
tons, which, at the current rate of extraction, could last
twenty-one years.

NICUESA, Diego de, d. ca. 1511.   Conquistador. He was granted
*Castilla del Oro in 1508. His expedition rescued Alonso de
*Ojeda off *Cartagena in 1509. Nicuesa tried to assume
command of *Santa María la Antigua del Darién in 1510 but
was repelled by *Nuñez de Balboa's followers and forced to
sail away. He disappeared at sea.

NIETO, Juan José, 1804-1866.   General, *Liberal political leader,
born Loma de Muerte, between Barranoa and Turbura (*Bolívar), June 24. He was anti-Bolivarian, 1828-1830, a supporter of General *Obando in the 1830s, and federalist leader
in both the War of the *Supreme Commanders, 1840-1841,
and the *rebellion of 1859-1862. He served in numerous
political posts in the city and province of *Cartagena, including
the governership of the province and the presidency of the

state of *Bolívar, 1860-1863. Nieto is credited with having published the first novel by a Colombian, *Ingermina, o la hija de Calamar* (Kingston, Jamaica, 1844), the story of an Indian girl who falls in love with Alonso de *Heredia. He was also the author of *Derechos y deberes del hombre en sociedad* (1834), an essay in political philosophy, and *Geografía histórica, estadística y local de la provincia de Cartagena* (1839), the first known geography of the Cartagena region.

NINETEENTH OF APRIL MOVEMENT, see: MOVIMIENTO DIECINUEVE DE ABRIL

NINETEENTH OF DECEMBER CONSPIRACY, 1905. An abortive plot to overthrow the government of General Rafael *Reyes. Luis Martínez Silva, Estimio Sánchez, Jorge Moya Vásquez, Felipe Angulo, and Manuel María Valdivieso were convicted of conspiring against the government after their plans were discovered.

NINTH OF APRIL RIOTS, see: BOGOTAZO

NITRATE WAR, see: PACIFIC, War of the

NON-ALIGNED NATIONS. A group of nations that claimed no fixed alliance in the East-West struggles of the Cold War or other international disputes. Colombia was officially accepted as a member of the Non-Aligned Nations at the group's meeting in New Delhi (India) in March 1983. Spokesmen for the *Betancur administration had previously stated that Colombia would not be a satellite of any specific nation and would pursue an independent foreign policy that included joining the Non-Aligned Nations, opposing U.S. and Soviet penetration of Central America, and neutralization of the Falkland Islands.

NORTE DE SANTANDER, Departamento de. Located in northeastern Colombia on the Venezuelan border, the department covers 21,658 square kilometers lying between 6° 58' and 9° 18'N latitude and 72° 2' and 73° 35'W longitude. The terrain is mountainous in the west with flatlands in the east; 10,622 square kilometers have tropical climate; 5,896 temperate; 3,461 cold; and 1,679 are wasteland. Major rivers include Borra, Chacira, Catatumbo, Cucutilla, Chitagá, Guarmito, and Zulia. Population is 871,966 people (1985 estimate), with a population density of about forty persons per square kilometer. *Cúcuta is the capital city. The department engages heavily in agricultural cattle ranching. Based on DANE, *Colombia estadística 86,* principal agricultural products, with tonnage produced in 1984, include plantains 67,200 tons; *potatoes, 63,000; rice, 52,340; *yuca,* 38,500; *sugar, 36,800; *tobacco, 14,000; *corn, 10,185; sorghum, 3,200; *cacao, 1,720; beans, 1,480; wheat, 410; and barley, 187. Early farmers were attracted to the region by cacao, and the department was prominent in the early stages of coffee cultivation. *Livestock slaughtered in 1984 included 77,567 head of cattle and 13,653 hogs. Mineral products include *iron, *copper, marble, mica, talc, and *coal. *Petroleum is important in the *Catatumbo region and the Zulia River Valley. There is incipient industrial-iztion, mostly concentrated in Cúcuta, *Ocaña and *Pamplona. There were ninety-seven businesses employing ten or more people recorded in 1983. Commerce is important especially because of border connections with Venezuela. Ambrosius *Dalfinger is said to have been the first Europoean conqueror to explore the area, but effective conquest did not occur until Pedro de Ursúa arrived in 1549. The department, created in 1910, has been important historically for movement between Colombia and Venezuela.

NORTHEASTERN RAILROAD. A line intended to connect *Bogotá and *Santa Marta via *Boyacá and *Santander. Under a contract with Francisco Pineda López, work began in 1921 and the line was completed as far as *Sogamoso in 1931. In 1952, following completion of the steel mill at *Paz del Río (Boyacá), the line was extended from Sogamoso to the foundry, but the original Bogotá-Caribbean plan was never implemented.

NORTHERN RAILROAD. The Ferrocarril del Norte, a line intended to connect *Bogotá with the *Magdalena River via *Boyacá and *Santander. The first section of the Northern Railroad, also known as the Puerto Wilches Railroad, joined *Bucaramanga and the Magdalena River at *Puerto Wilches. It was authorized in 1870 and begun in 1881, but little was accomplished. Work was resumed in 1908, but scarcely more than 21 kilometers were finished by 1920. The line was finally extended to the outskirts of Bucaramanga in 1941. The second section, from Bogotá to Bucaramanga, was authorized in 1871, surveyed in 1872, contracted in 1873, and completed to *Zipaquirá by 1898. It was extended to Nemocón (5° 4'N, 73°

53'W) by 1907, to Barbosa (6° 26'N, 75° 20'W) via *Chiquinquirá by 1935, and finally to Güepsa (6° 2'N, 73° 34'W) in 1945. The remaining sections to connect Bucaramanga were never completed, and part of the line north of Barbosa was closed after construction.

NOVEL, The, see: LITERATURE

NUDO DE LOS PASTOS.   A name given to the main trunk of the *Andes Mountains as they enter Colombia from Ecuador. The Andes divide into three major ranges, or Cordilleras, as they move northward in the Department of *Nariño (see: CORDILLERA CENTRAL, CORDILLERA OCCIDENTAL, and CORDILLERA ORIENTAL).

NUEVA ANDALUCIA.   New Andalusia is the name applied to a grant of land on the Caribbean Sea running eastward from the *Golfo de Urabá along the Colombian and Venezuelan coasts. The territory was entrusted to Alonso de *Ojeda in 1508, but his attempts to colonize the area were unsuccessful, and the term fell into disuse.

NUEVA CALEDONIA, see: DARIEN, Scottish colony of

NUEVA CASTILLA.   New Castile, also the Government of San Juan. It was a governmental area created in 1536, extending from the Pacific Coast of *Panama to the *San Juan River in the *Chocó. It was governed by Pascual de *Andagoya, 1539-1548, and ceased to appear as an independent entity after his death. References to New Castile are few; the area is most often referred to as the Government of San Juan.

NUEVA GRANADA, see: NEW GRANADA

NUEVA GRANADA, Estados Unidos de, see: ESTADOS UNIDOS DE NUEVA GRANADA

NUEVA GRANADA, Provincias Unidas de, see: PROVINCIAS UNIDAS DE NUEVA GRANADA

NUEVA GRANADA, Reino de, see: NUEVO REINO DE GRANADA

NUEVA GRANADA, República de, see: REPUBLICA DE NUEVA GRANADA

NUEVA GRANADA, United Provinces of, see: PROVINCIAS UNIDAS DE NUEVA GRANADA

NUEVA GRANADA, United States of, see: ESTADOS UNIDOS DE NUEVA GRANADA

NUEVE DE ABRIL, see: BOGOTAZO

NUEVO FRENTE REVOLUCIONARIO DEL PUEBLO. A *guerrilla movement reported in late November 1985 as having been formed by dissidents of the *Movimiento Diecinueve de Abril.

NUEVO LIBERALISMO. New Liberalism, a militant or radical splinter group of the *Liberal Party, originally organized in 1982 to oppose the candidacy of Alfonso *López Michelsen for reelection to the presidency. New Liberalism published a twelve-point program calling for radical reorganization of *Congress, state intervention in urban development, reclamation of natural resources and businesses from foreign control, restoration of moral values, defense of *Indian rights and human rights in general, support for progressive unionism, reform of national television, and an end to traditional elite control of national life. Luis Carlos *Galán was Nuevo Liberalismo's candidate for the presidency in 1982, and he won about 10% of the popular vote. The faction remained active in 1986, but did not run a separate presidential candidate. The movement declined after Galán returned to the fold of the official Liberal Party in 1988. Nevertheless, some members continued to support Galán until his death in 1989 and then to work for his succsssor, Julio César Gaviria, in the elections of 1990.

NUEVO REINO DE GRANADA. The New Kingdom of Granada, a name given to the territory conquered by Gonzalo *Jiménez de Quesada because the area reminded him of Granada, Spain. Santa Fe de *Bogotá was named after the city of Santa Fe, of the Catholic Kings, in Granada. The name was later applied to the area governed from Bogotá, 1538-1563, and still later was given to the viceroyalty established in the 18th century.

NUEVO REINO DE GRANADA, Presidencia del, see: PRESIDENCIA DEL NUEVO REINO DE GRANADA

NUEVO REINO DE GRANADA, Virreinato del, see: VIRRE-
INATO DEL NUEVO REINO DE GRANADA

NUEVOS, Los.   The name given to a group (or "generation") of
progressive, reformist-oriented intellectuals who frequented
the Café Windsor (owned by Agustín and Luis Eduardo Nieto
Caballero) in *Bogotá during the 1920s and 1930s. Including
widely varying political ideologies, the *tertulia of Los Nuevos
reacted against the classicism and the archaic forms of thought
and literature of the *Modernists and the *Centenary Generation. Members of Los Nuevos sought to modernize Colombia
both materially and spiritually. Originating in the years from
1919-1921, Los Nuevos included figures such as Jorge
*Zalamea Borda, Ricardo Rendón, Germán *Arciniegas, Ra-
fael Maya, Luis *Tejada, Luis Vidales, José Mar, Germán Pardo
García, Gabriel *Turbay, Jorge Eliécer *Gaitán, Felipe Lleras
Camargo, Alberto *Lleras Camargo, Octavio Amórtegui,
Carlos Lozano y Lozano, José Umaña Bernal, Juan Lozano
y Lozano, León de *Greiff, José Restrepo Jaramillo, Gregorio
Castañeda Aragón, José Antonio *Osorio Lizarazo, and
the subgroup known as Los Leopardos (Augusto Ramírez
Moreno, Eliseo Arango, José Camacho Carreño, and Silvio
Villegas).

NUÑEZ, Rafael, 1825-1894.   Journalist, legislator, philosophical
poet, President of Colombia 1880-1882, 1884-1886, and
1887-1894. Born *Cartagena, September 28; died Cartagena,
September 18. On the national level, Núñez was Minister of
the Interior, 1853; Minister of War, 1855; Minister of Finance,
1856-1857 and 1861-1862; consular representative in The
Havre and Liverpool, 1865-1874, and a member of both
houses of the national *Congress. He was also President of
*Bolívar, 1876 and 1878-1879. He was leader of the *Nation-
alists who sponsored the *Regeneration, including the *Constitution of 1886 and a return to protective tariffs in economic
affairs. Núñez was the author of a book of poetry, Versos; the
words to the *national anthem; a series of essays collected
under the title of La Reforma Política; and a collection of
articles on social criticism called Ensayos de crítica social, the last
of which he published in France.

NUÑEZ DE BALBOA, Vasco, 1470-1519.   Conquistador, explorer; born Jerez (Spain), August 17; beheaded by Pedro
Arias Dávila (*Pedrarias) in Acla (Panama), September 25.

Usually referred to simply as Balboa, he sailed to Colombia with Rodrigo de *Bastidas in 1500 and again with Martín *Fernández de Enciso in 1510. After the founding of *Santa María la Antigua del Darien, he expelled Fernández de Enciso and refused to recognize the authority of Diego de *Nicuesa. He explored much of the Isthmus of Panama, sighting the Pacific Ocean on September 25, 1513. For this he was named *Adelantado del Mar del Sur, but differences with Governor Pedro Arias Dávila eventually led to his execution.

-O-

O.A.S., see: ORGANIZATION OF AMERICAN STATES

OBALDIA, José de, 1806-1889.   Lawyer, orator, legislator, born Santiago de Veraguas (Panama), July 19; died David (Panama), December 28. In addition to serving in *Congress, he was Vice President of *New Granada, 1851-1854, and acting President briefly in 1854 while opposing the *Melo dictatorship. He also served as Governor of *Panama, and he returned to his native state after 1855.

OBANDO, see: INIRIDA

OBANDO, José María, 1795-1861.   General, President of *New Granada, 1853-1854. Born Güengüe, *hacienda* García (*Cauca), August 8; shot at Cruzverde (*Cundinamarca), April 21 during the *rebellion of 1859-1862. He was first a royalist, 1810-1822, and then a patriot military officer, 1822-1828. In the Cauca he led the resistance to the dictatorships of *Bolívar and *Urdaneta, 1828-1831. He was elected Vice President of Colombia, 1831-1832, and was an unsuccessful candidate for the presidency in 1836. Obando rebelled against the *Márquez government, 1840-1841, and was forced into exile, 1841-1849. Elected President of New Granada, 1853-1857, he was removed from office by the *Melo coup d'état in 1854. He joined the *rebellion of 1859-1862 against the *Confederación Granadina and was killed in the movement. Obando was a controversial popular leader who was frequently accused of having ordered the assassination of General *Sucre in 1830.

OBANDO–POSADA GUTIERREZ–ARTETA TREATY OF 1832. Signed *Pasto, December 8, 1832, by Generals José María *Obando and Joaquín *Posada Gutiérrez, *New Granada, and Pedro José Arteta, Ecuador. A treaty of recognition, alliance, boundaries, and obligations, the agreement forced Ecuador to repudiate the annexations of *Pasto, *Popayán, *Buenaventura, and *Chocó, accepting New Granada's position on the boundary at the Tulcán River. Ecuador, however, remained in control of the Archipelago Colón (the Galapagos Islands).

OBREGON, Alejandro, 1920-. Painter and muralist of Colombian-Spanish parents, born in Barcelona (Spain). After spending his childhood in *Barranquilla, he studied art in Boston (U.S.A.) and Barcelona, 1940-1944, following which he became a professor of art in the School of Fine Arts in *Bogotá. He worked in Paris from 1949 to 1954, and his works have been shown in numerous international exhibitions in the United States, Europe, and Brazil. In addition to paintings, he has also produced theatrical sets for ballets and murals for public buildings. At times his style has been called "magic expressionism." A rooster and a flower are often repeated motifs in his work, which focus on angels, condors, and landscapes. Overall, he has been described as one of the foremost practitioners, perhaps even the initiator, of modern art in Colombia.

OBSERVATORIO NACIONAL. The National Observatory, *Bogotá, built 1802-1803. It was first opened and directed by José Celestino *Mutis, and then by Francisco José de *Caldas, 1805-1810. It is now a historical monument.

OCAÑA. Rural mountain community of 51,922 people (1985 estimate) located at 8° 14'N, 73° 21'W, in the Department of *Norte de Santander. Although the altitude of the city itself is 1,202 meters, Ocaña is located in the *Cordillera Oriental, and surrounding peaks reach as high as 2,600 meters. The average temperature is 22°C. Principal economic activities include agriculture, cattle ranching, small industries, and mining. The settlement was first established by Francisco Hernández de Contreras in 1572 with the name Santa Ana de Hacarí and then moved to its present location in 1576 and the name changed to Ocaña. It was the scene of the 1828 *CONGRESS OF OCAÑA.

OCAÑA, Battle of. September 9, 1841, in the Department of *Norte de Santander. General Pedro A. *Herrán, for the government, defeated the rebellious forces of General Lorenzo Hernández. It was a major victory in the coastal campaign during the War of the *Supreme Commanders, 1840-1842.

OCAÑA, Congress of, see: CONGRESS OF OCAÑA

OCCIDENTE. A conservative daily newspaper founded in *Cali on November 19, 1961, by Alvaro H. Caicedo, Luis E. Palacios, Francisco Barberi Zamorano, and associates. In 1966 *Occidente* offices were established in *Bogotá as well as Cali, and circulation has been estimated as high as 100,000 copies per issue.

OCHOA VASQUEZ, Jorge Luis. Drug dealer, listed by *Forbes* magazine, 1988-1990, as a billionaire. The Ochoa Vásquez brothers—Jorge Luis, Fabio, and Juan David—as well as numerous cousins are said to be important members of the Medellín Cartel. Ancestors of the Ochoa Vásquez brothers (and sister Marta Nieves Ochoa Vásquez) established themselves in Antioquia in the 16th century, and the family is known for cattle ranching and horse breeding. Jorge Luis is said to have been seriously involved in the drug trade since 1977. He was arrested in Spain in 1984, but eventually released to return to Colombia in 1986. Fabio Ochoa Vásquez surrendered to authorities on December 19, 1990, under favorable terms offered by the *Gaviria administration, and Jorge Luis did the same on January 15, 1991. See also: MEDELLIN CARTEL; MUERTE A SECUESTRADORES

OIL, see: PETROLEUM

OJEDA, Alonso de, 1466-1516. Conquistador. He accompanied *Columbus on his second voyage, 1493-1494, and sailed from the vicinity of the equator to Cape Vela, 1499-1500. He was Governor of *Coquibacoa, 1501-1502. Then, named Governor of *Nueva Andalucía in 1508, he made an unsuccessful attempt to colonize *Cartagena Bay and had to be rescued by Diego de *Nicuesa, 1509. Having been named Governor of *Urabá on June 9, 1509, Ojeda founded *San Sebastián de Urabá in 1510 and then sailed to Santo Domingo to secure aid. He later encountered legal difficulties and died in relative obscurity in Spain.

OLAYA HERRERA, Enrique, 1880-1937. Lawyer, journalist, diplomat, President of Colombia, 1930-1934. Born Guateque (*Boyacá), November 12; died Rome (Italy), February 18. He was three times Minister of Foreign Relations and diplomatic representative to Venezuela, Chile, Argentina, the United States, and the *Vatican. He opposed the government of General Rafael *Reyes and organized the Republican Union (*Unión Republicana) in 1909. Mildly reformist, as President he governed with a coalition of *Liberals and *Conservatives known as the National Concentration (*Concentración Nacional). He stimulated public housing, welfare, and *education programs, attempted land distribution, and fostered *petroleum exploration. His administration was confronted by the problems of a world depression and by the *Leticia Dispute with Peru.

OLAYA HERRERA–TEZANOS PINTO TREATY, see: PUTUMAYO DISPUTE

OLD PROVIDENCE. Traditional English name for the island of *PROVIDENCIA to distinguish it from Providence, Rhode Island, and New Providence in the Bahamas.

O'LEARY, Daniel F., 1800-1854. General, diplomat, born Cork (Ireland), October 14; died *Bogotá, February 24. He came to *New Granada as a member of the *Legión Británica in 1818, and his first appointment was as assistant to General José Anzoátegui. However, O'Leary is best remembered as an aide-de-camp, personal secretary, and partisan of Simón *Bolívar. In 1829 he fought against the rebellion of General José María *Córdoba, who opposed the Bolivarian dictatorship. Following the Liberator's death in 1830, O'Leary left the country, but he returned to New Granada, 1844-1854, as minister from Great Britain. He is the author of a series of *Memorias*, which are, in addition to obvious autobiographical materials, a primary research source for the career of Bolívar.

OLIGARCHY. *Oligarquía* is generally used in Colombia as elsewhere in Latin America to designate the land-owning elite and their allies: oligarchy, or the oligarchs. But *oligarquía* is also a term of opprobrium used particularly in Colombian political history by *Independent Liberals to describe *Radical Liberals. It implied a domination of the party by a small clique. Especially in the election of 1876, the Oligarchs or Radicals supported Aquileo *Parra, the official administration candidate, while Independent Liberals tended to support Rafael *Núñez.

OLIMPO RADICAL. The Radical Olympus, a group of more partisan, doctrinaire *Liberals, 1860-1890. The Radical Olympus included such figures as Francisco J. *Zaldúa, Manuel *Murillo Toro, Aquileo *Parra, Santiago *Pérez, Felipe Zapata (1838-1902), Felipe Pérez (1836-1891), Salvador Camacho Roldán (1827-1900), Miguel Samper (1825-1899), Tomás Cuenca (1840-1870), Nicolás Esguerra (1838-1923), Luis A. Robles (1849-1899), and Medardo Rivas (1825-1901).

OLONES, El. Sobriquet of Jean David *Nau.

ONE HUNDRED YEARS OF SOLITUDE. Cien años de soledad is the best-known novel of Gabriel *García Márquez. It tells the surrealistic story (in the style known as *MAGICAL REALISM) of several generations of a Colombian family in a small, relatively isolated village, probably based on Aracataca (10° 36'N, 74° 12'W, *Magdalena) from the author's own experiences. The comic work is a study in futility that questions the meaning of Colombian life. At times based on actual events from Colombian history and sometimes completely fictitious, the magnificent failures of the Buendía family are symbolically chronicled as the results of its isolation from larger, more meaningful events and the egocentric preoccupations of the main characters—100 years that do not deserve to be repeated. The novel became a best-seller in Europe, North America, and Brazil, one of the first Spanish American works to do so, and is perhaps the most successful example of the boom in Hispanic American fiction in the late 1960s and 1970s.

OPERACION ANORI, see: ANORI, Campaign and Battle of

OPERACION COLOMBIA. The *Movimiento Diecinueve de Abril's name for the theft of 5,000 weapons from the *CANTON DEL NORTE arsenal on New Year's Eve 1978.

OPERATION FRIENDSHIP, see: DE NICOLO, Javier

ORACION DE LA PAZ. Literally, the "Oration (or "Prayer") for Peace," also known as the "Manifestation of Silence." A reference to the public demonstration led by Jorge Eliécer *Gaitán in *Bogotá, February 7, 1948. Gaitán's followers were asked to wear black and to maintain a "sacred silence" in honor of those who had died in political violence. An estimated 100,000 people gathered in the Plaza Bolívar in the late afternoon. Gaitán delivered a brief address—the "Oration for Peace"—in which he appealed to the administration of President *Ospina Pérez to respect the constitution, to end political violence, and to restore peace. He then dispersed members of the crowd quietly to their homes. It was the last mass demonstration that Gaitán led before he was assassinated.

ORATORIO, Battle of. August 18, 1860, *Santander. Confederation forces under General Pedro A. *Herrán, in the presence of President Mariano *Ospina Rodríguez, defeated and captured President Antonio María Pradilla of the State of Santander during the *rebellion of 1859-1862.

ORDINANCES OF 1616. Issued June 23, by Francisco de Herrera Campuzano for the regulation of Indian labor. There were forty-four clauses, including provision for religious instruction of the *Indians and protection of their families. There were stipulations regarding adequate food supplies for Indian laborers, and there were limitations on working requirements and regulations for the prompt payment of salaries.

ORGANIZATION OF AMERICAN STATES (O.A.S.). International association, headquartered in Washington, D.C., for promoting cooperation and defense in the Western Hemisphere. It was established at the close of the Ninth *International Conference of American States held in *Bogotá in 1948 as a successor to the Pan American Union (which survives as the secretariat of the O.A.S.). The Spanish name of the organization is Organización de los Estados Americanos (O.E.A.), and practically all American nations except Canada have been members, although the present Cuban government has been excluded. Colombia was a charter member and has been an active supporter of the organization since its foundaton.

ORTIZ, Tomás de, d. 1532. *Dominican. A missionary, one of 27 friars who arrived in 1529 to convert the *Indians of the Atlantic Coast. He was appointed the first Bishop of *Santa Marta in 1531.

OSORIO, Luis Enrique, 1896-1966.   Author, playwright; perhaps the most popular Colombian dramatist of the 20th century. He initially studied civil engineering and then law, but completed degrees in neither. He made numerous trips to Europe, and his first works were reflective of French influence. His first play, *Flor tardía*, was produced in 1917, but his early career was eclipsed by the success of his contemporary, Antonio *ALVAREZ LLERAS. In 1943, however, he established the Compañía Bogotana de Comedias, and therefter he achieved both popularity and commercial success. Many of his works used variations of the "eternal triangle" as a principal theme as well as political satire. Osorio wrote for public tastes, and some have called his writing style a new kind of *costumbrismo*. But while enjoying box office success, his writing deteriorated until his later plays, such as *Así sós, camisón rosao* (1949), were weak in both plot and characterization.

OSORIO BENITEZ, Miguel Angel, (PORFIRIO BARBA JACOB), 1883-1942.   Poet, journalist, born in Santa Rosa de Osos (*Antioquia), June 29; died in Mexico, January 14. Osorio Benítez used the pseudonyms Maín Ximénez (ca. 1900-1906), Ricardo Arenales (1906-1917), and Porfirio Barba Jacob (after 1917), as well as his own name. He spent long portions of his life in exile from Colombia. His poetry was meditative, deeply personal, and autobiographical. It has been described as a protest against conventional morality. "En la muerte del poeta" (1919-1920) is a typical meditative, autobiographical piece. *Antorchas contra el viento* (1944) and *Poemas intemporales* (1957) are among his best-known works. His *Obras completas* were published in *Medellín in 1962.

OSORIO LIZARAZO, José Antonio, 1900-1964.   Author, born *Bogotá, December 30; died October 12. Osorio Lizarazo was the author of more than twenty works, covering a wide range of subjects. He is considered by some as one of the first novelists to describe the urban life of modern Colombia. In his series of novels, *La cara de la miséria* (1926), *La casa de la vecinidad* (1930), *Hombres sin presente* (1938), *Garabato* (1939), *El día del odio* (1952), and *El Pantano* (1952), he described the daily life of lower- to middle-class urban dwellers in 20th-century Bogotá. He is also known for his descriptive analysis of Colombia in general: *Colombia, dónde los andes se disuelven*, published in Chile in 1955.

OSPINA. For President 1857-1861, see: OSPINA ROD-RIGUEZ, Mariano; for 1946-1950, see: OSPINA PEREZ, Mariano; and for 1922-1926, see: OSPINA VASQUEZ, Pedro Nel

OSPINA, Iván Marino, d. 1985. Sometime commander of the *Movimiento Diecinueve de Abril, in which he was known as Felipe. Born in Tuluá (4° 5'N, 76° 12'W, *Valle del Cauca), he joined the *Juventud Comunista in 1960, and was sent to Komsomol (the cadre training school in the Soviet Union). He returned in 1963 and joined the *Fuerzas Armadas Revolucionarias de Colombia (FARC) from 1966 to 1972. He eventually left FARC because the group's ideology was too narrow for him. He was second in command to Jaime *Bateman Cayón and became the M-19 leader when the latter died in April 1981. In February 1985, however, he was replaced as commander by Alvaro *Fayad Delgado, and subsequently killed in combat on August 28, 1985.

OSPINA PEREZ, Mariano, 1891-1976. Engineer, legislator, *Conservative leader, President of Colombia, 1946-1950. Born *Medellín, November 24; died *Bogotá, April 14. He studied engineering at San Ignacio and the School of Mines in Medellín and then in the United States and Belgium. He served as rector of the School of Mines and taught in Bogotá. He was several times a deputy to the *Antioquia Assembly, a member of both houses of the national *Congress, and Minister of Public Works, 1926. He was also director of the National Federation of Coffee Growers (*Federación Nacional de Cafeteros). As President, he first attempted to govern with a coalition cabinet, but ended by dissolving Congress to avoid impeachment. His presidency was marred by partisan repression, the *Bogotazo, and the beginning of La *Violencia. During his term in office, the *Currie mission studied economic problems in Colombia and the Ninth *International Conference of American States met in Bogotá. After 1950, Ospina Pérez was the leader of the *Unionist Conservatives, a faction of the Conservative Party. He was a grandson of former President Mariano *Ospina Rodríguez and a nephew of former President Pedro Nel *Ospina Vásquez.

OSPINA RODRIGUEZ, Mariano, 1805-1885. Lawyer, educator, journalist, President of *New Granada, 1857-1861. Born Guasca (*Cundinamarca), October 18; died *Medellín, January

11. A *Septembrino* in 1828 and a supporter of the revolt of José María *Córdoba against *Bolívar in 1829, Ospina Rodríguez was Minister of the Interior, 1842-1845, and Governor of *Antioquia, 1845-1847 and 1854-1855. He was co-editor of *La Civilización,* 1849-1851, and co-author of the first *Conservative Party platform (October 4, 1849). His presidential administration sanctioned the *Constitution of 1858, negotiated the *Herrán-Cass Treaty over claims resulting from the *Panama Riot of 1856 as well as a treaty of peace, extradition, and commerce with Ecuador; attempted to resolve a government financial crisis; and began issuance of modern postage stamps (see: POSTAL SERVICE). Nevertheless, highly partisan actions, such as the law of public elections (1859), provoked the *rebellion of 1859-1862 and led to the collapse of the *Confederación Granadina. Ospina Rodríguez was in exile in Guatemala, 1861-1871, and then returned to live in Medellín.

OSPINA VASQUEZ, Pedro Nel, 1858-1927. Military commander, engineer, legislator, President of Colombia, 1922-1926. A son of ex-President Mariano *Ospina Rodríguez, he was born in the Presidential Palace, *Bogotá, September 18; died *Medellín, July 1. He was educated at the *Universidad de Antioquia, with additional engineering studies in the United States, Germany, and France. He was rector of the School of Mines in Medellín, a delegate to the *Asamblea Nacional Constituyente y Legislativa in 1910, and diplomatic representative in the United States and Europe. His presidential administration initiated governmental reorganization, invited the *Kemmerer mission and other technical teams to study Colombian institutions, stimulated *railroad and industrial growth, and provided limited aid to *education and public works.

OSPINISTA. Supporter of Mariano *Ospina Pérez.

OTALORA, José Eusebio, 1828-1884. General, lawyer, legislator, diplomat, President of Colombia, 1882-1884, following the death of President Francisco Javier *Zaldúa. Born Fómeque (*Cundinamarca), December 16; died *Tocaima (Cundinamarca), May 8. He studied law at the *Colegio Mayor de San Bartolomé, graduating in 1851. He was a delegate to the Convention of *Rionegro, 1863; Treasurer of the Republic, 1864; consul in London, 1866; President of *Boyacá, 1878-

1880; and Minister of Finance, 1880-1882. As President of Colombia, 1882-1884, he presided over a relatively uneventful administration, although he confronted a severe financial crisis and was responsible for limited stimulus to *railroad building.

OTERO, Luis, d. 1985. Member of the high command of M-19 (*Movimiento Diecinueve de Abril), killed in the *army's storming of the *Palacio de Justicia in November 1985.

OYON, Alvaro de, d. 1553. Conquistador. He was the leader of a rebellion in the region around La Plata (2° 23'N, 75° 56'W) and Timaná (1° 58'N, 75° 55'W), both in the Department of *Huila. He attacked *Popayán but was defeated, captured, and executed. These events were loosely incorporated into the poem *Gonzalo de Oyón* by Julio *Arboleda in the 19th century.

-P-

P.C.C., see: PARTIDO COMUNISTA DE COLOMBIA

P.S.D.C. The Partido Social Democratico Cristiano. See also: DEMOCRACIA CRISTIANA

P.S.R., see: PARTIDO SOCIALISTA REVOLUCIONARIO

PABON NUÑEZ, Lucio, 1913-1988. *Conservative Party leader, statesman, legislator, educator, diplomat; born San José de Convención (*Norte de Santander), October 21; died July, 1988. He received his secondary education from the Colegio José Eusebio Caro in *Ocaña and the *Colegio Mayor de San Bartolomé and his university training from the *Universidad Javeriana, both in *Bogotá. He was awarded the doctorate in economics and legal studies. In his political career he was a member of the Conservative Party Directorate, 1951-1981, and its president, 1969-1979. He was a member of both houses of the *Congress, 1943-1987, and a member of the *Asamblea Nacional Constituyente, 1953-1957, as well as its president, 1956-1957. He was Minister of Education and Minister of War, but is most remembered as Minister of *Gobierno* (Interior) for the *Rojas Pinilla regime, 1953-1957. He held diplomatic appointments in Portugal, Spain, Argentina, Venezuela, and El Salvador; he was active in public affairs in the Department of Norte de Santander; he was on the faculty of a number of educational institutions, including the *Universidad Javeriana, Universidad La Gran Colombia, and the *Universidad de Santo Tomás; and he was the author of numerous books and pamphlets.

PABON PABON, Rosemberg.   "Comandante Uno" from the *Movimiento Diecinueve de Abril; the man who planned the seizure and occupation of the *DOMINICAN EMBASSY in February 1980. In March 1981, he was captured following the defeat of the *Columna Antonio Nariño.

PACHO, Obelisk of.   Pre-Hispanic monolith near Pacho (5° 8′N, 74° 10′W), *Cundinamarca. Approximately 25 meters tall, it is formed of two large outer stones with a mass of calcareous rock cut in four angles between them at the bottom. Several stones of decreasing size rest on this base. Their use or significance is not well understood.

PACIFIC, War of the.   A war between Chile, on the one hand, and Peru and Bolivia, on the other, 1879-1883. The conflict originated in a dispute between Chile and Bolivia over what was then the Bolivian-controlled part of the Atacama Desert. Peru entered as an ally of Bolivia. The war resulted in the loss of Bolivia's territory on the Pacific Coast and a long-standing dispute between Peru and Chile over the territories of Tacna and Arica. The *Trujillo administration in Colombia declared complete neutrality, preventing belligerents from conducting operations in Colombia, while allowing all parties free access to the Isthmus of *Panama. This interpretation of neutrality was strongly disliked by Chile, and its objections led to the signing of the *Chile-Colombia Treaty of 1880.

PACIFIC RAILROAD.   The Ferrocarril del Pacífico, originally a line connecting the Pacific port of *Buenaventura to *Cali. It was built by Francisco J. *Cisneros during the years 1878-1882. President *Murillo Toro had used the phrase in 1872 to describe a plan he hoped would connect the Pacific and Atlantic Oceans via Buenaventura, *Cali, *Cundinamarca (*Bogotá), *Boyacá, and *Santander. An attempt to realize Murillo Toro's dream was made in 1913 when *Congress created the Pacific Railroad by consolidating the existing Buenaventura-Cali line with the *Tolima, *Girardot, and *Sabana systems, but projected construction between *Armenia and *Ibagué across the *Cordillera Central was never completed. Branch lines from Cali, south to *Popayán and north to *Cartago, were begun in 1914, and the Pacific Railroad ultimately became a regional system serving an east-west axis from Buenaventura to Armenia and a north-south one from Cartago to Popayán.

PACT OF 1860, see: PACTO PROVISORIO, 1860

PACT OF UNION, see: PACTO DE UNION, 1861

PACTO ANDINO, see: ANDEAN COMMON MARKET

PACTO DE UNION, 1861.   A pact creating a provisional union known as the *Estados Unidos de Nueva Granada, 1861-1863. Adopted September 20, 1861, it was couched in terms of a formal treaty among the sovereign states of *Bolívar, *Boyacá, *Cauca, *Cundinamarca, *Magdalena, *Santander, and *Tolima. It permitted the individual states to determine the validity of national legislation, to amend the pact, and to choose electors for presidential elections as desired. The national government was limited in scope and was required to use state officials for law enforcement whenever possible.

PACTO PROVISORIO, 1860.   A provisional pact forming the United States of New Granada (*Estados Unidos de Nueva Granada). Signed September 10, 1860, by representatives of Generals T. C. de *Mosquera, of *Cauca, and by Juan José *Nieto, of *Bolívar, it created a temporary government pending a constitutional convention. It was superseded by the *Pacto de Unión de 1861.

PADILLA, José, 1778-1828.   Admiral active in patriot causes, 1811-1828. Born *Riohacha (Guajira), March 19; executed in *Bogotá, October 2. Padilla joined the Spanish navy as a young man and fought in the war against England until he was captured at the Battle of Trafalgar (1805). After returning to Spain, 1808-1811, he joined the patriot forces fighting for independence in Colombia. He was active in naval campaigns along the Caribbean Coast and participated in the Battle of Maracaibo, July 24, 1823. He was made Brigadier General in

1823 and Major General in 1828. He was implicated in conspiracies against the government and the *Liberator in *Cartagena and Bogotá, for which he was tried and executed following the attempt to assassinate *Bolívar on September 25, 1828. See also: MARACAIBO, Battle of

PADILLA BALLOTS.   Also called the Registry of Padilla, a set of contested ballots, signed in blank by the voters of Padilla, *Magdalena, and entrusted to the care of General Juanito Iguarán. These blank votes eventually gave the victory to Rafael *Reyes in the presidential elections of 1904.

PAECES.   The Paeces, or Páez Indians, were a pre-Columbian Indian group that inhabited the *Cordillera Central in the Departments of *Cauca and *Huila in what is known as the *Tierradentro region. Although pacified and forced to coexist with the Spanish, the Paeces were never completely conquered, and descendants of the group still inhabit the region today. Subsistence agriculture based on *corn, sweet potatoes, and squash predominates, but the region has considerable *mineral resources and some *sugar cane is grown in the warmer valleys.

PAEZ INDIANS, see: PAECES

PAIS, EL.   Conservative daily newspaper of *Cali, founded April 23, 1950, by the Lloreda brothers: Alvaro, Alfredo, and Mario. Circulation has been estimated at 65,000 copies daily.

PAJAROS.   Terrorists, professional or otherwise, often assassins, prominent in the *Violencia period. They were hired or appointed to ensure, forcibly and illegally, compliance with the wishes of the individuals or groups (private or public) who employed them.

PALACIO DE JUSTICIA, Attack on the.   *Bogotá, November 6-7, 1985. Approximatetly thirty-five members of the *Movimiento Diecinueve de Abril (M-19), led by Luis Otero, Andrés Almarales, Alfonso Jacquim, Guillermo Elevecio Ruiz, and Ariel Sánchez, seized the Palace of Justice on the Plaza Bolívar in *Bogotá at 11:40 A.M. on November 6, taking hostage twelve judges and numerous clerical workers. M-19 demanded the appearance of President *Betancur, supposedly to stand trial for failure to carry out completely provisions of the truce agreements signed in 1984 (see: URIBE [La], Agreements of). Allegations have been made that the attack was also inspired by leaders of the *drug trade who wanted to destroy court records regarding cases of possible extradition to the United States. The attack ended tragically on November 7 when military forces recaptured the building. More than 100 people, including the justices and most of the guerrillas, were killed, and the Palace of Justice itself was destroyed in the process.

PALACIO DE NARIÑO. The Presidential Palace in *Bogotá. It came under attack from mortar fire by the *Movimiento Diecinueve de Abril in July 1982. The attack was probably intended to prove M-19's continuing ability to operate in the capital rather than to do serious damage.

PALENQUE. A wooden stockade. Historically, *palenques* were the defenses built around the communities formed by *cimarrones* (*maroons), or runaway slaves. These *palenques,* or *cimarrón* communities, were illegal refuges, but they existed throughout *New Granada during most of the colonial period. The escaped slaves became self-supporting by *agriculture, brigandage, or other means; after a time, they might have had their free status recognized by law. The Bayano *palenque* in *Panama, ca. 1556, is one of the earliest on record, but *palenques* existed at Zaragoza (7° 30'N, 74° 52'W, *Antioquia) in 1599, *Matuna (*Bolívar) in 1600, Tolú (9° 32'N, 75° 35'W, Bolívar) in 1621 and 1748, Negua (*Chocó) in 1688, Norosí and Tisquisio on the lower *Cauca River, and elsewhere. Orlando Fals Borda estimates that twenty-one *palenques* were established in the Province of *Cartagena between 1599 and 1788. The government of Cartagena destroyed several of these villages in a campaign, 1693-1694. Perhaps the most famous of the *palenques* was *San Basilio at Tolú. Javier Ocampo López also records *palenques* at *Santa Marta, Santa Cruz de Masinga, and the *Sierra Nevada de Santa Marta, as well as the Palenque de Castillo in the Patía Valley (*Nariño). See also: BIOHO, Domingo; LEONOR, THE BLACK QUEEN

PALMIRA. Industrial town, on the *Pan American Highway, northwest of *Cali at 3° 33'N, 76° 16'W, in *Valle del Cauca department. Population in 1985: 214,395.

PALMIRA, Battle of. August 31, 1854, at *Palmira. The constitutional forces of Colonels Manuel Tejada and Pedro Antonio

Vergara defeated Major José Manuel Calle, representing the *Melo dictatorship.

PALO RIVER, Battle of the. July 5, 1815, *Cauca. Lieutenant Colonel Aparicio Vidaurrázaga, royalist, was defeated by the patriot forces of General José María Cabal and Colonel Manuel Roergas de Serviez.

PALONEGRO, Battle of. May 11-26, 1900, on a ridge of the *Cordillera Oriental between Lebrija (7° 7'N, 73° 13'W) and *Bucaramanga. General Próspero Pinzón, for the government, defeated the rebellious forces of General Gabriel Vargas Santos. It was the most decisive engagement of the War of the *Thousand Days.

PAMPLONA. City of 33,137 people (1985 estimate) located at 7° 23'N, 72° 39'W in the Department of *Norte de Santander. Pamplona itself sits in a highland valley at an altitude of 2,287 meters, but surrounding peaks in the *Cordillera Oriental reach as high as 3,800 meters. The average temperature is 16°C. Major economic activities include agriculture, cattle raising, and light industry. Historically the city was a commercial center important for its *gold and *silver mines. *Iron, *copper, lime, and *coal are also found in the area. Approximately 75 kilometers from *Cúcuta, modern Pamplona is an educational and tourist center as well. The city was founded in April 1549 by Pedro de *Ursúa and Ortún Velasco, who became its first governors.

PAMPLONA, Battle of. August 22, 1854, *Norte de Santander. It was a crucial victory for the constitutionalist forces under General Juan José Reyes Patria against Colonel Dámaso Girón, agent for the *Melo dictatorship.

PAN AMERICAN HIGHWAY. Colombia's section of the highway is the nation's western trunk highway through *Medellín and *Cali (see: HIGHWAYS). Owing to the "Darien gap" (see: DARIEN), it is still not linked with the North American portion of the Pan American Highway (known as the Inter-American Highway) in Central America.

PAN AMERICAN UNION. The forerunner of the *ORGANIZATION OF AMERICAN STATES

PANAMA.   The Isthmus of Panama was explored by Rodrigo de
*Bastidas in 1501, and Christopher *Columbus in 1502. An
independent Real *AUDIENCIA DE PANAMA was created
in 1538. It functioned 1538-1543, 1563-1718, and 1722-1751.
Panama was a dependency of Guatemala 1543-1563, con-
trolled from the *Virreinato del Perú 1563-1739, and finally a
part of the *Virreinato del Nuevo Reino de Granada after
1739. Colonial Panama consisted of the provinces of Veragua,
Panama, and *Darién. During the wars for independence,
Panama remained loyal to Spain. The last titular *viceroy died
in Panama in 1820 and was succeeded by the Governor of
Veragua, who retained his authority until November 28, 1821.
On that date a *cabildo abierto declared the provinces of the
Isthmus a part of the *República de Gran Colombia. With the
breakup of Gran Colombia, José Domingo Espinar declared
the Isthmus independent on September 26, 1830, but it was
reincorporated on December 11. Espinar's successor, Juan
Eligio Alzurú, again attempted, unsuccessfully, to establish
independence, July 9 to August 29, 1831. Nearly a decade
later, Tomás *Herrera proclaimed the independence of the
Estado Libre del Istmo, November 18, 1840, but decreed it
reincorporated into New Granada on December 31, 1841. In
1855, Panama became a state within the *República de Nueva
Granada by the Act of Panama. It was practically self-
governing until the centralist Colombian *Constitution of
1886 reduced it to a mere *department. Unhappiness over this
loss of local autonomy, the disastrous War of the *Thousand
Days, and the Colombian *Senate's rejection of the *Herrán-
Hay Treaty led to another bid for independence on November
3, 1903, which, bolstered by assistance from the United States,
proved successful. Panama has been independent of Colombia
since then (see: PANAMANIAN REVOLUTION OF 1903).

PANAMA, Congress of 1826, see: CONGRESS OF PANAMA,
1826

PANAMA, Congress of 1880, see: CONGRESS OF PANAMA,
1880

PANAMA, Isthmus of, see: PANAMA

PANAMA, Relations with.   Colombia's recognition of the newly
independent Republic of Panama was formally conceded in the
*Urrutia-Thomson Treaty of 1914. The boundary between

them was negotiated in the *Victoria-Vélez Treaty of 1924. Relations have generally been very good. President *López Michelsen supported Panama in its request for a new canal treaty with the United States, eventually concluded in the 1970s. The *drug trade, however, has created some potentially difficult problems in very recent years.

PANAMA CANAL COMPANY, see: COMPAGNIE UNIVER-SELLE DU CANAL INTER-OCEANIQUE DE PANAMA

PANAMA CITY. The original city, Old Panama, founded by *Pedrarias in 1519, was captured by Henry *Morgan in 1671 and so thoroughly devastated that it was rebuilt on a new site (8° 57'N, 79° 30'W) on a peninsula 4 miles west of the old one. This settlement proved able to resist a new attack, by Bartholomew Sharpe, April 23, 1680. Simón *Bolívar envisioned Panama as the eventual capital of *Gran Colombia, and the idea was revived by General *Mosquera in May 1863. The idea was rejected at least in part because of the lowland city's then unhealthy climate.

PANAMA-COLOMBIA TREATY OF 1924, see: VICTORIA-VELEZ TREATY

PANAMA ELECTRIC LIGHT COMPANY. The first electric company established in Colombia. It was a U.S.-based company organized in New York in 1886. The company was represented in the Isthmus of *Panama and Colombia by Ramón Santo Domingo Vila and eventually became known as the Compañía de Luz Eléctrica de Panamá. It began operation on September 21, 1889, but an accident soon interrupted production, which was not restored permanently until January 1890. The coal-burning plant suspended service for repairs, 1900-1903.

PANAMA RAILROAD. A railway connecting *Colón on the Caribbean Sea to *Panama City on the Pacific Ocean, it was the first transcontinental railroad built in the Western Hemisphere. It was constructed in the years 1850-1855 by the Panama Railroad Co., a firm chartered by the New York State legislature in 1849. The first railroad built in Colombia, the Panama line was a great aid to transportation and a very profitable investment for its owners, who eventually sold much of their stock to the French Panama Canal Company

(*Compagnie Universelle de Canal Inter-Oceanique de Panama).

PANAMA RIOT OF 1856. Also known as the Watermelon Riot, the incident was touched off by a dispute between a traveler, Jack Oliver (U.S.), and a black merchant, José Manuel Luna (*New Granada), in *Panama City over payment for a piece of watermelon, April 15, 1856. Numerous deaths and arrests resulted. Diplomatic relations were strained, and the United States pressed claims for damages. Many of these claims were finally accepted in the *Herrán-Cass Treaty of 1857.

PANAMA ROAD. One of the first roads opened in what was to become the Viceroyalty of *New Granada. The road, which ran from Nombre de Dios (9° 34′N, 79° 28′W) on the Caribbean Sea to *Panama City on the Pacific Ocean, was laid out in 1532. It was the only good road in the Isthmus of Panama, and it utilized essentially the same route later followed by the *Panama Railroad and the Panama Canal.

PANAMANIAN REVOLUTION OF 1903. November 3-6. Panamanian leaders, encouraged by the United States, proclaimed their independence from Colombia and established the Republic of Panama. Despite Colombian protests, the United States recognized the new nation immediately and, on November 18, secured a treaty from Panama giving the U.S. rights to construct a transisthmian canal. Colombia received belated indemnification by means of the *Urrutia-Thomson Treaty with the United States, 1914.

PANCHES. A group of *Indians occupying the *Magdalena River Valley in parts of *Cundinamarca and *Tolima at the time of the European conquest. The Panches have been studied archeologically through a series of sites from El Peñón (*Cundinamarca) to *Espinal (Tolima). A subgroup of the *Caribs, they were closely related ethnically to the *Pijaos and Pantágora Indians. They were organized into loosely affiliated chiefdoms that cooperated closely in warfare. They were a bellicose people who practiced cannibalism. Their economy was based on hunting, gathering, and agriculture. Skeletal remains show deliberate cranial reformation. The Panches were hostile to their eastern neighbors, the *Chibchas, and fiercely resisted the Spanish conquest begun by the brothers Gonzalo *Jiménez de Quesada and Hernán *Pérez de Quesada in the late 1530s. The majority of the Panches were exterminated in attacks directed by Captain Antón de Olalla and Juan Ruiz de Orjuela in 1550. Those who survived these attacks either died from overwork or disease or were absorbed by other groups.

PANTANO DE VARGAS, BATTLE OF.　July 25, 1819, approximately 5° 45'N, 73° 5'W, in the Department of *Boyacá. Generals Simón *Bolívar and Francisco de Paula *Santander and Colonel James Rook, with about 2,500 troops, won a heroic victory against the royalist forces of acting Colonel José María Barreiro, estimated at about 3,800 men. Colonel Juan José Rondón and his troops were cited for valor in the assault that culminated in the final victory. A difficult battle waged in a narrow valley with swampy terrain, it was a prelude to the Battle of *Boyacá.

PAPACY.　(Also the Vatican or the Holy See.) Official recognition of the independence of Colombia and the establishment of formal Church-State relations between Colombia and the Papacy occurred on November 26, 1835. *New Granada was the first of the Spanish American nations to be so recognized. The first Papal Internuncio, Monsignor Cayetano Baluffi, was sent to New Granada in 1836. In his work, *El Concordato de Colombia con la Santa Sede, Julio 12 de 1973* (Bogotá, 1973), Alfredo Vásquez Carrizosa, lists the diplomatic representatives from the Papacy to Colombia and vice versa, 1837-1973.

Representatives from the Vatican to Colombia before 1973 are listed below by year of appointment, name, and diplomatic title (if other than Apostolic Delegate and Envoy Extraordinaire before 1916 or Apostolic Nuncio between 1916 and 1945). No title is given after 1945.

1837	Cayetano Baluffi, Apostolic Internuncio
1843	Nicolás Savo, Chargé d'affaires
1847	Sebastián Buscioni, Chargé d'affaires
1851	Lorenzo Barili
1856	Miecislao Ledóchowski
1883	Juan Bautista Domingo F. Agnozzi
1887	Luis Matera
1891	Antonio Sabatucci
1895	Enrique Sibilia, Chargé d'affaires
1898	Antonio Vico
1903	Alejandro Solari, Interim Chargé d'affaires
1904	Francisco Ragonesi

1913	Carlos Montagnini
1913	Felipe Cortesi, Interim Chargé d'affaires
1914	Alberto Vasallo de Torregrossa
1916	Enrique Gasparri
[1916]	*Representatives become Apostolic Nuncios*
1920	Vicente Misuraca, Interim Chargé d'affaires
1922	Roberto Vicentini
1924	Juan Panico, Interim Chargé d'affaires
1926	Pablo Giobbe Zuchetti
1927	Federico Lunardi, Interim Chargé d'affaires
1928	Pablo Giobbe Zuchetti
1935	Juan Galleri, Interim Chargé d'affaires
	Title of Apostolic Nuncio no longer appears
1945	Guiseppe Beltrami
1950	Antonio Samoré
1953	Paolo Bertoli
1959	Guiseppe Paupini
1969	Angelo Palmas

Vásquez Carrizosa lists approximately forty different Colombians who have been diplomatic representatives to the Vatican, seven of whom have also served as President of Colombia. See also: CONCORDAT OF 1887; CONCORDAT OF 1942; CONCORDAT OF 1973

PAPAL VISITS.   Two Popes have visited Colombia, Pope Paul VI and Pope *John Paul II. Paul VI (Giovanni Batista Montini, 1897-1978), head of the Church from 1963-1978, was the first Pope to visit any place in Latin America. He arrived in *Bogotá, August 22, 1968, for a three-day visit timed to coincide with the meeting of the Conference of Latin American Bishops (*Consejo Episcopal Latinoamericano) in *Medellín and the 39th *International Eucharistic Conference. During his stay he was flown to nearby Mosquera (4° 42'N, 74° 14'W, *Cundinamarca) for a brief visit to the rural countryside. John Paul II (Karol Wojtyla, b. 1920), became Pope in 1978. He toured Colombia in 1986. His visit took him to *Bogotá (July 1-2), *Chiquinquirá and *Cali (July 3), *Tumaco and *Popayán (July 4), *Pereira, Chinchiná (4° 59'N, 75° 36'W), and Medellín (July 5), *Armero, Lérida (4° 52'N, 74° 55'W), *Bucaramanga, and *Cartagena (July 6), and *Barranquilla (July 7). Pope John Paul II delivered a number of public addresses that stressed morality, social justice, peace, and the defense of traditional Catholic values.

PAPEL PERIODICO DE LA CIUDAD DE SANTAFE DE BOGOTA.   The first major newspaper published in *New

Granada (Colombia). There were approximately 270 numbers during its run from February 1791 to February 1797. It was edited by Manuel del Socorro *Rodríguez.

PAPEL SELLADO.   A specially stamped paper necessary for all legal transactions. A source of government revenue, it was instituted by the colonial administration in 1640 and continued by republican governments after 1819. Its usage was eliminated in the late 1970s.

PAPER MONEY CRISIS OF 1885-1905.   Colombian *currency suffered a drastic fall in value between 1885 and 1903. Civil wars, high interest rates, a drop in agricultural prices, a shortage of *gold, and a policy of permitting the plural emission of bills have all been cited as contributing causes. By a series of decrees, 1885-1887, the *Núñez administration gave priority for the issuing of new bills to the *Banco Nacional, declared the notes of this bank the primary circulating medium of Colombia, and required that these notes be accepted as payment for all government debts. Núñez saw no problem so long as the government followed his "dogma of the 12 million," establishing at 12 million *pesos the maximum amount of bank notes in circulation at any one time. His principle was violated, however, by a series of *clandestine emissions, 1889-1894. The situation was further complicated by emergency issues during the *rebellion of 1895 and the War of the *Thousand Days, 1898-1903. Finally in 1903, new regulations established gold as the standard for Colombian currency and arranged for the retirement of the paper bills. A point of reasonable stability had been reached by 1905, but the problem was not completely resolved until after 1909. See also: GOLD STANDARD

PARAMO DE PISBA, Passage of the, see: PISBA, Passage of the Páramo de

PARDO BUELVAS, Rafael.   The so-called judgment of Pardo Buelvas occurred in *Bogotá, September 12, 1978. *Autodefensa Obrera first judged and then executed Pardo Buelvas for his allegedly criminal handling of the General Strike (*Paro Cívico) of September 14, 1977. Government actions against the strikers had resulted in numerous deaths, and the then Minister of Government, Pardo Buelvas, had seemed insufficiently concerned about or unsympathetic toward those who died. To commemorate the anniversary of the strike, ADO judged Pardo Buelvas guilty of mismanaging the goverment's handling of the affair and pronounced him responsible for the deaths that had occurred. ADO members shot Pardo Buelvas in the bathroom of his home on September 12 as a result of the judgment. See also: PARO CIVICO DE 1977

PARDO-GALVEZ TREATY OF 1858. Signed in *Bogotá, March 8, by Juan Antonio Pardo, *New Granada, and Pedro Gálvez, Peru. A treaty of friendship, commerce, navigation, consular duties, and extradition, the agreement was indicative of a détente in Peruvian-Colombian relations during the 1850s. The treaty was supplemented by an additional act on February 8, 1859.

PARDO LEAL, Jaime, d. 1987. President of *Unión Patriótica and the UP's unsuccessful presidential candidate in 1987 when he received 312,494 votes (4.4%). On October 11, 1987, he was shot in Bogotá, shortly after presenting evidence of army involvement in assassinations of six UP supporters. Although the Justice Minister blamed the death on drug traffickers, UP supporter protests and clashes with police followed. Pardo Leal was succeeded by Bernardo Jaramillo Ossa, who was also assassinated, in 1989 (see also: PIZARRO LEONGOMEZ, Carlos).

PAREJO GONZALEZ, Enrique. Succeeded assassinated Rodrigo *Lara Bonilla as Justice Minister, April 30, 1984. In August 1986, he was appointed ambassador to Hungary. On February 13, 1987, he was shot in Budapest, Hungary, and seriously wounded, apparently in revenge for his anti–drug traffic actions while Justice Minister. See also: DRUG TRADE

PARIS, Treaty of, 1881. Signed January 30 in Paris, by Luis Carlos Rico, Colombia, and the Marqués de Molins, for Spain. It was a treaty of peace, friendship, and commerce that formally recognized the independence of Colombia. It established a most-favored-nation status for Spanish-Colombian commercial relations.

PARNASILLO, El. A literary society, or *tertulia, active in *Bogotá, 1825-1830. Its most consistent members were Ignacio Gutiérrez Vergara, Agustín Gutiérrez Moreno, and Andrés and Juan Antonio Marroquín.

PARO CIVICO DE 1977. General strike of 1977, September 14, in *Bogotá and elsewhere. A general strike was called to protest rising costs of living and deterioration of workers' living standards. Officials of the administration of Alfonso *López Michelsen, specifically the Minister of Government, Rafael *Pardo Buelvas, ordered government troops to maintain or to restore order. Military forces fired on the strikers, and estimates of the number dead range from eighteen to fifty. See also: PARDO BUELVAS, Rafael

PARRA, Aquileo, 1825-1900. Businessman, legislator, major *Liberal politician, 1860-1900, President of Colombia, 1876-1878. Born Barichara (*Santander), May 12; died Pacho (*Cundinamarca), December 4. A *Radical Liberal, he attended the Convention of *Rionegro in 1863 and was active in Santander politics, 1857-1871, and again after 1878. He was Minister of Finance, 1872-1875. His presidential administration sanctioned reform of the *Constitution of 1863 with regard to presidential elections, suppressed the Conservative *Rebellion of 1876-1877, and enacted a number of punitive anti-clerical laws, 1877.

PARTIDO COMUNISTA DE COLOMBIA (P.C.C.). Founded in July 1930, by members of the *Partido Socialista Revolucionario, influenced by a commission of the Third International. Guillermo Hernández Rodríguez was the P.C.C.'s first General Secretary. Its first Central Committee was composed of Tomás Uribe Márquez, Jesús Cuervo, David Forero, Elvira Medina, Manuel Abella, Luis E. Cortés, Fideligno Cuéllar, Servicio Tulio Sánchez, Rafael Baquero, Pedro Abella, Pablo Emilio Sabogal, José Gonzalo Sánchez, Angel M. Cano, Jorge de Bosque, María *Cano, José G. Russo, Esteban Sánchez, and the General Secretary. The P.C.C.'s first public demonstration, a march in *Bogotá, took place on July 17, 1930. The party split into rival factions in 1947. Diego Montaña Cuéllar assumed control of a faction (Movimiento Reorgánico) demanding major reform. Augusto Durán headed a group that advocated collaboration with the administration of *Ospina Pérez, and the bulk of the party stayed with the leadership of Gilberto Vieira. In the 1960s, the party divided between the pro-Soviet and the pro-Maoist factions. The P.C.C. sponsors the *Voz Proletaria*, a weekly newspaper, and a series of *Documentos políticos*. The P.C.C. was the ideological parent of the *Fuerzas Armadas Revolucionarias de Colombia. See also:

PARTIDO SOCIALISTA REVOLUCIONARIO; SOCIAL-ISM

PARTIDO CONSERVADOR COLOMBIANO, see: CONSERVATIVE PARTY

PARTIDO CONSERVADOR SOCIAL. The current name of the *CONSERVATIVE PARTY.

PARTIDO LIBERAL, see: LIBERAL PARTY

PARTIDO NACIONAL. A loose alliance of *Independent Liberals and *Conservatives who backed the *Regeneration led by Rafael *Nuñez, 1880s-1890s. The term was also applied to an abortive effort by General T. C. de *Mosquera to organize a third party in the 1850s.

PARTIDO SOCIAL DEMOCRATICO CRISTIANO, see: DEMOCRACIA CRISTIANA

PARTIDO SOCIALISTA REVOLUCIONARIO. The P.S.R., or Revolutionary Socialist Party, founded in November 1926, by the Third Socialist Congress (Tercer Congreso Nacional Obrero). The P.S.R. had evolved at least partially from a group calling itself the Communist Party, founded in 1924 by a Russian immigrant named Vicente Staviskya. The P.S.R.'s first formal Executive Committee was composed of Eugenio Molina Palacios, Guillermo Hernández Rodríguez, and Francisco de Heredia. Tomás Uribe Márquez was its first Secretary General. According to Ulíses Casas, important figures who adhered to the newly founded P.S.R. included Luis Alberto Bravo, Francisco Socarrás, Hernando Echeverri, Enrique Acero Pimentel, Juan Francisco Mújica, Antonio Vicente Arenas, Luis Fabio Lince, Roberto García Peña, Darío Samper, and Diego Montaña Cuéllar. Raúl *Mahecha and María *Cano were also important figures in the early movement. The P.S.R. supported the Third International, and, in 1929, selected Alberto Castrillón as its candidate for the presidency of Colombia in the 1930 elections. The P.S.R. was also responsible for creating the Communist Party (P.C.C.) in 1930. See also PARTIDO COMUNISTA DE COLOMBIA; SOCIALISM

PASTO. Capital of *Nariño, located at 1° 13'N, 77° 17'W, approximately 995 kilometers southwest of Bogotá in the

Atriz Valley at the foot of the volcano Galeras (4,276 meters).
The altitude of Pasto is 2,594 meters; the average temperature,
14°C; and the population 244,559 people (1985 estimate).
Pasto is an important commercial and transportation junction,
with connections northward to Popayán and the interior, south
to Ecuador, west to *Tumaco and the Pacific Ocean, and east to
*Mocoa. The settlement was originally established July 17,
1539, by Lorenzo de *Aldana on a site known as Guacanquer,
and then transferred to its present location by Pedro de Puelles
on June 24, 1540. Known by variations of the names San Juan
de Villaviciosa and San Juan de Pasto, it was elevated to the
status of city and granted a coat of arms in 1559. In the 19th
century Pasto was a center of fierce royalist resistance and the
site of the 1839 Rebellion of the *Minor Convents.

PASTO, Barniz de.   Important folk art and commercial product
peculiar to the Department of *Nariño. It is a lacquerware
characterized by wood and resin inlay, first recorded in Madrid
around 1664.

PASTO COUP OF 1944.   An abortive coup d'état, July 10, in
which Colonel Gil Diógenes seized President Alfonso *López
Pumarejo and some cabinet officers while they were attending
army maneuvers in Pasto. His appeals to the rest of the *army
and the *Banco de la República for support were refused, and
the coup collapsed.

PASTRANA BORRERO, Misael, 1923-.   Lawyer, industrialist,
diplomat, President of Colombia, 1970-1974. Born *Neiva,
November 14, he received his law degree from the Javeriana
University in Rome (Italy), July 19, 1945. A leader of the
*Conservative Party, Pastrana Borrero was secretary to Presi-
dent *Ospina Pérez, 1947-1950. He has been Minister of
Development, Minister of Public Works, Minister of Government, and Acting Minister of Finance. He has held diplomatic
posts in the *United Nations, the *Organization of American
States, and Rome (the *Vatican). He was elected President of
Colombia in 1970 as the last official candidate of the *Frente
Nacional, and his administration was marred in its early stages by
severe political tensions and confrontations with university
students. His economic policy encouraged the construction
industry as the leading sector of Colombia's *economy and
encouraged private investment under the Unidades de Poder
Adquisitivo Constante (UPAC) scheme. Government policy

came to stress increasing agricultural production rather than land redistribution. In general, the period of Pastrana's presidency was marked by slow economic growth with high inflation.

PATERSON, William, 1658-1719. Scotsman, founder of the Bank of England. He was the moving spirit behind the Scottish colonization of Darien (see: DARIEN, Scottish colony of).

PATRIA BOBA, La. Literally, "the Foolish Fatherland"; the term is used to describe the period from 1810 to 1816 when the regions of present-day Colombia formed several small republics and fought among themselves instead of providing a united front against Spanish forces. Lack of unity and dispersed resources facilitated the Spanish *Reconquista,* 1816-1819. A similar use of *patria* occurs in the Chilean and Uruguayan phrase *patria vieja,* referring to the first, abortive attempts to achieve independence from Spain in those countries. See also: PROVINCIAS UNIDAS DE NUEVA GRANADA

PATRIOTIC UNION, see: UNION PATRIOTICA

PATRON DE ORO, see: GOLD STANDARD

PATRONATO LAW. The Law of Ecclesiastical Patronage, passed July 28, 1824. A legislative act that assumed in the name of Colombia the prerogatives previously exercised by the Spanish monarchs. It established the union of Church and State, which was intermittently enforced until 1886. Originally a series of privileges granted the Catholic monarchs, Ferdinand and Isabella, between 1492 and 1508, the patronage gave the secular authorities the right to approve clerical appointments, collect religious taxes, and edit or refuse to circulate papal documents in their domains. See also: SEPARATION OF CHURCH AND STATE

PAUL VI. The first Pope to visit Latin America. See also: PAPAL VISITS

PAUL Y VERGARA, José Telésforo, 1831-1889. Archbishop of Bogotá, 1885-1889; born *Bogotá, January 5; died La Mesa (*Cundinamarca), April 8. A member of the *Jesuit order, he completed his education and was ordained in Spain. He returned to Colombia in 1858 and served as Bishop of *Panama, 1876-1884, before becoming Archbishop of Bogotá. His administration reorganized ecclesiastical finances, 1885; approved the *Constitution of 1886; and negotiated the *Concordat with the Papacy, 1887.

PAYAN, Eliseo, 1825-1895. General, legislator, *Liberal political leader from *Valle del Cauca. Born *Cali, August 1; died *hacienda* of San Pedro near *Buga, June 30. He received his doctorate of law from the Colegio de Santa Librada in Cali. He was a delegate to the Convention of *Rionegro in 1863, Minister of War in 1880, Vice President, 1886-1888, and acting President of Colombia, January 6 to June 4, 1887, and December 13, 1887, to February 8, 1888. His administration encouraged *railroad construction and reorganized the *army. He was removed from office by President Rafael *Núñez who was displeased when Payán issued a decree that liberalized official supervision of the press.

PAZ DEL RIO. A small community on the River Chicamocha, located at 6°N, 72° 45'W in the *Cordillera Oriental in the Department of *Boyacá. The altitude is 2,200 meters; the average temperature, 16°C; and the population, 3,724 people (1985 estimate). It is the site of Acerías Paz del Río S.A., the only integrated steel-producing operation in Colombia. The system, which began production in 1955, is believed to be one of the most compact in the world, with *iron ore, *coal and limestone mines, and processing facilities all located within a 20-mile radius. Acerías Paz del Río S.A. was Colombia's first major steel mill, but important although less comprehensive mills have also been built at *Medellín (Empresa Siderúgica), *Cali (Siderúgica del Pacífico), and *Bogotá (Siderúgica del Muña). Smaller, less important iron foundries were known in the 19th century and before.

PEACE COMMISSION OF 1981. A committee apppointed by President *Turbay Ayala to recommend measures for ending the guerrilla violence (see: GUERRILLA MOVEMENTS). The Peace Commission was composed of twelve members, including former president Carlos *Lleras Restrepo (who headed the commission), Gerardo Molina (a reformist candidate for the presidency of Colombia), the commander of the *armed forces, the head of the national *police, and two bishops. Few of the commission's recommendations were actually implemented by the Turbay Ayala administration, but they formed a point of reference for the *Betancur administration, which followed.

PEACE LIBERALS. A name given to that faction of the *Liberal Party that opposed rebellion against the *Nationalist-*Conservative governments of the 1890s. Led by Aquileo *Parra and members of the older Radical Olympus (*Olimpo Radical), the Peace Liberals were ultimately unsuccessful in avoiding the rebellion that became the War of the *Thousand Days in 1899. They were opposed by Liberals who supported revolt, eventually led by men like Rafael *Uribe Uribe. Charles Bergquist has argued that the Liberal split also had a rural (pro-war)—urban (pro-peace) dimension.

PEDRARIAS. Also, Pedro Arias de Avila and Pedro Arias Dávila, 1440-1531.) Governor of *Panama, 1514-1526, he was responsible for the execution of Vasco *Núñez de Balboa and the founding of *Panama City, 1519. His administration is remembered as controversial, although not particularly progressive. He moved to Nicaragua in 1526 and died there a few years later.

PEDRERA (La), Battle of. An attack July 10, 1911, by Peruvian forces under Lieutenant General Oscar Benavides on Colombian troops at La Pedrera near Puerto Córdoba on the Caquetá River in the Department of *Amazonas during boundary disputes in the Putumayo region. See: PUTUMAYO DISPUTE

PENINSULAR. The name was used to distinguish Spaniards born in Europe from those of the same ancestry born in America. The latter were known as *creoles. Peninsulars always considered themselves socially superior to creoles, and policies of the Crown and Empire tended to discriminate against creoles in favor of Peninsulars. The discrimination became a deliberate part of Crown policy in the 18th century under the Bourbon monarchs, and it is often cited as one of the tensions contributing to the movement for independence from Spain. *Godo, Gachupín, and *Chapetón are related words designating one of Spanish or royalist origin in a pejorative manner.

PERALONSO, Battle of. December 15-16, 1899, *Norte de Santander. Also called La Amarilla and La Laja (after ravines along the Peralonso River), the battle was the first *Liberal victory in the War of the *Thousand Days. General Benjamín Herrera, rebel, defeated the government forces under General Vicente Villamizar.

PERDOMO, Ismael, 1872-1950. He was first Bishop of *Ibagué, 1903, and then Archbishop of *Bogotá, 1928-1950. He showed constant concern for *education and social problems, which resulted in the founding of Catholic social action groups. He brought more than thirty *religious orders to Colombia, convoked numerous religious conferences and congresses, and opposed communist movements. In politics, he is remembered for his vacillation between the *Conservative candidates Guillermo *Valencia and Alfredo Vázquez Cobo in the 1930 presidential elections, endorsing first one and then the other, which some say divided the Conservative vote and allowed the election of Enrique *Olaya Herrera, the Liberal candidate, as President.

PEREIRA. Capital of *Risaralda, located at 4° 49'N, 75° 42'W in the *Cordillera Central 344 kilometers from Bogotá. Altitude is 1,411 meters above sea level (some sources say 1,467 meters); average temperature, 21°C; and population, 390,190 people (1985 estimate for the greater metropolitan area), making it the eighth largest city in Colombia. Pereira is a commercial and industrial center for a major coffee-producing region. Some authorities say Pereira was founded in 1863 by Remigio A. Cañarete, Fermín López, Nepomuceno Buitrago, José María Ormaza, José Hurtado, Elías Rocío, Tomás Cortés, and Guillermo Pereira Gamba on land donated by the last beside the Otún River on the site of old *Cartago. The name dates from 1869 in memory of Dr. José Francisco Pereira Gamba (1789-1863), father of the donor of the land and the man who conceived the idea of founding a new city on the site of the old. Other sources say the city was founded as late as 1876. Pereira became the capital of Risaralda when the department was created in 1966.

PEREZ, Lázaro María, 1822-1882. Playwright, politician. He took part in the War of the *Supreme Commanders, served as *Senator for *Panama in the 1880s, and finally became Colombian minister to Germany, where he died.

PEREZ BRITO, Benito. Appointed *Viceroy of New Granada by the Regency Council of Cadiz (*Consejo de Regencia), he established his government in *Panama City, March 21, 1812, but remained largely inactive and resigned on November 1 of the same year.

PEREZ DE QUESADA, Hernán, d. 1544.   Conquistador, brother of Gonzalo *Jiménez de Quesada. He was governor of *Bogotá, 1539-1541, and successfully contested jurisdiction of the city with Jerónimo *Lebrón in 1540. Pérez de Quesada was responsible for the killing of numerous Indian chieftains around Bogotá prior to an expedition he led in search of *Eldorado through the *Llanos, *Caquetá, and *Pasto in 1541. He was imprisoned by Alonso Luis de *Lugo and died under arrest en route to Spain.

PEREZ MANOSALBAS, Santiago, 1829-1900.   Lawyer, educator, journalist, author, President of Colombia, 1874-1876. Born hacienda San José near *Zipaquirá, May 23; died Paris (France), August 5. A member of the *Chorographic Commission in the 1850s and a leader of the *Twenty-third of May Conspiracy, 1867, he was Minister of the Interior, 1868-1870, before becoming President in 1874. His administration continued the expansion of public *education and emphasized *railroad construction, particularly the *Northern Railroad from *Bogotá through *Boyacá and *Santander to the lower *Magdalena River. His presidency was marred by a serious split in the *Liberal Party between partisans of Aquileo *Parra and Rafael *Núñez in the elections of 1876. Pérez was a well-known author whose works included plays, novels, poetry, a grammar book, and numerous newspaper essays. A member of the *Radical Liberals, he was expelled from Colombia by acting President *Caro in 1893 and spent his last years in exile.

PEREZ-O'LEARY CONVENTION.   Signed by Felipe Pérez, Colombia, and Charles O'Leary, Great Britain, in 1873. The agreement regulated the *foreign debt owed to British creditors. It was honored by Colombia until 1879, when President *Trujillo had to suspend payments because of a treasury deficit.

PERU, Relations with.   The *army of *Gran Colombia was largely responsible for the final liberation of Peru from Spanish rule, 1822-1826 (see: AYACUCHO, Battle of; CALLAO; JUNIN, Battle of), but this was followed by a conflict over boundaries and war debts, 1828-1829 (see: PERU, War of 1828-1829 with). The dispute was settled during a period of détente in the 1850s (see: ANCIZAR-SANCHEZ TREATY; LLERAS–PAZ SOLDAN TREATY). Boundary questions became acute again in the early 20th century (see: PUTU-MAYO DISPUTE) and eventually led to war in the 1930s (see: LETICIA DISPUTE). In 1969 both countries became founding members of the *ANDEAN COMMON MARKET.

PERU, War of 1828-1829 with. July 3-March. It was a conflict over war debts and boundary claims. The major engagement, *Tarquí (Ecuador), was followed by the *Girón Convention and the *Gual-Larrea Treaty of 1829.

PERU, War of 1932-1933 with, see: LETICIA DISPUTE

PERU-COLOMBIA TREATY OF 1820, see: MOSQUERA-MONTEAGUDO TREATY

PERU-COLOMBIA TREATY OF 1829, see: GUAL-LARREA TREATY

PERU-COLOMBIA TREATY OF 1830, see: MOSQUERA-PEDEMONTE TREATY

PERU-COLOMBIA TREATY OF 1866, see: MOSQUERA-FREYRE TREATY

PERU-COLOMBIA TREATY OF 1906, see: PUTUMAYO DISPUTE

PERU-COLOMBIA TREATY OF 1909, see: PUTUMAYO DISPUTE

PERU-COLOMBIA TREATY OF 1911, see: PUTUMAYO DISPUTE

PERU-COLOMBIA TREATY OF 1922, see: LOZANO-SALOMON TREATY

PERU-COLOMBIA TREATY OF 1934, see: RIO DE JANEIRO, Treaty of

PERU–NEW GRANADA TREATY OF 1853, see: LLERAS–PAZ SOLDAN TREATY

PERU–NEW GRANADA TREATY OF 1854, see: ANCIZAR-SANCHEZ TREATY

PERU–NEW GRANADA TREATY OF 1858, see: PARDO-GALVEZ TREATY

PESO. Can be translated as "weight," or possibly "weighs." The Colombian monetary unit. The name originated in colonial times to describe a 28.5-gram weight of uncoined *gold (or the equivalent in *silver), worth eight *reales, used to make up for the chronic shortage of coin (see: CURRENCY). Later, coins, known in English as "dollars," and denoted by the same "$" sign, were minted for this amount. The introduction of paper money allowed the Colombian *peso* to fall far below the U.S. dollar (see also: EXCHANGE RATE).

PETITION OF THE TWENTY-ONE, see: *MOTIVOS DE DISIDENCIA*

PETROLEUM. The first modern attempt to produce petroleum in Colombia was made in 1866 by Manuel Palacio at Tubará, a site near *Barranquilla, and Jorge *Isaacs reported finding petroleum deposits in the *Golfo de Urabá region in 1887. The first major commercial ventures, however, were the *DE MARES CONCESSION and the *BARCO CONCESSION, both authorized in 1905. Neither concession began immediate production, and both eventually reverted to the state after producing for a specified period of time (De Mares in 1951 and Barco in 1955). These were then placed under the control of *ECOPETROL, the Colombian petroleum agency, founded in 1951. Petroleum production began in 1921; exportation began in 1926. Production figures cited by Enrique Caballero (*Historia económica de Colombia*), in 42-gallon barrels for selected years, are as follows: 1921 (the first year of production)—66,750; 1929—20,384,547; 1939—23,863,248; 1949—29,707,462; 1959—53,574,112; 1969—71,315,089; and 1979—44,875,063. Production began to decline in 1972, and exportation was suspended in 1975. New discoveries, such as the Cravo Norte field in *Arauca 1983-1985, brought production back up to 68 million barrels. In 1989 Colombia reported self-sufficiency in crude oil and a small surplus for export. Reserves are now estimated at 2.2 billion barrels, and oil *export earnings are close to $500 million a year. Major petroleum refineries have been built at *Barrancabermeja

(Santander), La *Dorada (Caldas), Guamo (4° 2'N, 74° 58'W, *Tolima), Tibú (*Norte de Santander), and Mamonal (*Bolívar). *Cali is a center of petrochemical industries.

PHILOTEMIC SOCIETY, see: SOCIEDAD FILOTEMICA

PICHINCHA, Battle of.   May 24, 1822, Quito, Ecuador. Generals Antonio José de *Sucre and Andrés de Santa Cruz, patriots, defeated royalist Field Marshal Melchor Aymerich. The battle freed most of Ecuador from Spanish control.

PIEDRA Y CIELO.   Literary publication begun in 1939 by Jorge Rojas (1911-). The review was a voice for young, progressive authors who sought to modernize Colombian intellectual life. Writers for the periodical introduced into Colombia ideas and methods current in Spain and Europe at the time. *Piedra y cielo* has been seen as one of the major sources for the evolution of contemporary writing styles in Colombia.

PIJAOS.   Fierce *Indians of the *Cordillera Central in *Huila, *Tolima, and parts of *Cauca and *Magdalena. They revolted against Spanish rule from 1557 to 1618 and frequently disrupted communications between *Bogotá and *Popayán. They menaced much of the central *Cauca Valley until they were finally subjugated by the Spanish in the War of the Pijaos, 1605-1618. See also: BORJA, Juan de; CALARCA

PIJAOS, Sierra de los.   A name given to the *Cordillera Central because the Pijao Indians occupied large portions of these mountains.

PINZAQUI, Treaty of.   Signed on December 30, 1863, in Pinzaquí, Ecuador, by General Juan José *Flores, for Ecuador, and General Antonio González Erazo, Colombia. It reaffirmed the settlement of disputes in the *Pombo–Gómez de la Torre Treaty of 1856 and created a Colombian-Ecuadoran alliance (by supplement of January 1, 1864). It was put into effect, but it was never fully ratified by Colombia.

PIRACY.   Spain's long lines of communication with her American possessions were fair game in time of war. Depredations by French privateers began in 1523, forcing Spanish ships to seek safety in numbers, and leading in the 1560s to the institution of the regular *flota* system. Martin *Cote led the way in incursions ashore; the English John *Hawkins showed how illicit trading could be almost as profitable as plunder, and Francis *Drake showed the way round the tip of South America into the unprotected Pacific. Early in the 17th century Dutch privateers became an important threat, too. From the Spanish point of view all such interlopers were "pirates" whether they were intent on destruction, plunder, or smuggling, and whether they were acting as agents of their governments or on their own account. But the term "pirate" is best reserved for the buccaneers of the latter 17th century—maritime outlaws lacking any national allegiance and seeking solely their own gain. The line is, however, a fine one. The Frenchmen Jean Baptiste *Ducasse and the Baron de *Pointis may have had tacit official support. The Welshman Henry *Morgan graduated from pure piracy to become governor of Jamaica. Increasing revenue loss to contraband depleted the Spanish treasury, and the increasing need for defense against pirate raids forced them to spend more and more on colonial defense. This in turn caused a need for new *taxation, such as the *sisa and the *Armada de Barlovento ("Windward Fleet" tax). It was also one of the things contributing to the *Cartagena Fortifications.

PISBA, Passage of the Páramo de. A reference to the rugged terrain northwest of Pisba (5° 46'N, 72° 28'W), in the *Cordillera Oriental between the Department of *Boyacá and the Intendancy of *Casanare, and to the crossing of it by *Bolívar's troops June 23 to July 6, 1819. The community of Pisba sits at 2,000 meters, but surrounding peaks range as high as 4,000 meters, and the average temperature is 17°C. Spanish leaders considered it unlikely that an attack could be made by crossing the mountains because of the climate and the terrain. The costly, difficult crossing of the mountains from Pore (5° 43'N, 72°W) to Socha (6°N, 72° 42'W, Boyacá) gave the patriot forces surprise and tactical advantages over the Spanish army. The passage of the Páramo de Pisba was a prelude to the patriot victories at the *Pantano de Vargas and the Battle of *Boyacá.

PISCO, Ambrosio, d. 1785   An ill-fated member of the *Comuneros Revolt, titular leader of the *Indians of the provinces of Santa Fe, *Tunja, *Vélez, and *Sogamoso. Pisco was a successful *mestizo merchant from Güepsa (6° 2'N, 73° 34'W, *Santander), where he raised cattle and mules and administered the *tobacco and *aguardiente state monopolies (*estanco). In addition he had dry-goods stores in Moniquirá (5°

53'N, 73° 35'W) and *Bogotá. Pisco claimed descent from the pre-conquest *Zipas. During the Comuneros Revolt, he was drafted, for different reasons, by both Indians and *creoles to join their respective movements. He eventually assumed the role of advocating the restoration of traditional Indian rights, and he appeared to many to be imitating the actions of Tupac Amarú, who headed a more ferocious Indian rebellion in Peru, 1780-1781. Pisco was arrested and imprisoned following the truce negotiated for the Comuneros from June 4-8, 1781, and died in prison in 1785.

PIZANO RESTREPO, Roberto, 1896-1929.   Painter, educator, critic; born *Bogotá, October 21; died Bogotá, April 9. Pizano Restrepo studied art at the Academy of San Fernando in Madrid and in the studio of Fernando Alvarez de Sotomayor and traveled in France and Italy before returning to Colombia in the early 1920s. He served as director of the School of Fine Arts (Escuela de Bellas Artes) in Bogotá and is credited with introducing influences of such masters as Joaquín Sorolla, Ingacio Zuloaga, and others into Colombian art. In addition to his own painting, which included such popular scenes as *Misa del Pueblo, En el hospital,* and various portaits, he was the author of a critical study entitled *Gregorio Vásquez Arce y Ceballos, pintor de la ciudad de Santa Fe de Bogotá, cabeca y corte del Nuevo Reino de Granada* (Paris, 1926), which did much to revive the memory of Colombia's most distinguished colonial painter. See also: VASQUEZ ARCE Y CEBALLOS, Gregorio

PIZARRO, Francisco, ca. 1470-1541.   Conqueror of Peru. He arrived in *New Granada in 1509, accompanied Alonso de *Ojeda's expedition to *San Sebastián de Urabá in 1510, and was with *Nuñez de Balboa when he sighted the Pacific Ocean in 1513. He explored the Pacific Coast of Colombia, 1524-1533, and carried out the conquest of Peru, 1533-1541.

PIZARRO, José Alfonso, d. 1755.   Viceroy of *New Granada, 1749-1753. He was responsible for pacification of the coastal *Indians; creation of the *aguardiente *estanco (state monopoly), 1749; nationalization of the mint (*Casa de Moneda) in *Bogotá, 1750; and the encouragement of *Jesuit activities.

PIZARRO LEONGOMEZ, Carlos, 1950-1990.   Leader of the *Movimiento Diecinueve de Abril who was assassinated aboard an Avianca jetliner, April 26, 1990. The son of an admiral (and former commander-in-chief of the Colombian *armed forces), Pizarro joined M-19 on its creation and became its leader on the death of Alvaro *Fayad Delgado, March 12, 1986. After protracted negotiations with the *Barco government, January-October 1989, Pizarro secured the conversion of his clandestine guerrilla group into a legitimate political party, which adopted him as its candidate for the May 1990 presidential elections. In late 1989 he ran for mayor of *Bogotá and won only 8% of the votes. Following the assassination of Bernardo Jaramillo Ossa, the *Unión Partiótica presidential contender (March 22, 1990, at the Bogotá airport), Pizarro appeared to stand a good chance of uniting most of the left behind his candidacy. Official opinion seemed to accept the claim by anonymous telephone callers that both Jaramillo and Pizarro were victims of the so-called Medellín drug cartel (see: DRUG TRADE). Pizarro had belonged briefly to the *Fuerzas Armadas Revolucionarias de Colombia in 1970, before joining the M-19. While working with the M-19 he had been captured in *Santander in September 1979 and then released in November 1982. He was the great-grandson of Adolfo *León Gómez, and his name is often written as "Pizarro León Gómez."

PLAN DE ESTUDIOS, 1826. A national *education program adopted March 18. It created a department of public instruction, a national academy with provincial affiliates, and a system of primary and secondary schools and national *universities. It was controversial because the prescribed textbooks were strongly influenced by the ideas of Jeremy Bentham (see: BENTHAMISM). With modifications, it lasted until 1841, although it was never fully implemented. See also: EDUCATION

PLAN DE ESTUDIOS, 1842. A series of decrees that completely replaced the educational programs in effect since 1826. Reacting vigorously to the *Benthamistic influences in the previous plan and to the War of the *Supreme Commanders, 1840-1842, the program emphasized the practical and applied arts and dictated rigid Catholic indoctrination for all students. It was resented by more liberal thinkers, but it lasted until 1850. See also: EDUCATION

PLAN DE ESTUDIOS, 1850, see: FREEDOM OF STUDIES LAW

PLAN DE ESTUDIOS, 1867, see: UNIVERSIDAD NACIONAL DE COLOMBIA

PLAN NACIONAL DE DESARROLLO. The *Constitution of 1991 provides for a Plan of National Development designed and administered by a National Planning Council (Consejo Nacional de Planeación) whose members are appointed by the *President for eight-year terms. The plan is intended to establish long-range economic goals and to decide how existing resources can best be used to achieve goals in fields such as health, education, and general maintenance of a wholesome environment.

PLATA (La), Battle of. *Huila, June 10, 1816; a patriot force of approximately 150 men under Colonel Liborio *Mejía and Colonel Pedro Monslave was defeated along the La Plata River by royalist troops (about 400 men) led by Carlos Tolrá. Colonel Mejía and others were taken prisoner. Together with the Battle of *Cuchilla del Tambo, it sealed the victory of the Spanish army in the *Reconquista of the *Cauca.

PLATINUM. Although platinum was found in conjunction with *gold deposits from the 1500s on, its refinement and use was not understood until the late 18th century. Before 1786, platinum was a waste by-product of the gold-refining process and a hazard to the Crown because it was used to adulterate gold. The Bogotá mint (*Casa de Moneda) declared it fraudulent to mix gold and platinum in 1707 and increased the penalties for the crime in 1720. The first important samples of platinum were sent to Spain in 1740. It was recognized as a separate chemical element by English and Swedish scientists in 1751, and large quantities were exported to Spain for experimentation in the following decade. Finally, in 1786, a French scientist discovered a simple method for refining platinum, and it became a new revenue source for the Spanish monarchy. The *Chocó remained the world's sole producer of platinum until the 1820s when deposits were also located in Russia. Platinum is now mined in *Cauca, Chocó, and *Valle del Cauca, and Colombia is the world's fifth largest producer.

PLOTS AND CONSPIRACIES, see: ECHAVARRIA CONSPIRACY; NINETEENTH OF DECEMBER CONSPIRACY; PASTO CONSPIRACY; SARDA CONSPIRACY; TENTH OF FEBRUARY, Conspiracy of; THIRTY-FIRST OF JULY

MOVEMENT; TWENTY-FIFTH OF SEPTEMBER CON-
SPIRACY; TWENTY-THIRD OF MAY CONSPIRACY.
See also: DEATH SQUADS

POETRY, see: LITERATURE

POINTIS, Jean Bernard Desjeans, Baron de, 1645-1707. A
French naval officer who captured *Cartagena with Jean *Ducasse in 1697. His siege, which began April 13, succeeded in
capturing the city by May 2. Although Baron de Pointis
himself left the port on May 25, his men continued to terrorize
Cartagena until June 3. He is said to have carried off more than
10 million pesos and eighty pieces of artillery. He later
published an account of the exploit, entitled *Rélation de l'ex-
pédition de Cartagene* (1698).

POLICE. A police force was organized in Bogotá by Viceroy
*Ezpeleta in 1791. The modern national police force (*Policía
Nacional*) was created under French advice in 1891. The
growth of *guerrilla movements and the *drug trade has led to
an increase in strength from 55,197 personnel in 1980 to
70,075 people in 1986. Nevertheless, in 1986 there were no
police assigned to 52 of Colombia's 990 *municipalities, none
in 1,515 of its 2,002 *corregimientos,* and none in 1,548 of its
4,918 *inspecciones.* Under the *Constitution of 1991, the National Police is a branch of the nation's *armed forces.

POLITICAL PARTIES. The two traditional parties are the
*CONSERVATIVE PARTY and the *LIBERAL PARTY.
These made a temporary alliance formally as the *FRENTE
NACIONAL in the 1958-1974 period, and various factions
have made less formal temporary alliances at other times, such
as the *Union Republicana of 1901-1910 and the *Concentra-
ción Nacional of the 1930s. Factions and splinter groups of the
two traditional parties have included the *HISTORICOS;
*INDEPENDENT CONSERVATIVES; *INDEPENDENT
LIBERALS; *MINISTERIALES; *MOVIMIENTO REVOLU-
CIONARIO LIBERAL; *NUEVO LIBERALISMO; *NA-
TIONALISTS; *OLIMPO RADICAL; *PARTIDO
NACIONAL; *PROGRESISTAS; *RADICALS; *UNION-
IST CONSERVATIVES; and *UNIR. Newer parties include
*ALIANZA NACIONAL POPULAR; *DEMOCRACIA
CRISTIANA; *FRENTE UNIDO DEL PUEBLO; *MOVI-
MIENTO NACIONAL POPULAR; *PARTIDO

COMUNISTA DE COLOMBIA; *PARTIDO SOCIALISTA REVOLUCIONARIO; *UNION DEMOCRATICA DE LA IZQUIERDA; and the *UNION PATRIOTICA. See also: GUERRILLA MOVEMENTS; SOCIALISM

POLITICAL SUBDIVISIONS, see: ADMINISTRATIVE SUB-DIVISIONS

POLONIA, Battle of la. September 29, 1840, *Santander. Rebel forces under Colonel Manuel *González defeated government troops led by Colonel Manuel María Franco and Major Alfonso Acevedo. Their defeat produced a panic in the *Márquez administration.

POMBO, Rafael, 1833-1912. Poet, translator, mathematician, engineer, diplomat, journalist; born *Bogotá, November 7; died Bogotá, May 12. His works covered a surprisingly wide variety of themes, but he is best remembered for his *Cuentos pintados,* stories for children; his *Fábulas y verdades,* bits of philosophy expressed in fables; and his poetry, including works such as *Hora de tinieblas* (ca. 1856), *Noche de diciembre* (1874), and *De noche* (1890). Pombo's work was honored in a public tribute in the *Teatro Colón in Bogotá on August 20, 1905, after which he withdrew from active public life. See also: *ESTER*

POMBO–GOMEZ DE LA TORRE TREATY OF 1856. Signed in *Bogotá on July 9 by Lino de Pombo, *New Granada, and Colonel Teodoro Gómez de la Torre, Ecuador. A treaty of friendship, commerce, and navigation, it recognized New Granada's claims to *Cauca and *Nariño as a basis for a boundary settlement. It replaced the *OBANDO–POSADA GUTIERREZ–ARTETA TREATY OF 1832, which Ecuador had respected but never formally ratified.

POMBO-MICHELENA TREATIES OF 1833. Signed December 14 and 23 in *Bogotá, by Lino de Pombo, *New Granada, and Santos Michelena, Venezuela. The first was a general treaty of friendship, commerce, alliance, navigation, and boundaries, which was rejected by both nations. It was eventually replaced by the *Pombo-Romero Treaty of 1842. The second agreement apportioned the national debt of Gran Colombia among New Granada, 50%; Venezuela, 28.5%; and Ecuador, 21.5%, on the basis of population. It was bitterly denounced in New Granada and was not ratified until 1837.

POMBO-ROMERO TREATY OF 1842. Signed in Caracas by Lino de Pombo, *New Granada, and Juan José Romero, Venezuela, on July 23, 1842. A treaty of friendship, commerce, and navigation, it replaced the *Pombo-Michelena Treaty of 1833. The agreement facilitated initial boundary settlements, leaving the territories of the *Guajira Peninsula and San Faustino to New Granada (see: BORDERS).

PONTIFICIA UNIVERSIDAD JAVERIANA, see: UNIVERSIDAD JAVERIANA

POPAYAN. Capital of the Department of *Cauca, situated at 2° 27'N, 76° 37'W, at an altitude of 1,760 meters. Average temperature is 19°C, and the population is 156,530 people (1985 estimate). Popayán is an agricultural and commercial center, with limited industrialization. Although 1536 is the date most frequently cited, the city was founded first by Juan de Ampudia in 1535 in the Valley of Pubenza on the Molino River. It was more officially established by *Belalcázar, January 13, 1537, and a *cabildo* was installed August 15, 1537. The settlement was granted a coat of arms in 1538, and a bishopric was established there in 1547. Popayán became a seat of colonial government, and it has been an important administrative, religious, and cultural center for more than four and a half centuries. It was the birthplace of several presidents and archbishops of Colombia and numerous other well-known figures, and is now a city known for its traditional Holy Week observances and its preservation of colonial art and architecture.

POPAYAN MINT, see: CASA DE MONEDA DE POPAYAN

POPAYAN STYLE. Also known as the Cauca Style; an archeological term applied to a set of artifacts discovered at the *hacienda* La Marquesa near *Popayán (Cauca). This style appears relatively isolated from other cultural groups in Colombia. Articles such as a golden pectoral that resembles the *tuimis,* or ceremonial knives, from Peru and pottery jars with pointed or conical-shaped bottoms suggest possible Incan or other Peruvian influences.

POPULATION. The first census of the colonial period dates from the 18th century. The first census of the *Virreinato del Nuevo Reino de Granada in 1770 recorded some 806,209 people, and in 1778 there were supposedly 828,775. In 1803, there were approximately 2 million, but the census of 1825, during the *República de Gran Colombia, showed a figure of 1,223,598. The first census of modern Colombia (*New Granada), taken in 1835, showed 1,686,038 people. In 1851 there were 2,243,054 people; in 1864, there were 2,694,487 people; in 1905, 4,143,632 people; in 1928, 7,851,000 people; in 1938, 8,997,307 people; in 1951, 11,962,360 people; in 1964, some 17,484,509 people; and 22,525,670 people in 1973. The 1985 census showed a population of 27,837,932, and estimates for 1986 placed the population at approximately 30 million. See also: BLACKS; CENSUSES; CREOLES; IMMIGRATION; INDIANS; JEWS; MESTIZOS

PORTOBELLO (Puerto Bello).   Long the Caribbean counterpart of *Panama City, it was the leading entrepôt on the northern coast of the Isthmus. Located 20 miles northeast of *Colón at 9° 33′N, 79° 37′W, the city was founded in 1597 on the site of a harbor named by *Columbus. Francis *Drake died off shore and was buried in the harbor, and Henry *Morgan sacked the city in 1688. Admiral *Vernon took it again in 1739. After independence Portobello was abandoned in favor of the slightly more convenient harbor at *Chagres, but even the latter was largely deserted for commercial purposes after the *Panama Railroad was built, 1848-1855. The new entrepôt became the rebuilt city of Colón at Navy Bay where the railroad terminated. The name is also written "Portobelo."

PORTUGUESE REBELLION, 1641-1642.   A short-lived movement among some of the Portuguese residents along the Atlantic Coast following the separation of the Portuguese monarchy from the Spanish monarchy in 1640. The most notable of the isolated incidents was an alleged plot by the Count of Castilmillor in *Cartagena. Castilmillor was accused of conspiracy, arrested, tried, convicted, and condemned to death. He was able to escape from *New Granada before the sentence could be carried out.

POSADA GUTIERREZ, Joaquín, 1797-1881.   General, *Conservative, diplomat, and historian. Born in *Cartagena (some say in 1791), he became a militia lieutenant in April 1821 and fought under *Urdaneta at Quisiro, Altagracia, Monteclaro, Juritiva, and Misión. In 1830 he issued a declaration in *Honda in support of Urdaneta, but transferred his allegiance to

Vice President *Caycedo in March 1831. He negotiated a treaty of limits with Ecuador, which was rendered void by the invasion of General Juan José *Flores in 1832. Posada Gutiérrez was also involved in the *Obando–Posada Gutiérrez–Arteta Treaty of 1832 and the *Ecuador–New Granada Treaties of 1840-1841. He fought for the government against the *rebellions of 1840-1842, 1854, and 1859-1862, signing the *Manizales Agreements with rebel commander General T. C. de *Mosquera. Posada Gutiérrez also had the honor of escorting the body of the *Liberator back to his native Caracas, and wrote an important autobiographical memoir, the *Memorias histórico-políticas*. He died in *Bogotá.

POSADA GUTIERREZ–DASTE TREATY, see: ECUADOR–NEW GRANADA TREATIES OF 1840-1841

POST-NUEVOS GENERATION. The Post-Nuevos were a group of writers, artists, and political leaders who shared the modernizing impulse of Los *Nuevos at the same time that they criticized the latter group for not taking reform seriously. According to Carlos Uribe Celis, the Post-Nuevos, who came into being as a group about 1927, were divided into two subgroups: the *Bachués* and the Albatross Group. The *Bachués* took their name from a statue of the *Chibcha goddess *Bachué created by sculptor Rómulo Rozo in 1929. The *Bachués,* who stressed nationalism and *Indian themes, included Darío Achury Valenzuela, Rafael Azuela Barrera, Darío Samper, Pedro Nel *Gómez, Luis Alberto *Acuña, and others. The Albatross Group stressed the more universal and cosmopolitan aspects of reform and modernization in opposition to the nationalist and Indian emphasis of the *Bachués.* Members of the Albatross Group included Antonio García, Eduardo Umaña Bernal, Clímaco Sepúlveda, and Jorge Padilla. All of the Post-Nuevos considered themselves more progressive than Los Nuevos, who dominated the first half of the 1920s. See also: NUEVOS, Los; GENERATIONS

POSTAL SERVICE (Servicio de Correos). Mail delivery was established as a function of the central government in 1718, but the service was not given formal organization until 1750. The first routes ran from *Bogotá to *Cartagena, *Socorro, and *Popayán. Under Viceroy *Solís Folch de Cardona, service was extended to *Antioquia, Guayaquil, *Chocó, and Caracas. Service between *Santa Marta and Maracaibo was established in 1757, and other routes connecting points within the viceroy-alty were established thereafter. Modern postal service in Colombia dates from 1859. Airmail service began in 1919. The post office became the Ministerio de Correos y Telégrafos in 1923.

POTATOES. The potato is an edible tuber of a widely cultivated plant that, along with *yuca and *corn, provides one of the main food staples of Latin Americans, especially in the highlands of South America. The potato was native to the Western Hemi-sphere and was exported to the rest of the world after the Spanish penetration of the Americas. Domestication of the potato by *Indians is attributed to the Lake Titicaca region in the mountains of Peru and Bolivia. A Rockefeller Foundation report in 1972 recorded that as many as 2,500 samples of different kinds of potatoes (representing 200 species) had been collected at an agricultural research station at Tibaitatá (*Cundinamarca) near *Bogotá, and that new varieties were continually being developed. Potatoes are used in daily diets throughout Colombia. They are most often referred to simply as *papas,* but *ajiaco,* a kind of potato soup identified as a Colombian regional dish, is made with *papas criollas.* °*ame* is a term often used for yam, or sweet potato.

PRADO-TANCO TREATY, see: PUTUMAYO DISPUTE

PRE-CENTENARY GENERATION. Also known as the Gener-ation of '86 and Generation of '96. A name used by Carlos Uribe Celis to describe the group of intellectuals and political leaders active in the last two decades of the 19th century, or from the *Regeneration (1885/1886) on into the early part of the 20th century. Included in this group were Carlos Martínez Silva, Carlos Arturo Torres, Fidel Cano, Rafael *Uribe Uribe, Tomás *Carrasquilla, Baldomero *Sanín Cano, Max Grillo, Guillermo *Valencia, Marco Fidel *Suárez, Tomás O. East-man, José Asunción *Silva, Víctor Londoño, Epifanio Garay, and Luis Zea Uribe. This classification of Uribe Celis coincides roughly with Generations IV and V of Abel Naranjo Villegas (see: GENERATIONS).

PRECURSOR, El, see: NARIÑO, Antonio

PRESBYTERIAN CHURCH. The oldest Protestant denomina-tion in Colombia outside of *San Andrés y Providencia. It was founded in *Bogotá in 1856 by the Reverend H. B. Pratt, who built its first chapel in 1861. A new building was erected in 1927. See also: PROTESTANTISM

PRESIDENCIA DE PANAMA. The name of the colonial government of *PANAMA.

PRESIDENCIA DE QUITO. The name of the colonial government in what is now Ecuador.

PRESIDENCIA DEL NUEVO REINO DE GRANADA. The Presidency of the New Kingdom of Granada, created 1563-1719 and reestablished 1723-1739. During the 17th century, the Presidency was dependent upon the Viceroyalty of Peru and had jurisdiction over the provincial governments of *Cartagena, *Santa Marta, *Antioquia, La Grita, Los Muzos, La Guayra, La Plata (2° 23'N, 75° 56'W), Timaná (1° 58'N, 75° 55'W), and part of *Popayán, as well as the Indian settlements at Funza (4° 43'N, 74° 13'W), *Tocaima, and *Mariquita. Presidents of the New Kingdom of Granada from 1564 to 1739 were:

Andrés Díaz Venero de Leiva, 1564-1574
Francisco Briceño, 1575
The Audiencia, 1575-1578
Lope Díez Aux de Armendáriz, 1578-1580
Juan Bautista Monzón, 1580-1582
Juan Prieto de Orellana, 1582-1584
Francisco Guillén Chaparro, 1585-1590
Antonio *González, 1590-1597
Francisco de *Sande, 1597-1602
The Audiencia, 1602
Núño Núñez de Villavicencio, 1603-1605
Juan de *Borja, 1605-1628
The Audiencia, 1628-1630
Sancho Girón, Marqués de Sofraga, 1630-1636
Martín Saavedra y Guzmán, Barón de Prado, 1637-1644
Juan Fernández de Córdoba y Coalla, 1644-1654
Dionisio Pérez Manrique, Marqués de Santiago, 1654-1659, 1660-1662
Juan Cornejo, 1659-1660
Diego de Egúes y Beaumont, 1662-1664
The Audiencia, 1664-1666
Diego del Corro y Carrascal, 1666-1667
Diego de *Villalba y Toledo, 1667-1671
Melchor Liñán y Cisneros, 1671-1674

The Audiencia, 1674-1678
Francisco del Castillo de la Concha, 1678-1685
Sebastián de Velasco, 1685-1686
Gil de Cabrera y Dávalos, 1686-1703
Diego Córdoba Lasso de la Vega, 1703-1712
The Audiencia, 1712
Francisco de Meneses de Saravia y Bravo, 1712-1715
The Audiencia, 1715-1717
Nicolás Infante de Venegas, 1717
Francisco del Rincón, 1718
Antonio de la Pedrosa y Guerrero, 1718-1719
The Viceroyalty, 1719-1723
Antonio Manso y Maldonado, 1725-1731
The Audiencia, 1731-1733
Rafael de *Eslava, 1733-1737
The Audiencia, 1737
Antonio González Manrique, 1738
Francisco *González Manrique, 1739-1740

PRESIDENT OF THE REPUBLIC.   The chief executive of the nation; under the *Constitution of 1991, this official is also known as the Chief of State (*Jefe del Estado*), Chief of the Government (*Jefe del Gobierno*), and Supreme Administrative Authority (*Suprema Autoridad Administrativa*). The president is elected by a simple majority of the popular vote for one 4-year term of office and can not be reelected. The President must be at least 30 years old and a native-born Colombian citizen in good standing. He may not leave the country during his term in office or for one year afterward without permission of the *Congress. The Chief Executive's major duties are to enforce the laws of Colombia, to appoint ministers of state and other public officials, to conduct foreign relations, to maintain public order, to serve as commander in chief of the armed forces, to provide for national defense, to conduct war when necessary, and to supervise public finances. There is a *Vice-President who assumes the presidential role when specifically empowered to do so.

PRESIDENTS OF COLOMBIA.   Allowing for variation in the official title of the republic before 1886, titular presidents and other chief executives of Colombia since 1810 are listed below with the years they were in office. The abbreviations P for President, V-P for Vice-President, and PD for Presidential Designate are used. Officials acting as chief executive have been designated by #.

#José Miguel Pey, VP of the Supreme Junta, 1810-1811
Jorge Tadeo Lozano, P of Cundinamarca, 1811
Antonio *Nariño, P of Cundinamarca, 1811-1812
Camilo *Torres, P of the United Provinces, 1811-1814
Manuel Benito de Castro, P of Cundinamarca, 1812
Antonio Nariño, P-Dictator of Cundinamarca, 1812-1813
Manuel Bernardo de *Alvarez, P-Dictator of Cundinamarca, 1813-1814
José *Fernández Madrid, José María Castillo y Rada, and Joaquín Camacho, Triumvirate of the United Provinces, 1814-1815
Custodio *García Rovira, José Miguel Pey, and Manuel Rodríguez Torices, Triumvirate of the United Provinces, 1815 (Antonio *Villavicencio replaced García Rovira)
Camilo Torres, P of the United Provinces, 1815-1816
José Fernández Madrid, P of the United Provinces, 1816
Custodio García Rovira, P of the United Provinces, 1816
#Liborio Mejía, VP of the United Provinces, 1816
Fernando Serrano, P of New Granada, 1816
Pablo *Morillo, Military Governor of New Granada, 1816
Juan *Sámano, Military Governor of New Granada, 1816-1818, Viceroy of New Granada, 1818-1819
Simón *Bolívar, P of Gran Colombia, 1819-1828; Dictator of Colombia, 1828-1830
#Francisco de Paula *Santander, Acting Chief Executive, VP of Colombia, 1819-1827
#Domingo *Caycedo, VP of Colombia, 1830
Joaquín *Mosquera, P, 1830
Rafael *Urdaneta, Dictator, 1830-1831
Juan García del Rio, Jerónimo de Mendoza y Galavís, José Miguel Pey, Plural Executive, 1831
#Domingo Caycedo, VP, 1831
José María *Obando, VP, 1831-1832
#José Ignacio de *Márquez, VP of New Granada, 1832
Francisco de Paula Santander, P of New Granada, 1832-1837
José Ignacio de Márquez, P, 1837-1841
#Domingo Caycedo, VP, 1840
Pedro Alcántara *Herrán, P, 1841-1845
#Juan de Dios Aranzazu, P of the Council of State, 1841
#Domingo Caycedo, VP, 1841-1842
Tomás C. de *Mosquera, P, 1845-1849
#José Joaquín Gori, VP, 1847
#Rufino Cuervo, VP, 1847
José Hilario *López, P, 1849-1853
#José de Obaldía, VP, 1851-1852
José María Obando, P, 1853-1854
José María *Melo, Dictator, 1854; Francisco Antonio Obregón Muñoz, Acting Dictator, 1854
#Tomás *Herrera, interim P, 1854

#José de Obaldía, VP, 1854-1855
Manuel María *Mallarino, P, 1855-1857
Mariano *Ospina Rodríguez, P, 1857-1861
#Bartolomé *Calvo, Attorney General, 1861
Tomás C. de Mosquera, Provisional P, 1861-1863
#Ignacio Gutiérrez Vergara, PD, 1861-1862
#Leonardo Canal, PD, 1862
#Manuel del Río y de Narváez, PD, 1862-1863
#Santos *Gutiérrez, Froilán Largacha, José Hilario López, and
    Tomás C. de Mosquera, Provisional Junta of Government, 1863
Tomás C. de Mosquera, P of the United States of Colombia,
    1863-1864
#Juan Agustín Uricoechea, Attorney General, 1864
Manuel *Murillo Toro, P, 1864-1866
Tomás C. de Mosquera, P, 1866-1867
#José María Rojas Garrido, PD, 1866
#Santos *Acosta, PD, 1867-1868
Santos Gutiérrez, P, 1868-1870
#Salvador Camacho Roldán, PD, 1868-1869
#Santiago *Pérez, PD, 1869
Eustorgio *Salgar, P, 1870-1872
Manuel Murillo Toro, P, 1872-1874
Santiago Pérez, P, 1874-1876
Aquileo *Parra, P, 1876-1878
#Sergio Camargo, PD, 1877
#Manuel María Ramírez, PD, 1877
Julián *Trujillo, P, 1878-1880
Rafael *Núñez, P, 1880-1882
Francisco Javier *Zaldúa, P, 1882
#Clímaco Calderón, PD, 1882
#José Eusebio *Otálora, PD, 1882-1884
Rafael Núñez, P, 1884-1886.
#Ezequiel Hurtado, PD, 1884
#José María Campo Serrano, PD, 1886-1887
#Eliseo *Payán, VP, 1887
Rafael Núñez, P, 1887-1894
#Eliseo Payán, VP, 1887-1888
#Carlos *Holguín, PD, 1888-1892
#Miguel Antonio *Caro, VP, 1892-1898
#Antonio Cuervo, PD, 1893
#Guillermo Quintero Calderón, PD, 1896
Manuel Antonio *Sanclemente, P, 1898-1900
#José Manuel *Marroquín, VP, 1898
José Manuel Marroquín, P by coup d'état, 1900-1904
Rafael *Reyes, P-Dictator, 1904-1909
#Euclides de Angulo, PD, 1908
Jorge *Holguín, PD, 1909
Ramón *González Valencia, VP, 1909-1910

Carlos Eugenio *Restrepo, P, 1910-1914
José Vicente *Concha, P, 1914-1918
Marco Fidel *Suárez, P, 1918-1921
#Jorge Holguín, PD, 1921-1922
Pedro Nel *Ospina, P, 1922-1926
Miguel *Abadía Méndez, P, 1926-1930
Enrique *Olaya Herrera, P, 1930-1934
Alfonso *López Pumarejo, P, 1934-1938
Eduardo *Santos, P, 1938-1942
Alfonso López Pumarejo, P, 1942-1945
#Carlos Lozano y Lozano, PD, 1942
#Darío *Echandía, PD, 1943-1944
#Alberto *Lleras Camargo, PD, 1945-1946
Mariano *Ospina Pérez, P, 1946-1950
Laureano *Gómez, P, 1950-1953
#Roberto *Urdaneta Arbeláez, PD, 1951-1953
Gustavo *Rojas Pinilla, Dictator, 1953-1957
#Gabriel París, interim Dictator, 1955
Military Junta, 1957-1958 (Gabriel París, Rafael Navas Pardo,
    Deogracias Fonseca, Luis Enrique Ordóñez, Rubén Piedrahita)
Alberto Lleras Camargo, P, 1958-1962
Guillermo León *Valencia, P, 1962-1966
#José Antonio Montalvo, PD, 1963
Carlos *Lleras Restrepo, P, 1966-1970
#Darío Echandía, Minister of Justice, 1967
#Julio César *Turbay Ayala, PD, 1968
Misael *Pastrana Borrero, P, 1970-1974
#Rafael Azuero Machola, PD, 1973
Alfonso *López Michelsen, P, 1974-1978
#Julio César Turbay Ayala, PD, 1975
#Indalecio *Liévano Aguirre, PD, 1975
Julio César Turbay Ayala, P, 1978-1982
#Víctor Mosquera Chaux, PD, 1981
Belisario *Betancur Cuartas, P, 1982-1986
Virgilio *Barco Vargas, P, 1986-1990
Julio César *Gaviria, P, 1990-1994

PRESS, The, see: CENSORSHIP; NEWSPAPERS; PRINTING; PUBLISHING

PRIAS ALAPE, Jacobo (d. 1960). Peasant and guerrilla leader, also known as Fermín Charry Rincón and Charro Negro. He was active in organizing agricultural communities and guerrilla movements in southern *Tolima, *Huila, and *Cauca during the 1950s, and he was responsible for the founding of *Marquetalia in 1955. Affiliated with communist-oriented guerrillas (see: PARTIDO COMUNISTA DE COLOMBIA), Charro

Negro was assassinated January 11, 1960, at the village of Gaitanía, by rival guerrillas more closely associated with the *Liberal Party and the government.

PRINTING.   The first documented press in *New Granada was established by the *Jesuits in October 1737. The press in *Bogotá was the ninth in the hemisphere after Mexico and Peru in the 16th century; the United States (Cambridge, Massachusetts), Guatemala, and Paraguay in the 17th century; and Cuba (1707), Jamaica (1718), and Barbados (1730). After the expulsion of the Jesuits in 1767, the press seems to have lain idle until it was reactivated by the government in 1777 as the Royal Printing Office (*Imprenta Real*). The first secular printer, Antonio Espinosa de los Monteros, arrived in New Granada in 1777, and the first secular press was started in Bogotá in 1779 (see: PUBLISHING). The first *newspapers, *Aviso de Terremoto* and *Gaceta de Santafé de Bogotá,* were published in 1785.

PROGRESISTAS.   Literally, "Progressives"; the term was used to describe more doctrinaire *Liberals in the late 1830s.

PROTESTANTISM.   The first permanent Protestant denomination established in Colombia (other than in *San Andrés y Providencia) was the *Presbyterian Church, founded in 1856. It was followed by the Gospel Missionary Union, 1910; the Scandinavian Missionary Alliance, 1922; the Seventh-Day Adventists, 1925; the Cumberland Presbyterian Mission, 1926; the National Baptist Convention, 1929; the United Evangelical Lutheran Church, 1930; the World-Wide Evangelical Crusade, 1933; the Pentecostal Assemblies of Canada, 1934; the Wesleyan Methodist Church, 1940; the Christian Missionary Alliance, 1942; and the Southern Baptist Convention, 1942. Fourteen additional groups entered Colombia, 1942-1950.

It was partially this rapid influx in the 1930s and 1940s that gave rise to the so-called Protestant persecution of the period from 1948-1959, during which the Evangelical Confederation of Colombia and others claimed that at least 42 Protestant buildings were violently destroyed, 200 Protestant schools were forced to close, and at least 115 Protestant supporters were murdered (estimates vary). Numerous Protestant mission stations were closed by the government following a treaty with the *Papacy in 1953. Anti-Protestant movements were supported, at least passively, by some Catholic clergymen. This

Protestant persecution coincided with the early stages of *La *Violencia*. Less than 10% of the population is Protestant.

PROVIDENCIA. The more northerly of the two main islands of the Archipelago San Andrés y Providencia, known in English as *OLD PROVIDENCE. See also: SAN ANDRES, PROVIDENCIA Y SANTA CATALINA, Departamento de

PROVINCE. From the Spanish *provincia,* a territorial division of the late colonial period. *Gran Colombia in 1824 consisted of twelve *departments (Apure, Azuay, *Boyacá, *Cauca, *Cundinamarca, Ecuador, Guayaquil, Istmo, *Magdalena, Orinoco, Venezuela, and Zulia) divided into thirty-six *provincias*. After the breakup of *Gran Colombia, *New Granada was left with twenty-three provinces, but decentralization under *Liberal rule had increased this to thirty-six by 1853. Between 1855 and 1857 the provinces were gradually amalgamated into *states, beginning with the amalgamation of the four isthmian provinces into the state of *Panama.

PROVINCIAS UNIDAS DE NUEVA GRANADA. A union of governments from present-day Colombia formed by the *PACTO DE LA CONFEDERACION DE LAS PROVINCIAS DE LA NUEVA GRANADA in 1811. *Antioquia, *Cartagena, *Pamplona, *Tunja, and eventually *Casanare, *Cundinamarca, and *Popayán struggled to form a viable state during the *PATRIA BOBA period, but they were weakened by internecine warfare and finally succumbed to the Spanish *Reconquista,* 1816-1819.

PUBLIC HEALTH. European diseases brought by the Spaniards were one of the principal reasons for the decline of the aboriginal population (see: EPIDEMICS; INDIANS). In 1850, the *Freedom of Studies Law abolished all qualifications for the practice of medicine (as well as other professions), but the new *Universidad Nacional, founded in 1867, stressed practical training, and by 1870 the student body of 132 pupils had 51 medical students. In 1873 the *Academia Nacional de Medicina was established. "Health" was first included in the title of a government ministry in 1923, although a separate health ministry was not set up until 1946 (see: MINISTRIES). Since its creation in 1927, the *Federación Nacional de Cafeteros has been instrumental in improving rural health services, and the *Frente Nacional governments of the 1960s increased the Health Ministry budget substantially and had ambitious plans for improving health care. Nevertheless, Colombian medical and health care remains poor even by Latin American standards. There are more doctors than nurses, more specialists than general practitioners, a greater concentration of health care providers in the larger cities than elsewhere, and a chronic drainage by emigration to the United States and other developed countries. Affiliation with social security is mandatory only for large firms and institutional employers, and the government has often failed to fund its share of the program. The national birth rate has shown a remarkable decline in recent years, but infant mortality remains high. Tuberculosis is becoming less prevalent, but malnutrition and alcoholism remain serious problems.

PUBLISHING.   The first book known to have been produced in *New Granada following the introduction of *printing is the *Septenario al corazón doloroso de María Santísima . . .* , a devotional work by Juan de Ricaurte y Terreros, printed by Father Francisco de la Peña at the *Jesuits' press in 1738. The first secular printer, Antonio Espinosa de los Monteros, arrived in the Viceroyalty in 1777, and set up his press in *Bogotá in 1779. One of the most influential publications of the early printers in the city was a Spanish version of *The *Rights of Man* from Antonio *Nariño's Imprenta Patriótica in 1793, a mere four years after the Paris original. The edition was exhausted so rapidly that Nariño's consequent prosecution for seditious libel failed for lack of evidence. The authorities could not find a single copy to produce in court.

Book publishing (as distinct from pamphleteering and newspaper printing) was of little importance in the tumultuous years of the Colombian 19th century. The nation's tiny book market was supplied largely by imports from France. Even Colombian authors sought Paris publication, notably from the Spanish-language department of Garnier Frères. From about 1912 Barcelona made itself the major center of publishing for the Hispanic American market. The virtual cessation of book exporting from Madrid and Barcelona during the 1936-1939 Spanish Civil War gave a boost to publishers in Argentina, Mexico, and Chile, eager to fill the sudden void this had created in Spanish-language publishing. It benefited Colombian publishers hardly at all. Basically this was because there was, in a sense, no national book trade at that time. Instead there were three separate, self-contained, regional markets centered on Bogotá, *Medellín, and *Cali. Bookshops did a little local publishing to achieve a modicum of prosperity, but they were unable to take advantage of the new conditions to expand internationally. By the 1960s, the Spanish publishing industry had totally recovered its pre-war dominance of the Spanish-language book trade worldwide. Its annual production exceeded 20,000 new titles or editions; Argentina was producing some 4,500, Mexico 3,000, Chile 1,100, and Castro's Cuba almost as many. Colombia was in sixth place with an average of barely 900. (For the development of Colombian publishing up to this time, consult Tito Livio Caldas, *Industria editorial, cultura y desarrollo en Colombia,* Bogotá, 1970.)

Since the early 1970s, however, there has occurred a remarkable growth, gradual at first, but later accelerating, as Colombia has transformed itself into the major Hispanic American book publishing country. From the 848 new editions of 1972 output has grown to 1,272 in 1975, 5,492 in 1980, and 15,041 in 1983. Although there has been some increase in edition size, the range of titles produced in the other Spanish-speaking countries has advanced little over 1969 levels. (Mexico, for example, issued 4,505 titles in 1983, and Argentina only 4,216.) Indicative of Colombia's new worldwide importance is the fact that its book exports to the United States are now quite sizable: $US5,383,768 worth in 1987, up 29.3% over 1986.

One of Colombia's premier publishing houses is the *Instituto Caro y Cuervo. The first commercial publishing house to achieve a reputation beyond the country's borders was Ediciones Tercer Mundo, founded in 1961, emphasizing politics, sociology, and literature. Colombia's new importance as an international publishing center has encouraged a number of foreign houses to establish Colombian subsidiaries, such as Plaza y Janés of Barcelona and Kapelusz of Buenos Aires.

Thanks to a skilled and relatively inexpensive labor force, there is one publishing area where Colombia has achieved absolute world preeminence: that of pop-up books, traditionally associated with children's publishing, but now increasingly used elsewhere (for example, in medical texts) to provide a means of three-dimensional illustration.

The Colombian capital is also the location of UNESCO's regional agency for books and reading, CERLAL (*Centro Regional para el Libro en América Latina y el Caribe).

PUERTO BELLO, see: PORTOBELLO

PUERTO BERRIO.   River port on the *Magdalena, 6° 29'N, 74° 24'W, for *Medellín (130 kilometers west-southwest) and almost all *Antioquia. It is also the hub of the national *railroad network. Population has grown from 5,487 in 1938 to 12,750 in 1985.

PUERTO CARREÑO.   Capital of *Vichada, located at 6° 12'N, 67° 23'W, approximately 873 aerial kilometers from Bogotá and 850 kilometers by land from *Villavicencio. Altitude is 90 meters; average temperature, 28°C; and population, 3,377 people (1985 estimate). Puerto Carreño is an important border town between Colombia and Venezuela at the junction of the Meta and Orinoco Rivers.

PUERTO HORMIGA.   An archeological site in the Department of *Bolívar. Until more recent finds at El *Abra, El *Tequendama, and *Monsú, Puerto Hormiga was often cited as the oldest recorded location for human habitation in Colombia. It dates from approximately 3000 B.C. Among the other oldest sites in Colombia are Canapote, 2200 B.C., Barlovento, 1550 B.C., and Momil, 700 B.C., all in Bolívar; Malambo, 1200 B.C., in *Atlántico; and *San Agustín in Huila.

PUERTO INIRIDA, see: INIRIDA

PUERTO WILCHES.   River port on the *Magdalena River, located at 7° 21'N, 73° 54'W, in the Department of *Santander, 88 kilometers west-northwest of *Bucaramanga. Altitude is 75 meters and the average temperature 28°C. The community of 8,195 people (1985 estimate) is a commercial center for agriculture, cattle raising, fishing, and forestry products, with some petroleum resources. It is a *railroad center on the *Atlantic Railroad, and it is the Department of Santander's main outlet for its *exports. It was established as a seat of minor local government (*corregimiento*) on May 12, 1882, by General Solón *Wilches.

PUERTO WILCHES RAILROAD, see: NORTHERN RAILROAD

PUTUMAYO, Departamento del.   Located in southern Colombia on the Ecuadoran-Peruvian frontier, the department covers 24,855 square kilometers of tropical forest and lowlands lying between latitudes 0° 40' and 1° 25'N, and longitudes 74° 15' and 77° 15'W. Average temperatures are in the 27°-30°C range. Major rivers include the Caquetá and Putumayo. The estimated population in 1973 was 67,336 people, of which about 45% was concentrated in Puerto Asís (O° 29'N, 76° 32'W). The capital city is *Mocoa. Agriculture is predominantly subsistence, with 6,600 hectares planted in *corn; 4,000 in *yuca; 1,700 in *sugar; 1,300 in plantains; 200 in beans; and 200 in *potatoes. There were 80,000 head of cattle in 1985, and about 7,113,258 barrels of *petroleum were produced in 1981. *Fishing, forest reserves, and *copper are potentially important. The *Intendancy of Putumayo was created in 1968 and then elevated to a department in 1991.

PUTUMAYO DISPUTE. A reference to territorial disputes in the region drained by the Putumayo River, which originates in *Nariño and forms much of the present boundary between Ecuador and Peru and the Departments of *Putumayo and *Amazonas. The development of the *rubber trade in the upper Amazon at the beginning of the 20th century led to disputes over occupation and boundaries affecting Colombia, Peru, Ecuador, Bolivia, and Brazil. Attempts to settle these between Colombia and Peru led to a series of treaties in 1906, 1909, and 1911. The first of these, the Treaty of 1906, was signed by Luis Tanco Argáez, Colombia, and Javier Prado Ugarteche and Hernán Velarde, Peru. It recognized disputed areas of the Putumayo. Both countries agreed to withdraw from the areas pending the settlement of ownership by arbitration. The treaty was revoked by Colombia in 1907, and both nations continued penetration of the areas. Conflicts between settlers and *Indians led to the second agreement. The Treaty of 1909, signed on April 21 by Tanco Argáez, Colombia, and Melitón Porras, Peru, expressed regret for any unfortunate incidents that had occurred in the area and again submitted the dispute to arbitration. This also was never carried out, and two years later, on July 10, 1911, Peruvians under Lieutenant Colonel Oscar Benavides attacked Colombian forces at La *Pedrera (Puerto Córdoba). A third treaty was signed later that month, on July 19, by Enrique *Olaya Herrera, Colombia, and Ernesto de Tezanos Pinto, Peru, providing for a limitation of troops and the avoidance of hostilities pending a final settlement of the dispute. Although this was the last of the "Putumayo Treaties," the later *LETICIA DISPUTE grew out of the same general region.

-Q-

QUEMUNCHATOCHA, 1471-1538. Ruling *Zaque of the *Chibchas when the Spanish arrived. He died soon after capture by the Spanish and was succeeded by *Aquimin.

QUESADA, Gonzalo Jiménez de, see: JIMENEZ DE QUESADA, Gonzalo

QUESADA, Gonzalo Ximénez de, see: JIMENEZ DE QUESADA, Gonzalo

QUESADA, Hernán Pérez de, see: PEREZ DE QUESADA, Hernán

QUEVEDO, Juan de, d. 1519. *Franciscan, the first bishop of colonial *New Granada. He accompanied the expedition of *Pedrarias, 1514. He served first at *Santa María la Antigua del Darién, where he built a cathedral. He then moved to Acla (*Panama), where he tried to mediate between Pedrarias and *Núñez de Balboa. He returned to Spain in 1519.

QUIBDO. Capital of the Department of *Chocó located at 5° 41'N, 76° 40'W, on the *Atrato River, approximately 718 kilometers from Bogotá. The altitude is 43 meters; the average temperature, 29°C; and the population, 47,898 people (1985 estimate). Quibdó is a center of river traffic in a region where *gold, *silver, and *platinum mining have been important. It was first founded by the *Jesuits Francisco de Orta and Pedro Cáceres in 1654 with the name Citará, and then refounded on its present site by Manuel Cañizales in 1690. It was formally given the name San Francisco de Quibdó by Francisco Berro in 1702, and the name Quibdó came from an Indian chieftain of the region. The city was made the capital of Chocó on January 15, 1948.

QUIJANO OTERO–CASTRO TREATY OF 1880. Signed December 25, by José María Quijano Otero, Colombia, and José María Castro, Costa Rica. It was an agreement by which the two nations submitted their boundary disputes to arbitration. On September 11, 1900, the President of France issued a judgment that gave Colombia control of the archipelago of

San *Andrés y Providencia, although other points were not satisfactorily settled.

QUIMBAYA STYLE. A type of pre-conquest Indian *goldwork typical of the *Quindío region. It is characterized by the use of gold, *silver, *platinum, and *copper alloys, restrained decoration, and the employment of multiple techniques, including casting by the lost-wax process, molding, hammering, and soldering. Plating, gilding, repoussé, false filigree, and three-dimensional forms with smoothly flowing contours are common. Both anthropomorphic and zoomorphic figures show extremely realistic details, and there is great variety in the types of body ornaments used. The term "Quimbaya" is also used to describe pre-conquest ceramic work found in western Colombia. In this case it is a generic term, not well defined, encompassing a number of individual styles.

QUIMBAYAS. A group of Indians inhabiting parts of the Departments of *Risaralda, *Caldas, *Quindío, and *Valle del Cauca in 1500. The Quimbayas lived in sedentary villages with recognized social classes ruled by numerous local chieftains. Their economy was based on agriculture (*corn, *potatoes, beans), *fishing, and commerce in *gold, *salt, textiles, and sisal. There is some evidence that the Quimbayas practiced ritual cannibalism. Comparable in many ways to the *Chibcha and *Tairona Indians, the Quimbayas were conquered, starting in 1540, by Jorge *Robledo and his subordinates. Although the Quimbayas offered relatively little resistance at first, they rebelled in 1542; nevertheless, by some accounts, they were virtually eliminated as a distinct ethnic group by 1557.

QUINDIO, Cordillera del. The "Mountains of the Quindío," a part of the *Cordillera Central. The pass of the Quindío was a vital communications link, important historically as one of the few accessible passages across the central mountains. The Nevado del Quindío, covering parts of the Departments of *Quindío, *Risaralda, and *Tolima, is located at 4° 40′N, 75° 25′W and is frequently said to be 5,150 meters high, although recent measurements list it as only 4,800 meters.

QUINDIO, Departamento del. Located in central Colombia on the western slopes of the *Cordillera Central, the Quindío is the smallest department in the republic, covering only 1,845 square kilometers lying between 4° 4' and 4° 44'N latitude, and 75° 24' and 75° 52'W longitude. The terrain is mountainous, with 20 square kilometers in tropical climate; 1,100 in temperate zones; 404 in cold; and 321 in wasteland. Major rivers include San Juan, Quindío, Barbas, Barragán, Rojo, Santo Domingo, Roble, Espejo, Navarro, Boquerón, and La Vieja. The population is 375,762 people (1985 estimate), with a population density of 203.7 people per square kilometer. *Armenia is the capital city. *Coffee cultivation is a primary economic activity. Based on DANE, *Colombia estadística 86,* other principal agricultural products, with tonnage produced in 1984, include plantains, 227,200 tons; *yuca,* 82,500; *potatoes, 4,350; sorghum, 3,388; *sugar, 2,300; *cacao, 130; beans, 126; soybeans, 100; and peanuts, 30. *Livestock slaughtered in the department in 1984 included 49,908 head of cattle and 27,334 hogs. There is some mining, especially of *gold, *silver, and *copper. In 1983 there were forty-three businesses employing ten or more people. Although the area was technically conquered by *Belalcázar, *Robledo, Francisco de Cieza, and others in the 16th century, the region was largely unsettled until the *Antioqueño* colonization of the 19th century. Taking its name from the well-known pass through the Cordillera Central, the department was created in 1966 from territory previously in the Department of *Caldas.

QUININE. *Quina,* as it is called in Spanish, is an anti-malaria drug obtained from the bark of the *cinchona tree. The export of the bark of wild trees became important in *Tolima and *Cundinamarca in the 1850s, but from the 1870s *Santander sought to develop cinchona exports to compensate for the decline in the *tobacco industry. The value of Colombia's cinchona and processed quinine exports grew from 3% of the total exports in the late 1860s to 32% in 1881 shortly before the bubble burst.

QUINQUENIO. A term applied to the five-year authoritarian government of General Rafael *Reyes, 1904-1909.

QUINTADA, La, see: QUINTIN LAME, Manuel

QUINTA DE BOLIVAR. Literally, the "Garden of *Bolívar," but, more precisely, a private estate. Built around 1800 at the then edge of *Bogotá, it was the residence of Simón Bolívar, 1826-1830. The house and grounds were declared a national monument in 1918 and presently serve as a public museum. See also: BOLIVAR'S SWORD, Theft of

QUINTIN LAME, Manuel, 1880-1967. Advocate of Indian rights, born on the *hacienda* San Isidro (about 50 kilometers east of *Popayán, October 26; died Ortega (*Tolima), October 7. Although baptized Juan Quintín Lame, he always used the name Manuel, and gave his birth date as October 31, 1883. He served in the *army for the government, 1899-1904, and claimed to have achieved the rank of lieutenant colonel. However, he is better known for his militant opposition to what he considered the neglect or persecution of Indian groups by the state. He was active in organizing Indian groups in the Department of *Cauca, 1910-1921, especially among the *Páez Indians, who named Quintín Lame chief, representative, and defender of the rights of the Indians of Pitayó, Jambaló, Puracé, Poblazón, Calibío, Pandiguando, and other towns in the Cauca. During this period, which came to be known as *La Quintada,* he was accused of leading at least four rebellions between 1914-1917. He was imprisoned from 1915-1916, although he was released after a formal investigation. Nevertheless, he spent 1917-1921 in jail as a result of an Indian-government conflict at Inzá. In 1922 he shifted his activities to Tolima, where he founded San José de Indias (formerly Llanogrande) and was active in demanding *resguardo* and other Indian rights for the next two decades. Quintín Lame believed in the racial purity and the superiority of Indians over whites. He defended Indian claims in land disputes and sought to improve working conditions. Although a militant defender of Indian rights, he rejected Marxist ideologies and refused to collaborate with José Gonzalo Sánchez and Eutiquio Timoté in the 1930s. He was the author of *Los pensamientos del Indio que se educó dentro de las selvas colombianas* (1939).

QUINTIN LAME GUERRILLAS, see: COMANDO QUINTIN LAME; COORDINADORA GUERRILLERA "SIMON BOLIVAR"

QUITO REBELLION. August 10, 1809. A protest movement preliminary to the *independence movement, it had repercussions in *Bogotá, the capital of the *viceroyalty, where a *Junta of Notables was called to discuss possible responses. The deliberations in Bogotá eventually resulted in the *Memorial de

Agravios (Declaration of Grievances), November 20, 1809. The events in Quito increased tension between the *creoles and the Spanish officials in *New Granada.

-R-

RADICAL OLYMPUS, see: OLIMPO RADICAL

RADICALS. A term applied at various times to doctrinaire *Liberals. The term was used especially for the supporters of Vicente *Azuero in the elections of 1836 and 1840; the *Gólgotas in the 1850s; and those who opposed the *Independent Liberals and the *Regeneration during the period of 1870-1900.

RADIO BROADCASTING. Radio telegraph was introduced in Colombia in 1915, and a system of transmitters belonging to the Marconi Wireless Company was offically inaugurated by President Pedro Nel *Ospina in Engatativá (4° 43'N, 7° 39'W, *Cundinamarca) on April 2, 1923. In addition to the station (Morato) in Engatativá, transmitters operated from *Barranquilla, *Cali, *Medellín, *Cúcuta, and *San Andrés y Providencia. Public radio broadcasting was officially inaugurated by President *Abadía Méndez on August 7, 1929, from Station HJN (Radio Nacional). The station was under the direction of Daniel Samper Ortega, and Luis Ramírez Arana was technical chief. The first privately owned station was begun on December 8, 1929, as Station KHD (later known as La Voz de Barranquilla). Elías Pellet Buitrago was the first owner-operator, although much of the advanced preparation is credited to Jesús Amórtegui. The first commercial radio station was established by Gustavo Uribe Thornschmidt and Roberto Jaramillo in January 1930, as Station HKF (Colombian Radio and Electric Corporation). Other stations were founded in 1930 by Jesús Amórtegui, HKA (Voz Colombiana); Pompillo Sánchez, KHB (Voz de *Tunja); Antonio Barona, HKJ (Cali); Miguel A. Rivas, HKK (Cali); Alberto Hoyos, HKT (*Manizales); and the Observatorio Meterelógico de San Bartolomé de la Merced, Station HKE. Commercial broadcasting was relatively limited until President *Olaya Herrera issued Decree No. 423, February 28, 1931, which greatly facilitated licensing and operation. A 1932 estimate indicated that there were about 5,000 radio receivers in all of Colombia. By 1952 this had grown to 500,000, increasing to 2,084,287 in 1959, and to 5,250,000 in 1964. According to Reynaldo Pareja, the growth of radio broadcasting can also be gauged by the increasing number of transmitters within the national territory: 17 in 1934, 44 in 1939, 70 in 1941, 109 in 1955, and 344 in 1977. The three most important national broadcasting systems (*cadenas*) were founded between 1948 and 1956. These were the Cadena Radial Colombiana (CARACOL), established September 1, 1948; Radio Cadena Nacional (R.C.N.), founded February 11, 1949; and TODELAR, organized 1952-1956 by Bernadro Tobón de la Roche. On political issues, R.C.C. and TOLEDAR have tended to favor the *Conservative Party, while CARACOL has been inclined to the *Liberal Party. See also: TELEVISION

RAILROADS.   *New Granada's most important communication link was the *Panama Road, a mule trail from Nombre de Dios (9° 34′N, 79° 28′W) across the Isthmus to *Panama City. This connection between the Caribbean and the Pacific carried all of Spain's trade with the west coast, from Chile to California, during the colonial period. It was not surprising that the standard-gauge (4 ft., 8.5 in.) *Panama Railroad that replaced it as the main commercial link was Colombia's first railroad. After its completion in 1855, no further railroads were built for another fourteen years. New lines, built when agricultural exports demanded improved transportation facilities, were all narrow gauge. This lowered the construction costs and permitted sharper turns in the mountains. Unfortunately, some were meter gauge and others three feet. Uniformity was not imposed until 1924 when the narrower yard gauge (.914m) was made standard. A start was made in 1869 with the *Bolívar Railroad, which connected *Barranquilla with its seaport, and three years later the *Santa Marta Railway was begun to link the port of that name with Colombia's great fluvial artery, the *Magdalena River. Then the growing importance of *coffee stimulated the improved transportation in the interior highlands. The *Antioquia Railroad between *Medellín and Puerto Berrío (6° 29′N, 74° 24′W) was begun in 1875, the *Pacific Railroad connecting *Cali and the Pacific in 1878, and the *Cúcuta Railroad (providing an outlet for *Norte de Santander) in 1880. The 1880s saw the first lines based in *Bogotá: the *Cundinamarca Railroad, the *Girardot Railroad, and the

*Northern Railroad. The *Dorada Railway connected *Honda
and La Dorada on the Magdalena, and the *Calamar Railroad
was intended to replace the *Dique Canal. After the *Tolima
Railroad and the *Southern Railroad in 1892, there were no
completely new projects until the *Northeastern Railroad in
1921, but Colombia's rugged terrain ensured that nearly all the
lines took years to build. The *Tolima line from *Ibagué to
*Ambalema took from 1893 until 1930. Between 1913 and
1926 track mileage doubled; between 1920 and 1927 it increased 87%, from 1,218 kilometers to 2,281. Construction
was made possible largely by foreign capital: American in the
case of the Panama line, British for most of the rest. British
investment grew from £1,170,000 in two lines in 1875 to
£6,139,000 in eleven out of fourteen lines in 1913. When
*foreign investment dried up in the Great Depression of the
1930s, railroad building practically ceased, and Colombia was
left with a number of unconnected systems. To some degree
this was intentional because of the heavy reliance on river
transport. The Pacific and Antioquia lines were linked up by
the 1946 completion of the *Western Trunk Railroad, but the
long-dreamed-of plan to integrate all the major lines into one
national network was achieved only with the 1961 completion
of the *Atlantic Railroad. This great engineering feat, which
took nine years, was financed by the World Bank. The Colombian rail system has no international connection. The isolated
Cúcuta Railroad did have direct cross-border traffic onto
Venezuelan tracks, but the line closed down in 1958. The
*Nariño Railroad, originally intended to lead into Ecuador,
was never completed. Administratively, Colombian railroads
were joined by the 1954 establishment of a single state
enterprise to take over and run them, the *Ferrocarriles
Nacionales de Colombia.

   The present-day network is a Y-shaped system, pivoted on
*Puerto Berrío. From there the tail of the Y stretches north-
ward along the course of the Magdalena, past *Puerto Wilches
(where a branch leads off to *Bucaramanga) to the Caribbean at
*Santa Marta. The Y's southeastern arm continues up the
Magdalena Valley through La Dorada (where there is a branch
to Ambalema) to *Bogotá. From Bogotá, branches radiate
south to Girardot, north to Barbosa (6° 26′N, 75° 20′W), and
northeast to *Paz del Río. The southwestern arm of the Y
crosses the mountains from Puerto Berrío to *Medellín and
then runs up the Cauca Valley to *Cali and over the *Western
Cordillera to the Pacific at *Buenaventura.

There are still only 3,700 rail kilometers as compared with ten times that length—38,200—in highways. Passenger traffic reached its peak, approximately 9 million people, in 1962. Although it has been declining since then, in part because of poor maintenance, the system remains important. There were about 2 million passengers in 1970. Rails were still moving about 18% of Colombia's freight traffic in 1975.

RAMADA, La.   Indian site. See also: TAIRONAS

RAMIREZ, José Tomás.   Builder of the *COLISEO RAMIREZ, Bogotá's first theater.

RAMIREZ VILLAMIZAR, Eduardo, 1923-.   Artist, sculptor; born *Pamplona (Norte de Santander). Ramírez Villamizar studied architecture and design at the *Universidad Nacional. He is known for his abstract art, which stresses pure form with a sparsity of color. His works have been shown at many places in the United States and Europe as well as Latin America.

RAQUIRA.   A small village (689 people in 1985) located at 5° 32'N, 73° 38'W in the Cordillera Oriental in the Department of *Boyacá. The village, approximately 75 kilometers from *Tunja, was a pre-conquest subordinate of the *Zaque of Hunza, and has been known for its ceramic work from pre-Hispanic times to the present.

RAYO AFFAIR.   Occurred in 1867 when the Peruvian steamship Rayo was released in New York after representatives of the *Mosquera administration declared it to be a Colombian ship. Mosquera acted in accordance with the secret treaty he had negotiated with Peru, August 28, 1866. News of the affair and the arrival of the Rayo at *Cartagena exposed the secret diplomacy and led to charges of abuse of authority against Mosquera. He was removed from office on May 23, and the secret treaty was repudiated. After three years of negotiations while the Rayo sat in Cartagena Bay, the ship was returned to Peruvian officials.

RAYO REYES, Omar, 1929-.   Painter, engraver, caricaturist; born January 20 in Roldanillo (*Valle del Cauca). His works were exhibited in local shows 1945-1952, after which he traveled in Latin America and later studied in Mexico (1959-1960) before moving to New York in 1961.

He is well known in Colombia as a caricaturist and magazine illustrator. His more mature works include abstract geometric art, op art, and printmaking through what is called a process of intaglio. He was the founder of the Museo Rayo in Roldanillo.

REAL. A colonial and early-independence-period coin worth an eighth of a *peso,* although sums considerably larger than a *peso* were often expressed in *reales.* *Decimalization of the currency in 1857 involved introducing the *granadino* of ten *reales,* making the *real* worth ten *centavos.*

REBELLION OF 1830-1831. August 10 to April 28. General Rafael *Urdaneta attempted to establish a viable dictatorship but failed. The major military engagement of the period was the Battle of *Santuario. The dictatorship ended with the accords of *Juntas de Apulo, April 28.

REBELLION OF 1839, see: MINOR CONVENTS, Rebellion of the

REBELLION OF 1840-1842, see: SUPREME COMMANDERS, War of the

REBELLION OF 1851-1852. May 1851 to January 1852. A *Conservative rebellion, it was centered mainly in *Nariño, *Valle del Cauca, *Antioquia, *Tolima, and *Cundinamarca. Major military engagements occurred at *Buesaco, *Garra-pata, *Gachetá, and *Rionegro.

REBELLION OF 1854. The dictatorship of General José María *Melo, April 17 to December 4. Major military engagements included *Zipaquirá, *Tíquisa, *Pamplona, *Palmira, *Bosa Bridge, and *Bogotá.

REBELLION OF 1859-1862. Begun first as civil wars within the states of *Santander (1859), *Bolívar (1859), and *Cauca (1860), the war became a general revolt against the *Ospina administration in 1860. Significant military engagements included La *Concepción, *Oratorio, *Hormezaque, *Tunja, El *Derrumbado, *Manizales, *Segovia, *Bogotá, *Subachoque, *San Agustín (Bogotá), Los *Arboles, *Tulcán (Ecuador), and *Santa Bárbara de Cartago. General *Mosquera overthrew the government of the *Confederación Granadina in July 1861, culminating the only successful rebellion of the 19th century.

REBELLION OF 1876-1877. A *Conservative rebellion, July-April, it occurred in *Cauca, *Tolima, *Antioquia, *Santander, and elsewhere. Major military engagements included Los *Chancos, *Garrapata, La *Donjuana, and *Manizales.

REBELLION OF 1884-1885. August 17, 1884, to August 26, 1885. It was a *Liberal revolt that began first in *Santander and then spread throughout the nation. Major military engagements took place at *Sonsó, *Barranquilla, *Roldanillo, *Salamina, *Santa Bárbara de Cartago, *Cogotes, *Jericó, *Colón, *Cartagena, La *Humareda, *Neiva, and *Salado. The war was ended by the armistice of Los Guamos.

REBELLION OF 1895. January 22 to March 15. Unsuccessful *Liberal revolts occurred in *Cundinamarca, *Tolima, *Boyacá, *Panama, *Santander, and elsewhere. Major military engagements included La *Tribuna and *Enciso.

REBELLION OF 1899-1903, see: THOUSAND DAYS, War of the

REBELLION OF NEIVA, 1767. The rebellion during the month of July was an unsuccessful protest against tax collecting procedures and new regulations regarding *tobacco production. It was led by Juan Asencio Perdomo, who was arrested and imprisoned. He died in jail two years later.

REBELLION OF PASTO, see: PASTO CONSPIRACY

REBELLION OF QUITO, see: QUITO REBELLION

REBELLION OF THE COMUNEROS, see: COMUNEROS REVOLT

REBELLION OF THE MINOR CONVENTS, see: MINOR CONVENTS, Rebellion of the

REBELLION OF THE PORTUGUESE, see: PORTUGUESE REVOLT

REBELLIONS, see: GUERRILLA MOVEMENTS; PLOTS AND CONSPIRACIES; RIOTS

RECONQUISTA. The Spanish reconquest; the name given to the period from 1815-1819, when royalist forces attempted to suppress the *independence movements and restore the *viceroyalty.

RECOPILACION DE LEYES DE LOS REYNOS DE LAS INDIAS. The 1681 codification of the *LAWS OF THE INDIES.

RECOPILACION GRANADINA. A compilation of the national laws published in 1845. It was supplemented under Presidents *López and *Pérez and superseded completely by the *Codificación Nacional* after 1912.

RED BASTION. A socialist-inspired peasant settlement at Lomagrande in the Sinú region of the Department of *Córdoba in the 1920s. See also: ANDAMO, Vicente

RED CROSS. The Colombian Red Cross (Cruz Roja Colombiana) was founded in 1915.

REGENERATION. A movement spanning the years 1869-1900, most influential between 1877 and 1889. Headed by Rafael *Núñez, supported by the *Nationalists, the Regeneration attempted administrative reforms and internal improvements. It was responsible for the *Constitution of 1886.

REIGN OF TERROR. A term applied to various portions of the period from 1815-1819, when more than 300 patriot supporters were executed by the Spanish. It is applied especially to the year 1816 in *Bogotá, when General *Morillo established a military administration (*Consejo de Guerra Permanente), a tribunal to punish treason (*Consejo de Purificación), and a board of confiscations (*Junta de Secuestros), and executed such patriot leaders as Manuel Bernardo *Alvarez, Francisco José de *Caldas, Antonio *Villavicencio, Camilo *Torres, Liborio *Mejía, and Custodio *García Rovira. In addition, the *Inquisition was reestablished and priests were tried in military rather than ecclesiastical courts.

REINOSO. A term dating from the colonial period used to describe an inhabitant of the *Nuevo Reino de Granada. The term continued to be used with this meaning in Ecuador well into the 19th century. In Venezuela the term came to mean a person from Colombia, and in Colombian usage it described a person from the cold eastern highlands.

RELIGIOUS ORDERS, Feminine. At least ninety orders of religious women have established themselves in Colombia since 1573. According to the calculations of Gustavo Pérez and Isaac Wust, *La iglesia en Colombia, estructuras eclesiásticas* (Bogotá, 1961), there were 12,058 nuns in thirty-one different orders working in the nation in 1960. Of these, the Dominican Sisters of Charity of the Virgin of Tours and the Daughters of Charity of St. Vincent de Paul were the largest. Listed chronologically by date of founding and by Spanish name the feminine orders known to have existed in Colombia from 1573 to 1960 are as follows:

1573	Orden de *Santa Clara de Tunja
1583	Orden de Monjas Franciscanas de la Concepción (*Concepcionists)
1606	Orden de la Bienaventurada Virgen María del Monte Carmelo (Carmelitas Descalzas)
1645	Orden de Santa Inés de Montepuciano (*reestablished in 1865*)
1739	Religiosas Terciarias Recoletas de San Agustín (*added to the* Congregación Misioneras de María Agustinas Recoletas *in 1953*)
1783	Orden de la Compañía de María Nuestra Señora (Enseñanza)
1873	Hermanas de la Caridad Dominicanas de la Presentación de Tours
1880	Hermanas Terciarias Dominicanas de Santa Catalina de Sena
1882	Hijas de la Caridad de San Vicente de Paúl
1885	Hermanas Betlemitas Hijas del Sagrado Corazón de Jesús
1889	Congregación de Hermanitas de los Pobres
1890	Congregación de Nuestra Señora de la Caridad del Buen Pastor
1892	Orden de la Visitación de Santa María
1893	Congregación de las Hermanitas de los Ancianos Desamparados
1893	Congregación de las Hermanas Terciarias Franciscanas de María Inmaculada
1895	Congregación de las Hermanas Franciscanas Misioneras de María Auxiliadora
1897	Congregación de Hijas de María Auxiliadora
1897	Congregación de Hermanas de San José de Tarbes
1903	Congregación de Siervas del Santísimo y de la Caridad
1905	Congregación de Hijas de los Sagrados Corazones de Jesús y María
1905	Congregación de Religiosas Terciarias Capuchinas de la Sagrada Familia

1905	Congregación de Hijas de la Sabiduría
1907	Sociedad del Sagrado Corazón de Jesús
1907	Congregación de Hermanas de la Providencia y de la Inmaculada Concepción
1910	Congregación de Hermanas de la Sagrada Familia
1912	Congregación de las Hermanas de Santa Mariana de Jesús
1912	Congregación de Hermanitas de los Pobres de San Pedro Claver
1914	Congregación de Hermanas Misioneras de María Inmaculada y Santa Cantalina de Sena
1918	Congregación de Hermanas Siervas de Cristo Sacerdote
1918	Congregación de Siervas de la Sagrada Familia
1922	Instituto de Hermanas de San José de Gerona (Veladoras de Enfermos)
1925	Congregación de Hermanas Carmelitas Descalzas Misioneras
1929	Instituto de Religiosas Adoratrices, Esclavas del Santísimo Sacramento y de la Caridad
1929	Congregación de Misioneras Activas de Santa Teresita del Niño Jesús
1929	Congregación de Mercedarias del Santísimo Sacramento
1931	Congregación de Hermanas de la Caridad de Santa Ana
1932	Congregación de Hermanas de San Juan Evangelista
1934	Congregación de Religiosas Esclavas del Sagrado Corazón de Jesús
1936	Congregación de Siervas de María, Ministras de Enfermos
1937	Congregación de Hermanas del Niño Jesús Pobre
1937	Instituto de Hermanas Catequistas de María Inmaculada
1938	Congregación de Siervas del Sagrado Corazón de Jesús
1938	Congregación de Hijas de Nuestra Señora de Nazareth
1939	Congregación de Misioneras Contemplativas de Santa Teresita del Niño Jesús
1939	Compañía del Niño Dios
1939	Congregación de Hermanas Misioneras de Santa Rosa de Lima
1940	Congregación de las Hermanitas de la Asunción
1943	Congregación de las Hermanitas Agustinas Misioneras de Ultramar
1943	Congregación de las Hermanas de la Anunciación
1943	Congregación de las Misioneras de María Agustinas Recoletas
1945	Pío Sodalicio de Hermanas del Rosario Perpétuo y de Santa Isabel de Hungría
1945	Pía Unión de Hermanas Misioneras de la Prensa Católica
1946	Congregación de Siervas de la Madre de Dios
1947	Congregación de Siervas de María Reparadora
1947	Congregación de Hijas del Corazón Misericordioso de María

1947	Sociedad de las Hijas del Corazón de María
1948	Congregación de Hermanas del Sagrado Corazón de María (Mary Mount)
1948	Pía Sociedad de Hijas de San Pablo
1949	Congregación de Hermanas Hospitalarias del Sagrado Corazón de Jesús
1950	Congregación de las Hermanas del Divino Salvador
1950	Instituto Apostólico de María Inmaculada para la Enseñanza
1950	Instituto de Hermanas Misioneras de la Consolata para las Misiones Extranjeras
1950	Sociedad Sacerdotal de la Santa Cruz y *Opus Dei*
1951	Congregación de Hermanitas de los Pobres de Maiquetía
1951	Congregación de Hijas de María Inmaculada para el Servicio Doméstico y Protección de la Joven
1951	Congregación de Hijas de Nuestra Señora de la Misericordia
1952	Congregación de Misioneras Hijas de la Sagrada Familia de Nazareth
1952	Congregación de Siervas del Santísimo Sacramento (Caracas)
1952	Congregación de las Hermanas Franciscanas Misioneras de María
1952	Instituto Secular Hijas de María Reina Apóstoles
1953	Instituto de Religiosas de Nuestra Señora de la Paz
1953	Obra Misionera de Jesús y María
1955	Congregación de Hijas de San José
1955	Congregación de Hermanas de San Francisco Javier
1955	Congregación de Religiosas Siervas de San José
1955	Pío Instituto de las Hijas de María, Religiosas Escolapias
1955	Fraternidad de las Hermanitas de Jesús (P. Foucauld)
1955	Congregación de Oblatas de Betania
1955	Asociación de Misioneras Seglares
1955	Congregación de Pías Discípulas del Divino Maestro
1956	Congregación de Hermanas de San Antonio de Padua
1957	Congregación de Hermanas del Santo Angel de la Guarda
1957	Hermanas Misioneras Claretianas
1957	Hermanas Hospitalarias del Sagrado Corazón
1958	Congregación de Hermanas de la Providencia y la Inmaculada Concepción
1960	Congregación de las Hermanas de la Caridad (Cardenal Concha)
1960	Congregación de Misioneras Franciscanas de María
1960	Congregación de Siervas del Sagrado Corazón de Jesús y de los Pobres
1960	Congregación de Hijas de Cristo Rey
1960	Congregación de Hermanas Redentoristas

RELIGIOUS ORDERS, Masculine. Since 1509, at least thirty-four orders of religious men have been established in Colombia. According to Gustavo Pérez and Isaac Wust, *La iglesia en Colombia, estructuras eclesiásticas* (Bogotá, 1961), the total number of men in religious orders in the nation in 1960 was 3,526, including monks and lay brothers. The Brothers of Christian Schools and the Society of Jesus (*Jesuits) were the two largest orders at that time. Listed chronologically by the date of founding in Colombia, and by Spanish name, the masculine religious orders known to have existed in Colombia from 1509 to 1954 are as follows:

1510	Orden de Frailes Menores (*Franciscans)
1529	Orden de Hermanos Predicadores (*Dominicans)
1537	Orden de Santa María de la Merced de la Redención de Cautivos (*Mercedarians)
1575	Orden Hermanos Ermitaños Agustinos (*Augustinians)
1596	Orden Hospitalaria de San Juan de Dios
1604	Compañía de Jesús (*Jesuits)
1604	Orden de Recoletos de San Agustín (Candelarios)
1646	Orden de Frailes Menores (*Capuchins)
1824	Instituto del Oratorio de San Felipe Neri (Oratorianos)
1870	Congregación de la Misión (Lazaristas o Vicentinos)
1883	Congregación de Jesús y María (Eudistas)
1884	Congregación del Santísimo Redentor (Redentoristas)
1889	Instituto de Hermanos Maristas de la Enseñanza
1890	Congregación de los Hermanos de las Escuelas Cristianas
1890	Pía Sociedad Salesiana
1895	Sociedad del Divino Salvador (Salvatorianos)
1903	Compañía de María Montfortiana (Montfortianos)
1909	Congregación de Misioneros Hijos del Corazón Inmaculado de María (Claretianos)
1911	Orden de los Hermanos de la Bienaventurada Virgen María del Monte Carmelo (Carmelitas Descalzos)
1924	Instituto Español de San Francisco Javier para Misiones Extranjeras (Misioneros de Burgos)
1927	Instituto de Misiones Extranjeras de Yarumal (Padres Javieres)
1927	Congregación de Clérigos Descalzos de la Cruz y Pasión de Nuestro Señor Jesucristo (Pasionistas)
1928	Congregación de Religiosos Terciarios Capuchinos de Nuestra Señora de los Dolores (Terciarios Capuchinos)
1946	Agustinos de la Asunción (Asuncionistas)
1947	Pía Sociedad de San Pablo Apóstol (Padres de San Pablo)

1947	Instituto de la Consolata
1948	Orden de los Clérigos Regulares Pobres de la Madre de Dios de las Escuelas Pías (Escolapios)
1949	Sacerdotes de San Sulpicio
1950	Sociedad Sacerdotal de la Santa Cruz y *Opus Dei*
1951	Congregación de Presbíteros del Santísimo Sacramento (Padres Sacramentinos)
1952	Pía Unión de Jesús Adolescente
1952	Hermanos de Jesús Nazareno
1954	Fraternidad Sacerdotal
1954	Orden de San Benito (Benedictinos)

REPARTIMIENTO. A system whereby Crown officials regulated the Indian work force, also called the *mita*. The *Indians were required to work for Spanish overlords as many as 300 days a year. According to law, the work assignments were to be on a rotational basis and the Indians were to be salaried employees, but numerous abuses occurred in practice. Forced labor was prohibited as early as 1530 in regulations published by Friar Tomás de *Ortiz, "protector and defender of the Indians of *Santa Marta." The Crown prohibited forced levies in 1542, 1549, and again in 1581, but it was never successful in eliminating them. Indian service in *New Granada's mines was ordered by President Antonio *González, 1590-1597, and reaffirmed under President *Borja, 1612, 1616, and so on. The *repartimiento* became the predominant form of Indian service in the 17th and 18th centuries following the decline of the *encomienda*. See also: MITA

REPUBLICA, La. A Bogotá daily *newspaper founded March 1, 1954, under the auspices of Mariano *Ospina Pérez, Hernán Jaramillo Ocampo, José Restrepo Restrepo, Luis Córdoba Mariño, and Alvaro de Angulo. Manuel Mosquera Garcés served as director of the paper until 1956, and Silvio Villegas from 1956 to 1966. Former President Ospina Pérez maintained his connection with the publication until shortly before his death. *La República* has been described as "the workingman's daily" and has earned a reputation as a major source of economic news. It was one of the few papers not subjected to press censorship under the *Rojas Pinilla dictatorship. Circulation is estimated at 20,000 copies.

REPUBLICA DE COLOMBIA, 1819-1830, see: REPUBLIC DE GRAN COLOMBIA, 1819-1830

REPUBLICA DE COLOMBIA, 1886-1991. A centralistic republic, established by the *Constitution of 1886, it was originally composed of the departments of *Antioquia, *Bolívar, *Boyacá, *Cauca, *Cundinamarca, *Magdalena, *Panama, *Santander, and *Tolima. The name remained constant after 1886, although Panama separated itself from Colombia in 1903.

REPUBLICA DE COLOMBIA, 1991-. A unitary but decentralized republic established by the *CONSTITUTION OF 1991. For a list of the heads of state since 1810, see: PRESIDENTS OF COLOMBIA. See also: ADMINISTRATIVE DIVISIONS; AREA; BORDERS; CLIMATIC ZONES; ECONOMY, The; GEOGRAPHY; HOLIDAYS, Public; POPULATION; TIME

REPUBLICA DE GRAN COLOMBIA, 1819-1830. Gran Colombia is a name normally applied to the Republic of Colombia composed of parts of present-day Venezuela, Colombia, Ecuador, and *Panama, 1819-1830, to distinguish it from the modern *República de Colombia (1886-1991). It was created by the *Congress of Angostura (1819) and defined by the *Congress of Cúcuta and the *Constitution of 1821. There were twelve departments (Apure, Azuay, *Boyacá, *Cauca, *Cundinamarca, Ecuador, Guayaquil, Istmo, *Magdalena, Orinoco, Venezuela, and Zulia) and twenty-six provinces (see: MAP: TERRITORIAL DIVISIONS OF GRAN COLOMBIA). Although not legally superseded until the *Constitution of 1830, Gran Colombia was disintegrating after 1827. Simón *Bolívar was the President of the republic; Francisco de Paula *Santander, Vice-President; General José Antonio Páez, chief military commandant in Venezuela; and General Juan José *Flores, the major army commander in Ecuador (after 1827). Although the term "Gran Colombia" is said to have been coined by historians after the 1819-1830 period, it is used throughout this dictionary in keeping with what has become customary usage.

REPUBLICA DE NUEVA GRANADA. Established by the *Constitution of 1832, superseded by the *Constitution of 1858, the Republic of *New Granada included the territories of present-day Colombia and *Panama. Its presidents were General Francisco de Paula *Santander (1832-1837); José Ignacio de *Márquez (1837-1841); Generals Pedro A. *Herrán (1841-1845), T. C. de *Mosquera (1845-1849), José Hilario *López

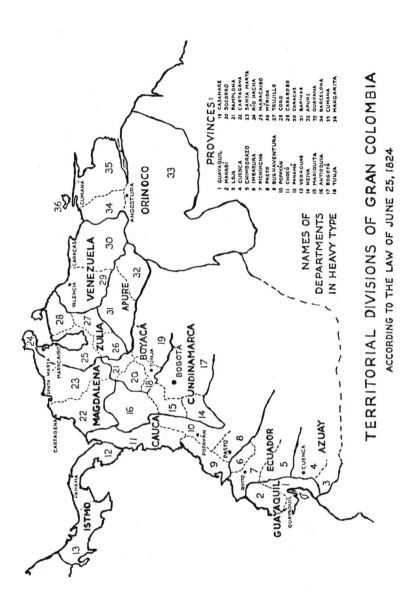

TERRITORIAL DIVISIONS OF GRAN COLOMBIA

ACCORDING TO THE LAW OF JUNE 25, 1824

NAMES OF
DEPARTMENTS
IN HEAVY TYPE

PROVINCES:

1 GUAYAQUIL
2 MANABÍ
3 LOJA
4 CUENCA
5 CHIMBORAZO
6 IMBABURA
7 PICHINCHA
8 PASTO
9 BUENAVENTURA
10 POPAYÁN
11 CHOCÓ
12 PANAMÁ
13 VERAGUAS
14 NEIVA
15 MARIQUITA
16 ANTIOQUIA
17 BOGOTÁ
18 TUNJA
19 CASANARE
20 SOCORRO
21 PAMPLONA
22 CARTAGENA
23 SANTA MARTA
24 RÍO HACHA
25 MARACAIBO
26 MÉRIDA
27 TRUJILLO
28 CORO
29 CARABOBO
30 CARACAS
31 BARINAS
32 APURE
33 GUAYANA
34 BARCELONA
35 CUMANÁ
36 MARGARITA

(1849-1853), and José María *Obando (1853-1854). Manuel María *Mallarino was acting President, 1855-1857, and Mariano *Ospina Rodríguez was President in 1858 when the *Confederación Granadina was formed.

REPUBLICAN GENERATION. The group of cultural leaders who, in the terms of Abel Naranjo Villegas, developed or were prominent from 1905 to 1920. This coincides with the Republican Generation of Ernesto Cortés Ahumada, who uses 1900 as the key date for this group. According to Naranjo Villegas, the Republican Generation was characterized by intellectual skepticism and an experiential and intuitive sense of living. Representative figures of the generation include Miguel *Abadía Méndez, Aristóbulo Archila, Miguel Arroyo Díez, Gerardo Arrubla, Eduardo *Caballero Calderón, Ramón Eduardo Lemaitre, José Joaquín Gómez, Max Grillo, Jesús María Henao, Alejandro López, Luis María *Mora, Mariano Ospina Vásquez, Carlos E. *Restrepo, Eduardo Rodríguez Piñeres, José Asunción *Silva, Clímaco Soto Borda, Carlos Arturo Torres, and Guillermo *Valencia. See also: GENERATIONS

REPUBLICAN SCHOOL, see: ESCUELA REPUBLICANA

REPUBLICAN UNION, see: UNION REPUBLICANA

RESGUARDOS. A term designating lands communally held by *Indians; an institution somewhat analogous to Indian reservations in the United States. *Resguardos,* or lands allotted to an Indian community, were created in *New Granada by decree of President Antonio *González in 1593. During most of the 19th century, reform legislation attempted to eliminate these corporately controlled lands in favor of personal private property. This well-intentioned effort worsened rather than improved Indian living standards. After 1890, the emphasis returned to protection of the Indian *resguardos,* which are now supervised by the *División de Asuntos Indígenas. In 1964, official estimates showed 79,991 of Colombia's Indians living in some 70 *resguardos.* Within a *resguardo,* Indian lands were often divided into three parts: one for allocation to individual families, one for public works, and one for common pasture. Textile factories (*obrajes*) might be found on the *resguardo,* and portions of the land might be rented to persons outside the Indian community as well.

RESIDENCIA. The "Residence." In colonial Spanish America, the Residence was a review of administrative actions required by law for royal officials at the end of their terms. The *juez de residencia,* or judge, received complaints against the departing official and determined whether he was to be held responsible for any misconduct in office. The Residence served the same function as the *Visita,* but it differed in the fact that the former was predictable while the latter was generally unexpected.

RESTREPO, José Manuel, 1781-1863. Lawyer, statesman, active in patriot causes from 1810; born Envigado (*Antioquia), December 31; died *Bogotá, April 1. Restrepo was a member of the Congress of the *Provincias Unidas, the *Congress of Cúcuta, and the *Congreso Admirable, as well as Minister of Interior, 1821-1830, but he is best remembered as a diarist (*Diario político y militar . . . ,* 1819-1858) and historian (*Historia de la revolución de Colombia,* 1740-1832, and *Historia de la Nueva Granada,* 1832-1854).

RESTREPO RESTREPO, Carlos Eugenio, 1867-1937. Educator, legislator, journalist, diplomat, President of Colombia 1910-1914; born *Medellín, September 12; died Medellín, July 6. He was a leading spirit of the *Unión Republicana, 1909-1910, Minister of Government for President *Olaya Herrera, and ambassador to the *Vatican. His administration authorized publication of the *Codificación nacional,* 1912; favored protection of industry and *petroleum development; promoted programs for national hygiene and the prevention of tropical diseases; and provided retirement benefits for public school teachers. It also engaged in negotiations leading to the *Urrutia-Thomson Treaty of 1914.

REVOLLO BRAVO, Mario, 1919-. Archbishop of Bogotá; born June 15 in Genoa, Italy. He was educated at the Pontificia Universitas Gregoriana and the Instituto Bíblico, both in Rome, and the Seminario Mayor in *Bogotá. He was ordained on October 31, 1943, and appointed Auxiliary Bishop in Bogotá in 1973. He also served as Archbishop of Nueva Pamplona and was President of the Colombian Episcopal Conference from 1978 to 1984. He became Archbishop of Bogotá in 1984.

REVOLUTIONARY SOCIALIST PARTY, see: PARTIDO SOCIALISTA REVOLUCIONARIO

REYES, Rafael, 1850-1921. General, legislator, explorer, diplomat, President-Dictator, 1904-1909, the *quinquenio.* Born Santa Rosa de Viterbo (*Boyacá), October 24; died *Bogotá, February 16. General Reyes served as Minister of Development and was representative to France, Switzerland, Great Britain, Costa Rica, and El Salvador, but lived abroad in exile most of his life after 1909. He was elected President in 1904, but at the close of *Congress, 1904, he created his own extra-legal National Assembly (*Asamblea Nacional) through which he ruled. His slogans were "Peace, concord, and work" and "Less politics, more administration." He formed a bipartisan cabinet, 1904, and sanctioned the Acto Reformatorio No. 8, April 13, 1905, and Law 42 of April 28, 1905, which provided for representation of political minorities. He further sought to reduce political factionalism by professionalization of the *armed forces. Economically, his government adopted policies aimed at sound fiscal administration, *currency stabilization, restoration of the *gold standard, and reestablishment of foreign credit. It also encouraged *railroad construction, river transportation, and export agriculture. Reyes initiated an unpopular territorial reorganization, 1908-1909, and conducted equally unpopular negotiations with the United States over *Panama. Public pressure and assassination threats forced his resignation on June 13, 1909. General Reyes was also known for his exploration of the *Amazon region and travel accounts, such as *A través de la América del Sur, exploraciones de los hermanos Reyes* (Mexico and Barcelona, 1902) and *Las dos Américas; excursiones por varios países de las dos Américas* (New York, 1914).

RIBERO, Juan de, 1681-1736. A *Jesuit missionary, he was the author of *Historia de las misiones de los llanos de Casanare y de los ríos Orinoco y Meta,* first published in *Bogotá, 1883.

RICARDO FRANCO FRONT. Militant, Marxist-oriented *guerrilla group organized in 1983 as a dissident offshoot of the *Fuerzas Armadas Revolucionarias de Colombia (FARC). Major leaders of the group, which operated largely in the Departments of *Cauca and *Valle del Cauca, were Javier Delgado (alias José Fedor Rey) and Hernando Pizarro Leongómez (d. 1986), a brother of Carlos *Pizarro Leongómez, and Omar González. The group, named after a FARC member killed in action in the *Magdalena River valley, staged its own independent actions and cooperated with parts of the *Movimiento Diecinueve de Abril and the *Comando Quintín Lame,

1984-1985, before suffering a series of military reversals and an internal purge of 150 to 200 of its own members known as the Tacueyo massacre. The Front refused to sign the peace agreements offered by the *Betancur government and joined the *Coordinadora Guerrillera "Simón Bolívar" in 1985. It was expelled from the latter, however, in December of that year as a result of the Tacueyo executions. See also: GUERRILLA MOVEMENTS

RICAURTE, Antonio, 1786-1814.   Captain; patriot military officer with *Nariño and *Bolívar, 1812-1814. Born Villa de *Leiva (Boyacá), June 10. He joined the patriot cause in 1810 and participated in the *Campaña Admirable in 1813. Charged with defending an ammunition depot during the Battle of *San Mateo (Venezuela), March 25, he ordered the small patriot force to withdraw as larger Spanish forces moved in to take control of the supplies. Ricaurte sacrificed himself by setting fire to the ammunition, which exploded, leaving the Spanish in disarray just as they were about to seize control.

RIGHTS OF MAN, The.   Customary way of referring to the *Declaration of the Rights of Man and of the Citizen (Déclaration des Droits de l'Homme)*, adopted by the Constituent Assembly of France on August 27, 1789. The *Declaration* asserted that human beings were entitled to liberty, equality, property, security, freedom of opinion, and fairness in taxation. Citizens had the right to resist oppression and illegal imprisonment, and public officials were held accountable for their actions. *Rights of Man* was a closely related title used by Thomas Paine in 1791 for his two-volume discussion of the *Declaration* and the French Revolution. The text of the original document was translated into Spanish as the *Declaración de los derechos del hombre y del ciudadano* and published in Bogotá by Antonio Nariño in 1793. See also: NARIÑO, Antonio; TERTULIA

RIO DE JANEIRO, Treaty of.   Signed May 24, 1934, in Rio de Janeiro, Brazil. The treaty contained an apology from Peru for the *Leticia Dispute, a reaffirmation of the *Lozano-Salomón Treaty of 1922, and provisions for negotiating treaties regarding customs, commerce, river navigation, settlement, transportation, and policing of the frontiers.

RIO PALO, Battle of, see: PALO RIVER, Battle of the

RIOFRIO, Battle of. May 4-5, 1841, Huila. General Joaquín *Posada Gutiérrez, for the government, defeated rebel forces under Colonel Pedro Antonio Sánchez during the War of the *Supreme Commanders, 1840-1842.

RIOHACHA. Capital of La *Guajira, located at 11° 33'N, 72° 55'W, on the Caribbean Sea at the mouth of the Ranchería River at the foot of the *Sierra Nevada de Santa Marta. The altitude is 3 meters; average temperature, 28°C; and population, 75,584 people (1985 estimate). Riohacha, founded in 1545, serves as a local center for agriculture, commerce, and fishing. It was part of the Department of *Magdalena until Guajira became a separate intendancy in 1954, and it became capital of the department in 1964. Although a seaport, Riohacha does not have a harbor that permits major maritime vessels.

RIONEGRO. Rural community in the Department of *Antioquia, located at 6° 9'N, 75° 23'W, most often remembered as the site of the 1863 constitutional convention (see: RIONEGRO, Convention of). Altitude is 2,120 meters; average temperature, 17°C; and the population, 32,804 people (1985 estimate). Rionegro is essentially an agricultural and commercial center with some light industries (food processing and textiles). The city was founded in 1663.

RIONEGRO, Battle of. September 10, 1851, *Antioquia. General Tomás *Herrera, for the government, defeated the rebel forces of *Conservative General Eusebio Borrero. It was the last major engagement in the *rebellion of 1851-1852.

RIONEGRO, Convention of. Constitutional assembly, February 4 to May 19, 1863, at *Rionegro, Antioquia. The convention was overwhelmingly *Liberal in ideology and politics with little *Conservative representation. It drew up the *Constitution of 1863 and elected General T. C. de *Mosquera provisional President until 1864.

RIOTS, see: BOGOTAZO; DAYS OF MAY; PANAMA RIOT, 1856; PARO CIVICO DE 1977; TRECEMARCISTAS

RISARALDA, Departamento de. Located in central western Colombia on the *Cauca River between the *Cordilleras Occidental and Central, the department covers 4,140 square kilometers between 4° 39' and 5° 30'N latitude, and 75° 23' and 76° 18'W longitude. The terrain is mountainous, with 366 square kilometers in tropical climate; 2,157 temperate; 1,314 cold; and 303 wasteland. Major rivers include the Apía, Barbas, Campoalegre, Cañaveral, *Cauca, Guare, Guática, La Vieja, Llorando, Mapa, Quindío, and Risaralda. High points in the department include the Nevado de Santa Isabel, 5,100 meters; Tamaná, 4,200; Tatamá, 3,950; Caramanta, 3,900; Alto de Serna, 3,650; and Alto de las Palomas, 3,519. Population is 623,756 people (1985 estimate), with a population density of 150.7 people per square kilometer. The capital city is *Pereira. Risaralda is a major *coffee-producing region. According to DANE, *Colombia estadística 86,* other principal agricultural products, with tonnage produced in 1984, include *sugar, 663,000 tons; plantains, 103,800; *yuca, 19,600; *corn, 3,380; sorghum, 2,450; soybeans, 2,190; *cacao, 280; and beans, 245. Mineral production includes *gold, *silver, *lead, *zinc, and *coal mining. In 1983 there were 162 businesses employing 10 or more people in the department. Although the region was conquered by Jorge *Robledo and others in the 1500s, it was essentially unsettled until colonized by people from Antioquia (see: ANTIOQUEÑO COLONIZATION) and *Valle del Cauca in the 19th century. Risaralda was created on December 1, 1966, from territory formerly in the Department of *Caldas. Pereira, founded in 1863, is the eighth largest city in Colombia.

RIVER TRANSPORT, see: WATERWAYS

RIVERA, José Eustacio, 1888-1928. Poet, author, lawyer, diplomat, explorer of the *Llanos; born *Neiva, February 19; died New York, December 1. After receiving his law degree from the *Universidad Nacional in 1917, he practiced law. He lived and traveled in the Llanos, 1918-1920, with visits to *Sogamoso, Orocué (4° 48'N, 71° 20'W) and *Casanare), and again 1922-1923 (San Fernando de Atabapo, Manaos, and *Caquetá). He served on several official commissions and was a member of the delegation sent to the Conference on Immigration and Emigration in Havana, Cuba, in 1928. From Havana he went to New York where he eventually became ill and died. He was an advocate of the reform of working conditions in the *rubber trade and other laborers of the Llanos after 1923. His works include *Tierra de promisión* (1921) and fifty-six sonnets on the nature of tropical Colombia, but he is perhaps best remembered as the author of *La *vorágine* (1924), a novel describing the futile struggle of a small party against the rampant nature of the tropical rain forests in the *Vaupés.

ROADS, see: HIGHWAYS

ROBLEDO, Jorge, d. 1546. Conquistador. He was sent to southern Colombia from Peru in 1536 and explored much of the *Cauca Valley, 1539-1540. He founded *Anserma, 1539; authorized the founding of *Cartago, 1540; and established *Santa Fe de Antioquia, 1541. Arrested by Alonso de *Heredia in a jurisdictional dispute, 1542, he was sent to Spain to stand trial for usurpation of authority. Acquitted, he returned to *New Granada with his wife in 1544. He later contested the jurisdiction of *Antioquia and the northern Cauca Valley with *Belalcázar, who managed to capture and execute Robledo in 1546.

RODAS, Gaspar de, 1520-1607. Conquistador. He arrived in the Indies in 1540 and came to Colombia with *Belalcázar in 1541. He was the first Governor of *Dos Ríos, 1547-1579, and then the first Governor of *Antioquia, when royal administration was established there in 1579.

RODRIGUEZ, Manuel del Socorro, 1756-1819. Cuban-born director of the National Library (*Biblioteca Nacional) after 1790. He founded the *Tertulia *Eutropélica. The first major journalist of Colombia, he edited the *Papel Periódico de la Ciudad de Santafé de Bogotá*, 1791-1797; *El Redactor Americano*, 1806-1809; and *El Alternativo del Redactor Americano*, 1807-1809.

RODRIGUEZ FREILE, Juan, 1566-1642. A native of *Bogotá, he was the author of *El carnero, conquista y descubrimiento del Nuevo Reino de Granada* . . . Written in a novelistic and moralizing style, much of the work focuses on events of the decades of the 1570s and 1580s, largely in Bogotá. *El carnero* remained in manuscript form until published by Felipe Pérez in 1859. The name can also be spelled "Rodríguez Fresle" and "Rodríguez Freyle."

RODRIGUEZ VARGAS, Gustavo. Leader of the Gustavista faction of the *Conservative Party.

ROJAS, Ernesto. "Comandante" Rojas was the *guerrilla code name of Jairo de Jesús Calvo Ocampo, leader of the *Ejército

Popular de Liberación. He was killed in a clash with police February 16, 1987. He was succeeded by Francisco Caraballo.

ROJAS DE MORENO DIAZ, María Eugenia, 1934-. Legislator, political leader, born in *Vélez (Santander). She was the daughter and main spokeswoman of General Gustavo *Rojas Pinilla, 1950s-1970s. Educated at the Colegio de las Esclavas del Sagrado Corazón in Bogotá, she was a major figure in *ANAPO and a frequent member of *Congress after 1950. She was appointed head of the *Secretariado Nacional de Asistencia Social in 1954 and was the insulted party in the events leading to the *bullring massacre in 1956. She was a candidate for the presidency in 1974 and Director of the Instituto de Crédito Territorial under the administration of Belisario *Betancur.

ROJAS PINILLA, Gustavo, 1900-1975. General, Dictator of Colombia, 1953-1957. Born *Tunja, March 12; died at his estate in Melgar (*Tolima), January 17. He was educated in the Escuela Militar de Cadetes, *Bogotá, and then studied engineering in the United States, 1924-1927. In addition to serving in the Colombian-Peruvian conflict, the *Leticia Dispute, in the 1930s, he was a military commander, head of the Third Brigade in Cali during the *Bogotazo and La *Violencia, as well as a member of the Inter-American Defense Board. He deposed President Laureano *Gómez on June 13, 1953. His administration attempted authoritarian reform and economic development. It used Peronist-inspired tactics with third-party and organized-labor movements. General Rojas Pinilla was overthrown on May 10, 1957, and later tried by a national tribunal, which stripped him of his political rights. Nevertheless, he returned to politics as leader of *ANAPO, which he made a major protest party, 1960-1974, nearly winning the presidential elections of 1970.

ROLDAN-PASSMORE RENEGOTIATION. A renegotiation in 1895 of Colombia's foreign debt, which could not be fulfilled because of the disruption caused by the War of the *Thousand Days. See: FOREIGN DEBT

ROLDANILLO, Battle of. February 15, 1885, 4° 24'N, 76° 9'W, *Valle del Cauca. General Rafael *Reyes, for the government, achieved a decisive triumph over the rebellious forces under General Guillermo Márquez.

ROMAN CATHOLIC CHURCH, see: CATHOLIC CHURCH

ROMANTICISM. A literary movement that prevailed in Colombia and elsewhere during the 19th century. It exalted nature, the emotions, the unique, and the individual, frequently with tragic overtones. In Colombia, José María *Grueso, Luis *Vargas Tejada, José Eusebio *Caro, Miguel Antonio *Caro, Julio *Arboleda, and Gregorio *Gutiérrez González were among the leading romantic poets. The best-known romantic novel is *María by Jorge *Isaacs.

ROOT-CORTES-AROSEMENA AGREEMENTS. A series of treaties, signed by Elihu Root (for the United States), Enrique Cortés (for Colombia), and Carlos Arosemena (for *Panama) in Washington, D.C., January 9, 1909. The agreements, which were never fully ratified, included treaties between the United States and Panama, the United States and Colombia, and Panama and Colombia. The treaties provided for recognition of Panamanian independence, Panama's assumption of a portion of Colombia's national debt, trade concessions for Colombian goods in Panama, and settlement of the Panamanian-Colombian boundary by accepting Colombia's claims in most areas and arbitration of the boundary in the disputed Jurado region (now part of a *municipio* of the same name in the Department of Chocó). The treaties were ratified by Panama and the United States but failed to achieve approval in Colombia where they became a catalyst for uniting opposition to the pro–United States administration of General Rafael *Reyes.

ROSARIO, Colegio Mayor de Nuestra Señora del, see: COLEGIO MAYOR DE NUESTRA SEÑORA DEL ROSARIO

ROSCA, Fall of the Conservative, 1929. A reference to the events of June 6-8, in *Bogotá, which brought about the removal from office of the Minister of War, Ignacio Rengifo; the Minister of Public Works, Arturo Hernández; the National Chief of Police, General Carlos Cortés Vargas; the Governor of *Cundinamarca, Ruperto Melo; and the Governor of *Santander, Narciso Torres Meléndez (all described by the term *rosca,* which in Colombian usage is a gang of insiders or group of followers). The incidents began when Governor Melo removed Luis Augusto Cuervo from his position as Mayor of Bogotá for his firing of two *Conservative subordinates. June 6 saw a public strike, protesting Cuervo's removal and administration policies in general. The strike was put down by force. On June 7, university students resumed the protest and government forces fired on them, killing Gonzalo Bravo Pérez. On June 8, a *junta of notables, including Miguel Jiménez López, Lucas Caballero, and Silvio Villegas, supported by Jorge Eliécer *Gaitán, succeeded in restoring Cuervo to his position and removing the officials held responsible for the violence. Rengifo and Cortés Vargas were also those whom the public held responsible for the violent suppression of the *United Fruit Company strike in the banana zone less than a year earlier.

ROYAL ROAD, see: CAMINO REAL

RUANA.   A woolen poncho worn by all classes in Colombia but associated particularly with the lower classes. In social terms, it means a member of the lower class. See *CACHACO* for contrast, especially in the 1850s.

RUBBER TRADE.   Commercial tapping of wild rubber trees in the *Amazon rain forest began in the 1820s and was greatly boosted by the 1839 discovery of vulcanization. Destructive exploitation of nearby trees forced the industry to push farther and farther westward until, following the boost in demand caused by Dunlop's 1888 invention of the pneumatic tire, it became profitable to develop tapping beyond Brazil's western frontier, in the Bolivian, Peruvian, and Colombian parts of Amazonia. In an attempt to avoid direct confrontation in the region, Peru and Colombia agreed to pull their military forces back from their disputed border (see: PERU-COLOMBIA TREATY OF 1906). But this created a wild-West-style power vacuum that Peruvian rubber baron Julio *ARANA DEL AGUILA moved in to exploit. Although many Colombians had entered the area after the late 1890s, particularly those seeking a new crop after the collapse of the *cinchona (quinine) boom, Arana crippled their efforts through his control of access to the markets of Iquitos (Peru) and Manaus, or Manáos (Brazil), and often by direct armed aggression. Even after the collapse of Arana's empire and the effective recovery of Colombian sovereignty over the lower *Putumayo (see: PUTUMAYO DISPUTE), Colombian rubber output was only a fraction of that of its neighbors: In 1913 it was 37 tonnes compared to Peru's 2,568, Bolivia's 4,057, and Brazil's 39,970.
    Whereas the Peruvians (and Arana in particular) used terror to recruit their Indian tappers (30,000 died working for Arana

in ten years), the Colombian government encouraged missionary activity by the *Capuchins to conquer the forest *Indians and provide the necessary labor supply. But with the maturity of new plantations in the Far East, the boom in wild rubber collapsed in 1912, and the Colombian industry became of minimal economic importance. Today Colombia imports almost all its rubber.

RUIDO, El.   A reference to the loud, but essentially unexplained, roaring noise that accompanied the *earthquakes of 1687.

RUSSELL AFFAIR.   A diplomatic dispute, 1836-1837. The trial and imprisonment of British Consul Joseph Russell in *Panama resulted in a British blockade of *New Granada's ports, January 21, 1837. A negotiated settlement with payment of damages revealed New Granada's international weakness, as had the *Barrot Affair shortly before. See also: UNITED KINGDOM, Relations with

-S-

SABANA.   A savannah, or largely treeless plain. Originally *zavana*, the word is reputedly *Carib.

SABANA DE BOGOTA.   Plains or plateau of Bogotá. The flatland surrounding the city of *Bogotá, approximately 2,600 meters above sea level.

SABANA RAILWAY.   The Ferrocarril de la Sabana, also known as the Cundinamarca Railroad. A line connecting *Bogotá with the *Magdalena River was authorized as early as 1865 but little progress was made toward actual construction. During the early 1880s at least three routes were simultaneously in various stages of construction: Bogotá to La *Dorada; Bogotá to *Honda; and Bogotá to *Girardot. Under a contract negotiated in 1881, construction from Bogotá to *Facatativá was completed from 1882-1889. Nothing else was accomplished until the Girardot Railroad joined the *Sabana line at Facatativá in 1908, initiating service to the upper Magdalena. Extension of the line from Facatativá to Puerto Salgar (5° 28'N, 74° 39'W), opposite La Dorada, 1928-1938, opened communications with the lower Magdalena. The lines converging at the Facatativá junction were built on different gauges, a situation that created technical problems until government intervention forced standardization in 1924.

SAC, see: SOCIEDAD DE AGRICULTORES DE COLOMBIA

SACO, see: SERVICIO AEREO COLOMBIANO

SAENZ, Manuela, 1797-1856. A native of Paita, Peru, she was first married to Dr. James Thorne but deserted him to become the companion of *Bolívar in 1822. She lived in *Bogotá, 1827-1834, and was known as the "Liberator of the *Liberator" for her actions in distracting Bolívar's would-be assassins on September 25, 1828. Manuela was also known for her eccentric behavior, which included wearing men's clothing and having two black slaves accompany her in public. She was accused of fomenting political rebellion and then expelled from Bogotá in 1834. She died in relative obscurity, probably in Paita.

SAGIPA. Also Saquesazipa, the last *Zipa of the *Chibchas, 1538. He first resisted the Spanish but then formed an alliance with them against the *Panche *Indians in the west. He was betrayed by the Spanish at Bojacá and ordered to stand trial for usurpation of authority. He was first tortured by his captors, who hoped to get *gold from him, and then executed by them.

SAGUANMACHICA. The earliest known *Zipa of the *Chibchas, 1470-1490. His reign was troubled by numerous civil and foreign wars. He fought the *Zaque at Chocontá (5° 9'N, 73° 42'W, *Cundinamarca) where both were killed.

SAINT ANDREW, see: SAN ANDRES

SALADO, Battle of. August 23, 1885, *Cesar. General Guillermo Quintero Calderón and Antonio B. Cuervo, for the government, fought an inconclusive battle with rebel forces under General Foción Soto. It was followed by the armistice of Los Guamos, August 26, and was the last major engagement of the *Rebellion of 1884-1885.

SALAMINA, First Battle of, 1841. May 5, at 5° 25'N, 75° 30'W, *Caldas. General Braulio Henao, for the government, defeated the rebellious forces of Colonel José María Vesga, who was captured during this encounter in the War of the *SU-PREME COMMANDERS.

SALAMINA, Second Battle of, 1885.   February 5, at 5° 25'N, 75° 30'W, *Caldas. Government forces, under General Juan N. Mateus, defeated rebellious troops from *Antioquia. The battle resulted in the subsequent occupation of *Manizales and the signing of a truce on February 25. See: REBELLION OF 1884-1885

SALAVARRIETA, Policarpa, ca. 1795-1817.   "La Pola," patriot heroine, born *Guaduas (Cundinamarca), February 22. She was arrested for espionage and subversion against the Spanish Crown, imprisoned in the *Colegio Mayor de Nuestra Señora del Rosario, and then hanged with seven others in *Bogotá on November 14.

SALGAR, Eustorgio, 1831-1885.   General, lawyer, legislator, President of Colombia, 1870-1872. Born *Bogotá, November 1; died Bogotá, November 25. He received his law degree in 1851, and served as political chief (*jefe político*) in *Zipaquirá, 1851-1852; legislator in the Zipaquirá assembly, 1852-1853; Senator, 1858-1859; Governor of *Cundinamarca, 1860-1861; Minister of Finance, 1863; Minister of War, 1876; Minister of Foreign Relations, 1877-1878 and 1884; and Minister of Government, 1884. Known as the "Gentleman President" because of his manner of conduct in the presidency, 1870-1872, his administration was most distinguished by its interest in the development of public *education. It established a department of public instruction that coordinated a national system of primary and normal schools, published a journal called *La Escuela Normal,* and contracted for a German mission to study Colombian education (see: GERMANY, Relations with). The administration also patronized a national industrial exposition held at Bogotá in 1871.

SALT CATHEDRAL, see: CATHEDRAL OF SALT

SALT PRODUCTION.   Colombia has almost inexhaustible salt deposits that have been exploited since pre-Hispanic times. The most well-known site is *Zipaquirá, but Nemocón (5° 4'N, 73° 53'W, *Cundinamarca), Sesquilé (5° 3'N, 73° 48'W, *Cundinamarca), Cumaral (4° 14'N, 73° 30'W, *Meta), and

Upín are next in importance. Most Colombian salt lies within the Departments of *Cundinamarca, *Boyacá, and *Meta. Salt was a prime commercial product among the *Chibchas and *Quimbayas at the time of the conquest, and salt revenues have been important to both the colonial and republican governments since then. *Humboldt is said to have recommended the use of mine shafts and tunnels for production at Zipaquirá, and these were introduced in 1816. Administration of salt revenues was entrusted to the *Banco de la República in 1931.

SAMANO Y URIBARRI, Juan, 1753-1821. Field Marshal. He was military governor of *New Granada, 1816-1818, and the last effective *viceroy, 1818-1819. He fled Bogotá after the Battle of *Boyacá. Along with General Pablo *Morillo, Sámano is the official held most responsible for the *reign of terror during the Spanish *Reconquista.

SAMPER AGUDELO, José María, 1828-1888. Author, journalist, politician, diplomat; born *Honda (Tolima), March 31; died Anapoima (*Cundinamarca), June 22. After earning his law degree, he was associated with *Liberal politics in the 1850s and 1860s, during which time he held numerous government posts in Colombia, South America, and Europe. He later converted to the *Conservative Party and is best remembered for his career as a prolific writer. Among his best-known historical works are his autobiographical *Historia de una alma* (1881), *Apuntamientos para la historia política y social de la Nueva Granada desde 1810 . . .* (1856); and *Ensayo sobre las revoluciones políticas y la condición social de la República Hispanoamericana* (1861). In addition to contributions to numerous *newspapers, he was also the author of at least one play, *Un alcalde a la antigua y dos primos a la moderna,* and three collections of poetry. He was married to Soledad *Acosta de Samper.

SAN AGUSTIN. Archeological site, *Huila, 4 miles from the municipal seat of the same name, located at 1° 53'N, 76° 16'W, near Pitalito, 1° 51'N, 76° 2'W. It is composed of a principal park with numerous outlying sites on the eastern side of the Macizo Colombiana (see: CORDILLERA CENTRAL). Typical altitudes in the region of the park range from 1,318 to 1,695 meters. Major sites include Alto de los Idolos, El Tablón, and Lavapatas, all known for their profusion of three-dimensional, monolithic sculptures and architecture. The ruins of San Agustín were first recorded in 1757 by Fray Juan de *Santa Gertrúdis, although the site seems to have been occupied long after the Spanish appeared on the scene. Carbon 14 dating shows occupation at the site from 555 B.C. to A.D. 1630, but habitation may have begun much earlier. The culture seems to have been organized into chiefdoms, with well-defined social classes and an influential priesthood. The economy was based on *corn, *agriculture, hunting, and gathering. Ritual cannibalism has been suggested. Five pottery styles have been distinguished at San Agustín: Horqueta and Primavera (pre-Christian era), Isnos (about the time of Christ), and Sombrerillos and Potrero (post-Christian era). The site shows Mesoamerican influences.

SAN AGUSTIN, Battle of. February 25-28, 1862, *Bogotá. General Leonardo Canal, *Conservative, unsuccessfully besieged supporters of General *Mosquera in the Monastery of San Agustín.

SAN ANDRES. Capital of the Department of *San Andrés, Providencia y Santa Catalina, located on San Andrés Island, at 12° 35'N, 81° 42'W, on a bay of the same name. San Andrés Island is approximately 13 kilometers long and 3 kilometers wide, with a ridge of north-south mountains that reach an altitude of 85 meters. San Andrés city is 2 meters above sea level with a population of 33,190 people (1985 estimate). The average temperature is 27°C. The principal industry is tourism. San Andrés was declared a free port in 1953. An airport was opened in 1955, and construction of modern port facilities was authorized in 1962. See also: SAN ANDRES, PROVIDENCIA Y SANTA CATALINA, Departamento de

SAN ANDRES, PROVIDENCIA Y SANTA CATALINA, Departamento de. An archipelago (44 square kilometers) in the Caribbean Sea, 480 kilometers northwest of the Colombian mainland, 250 kilometers north of *Panama, 400 kilometers southwest of Jamaica, and 180 kilometers east of Nicaragua. The two principal islands, 90 kilometers apart, are San Andrés (occasionally anglicized as St. Andrew) located between 12° 29' and 12° 36'N, and 81° 41' and 81° 43'W, and Providencia (Old Providence), between 13° 9' and 13° 23'N, and 81° 21' and 81° 23'W. Providencia is about 7 kilometers long and 4 kilometers wide. El Pico mountain on the island is 550 meters high. Santa Catalina is a small island off Providencia at 13°

23'N, 81° 22'W. On the latter island, agriculture and cattle ranching predominate; the maximum altitude is 133 meters (see also: SAN ANDRES). There are also several small keys (*cays* or *cayos*). Average temperature is 27°-29°C, and mountain ridges on the islands reach as high as 550 meters. The main industry is tourism, but there is also incipient development of coconut and vegetable oil production, commerce, and *fishing. There may also be *petroleum deposits, an alleged reason for the renewed Nicaraguan interest. The capital is the city of San Andrés. The islands were sighted by *Columbus in 1492, and appear to have been first recorded on known maps in 1527, when the more northerly one was called Santa Catalina. Its present name was bestowed by the English Puritan settlers of Lord Rich's Providence Island Company, who seized the archipelago in 1629, and rapidly made it the most notorious pirate lair in the western Carribbean, at one time serving as headquarters for Henry *Morgan. The islands were returned to Spain in 1689 and formed part of the *Virreinato de Nueva Granada after 1739. The English once again seized control of them, 1806-1808, but they became part of *New Granada with the 1803 incorporation of the *Mosquito Coast. During the wars for independence they became an important supply and staging point. They were formally incorporated into the Republic of *Gran Colombia in 1822 and were part of the Department of *Bolívar until 1866. In 1868 they became a national territory, and in 1912 the *Intendancy of San Andrés y Providencia, and that is the way the archipelago has most often been referred to since then. The Department of San Andrés, Providencia y Santa Catalina was established in 1991. An archaic English survives as the local vernacular. Colombian sovereignty was recognized by Nicaragua only with the *Esguerra-Bárcenas Meneses Treaty of 1928. This was abrogated by the Sandinista government of Nicaragua soon after it came to power, February 5, 1980. In response, the Colombian government sent warships to the area. In April 1985, the Nicaraguan government, claiming legal defects in the treaty, plus the fact that the islands lay within its 200-mile territorial waters, announced that it would appeal to international law. Ownership of the islands had also featured in 19th-century negotiations with Costa Rica. These had culminated in the *Quijano Otero–Castro Treaty of 1880 and resultant arbitration by the President of France. His award, although never accepted by Costa Rica, had confirmed Colombian sovereignty over San Andrés y Providencia. In 1985 the 44-square kilometer archipelago had an estimated population of 35,515, with an overall population density of 829.9 per square kilometer.

SAN BARTOLOME, Seminario y Colegio Mayor, see: COLEGIO MAYOR DE SAN BARTOLOME

SAN BASILIO, Palenque de. Established at Tolú (9° 32'N, 75° 35'W, *Bolívar) in 1621 by remnants of the Palenque de *Matuna (1600-1621), San Basilio was the most famous runaway slave (*maroon) community in colonial New Granada. Members of the *palenque* harassed the Tolú, *Mompós, Tenerife (9° 54'N, 74° 52'W) area until the Governor of Cartagena, Martín de Zevallos, launched a campaign to destroy them from 1692-1694. Some say the *palenque* lasted until a truce was negotiated, 1712-1713, recognizing the independent status of the former slaves; others say the *palenque* lasted until 1719. See: PALENQUE

SAN FELIPE DE BARAJAS CASTLE. The dominant structure in the *CARTAGENA FORTIFICATIONS.

SAN JOSE DEL GUAVIARE. The capital of the Department of *Guaviare, San José is situated 2° 34'N, 72° 38'W, at an altitude of 240 meters. It has an average temperature of 24°C. It is a port city on the Guaviare River. Estimated population in 1985 was 12,351 people.

SAN JUAN, Gobierno de, see: NUEVA CASTILLA

SAN JUAN RIVER. An inland waterway rising on the western slopes of the *Cordillera Occidental at 5° 25'N, 75° 57'W, in the Cerro de Caramanta in the Department of *Risaralda. It flows west 376 kilometers to the Pacific Ocean at 4° 5'N, 77° 26'W, and at least 230 kilometers are navigable. The San Juan is frequently cited with the *Atrato River as a possible route for an interoceanic canal. It was explored by Pascual de *Andagoya in 1518 and named for San Juan Bautista (St. John the Baptist). See also: INTEROCEANIC CANAL

SAN MATEO, Battle of. March 25, 1814, Venezuela. Patriot forces under Simón *Bolívar defeated royalist forces under José Tomás Bóves. The battle was marked by the heroic self-sacrifice of Captain Antonio *Ricaurte, whose efforts saved the patriot forces from disaster.

SAN PEDRO, Hospital of. Founded by Archbishop Juan de los *Barrios in 1564, it was run by the monks of the Order of San Juan de Dios. New buildings were constructed for the hospital, 1723-1739. It was the only major hospital in *Bogotá during the colonial period and continued to operate in the 19th century.

SAN PEDRO ALEJANDRINO. A private estate located near *Santa Marta. It is remembered as the place where *Bolívar died in 1830. It is presently a public museum.

SAN SEBASTIAN DE URABA. Short-lived settlement founded by Alonso de *Ojeda in 1510 on the eastern shore of the *Golfo de Urabá. It lasted less than a year, but survivors of the settlement moved to *SANTA MARIA LA ANTIGUA DEL DARIEN.

SANCLEMENTE, Manuel Antonio, 1813-1902. Lawyer, *Conservative legislator, President of Colombia, 1898-1902. Born *Buga (Valle del Cauca), September 19; died Villeta (*Cundinamarca), March 19. He received his doctorate in jurisprudence in *Popayán in 1837. He was later a justice of the *Supreme Court (1854-1857) and practiced law in *Panama (1860s). In addition he was Minister of War and Government for the *Ospina administration, 1857-1861, and Minister of Government for the *Caro administration, 1894. As President, he withdrew from active administration initially because of age and poor health, but he then assumed command to stop conciliatory policies proposed by Vice President José Manuel *Marroquín. He exercised authority illegally from Villeta and other sites where he was at times incapacitated and virtually a prisoner of *Nationalist Conservatives who acted in his name. He was formally deposed in the *THIRTY-FIRST OF JULY MOVEMENT.

SANDE, Francisco de, d. 1602. A rather arbitrary President of *New Granada, 1597-1602. He is most often remembered as *el emplazado* ("the summoned") because an official he had falsely accused declared that Sande would die within nine days of the time that he indicated. Sande died September 12, 1602, within the specified nine days.

SANIN CANO, Baldómero, 1851-1957. Educator, critic, journalist; born *Rionegro (Antioquia), June 27; died *Bogotá,

May 12. Sanín Cano has been called the first authentic Colombian literary critic. In addition to numerous educational appointments, he was secretary in charge of the Ministry of Finance, 1905-1908; a member of various legislatures including the *Asamblea Nacional, 1905-1907, and the *House of Representatives in the 1920s; and diplomatic envoy to Argentina and Peru. He is best known for his efforts to place Colombian and Latin American intellectual life in its broader world context, for readers within Colombia as well as those in Europe and elsewhere in America. Among his many books and essays are *Colombia hace 60 años* (1888); *La administración de Reyes, 1904-1909* (1909); *La civilización manual y otros ensayos* (1925); *De mi vida y otras vidas* (1949); and *El humanismo y el progreso del hombre* (1955).

SANTA BARBARA DE CARTAGO, First Battle of, 1862. September 18, *Valle del Cauca. General Santos *Gutiérrez, for the *Mosquera government, defeated Generals Braulio Henao and Rafael M. Giraldo during the *rebellion of 1859-1862.

SANTA BARBARA DE CARTAGO, Second Battle of, 1885. February 23, *Valle del Cauca. An invading army from *Antioquia under Generals Valentín Daza and Manuel Angel was defeated by *Liberal General Eliseo *Payán, acting for the government during the *rebellion of 1884-1885.

SANTA CLARA DE TUNJA, ORDER OF. The first order of *religious women founded in Colombia. It was established in *Tunja in 1573 by Juana Macías de Figueroa. At first under the supervision of the *Franciscans, it was granted autonomy in 1580. Twenty-six nuns were reported at the convent in 1595.

SANTA FE, see: SANTA FE DE BOGOTA

SANTA FE DE ANTIOQUIA. A city in the Department of *Antioquia, now known simply as Antioquia, founded December 4, 1541, by Marshal Jorge *Robledo, some say as Antiochia. Because of Indian attacks, it was moved to its present site (6° 34'N, 75° 50'W) in 1547 and given a new name, Santa Fe, by Gaspar de *Rodas. Santa Fe de Antioquia served as the capital of the Province of Antioquia, 1584-1830, until the government was moved to Medellín. It was also the site of the first parish church established in the province (September 8, 1547), and the head of a diocese created in 1808. The first

Bishop of Santa Fe de Antioquia actually resided in the city until 1828. The city is now an interesting example of well-preserved colonial architecture.

SANTA FE DE BOGOTA. The original name for *Bogotá (4° 35′N, 74° 4′W), which persisted as its full official designation until 1819 when the shorter form was adopted by the *Congress of Angostura. Santa Fe de Bogotá was founded August 6, 1538, by the conquistador Gonzalo *Jiménez de Quesada and named after the Catholic Sovereigns' city of Santa Fe in his native Granada, Spain. The city's first *cabildo (with jurisdiction over the surrounding area) met April 29, 1539. The settlement was elevated to the rank of city with a coat of arms in 1548, the royal *Audiencia was established there in 1549, and it became an archepiscopal see in 1563. The *VIRREINATO DEL NUEVO REINO DE GRANADA, established in the 18th century, may also be referred to (inaccurately) as the Viceroyalty of Santa Fe de Bogotá. See also: AUDIENCIA DE SANTA FE DE BOGOTA, Real; BOGOTA; DISTRITO ESPECIAL DE BOGOTA; SANTA FE DE BOGOTA, Archbishopric of

SANTA FE DE BOGOTA, Archbishopric of. Seat of the principal religious authority in Colombian history. The name was changed simply to the Archbishopric of *Bogotá in 1953. Although other bishoprics were founded first, such as *Darien (1514), *Santa Marta (1531), *Cartagena (1533), and *Popayán (1547), Bogotá became the principal clerical see after its creation in 1563. Friar Juan de los *Barrios was the first Archbishop. Archbishop Crisanto *Luque Sánchez was appointed the first Colombian Cardinal in 1953. The present ecclesiastical structure includes eight archbishops and twenty-six bishoprics. Archbishops of Bogotá from 1564 to 1984 were:

Juan de los *Barrios, 1564-1569
Luis *Zapata de Cárdenas, 1573-1590
Bartolomé *Lobo Guerrero, 1599-1609
Pedro Ordóñez y Flórez, 1613-1614
Hernando *Arias de Ugarte, 1618-1625
Julián de Cortázar, 1627-1630
Bernardino de Almansa, 1631-1634
Cristóbal de *Torres, 1635-1654
Juan de *Arguinao, 1661-1678
Antonio Sanz Lozano, 1681-1688
Ignacio de *Urbina 1690-1703

Francisco de Cossío y Otero, 1706-1714
Francisco del Rincón, 1718-1723
Antonio Claudio *Alvarez de Quiñones, 1731-1736
Juan de Galavís, 1739
Diego Fermín de Vergara, 1741-1744
Felipe de Azúa, 1745-1754
José Javier de Arauz, 1754-1764
Francisco Antonio de la Riva Mazo, 1768
Agustín Camacho y Rojas, 1771-1774
Agustín de Alvarado y Castillo, 1775-1779
Antonio *Caballero y Góngora, 1779-1788
Baltasar Jaime Martínez Compañón, 1791-1797
Fernando del Portillo y Torres, 1800-1804
Juan Bautista Sacristán, 1804-1817
Francisco *Caycedo y Flórez, 1827-1832
Manuel José *Mosquera, 1835-1853
Antonio *Herrán, 1855-1868
Vicente *Arbeláez, 1868-1884
José Telésforo *Paúl, 1885-1888
Ignacio León Velasco, 1889-1891
Bernardo *Herrera Restrepo, 1891-1928
Ismael *Perdomo, 1928-1950
Crisanto *Luque Sánchez, 1950-1959
Luis *Concha Córdoba, 1959-1973
Aníbal *Muñoz Duque, 1973-1984
Pedro *Revollo Bravo, 1984-

SANTA FE DE BOGOTA, Real Audiencia de, see: AUDIENCIA DE SANTA FE DE BOGOTA, Real

SANTA FE DE BOGOTA, Virreinato de, see: VIRREINATO DEL NUEVO REINO DE GRANADA

SANTA GERTRUDIS, Juan de, d. 1799. Missionary friar who traveled in *New Granada, 1756-1767. He was the author of *Maravillas de la naturaleza,* an account of his experiences in New Granada (not published, however, until 1956).

SANTA MARIA LA ANTIGUA DEL DARIEN. First important settlement on the mainland, it was founded on the western side of the *Golfo de Urabá in 1510 by the expedition of Martín *Fernández de Enciso and survivors from *Ojeda's outpost at *San Sebastián de Urabá. Soon after it was established, Vasco *Núñez de Balboa seized command of the colony and became its first important leader. Santa María, or Antigua as it is also called, functioned as the base for the exploration of the Pacific

Coast and the exploration and settlement of other parts of the Isthmus of *Panama until it was abandoned in 1519 when *Pedrarias moved the colonial government to *Panama City.

SANTA MARTA. Capital of *Magdalena, located at 11° 15'N, 74° 13'W, on the Caribbean Sea, 1,197 kilometers from *Bogotá and 88 kilometers from *Barranquilla. The altitude is 6 meters; average temperature, 27°C; and the population, 215,540 people (1985 estimate). Tourism is the major industry, but Santa Marta is also a center of maritime commerce, the end of the *Atlantic Railroad, and the terminus of the Zulia oil pipeline. Santa Marta is sometimes said to be the oldest continuously settled city on the continent. It was founded by Rodrigo de *Bastidas on July 29, 1525, and was the seat of the first bishopric in present-day Colombia, 1534. It holds an annual festival of the sea (*Fiesta del Mar*).

SANTA MARTA RAILWAY. The Ferrocaril de Santa Marta, also called the Magdalena Railroad, was a line intended to connect *Santa Marta with the *Magdalena River. Authorized from Santa Marta to Cerro de San Antonio (10° 20'N, 74° 52'W) in 1871, its destination was later changed to El Banco (9°'N, 73° 59'W). Construction began in 1882, progressing through Ciénaga (11° 1'N, 74° 15'W) in 1887 and the Sevilla River in 1894. Work was terminated at Fundación (10° 31'N, 74° 11'W) in 1906. The line was used predominantly by *banana producers.

SANTANDER, Departamento de. Located in eastern Colombia in the *Cordillera Oriental, the department covers 30,537 square kilometers of mountainous terrain interrupted by river valleys and plateaus, between 5° 42' and 8° 8'N latitude, and 72° 26' and 74° 32'W longitude. Approximately 15,318 square kilometers have tropical climate; 7,352, temperate; 5,180, cold; and 2,687 are wasteland. Major rivers include the *Magdalena, Carare, Lebrija, Opón, Sogamoso, Cáchira, Barichara, Chucurí, and Ermitaño. Population is 1,427,110 people (1985 estimate), with a population density of 46.7 people per square kilometer. The capital city is *Bucaramanga. According to DANE, *Colombiana estadística 86,* principal agricultural products, with tonnage produced in 1984, include *yuca,* 270,000; plantains, 72,600; *sugar, 61,830; *potatoes, 48,260; *corn, 37,990; *African palm, 23,800; *tobacco, 13,260; *cacao, 12,670; beans, 4,275; hemp, 4,200; wheat,

3,375; sorghum, 3,070; barley, 760; and sesame, 48. There were 228,382 head of cattle and 58,572 hogs slaughtered in 1984. Mining resources include *gold, *silver, *petroleum, *coal, and other industrial *minerals. Industries include textiles, candies, tobacco products, agricultural machinery, chemicals, and sewing machines. Forestry reserves are significant. There were 368 businesses employing ten or more workers in 1983. The Salto del Mico, perhaps the highest waterfall in Colombia, is in the department. Early conquerors of Santander included Antonio de Lebrija (1529) and *Dalfinger (1532), and colonization is said to have begun with Martín Galeano, who founded *Velez on June 3, 1539. Other early settlements were Malaga (6° 42'N, 72° 44'W), 1542; Guaca (6° 53'N, 72° 51'W), before 1553; and Puente Nacional (5° 53'N, 73° 41'W), 1569. During the colonial period, Santander was one of the main centers of the *Comuneros Revolt in the 1780s. The State of Santander was established in 1857, and the Department of Santander in 1886. The department was reduced in size by some 21,658 square kilometers in 1911 when *Norte de Santander was separated from it to become a department in its own right.

SANTANDER, Francisco de Paula, 1792-1840.   General, patriot, military officer, 1810-1819; Vice President, acting President of *Gran Colombia, 1821-1827; and President of *New Granada, 1832-1837. Born Villa del Rosario de Cúcuta (*Norte de Santander), April 2; died *Bogotá, May 6. Santander, known as the "Man of Laws," is frequently cited as the precursor of the Colombian *Liberal Party. Active in the *independence movement, General Santander participated in the Battle of *Boyacá, 1819. As acting President in the 1820s and again as President, 1832-1837, he played an important role in establishing the administrative structure of the government of republican Colombia. He resisted the proposed *Bolivian Constitution of 1826 and *Bolívar's dictatorship, 1828-1830. He was exiled from Colombia following the attempt by many of his followers to assassinate Bolívar in the *Twenty-fifth of September Conspiracy, 1828, but later recalled to be the first President of *New Granada. He was leader of the congressional opposition, 1837-1840. Both of his administrations faced major organizational tasks and difficulties in achieving financial stability. Both supported public *education programs with strong influences of *Benthamism. Particularly in the 1830s, his policies appeared partisan to many and contributed to serious political tensions. He was the author of the autobiographical *Apuntamientos para las memorias sobre Colombia i la Nueva Granada* (Bogotá, 1837).

SANTO DOMINGO, Relations with.   *New Granada was under the jurisdiction of the *Audiencia de Santo Domingo until the *Audiencia de Santa Fe de Bogotá began functioning in 1550. The Santo Domingo Audiencia continued its hold over Venezuela until 1780. On November 30, 1821, Santo Domingo declared itself independent of Spain and a part of the Republic of *Gran Colombia as the Estado de Haiti Española (State of Spanish Haiti). The union was not consummated, however, because the territory was annexed by President Jean Pierre Boyer of Haiti in 1822. When the Spanish part of the island eventually threw off Boyer's rule on January 27, 1844, it became the Dominican Republic. See: DOMINICAN REPUBLIC, Relations with

SANTO TOMAS UNIVERSITY, see: UNIVERSIDAD DE SANTO TOMAS

SANTOS, Antonia, 1785-1819.   Patriot heroine, martyr, born Charalá (*Santander). She was a member of a guerrilla band whose actions in Coromoro (6° 18'N, 73° 3'W, Santander) are said to have distracted the Spanish while *Bolívar and the patriot army crossed the *Cordillera Oriental during the *Campaña Libertadora of 1819. She was arrested and executed by the Spanish in *Socorro (Santander), July 28.

SANTOS, Eduardo, 1888-1974.   Lawyer, *Liberal, longtime editor of *El *Tiempo,* President of Colombia, 1938-1942. Born *Bogotá, August 28; died Bogotá, March 27. He received his law degree from the *Universidad Nacional in 1908 and then served in the Colombian legation in Paris, 1909-1911, as chief of the Foreign Relations Archive, 1911-1913, and Minister of Foreign Relations, 1934. He was also Governor of *Santander, 1931, and President of the *Academia Colombiana de Historia. Only moderately reformist, his presidential administration slowed many of the reforms initiated by the *López Pumarejo administration, 1934-1938 (See: GRAN PAUSA). It supported the Allied Powers in *World War II and cultivated close ties with the United States. His administration was generally efficient and made some attempt at internal development.

SANTOS GIL, Pest of. *El peste de Santos Gil,* a reference to the typhus, or typhoid, *epidemic of 1633 in Bogotá. It was so named because numerous people appeared before the notary public Santos Gil to make their wills, many leaving property to him for want of other heirs.

SANTOS LUGARES. Literally, "Holy Places." Historically, the phrase "to visit Holy Places" was a reference to the contraband trade in the Antilles.

SANTUARIO, Battle of. August 27, 1830, *Cundinamarca. General *Urdaneta and his rebellious troops defeated the government forces of Colonel Pedro Antonio García. The battle facilitated the establishment of the *Urdaneta dictatorship, 1830-1831.

SAQUESAZIPA, see: SAGIPA

SARDA CONSPIRACY. A plot by Spanish-born General José María Sardá (d. 1834) and others to overthrow President *Santander and his government in 1833. It was exposed, but the deaths of Sardá and other conspirators in questionable circumstances created much ill will for Santander.

SATENA. An official air service created by Decree No. 940 in 1962 for the purpose of serving locations in the national territories of *Arauca, *Vichada, *Vaupés, *Caquetá, *Putumayo, and *Amazonas. Its objective was to encourage colonization and development in sparsely populated areas. See also: AIR TRANSPORT

SCADTA, see: SOCIEDAD COLOMBO-ALEMANA DE TRANSPORTES AEREOS

SCIENTIFIC COMMISSION OF THE ACADEMY OF SCIENCES OF PARIS. Composed of French scientists Charles Marie de *La Condamine, Peter Bouguer, and Louis Godin, accompanied by Spanish agents Jorge *Juan and Antonio de *Ulloa, the expedition traveled through the *viceroyalty from *Cartagena to Quito and down the *Amazon River, 1735-1743. It marked the equator by erecting two pyramids near Quito in 1740. La Condamine published an account of his experiences in 1745.

SECRETARIA. The title used to designate a major department of state (for example, *Secretaría de Guerra*) before 1886. Since then the term has been replaced by *Ministerio*. See also: MINISTRIES

SECRETARIADO NACIONAL DE ASISTENCIA SOCIAL. SENDAS was founded September 1954, by the *Rojas Pinilla government. It was a social assistance agency, originally directed by María Eugenia *Rojas de Moreno Díaz, intended to secure political support through public aid to peasants and small farmers.

SECURITY STATUTE OF 1978, see: ESTATUTO DE SEGURIDAD, 1978

SEGOVIA, Battle of. November 19, 1860, in the Department of *Cauca. General *Mosquera gained access to the *Cordillera Central while General Joaquín París and the army of the *Confederación Granadina were forced to flee during the *rebellion of 1859-1862.

SEMANARIO DEL NUEVO REINO DE GRANADA, El. One of Bogotá's earliest *newspapers, edited by Francisco José de *Caldas, 1808-1811. See also: NEWSPAPERS, 1785-1809

SENA, see: SERVICIO NACIONAL DE APRENDIZAJE

SENADO. The Senate, one of the houses of Congress (see: CONGRESS).

SENDAS, see: SECRETARIADO NACIONAL DE ASISTENCIA SOCIAL

SEPARATION OF CHURCH AND STATE. The union of Church and State was established during the colonial period and continued under the Law of the *Patronato,* 1824. Separation of Church and State was first legislated on June 15, 1853. Modified and repealed at various times from 1855 to 1886, it was permanently secured from 1886-1887. The act of 1853 was the first of its kind in Latin America.

SEPTEMBRINOS. "Septembrists," participants in or supporters of the *TWENTY-FIFTH OF SEPTEMBER CONSPIRACY to assassinate *Bolívar in 1828.

SERRANIA DE BAUDO. A mountain range on the Pacific Coast in the Department of *Chocó. High point in the range may be the Alto de Buey (1,810 meters).

SERVICIO AEREO COLOMBIANO. SACO was formed June 15, 1933, by Ernesto Samper Mendoza to link *Bogotá *Medellín, and *Cali with air service. Samper was killed when his plane crashed into another on takeoff, June 24, 1934. An agreement was made to merge SACO and *SCADTA in October 1939, but legal formalities were not completed until October 3, 1940, by which time SCADTA had become *AVIANCA. See also: AIR TRANSPORT

SERVICIO NACIONAL DE APRENDIZAJE. The National Service of Apprenticeship, or SENA. An organization established by law in 1957 to provide professional training for numerous skilled or semiskilled occupations, to aid in securing employment for trained personnel, and to conduct research programs to improve services in given occupations. Dr. Rodolfo Martínez Toro, of *Cartagena, was the man most responsible for its establishment.

SEVENTH OF MARCH, Election of the. March 7, 1849. *Congress declared José Hilario *López elected President of *New Granada. Vociferous crowds, which surrounded the building and filled the hall where Congress met, were accused of forcing legislators to vote for López in order to avoid violence.

SHEEP RANCHING, see: LIVESTOCK

SHIPPING, see: MERCHANT MARINE

SICARIO. A death-squad gunman. See also: DEATH SQUADS

SIERRA DE ABIBE, see: ABIBE, Sierra de

SIERRA DE LOS PIJAOS, see: CORDILLERA CENTRAL

SIERRA NEVADA DE SANTA MARTA. A mountain range on the Caribbean Coast, the Sierra Nevada extends 17,000 square kilometers, covering parts of the Departments of *Magdalena, *Cesar, and the *Guajira. It rises precipitously from the coast to the Peaks of Bolívar (5,775 meters) and Colón (5,770 meters), which are the highest points in Colombia. The range is located between the *Guajira Peninsula and the *Magdalena River. It was the home of the *Tairona Indians before the Spanish conquest.

SIERRA NEVADA DE SANTA MARTA STYLE. A type of pre-conquest Indian goldwork found on the Atlantic Coast, also know as the *Tairona Style. It is characterized by the use of *gold and *copper alloys worked with a mixture of techniques, including the lost-wax process, molding, soldering, casting, hammering, and repoussé, with frequent decoration of cast and braided threads. Typical pieces include nose rings, earrings, bells, rattles, anchor-shaped objects, and anthropomorphic figures reminiscent of the *Quimbaya, *Darien, and *Sinú styles.

SIGLO, EL. *Conservative *Bogotá daily *newspaper founded by Laureano *Gómez on February 1, 1936. It was edited in the early years by his chief lieutenant, José de la Vega, with a militant defense of Conservatism, criticism of *Liberal policies, and a pro-Axis line in its editorials on foreign affairs. Publication was suspended and Gómez was temporarily exiled in the wake of the attempted coup d'état against President *López Pumarejo in 1944. Its facilities were destroyed by fire during the *Bogotazo, and publication was suspended again during the *Rojas Pinilla government. In addition to President Gómez, directors of El Siglo have included President Belisario *Betancur and presidential candidate Alvaro *Gómez Hurtado. Its present circulation is about 65,000 copies.

SILVA, José Asunción, 1865-1896. Poet, essayist, born *Bogotá, November 27. He enjoyed a short stay in Paris (1884) and was also secretary to the Colombian legation in Caracas (1894), but essentially he followed a business career at which he ultimately failed. In literature he is called the precursor of *modernism in Colombia and Latin America. He was the author of eighty-five compositions in verse and numerous prose pieces. His major works, many of which were published posthumously, include the poem "Nocturno" (1894), the anthology, *Versos,* and the novel *De sobremesa.* After a number of personal misfortunes, Silva committed suicide.

SILVER. Mined in *Chocó, *Nariño, *Quindío, *Santander, *Tolima, *Antioquia, *Risaralda, and *Valle del Cauca. Output, which was recorded as 2.8 metric *tons in 1977 and 6.2

tons in 1985, may be compared to Chile's annual production of around 500 tons.

SIMON, Pedro, b. 1581.   A Franciscan priest who came to *Bogotá in 1604. He accompanied President Juan de *Borja on his campaigns against the *Pijaos and served as Provincial of the Franciscan Monastery in Bogotá after 1623. He was the author of *Noticias historiales de las conquistas de Tierra Firme en las indias occidentales,* first published in Cuenca, Spain, in 1627. Earlier authorities give 1574 as Simón's birth date, but recent scholarship suggests 1581. His exact date of death is unknown.

SIMON BOLIVAR HIGHWAY.   Name given to the Colombian portion of the 3,800 kilometer road from Caracas (Venezuela) to Guayaquil (Ecuador).

SINCELEJO.   Capital of *Sucre, located at 9° 18'N, 75° 24'W. The altitude is 213 meters; the average temperature, 26°C; and the population, 133,911 people (1985 estimate). An agricultural, cattle-ranching, and commercial center, Sincelejo is situated amid flat to rolling plains, which have become the richest cattle-raising region of Colombia. The city is located 195 kilometers from *Cartagena and 971 kilometers from Bogotá. It was founded on an old Indian site on October 4, 1535, with the name San Francisco de Asís de Sincelejo, but modern Sincelejo was stimulated by the colonizing efforts of Antonio de la Torre Miranda in the 1770s. It is remembered locally for the "Priests' Revolution" (*Revolución de las Curas*), when the priests of Chimú (Jorge Vásquez), Sampués, and Sincelejo publicly proclaimed their allegiance to Ferdinand VII on September 6, 1812. Sincelejo became the capital of the Department of *Sucre in 1966, although it had been capital of a short-lived Province of Sincelejo, 1898-1908, and of the Department of Sincelejo, 1908-1910.

SINDICATO OBRERO.   SO is the *Petroleum workers' union founded in *Barrancabermeja by Raúl *Mahecha in 1926. It was the successor of the *Sociedad Unión Obreros, which had been destroyed after the 1924 strike against the Tropical Oil Company (*TROCO). In additon to oil workers, SO also attracted support from local merchants who resented TROCO's company-store trading policies. SO led a major strike against TROCO on January 8, 1927. Tropical Oil fired more than 5,000 workers, and police and army troops used force to break the strike and to destroy the union. This event, together with the banana zone strike (*United Fruit Company Strike) of 1928, led to bitter resentment against both foreign businesses and the administration of President *Abadía Méndez. See also: UNION SINDICAL OBRERA

SINU. A name used to designate the people who inhabited the chiefdoms of Zenufana, Finzenú, and Panzenú in the Sinú, San Jorge, Nechí, and lower *Cauca River valleys. The territory of the Sinú spread across most of the present-day Department of *Córdoba and parts of *Antioquia and *Sucre. Each chiefdom was ruled by a separate leader—male or female—each a sibling of the other rulers. Agriculturally, Sinú society was based on *corn and *yuca cultivation, practiced on artificially created mounds or ridges. *Gold mining, *salt mining, and trade were also important economic activities. The name was also applied to the elaborate Indian burial grounds of these people near the Sierra de *Abibe on the lower portions of the Sinú River, where the conquistadors found considerable wealth in the guacas, or tombs of the Indians. Although Juan de la *Cosa (1510), Martín *Fernández de Enciso, and Francisco de Becerra (1529) all made incursions into the Sinú territory, conquest of these people was carried out by Pedro de *Heredia, Alonso de *Heredia, Francisco *César, Juan *Vadillo, and others after 1533. See also: SINU STYLE

SINU STYLE. A type of pre-conquest Indian *goldwork. It is characterized by techniques of molding, tempering, and the lost-wax process, with frequent decoration in false filigree or cast threads. The molds used in casting were possibly made from a fabric or netting of vegetable fibers. The most commonly found items in this style are large, semicircular ear and nose pieces, anthropomorphic and zoomorphic figures (including large-nosed birds, jaguars, frogs, and deer), scepter or staff heads, collars, and breastplates. Some suggest that the *Darién Style is a subcategory or derivative of the Sinú Style.

SISA. An excise tax, authorized by the Crown in 1625, imposed in *New Granada by President *Saavedra y Guzmán, 1637-1644, to cover the cost of new weapons. It was collected at various times thereafter and was frequently confused in practice with the *alcabala.

SITGES ACCORD. An agreement concluded July 20, 1957, in Sitges, Spain, between Alberto *Lleras Camargo and Laureano *Gómez, following the Pact of *Benidorm. It provided for collaboration of the *Liberal and *Conservative parties for a period of twelve years, alternation of the presidency between the parties, and parity in the appointment of national officials. These arrangements, ratified by a national referendum, December 1957, led to the formation of the first National Front (*Frente Nacional) government, with Lleras Camargo as President in 1958.

SLAVERY, see: AFRICAN SLAVERY; INDIAN SLAVERY

SO, see: SINDICATO OBRERO

SOCIAL CONSERVATIVE PARTY. The Partido Conservador Social, a name adopted by the main line of the Conservative Party in the mid-1980s. See also: CONSERVATIVE PARTY

SOCIALISM. Socialism as a new ideology appeared in Colombia in 1919 in the wake of the Russian Revolution. A Workers Assembly (Asamblea Obrera) created the first Socialist Party in *Bogotá, May 20, 1919, based on a program adopted from January-February 1919. The first national congress of this Socialist Party was held in August of the same year. A Socialist Congress in *Honda in 1920 produced the first socialist candidates for office in the elections of that year. The First Socialist Congress (Primer Congreso Nacional Obrero) was held May 1, 1924; the Second began on July 25, 1925; and the Third opened November 21, 1926 (all in Bogotá). Prominent leaders of the First Congress were Tomás Uribe Márquez, Francisco de Heredia, José María Olózaga, Nefatlí Arce, and Rodolfo von Wedell. Presiding over the Second Congress were Carlos F. León (President), Ismael Gómez (Vice President), Manuel *Quintín Lame (Second Vice President), and Gerardo Gómez (Secretary). Officers of the Third Congress were Ignacio *Torres Giraldo (President), María *Cano (Vice President), Raúl Eduardo *Mahecha (Second Vice President), and Tomás Uribe Márquez (Secretary). According to Carlos Uribe Celis and other authors, important figures of the early socialist movement also included Roberto García Peña, Francisco Socarrás, Moisés Prieto, Diego Montaña Cuéllar, Darío Samper, Felipe Lleras Camargo, José Mar, Guillermo Hernández Rodríguez, Alberto Castrillón,

Luis *Tejada, Armando Solano, León de *Greiff, and Silvestre Savidiski. The Second Congress proclaimed its adherence to the Third International and founded the Confederación Obrera Nacional (which may be the first socialist labor union in Colombia). The Third Congress founded the Revolutionary Socialist Party (see: PARTIDO COMUNISTA DE COLOMBIA; PARTIDO SOCIALISTA REVOLUCIONARIO).

SOCIALIST PARTY, see: PARTIDO SOCIALISTA REVOLUCIONARIO

SOCIALIZADORA GENERATION. The "Socialist," or "Socializing," Generation, a group of cultural leaders who, in the terms of Abel Naranjo Villegas, developed or were prominent in the period 1950 to 1980. Naranjo Villegas characterizes the generation as anti-bourgeois with marked tendencies in opposing directions: one, a reformist and often Marxist impulse toward the left, and the other, an anti-reform often fascist-like movement toward the right. Violence in politics was common. Ernesto Cortés Ahumada divides the period into two generations: the Bi-Front (or perhaps more accurately, the United Front) Generation (key date, 1945) and the Urban-Social Generation (key date, 1960). Representative figures of the Bi-Front Generation include Gilberto *Alzate Avendaño, Rafael Azula Barrera, Virgilio *Barco, Eduardo Carranza, Jaime Duarte French, Luis Duque Gómez, Ramón de la Espriella, Joaquín Estrada Monsalve, Gabriel Giraldo Jaramillo, Carlos *Lleras Restrepo, Alfonso *López Michelsen, Otto Morales Benítez, Victor Mosquera Chaux, Alejandro *Obregón, Lucio *Pabón Núñez, José Manuel Rivas Sacconi, Horacio Rodríguez Plata, Alberto Ruiz Novoa, Julio César *Turbay Ayala, Guillermo León *Valencia, Gilberto Vieira, and Manuel Zapata *Olivella. Representative figures of the Urban-Social Generation might include Horacio Gómez Aristizábal, Belisario *Betancur, Orlando Fals Borda, Pedro Gómez Valderamma, Misael *Pastrana Borrero, Eduardo Santa, Fernando Soto Aparicio, Camilo *Torres, and the poets Amilkar U. and X-504.

SOCIEDAD BIBLICA. The Bible Society, founded March 20, 1825, by James Thompson, agent for the British and Foreign Bible Society, with the collaboration of numerous government officials and clergymen. It quickly became the center of a theological dispute between Protestants and Catholics. The

Society lasted at least until 1838; it had more than 2,000 Bibles for distribution. See also: PROTESTANTISM

SOCIEDAD CATOLICA. The Catholic Society, an ultra-conservative political pressure group formed in 1838 by Ignacio Morales. It published the *newspaper *El Investigador Católico* (1838-1839), and tried to influence election results, but the society was not supported officially by the *Márquez administration or by the *Archbishop of Bogotá. It was largely unsuccessful, although it did exacerbate political tensions.

SOCIEDAD COLOMBIANA DE INGENIEROS. Colombian Society of Engineers. It was founded in 1887 and was later declared a government consultative organ.

SOCIEDAD COLOMBO-ALEMANA DE TRANSPORTES AEREOS. Colombia's second airline and the first to offer regularly scheduled service, SCADTA was formed in *Barranquilla on December 5, 1919, with a $100,000 capital investment by a combination of Colombians (Ernesto Cortissoz, Rafael María Palacio, Jacobo A. Correa, Cristóbal Restrepo J., and Aristides Noguera) and Germans (Albert Tietjen, Stuart Hosie, and Werner Kaemmerer, who was the engineer and prime mover of the project). The first pilots were *World War I veterans Wilhelm Schnurbusch, Fritz Hammer, and Helmuth von Krohn. They flew Junkers F-13 five-seat float planes. The first service began September 19, 1921, between Barranquilla and *Girardot, reducing the journey from ten days by river steamer to eight hours. An international service from *Buenaventura to Guayaquil, Ecuador, began June 10, 1928, but the Depression led SCADTA to sell 85% of its stock to Pan-American in 1930-1931. International flights were then taken over by Pan Am, and American Ford and Boeing Aircraft were introduced. A joint SCADTA–Pan Am mail service from New York to Bogotá began in July 1931. Between September 1932 and July 1933, SCADTA kept Colombian *army outposts supplied by air during the *Leticia Dispute with Peru. The approach of *World War II led Pan Am to dismiss all Germans working for SCADTA on June 8, 1940. Six days later the airline's name was changed to *AVIANCA. See also: AIR TRANSPORT

SOCIEDAD DE AGRICULTORES DE COLOMBIA. The SAC is an organization, founded December 15, 1871, to promote the interests of farm owners and agriculturalists. It is perhaps the oldest special-interest group in Colombia. The society was made a government consultative agency in 1909. It has published the *Revista Nacional de Agricultura* since 1906.

SOCIEDAD DE AMIGOS DEL PAIS, see: AMIGOS DEL PAIS, Sociedad de

SOCIEDAD DE ARTESANOS. The Artisans' Society, founded November 18, 1847, by Ambrosio López and others. An early labor association formed to protest free trade, it undertook welfare programs, particularly *education and political agitation. It declined in importance after 1851.

SOCIEDAD DE INTERCONEXION ELECTRICA S.A. The Society for Electrical Interconnection, a corporation formed in 1967 to supervise and direct Colombia's program of electrical distribution. The association had two major objectives: to achieve total integration of all electrical systems and to enlarge the generating capacity of the nation. See also: INSTITUTO COLOMBIANO DE ENERGIA ELECTRICA

SOCIEDAD DEMOCRATICA. The Democratic Society, a name given to political action groups, especially from 1849-1854. Members tended to reflect moderate liberal philosophies and to represent the working classes. They were opposed by analogous conservative groups. The Democratic Society was in some ways the successor of the Artisans' Society (*Sociedad de Artesanos). See also: DRACONIANOS; ESCUELA REPUBLICANA; SOCIEDAD FILOTEMICA; SOCIEDAD POPULAR

SOCIEDAD FILOTEMICA. The Philotemic Society, founded in October 1850. A response to the Republican School (*Escuela Republicana), the society was *Conservative and aimed specifically to neutralize the radical opposition of the *Golgótas and their supporters. See also: SOCIEDAD DEMOCRATICA

SOCIEDAD POPULAR. The Popular Society, a name given to conservative political action groups, 1849-1854. They opposed the *Sociedad de Artesanos, the *Sociedad Democrática, and the *Escuela Republicana. Popular Societies tended to oppose the policies of the *López and *Obando presidencies. The first Popular Society was founded on December 17, 1849, in *Bogotá. See also: SOCIEDAD FILOTEMICA

SOCIEDAD UNION OBREROS. SUO was a *trade union established in February 1923 among *petroleum workers in *Barrancabermeja. Founded by Raúl *Mahecha, SUO led its first strike against the Tropical Oil Company (*TROCO) on October 5-13, 1924. Although the government intervened on behalf of the workers, the union was destroyed immediately after the strike when TROCO fired more than 1,200 workers including the union leaders. See also: SINDICATO OBRERO; UNION SINDICAL OBRERA

SOCIETY OF JESUS, see: JESUITS

SOCORRO. Agricultural, commercial, industrial, cattle-raising center in the *Cordillera Oriental in the Department of *Santander, situated at 6° 28'N, 73° 16'W, approximately 121 kilometers from *Bucaramanga. Altitude is 1,230 meters; average temperature, 22°C; and the population, 17,500 (1985 estimate). The Socorro region was first conquered by Martín Galeano in about 1540, and the city was established on the Suárez River in 1671. It was made a parish of the Church in 1683 and given the title Villa de Nuestra Señora del Socorro on October 25, 1771. It functioned as an important regional commercial and administrative center throughout the colonial period. It is famous as the place where the *Comunero Revolt began. Socorro was also used at various times as the name of a province or department and was the capital of the State of Santander, August 1862 to March 1886.

SOGAMOSO. Municipal center located at 5° 43'N, 72° 56'W in the *Cordillera Oriental in the Department of *Boyacá, 78 kilometers from *Tunja. The city itself sits in a mountain valley (the Valley of Sogamoso) with an altitude of 2,569 meters but surrounding peaks—such as Toldo (3,650 meters) and El Motón (3,600 meters)—are much higher. The average temperature is 14°C, and the population, 64,398 people (1985 estimate). Pre-conquest Sogamoso was the site of a *Chibcha temple (see: SOGAMOSO, Temple of). Modern Sogamoso is a commercial center for agriculture, cattle raising, and light industry. It has railroad connections and is near *coal, asphalt, and marble deposits.

SOGAMOSO, Temple of. Also known as the temple of Suamo, it was a pre-Hispanic sanctuary of the sun, seat of the sacred *Iraca, or *Chibcha high priest. The cult of the temple, which revered *Bochica, is said to have been established by *Garan-chacha. The location of the temple was also referred to as the valley of the Iraca and the valley of *Sugamuxi. The temple was destroyed by fire during the Spanish conquest. See also: NEMQUETABA

SOLIS FOLCH DE CARDONA, José, 1716-1770. Viceroy of *New Granada, 1753-1761. He established the ceremony for the reception of new viceroys; assisted the Spanish-Portuguese *Boundary Commission, 1750-1753; enlarged the mint (*Casa de Moneda), 1753-1756; and inaugurated the first aqueduct in *Bogotá, 1757. He undertook numerous public works, such as the roads to Opón and the *Llanos, and aided missionary work among the Indians in the *Guajira, the *Chocó, and the Llanos. He is known as the "friar-viceroy" because he entered the *Franciscan order upon leaving office. He is also remembered for the scandal of Las *Marichuelas.

SOLIS Y VALENZUELA, Pedro de, 1624-1711. Probably the son of Pedro Valenzuela (d. 1660), a conquistador, and Juana Vásquez de Solís. Author of *El desierto prodigioso y prodigio de desierto,* written about 1650, but not published until 1977. First attributed to the author's brother (Fernando *Fernández Solís de Valenzuela), the work consists of twenty-two chapters containing poetry, dramatic pieces, religious meditations, and prose selections of various types. It has been described as the antecedent of the novel or prose fiction in Colombia. He was also the author of a biography of Archbishop Bernardo de Almansa published in Madrid in 1647. See also: *LAUREA CRITICA, La*

SONSO, Battle of. January 23, 1885, *Valle del Cauca. The rebellious forces of General Francisco Escobar and Colonel Guillermo Márquez were defeated by General Juan Evangelista Ulloa for the government during the *rebellion of 1884-1885.

SOUTHERN RAILROAD. A minor line running from *Bogotá to Santa Isabel (Sibaté, 4° 30'N, 74° 16'W) in *Cundinamarca. It was first authorized in 1892 as a line from Bogotá to Soacha (4° 35'N, 74° 17'W). An extension to Sibaté was approved in 1898, and work was completed in 1906. A branch to the *Tequendama Falls (4° 35'N, 74° 18'W) was begun in 1913.

SPAIN, Relations with. Colombia's *independence movement lasted from 1810 until 1826. It included an 1820 proposal, supported by Colombian minister Francisco A. *Zea, for a permanent federation of the independent states of Spain and Colombia and a perpetual defensive alliance between them, accompanied by the immediate withdrawal of Spanish troops from Colombia. The scheme was rejected in favor of unconditional independence. Friendly relations were restored by informal agreement in 1838, but Spain's war with Peru and Chile, 1865-1866, led President *Mosquera into a secret treaty with Peru against what seemed to be a general threat to South American independence. The unsettled state of Spanish internal affairs after 1868 delayed the signing of a treaty of peace, friendship, and commerce, which formally recognized Colombian independence until 1881 (see: PARIS, Treaty of). In the 20th century, Spain's adoption of a Liberal Republic in 1931 was a limited inspiration to the Colombian *Liberals who achieved power in 1930, but the Civil War of 1936-1939 split Liberal opinion. Only the most radical progressives favored the Republican side, while Conservatives and most senior clergy were vociferous supporters of the Nationalists. For some, the *Bogotazo of 1948 was a reenactment of the Spain of 1936.

SPANISH. The official language of *Colombia. As befits the conservative Hispanic nature of Colombian society, the local variety, especially among the upper classes of *Bogotá, is closer, perhaps, to the Castilian norm than is Spanish anywhere else in the Americas, with little more than the seseo (the pronunciation of z or c before a front vowel as s) to distinguish it. Among the older generation even lleísmo (the pronunciation of ll as a palatal l) still persists to some extent. The prestige of the *Instituto Caro y Cuervo testifies to the *Bogotano's concern with linguistic standards. English survives to some extent as a local vernacular in *San Andrés y Providencia.

SPANISH-COLOMBIAN FEDERATION PROJECT. A proposal supported by Colombian minister Francisco A. *Zea in 1820. It would have provided for an immediate withdrawal of Spanish troops from Colombia, a permanent federation of the independent states of Spain and Colombia, and a perpetual defensive alliance between the two countries. The scheme was rejected by Colombia in favor of unconditional independence.

SPANISH EMPIRE IN AMERICA, Administration of the. Spain was the first European nation to develop a major empire in the Western Hemisphere. The imperial system it devised was centralized, hierarchically organized, autocratic, bureaucratic, idealistic, regulated, and regimented. The colonies were intended to support and to be subordinate to the mother country. In the whole of Spanish America, the evolution of the system might be traced through its legal codes (the Laws of Burgos, 1512; the *New Laws of the Indies, 1542; the Recopilation of All the *Laws of the Indies, 1680; and the so-called Bourbon Reforms of the 18th century), but an equally useful tripartite periodization has been suggested, using 1500-1542 as the early conquest period, 1543-1700 as the high colonial (or Hapsburg) era, and 1700-1810 as the late colonial (or Bourbon) era. *New Granada (Colombia) was the third of four *viceroyalities created in the empire (Mexico, 1535; Peru, 1544; New Granada, 1739; and Rio de La Plata, 1776), and royal government was never so highly organized in New Granada as in Mexico or Peru.

Throughout the colonial period, overlapping jurisdictions were chronic, and almost any official might find himself exercising executive, legislative, judicial, military, and fiscal authority simultaneously. Within this admitted confusion, however, it is possible to suggest a picture of the imperial administrative structure. Ultimate authority lay with the Spanish monarch at the apex of the governmental hierarchy, but normal functions were handled by two official bureaucracies. Commercial affairs were entrusted to the House of Contracts (*Casa de Contratación, founded 1503). All other realms of life except religious matters were handled by the Council of the Indies (*Consejo de Indias, formally established in 1524). Religious issues fell under the jurisdiction of the Spanish secular clergy or approved *religious orders, all of which took political direction from the Crown, even though doctrinal matters remained the prerogative of the *Papacy. Policies emanated from these bodies in the Peninsula and were dispersed to officials in the colonies.

Within the colonies, the highest-ranking officials were *viceroys (*virreyes*), *presidents (*presidentes*), and judges (*oidores*) of the audience (*audiencia*), respectively. Because there were always more audiences than viceroyalties, and therefore more judges than viceroys, the judges of the audience were often the effective rulers of an area. Beneath these officials were a host of other appointees (*adelantados, gobernadores, corregidores, and so on.) with much more specific obligations and restricted powers. On the local level, government was shared by a town council (*cabildo*) and a mayor (*alcalde*). All royal officials were subject to an investigation (*residencia*) of their actions at the close of their term in office, and a special investigation, or visit (*visita*), could be launched at any time by a special commisioner called a visitor (*visitador*). During the course of a *visita,* the visitor's authority superseded all other officials in the area. Suffice it to say that religious matters were handled by separate but parallel hierarchies at all levels of government.

The evolution of administrative growth in Colombia can be seen in an initial period of conquest and government by audiences (1500-1563), a period of rule by presidents and audiences (1563-1739), and the period of the viceroyalty (1739-1810). A branch of the *Inquisition was established in *Cartagena in 1610, and Cartagena's function as a fortified commercial-defense center gave the Caribbean Coast an importance lacking in much of the rest of the colony.

The Bourbon reforms introduced in the 18th century were intended to increase royal control, make government more efficient by modernizing the bureaucracy, and to produce greater revenue by new technology and economic diversification. The *intendancy system was devised to accomplish this, but it was never fully implemented in Colombia. Free trade was permitted within the empire after 1789. On the whole, however, it has been said that the reforms failed to achieve the maximum results desired for the Crown while provoking hostile resentment from the colonists. Long distances, costs, insufficient personnel, and local interests had long balanced in practice the extreme regimentation of official policy. Colonists were accustomed to the practice of *Obedezco pero no cumplo* ("I obey, but I do not comply"). In effect, the king ruled in theory, but local custom just as often prevailed in practice. By the end of the 18th century, the gulf between theory and practice had become too wide to withstand the Bourbon attempt at greater centralization of power in and exploitation of the colonies.

SPEYER, Georg Hohermuth von, 1508-1540. A German explorer (whose name is also written "George Hohermuth von Speyer-am-Rhein" and "George Formut"), he was named Governor of the Welser territory in Venezuela in 1535. He explored the Colombian-Venezuelan border areas from Coro to the Casanare River and back again, 1535-1537. He died in Coro while planning a second expedition.

STEEL PRODUCTION. Colombia's steel production was 200,000 metric tons in 1965. It doubled to 402,000 tons by 1980 and reached 499,000 tons in 1984, only to fall to 277,000 tons in 1985. The 1985 total may be compared to the 1,786,000 tons produced in Venezuela and the *Andean Common Market's overall total of 2,393,000 tons. Colombia's most important steel complex is *PAZ DEL RIO. See also: IRON AND STEEL

STONE AGE SETTLEMENTS. According to Lucía Rojas de Perdomo, Stone Age, or *paleoindio,* cultures were characterized by hunting and gathering bands who sometimes utilized cave dwellings, in a stage of cultural evolution prior to the development of pottery. The oldest sites recorded in Colombia are El Abra and El Tequendama, both of which seem to be cultural ancestors of settlements studied at Nemocón and Sueva (all in the Department of *Cundinamarca). El Abra has yielded carbon 14 dates of 12,400 years ago (ca. 10,450 B.C.) and El Tequendama, 9,000 years ago (ca. 7050 B.C.). Nemocón and Sueva have C14 dates of about 7,530 years ago (ca. 5580 B.C.). Numerous other Stone Age sites have been reported in other departments. See: ABRA, El; TEQUENDAMA, El

STRIKES, see: DAYS OF MAY; PARO CIVICO DE 1977; ROSCA, Fall of the Conservative; TRADE UNIONS; TROPICAL OIL STRIKES; UNITED FRUIT COMPANY STRIKE. See also: SINDICATO OBRERO; SOCIEDAD UNION OBREROS

SUAMO. Another form of *SOGAMOSO.

SUAREZ, Marco Fidel, 1855-1927. Educator, linguist, diplomat, essayist, President of Colombia, 1918-1921. Born Hatoviejo (*Antioquia), April 23; died *Bogotá, April 3. He was educated at La Ceja, a seminary in *Medellín, and taught in Hatoviejo and, after moving to Bogotá in 1879, at the Colegio del Espíritu Santo. In various capacities, he served the Academy of Language (*Academia Colombiana de la Lengua), the National Library (*Biblioteca Nacional), and the Universidad Católica. In public office he was both Representative and Senator in *Congress; Minister of Foreign Relations, 1892-1895 and 1914-1917; Minister of Government, 1893; Minister of Public Instruction, 1899, 1911-1912; Minister of Finance,

1899; and Minister of the Treasury, 1899. His presidential administration approved laws regarding sanitary housing, and income and property taxes. It created a national school of veterinary medicine; undertook judicial reform; facilitated the establishment of telephone service; and presided over the introduction of commercial aviation (see: *AIR TRANS-PORT). He is remembered in international affairs for the *Suárez Doctrine. President Suárez was forced to resign by social and political pressures during a financial crisis in 1921. He was the author of a series of literary and political essays, *Sueños de Luciano Pulgar,* and a prayer, *Oración a Jesucristo,* among other things. He is often described as the Abraham Lincoln of Colombia because of his humble background.

SUAREZ DOCTRINE.   A reference to the viewpoint of Marco Fidel *Suárez, Colombian internationalist, who stressed the special links of friendship between the Bolivarian republics. Although more often regarded as a general principle of conduct, the concept was specifically enunciated on April 4, 1920, by President Suárez in a speech on the Rumichaca Bridge, which connects Ecuador and Colombia.

SUAREZ–LOSADA DIAZ TREATY OF 1916.   Signed *Bogotá, November 3, by Marco Fidel *Suárez, Colombia, and Demetrio Losada Díaz, Venezuela. The treaty submitted to arbitration by Switzerland the question of whether the arbitrament given in 1891 could be applied in part or only in its totality. The decision in 1922 favored the Colombian interpretation of partial application. This allowed the observance of the 1891 decision where actual boundaries had been drawn even though there were areas where this had not been accomplished. Efforts to delineate the remaining boundaries were undertaken immediately. A further agreement signed in 1928 facilitated work throughout the 1930s.

SUAREZ–MUÑOZ VERNAZA TREATY OF 1916.   Signed July 15, in *Bogotá, by Marco Fidel *Suárez, Colombia, and Alberto Muñoz Vernaza, Ecuador. The treaty resolved all existing territorial disputes between the two nations, thereby establishing the international boundary between them. Free navigation of jointly held rivers was guaranteed in perpetuity.

SUAREZ RENDON, Gonzalo, d. 1583.   Captain, conquistador. A member of *Jiménez de Quesada's expedition, 1536-1539, he was the founder of *Tunja, 1539, and Governor of *Bogotá, 1541-1543. He later settled in Tunja, where he lived until his death.

SUBACHOQUE, Battle of. April 25, 1861, at 4° 56'N, 74° 11'W, *Cundinamarca. General T. C. de *Mosquera, rebel, defeated General Joaquín París, overthrowing acting President Bartolomé *Calvo and the *Confederación Granadina during the *rebellion of 1859-1862.

SUBSOIL MINERAL RIGHTS. By traditional Spanish law, control of subsoil *mineral deposits was reserved for the Spanish Crown. Even though control of land surface might pass into private ownership, subsoil resources remained a monopoly of the monarchy. This practice was frequently continued by Colombia and other Latin American nations when they became independent. In Colombian history, the practice did not become a major issue until the 20th century, when *petroleum production began, but it was a troublesome problem, 1919-1929 (see: DECREE 150; DECREE 1225 BIS; LAW 120). The most recent statement of subsoil ownership by the state is found in Article 332 of the *Constitution of 1991.

SUCRE, Antonio José de, 1795-1830. General, Grand Marshal of *Ayacucho. A patriot military leader, 1811-1824, he was second in command to *Bolívar. He held major responsibilities during the Battles of *Pichincha (Ecuador), *Junín (Peru), and *Ayacucho (Peru). He was President of Bolivia, 1826-1828. Sucre was assassinated on June 4, 1830, at *Berruecos (*Nariño). His death had repercussions in Colombian politics until 1849.

SUCRE, Departamento de. Located on the Caribbean Coast, the department covers 10,917 square kilometers of tropical plains and swamps lying between 8° 17' and 10° 8'N latitude, and 74° 31' and 75° 43'W longitude. Average temperatures range from 27° to 30°C. The *Cordillera Occidental ends within the department, and toward the south there is a marshy lowland known as the Depresión Momposina. Major rivers include the *Cauca and San Jorge. Population is 523,525 people (1985 estimate), with a population density of forty-eight persons per square kilometer in the department. The capital city is *Sincelejo. Within the department cattle raising predominates. According to DANE, *Colombia estadística 86,* principal agricultural products, with tonnage produced in 1984, include yams, 48,000 tons; rice, 22,110; *corn, 19,700; sorghum, 16,600; plantains, 15,600; *cotton, 10,500; *yuca, 10,000; *tobacco, 3,600; coconuts, 1,998; sesame, 180; and *cacao, 10. In 1983 there were 32,874 head of cattle and 2,743 hogs slaughtered. There were ten businesses employing more than ten workers. There is also cement manufacturing and important *hydroelectric production. At the time of the conquest the region was occupied by the Zenu (See: SINU) and Turbaco Indians. Among the first explorer-conquerors in the area were Alonso de *Ojeda, Juan de la *Cosa, and Francisco *César. The present Department of Sucre was created in 1966 from territory previously in the Department of *Bolívar.

SUGAMUXI. A posthumous name for *NEMQUETABA; also said to be the name of the last *Iraca of the *Chibchas.

SUGAR. Cultivation of sugarcane in Colombia dates from the early conquest era. Sebastián de *Belalcázar is credited with importing sugarcane to grow on his estate "La estancia" in Yumbo, near *Cali. Although grown throughout the colonial period, development of sugarcane as an important export crop occurred only in the 19th century through the efforts of families such as the Caicedos, Eders, Cabales, Becerras, and Isaacs. Colombia remained a relatively minor exporter of sugar until the 1960s. One authority says, for example, that in 1959, there were 11,000 sugar workers in Colombia, while ten years later there were 28,000. The Cuban sugar crisis, the growth of the *Corporación Autónoma Regional del Cauca, and the formation of ASOCA°A (the *Asociación Nacional de Cultivadores de Caña de Azucar) all stimulated the development of sugar production. In the period from 1961 to 1968, Colombia expanded to become the third largest sugar exporter in Latin America, surpassed only by Brazil and Cuba. The nation's four largest milling companies (Manuelita, Río Paila, Central Castilla, and Providencia) are located in the *Cauca Valley. Manuelita, founded in 1901, is the oldest of these firms; Río Paila, established in 1926, is the largest.

SUMAPAZ, Agricultural Colony of. The *Colonia Agrícola de Sumapaz* was the largest organization formed by squatters and small colonists in the 1930s. Located in southwestern *Cundinamarca, the colony was founded by Erasmo Valencia, Juan de la Cruz Varela, and others around 1930 to defend the interests of peasants, colonists, and squatters who thought their lands were under attack from entrepreneurs and large estate owners. More than an estimated 6,000 squatters formed a society that conducted its own judicial and administrative affairs and flew its own independent flag. Chief aims of the colony were the defense of the community and the property rights of its members. A number of violent clashes occurred with government authorities before the community declined in the latter part of the decade as a result of government land redistribution programs and the Land Reform Act (*Law 200) of 1936. The Agricultural Colony of the 1930s is often said to have been the forerunner of the independent republics such as *Marquetalia, Ríochiquito, El Pato, and Guayabero in the same region during the 1960s.

SUMAPAZ, Region. A region in the *Cordillera Oriental at the junction of the Departments of *Cundinamarca, *Huila, and *Meta. The terrain is very mountainous and is distinguished by peaks such as El Nevado, 4,500 meters; Las Oseras, 3,830; Ramírez, 3,780; and El Rayo, 3,720. The Sumapaz River originates in the mountains at 3° 43'N, 74° 30'W. The area is essentially one of subsistence farming and forestry.

SUO, see: SOCIEDAD UNION OBREROS

SUPREME COMMANDERS, War of the. The *Guerra de los Supremos*, 1840-1842. It began with General José María *Obando in *Nariño and *Cauca in 1840 with subsequent uprisings by Colonel Salvador *Córdoba in *Antioquia, Manuel *González in *Santander, Juan José Reyes Patria in *Boyacá, Francisco Carmona in *Santa Marta, Juan A. *Gutiérrez de Piñeres in *Cartagena, General Tomás *Herrera in *Panama and elsewhere. The rebellion was characterized by a number of simultaneous, although largely uncoordinated, federalistic revolts. Significant military engagements included La *Polonia, *Huilquipamba, *Buenavista, *Itagüi, *Riofrío, *Aratoca, *Tescua, *Salamina, *La Chanca, and *Ocaña.

SUPREME COURT. The Supreme Court of Justice (*Corte Suprema de Justicia*), the Constitutional Court (*Corte Constitucional*), and the *Council of State (*Consejo de Estado*) form the national judiciary under the *Constitution of 1991. The Supreme Court is the court of final appeals for ordinary legal matters, annulments or contractual disputes, and it tries members of Congress, diplomatic agents, and other public officials for misconduct in office. The Council of State hears cases involving administrative issues and proposes laws regarding administrative practices. The Constitutional Court is charged with seeing that laws, treaties, or other public policies do not violate the constitution and with ruling on the propriety of proposed constituent conventions, referenda, or plebescites. The Supreme Court and the Council of State appoint justices to fill their own respective membership from lists of nominees submitted by a special judiciary council (*Consejo Superior de Judicatura*). A candidate for election to any of the three judiciary courts must be a native-born citizen in good standing, without a criminal record, as well as a professional lawyer with ten years' experience in the practice of law or related public service or a professor of law. Justices are elected for eight years and cannot be reelected. Under previous documents, such as the *Constitution of 1886, the national judiciary was much simpler in structure and the term "Supreme Court" normally referred to a single body.

SUPREME COURT MASSACRE, see: PALACIO DE JUSTICIA, Attack on the

SUPREME JUNTA OF GOVERNMENT, see: JUNTA SUPREMA DE GOBIERNO

SYMBOLISM, see: DECADENTISM

-T-

TAIRONA STYLE, see: SIERRA NEVADA DE SANTA MARTA STYLE

TAIRONAS. A pre-conquest *Indian civilization inhabiting the Atlantic Coast and the slopes of the *Sierra Nevada de Santa Marta, the Taironas were divided into two major groups. The Province of Tairona, with Taironaca as its capital, was located on the northern slopes of the Sierra Nevada, and the Province of Betoma, with Pocigueyca as its capital, was located on the western slopes. Among the best-known sites of the Taironas were Pueblito (Chairama) on the Piedras River, Taironaca on the Don Diego River, Ciudad Perdida (Buritaca-200) on the Buritaca River, Cincorona, and Ciudad Antigua. Early Spanish settlers called the region La Ramada. The most extensive archeological studies have been carried out at Pueblito, Ciudad Perdida, and La Aguja (near *Santa Marta). Tairona civilization had highly developed social organization, ceramic and goldwork, weaving, and urban/agricultural engineering. Its economy was based on *fishing, *agriculture (*corn, *yuca, and *cotton), and commerce. The Taironas were, by some definitions, the most highly developed of Colombia's pre-conquest Indians. Remains of architectural and engineering achievements of the Taironas include paved roads; stone stairways and retaining walls; bridges; canals, aqueducts, and drainage systems; agricultural terraces; raised platforms for housing construction; and public plazas for ceremonial centers. Although the origins of the Tairona civilization may be earlier, a great many of the Tairona ceramics date from about 1000 B.C. Conquest of the Taironas was begun by Pedro de *Badillo and others in expeditions from nearby *Santa Marta, 1526-1528, but not completed for nearly a century, until the governorship of Diego de Argote around 1618. The present-day Kogi, Sanka, and Ika Indians are descendants of the Taironas. See also: CHIBCHAS; CIUDAD PERDIDA; SIERRA NEVADA DE SANTA MARTA STYLE

TAMARA DE MARQUETALIA, see: MARQUETALIA

TANCO ARGAEZ–PORRAS TREATY, see: PUTUMAYO DISPUTE

TANCO ARGAEZ–PRADO UGARTECHE–VELARDE TREATY, see: PUTUMAYO DISPUTE

TARQUI, Battle of. February 27, 1829. General Antonio José de *Sucre, Colombia, defeated the Peruvian army under President José de la Mar at the Portete de Tarqui, near Cuenca, Ecuador (see: PERU, War of 1828-1829 with).

TAXATION. The Spanish administration brought with it to the New World the biblical *tithes (diezmos) on agricultural income, the Roman gabella sales tax (*alcabala in Spanish), and the Moorish *almojarifado (almojarifazgo), or customs duty. The *Indians were required to contribute their labor, at first to the individual Spaniard to whom they were assigned (the *encomienda* system), and later to the state through the *mita*, but eventually they were allowed to commute these into a monetary *tributo*. The increasing fiscal difficulties of the Spanish state led to new burdens, such as the *sisa* (an excise tax) and the *camellón*. To pay for coastal defense in a period of increasing *piracy, a special Windward Fleet tax (*Armada de Barlovento*) was levied on a number of everyday commodities. And to discourage various petty vices, the sale of dice, playing cards, *aguardiente,* and *tobacco was limited in the mid-18th century to the *estanco,* a high-priced government monopoly. Although the wish to escape such burdens was a major motivation for the break with Spain, the financially hard-pressed governments of the independence period dared not immediately dispense with them all. The *tributo* persisted until 1833, tithes and the tobacco *estanco* until mid-century. Revenue from salt was also important, and in 1863, 15% of it was formally pledged to secure a new £200,000 loan. But the main recourse of independent Colombia was to customs duties. These were generally contemplated solely in their function as revenue raisers. A consistent policy of protective tariffs to aid *manufacturing dates from 1950. The most important fiscal innovation since independence was the 1918 introduction of *income tax. See also: PAPEL SELLADO

TEATRO COLON. The Colón Theater, probably the oldest theater continuously in service in *Bogotá. Located on Calle 10, between Carreras 5 and 6, it was begun in 1885 on the site of the old Coliseo Ramírez, Bogotá's first theater, when President Rafael *Núñez expropriated the Teatro Maldonado (see: COLISEO RAMIREZ) by decree of September 14, in order to create a national theater. A group of Italian artists was hired to construct and decorate the building, including Pedro Cantini, César Sighinolfi, Luis Ramelli, and Felipe Mastellari. The stage curtain was designed by A. Gatti. By Law 25 of October 6, 1892, the theater was named *Colón in honor of Christopher Columbus. It was first used on August 8, 1892, for a dinner in honor of Carlos *Holguín, but it was publicly inaugurated on October 12, 1892. The performance of the opera *Hernani* by the Company of Augusto Azzali, in 1895, however, marks the real beginning of its history as a theatrical center.

TEJADA CANO, Luis, 1888-1924. Journalist, author, political leader; born Barbosa (*Antioquia), February 7; died *Girardot,

September 17. Luis Tejada was a columnist who wrote some 150 "chronicles," or short interpretative essays on the history and politics of Colombia. Known as *gotas de tinta* ("ink drops"), the columns appeared in *El *Espectador* and *El Sol,* in *Bogotá. Some of these chronicles were collected in his only major book, *Libro de crónicas* (1924). Tejada was President of the Executive Committee of the Communist Group in Bogotá, and he helped organize an early socialist group in *Pereira known as La Golconda (not to be confused with the *Golconda Movement of the 1960s).

TEJIDOS UNICA.   One of Colombia's major textile firms. Unlike COLTEJER (*Compañía Colombiana de Tejidos), FABRICATO (*Fábrica de Hilados y Tejidos de Hato), and Tejicondor, all located in Medellín, Tejidos Unica is located in *Manizales. It was founded in 1932.

TELEVISION.   Black-and-white television was introduced in Colombia on June 13, 1954, by the government of General *Rojas Pinilla to commemorate the first anniversary of the establishment of his dictatorship and to generate continued support for his policies. The broadcast originated in the presidential offices in the Palace of San Carlos (*Bogotá) and early telecasts continued to be controlled by an official press agency (Oficina de Información y Prensa del Estado). Transmitting equipment was purchased from Germany and the United States, German and Cuban specialists were used to train broadcasting personnel, guest performers were invited from numerous countries, and the *Banco de la República was authorized to make available an initial quota of 40,000 imported television sets at cost. Experiments with commercial broadcasting from 1955-1957 were only temporarily successful, and nongovernmental programming had to await the fall of the Rojas Pinilla regime. CARACOL (one of the major radio broadcasting companies), Punch Limitada (founded in 1956 by Alberto Peñaranda), and Radio Television Interamericana (R.T.I.) took the lead in developing regular telecasts. During the period from 1965-1970, a major innovating figure was Consuelo de Montejo, whose independent "Teletigre" drew larger audiences than the major networks. Color television was introduced in 1979, and a national supervisory agency, INRAVISION (Instituto Nacional de Radio y Televisión) was created under the administration of Guillermo León *Valencia in 1962. In the 1980s there were three national channels, all based in Bogotá and under the supervision of INRAVISION. Commercial companies were allowed to hire time on the state-controlled channels for programs supported by advertising revenue. Telecasts have become more important than radio broadcasts commercially even though the size of radio audiences remains larger. See also: RADIO BROADCASTING

TENERIFE, Battle of. June 27, 1820, Department of *Magdalena, on the *Magdalena River (9° 54'N, 74° 52'W). Lieutenant Colonels José María *Córdoba and Hermógenes Maza captured Tenerife from royalist forces, giving the patriot armies access to the Caribbean Sea. It set the stage for the siege of *Cartagena.

TENTH OF FEBRUARY, Conspiracy of.   An abortive attempt to assassinate General Rafael *Reyes in *Bogotá in 1906. The affair resulted in the executions of Juan Ortiz E., Carlos Roberto González, Fernando Aguilar, and Marco Tulio Salgar. Others were imprisoned.

TEQUENDAMA, El.   Also referred to as Tequendama Man, after the remains found at an archeological site, El Tequendama, near Soacha (4° 35'N, 74° 17'W, *Cundinamarca), where the earliest recorded human remains found in Colombia were discovered. Lithic artifacts found at the site were similar to those of El Abra. A series of human skeletal remains were dated from 9,000 years ago (ca. 7050 B.C.) to 5,805 years ago (ca. 3855 B.C.). The Tequendama site shows evidence of occupation from these dates to those of the *Chibcha era. See also: ABRA, El; STONE AGE SETTLEMEMTS

TEQUENDAMA FALLS.   A well-known, picturesque waterfall on the Bogotá River on the western edge of the *Sabana de Bogotá near Soacha (*Cundinamarca). The falls are 157 meters high at 4° 35'N, 74° 18'W, some 2,467 meters above sea level. They are said to have been created by the god Bochica and are one of the best-known tourist sites in Colombia. See: BOCHICA; CHIBCHACHUN

TERTULIA.   Literally, a "party" or "soirée," but more specifically a literary society or discussion group popular in the late 18th century and afterward. *Tertulias* most often cited in Colombian colonial history are the *Arcano de la Filantropía, organized around 1789 by Antonio *Nariño; the Tertulia del *Buen

Gusto, presided over by Manuela Santamaría de Manrique; and the Tertulia *Eutropélica, founded by Manuel del Socorro *Rodríguez, 1790. It was probably for discussion by one of these groups that Nariño published *The *Rights of Man* in 1793 (see also: AMIGOS DEL PAIS, Sociedad de). In the 19th century, major *tertulias* included El *Parnasillo and El *Mosaico, and in the 20th century, La *Gruta Simbólica and Los *Nuevos.

TESCUA, Battle of.   April 1, 1841, *Norte de Santander. General T. C. de *Mosquera, for the government, defeated the rebellious forces of General Francisco Carmona. It was a major victory for the government during the War of the *Supreme Commanders, 1840-1842.

TEXTILES, see: MANUFACTURING INDUSTRY

THEATER, see: COLISEO RAMIREZ; *ESTER;* EZPELETA GALDEANO, José de; LITERATURE; TEATRO COLON

THIERRY CONCESSION.   A privilege granted in 1835 to Charles de Thierry for construction of a canal across the Isthmus of *Panama via the Chagres River. It later passed to Augusto Salomón and Co., but it was never satisfactorily implemented. However, it did serve to stimulate French interests in a canal (see: COMPAGNIE UNIVERSELLE DU CANAL INTER-OCEANIQUE DU PANAMA).

THIRTY-FIRST OF JULY MOVEMENT.   Action of *Conservatives and *Liberals that deposed ailing President Manuel Antonio *Sanclemente and installed Vice President José Manuel *Marroquín in his place on July 31, 1900. The incident marked the demise of the *Nationalist Conservatives.

THOMSON-URRUTIA TREATY, see: URRUTIA-THOMSON TREATY

THOUSAND DAYS, War of the.   Also called the Three Years War, it lasted from October 17, 1899, to June 1, 1903. Liberals revolted against the rigidly partisan governments of President *Sanclemente and Vice President *Marroquín. Major military engagements included *Peralonso and *Palonegro. The rebellion was settled by the Treaties of Nerlandia, the *Wisconsin, and Chinácota.

THREE YEARS WAR, see: THOUSAND DAYS, War of the

TIEMPO, EL. One of Latin America's outstanding daily newspapers. It was founded by Alfonso Villegas on January 20, 1911, with an announced intention of rising above partisan politics in support of the *Unión Republicana of the time. However, the paper is more commonly identifed as a *Liberal Party paper because Eduardo *Santos was its owner-operator from 1913 to 1974, and his heirs continue to operate it. Among others, its directors have included Roberto García Peña, Germán *Arciniegas, Alberto *Lleras Camargo, and Carlos *Lleras Restrepo. The paper is known for its regularity, with publication having been interrupted only briefly in 1948 after the *Bogotazo,* in 1952 after vandals destroyed the offices, and in 1955 by the government of *Rojas Pinilla. It was published under the name *El Intermedio* from 1955 to 1957. Circulation, between 200,000 and 300,000, is rivaled only by *El *Espectador.*

TIERRADENTRO. The Tierradentro region lies in the Cordillera Central in northern *Cauca and southern *Huila, where the Páez River and the Negro de Narváez River meet. At the time of the conquest it was the home of various tribes of the Páez Indians (*Paeces) including the Huilas, Guanacas, Nátagas, Iquiras, Jaguaraes, Bachéas, Pataes, and Guaguas, many of whose descendants still live in the area. The origin of the pre-Hispanic archeological complex in the northern *Cauca known as Tierradentro is not clear, although carbon 14 dates establish occupation of the site from A.D. 610 to 850. One theory attributes the site to the Paéz Indians even though they were not directly inhabiting it at the time of the conquest. Tierradentro is distinguished by inverted bowl-shaped subterranean chambers (tombs), some with supporting columns and niches, decorated with predominantly black-and-white geometric designs. Lithic statuary (2-6 meters high) at the site may be unrelated to the tombs. Ceramics do not show a distinctly differentiated style but display influences from *SAN AGUSTIN, Mesoamerica, and other cultures. The economy seems to have been based on *agriculture (*corn and tubers), hunting, *fishing, and *salt mining. Tierradentro was contemporaneous with San Agustín, but the relationship is not clear. Exploration of the region was begun by Sebastián de *Belalcázar in 1539, but fierce resistance from the Paéz delayed complete domination until after the War of the *Pijaos, 1605-

1618. The earliest Spanish record of Tierradentro may be the description of Fray Juan de *Santa Gertrúdis in 1756.

TIME. Spanish America adopted the Gregorian calendar in October 1583, making dates from colonial sources—followed in this *Dictionary*—ten days later than the corresponding Anglo-American dates through February 1700, and eleven days later from March 1700 until the British Empire abandoned the old Julian calendar in September 1757. Colombia is five hours behind Greenwich Mean Time, which makes it the same as Atlantic time.

TIN. A small amount of tin is mined in the Department of *Cauca.

TINTERILLO. Literally, "one who uses ink," or derisively, an ink spiller. Historically, the term was one of opprobrium, describing a person with the mentality of a petty bureaucrat, or someone who perverted the course of justice; a pettifogger, especially in *Bogotá.

TIQUISA, Battle of. May 21, 1854, *Cundinamarca. General *Melo, dictator, defeated the constitutionalist forces of General Marcelo Buitrago.

TIROFIJO. "Sure Shot." A nickname for Pedro Antonio *MARIN. See also: FUERZAS ARMADAS REVOLUCIONARIAS DE COLOMBIA; GUERRILLAS; MARQUETALIA

TISQUESUSA. *Zipa of the *Chibchas, 1514-1538. Known as the Lord of Bacatá (Bogotá), he burned the seat of his government, Muequetá (Funza, 4° 43′N, 74° 13′W, *Cundinamarca) as *Jiménez de Quesada and the Spanish approached. He fled to *Facatativá but was discovered and fatally wounded.

TITHES. *Diezmos* in Spanish, the biblical 10% tax on agricultural income for Church support came to the New World with the Spanish conquest. It impinged on cereals, vegetables, *cotton, silk, fruit trees, *livestock, *sugar, milk, cheese, and other produce, and was collected by the secular authorities as an aspect of the close relationship between the Crown and the established Church. Governments after independence continued to collect it as part of the royal *patronato* they claimed to have inherited. It became politically controversial as many

Liberals sought complete *separation of Church and State. Its abolition was necessarily included in the disestablishment legislation of June 1853.

TOBACCO. Tobacco was native to the Western Hemisphere, and small amounts were produced from the earliest periods of colonial settlement. Colombian tobacco was exported at least as early as 1700, but with the 1766 creation of the *ESTANCO, its supply became a government monoply, and the colonial regime preferred importing it from the *Casa de Contratación. Local production was discouraged in favor of importation from the Portuguese colony of Brazil. After independence, the smallness of the profit that growers could make selling it to the *estanco* continued to discourage its cultivation until government control was abolished in 1850. After that, production increased rapidly, particularly around *Ambalema in northern *Tolima and then in the 1860s in *Bolívar and in *Cauca during the 1870s. Exports peaked in 1867 (51% of total Colombian exports) only to fall precipitously after 1870. By 1877 tobacco accounted for only 10% of export earnings, and production reached a crisis in 1887. This was due to the declining quality of the Colombian crop and competition from European colonies in the Far East. Colombia continues to grow and export tobacco, but the product has never regained the importance it enjoyed in the mid-19th century. Government regulation was reestablished in 1893. In 1985 some 42,800 metric *tons were produced as compared with 411,000 tons in Brazil, 56,000 in Mexico, and 46,000 in the Dominican Republic.

TOCAIMA. City in *Cundinamarca located at 4° 28'N, 74° 38'W, on the western slopes of the *Cordillera Oriental, approximately 102 kilometers from Bogotá. The surrounding terrain is plains to rolling hills. Altitude is 400 meters; average temperature, 26°C; and population, 7,592 people (1985 estimate). Tocaima is a railroad station serving an agricultural, cattle-raising, and mining community. The original settlement founded by Hernán (sometimes written "Fernán") Vanegas Carillo de Manosalva, Alonso de Vera, Asencio Salinas, and Lope de Acuña on the *Bogotá River in 1544 was destroyed by flood, but the permanent settlement was reestablished on its present location in 1581. Tocaima is known for its thermal springs, which make it a popular tourist site.

TOLEDO PLATA, Carlos, d. 1984. Physician and *ANAPO congressman who went underground in 1979, joining the *Movimiento Diecinueve de Abril. He was captured while commanding the *Columna Antonio Nariño. Later amnestied and ostensibly no longer involved with *guerrilla activities, he was assassinated in 1984.

TOLIMA, Departamento de. The department is located in central Colombia on the *Cordilleras Central and Oriental. It covers 23,562 square kilometers of mountainous terrain between 2° 59' and 5° 18'N latitude, and 74° 29' and 76° 5'W longitude. Of the total territory, some 9,771 square kilometers have tropical climate; 5,848 are temperate; 4,905 cold; and 3,038 wasteland. Major rivers include the Aico, Alvarado, Ambeima, Amoyá, Anaime, Atá, Cabrera, Combeima, Cunday, Gualí, Guamo, Luisa, *Magdalena, Ortega, Sumapaz, Toche, Venadillo, and Saldaña. High points in the department include the Nevado de Huila, 5,750 meters, and the *Nevado del Ruiz, 5,400; and the peaks of Tolima, 5,215; Quindío, 5,150; and Santa Isabel, 5,100. The population is 1,028,239 people (1985 estimate), with a population density of 43.6 people per square kilometer. The capital city is *Ibagué. According to DANE, *Colombia estadística 86,* principal agricultural products, with tonnage produced in 1984, include rice, 439,204; sorghum, 137,561; plantains, 111,000; *potatoes, 72,900; *cotton, 70,200; *yuca,* 63,000; *corn, 35,250; *sugar, 34,000; sesame, 3,091; peanuts, 3,000; soybeans, 2,293; beans, 2,140; *cacao, 2,100; and *tobacco, 1,300. There were 136,104 head of cattle and 41,316 hogs slaughtered in the department in 1984, and there were 109 businesses employing 10 or more people in 1983. *Gold, *silver, *iron, *lead, *coal, *petroleum, calcite, quartz, and *mercury are produced in the department, and *coffee cultivation is important. The first Spanish conquerors in the region were Sebastián de *Belalcázar (1538) and Hernán *Pérez de Quesada (1541). During the period from 1550 1560, Andrés López de Galarza founded *Ibagué (October 14, 1550), and Francisco Núñez de Pedrozo established *Mariquita (August 8, 1551) and *Honda (August 24, 1560). Tolima was the scene of the *Pijao wars of the 16th and 17th centuries. Present-day Tolima was composed of the Provinces of *Neiva and *Mariquita during the colonial period. Mariquita declared its independence from Spain on December 20, 1814, and joined the republican government based in Bogotá on August 17, 1819. In 1824, the territory was again the Province of Mariquita (with jurisdiction over the cantons of Mariquita, Honda, Ibagué, and La Palma) and the Province of Neiva (with the cantons of Timaná, La Plata, and Purificación). The State of Tolima was first established on April 12, 1861, by General T. C. de *Mosquera, from the former provinces of Mariquita and Neiva. The department was originally created in 1886, but it was reduced in size by 19,890 square kilometers when the Department of *Huila was separated from the southern part of Tolima in 1905. Ibagué became the capital of Tolima in 1887. The Department of Tolima has always been important strategically as a link between north-south and east-west communication routes.

TOLIMA RAILROAD.   Originally a line connecting *Girardot on the *Magdalena River with *Ibagué. It was authorized in 1892 and begun by Carlos Tanco in 1893. Construction progressed from *Girardot to *Espinal by 1907, to Chicoral in 1914, and finally to Ibagué in 1921. An extension of the line south from Ibagué to *Huila and *Caquetá via Espinal was authorized in 1911. Service from Ibagué to *Neiva was completed in 1938, but the projected connection to Caquetá was never built. In the same way, the Tolima line was incorporated into the proposed *Pacific Railroad in 1913, but construction between Ibagué and *Armenia, across the *Cordillera Central, was never completed. An extension northward from Ibagué to *Ambalema joining the Tolima and La *Dorada railways was built from 1921-1930. See also: RAILROADS

TOLIMA STYLE.   A type of pre-conquest Indian *goldwork typical of the Department of *Tolima. The style is characterized by the techniques of casting with the lost-wax process or by cutting and hammering from flat sheets. Finished works tend to be highly polished. The most unique pieces in the Tolima style are flat geometric figures in a basic cruciform or anchor shape.

TON, see: WEIGHTS AND MEASURES

TORRES, Camilo.   For the patriot martyr of the 19th century, see: TORRES Y TENORIO, Camilo. For the priest and revolutionary of the 20th century, see: TORRES RESTREPO, Camilo.

TORRES, Cristóbal de, 1573-1654.   *Dominican, Archbishop of *Bogotá, 1635-1654. He is remembered for numerous philanthropic acts and is the author of several inspirational works. He entrusted *San Pedro Hospital to the monks of San Juan de Dios; opened the *Universidad de Santo Tomás, 1639; and inaugurated the *Colegio Mayor de Nuestra Señora del Rosario, 1653.

TORRES, Diego de, 1549-1590. A *mestizo *encomendero* known as the **cacique,* or chief, of Turmequé (5° 20'N, 73° 30'W, *Boyacá). He was the son of a Spanish conqueror, Juan de Torres, and Catalina de Moyachoque, a sister of the chief of Turmequé. After inheriting an **encomienda* at Turmequé from his father in 1570, Torres was the object of numerous efforts to deprive him of jurisdiction over the *Indians and of repeated attempts to convict him of fomenting rebellion among them. He was acquitted of all major charges in 1587.

TORRES, Manuel, 1767-1822. The first diplomatic representative from a Latin American nation (the *República de Gran Colombia) to be formally received by the United States government. Torres maintained a permanent residence in Philadelphia from 1796 to 1822 and was active in securing aid for patriot causes. By one account his actions as a purchasing agent secured 11,000 muskets, 250,000 flints, and 25,000 firelocks for use in the *independence movement. Moving between Philadelphia and Washington, D.C., he worked to achieve the recognition of Colombia's independence from Spain, and he died shortly after the United States extended recognition. See also: UNITED STATES, Relations with

TORRES GIRALDO, Ignacio, 1893-1968. Author, labor and political leader, socialist ideologue; born May 1; died *Cali, November 15. He was active in forming labor cooperatives in Cali and *Medellín, 1925-1927, and was Secretary General of the National Confederation of Labor (Confederación Obrera Nacional), 1925-1926. He was a member of the general directorate of the *Partido Socialista Revolucionario (P.S.R.), founded in 1926, and Secretary General of the *Partido Comunista de Colombia (P.C.C.), 1935-1939. He was associated with María *Cano, Tomás Uribe Márquez, Raúl *Mahecha, and other early socialist leaders. After 1942, he devoted much of his time to writing and left a large number of works, some of which were published after his death. Among these were *Los inconformes* (5 vols.; 1967-1974); *Síntesis de la historia política de Colombia* (1972); *La cuestión indígena* (written in 1947, published in 1973), *La cuestión sindical de Colombia* (1975); and other works in which he wrote about the masses, social conflicts, and anti-imperialism in Colombian history.

TORRES MENDEZ, Ramón, 1809-1895. *Costumbrista* artist; portrait painter, miniaturist. Originally apprenticed as a printer, and wounded at the Battle of *Santuario, he became a professor of drawing at the *Universidad Nacional. He painted some 600 portraits and 200 other works. He is best known for his series of drawings and watercolors of Colombian life in the mid-19th century published and several times republished under the title *Cuadros de costumbres.* These works show clothing, social classes, occupations, transportation, and other activities of daily life.

TORRES RESTREPO, Camilo, 1929-1966. Priest, sociologist, revolutionary. Educated in Louvain, he was ordained in 1954. He was chaplain and lecturer at the *Universidad Nacional, 1959-1962. In the mid-1960s he attempted to organize the United Front (*Frente Unido del Pueblo), an initially reformist alliance that eventually advocated violence. Laicized in 1965, he joined a guerrilla movement shortly thereafter. Camilo Torres Restrepo was killed on February 15, 1966, at a site called Patio Cemento (*Santander) in a clash between government troops of the Fifth Brigade under the command of then Colonel Alvaro Valencia Tovar and guerrilla forces of the *Ejército de Liberación Nacional with whom Torres was fighting.

TORRES Y TENORIO, Camilo, 1766-1816. Patriot martyr executed by the Spanish in Bogotá, October 5. Born *Popayán, November 22, Camilo Torres y Tenorio was a member of the *Junta of Notables called to discuss the *Quito Rebellion in 1809 and the author of the *Memorial de Agravios* (Declaration of Grievances), which developed from it. A member of the *cabildo* and signatory of the *Acta del 20 de Julio de 1810, he was a major author and signer of the *Acta de la Confederación de las Provincias Unidas, 1811. He opposed *Cundinamarca and the governments of Antonio *Nariño and Manuel *Alvarez, 1811-1814. He was President of the *Congreso de Leiva and the chief executive of the United Provinces (*Provincias Unidas de Nueva Granada), 1812-1814.

TORREZAR DIAZ PIMIENTA, Juan de, d. 1782. Governor of *Cartagena, 1774-1782. He was Viceroy of *New Granada, April-July 1782.

TRADE UNIONS. Societies of artisans had existed in colonial times, but they were little more than mutual aid associations. The *Sociedad de Artesanos, 1847-1851, aimed to prevent the competition of European goods and *immigration, and its successor, the *Sociedad Democrática, was active in *Liberal politics into the 1860s. Their influence helped secure some of the reforms of the *López and *Obando presidencies and the dictatorship of José María *Melo in 1854, but they were hardly labor unions in the modern sense. Contemporary labor unions began to develop in the early part of the 20th century, and the Sociedad de Artesanos de Sonsón (Antioquia), accorded legal status on August 31, 1909, may be the first association to achieve official recognition. The worldwide labor unrest at the end of *World War I found expression in Colombia in a wave of strikes among dockworkers, railroad men, *United Fruit Company employees, and petroleum workers. The *Sindicato Obrero was formed in 1926, many mutual aid societies evolved into trade unions, and legislation in 1919 acknowledged the right to strike. The bloody *United Fruit Company Strike of 1928 helped discredit the repressive tactics of the *Conservative government and persuaded Liberals of the need to contest communist domination of the unions. As a result, unions were given national legal status in 1931 (Law No. 83) under the administration of President Enrique *Olaya Herrera. The Confederación Sindical de Colombia of 1934 (which in 1938 became the *Confederación de Trabajadores de Colombia—C.T.C.) was the country's first effective union federation. Its ties with the *Liberal Party led to the formation of a number of rival organizations, including the Church-supported *Unión de Trabajadores Colombianos (U.T.C.), 1946; the ephemeral communist-supported *Confederación de Trabajadores Colombianos Independientes, 1950, and its successor the *Confederación Sindical de Trabajadores de Colombia (C.S.T.C.), 1964; and the Peronist-inspired *Confederación Nacional de Trabajadores (1953-1955). Personal rivalries split the U.T.C. and boosted the fortunes of the Antioquia-based *Confederación General de Trabajo (C.T.G.), 1971. All four trade union federations came together, to support the general strike (*Paro Cívico) of 1977 and formed a coordinating council, the *Consejo Nacional Sindical (C.N.S.). The C.N.S. has managed in some cases to get individual unions of rival federations to work together, for example, in the soft drink and textile industries. *Petroleum workers' unions have included the *Sociedad Unión Obreros (1923), the *Sindicato Obrero

(1926), and the *Unión Sindical Obrera (1934). Labor associations in Colombia are found at local, regional, and national levels. Using a 1984 labor census, author Paul Osterling found that there were 873,442 workers belonging to 2,172 different unions. Approximately 51% of these workers belonged to independent unions, but the other 49% were affiliated with one of five national confederations: the C.T.C., the U.T.C., the C.S.T.C., the C.G.T., or the *Central Unitaria de Trabajadores (organized in 1986). The Confederación Sindical and the Central Unitaria are sometimes described as leftist or socialist groups, while the other confederations are labeled variously as moderate, reformist, or reactionary. Despite numerous attempts at cooperation, organized labor has remained a relatively divided group and never functioned as a strong, unified political force. See also: LABOR LEGISLATION; STRIKES

TRANSPORTATION, see: AIR TRANSPORT; HIGHWAYS; MERCHANT MARINE; RAILROADS; WATERWAYS

TREASURE FLEET, see: FLOTA SYSTEM

TREATIES. See entries under the names of the country with which the treaty was signed, under the names of the individuals signing, or the place where signed.

TRECEMARCISTAS. "Those from the thirteenth of March"; a name given to those who participated in the public protests led by university students in *Bogotá on March 13, 1909. They protested the dictatorship of Rafael *Reyes and a proposed treaty with the United States over the Isthmus of *Panama. The events, the culmination of discontent with the Reyes government, led to the dictator's resignation.

TRIBUNA (La), Battle of. January 29, 1895, *Cundinamarca. General Rafael *Reyes, for the government, defeated the rebellious forces of General Siervo Sarmiento.

TRIBUNAL DE CONTADORES DE CUENTAS. Composed of eight officials, it was a royal accounting office established in *Bogotá in 1605. It was the third such office in Spanish America, after Mexico and Lima, and it functioned until abolished in 1819.

TRIBUTO. A special tax levied upon the *Indians, established in 1523. Originally it was a way of replacing service in the *encomendia* or *repartimiento* with a money payment. Maintained throughout the colonial period, it was abolished during the era of *Gran Colombia, in 1821, but was revived from 1828-1833.

TROCO, see: TROPICAL OIL STRIKES

TROPICAL OIL STRIKES. The Workers Labor Union (*Unión Sindical Obrera) and other groups were responsible for six major strikes against the Tropical Oil Company (TROCO) while it held the *De Mares Oil Concession (1919-1951). There were strikes in 1924, 1927, 1935, 1938, 1946, and 1948, the largest of which may have been in 1927 and the most successful in 1948. With some variation, the demands were similar in each case: salary increases, better food and health services, lower rents, the right to buy goods from businesses other than company stores, the eight-hour day, safe working conditions, the right to read newspapers, respect for private property of the workers, elimination of unpopular supervisors, and no punishment for workers belonging to labor organizations. The strike of 1924 was led by Raúl *Mahecha; in 1927 the leaders were Mahecha, María *Cano, Ignacio *Torres Giraldo, and Isaac Gutiérrez Navarro. The strike of 1935 was directed by Gilberto Vieira and Jorge Regueros Peralta; in 1938 the leaders were Gonzalo Buenahora, Diego Luis Córdoba, and Guillermo Rodríguez. Diego Montaña Cuéllar led the 1948 protest. In 1927, the strikers against TROCO in *Barrancabermeja were supported by pipeline workers and transportation workers in La *Dorada, Beltrán (4° 48'N, 74° 45'W, *Cundinamarca), *Honda, *Ambalema, *Girardot, Calamar (10° 15'N, 74° 55'W, *Bolívar) and *Cartagena. The strike of 1948 was supported by mass demonstrations in *Bogotá and in part by Jorge Eliécer *Gaitán's *"Oration for Peace," February 13. Nearly all of the strikes engendered repressive violence from the government, although the strike of 1948 was finally settled by arbitration in favor of the workers.

TRUJILLO, Julián, 1828-1883. General, *Liberal legislator, diplomat, President of Colombia 1878-1880. Born *Popayán, January 28; died *Bogotá, July 18. He received his law degree in 1849. In addition to his career as a military officer, he served as President of the *Cauca, 1867-1869 and 1873-1875, Minister to Ecuador, 1870, Minister of the Treasury, National Credit, and Finance, and President of *Antioquia, 1877. He supported the government in the *rebellions of 1854 and 1876 but opposed the *Ospina administration, 1860-1861. His presidential administration approved contracts for a transisthmian canal and a *railroad from *Buenaventura to the *Cauca River, and it organized a committee to dredge the *Magdalena River. It reorganized the national executive, creating seven secretariats for more efficient administration (see: MINISTRIES); it stimulated *iron smelting in Samacá (5° 30'N, 73° 29'W, *Boyacá) and Subachoque (4° 56'N, 74° 11'W, *Cundinamarca); and it decreed honors to several people, including generals Francisco de Paula *Santander, T. C. de *Mosquera, and Santos *Gutiérrez, as well as to the scientist Francisco José de *Caldas.

TUITION DECREE, see: ANTI-CLERICAL LAWS, 1861

TULCAN, Battle of. July 31, 1862, Ecuador. Julio *Arboleda, acting in the name of the defunct *Confederación Granadina, defeated and captured Ecuador's President Gabriel García Moreno, with whom he then negotiated an alliance against the *Mosquera government.

TUMACO. An island in the inlet of the Pacific Ocean at 1° 48'N, 78° 46'W, and a town built upon it. Tumaco is Colombia's most important west coast port after *Buenaventura. Some 250 kilometers (110 miles) northwest of *Pasto, it had an estimated population of 44,721 people in 1985.

TUMACO–LA TOLITA CULTURE. A pre-Columbian Indian culture that flourished between 400 B.C. and A.D. 500 along the Pacific Coast of southern Colombia and northern Ecuador, Tumaco–La Tolita has also been called simply *Tumaco (after its principal site in Colombia), Esmeraldas (after the Ecuadoran province in which La Tolita lies), and Atacames (after the inhabitants of the region at the time of the conquest). The more modern, inclusive term, however, is Tumaco–La Tolita. Three distinct epochs have been established for the culture's development: the Oriental Period, 400-100 B.C., characterized by portraits and creative art; the Transition Period, 100 B.C.-A.D. 100; and the Mesoamerican Period, A.D. 100-500, characterized by prototypes and conventional art. The Oriental Period is said to have resulted from contacts with China, Japan, or Southeast Asia, and the Mesoamerican Period shows signs of influence from Mexico and Central America. Tumaco–La Tolita artwork shows great diversity in realistic depiction of everyday life and is often characterized by a plain white-clay appearance and the use of molds. Life in the Tumaco–La Tolita sites seems to have died out for unexplained reasons by about A.D. 500, although its influences spread northward and can be seen in the *Nariño, *Calima, *Tierradentro, and *San Agustín cultures (See also: TUMACO STYLE). Although the Tumaco Indians resisted the conquest and work in Spanish-run mines, permanent European settlements were established in the area during the 1620s, and most of the Indians died from disease and overwork or fled to other regions.

TUMACO STYLE.   A subdivision of the Nariño Style; an archeological term used to describe one of the major pre-conquest Indian groups occupying the present-day Department of *Nariño (see: NARIÑO STYLE). The Tumaco people inhabited the Pacific Coast in the extreme southwestern part of Colombia and northern Ecuador. Carbon 14 dates in the Metaje sequence show occupation from 400 B.C. to 10 B.C., but older habitation is likely. Tumaco people are thought to have originated in Mesoamerica and immigrated to Colombia because of numerous cultural traits similar to those found in Mexico and Central America. In the case of the jaguar cult, there are also similarities with Chavín de Huantar in Peru. Tumaco culture is distinguished by the use of mounds, *tolas* or *tolitas,* for construction, cultivation, and burial. There were well-defined social classes, and the economy was mixed: *agriculture (primarily *yuca* with some *corn), *fishing, hunting, and pastoralism. A distinctive characteristic of Tumaco culture is its gray-white ceramic work, which depicts a complex variety of human figures (normal and deformed), masks, rituals (sexual, birth, and religious), plants, animals, composite figures (human bodies with reptile, jaguar, and other animal heads), figures with alter egos, storage vessels, houses, musical instruments, roller stamps, and shuttles. Molding was a common ceramic technique. Goldwork displays many of the same motifs.

TUNEL (El), Grupo Literario.   Founded in 1975, "The Tunnel" was a group of writers from *Montería and other places in the Department of *Córdoba whose work has been characterized as an attack on the superficiality and indolence of traditional writing from the region. The Authors associated with the group include Antonio Vélez (1942-), José Garcés González (1948-), Gustavo Tatis Guerra (1961-), Soad Luis de Farah (1952-), Gustavo Abad Hoyaos (1955-), Omar González Anaya (1945-), Guillermo Valencia Salgado, "Compae Goyo" (1929-), Carlos Morón Díaz (1943-), Nelson Castillo Pérez (1953-), and Leopoldo Bordella de la Espriella.

TUNJA. Capital of *Boyacá, located on the *Pan American Highway, 135 kilometers northeast of *Bogotá, at 50° 32'N, 73° 22'W. Tunja is 2,820 meters above sea level in mountainous terrain in the *Cordillera Oriental. The average temperature is 13°C, and the population in 1987 was about 77,000 people. Industries include food processing and manufacturing of construction materials. Founded on August 6, 1539, the city was established on the site of Hunza, the capital of the Chibcha *Zaque, by Captain Gonzalo *Suárez Rendón. It was elevated to the rank of city and given a coat of arms in 1541. Tunja was known as the "very noble and very loyal city" (*ciudad muy noble y muy leal*), and now preserves interesting examples of colonial architecture. In 1819 it was Simón *Bolívar's base from which he marched 16 kilometers to the Puente de Boyacá (Boyacá bridge) where the Battle of *Boyacá occurred.

TUNJA, Battle of. April 1-7, 1861. Colonel Santos *Gutiérrez, representing rebellious *Liberals, withstood the siege of forces from the *Confederación Granadina under General Manuel Arjona.

TUNJA, Stones of. Piedras de Tunja, also known as the Cercado de los *Zipas, located near *Facatativá. The area has been a national archeological park since 1946. It is the site of numerous painted and carved rocks with pre-Hispanic motifs, especially frogs, alligators, cruciforms, and serpents. Similar stones are found at Chinuata, Anacutá, Fusagasugá (4° 22'N, 74° 22'W), Pandi (4° 12'N, 74° 30'W), and other places.

TUNJO, see: MUISCA STYLE

TUQUERRES. Rural community located at 1° 6'N, 77° 37'W, in the Department of *Nariño, 72 kilometers southwest of *Pasto. Altitude is approximately 3,500 meters; average temperature, 11°C; population, 12,378 people (1985 estimate).

Túquerres is a commercial center on the crossroads between Pasto and Ipiales (on the border) and *Tumaco and *Mocoa. The surrounding countryside is devoted to agriculture, cattle raising, and mining. Exact origin of the settlement is unknown, but there are at least three accounts. By one, the city was founded on the settlement of an Indian chieftain named Túquerres in 1447. By another land was given for the settlement by Spanish priests; and, by the third, the town was founded by Miguel Muñoz in 1541. An agreement signed in Túquerres by General Joaquín *Posada Gutiérrrez, New Granada, and invading Ecuadoran commander Bernardo Daste, on November 3, 1841, would have ceded the town to Ecuador, but it was never ratified by *Congress.

TURBAY, Gabriel, 1901-1947. Doctor, legislator, orator, and diplomat. He served in both houses of *Congress, was Minister of Government in the administrations of Enrique *Olaya Herrera and Alfonso *López Pumarejo and held the position of Minister of Foreign Relations, 1937-1939. Turbay was an active *Liberal leader, often known as "the Turk" because of his Syrian ancestry. He was an unsuccessful candidate for the presidency in 1946.

TURBAY AYALA, Julio César, 1916-. Legislator, journalist, *Liberal political leader, President of Colombia, 1978-1982. He was educated at the Escuela Nacional de Comercio and has held numerous public positions including alderman for the city of Engatativá (4° 43'N, 73° 9'W, *Cundinamarca), 1939-1948, delegate to the *United Nations, 1947 and 1961, Minister of Labor, Minister of Mines and Engineering, Minister of Foreign Relations, 1958-1961, and ambassador to the United Kingdom. Turbay Ayala was a significant influence in the Liberal Party, especially after the formation of the *Frente Nacional. He was acting President in June 1968, March 1975, and August 1976. As President he proposed a "Plan of National Integration," which stressed regional autonomy, development of transportation, communications, energy production, and mining, and improved social conditions. His term was marked by high inflation, the signing of a contract for *coal mining in the El *Cerrejón (*Guajira) region, growth of the illegal *drug trade, and strong *army initiatives against the various *guerrilla movements (see: ESTATUTO DE SEGURIDAD, 1978).

TURBAYISTA. Supporter of Julio César *Turbay Ayala.

TURMEQUE, Cacique de, see: TORRES, Diego de

TWENTIETH OF JULY 1810. Traditional independence day in Colombia. A dispute over the use of a flower vase between a Spanish merchant, José González Llorente, and the family of Francisco Morales, *creoles, provoked public riots in *Bogotá and the *Acta del 20 de Julio de 1810, which formally launched the *independence movement.

TWENTY-FIFTH OF SEPTEMBER CONSPIRACY. An abortive effort to end the dictatorship of Simón *Bolívar in 1828. The would-be assassins, later known as *Septembrinos,* broke into the presidential palace, but Bolívar was able to escape with the aid of Manuela *Sáenz, who momentarily distracted the assailants while the Liberator jumped out of a window and took refuge under a bridge until friendly forces appeared the next morning. Numerous opponents were exiled or imprisoned following the attempt.

TWENTY-ONE, The. A group of Conservative congressmen, mostly Historicals (*Históricos), who opposed the policies of the *Caro administration in the 1890s. They were the authors of the *Motivos de disidencia,* 1896, which listed abuses that they believed needed correction.

TWENTY-THIRD OF MAY CONSPIRACY. A reference to the movement of May 23, 1867, headed by the Presidential Designate, Santos *Acosta, which removed President T. C. de *Mosquera from office for abuse of executive authority.

-U-

U.P., see: UNION PATRIOTICA

U.T.C., see: UNION DE TRABAJADORES COLOMBIANOS

ULLOA, Antonio de, see: JUAN AND ULLOA, Expedition of

UNIDAD DEMOCRATICA DE LA IZQUIERDA. A political organization founded in 1982 to unite reform-oriented groups. Gerardo Molina, head of the association, was also the party's candidate for president in 1982. Firmes, a group of politically oriented intellectuals (founded in 1976), also headed by Molina, the Partido Socialista de los Trabajadores, and the *Partido Comunista de Colombia (P.C.C.) all supported the Unidad Democrática.

UNION DE TRABAJADORES COLOMBIANOS (U.T.C.). A Catholic, confessional labor union organized by Jesuit Father Vicente Andrade (founded June 12, 1946) as a rival to the C.T.C. (*Confederación de Trabajadores de Colombia), which the U.T.C. claimed was communist dominated. Although officially nonpartisan, the U.T.C. became the government's favored union under the *Gómez administration. It became the most prominent labor union in Colombia, 1946-1957, a prominence that it maintained through the early 1980s. However, after the election of Tulio Cuevas as president of the union in 1963, the U.T.C. abandoned its nonpartisan stance and became more closely identified with the *Conservative Party. A crisis within the U.T.C. beginning in 1980 brought an end to the Cuevas era when he failed to secure reelection in 1983. In the early 1980s the U.T.C. was estimated to have about 350,000 members.

UNION NACIONAL. The name given to a coalition of political *Liberals, moderates, and *Conservatives during the 1946-1950 period. The National Union supported Mariano *Ospina Pérez in the elections of 1950.

UNION NACIONAL IZQUIERDISTA REVOLUCIONARIA (UNIR). A short-lived splinter group of the *Liberal Party founded by Jorge Eliécer *Gaitán.

UNION OF COLOMBIAN WORKERS, see: UNION DE TRABAJADORES COLOMBIANOS

UNION PATRIOTICA (U.P.). A political party formed on May 28, 1985, in the wake of the truce agreements of La *Uribe in 1984 by the *Fuerzas Armadas Revolucionarias de Colombia (FARC) and other dissident reform groups, including parts of the *Partido Comunista Colombiano. The formation of the U.P. was announced by the FARC in March 1985, and its first National Conference was held in Bogotá in November. The twenty-point platform, which the Patriotic Union enunciated, included popular election of mayors and governors, revision of

the electoral quotient system for elections, granting *municipalities 30% of national revenues, grants of free land to
peasants, constitutional reform, an increase in spending for
*education, and appointment of a civilian to be Minister of
Defense. Jaime Pardo *Leal was the U.P. candidate for President in the 1986 elections. The Patriotic Union won 3 million
votes, 6 seats in the *House of Representatives and 3 seats in
the *Senate in its first election campaigns. However, many of
its leaders, including Jaime Pardo Leal, fell victim to political
*death squads. Bernardo Jaramillo Ossa (March) and Carlos'
*Pizarro Leongómez (April) were both killed while campaign-
ing as presidential candidates in 1990. Pizarro Leongómez was
replaced by Antonio *Navarro Wolff, who eventually won
12.5% of the vote in the 1990 elections.

UNION REPUBLICANA. The Republican Union, sometimes
referred to as the Republican Party, 1909-1910. The union was
a temporary coalition of disparate interests organized by Carlos E. *Restrepo, *Conservative, and Enrique *Olaya Herrera,
*Liberal. It began to form several months before March 13,
1909, but became a formal reality with the events leading to
the resignation of President-Dictator *Reyes. The Republican
Union's program was formally published on November 3,
1909, and it called for a defense of the independence, sovereignty, and territorial integrity of Colombia, an obvious statement of opposition to a treaty the Reyes administration had
negotiated with the United States over *Panama (see: ROOT-
CORTES-AROSEMENA AGREEMENTS). It also called for
separation of powers, loyalty to the constitution and constitutional procedures, justice for all regardless of class or political
party, administrative decentralization, a program of primary
education designed for the Colombian masses, professionalization of the army, formation of capital for internal development,
and limitations on *taxation. The Republican Union, which
supported the constitutional convention of 1910, lasted until
about 1914.

UNION SINDICAL OBRERA (USO). The Workers Labor
Union, an independent labor union of oil workers centered in
*Barrancabermeja. Originally founded by Raúl *Mahecha in
1921 as the Sociedad Unión Obrera, the name was changed
and the USO formally recognized as a union by the Tropical
Oil Company and by the government in 1934. With notable
interruptions (1948-1957, for example), the USO has func-

tioned continuously since 1921, and it played an important role in the various *Tropical Oil Company strikes, especially those of 1935 and 1948. The USO serves workers of *ECOPETROL, the state petroleum agency.

UNIONIST CONFEDERATION OF COLOMBIAN WORKERS, see CONFEDERACION SINDICAL DE TRABAJADORES DE COLOMBIA

UNIONIST CONSERVATIVES.   A faction of the *Conservative Party, important after 1950. It was also called *Ospinista after its leader, ex-President Mariano *Ospina Pérez. The Unionists supported the *Frente Nacional, although they initially opposed the idea. Less doctrinaire in ideology than the Independent Conservatives, they tended to represent interests engaged in commerce and industry. In the late 1980s, a number of the Ospina Pérez supporters threw their support to Senator Gustavo Rodríguez Vargas, thereby becoming known as Gustavistas. See, for comparison: INDEPENDENT CONSERVATIVES

UNIR, see: UNION NACIONAL IZQUIERDISTA REVOLUCIONARIA

UNITED FRONT OF THE PEOPLE, see: FRENTE UNIDO DEL PUEBLO

UNITED FRONT OF REVOLUTIONARY ACTION, see: FRENTE UNIDO DE ACCION REVOLUCIONARIA

UNITED FRUIT COMPANY.   Commercial firm founded by the 1899 merger of the Tropical Trading Company and the Boston Fruit Company. This Boston-based company acquired interests in banana plantations in Colombia and Central America. In 1949 it was merged with United Brands. See also: BANANAS

UNITED FRUIT COMPANY STRIKE.   A movement started on October 6, 1928, when *banana workers around *Santa Marta went on strike for better living and working conditions. In December, the *army was used to suppress forcibly the workers, and numerous people were killed or injured. The violence was investigated by Jorge Eliécer *Gaitán, and it provoked sharp criticism of the administration of President *Abadía Méndez. The events of the strike have been incorporated into several works of fiction, including *La casa grande* by Alvaro Cepeda Samudio and *One Hundred Years of Solitude* by Gabriel *García Márquez.

UNITED KINGDOM, Relations with. Prior to the 1707 creation of Great Britain, England's relations with what is now *Colombia involved mostly smuggling and *piracy (leading to the 1629-1786 occupation of *San Andrés y Providencia), while Scotland was involved in the abortive attempt to plant a colony at *Darién, close to the present Colombia-Panama border. In 1713 the Treaty of Utrecht obtained for Great Britain the *asiento de negros:* the legal right to supply slaves to the Indies. This facilitated increased smuggling of other goods, particularly woolen cloth. Such commerce engendered an overoptimistic assessment of the Spanish American market and explains the enthusiastic British support for the early-19th-century movements for political independence and commercial liberation, although Napoleon's Continental System, denying European outlets for British goods, was also a factor. *Bolívar was given refuge in Jamaica; a number of other freedom fighters spent time in London exile. After the end of the Napoleonic Wars, many British and Irish veterans participated actively in the *independence movement in Colombia. A noteworthy example was the *Legión Británica, one of whose members, Daniel F. *O'Leary, became Bolívar's aide-de-camp. British loans buttressed the new republic financially beyond its capacity to repay (see: LONDON LOANS). Given the disturbed political development of 19th-century Colombia, it is not surprising that its international financial history should have been one of repeated defaulting, followed by enforced rescheduling. The onerous 1821 *Mackintosh Contract was the subject of the *Martin-Malmesbury Treaty of 1858, but it was not finally settled until the *Holguín-Avery Convention of 1905.

Direct British private investment began almost simultaneously with independence, some £631,500 having been invested in mining (mostly *gold) companies by 1825. Such was the preeminence of the London money market that capital from other countries was often channeled through it (for example, the French-owned but U.K.-registered New Emeralds Co., Ltd., of Colombia, in 1892). It is almost impossible to compute the precise extent of British contribution to the Colombian economy, but it undoubtedly surpassed that of any other country up until *World War I. It was particularly important in financing *railroads. Britain was also during this period Colombia's premier trading partner, with the balance heavily in the U.K.'s favor from the very beginning. In 1825, the best year of the post-independence decade, Colombia imported £451,000 worth of British goods, but sold the U.K. only £90,000 worth of exports in return. Typically, when Colombia finally achieved monetary stability in 1907, the *peso* was tied to the pound sterling.

Official diplomatic relations were established by the *Gual-Campbell Treaty of 1825, and Britain supported the *Congress of Panama in 1826. As a small and poorly organized nation, Colombia was easily intimidated by the great powers of the time. In her relations with Britain, the *Russell Affair of 1837 is the most notorious instance of this. The biggest bone of contention was the British claim, going back to the 17th century, to a protectorate over the *Mosquito Coast. This was resolved, in Colombia's case, by the *Clayton-Bulwer Treaty of 1850. The *Mosquera-Clarendon Treaty of 1866 regularized commercial and consular relations.

Although Latin Americans tended to look to France, and later to Germany, as their cultural and intellectual mentors, *Benthamism had an impact in the early 19th century, and British economic thought was also influential. *Lancasterian Schools provided a useful model in a country with a desperate shortage of trained teachers. Nineteenth-century British social conventions permeated the behavior of the elites throughout Latin America, but nowhere else, perhaps, have they persisted so long as in conservative Colombian society. Five o'clock tea has not lost its appeal, and London stockbroker–style dress of dark pin striped suit, rolled umbrella, and derby hat, was de rigueur for most upper-class males into the 1960s, often with the incongruity of a *ruana* in the cool of the evening. British preeminence ended with World War I. Its influence declined further as first the Great Depression of the 1930s and then a desperate shortage of hard currency in the immediate post–*World War II years forced the U.K. to concentrate her trade within the sterling area, now limited to the Commonwealth less Canada and Belize. Colombia's current trade with the U.K. is less than that with any other major E.C. country. Exports to the U.K. were worth US$42 million in 1980 and US$126 million in 1986. *Imports from the U.K. were worth US$112 million in 1980 and US$94 million in 1986.

UNITED KINGDOM–COLOMBIA TREATY OF 1825, see: GUAL-CAMPBELL TREATY

UNITED KINGDOM–COLOMBIA TREATY OF 1866, see: MOSQUERA-CLARENDON TREATY

UNITED KINGDOM–NEW GRANADA TREATY OF 1858, see: DE FRANCISCO MARTIN–MALMESBURY TREATY

UNITED KINGDOM–UNITED STATES TREATY OF 1850, see: CLAYTON-BULWER TREATY

UNITED NATIONS. An organization for international cooperation, formed at the close of *World War II. Colombia joined the United Nations on November 5, 1945, and has actively supported the world association since then. Most notably, it contributed military support to the United Nations peace forces first in *Korea, 1951-1954, and then in Egypt during the Suez Canal crisis, 1956-1958.

UNITED PROVINCES OF NEW GRANADA, see: PROVINCIAS UNIDAS DE NUEVA GRANADA

UNITED STATES, Relations with. The United States formally recognized the independence of Colombia (then the Republic of *Gran Colombia) in 1822. Allowing for momentary tensions and constitutional reorganizations, relations between the two nations have been essentially uninterrupted since then. Diplomatic relations between the United States and Colombia have always been concerned mainly with commerce and industry on the one hand and foreign rivalries and defense of strategic points on the other. Because the present-day Republic of Panama belonged to Colombia until 1903, events of the 19th century frequently focused on isthmian issues.

   Although there were repeated attempts to secure recognition and aid from the United States during the Colombian *independence movement, 1810-1822, the United States refused to support the Spanish American cause until after 1819, when it managed to purchase the Florida territory from Spain. At the same time, the Battle of *Boyacá was a significant victory for the patriots. These events, plus the continued efforts of Manuel *Torres and others in the United States, eventually culminated in the recognition of Colombian independence and the appointment of Richard C. Anderson as the first U.S. minister to the new nation. The anti-colonization statement issued by President James Monroe (the Monroe Doctrine) in 1823 had implications for Colombia, and the

*Gual-Anderson Treaty signed the following year became the first formal agreement ratified between the two nations. It continued in force even after the dissolution of Gran Colombia.

During the 1830s and 1840s, commercial disputes and fear of European influence emerged as the dominant issues. The Gual-Anderson Treaty admitted U.S. commercial goods to Colombia on a most-favored-nation basis. However, *Bolívar imposed a differential customs duty on all foreign commerce, and President *Márquez abrogated the commercial provisions of the treaty in 1837. Customs duties remained a controversial issue until free trade was established in Colombia in 1847. Throughout the period Colombia sought to establish itself as a respected independent nation while the United States kept an uneasy eye on the efforts of European nations to exert influence in the Western Hemisphere, especially in Central America and the Isthmus of *Panama. These factors led to the signing of the *Mallarino-Bidlack Treaty in 1846. Colombia granted the United States some reduction in tariffs in exchange for a pledge to defend Panama should the isthmus be threatened or disturbed. This 1846 treaty had a direct influence on the signing of the *Clayton-Bulwer Treaty between the United States and the United Kingdom in 1850.

Investors from the United States built the *Panama Railroad in the early 1850s, but U.S.-Colombian relations were strained in 1856 by the Watermelon Riot (see: PANAMA RIOT, 1856), responsibility for which the North American government placed on Colombia. Damage claims were accepted by the latter in the *Herrán-Cass Treaty of 1857. The next three major agreements between the two nations also dealt mainly with Panamanian problems. A license renegotiation for the Panama Railroad earned Colombia US$1 million in 1867. The *Herrán-Hay Treaty of 1903 was an unsuccessful attempt to negotiate transisthmian canal rights. Its failure contributed to the *PANAMANIAN REVOLUTION for independence that same year. Following the U.S. intervention (under the Mallarino-Bidlack Treaty) on behalf of the Panamanians, the *Root-Cortés-Arosemena Agreements of 1909 were an abortive effort to secure damages from the United States on behalf of the Colombian government. Settlement of the Colombian claims from 1903 was finally secured in the *Urrutia-Thomson Treaty, negotiated in 1914 and ratified in 1921.

Diplomatic relations remained formally correct but less than cordial during the first quarter of the 20th century. Aside from the delay in settling the Panamanian-claims issue, the United States followed an aggressive protective tariff policy and Colombia refused to follow the U.S. lead in *World War I, remaining neutral throughout. By the mid-1920s, however, the payment of Panamanian reparations by the U.S., Colombia's potential as a *petroleum producer, the establishment of commercial *air transport, a boom in *foreign investment, and eventually the Good Neighbor policy of the United States lead to a rapprochement. The U.S. became the chief source of foreign loans (see: NEW YORK LOANS). A commercial treaty indicative of improving relations was negotiated, although never ratified, in 1933 (*UNITED STATES–COLOMBIA TREATY OF 1933.)

In contrast to the government's policy during World War I, the administration of President Eduardo *Santos was a wholehearted supporter of U.S. policy leading up to and during *World War II. For example, German ownership of the Colombian airline *SCADTA was eliminated as a defensive measure before the U.S. entered the war. This cooperation has remained more or less true in the post–World War II period, especially during the Cold War and the East-West ideological struggle. In both the *United Nations and the *Organization of American States, the anti-communist policies of the United States have been supported, or unopposed, by Colombia, which, for example, sent troops to assist with the *Korean War of the early 1950s. The major exception to this pattern dealt with U.S. intervention in Latin American countries. Recalling her own bitter experience with the Panamanian Revolution of 1903, Colombia's response to events in Cuba since 1959 has been more ambivalent than the hard line of the United States, and Colombia was one of the *Contadora nations seeking alternatives to counteract U.S. unilateral initiatives in Central America during the 1980s.

Aside from these cases, however, Colombia has remained a nation essentially wedded to U.S. policies and closely dependent on the U.S. for trade and for aid in socioeconomic development (such as the Alliance for Progress) and for military assistance in combating domestic *guerrilla movements within Colombia since the 1950s (the *Violencia). In recent years, relations have been clouded by the rise of the illegal *drug trade from Colombia, which Colombian officials have been unable or unwilling to suppress in spite of repeated U.S. demands (see: EXTRADITION TREATIES). Moreover, the United States has been surpassed as the chief market for

Colombian exports (other than illegal narcotics) by the European Community.

UNITED STATES–COLOMBIA TREATY OF 1824, see: GUAL-ANDERSON TREATY

UNITED STATES–COLOMBIA TREATY OF 1903, see: HE-RRAN-HAY TREATY

UNITED STATES–COLOMBIA TREATY OF 1909, see: ROOT-CORTES-AROSEMENA AGREEMENTS

UNITED STATES–COLOMBIA TREATY OF 1914, see: URRU-TIA-THOMSON TREATY

UNITED STATES–COLOMBIA TREATY OF 1933. Signed December 15, 1933, this commercial treaty was considered by some a victory for the United States. It placed nine Colombian products, including *petroleum, on the free import list for United States markets, while Colombia reduced import duties on approximately 150 items, mostly manufactured goods, from the United States. For various reasons the treaty was never ratified by either nation.

UNITED STATES–COLOMBIA TREATY OF 1979, see: EX-TRADITION TREATIES

UNITED STATES–COLOMBIA TREATY OF 1982, see: EX-TRADITION TREATIES

UNITED STATES–NEW GRANADA TREATY OF 1846, see: MALLARINO-BIDLACK TREATY

UNITED STATES–NEW GRANADA TREATY OF 1857, see: HERRAN-CASS TREATY

UNITED STATES–UNITED KINGDOM TREATY OF 1850, see: CLAYTON-BULWER TREATY

UNITED STATES OF COLOMBIA, see: ESTADOS UNIDOS DE COLOMBIA

UNITED STATES OF NEW GRANADA, see: ESTADOS UNI-DOS DE NUEVA GRANADA

UNIVERSIDAD CENTRAL DE BOGOTA. State university created in 1826 by decree of Vice-President Francisco de Paula *Santander to take over the *Universidad de Santo Tomás. It was closed in 1850.

UNIVERSIDAD CENTRAL DEL CAUCA. State university located in *Popayán. Founded as part of the educational reforms of Vice President *Santander in 1827, the university currently has an estimated enrollment of 4,500 students, 450-500 teachers, and faculties in arts, humanities, engineering (civil and electrical), telecommunications, medicine, and nursing.

UNIVERSIDAD DE ANTIOQUIA. Located in *Medellín, established in 1822, the University of Antioquia is perhaps the third oldest university in Colombia still in operation (see also: UNIVERSIDAD DE SANTO TOMAS and UNIVERSIDAD JAVERIANA, Pontificia). Enrollment has been estimated at about 25,000. Principal faculties include humanities, engineering, medicine, veterinary medicine, dentistry, chemistry, pharmacy, and public health. Publications of the university include *Universidad de Antioquia* and *Noticiero Universitario de la Secretaría General.* The Inter-American School of Librarianship (Escuela Interamericana de Bibliotecnología) is an affiliate institution.

UNIVERSIDAD DE CALDAS. State university established in 1943 in *Manizales. Enrollment is about 3,800 students. Academic programs include arts and humanities, agriculture, medicine, nursing, veterinary medicine, and stockbreeding.

UNIVERSIDAD DE CARTAGENA. Located in the city of *Cartagena, founded in 1827. Along with the Pontificia *Universidad Javeriana, *Universidad de Santo Tomás, *Universidad de Antioquia, and the *Universidad Central del Cauca, it is one of the oldest universities in Colombia. Current enrollment is about 4,500. The university publishes the *Revista de la Facultad de Medicina,* and it offers programs in medicine, dentistry, nursing, pharmacy, and engineering.

UNIVERSIDAD DE CORDOBA. State university established in 1966 in *Montería. The university has between 2,500 and 3,000 students, approximately 221 lecturers, and major faculties in veterinary medicine, animal husbandry, agronomy, nursing, and education.

UNIVERSIDAD DE LA SALLE, see: UNIVERSIDAD SOCIAL CATOLICA DE LA SALLE

UNIVERSIDAD DE LOS ANDES. Private university established in *Bogotá in 1948. The original curriculum was patterned along the lines of universities in the United States. The university has about 4,000 students, approximately 150 faculty members, and affiliated centers specializing in electronics and computing, hydraulic research, and genetics.

UNIVERSIDAD DE MEDELLIN. Private university founded in 1950. Enrollment is about 5,000. Major faculties include law, business, industrial economics, statistics, public accounting, civil engineering, and education. The Institute of Postgradute Studies and Research (Instituto de Postgrados Estudios e Investigaciones) and the Institute of Penal Law and Criminology (Instituto de Derecho Penal y Criminología) are affiliated programs.

UNIVERSIDAD DE NARIÑO. Founded in *Pasto, June 2, 1827, as the Colegio de San Agustín. Authorization for the institution to become a university was granted in 1904, but continuous full-time university functions date from the 1960s. Major faculties include law, education, languages, and agronomy, and the university publishes *Anales, Foro Universitaria,* and *Numen Universitario 'A.'*

UNIVERSIDAD DE QUINDIO. State university established in *Armenia in 1962. Estimated enrollment is 3,300 students, and major faculties include humanities, mathematics, sciences, topography, and engineering.

UNIVERSIDAD DE SAN BUENAVENTURA. Although founded by *Franciscans in 1715, the institution did not achieve university status until 1961. It has major branches in *Cali and *Medellín, with approximately 1,600 students. Principal programs are in philosophy, theology, sociology, psychology, law, business, and education. The university publishes *Franciscanum.*

UNIVERSIDAD DE SANTO TOMAS. With origins claimed as far back as 1580, the University of Santo Tomás was definitively established in 1639 after litigation with the competing *Jesuits, 1608-1639. Run by the *Dominicans, with faculties of arts and theology, it granted four degrees (bachelor, licenciate,

512 / Universidad de Tolima

master, and doctor), although much of the actual teaching was done by two other institutions, the *Colegio Mayor de San Bartolomé and the *Colegio Mayor de Nuestra Señora del Rosario. Along with the *Universidad Javeriana, it was one of the two degree-granting universities of colonial *New Granada. In 1826, Santo Tomás was taken over by the government and converted into the *Universidad Central de Bogotá. The university, often called the Universidad Tomística, was reestablished in 1964, and currently has some 14,000 students. See also: UNIVERSIDAD JAVERIANA

UNIVERSIDAD DE TOLIMA. A state university founded in *Ibagué in 1945, but not granted university status until 1954. Major faculties include agricultural engineering, technology, forestry, commerce, and education. Estimated enrollment is 3,500 students.

UNIVERSIDAD DEL ATLANTICO. State undergraduate university in *Barranquilla founded in 1941. It has approximately 8,800 students, 592 lecturers, and programs in arts and humanities, chemistry and chemical engineering, pharmacy, dietetics, nutrition, and architecture.

UNIVERSIDAD DEL CAUCA, see: UNIVERSIDAD CENTRAL DEL CAUCA

UNIVERSIDAD DEL VALLE. A state university founded in *Cali in 1945. Principal divisions of the university include humanities, engineering, health, architecture, and sciences, with numerous departments in each. University publications include the *Boletín del Departamento de Biología, Revista División de Ingenería,* and *Acta Médica del Valle.* Estimated enrollment is 8,000 students.

UNIVERSIDAD JAVERIANA, Pontificia. The Universidad Javeriana was founded in *Bogotá in 1622 by the *Jesuits, acting on authorization granted by the *Papacy in 1621. The Jesuits ran the university until they were expelled in 1767. After that the *viceroy proposed converting the institution into a public university, but lack of funds prevented anything from being done. The school was run by laymen until the order was allowed to reenter Colombia at various times during the 19th century. The Javeriana has functioned more or less continuously since its establishment, although the present university may be said to date from 1932. It was one of two degree-granting institutions in the colonial period. See also: UNIVERSIDAD DE SANTO TOMAS

UNIVERSIDAD NACIONAL DE COLOMBIA. The National University, *Bogotá, established September 22, 1867, with faculties of law, medicine, natural sciences, engineering, applied arts, and literature. At various times it has had charge of the *Biblioteca Nacional (national library) and a museum, chemical laboratory, charity hospital, and military training program. Its organization has varied, but the university has been in continuous service since 1867. It is Colombia's biggest university, with an enrollment of 28,000 students.

UNIVERSIDAD PEDAGOGICA NACIONAL. The National Pedagogic University was established in *Bogotá in 1955. Principal departments include humanities, mathematics, chemistry, physics, biology, and industrial education. There are two affiliated programs, the National Pedagogic Institute (Instituto Pedagógica Nacional) and the Industrial Technical Institute (Instituto Ténico Industrial). The university publishes the *Revista Colombiana de Educación* and the *Documentación Educativa*. Estimated enrollment is 4,800 students.

UNIVERSIDAD SOCIAL CATOLICA DE LA SALLE. The La Salle Catholic University was founded in *Bogotá in 1965. It has approximately 3,450 students, 300 teachers, and major faculties in philosophy and letters, education, economics, civil engineering, architecture, information sciences, and optometry. There are also programs in social work, agricultural administration, mathematics and natural sciences, languages, and accounting.

UNIVERSIDAD TOMISTICA, see: UNIVERSIDAD DE SANTO TOMAS

UNIVERSITIES. Colonial *New Granada had two degree-granting institutions: the *Universidad Javeriana and the *Universidad de Santo Tomás. Francisco de Paula *Santander's reforms of 1826-1827 transformed the latter into the short-lived *Universidad Central de Bogotá and established two other universities: the *Universidad del Cauca in *Popayán and the *Universidad de Cartagena in *Cartagena. A *Universidad de Antioquia at *Medellín had come into existence a few years earlier. Part of the educational reforms of 1842 made the universities directly subject to the director general of public education, and the so-called *Freedom of Studies Law of 1850 downgraded them to non-degree-granting *colegios*. In 1867, however, a new national program created the technically oriented *Universidad Nacional de Colombia. The government of Rafael *Núñez increased state control and required students and faculty to state their religious affiliation. A post–*World War I campaign for reform culminating in 1935 achieved both greater institutional autonomy and construction of a separate campus (*ciudad universitaria*) for the Universidad Nacional. From 1941 onward the nation has experienced a steady increase in the number of new state-supported provincial universities and a considerable growth in private (mostly Church-run) institutions.

URABA, see: GOLFO DE URABA

URBAN SOCIAL GENERATION, see: SOCIALISTIC GENERATION

URBINA, Ignacio de, 1632-1703. Jeronimite friar, Archbishop of *Bogotá, 1690-1703. He made San Luis *Beltrán the patron saint of *New Granada. In 1702 he prohibited the sale of *chicha to the *Indians, but public pressure forced him to withdraw the injunction within a year.

URDANETA, Rafael, 1788-1845. Venezuelan general, patriot officer, legislator, diplomat, dictator of Colombia, 1830-1831. Born Maracaibo (Venezuela), October 24; died Paris (France), August 23. He moved to *Bogotá when he was twelve years old and studied at the *Colegio Mayor de San Bartolomé. He was Minister of War in the 1820s and tried to restore the Bolivarian dictatorship by assuming control of the government, 1830-1831, but he was unsuccessful because *Bolívar refused to cooperate. After leaving Colombia in 1831, he was Venezuelan minister to France and Spain.

URDANETA ARBELAEZ, Roberto, 1890-1972. Lawyer, legislator, active member of the *Conservative Party, acting President, 1951-1953. Born *Bogotá, June 27; died Bogotá, August 20. He received his law degree from the *Universidad Nacional in 1906 and his doctorate in 1913. He later taught at the National University as well. He served in both houses of the national *Congress; in addition he was Minister of Foreign Relations, 1931-1935; a delegate to the *United Nations, 1945-1947; Minister of War, 1949-1950; and delegate to various international conferences. He held presidential power under the administration of Laureano *GOMEZ before the events that led to the coup d'état of General *Rojas Pinilla.

URIBE (La), Agreements of.   Signed March 28, 1984, at La Uribe (*Meta) by representatives of the national government and the *Fuerzas Armadas Revolucionarias de Colombia. The agreements provided for a cessation of hostilities on both sides; lifting of the state of siege; popular election of local mayors; access to public communications for all political groups; punishment of extra-legal *death squads; cessation of disappearances and kidnappings; and reforms in housing, employment, health, *education, and agrarian life. Preceded by President *Betancur's "declaration of peace" (August 7, 1982) and a general amnesty law (Law 35, November 19, 1982), the agreements sought to end guerrilla violence and government repression. The La Uribe accords were signed first by the FARC, and then by representatives of the *Ejército de Liberación Nacional (*Medellín, April 24), the *Movimiento Diecinueve de Abril—or M-19 (Corinto, 3° 9'N, 76° 12'W, Cauca, April 24); and *Autodefensa Obrera (*Bogotá, April 23, and El Hobo, 2° 35'N, 75° 27'W, *Huila, April 24). The guerrilla organizations, especially M-19, demanded a national dialogue to address major social issues and were not satisfied with efforts to implement the promised reforms. Some say the agreements of La Uribe had ceased to be effective by May 1985, but the peace initiative was pursued nonetheless by President Betancur and by his successor, Virgilio *Barco, who achieved another settlement with the M-19 in March 1990.

URIBE CORDOVEZ–DILLON TREATY OF 1913.   Signed on May 20, by Carlos Uribe Cordovez, Colombia, and Luis M. Dillon, Ecuador. The agreement provided that the Ecuadorans would submit all existing Colombian claims to arbitration.

URIBE HOLGUIN, Guillermo (b. 1880).   Violinist, composer, conductor; born *Bogotá, March 17. After studying with various musicians in Colombia, France, and Belgium, he was named director of the Academia Nacional de Música (founded 1882) in 1910. He changed its name to the Conservatorio

Nacional de Música and remained as its director until 1935, and he was the founder of the Conservatorio's Sociedad de Conciertos Sinfónicos in 1920. One of the most prominent Colombian composers of the 20th century, Uribe Holguín is said to have written as many as 500 musical works, including pieces for orchestra, chamber groups, instrumental solos, chorus, religious occasions, and opera.

URIBE PIEDRAHITA, César, 1897-1951. Doctor, specialist in tropical medicine, author, born *Medellín, November 16; died *Bogotá, December 17. Uribe Piedrahita studied medicine at the *Universidad de Antioquia and Harvard University (U.S.A.). He was an educator at the *Universidad Nacional (*Bogotá), rector of the *Universidad Central del Cauca (*Popayán), and director of the Instituto Samper Martínez. As a novelist, he was the author of *Toá* (1933) and *Mancha de aceite* (1935). *Toá,* set in *Caquetá and *Putumayo, and *Mancha,* set in the Caribbean borderlands between Venezuela and Colombia, criticize the exploitation of workers in these frontier regions. The works are stridently anti-foreign and anti-imperialist in tone.

URIBE URIBE, Rafael, 1859-1914. General, *Liberal journalist and military leader, legislator, statesman, and diplomat; born on the *hacienda* El Palmar, near Valparaíso (*Antioquia), April 12; died *Bogotá, October 15. He began his military career in the *rebellion of 1876-1877 and was one of the chief leaders for the Liberals in the War of the *Thousand Days. A colorful and fiercely determined personality, Uribe Uribe was a successful *coffee producer near *Medellín; the author of a language treatise completed while in prison; Minister to Chile, Argentina, and Brazil; and, for a time, the only Liberal deputy in the *House of Representatives, 1895-1899. He was director of the newspapers *El Autonomista* and *El Liberal,* and his political writings included *De cómo el liberalismo político de Colombia no es pecado* (1912). He was assassinated in 1914 near the *Congress building in Bogotá, allegedly by two disgruntled workers.

URICOECHEA, Ezequiel, 1834-1880. Educator, scientist, and linguist. He was a professor of chemistry and mineralogy at the *Colegio Mayor de Nuestra Señora del Rosario, 1857-1867. Uricoechea produced numerous linguistic studies, including works on *Indian languages, *Spanish, and Arabic. He was the author of *Memorias sobre las antigüedades neo-granadinas* (Berlin, 1854), *Mapoteca colombiana* (London, 1860), and *Gramática, vocabulario, catecismo y confesionario de la lengua chibcha* . . . (Paris, 1871), as well as a contributor to *El *Mosaico* in Bogotá. He resided in Europe after 1868 and died in Beirut, Lebanon.

URRUTIA-THOMSON TREATY OF 1914. Signed on April 6 by Francisco José Urrutia for Colombia and Thaddeus Thomson for the United States. The treaty expressed regret for the actions of the United States in *Panama during the revolution of 1903 and paid Colombia a $25 million indemnity. Opposition in the United States delayed ratification of the agreement for seven years and forced deletion of the regret clause, but the treaty was finally approved in 1921.

URSUA, Pedro de, 1527-1561. Conquistador. He arrived in *New Granada in 1544 with Miguel *Díaz de Armendáriz. He was first Governor of *Bogotá, 1546; then founder of *Pamplona, 1549; and finally Governor of Pamplona, 1549-1550. While leading an expedition to explore the Amazon, he was assassinated by Lope de *Aguirre.

USO, see: UNION SINDICAL OBRERA

-V-

VAAL, Robert, see: VAL, Robert

VACCINATION EXPEDITION. An expedition led by Dr. José Salvani, 1804-1805. It introduced into *New Granada the method of immunization against smallpox with live vaccine, which had been perfected in Europe by Edward Jenner.

VADILLO, Juan. Conquistador. He was first sent to take the *residencia* for Pedro de *Heredia in *Cartagena in 1536. From 1538 to 1539, he led an expedition from the *Golfo de Urabá inland, up much of the *Cauca Valley, to *Cali. He later fled New Granada to escape legal problems, going first to Peru, then to *Panama, and finally to Spain, where he died. The name is also written "Badillo" and can easily be confused with Pedro de *Badillo.

VAL, Robert. Also spelled "Vaal" and "Bal." Buccaneer, pirate. He sacked *Santa Marta in 1543 and occupied *Cartagena in 1544. In the latter case, he is said to have secured 200,000 *pesos in *gold. Val was helped by a Spaniard named Juan Alvarez who was seeking revenge on Cartagena and its lieutenant governor, Alonso de Bejinés, who had ordered Alvarez whipped for alleged criminal actions a few months previous to the Val raid. Alvarez took revenge by killing Bejinés during the pirate attack (see also: PIRACY).

VALDEZ, Juan. A fictitious but widely recognized Colombian figure popularized through commercial advertising. Valdez, a symbolic characterization of the typical small *coffee grower, was created in 1960 by the *Federación Nacional de Cafeteros (National Federation of Coffee Growers) for an extensive international advertising campaign.

VALENCIA, Guillermo, 1873-1943. *Modernist poet, agriculturalist, journalist, diplomat, and *Conservative political leader, born *Popayán, October 20; died Popayán, July 8. He began his political career as a member of *Congress in 1895 and was Minister of Finance under *Reyes and again under Pedro Nel *Ospina, Minister of Public Instruction under *Marroquín and *Restrepo, and Minister of War for President *Concha. He held numerous diplomatic commissions in Europe and America and was a Conservative candidate for the presidency in 1918 and 1930. In literature, known as "The Master" (*El Maestro*), he was the author of *Anarkos, Ritos* (1899), *Mejoras poemas* (1919), *Catay* (1929), and other works. An edition of his complete works, *Obras completas,* was published in 1952. He is considered one of the best modernist poets in Colombia during the first half of the 20th century.

VALENCIA, Guillermo León, 1909-1971. Legislator, journalist, orator, leader of the *Conservative Party, President of Colombia, 1962-1966. Born *Popayán, April 27; died New York (U.S.A.), November 4; he was the son of Guillermo *Valencia, "The Master." He received his education at the *Universidad Central del Cauca in his native city, and he directed the periodical *La Claridad,* founded in Popayán in 1933. Ideologically he was a Hispanist and a supporter of the Spanish *Falange, 1940-1944. He was twice ambassador to Spain, 1952-1953 and 1966-1969, as well as ambassador to the *United Nations. His administration is not generally known as one of aggressive innovation, although it did claim to have ended *La *Violencia.*

VALENZUELA-CASTRO TREATY, 1865. Signed *Bogotá, March 28, by Teodoro Valenzuela, Colombia, and José María Castro, Costa Rica. The treaty proposed the annexation of Costa Rica to the *Estados Unidos de Colombia. Colombia ceded some thirty leagues of disputed territory to Costa Rica in exchange for the latter's recognition of the *Constitution of 1863. The treaty generated strong opposition in Colombia, and it was never ratified.

VALLE. Literally, "valley." Capitalized and unqualified, Valle is frequently used to mean the political division known as the Department of *VALLE DEL CAUCA. The Cauca Valley, however, is also used more broadly to mean the land and cultural milieu surrounding the *Cauca River. In a more limited fashion it refers to the actual land immediately adjacent to the Cauca River. In this case the Cauca Valley is about 200 kilometers long and about 15 kilometers wide.

VALLE DEL CAUCA, Departamento del. Located in western Colombia on the *Cauca River between the *Cordillera Occidental and the *Cordillera Central. The department covers 22,140 square kilometers between 3° 5′ and 5° 1′N latitude, and 75° 42′ and 77° 33′W longitude. The terrain is a mixture of lowland river valleys surrounded by mountains, with 10,337 square kilometers tropical; 7,606 temperate; 3,089 cold; 1,108 wasteland. Major rivers include the Cauca, Anchicayá, Dagua, Guapí, Jamundí, and La Vieja. High points in the department include the Farallones de Cali (4,200 meters). Population is 2,833,940 people (1985 estimate), with a population density of about 128 people per square kilometer. *Cali is the capital city. According to DANE, *Colombia estadística 86,* principal agricultural products, with tonnage produced in 1984, include *sugar, 8,731,800; sorghum, 183,900; plantains, 115,800; soybeans, 83,350; rice, 61,255; *corn, 46,524; *cotton, 28,000; *yuca, 26,000; *potatoes, 15,300; *tobacco, 2,340; beans, 2,230; coconuts, 1,660; *cacao, 800; wheat, 730; *African palm, 700; and peanuts, 107. Cattle raising is a major industry. There were 349,348 head of cattle and 152,798 hogs slaughtered in 1984. *Coal, *gold, *silver, *platinum, marble, granite, *iron, asbestos, and *salt are mined in the department. In 1983 there were 908 businesses employing 10 or more people. The area is highly industrialized, and tourism is important. The region was conquered by Juan de *Ampudia, Miguel López Muñoz, Pedro de *Añasco, Sebastián de *Belalcázar, and others, 1535-1536. Juan *Vadillo, Jorge *Robledo, and Lorenzo de Aldana joined the valley conquest in 1538, and Pascual de *Andagoya and Juan de Ladrilleros did so in 1539. The region was first governed from the Province of Quito, then from the Province of Popayán, and eventually became the Estado (State) del Cauca. In 1908 the Departments of Cali and Buga were separated from the *Cauca, but they were merged into a single Department of Valle del Cauca in 1910. The Valley of the Cauca has always been important agriculturally, and the Cauca River has been a vital south-north transportation link.

VALLEDUPAR.   The capital of *Cesar, located at the foothills of the *Sierra Nevada de Santa Marta on the Río Guatapurí. Valledupar is situated at 10° 29'N, 73° 15'W, at an altitude of 169 meters. It has an average temperature of 27°C and a population of 196,984 people (1985 estimate). The city was founded on January 6, 1550, by Captain Hernando de Santana and Juan de Castellanos. It was originally called Valle de Upar, after an Indian chieftain. The settlement lay on the route of many conquistadors. It followed María Concepción Lopera de Fernández de Castro in proclaiming independence and resisting Spanish rule, 1810-1813. Valledupar was first made the capital of the Province of Valledupar, 1850, and then of the Department of Valledupar in the State of Magdalena in 1886. Finally it became the capital of the Department of *Cesar in 1967. The city was the scene of continuous fighting during the War of the *Thousand Days, from which it required several years to recover.

VANGUARDIA LIBERAL, La.   *Liberal daily newspaper of *Bucaramanga that began publication on September 1, 1919, under the direction of Alejandro Galvís Galvís and Rodolfo Azuero. Present circulation is estimated at 34,500.

VARA.   A Spanish yard of 83.6 centimeters. Two varas made a braza, or fathom, of 1.67 meters. Ten thousand brazas equaled three leagues (leguas), the traditional measure of distance. The basis of land measure was the fanegada of 1,000 square varas (0.699 hectares). The vara and fanegada (or fanega) survive in modern Colombia, but with their values rounded down to 80 centimeters and 0.64 hectares respectively. See also: WEIGHTS AND MEASURES

VARGAS TEJADA, Luis, 1802-1829. Romantic poet, playwright, born *Bogotá, November 27; died in the eastern *Llanos, December 8. Vargas Tejada's poetry was patriotic, strongly libertarian, and anti-*Bolívar, especially during the latter's dictatorship. His plays included *Sugamuxi, Doraminta, Aquimín, Zaquesazipa,* and *Las convulsiones,* many of which used *Indian themes. He was a delegate to the *Congreso de Ocaña and a member of the *Twenty-fifth of September conspiracy to assassinate Bolívar, 1828. Forced to flee Bogotá as a consequence of this attempt on the Liberator, he was drowned while crossing a river in the Llanos.

VARGAS VILA, José María, 1860-1933. Novelist. Vargas Vila was the author of more than thirty novels, including *Flor de fango* (1895), *Ibis* (1900), *La caída del cóndor* (1913), and *La novena sinfonía* (1928). His work was markedly iconoclastic and controversial. His language was often unorthodox or experimental, and the quality of his work was uneven. His works were vociferously anti-clerical, opposed to the institutional *Catholic Church, and they were never popular with the ruling Conservative elite. Modern reassessments tend to give Vargas Vila greater respect than he enjoyed with his own contemporaries.

VASQUEZ ARCE Y CEBALLOS, Gregorio, 1638-1711. Probably the best known of Colombia's colonial artists, he painted predominantly religious motifs. More than 400 of his works survive, including 66 paintings and 105 drawings in the *Museo del Arte Colonial in *Bogotá. Several attempts were made to popularize Vásquez Arce y Ceballos in Europe, but all failed. See also: PIZANO RESTREPO, Roberto

VASQUEZ COBO–MARTINS TREATY, 1907. Signed April 24, by Enas Martins, Brazil, and Alfredo Vásquez Cobo, Colombia. The treaty provided for settlement of major portions of the Brazilian-Colombian *borders and, by supplementary agreement signed on August 21, 1908, it regulated transportation, navigation, and commerce between the two countries.

VASQUEZ DE ESPINOSA, Antonio, d. 1630. He was the author of *Compendio y descripción de las indias occidentales,* an early ethnogeographical description of the Colombian coastal area, first published from 1942-1948.

VATICAN, see: PAPACY

VAUPES, Departamento del. Located in southern Colombia on the Brazilian border, Vaupés covers 65,268 square kilometers of tropical lowland, between 1° 10' and 2°N latitude, and 69° 10' and 72° 10'W longitude. In the north the region is dry plains and in the south, tropical rain forest. Average temperatures are 28° to 30°C. Major rivers include the Vaupés, Inírida, Querari, Piraparana, and Apaporis. The estimated population in 1985 was 3,414 people, with a population density of less than one person per square kilometer. The capital city is *Mitú. Subsistence *agriculture is the main economic activity, with approximately 2,450 hectares in *corn and *yuca. There are 1,000 head of cattle in the department. There is also some *fishing, forestry, and *rubber production, as well as local handicrafts. The Vaupés was established as a *commissariat in 1963, and it became a department under the *Constitution of 1991.

VELEZ. A mountain community in the *Cordillera Oriental of about 7,738 people (1985 estimate) in the Department of *Santander. It is located at 6° 1'N, 73° 40'W, about 50 kilometers northeast of *Chiquinquirá on the *Tunja–Puerto Berrío Highway and 231 kilometers from *Bucaramanga. Altitude is 2,133 meters, and the average temperature 17°C. Major economic activities include agriculture, cattle raising, commerce, mining, and fishing. Vélez was founded June 3, 1539, by Martín *Galeano at the juncture of the Suárez and Ubasá Rivers and later moved to its present location. Estimated population in 1985 was 7,378 people.

VELEZ REBELLION. August-October 1740. Alvaro Chacón de Luna (d. 1744) and others protested special taxes levied to finance the defense of *Cartagena aginst Admiral *Vernon. The protest was unsuccessful and Chacón de Luna died in prison.

VENERO DE LEIVA, Andrés Díaz, d. 1576. The first President of the *Nuevo Reino de Granada, 1564-1574. He organized the administration of the presidency; encouraged *emerald mining; authorized various public works; and saw to the efficient administration of justice. He ordered improvements in the working conditions of the *Indians and opened schools for Indian children. His presidency was generally a laudable effort at colonial administration.

VENEZUELA, Relations with. Present-day Colombia and Venezuela formed part of the *Virreinato de la Nueva Granada during the late colonial period, and sections of each nation tried separately to achieve independence, 1810-1819. In 1811, the Republic of Venezuela and the Province (state) of *Cundinamarca formed an alliance to secure mutual assistance in the struggle with Spain (see: LOZANO-MADARIAGA TREATY). Both formed part of the *República de Gran Colombia until Venezuela separated, de facto, to become independent in 1829. The *POMBO-MICHELENA TREATIES, signed in 1833, were an effort to establish formal relations between New Granada and Venezuela, to define boundaries, and to settle debt questions. International frontiers (see: BORDERS) remained the chronic problem between the two nations throughout the 19th century (see: AROSEMENA-GUZMAN TREATY; POMBO-ROMERO TREATY; SUAREZ–LOSADA DIAZ TREATY) and until 1941 when the two declared all boundary questions settled (see: LOPEZ DE MESA–GIL BORGES TREATY). Renewed disputes, however, continue to trouble relations between the two nations. Venezuela is one of Colombia's major trading partners, but lack of consistency in Venezuelan economic policy has made cooperation difficult. Venezuela helped set up the *Flota Mercante Grancolombiana, but then withdrew from it. It first delayed joining the *Andean Common Market, then withdrew, and later rejoined. The most important problems in current Colombian-Venezuelan relations are immigration and claims to the Gulf of Venezuela. During the 1970s, it was estimated that some 500,000 Colombians had emigrated to Venezuela, often illegally, causing protests from the Venezuelan government. Petroleum potential in the Gulf of Venezuela (referred to as the Gulf of Coquivacoa by some Colombians) led Venezuela to assert its claims to jurisdiction over the region, and President *Barco tried unsuccessfully to resolve the dispute by placing it before the International Court of Justice.

VENEZUELA-COLOMBIA TREATY OF 1881, see: AROSEMENA-GUZMAN TREATY

VENEZUELA-COLOMBIA TREATY OF 1916, see: SUAREZ–LOSADA DIAZ TREATY

VENEZUELA-COLOMBIA TREATY OF 1941, see: LOPEZ DE MESA–GIL BORGES TREATY

VENEZUELA-CUNDINAMARCA TREATY OF 1811, see: LOZANO-MADARIAGA TREATY

VENEZUELA–NEW GRANADA TREATIES OF 1833, see: POMBO-MICHELENA TREATIES

VENEZUELA–NEW GRANADA TREATY OF 1842, see: POMBO-ROMERO TREATY

VENTANILLA SINIESTRA.   A phrase that became popular in the 1980s to describe the method used by banks in dealing with dollars from the black market. U.S. dollars were converted into Colombian pesos with no questions asked regardless of normal currency regulations. It was a way of encouraging drug dealers to return their profits from abroad to Colombia.

VERGARA Y VERGARA, José María, 1831-1872.   Poet, essayist, and literary historian, born *Bogotá, March 19; died Bogotá, March 9. Considered one of the most distinguished literary figures of the 19th century in Colombia, Vergara y Vergara was one of the founders of the *tertulia* and newspaper, *El *Mosaico* (1858-1872), and the *Academia Colombiana de la Lengua (1871). With José Benito Gaitán, he published an *Almanaque de Bogotá y guía de forasteros para 1867.* He was also the author of *Historia de la literatura en Nueva Granada, época colonial* (1867); a *costumbrista* novel, *Olivos y aceitunos todos son unos;* and numerous essays and poems. His collected works, *Obras escogidas,* were published in five volumes in 1931.

VERNON, EDWARD, 1684-1757.   English admiral. Sent by the British Admiralty at the outset of the War of Jenkins' Ear (the War of Austrian Succession) against the Spanish possessions in the Caribbean, he attacked La Guayra in October 1739, and then captured *Portobello, November 1739. He had only six ships, but the Spanish forts were ill prepared, with many guns dismounted, and the port was taken after two days. The victory was celebrated wildly throughout the British Empire. Laurence Washington was a member of the expedition, and his brother, later President George Washington, named his home Mt. Vernon (Virginia) after the admiral. Vernon attacked *Cartagena, March 6-24, 1740, bombarding it ineffectually on March 17, and returned with a large body of troops March-April 1741. The attack was unsuccessful due to sickness and inept leadership from General Wentworth, who commanded the land forces. Vernon threatened, but did not attack, Cartagena again in April 1742. He is ridiculed in Colombian history because he prematurely cast medals that proclaimed his anticipated but unrealized victory over the Spanish at Cartagena in 1741. The main result of the 1739 attack as far as Colombia was concerned was that alarmed Spanish officials reestablished the *Virreinato de la Nueva Granada so that the defenses of *Panama might be better maintained.

VESPUCCI, Amerigo, 1454-1512.   Italian sailor who became a *piloto mayor* (navigational official) of Spain. He was among the first to explore the Colombian coasts as a member of Alonso de *Ojeda's expedition in 1499. The Latin form of his name is most often cited as the probable source for the name "America."

VICE PRESIDENT OF THE REPUBLIC.   An official authorized by the *Constitution of 1991 to assume the role of the *President of the Republic when specifically asked to do so by the Chief Executive or when death or other circumstances make it impossible for the President to act. The Vice President is elected for four years, and qualifications for the office are the same as those needed to be elected President.

VICEROYALTY.   The *virreynato* was the major jurisdictional unit in Spain's American empire. There were originally two viceroyalties. New Spain (Nueva España), which was organized in 1535 with its capital at Mexico City, was intended to govern North America, and the *Virreinato del Peru, dating from 1544, with its capital at Lima, long had titular control of much of South America. In the 18th century, two others were created. The *VIRREINATO DEL NUEVO REINO DE GRANADA, with its capital at *Santa Fe de Bogotá, was permanently established in 1739 over the area that later became *Gran Colombia, and the Viceroyalty of the Rio de la Plata (capital at Buenos Aires) was created in 1776.

526 / Viceroys

VICEROYS. Viceroys (*virreyes*) of the Viceroyalty of the New Kingdom of Granada (*Virreinato del Nuevo Reino de Granada) from 1719 to 1819 were:

Antonio de la Pedrosa y Guerrero, 1718
Jorge *Villalonga, 1719-1723
(*presidency reestablished, 1723-1739*)
Sebastián de *Eslava, 1740-1749
José Alfonso *Pizarro, 1749-1753
José *Solís Folch de Cardona, 1753-1761
Pedro *Messía de la Zerda, 1761-1772
Manuel *Gurior, 1773-1776
Manuel Antonio *Flórez, 1776-1782
Juan de *Torrezal Díaz Pimienta, 1782
Juan Francisco *Gutiérrez de Piñeres, 1782
Antonio *Caballero y Góngora, 1782-1789
Francisco *Gil de Taboada y Lemos, 1789
José de *Ezpeleta Galdeano, 1789-1797
Pedro *Mendinueta y Muzquiz, 1797-1803
Antonio *Amar y Borbón, 1803-1810
Benito *Pérez Brito, 1812-1813
Pablo *Morillo, 1816
Francisco de *Montalvo y Ambulodi, 1816-1818
Juan *Sámano y Uribarri, 1818-1819

VICHADA, Departamento del. Located in northern Colombia on the Venezuelan border, Vichada covers 100,242 square kilometers between latitudes 2° 40′ and 6° 20′N, and longitudes 67° 20′ and 71° 5′W. The region is *Llanos with savannah vegetation and alternating wet and dry seasons in the north changing to tropical rain forest in the south. Average temperatures range from 28° to 30°C. April to October is the rainy season. Major rivers include the Meta, Tomo, Vichada, and Guaviare. The population is 3,377 people (1985 estimate), with a population density of less than one person per square kilometer. *Puerto Carreño is the capital city. Cattle raising is the principal commercial activity, with 150,000 head of cattle recorded in the department. Approximately 1,800 hectares are cultivated (rice, *corn, *yuca, and *cacao). Santa Rita is the main commercial center. There is also some *fishing and forestry development. A *Commissariat of Vichada was created in 1947. It became a department in 1991. Puerto Carreño, San José de Ocuné, and Santa Rita are all connected by highway to *Villavicencio (*Meta).

VICTORIA-VELEZ TREATY OF 1924. Signed in *Bogotá on August 20 by Nicolás Victoria, Colombia, and Jorge Vélez, Panama. The treaty established the permanent boundaries between the two republics.

VILLA DE LEYVA, see: LEIVA

VILLA ROSARIO DE CUCUTA, see: CUCUTA

VILLALBA Y TOLEDO, Diego de. President of the *Nuevo Reino de Granada, 1667-1671. He is remembered for building the bridge over the Río Gualí at *Honda and Puente Grande over the Río Bogotá.

VILLALONGA, JORGE DE, b. ca. 1665. The first effective Viceroy of *New Granada, 1719-1723. He established the *viceroyalty with orders to expand, but closely supervise, ecclesiastical work and to prohibit the cultivation of grapes and the growth of the cloth industry. He organized an appropriate court life; reestablished the *Audiencia of Quito; attempted to alleviate working conditions for the *Indians; ordered the construction of fortifications in *Cartagena; and probably recommended suppression of the viceroyalty. He was accused of engaging in contraband trade and other irregularities while in office.

VILLAVICENCIO. The capital of *Meta, located at 4° 9'N, 73° 39'W, approximately 126 kilomters from Bogotá. It has an altitude of 467 meters, an average temperature of 26°C, and a population of 173,932 people (1985 estimate). The city was founded in 1840 by Father Manuel Santos Martínez, Esteban Aguirre, and others, and given the name Gramalote. It was renamed for Antonio *Villavicencio in 1850. It is essentially a cattle-raising and commercial center with some beverage and food-processing industries, and is known as the gateway to the *Llanos (*puerta del Llano*).

VILLAVICENCIO, Antonio, 1775-1816. Patriot martyr. A commissioner sent by the Spanish Regency (*Consejo de Regencia) to deal with colonial problems in 1810. He sympathized with many *creole demands and released *Nariño from prison. Villavicencio's expected arrival in *Bogotá led to the events of the *TWENTIETH OF JULY 1810. He was one of the first to be executed by the Spanish during the *Reign of Terror, 1816-1819.

VIOLENCIA, La. "The Violence"; a reference to the period from the late 1940s to the mid-1960s, during which chaotic violence was common in Colombia. Incited, although not necessarily begun, by the assassination of *Gaitán in 1948, the Violence took the form of terrorization, murder, and destruction of property. Numerous social and political tensions contributed to the destructiveness, including anti-communism, anti-*Protestantism, partisan politics, economic deprivation, and personal vindictiveness. A series of simultaneous, although probably not coordinated, outbursts, the Violence persisted throughout the 1950s. Although it is difficult to fix exactly when the turbulence ended, a claim of the *Valencia administration, 1962-1966, was that it had resolved the problem. However, violence continued as a phenomenon in Colombian political life through the 1970s and 1980s. Various categorization schemes have been suggested for describing the Violence. One of these distinguishes four phases. Phase I, 1945-1953, was characterized by *Liberal-*Conservative political rivalry, with guerrilla warfare concentrated in the *Llanos. Phase II, 1954-1957, was largely anti-*Rojas Pinilla. Phase III, 1958-1982, was marked by revolutionary anti-*Frente Nacional, guerrilla-inspired movements dispersed throughout central and coastal parts of the nation. Phase IV, since 1982, has been the period of peace negotiations and intermittent violence. The effects of the Violence were profound in many ways, most obviously in the sharp increase in urban populations. People fled to the towns and cities in large numbers, sometimes driven off their land, but frequently for greater security.

VIRGIN OF CHIQUINQUIRA, see: CHIQUINQUIRA, Virgin Mary of the Rosary of

VIRREINATO DEL NUEVO REINO DE GRANADA. The Viceroyalty of the New Kingdom of Granada, first created from 1719-1723, later reestablished from 1739-1810 (1819). It encompassed much of present-day Colombia, Ecuador, Venezuela, and *Panama. The order of 1739 established the Viceroyalty with jurisdiction over the Captaincy General of *Panama, which included *Portobello, Veraguas, and

*Darién; the governments of *Chocó, Quito, *Popayán, and Guayaquil; the Provinces of *Antioquia, *Cartagena, *Riohacha, Maracaibo, Caracas, Cumaná, Guayana, and Río Orinoco; and the islands of Trinidad and Margarita. The capital city was *Santafé de Bogotá. Although Antonio *Amar y Borbón was the last effective Viceroy, 1803-1810, the viceroyalty persisted legally until 1819. The Captaincy General of Venezuela was created as a subdivision of the viceroyalty in 1777.

VIRREINATO DEL PERU. A viceroyalty organized in 1544 with its capital at Lima. Its jurisdiction included *New Granada until 1719, and again during the period from 1723-1739.

VISITADOR. Literally, a "visitor"; one who conducted a *visita,* or visit. In colonial Spanish America, the visitor was a specially appointed judge sent by the Crown without previous warning to investigate the administrative practices in a designated area. During the length of his investigation, or visit, the visitor's authority took precedence over all other secular officials. See also: RESIDENCIA

VORAGINE, La. Well-known regionalist novel of the Colombian rain forest published in 1924 by José Eustacio *Rivera. It tells the story of the systematic destruction of · characters pitted against, among other things, the merciless environment.

-W-

WAR OF THE SUPREME COMMANDERS, see: SUPREME COMMANDERS, War of the

WAR OF THE THOUSAND DAYS. Also known as the rebellion of 1899-1903 and the Three Years War, this civil conflict lasted from October 17, 1899, to June 1, 1903. *Liberals revolted against the rigidly partisan *Conservative governments of President *Sanclemente and Vice President *Marroquín. Major military engagements included *Peralonso and *Palonegro. The rebellion was settled by the treaties of Nerlandia, the *Wisconsin,* and Chinácota.

WARS, see: CHACO WAR; CIVIL WARS; INDEPENDENCE MOVEMENT; KOREAN WAR; PACIFIC, War of the; VERNON, Edward; WORLD WAR I; WORLD WAR II

WATERMELON RIOT, see: PANAMA RIOT, 1856

WATERWAYS. Rivers were long the only convenient access into the central highlands of Colombia. Most prominent of these were the *Magdalena River and the *Cauca River, but numerous others were also important. Their use accounts for the slow and incomplete development of *railroads. In recent times, the waterways account for only about 10% of freight movements. See also: DIQUE CANAL

WEIDEMANN, Guillermo, 1905-. Painter in oils and watercolors; born and educated in Munich, Germany. He immigrated to Colombia via *Buenaventura in 1939 and became a naturalized Colombian citizen in 1946. He has held numerous expositions in the United States, Europe, and Latin America. His early works featured the tropical environment and African-American themes, but his mature work abandoned these, evolving into essentially abstract art.

WEIGHTS AND MEASURES. The traditional Spanish measures of colonial times were replaced by the metric system in 1857. Some colonial terms survive, but they have been assimilated by rounding to the nearest convenient metric amount. Thus the *libra, the old Spanish pound of 461.92 grams, is nowadays understood as half a kilogram (500 grams), and the *vara, or Spanish yard of 83.6 centimeters, is understood as 80 centimeters. The galón (of 5 botellas) equals 3.75 litres, but U.S. measures persist in the *petroleum industry, where the barrel (barril) is divided into 42 gallons (galones) of 3.785 liters. Bulk *coffee is measured by the bag (saco) of 60 kilograms. See also: TIME

WELSERS. A German banking association based at Augsburg whose representatives, Hieronymus Sailer (or Sayler) and Heinrich Ehinger (or Eygner) of Constanz, were given permission to establish a colony in present-day Venezuela. Acting under a *capitulación, or contract, with the Spanish Crown, signed in Burgos, January 3, 1528, the Welsers sent out explorer-colonizers such as *Dalfinger, *Federmann, *Hutten, and *Speyer in efforts to develop their concession from 1528 until it was revoked by Charles V in 1548.

WESTERN CORDILLERA, see: CORDILLERA OCCIDENTAL

WESTERN TRUNK RAILROAD. The Ferrocarril del Occidente, a line intended to connect *Cartagena with *Popayán. It was authorized in 1922 and work began on two fronts in *Antioquia, roughly parallel to the *Cauca River, in 1925. The line was never completed, but it did connect the *Pacific Railroad from *Cartago to the *Antioquia Railroad in 1946. Other fragments of the line were discontinued for economic reasons.

WILCHES, Solón. Soldier-politician who was dismissed as commander-in-chief of the *army in 1875 for supporting Rafael *Núñez for the governorship of *Santander. Wilches fought for the government against the *rebellion of 1876-1877. As governor of Santander in the late 1870s he promoted the *Cúcuta Railroad. In 1882 he ran for president but lost to Francisco *Zaldúa. He ran again on Zaldúa's death, but was persuaded to withdraw in favor of Núñez.

WINDWARD FLEET TAX, see: ARMADA DE BARLOVENTO

WISCONSIN TREATY. Signed on November 21, 1902, aboard the United States battleship Wisconsin. The agreement was accepted by General Nicolás Perdomo, for the government, and General Benjamín Herrera, for the opposition. Its major provisions included a cessation of hostilities, an amnesty, and safe-conduct for all. Together with the Treaty of Nerlandia, October 24, and the Treaty of Chinácota, November 21, it ended the War of the *Thousand Days.

WORKERS' CIRCLE, see: CIRCULO DE OBREROS

WORKER'S LABOR UNION, see: UNION SINDICAL OBRERA

WORKER'S SELF-DEFENSE, see: AUTODEFENSA OBRERA

WORKER'S UNION, see: SINDICATO OBRERO

WORKERS' UNION SOCIETY, see: SOCIEDAD UNION OBREROS

WORLD WAR I, 1914-1918. Colombia declared its neutrality in a series of decrees, August-December 1914, and remained a nonparticipant throughout the war.

WORLD WAR II, 1939-1945. As in *World War I, Colombia declared complete neutrality in this international conflict on September 6, 1939. Nevertheless, as the struggle developed, it collaborated closely with the United States. It adhered to agreements at *Panama, establishing a neutral zone in the Western Hemisphere, and at Havana, providing for mutual defense of the American nations. The following year, in December 1941, Colombia severed diplomatic relations with Japan, Germany, and Italy. It supported the declarations of the Rio de Janeiro meeting early in 1942 and concluded both a military pact and a lend-lease agreement with the United States later that year. Although Colombia did not contribute actual combat forces to the war effort, it did declare war and supported the Allied Powers with strategic defense measures.

-Y-

YARI. A river in the Department of *Caquetá and the name given to a cocaine-processing center on an island in the river (approximately 6 square miles in size), which was raided by government forces, first on March 10 and again in April 1984. The Yarí facilities, located in southeastern Caquetá, were constructed in 1982 and made operational in 1983. Accounts vary, but the Yarí complex was composed of as many as 6 clusters of buildings, the largest of which were Tranquilandia, Coquilandia, and Villa Coca. It included as many as six airstrips and nineteen laboratories. At Tranquilandia, the headquarters for the processing center, authorities seized 2,500 kilograms (5,555 pounds) of pure cocaine. Total estimated value of the Yarí cocaine seizures was $1.2 billion. Controlling interest of the narcotics operation was said to be the *Medellín Cartel, including Pablo *Escobar Gaviria, the *Ochoa Vásquez family, and Gonzalo Rodríguez Gacha. A second series of raids in April uncovered a seventh base with three laboratories at La Loma, 75 kilometers northwest of Yarí. The La Loma complex was thought to have been occupied, at least for a while, by members of the *Fuerzas Armadas Revolucionarias de Colombia (FARC).

YOPAL. The capital of the Department of *Casanare, located at 5° 21'N, 72° 24'W, approximately 230 kilometers from *Tunja. Altitude is 350 meters; average temperature, 26°C;

and population, 12,684 people (1985 estimate). The terrain merges from the foothills of the *Cordillera Oriental to the *Llanos. Principal economic activities around Yopal are cattle raising and agriculture (*sugar, beans, plantains, citrus fruits, rice, *coffee, and *corn). Yopal is a name derived from an Indian word, *yopos,* meaning heart. The city was founded by Pedro Pablo González in 1935. Yopal was made the capital of Casanare in 1942 after Marroquín and El Morro had each briefly been the capital first.

YUCA. In Colombian usage *yuca* is the common name for a traditional *Indian tuber known by the scientific names *manihot esculenta, manihot utilisima,* and *manihot manihot* (family, Euphorbiaceae). It is one of Colombia's principal food products, largely grown by small farmers as a subsistence crop. The 1985 harvest of 1,729,000 metric *tons was surpassed in Latin America only by Brazil and Paraguay. *Yuca* is a synonym for plants or food products known elsewhere as mandioca, mandioc, manioc, casabe, and cassava. It is a starchy plant used in making breads, cakes, beverages, and other foods. As a commercial product it is the source from which tapioca and arrowroot are derived. In its natural state *yuca* is often divided into the categories of bitter manioc and sweet manioc. Sweet is readily edible, but bitter is posionous until properly processed. It has been suggested that cultivation of *yuca* plants originated with the *Arawak Indians in the interior of South America and was diffused toward the Atlantic and Caribbean through tributaries of the Orinoco River, such as the Apure, Arauca, and Meta in Colombia. The name is said to be descended from a *Carib Indian word, and *yuca* is often translated into English as yucca. Care should be taken when doing this, however, because yucca is also the name frequently given to a plant of the family Liliaceae, which has long, sharply pointed leaves, white waxy flowers, and little value in human diets. See also: CORN; POTATOES

YURUPARY, EL. Pre-Hispanic epic poem of the *Guaviare-*Vaupés region of Colombia and Brazil. The oldest piece of *Indian literature known from Colombia, it was first written down in the °engatú language by a Brazilian Indian, Maximiano José Roberto, and then translated into Italian and first published by Ermanno Stradelli in 1890. The first Spanish version published in Colombia appeared in 1983. *Yurupary* tells the story of creation and the events through which the deity of the same name brought civilization to the Tarian (Tariana) Indians. Héctor J. Orjuela has compared this work to the *Popol Vuh*, sacred book of the Quiché Maya.

-Z-

ZALAMEA BORDA, Jorge, 1905-1969.   Journalist, author, diplomat, *Liberal politician; born *Bogotá, March 8. He enjoyed a long career as a journalist with various Bogotá *newspapers, including *El* *Tiempo*, *El Liberal*, and *El* *Espectador*, and held numerous government posts, including Secretary of the Ministry of Education, 1936-1937, Secretary General of the Presidency, 1937-1938, member of the *House of Representatives, 1938-1940, and ambassador to Mexico, 1947. He is perhaps more widely remembered as a novelist and critic whose works include *La vida maravillosa de los libros* (1941), *Minerva en la rueca* (1949), *Las Metamorfosis de su Excelencia* (1949), and *El Gran Burudún-Burudá ha muerto* (1952).

ZALDUA, Francisco Javier, 1811-1882.   Lawyer, educator, legislator, judge; *Radical Liberal, President of Colombia, 1882. Born *Bogotá, December 3; died Bogotá, December 21. He received his law degree from *Colegio Mayor de San Bartolomé. He later served as rector of his alma mater and rector and professor at the *Universidad Nacional. He was Minister of Government, 1849-1850; a delegate to the Convention of *Rionegro, 1863; Minister of Interior and Foreign Relations, 1878; and elected President of Colombia, 1882-1884. His administration sought reconciliation of factions within the *Liberal Party, but it was paralyzed by fierce opposition in *Congress. Zaldúa died within a few months of his inauguration as President.

ZAMORA, Alonso de, 1635-1717.   *Dominican. A native of *Bogotá who wrote the *Historia del Nuevo Reino de Granada, y de la Provincia de San Antonino en la religión de Santo Domingo*, first published in Barcelona, 1701. It is a basic source for 16th- and 17th-century history, especially for Dominican expansion.

ZANCUDO, El.   A *gold- and *silver-mining center near Titiribí (6° 5'N, 75° 49'W) in the Department of *Antioquia. Founded in 1775, it became the wealthiest commercial enterprise in Colombia during the 1880s. The mine is located about 64 kilometers from *Medellín at an altitude of 1,500 meters in the *Cordillera Central. Half of all the shares of the Empresa Minera de El Zancudo y Sabaletas were controlled and managed by Carlos Coriolano *Amador and his wife, Lorenza Uribe Lema, who had inherited the mine from her father, José María Uribe Restrepo (1794-1854). Other important investors included Juan Bautista *Marinero y Trucco. El Zancudo's value was estimated at 50,000 *pesos in 1854, at 200,000 pesos in the late 1860s, and at more than 4 million pesos in 1885. The mining venture first began to experience serious financial difficulties in 1898, but recovered. After a third near failure, it was closed in 1945. The region around the mine is now a center for agriculture and cattle raising.

ZAPATA DE CARDENAS, Luis, ca. 1510-1590. *Franciscan; born Villa de Llerena (Extremadura, Spain); died *Bogotá, January 24. He followed a military career until the age of forty, when he entered the Franciscan order. He was Visitor of his order in Peru, 1561-1566, before being appointed to Bogotá in 1570. He was the second Archbishop of Bogotá, serving from 1573 to 1590. His administration founded the first convents for women (*Santa Clara in Tunja, 1573, and La Concepción in Bogotá, 1584); the first seminary in Colombia, 1582-1586; and the first pontifical university (Dominicans, 1580). It authenticated the miraculous Virgin of *Chiquinquirá and named saints Isabel of Hungary and Victor as patrons against killing frosts and saints Rocco and Sebastián as patrons against smallpox.

ZAPATA OLIVELLA, Manuel, 1920-. Author, physician, *black cultural leader; born Lorica (*Córdoba), March 17. He began medical studies at the *Universidad de Cartagena, completed his medical degree at the *Universidad Nacional in 1948, and practiced medicine until 1965, when he became chief of the Cultural Extension Division of the Ministry of National Education. After that he became a full-time student and promoter of cultural affairs, especially in the fields of folkloric dance and *literature. He founded and directed the journal *Letras nacionales* (1965-1985) and the Center for Afro-Colombian Studies (Centro de Estudios Afro-Colombianos) in 1975. His major works include *Tierra Mojada* (1947); *La calle 10* (1960); *Chambacú, corral de negros* (1967); *Teatro* (1972); *En*

Chimá nace un santo (1974); *Changó, El Gran Putas* (1983); and *El fusilamiento del diablo* (1986). His novel *Changó, El Gran Putas* won first prize at the Concurso de Literatura Negra in São Paulo, Brazil, in 1985.

ZAQUE. The ruler of the northern half of the *Chibcha territory. His capital was at *Tunja. Like that of the Zipa, the Zaque's throne passed matrilineally to his sister's children, the Zaque's nephews. The Zaque's realm was identified with the cult of the sun. His counterpart was the Zipa. *Quemunchatocha and *Aquimín are the only known Zaques. See also: ZIPA

ZEA Y DIAZ, Francisco Antonio, 1766-1822. Scientist, writer, and independence fighter. In 1794 he was sent to Spain to stand trial for complicity with Antonio *Nariño's publication of *The *Rights of Man*. Although absolved in 1799, he was forbidden to return to *New Granada. After scientific study in Paris, he was made director of the Gabinete Botánico in Madrid in 1805. Returning to Venezuela in 1815, he supported Simón *Bolívar in the *independence movement, and Bolívar appointed him his vice president. In 1820, under the government of *Gran Colombia, he was sent to Europe to help establish the new nation's credit. He was responsible for negotiating the *London Loan of 1820 (signed in March of 1822), which was bitterly attacked for its onerous conditions. Zea died at Bath, England, shortly after signing the loan.

ZINC. Some 100 metric *tons of zinc were produced in 1975, from mines in *Cundinamarca, *Risaralda, and *Cauca.

ZIPA. The ruler of the southern half of the *Chibcha territory. His capital was at Muequetá (Funza, 4° 43'N, 74° 13'W, *Cundinamarca). Inheritance of the throne seems to have been similar to that of the Zaque's household. The Zipa's realm was identified with the cult of the moon. *Saguamachica, *Nemequene, *Tisquesusa, and *Sagipa are the only known Zipas. See also: ZAQUE

ZIPAQUIRA. A city located 5° 23'N, 74°W, about 49 kilometers east of *Bogotá in the Department of *Cundinamarca. Zipaquirá has been an important mineral-processing center since pre-Hispanic times. The city is situated 2,611 meters above sea level with an average temperature of 14°C. The population is 55,119 people (1985 estimate). Sometimes called the *salt capital of the world, the city is most widely known for its mountain of salt (400,000 square meters) and salt mining (125,000 bags monthly). Salt was an important item of trade for the *Chibcha Indians before the Spanish conquest, and the mines at Zipaquirá, Nemocón (5° 4'N, 73° 53'W) and elsewhere have been exploited for more than 400 years. The original Indians working the mines were virtually annihilated by 1623, when only 321 workers remained. Major shaft excavations at the Zipaquirá mine were begun by the German engineer Jacob Wiesner in 1808. Soda and other minerals are also processed in Zipaquirá. See also: CATHEDRAL OF SALT; SALT PRODUCTION

ZIPAQUIRA, Battle of.   May 20, 1854, *Cundinamarca. Constitutional forces under General Manuel María Franco were defeated by Colonel Manuel Jiménez, agent of the *Melo dictatorship.

A BIBLIOGRAPHIC GUIDE
TO COLOMBIAN HISTORY

The following selections are intended as an introduction to the study of Colombian history. The essay lists works published in English and Spanish, but where editions exist in both languages, only the English version has been included. The citations do not indicate the number of times a work has been published, nor do they necessarily refer to the earliest, latest, or even the best editions, rather only to those for which the data was readily available. In cases where the volume of studies on a given theme makes more than a sampling of titles unfeasible, the latest editions published have often been cited on the assumption that these are the most likely to be accessible and that, with hope, these are the most up-to-date. With a very few exceptions, documentary collections have not been noted. Again with very few exceptions, all of the works cited in this guide are available in the United States, either in public or in private collections. The U.S. Library of Congress *National Union Catalog . . .* and/or the Online Computer Library Center (OCLC) can be used to determine the location of most individual titles.

For the sake of convenience and consistency, books are cited in the essay with author, title, and place and date of publication—e.g., David A. Bushnell, *The Santander Regime in Gran Colombia* (Newark, Del., 1954). Articles are referred to by author, title of the article, journal, volume and number, date of publication, and pages—e.g., J. León Helguera, "The Changing Role of the Military in Colombia," *Journal of Inter American Studies,* 3:3 (July 1961), 351-358. The place of publication is inserted in parentheses for periodicals other than those produced in the United States. The *Hispanic American Historical Review* (the most frequently cited journal) is abbreviated *HAHR* after the first citation. Unpublished masters' theses and doctoral dissertations are listed here by author, title, the university to which the work was submitted, and the date of submission—e.g., John W. Kitchens, "Colombian-Chilean Relations, 1817-1845: A Diplomatic Struggle for Pacific Coast Hegemony," Vanderbilt University, 1969.

The materials have been arranged in seven sections:

Generally speaking, works have been cited in full at the first mention and by short-title references thereafter.

I. BACKGROUND MATERIALS

There are several works that provide general background information on Colombia. Among the most recent and useful all-purpose surveys are Harvey F. Kline, *Colombia: Portrait of Unity and Diversity* (Boulder, Colo., 1983); and Howard I. Blutstein et al., *Area Handbook for Colombia* (3rd ed.; Washington, D.C., 1977). W. O. Galbraith, *Colombia: A General Survey* (London and New York, 1966), is also helpful, although somewhat dated. *Image of Colombia* (Washington, D.C., 1972) is an introductory pamphlet published by the Organization of American States, and Joaquín Paredes Cruz, *Colombia al día: Síntesis de la realidad nacional* (3rd ed.; Bogotá, 1984), is an informative almanac presentation of statistics and institutional data. The most recent edition of *The South American Handbook* (London, annually since 1924); Hilary Bradt, George Bradt, et al., *Backpacking in Venezuela, Colombia, and Ecuador: Treks in the Northern Andes* (Boston: Bradt Enterprises, 1979), and other travel guides offer helpful comments on day-to-day functions in the country. Seldon Rodman, *The Colombian Traveler* (New York, 1971), combines a historical sketch with travel information.

From a historical standpoint, the older works of Purl L. Bell, *Colombia: A Commercial and Industrial Handbook* (Washington, D.C., 1921); Phanor J. Eder, *Colombia* (London, 1913); Francis L. Petre, *The Republic of Colombia: An Account of the Country, Its People, Its Institutions, and Its Resources* (London, 1906); and John D. Powles, *New Granada: Its Internal Resources* (London, 1863), should be consulted. A number of recent works provide background on the economic situation in Colombia. See, for example, Fondo de Promoción de Exportaciones, *General Aspects of Colombian*

Economy (Bogotá, 1976); Harold Blakemore and Paul Clifford, *Pacific South America: Chile, Colombia, Ecuador, Peru—Business Opportunities in the 1980s* (London, 1981); Price, Waterhouse and Company, *Doing Business in Colombia* (New York, 1978); and British Overseas Trade Board, *Colombia,* "Hints to Business Men" Series (London, 1975, updated 1985 in the restricted-circulation "Hints to Exporters" Series).

For popular, illustrated, encyclopedic treatments, see *The World and Its Peoples: Venezuela, Colombia, Ecuador, Guiana, Uruguay* (New York, 1966); Martha Murray Sumwalt, *Colombia in Pictures* (Minneapolis, Minn., 1987); Gary MacEóin and the editors of *Life, Colombia and Venezuela and the Guianas* (New York, 1965); and *Peoples of the Earth,* Vol. 6, *Amazonia, Orinoco, and Pampas,* and Vol. 7, *Andes* (Danbury, Conn., 1974).

The basic collection of maps is that of the Instituto Geográfico Agustín Codazzi, *Atlas de Colombia* (Bogotá, 1969), but the more usable publications might be the Instituto's student edition, *Atlas básico de Colombia* (Bogotá, 1970); and the Esselete Map Service, *Primer atlas de Colombia* (Bogotá, 1985). For information on the socioeconomic life of Colombia, see the Banco de la República, Departamento de Investigaciones Económicas, *Atlas de economía colombiana* (4 vols.; Bogotá, 1959-1964), whose maps show geographical, political, ecological, demographical, agricultural, and mineralogical data. The multi-volume *Atlas lingüístico-etnográfico de Colombia,* Luis Flórez, dir. (Bogotá, 1981-), gives linguistic and ethnographical information. The Instituto Geográfico Agustín Codazzi's *Atlas regional Pacífico* (Bogotá, 1983), and *Atlas regional Orinoquia-Amazonia* (Bogotá, 1983), as well as Manuel Felipe Olivera, dir., *Conozca Cundinamarca atlas* (Bogotá, 1982), are all regional guides. Numerous sheet and road maps are also available. The major historical atlases are Eduardo Acevedo Latorre, *Atlas de mapas antiguos de Colombia: siglos XVI a XIX* (Bogotá, 1971); and Agustín Codazzi, *Atlas geográfico é histórico de la República de Colombia (antigua Nueva Granada) . . .* (Manuel María Paz and Felipe Pérez, eds.; Paris, 1889).

Preston E. James, C. W. Minkel, and Eileen W. James, *Latin America* (5th ed.; New York, 1986); Gilbert J. Butland, *Latin America: A Regional Geography* (New York, 1972); John P. Cole, *Latin America: An Economic and Social Geography* (Washington, D.C., 1965); and D. J. Robinson, "Venezuela and Colombia," in Harold Blakemore and Clifford T. Smith, eds., *Latin America: Geographical Perspectives* (London, 1971), all provide short overviews of Colombian geography in English. Alberto Pardo Pardo, *Geografía económica y humana de Colombia* (Bogotá, 1972); Ernesto

Guhl, *Colombia; bosquejo de su geografía tropical* (Bogotá, 1969); and Jesús Arango Cano, *Geografía física y económica de Colombia* (Bogotá, 1964), offer detailed descriptions of Colombian resources. From a historical viewpoint, José Manuel Forero, *Reseña histórica de la geografía de Colombia* (Bogotá, 1969), is a useful discussion of works by explorers and scientific groups in Colombia. The historian may also find interesting the more specialized studies of Raymond E. Crist, *The Cauca Valley, Colombia: Land Tenure and Land Use* (Baltimore, 1952); Crist and Ernesto Guhl, "Pioneer Settlement in Eastern Colombia," in Smithsonian Institution, *Annual Report of the Board of Regents,* 1956 (Washington, D.C., 1958), 339-355; Herbert G. Zandstra, *Caqueza: Living Rural Development* (Ontario, 1979); Ronald L. Tinnermeier, "New Land Settlement in the Eastern Lowlands of Colombia," University of Wisconsin, 1965; Edmund E. Hegen, *Highways into the Upper Amazon Basin: Pioneer Lands in Southern Colombia, Ecuador and Northern Peru* (Gainesville, Fla., 1966); B. Le Roy Gordon, *Human Geography and Ecology in the Sinú Country of Colombia* (Berkeley, Calif., 1957); James J. Parsons, *San Andrés and Providencia: English-Speaking Islands in the Western Caribbean* (Berkeley, Calif., 1956); Parsons, *Antioquia's Corridor to the Sea: An Historical Geography of the Settlement of Urabá* (Berkeley, Calif., 1967); and Parsons, *Antioqueño Colonization in Western Colombia* (Berkeley, Calif., 1968). In the last case, see also Keith H. Christie, "Antioqueño Colonization in Western Colombia: A Reappraisal," *Hispanic American Historical Review* (hereafter *HAHR*), 58:1 (May 1978), 260-283. For the mid-19th century, the standard compilation was that of the Comisión Corográfica, *Geografía física i política de las provincias de la Nueva Granada . . . ,* most recently printed in 4 volumes (Bogotá, 1957-1959).

In dealing with problems of nomenclature, changes of sites, and specific location, consult the United States Office of Geography, *Colombia: Official Names Approved by the U.S. Board on Geographical Names* (Washington, D.C., 1965); and the Instituto Geográfico Agustín Codazzi, *Diccionario geográfico de Colombia* (2nd ed., 2 vols.; rev. and enl.; Bogotá, 1980). The works of Eugenio J. Gómez, *Diccionario geográfico de Colombia* (Bogotá, 1953); and Alfredo D. Bateman, "Vocabulario geográfico de Colombia," *Cuadernos de geografía de Colombia,* 1-24 (Bogotá, 1955-1969), may also be useful. Earlier works include Tomás C. de Mosquera, *Diccionario geográfico de los Estados Unidos de Colombia* (Bogotá, 1868); and Joaquín Esguerra Ortiz, *Diccionario geográfico do los Estados Unidos de Colombia* (Bogotá, 1879). Eduardo Riascos Grueso's *Geografía guerrera de Colombia* (Cali, 1949) deals specifically with the location of 19th-century civil war battle sites.

Beyond the descriptive survey, there are studies that focus on the history and/or development of Colombia's specific natural resources. The International Bank for Reconstruction and Development, *The Basis of a Development Program for Colombia: Report of a Mission Headed by Lauchlin Currie* . . . (Washington, D.C., 1950); and Enrique Pérez Arbeláez, *Recursos naturales de Colombia: su génesis, su medida, su aprovechamiento, conservación y renovación* . . . (4 vols.; Bogotá, 1953-1957), are indispensable. See also Departamento Nacional de Planeación, *Plan de integración nacional* (Bogotá, 1980); and Rodolfo Méndez Q., *Introducción a la economía de los recursos nacionales de Colombia* (Bogotá, 1980). Much more specialized and technical, but still useful for background materials, are such works as Enrique Pérez Arbeláez, *Plantas útiles de Colombia* (Bogotá and Madrid, 1956); Aparicio Rang[h]el Galindo, *Forests of Colombia* (Bogotá, 1952); Rafael Romero Castañeda, *Frutas silvestres de Colombia* (2 vols.; Bogotá, 1961-1969); Khalil Choucair, *Fruticultura colombiana* (2 vols.; Medellín, 1962), and *Huertas y hortalizas* (Medellín, 1965); and S. M. Bukasov, *Las plantas cultivadas de México, Guatemala y Colombia* (English, Russian, Spanish versions; Turrialba, C.R., 1981). Rodolphe M. de Schauensee, *The Birds of Colombia and Adjacent Areas of South and Central America* (Narberth, Pa., 1964); Antonio Olivares, *Aves de Cundinamarca* (Bogotá, 1969); and Raymond A. Paynter, Jr., and Melvin A. Taylor, Jr., *Ornithological Gazetteer* (Cambridge, Mass., 1981), describe the nation's birds.

Andrés Uribe Campuzano, *Brown Gold: The Amazing Story of Coffee* (New York, 1954); and the Federación Nacional de Cafeteros de Colombia, *Manual del cafetero colombiano* (Medellín, 1969), cover the coffee industry generally, while the Federación's *Coffee in Colombia, 1979-1980* (Bogotá, 1980-1983) gives a more recent statement of affairs. Rafael Domínguez A., *Historia de las esmeraldas de Colombia* (Bogotá, 1965), provides a technically oriented summary of Colombia's most unique resource; and Peter W. Rainier, *Green Fire* (New York, 1942), is a personal memoir of a man who mananged the Chivor emerald mines in the 1920s. René de la Pedraja Tomán, *Historia de la energía en Colombia, 1537-1930* (Bogotá, 1985), is an introduction to energy production and consumption in Colombia; and although there is no thorough history, Jorge Villegas, *Petroleo, oligarquía e imperio* (Bogotá, 1968); Gilberto García G., *Petróleo colombiano* (Bogotá, 1961), and Marco J. Angarita Niño, *Economía e industria del petróleo en Colombia* (Bogotá, 1953), give summaries of development and potential for the oil industry. The works of Grant M. Scobie and Rafael Posada T., *The Impact of High-Yielding Rice Varieties in*

Latin America, with Special Emphasis on Colombia (Cali, 1977); Howard Stonaker, Ned S. Raun, and Juvenal Gómez, *Beef Cow-Calf Production Experiments on the Savannas of Eastern Colombia . . .* (Morrilton, Ark., 1984); Barbara Meyers, *A Commercial Use for Taro* (Washington, D.C., 1982); and Luis R. Saint, *Demand for Carbohydrate Foods in Colombia and Venezuela* (Washington, D.C., 1983), form a potpourri of resource studies.

Alberto Charry Lara, *Desarrollo histórico de la estadística nacional en Colombia* (Bogotá, 1954), is useful for understanding what statistical evidence is available for Colombia. The two publications of the Departamento Administrativo Nacional de Estadística (DANE)—the *Anuario general de estadística* (Bogotá, No. 1-, 1905-) and *Boletín mensual de estadística* (Bogotá, No. 1-, March 1951-)—or volumes such as *Colombia estadística 86* (Bogotá, 1986) are the most readily accessible summaries of current statistics. Miguel Urrutia Montoya and Mario Arrubla, eds., *Compendio de estadísticas históricas de Colombia* (Bogotá, 1970), contains historical statistics on selected subjects.

Descriptive and analytical viewpoints on the daily life of Colombians are available in a number of sociological-anthropological studies and a wide variety of travel accounts. T. Lynn Smith, *Colombia: Social Structure and the Process of Development* (Gainesville, Fla., 1967); Smith, *Tabio: A Study of Rural Organization* (Washington, D.C., 1945); Orlando Fals-Borda, *Peasant Society in the Colombian Andes: A Sociological Study of Saucío* (Gainesville, Fla., 1955); Fals-Borda, "A Sociological Study of the Relationships Between Man and the Land in the Department of Boyacá, Colombia," University of Florida, 1955; Ernesto Vautier and Orlando Fals-Borda, eds., *La vereda de Chambimbal: Estudio y acción en vivienda rural* (Bogotá, 1958); Gerardo Reichel-Dolmatoff and Alicia Reichel-Dolmatoff, *The People of Aritama: The Cultural Personality of a Colombian Mestizo Village* (Chicago, 1961); Andrew H. Whiteford, *Two Cities of Latin America* [Popayán, Colombia; Querétaro, Mexico]: *A Comparative Description of Social Classes* (New York, 1964); Whiteford's *Popayán Revisited: An Andean City at Mid-Century—A Traditional Urban Society* (East Lansing, Mich., 1977); and Miles Richardson, *San Pedro, Colombia: Small Town in a Developing Society* (New York, 1970), are all recommended. For ethnography and demography, see Rakesh Mohan and Nancy Hartline, *The Poor of Bogotá: Who They Are, What They Do, and Where They Live* (Washington, D.C., 1983); T. Lynn Smith, "The Racial Composition of the Population of Colombia," *Journal of Inter-American Studies,* 8:2 (Apr. 1966), 213-235; Norman D. Humphrey, "Race, Caste, and Class in Colombia," *Phylon,* 13:2

Bibliography / 545

(June 1952), 161-162; Robert C. West, *The Pacific Lowlands of Colombia: A Negroid Area of the American Tropics* (Baton Rouge, La., 1957); Aquiles Escalante, *El negro en Colombia* (Bogotá, 1964); José M. Iragorri V., *Evolución demográfica colombiana* (Bogotá, 1959); Peter J. Wilson and John Buettner-Janusch, "Demography and Evolution on Providencia Island, Colombia," *American Anthropologist,* 62:5, pt. 1 (Oct. 1961), 940-954; and Thomas G. Sanders, "The Blacks of Colombia's Chocó," *American University Fieldstaff Reports, West Coast of South America Series,* 17:2 (Jan. 1970), 1-7. See also the anthropological history of Virginia Gutiérrez de Pineda, *La familia en Colombia: Estudio antropológico* (Bogotá, 1963); Linda Greenow et al., *Family, Household, and Home: A Micro-Geographic Analysis of Cartagena* (New York, 1976); and Gloria Carvallo and Fernando Ramírez, *The Improvement of the Situation of Women and Its Impact on the Welfare of Children* (New York, 1980). Víctor Patiño, *La alimentación en Colombia y los paises vecinos* (Bogotá, 1984); and José Joaquín Montes Giraldo, *Medicina popular en Colombia: vegetales y otras sustancias usadas como remedios* (Bogotá, 1981), offer comments on local eating and medical customs. Jaime Sierra García, *Diccionario folclórico antioqueño* (Medellín, 1983), describes social life and customs in Antioquia. Alberto Montezuma Hurtado, *Nariño, tierra y espíritu* (Bogotá, 1982), is a collection of short pieces concerning Colombia's southern border department. For brief descriptive studies of local areas, DANE has published a number of works, such as *Monografía del municipio de Bucaramanga* (Bogotá, 1982); . . . *Buga* (Bogotá, 1982); . . . *Cúcuta* (Bogotá, 1983); . . . *Pamplona* (Bogotá, 1983); and . . . *Neiva* (Bogotá, 1984).

Representative selections of the travel and descriptive literature from the mid-19th century to the present might well include Eugene J. Stann, "The New Granadan Diary of William M. Blackford: 1843-1845," Vanderbilt University, 1968; Manuel Ancízar, *Peregrinación de Alpha por las provincias del norte de la Nueva Granada, en 1850-1851* (Bogotá, 1956); Isaac F. Holton, *New Granada: Twenty Months in the Andes* (New York, 1857; condensation reprinted Carbondale, Ill., 1967); James P. Jones and William W. Rogers, "Across the Isthmus in 1850: The Journey of Daniel A. Horn," *HAHR,* 41:4 (Nov. 1961), 533-554; Elisée Reclus, *Colombia* (trans. F. J. Vergara y Velasco; Bogotá, 1958); Ernst Röthlisberger, *El Dorado; Estampas de viaje y cultura de la Colombia suramericana* [1882-1886] . . . (trans. Antonio de Zubiaurre; Bogotá, 1963); Hiram Bingham, *The Journal of an Expedition Across Venezuela and Colombia, 1906-1907: An Exploration of the Route of Bolívar's Celebrated March of 1819 and of the Battlefields of Boyacá and Carabobo* (New Haven, Conn., 1909); William McFee, *Sunlight in New Granada* (Garden City, N.Y., 1925); Kathleen Romoli, *Colombia: Gateway to South America* (Garden City, N.Y., 1941); William R. Philipson, *The Immaculate Forest: An Account of an Expedition to Unexplored Territories Between the Andes and the Amazon* (London, 1952); Alain Gheerbrant, *The Impossible Adventure: Journey to the Far Amazon* (London, 1953); José Antonio Osorio Lizarazo, *Colombia dónde los Andes se disuelven* (Santiago de Chile, 1955); and Hernán Díaz, *Cartagena* (Bogotá, 1984). References to 42 travel and descriptive accounts in English may be found in A. Curtis Wilgus, *Latin America in the Nineteenth Century . . .* (Metuchen, N.J., 1973); and in Bernard Naylor, *Accounts of Nineteenth Century South America: An Annotated Checklist of Works by British and United States Observers* (London, 1969).

II. SURVEYS AND REFERENCE WORKS

There are few works providing an adequate synthesis of Colombian history. Those that do exist tend to be fragmentary and episodic rather than well conceived and balanced, and English-language works are relatively scarce.

From the national perspective, there has traditionally been only one standard survey of Colombian history from the pre-conquest era to the 20th century: Jesús María Henao and Gerardo Arrubla, *Historia de Colombia, para la enseñanza secundaria . . . ,* first published in Bogotá, 1911-1912, and continually reissued. The somewhat condensed version in English, *History of Colombia,* translated by J. Fred Rippy, first appeared in the United States in 1938 and was reissued in 1972. A much shorter but up-to-date survey is Javier Ocampo López, *Historia básica de Colombia* (Bogotá, 1978). Harry Bernstein, *Venezuela and Colombia* (Englewood Cliffs, N.J., 1964), and the Colombian chapters in most college textbooks lack depth by comparison. The three-volume *Manual de historia de Colombia,* edited by Jaime Jaramillo Uribe (3rd ed.; Bogotá, 1984), is a commendable collection of chapters by individual authors who provide a broad interpretive survey of a number of aspects of Colombian history. José Manuel Groot, *Historia eclesiástica y civil de Nueva Granada* (5 vols.; Bogotá, 1953), stops in the mid–19th century, but is an interesting, clerically oriented survey of earlier periods. José María Arboleda Llorente's one-volume *Historia de Colombia* (Popayán, 1952) is an extended outline with a similar Church orientation through 1950; and José María Quijano Otero, *Compendio de la historia patria* (Bogotá, 1872), is an equally brief outline of events prior to 1863. The multi-volume *Historia extensa de Colombia* (Bogotá, 1964-) attempts a modern, in-depth survey, but it remains incomplete. Eduardo Caballero Calderón, *Historia privada de los colombianos* (Bogotá, 1960); Orlando Fals-Borda, *Subversion and Social Change in Colombia* (trans. Jacqueline K. Skiles; New York, 1969); and Indalecio Liévano Aguirre, *Los grandes conflictos sociales y económicos de nuestra historia* (Bogotá, 1966), should be consulted for interpretive social history. Enrique Santos Molano and Jaime Zárate Valero, *Enciclopedia ilustrada de las grandes noticias colombianas, 1483-1983* (2nd ed.; Bogotá, 1984); Lucas Morán Arce, ed., *Enciclopedia de Colombia* (7 vols.; Bogotá, 1977); Edgar Bustamante, ed., *El gran libro de Colombia* (Bogotá, 1984); and Horacio Gómez Aristizábal, *Diccionario de la historia de Colombia* (Bogotá, 1983), are attempts to compile and synthesize materials over the broad sweep of Colombian history. Roberto Velandia, ed., *Enciclopedia de Cundinamarca* (5 vols.; Bogotá, 1979-1981), is a detailed compilation on the department that surrounds Bogotá; and Jaime Sierra García, *Cronología de Antioquia* (n.p., 1982), is an outline of events in Antioquia.

For detailed studies, the lack of good national surveys can be overcome somewhat by an appeal to a variety of regional or local histories. These are of uneven quality, periodization, and methodology, but are nonetheless potentially useful. Orlando Fals-Borda, *Historia doble de la Costa* (4 vols.; Bogotá, 1980-1986); Ernesto Restrepo Tirado, *Historia de la provincia de Santa Marta* (2 vols.; Bogotá, 1953); Eduardo Lemaitre, *Historia general de Cartagena* (4 vols.; Bogotá, 1983); Gabriel Porras Troconis, *Cartagena hispánica, 1533 a 1810* (Bogotá, 1954); Enrique Marco Dorta, *Cartagena de Indias; La Ciudad y sus monumentos* (Sevilla, 1951); José María Valdeblánquez, *Historia del departamento del Magdalena y del territoria de la Guajira, desde el año de 1895 hasta el de 1963* (Bogotá, 1964); Ernesto Hernández Benarides, *Urabá heróica* (2 vols.; Bogotá, 1956); Fernando Gómez Pérez and Gustavo Ramírez E., *Chocó, 500 años de espera* (Medellín, 1980); Enrique Ortega Ricaurte and Ana Rueda Briceño, eds., *Historia documental del Chocó* (Bogotá, 1954); Abel Naranjo Villegas, *Antioquia, del hidalguismo al puritanismo* (Bogotá, 1981); Luis Latorre Mendoza, *Historia e historias de Medellín, siglos XVII-XVIII-XIX* (Medellín, 1934); Jorge Restrepo Uribe and Luz Posada de Greiff, *Medellín, su orígen, progreso y desarrollo* (Medellín, 1981); Ernesto Tobón, *Crónicas de Rionegro* (Pereira, 1963); Gustavo Arboleda, *Historia de Cali, desde los orígenes de la ciudad hasta la expiración del período colonial* (Cali, 1928); José M. Arboleda Llorente, *Popayán a través del arte y de la historia* (Popayán, 1966); Alfredo Galeano Velasco, *Historia del departamento de Nariño, compendio 1492 a 1954* (Pasto, 1954); José Ignacio Arciniegas, *El Tolima: geografía histórico-socio-económico, 1979* (n.p., 1980); Alfonso Toro Patiño, *El Quindío: Perfil histórico y socio-económico* (Armenia, 1966); Erique Ortega Ricaurte and Carlota Bustos Losada, eds., *San Bonifacio de Ibagué del Valle de las Lanzas: documentos para su historia* (Bogotá, 1952); Rafael Gómez Picón, *Timaná, de Belalcázar a la Gaitana, parábola de violencia y libertad* (Bogotá, 1960); Roberto María Tisnés J., *Capítulos de historia zipaquireña, 1480-1830* (Bogotá, 1956); Ramón C. Correa, *Historia de Tunja* (3 vols.; Tunja, 1944-1948); Germán Colmenares, *La Provincia de Tunja en el Nuevo Reino de Granada: Ensayo de historia social, 1539-1800* (Bogotá, 1970); and Luis Enrique Valencia R., *Historia de Santa Rosa de Cabal* (Manizales, 1984), are a representative sampling. The title of Loren C. Turnage's *Island Heritage: A Baptist View of the History of San Andres and Providencia* (Cali, Colombia, 1975) is self-explanatory; see also Wenceslao Cabrera Ortiz, *San Andrés y Providencia: historia* (Bogotá, 1980).

John A. Peeler, *Latin American Democracies: Colombia, Costa Rica, Venezuela* (Chapel Hill, N.C., 1985), provides a comparative overview of representational government in Colombia and two of its close neighbors. For a description of how the national government is organized and an analysis of how it functions, see Jorge P. Osterling, *Democracy in Colombia: Clientelist Politics and Guerrilla Warfare* (New Brunswick, N.J., and Oxford, 1989). República de Colombia, *Codificación nacional de todas las leyes de Colombia desde el año de 1821, hecha conforme a la ley 13 de 1912, por la sala de negocios generales del Consejo de Estado* (Bogotá, Vol. 1-, 1924-), is the official summary of Colombian laws. Texts of the constitutions of Colombia are accessible in two standard compilations: Diego Uribe Vargas, *Las constituciones de Colombia: historia, crítica y textos* (2nd ed., rev. and enl., 3 vols.; Bogotá, 1985); and Manuel Antonio Pombo and José Joaquín Guerra, eds., *Constituciones de Colombia* (4 vols.; Bogotá, 1951). William M. Gibson, *The Constitutions of Colombia* (Durham, N.C., 1948), is an English version analogous to Pombo and Guerra. Luis Carlos Sáchica Aponte, *La constitución colombiana, cien años haciéndose* (Mexico, D.F., Mexico, 1982); Miguel Aguilera, *La legislación y el derecho en Colombia; Sinópsis histórica desde la conquista hasta el presente* (Bogotá, 1965); Eustorgio Sarria and Luis Carlos Giraldo W., *Constitución política de Colombia, 1886-1986: estudio, introducción, comentarios y jurisprudencia* (Bogotá, 1983); and Diego Renato Salazar, *Historia constitucional de Colombia* (Bogotá, 1980), provide historical overviews. Jorge Ortega Torres, *Constitución política de Colombia* (Bogotá, 1983); Luis Carlos Sáchica Aponte,

Constitucionalismo colombiano (7th ed.; Bogotá, 1983); Alfonso López Michelsen, *Introducción al estudio de la constitución de Colombia* (Bogotá, 1983); Diego Renato Salazar, *Constitución política de Colombia: concordada-comentada con jurisprudencia* (Bogotá, 1982); and Jaime Castro, *Constitución política de Colombia: concordancias, referencias históricas, índices y compilación* (Quito, 1982), are recent aids to understanding the constitution. Older interpretations by Francisco de Paula Pérez, *Derecho constitucional colombiano* (2 vols.; Bogotá, 1954); and José María Samper, *Derecho público interno de Colombia* (2 vols; Bogotá, 1951), are also available. For commercial laws, Dominic A. Perenzin and Kirkwood, Kaplan, Russin and Vecchi Ltda., *The Republic of Colombia Business-Legal Handbook* (Bogotá, 1975); Arthur Anderson and Co., *Tax and Trade Guide* (3rd ed.; Chicago, 1977); Deloitte, Haskins and Sells, *Taxation in Colombia* (New York, 1980); Ignacio Mejía Maya, *Guía administrativa* (5th ed.; Medellín, 1982); and Departamento Nacional de Pleaneación, *Foreign Investment in Colombia: Basic Rules* (Bogotá, 1980), might also prove helpful. For comments on legal services in general, see Dennis O. Lynch, *Legal Roles in Colombia* (Uppsala, Sweden, 1981); and Rubens Medina, *Government Liability Under the Laws of Colombia* (Washington, D.C., 1975).

Information on contemporary political developments can be found in *Latin American Caribbean Contemporary Record* (New York and London, 1983-), edited by Jack W. Hopkins, in what appear to be annual volumes: Vol. I, 1981-1982; Vol. II, 1982-1983; Vol. III, 1983-1984, etc. Similar information can be found in the essay by Malcom Deas, "Colombia," in *South America, Central America, and the Caribbean, 1986* (London, 1985), 215-235. Ciarán O. Maolain, ed., *Latin American Political Movements* (London, 1985), 57-74, provides brief sketches on 32 political groups operating in Colombia in the 1980s. Finally, the Organization of American States, Inter-American Commission on Human Rights, *Report on the Situation of Human Rights in the Republic of Colombia* (Washington, D.C., 1981); and Americas Watch Committee, *The Central Americanization of Colombia?* (New York, 1986), and *Colombia: Amnesty International Briefing* (New York, 1988), describe the state of personal liberty in the nation as a whole. Finally, Adolfo Triana Antorveza, *La organización del estado colombiano* (Bogotá, 1988), and the two legal dictionaries, *Diccionario jurídico*, by Alberto Duarte French (Bogotá, 1980), and *Diccionario jurídico penal*, by Gil Miller y Jaramillo (Bogotá, 1981), might also prove helpful.

The history of printing in Colombia has been described in several works. José Toribio Medina, *La imprenta en Bogotá y la Inquisición en Cartagena de Indias* (Bogotá, 1952), is a combination essay and bibliography of works for the years 1739-1821, although Eduardo Posada's *Bibliografía Bogotana* (2 vols.; Bogotá, 1917-1925) is the classic survey of this period. The more recent and wide-ranging study, however, is Tarcisio Higuera B., *La imprenta en Colombia, 1737-1970* (Bogotá, 1970). The two volumes by Gustavo Otero Muñoz, *Historia del periodismo en Colombia desde la introducción de la imprenta hasta el fin de la reconquista española, 1737-1819* (Bogotá, 1925), and *Historia del periodismo en Colombia* [1791-1890] (Bogotá, 1936), comment upon the editorial position and historical context of representative periodicals. The works by Antonio Cacua Prada, *Historia del periodismo colombiano* (Bogotá, 1983), and *Legislación de periodismo actual* (2nd ed.; Bogotá, 1982-1984?); as well as Gabriel Fonnegra, *La prensa en Colombia* . . . (Bogotá, 1984), supplement the work of Otero Muñoz with 20th-century materials.

Colombian writers have always been prolific in the field of belles lettres. Antonio Gómez Restrepo, *Historia de la literatura colombiana* (4 vols.; Bogotá, 1956), is probably the most extensive survey available, even though it omits most of the 20th century. Fernando Ayala Poveda, *Manual de literatura colombiana* (Bogotá, 1984), is a much shorter but more up-to-date survey, and the multi-author *Manual de literatura colombiana* (2 vols.; Bogotá, 1988) is very useful for the selected subjects covered, although it is not an integrated survey. In English one of the most usable overviews is that of Raymond L. Williams, "Colombia," in the *Handbook of Latin American Literature* (New York and London, 1987), 153-190. José María Vergara y Vergara, *Historia de la literatura en Nueva Granda, desde la conquista hasta la independencia, 1538-1820, con notas de Antonio Gómez Restrepo y Gustavo Otero Muñoz* (3 vols.; Bogotá, 1958), is an earlier work focusing on the colonial period; and Isidoro Laverde Amaya, *Ojeada histórico-crítica sobre los orígenes de la literatura colombiana* (Bogotá, 1963), contains useful comments on the 19th century. José A. Núñez Segura, *Literatura colombiana: Sinópsis y comentarios de autores representativos* (Medellín, 1961), is a good textbook approach, and Fernando Arbeláez, *Nuevos narradores colombianos: antología* (Caracas, 1968), is a panoramic view of contemporary styles and themes. Héctor M. Ardila A., *Hombres y letras de Colombia: 435 años de suceder literaria* (Bogotá, 1984); and Luis María Sánchez López, *Diccionario de escritores colombianos* (3rd ed., rev. and enl.; Bogotá, 1985), and the same author's *Diccionario de escritores antioqueños* (n.p., 1982), contain biographical data on numerous Colombian literary figures.

For more specialized aspects, the student may wish to consult the excellent monograph of Antonio Curcio Altamar, *Evolución de la novela en Colombia* (Bogotá, 1957); Donald McGrady, *La novela histórica en Colombia, 1844-1959* (Bogotá, 1962); Lucía Luque Valderrama, *La novela femenina en Colombia* (Bogotá, 1954); and Frank M. Duffey, *The Early Cuadro de Costumbres in Colombia* (Chapel Hill, N.C., 1956). Andrés Pardo Tovar, *La poesía popular colombiana y sus orígenes españoles* (Bogotá, 1966); and Javier Arango Ferrer, *Raíz y desarrollo de la literatura colombiana; Poesía desde las culturas precolombianas hasta la "Gruta Simbólica"* (Bogotá, 1965), deal with the history of poetry. The most recent survey of the theater is Fernando González Cajiao, *Historia del teatro en Colombia 1986* (Bogotá, 1986). See also Vicente Ortega Ricaurte, *Historia crítica del teatro en Bogotá* (Bogotá, 1927); Leon F. Lyday, "The Colombian Theatre Before 1800," *Latin American Theatre Review,* 4:1 (Fall 1970), 35-50; and Gonzalo Arcila, *Nuevo teatro en Colombia: actividad creadora, política cultural* (Bogotá, 1983). Gustavo Otero Muñoz, "Seudónimos de escritores colombianos," *Thesaurus* (Bogotá), 13 (1958), 112-131, is a helpful reference work. For understanding idiomatic language in Colombian authors, consult Mario Alario di Filippo, *Lexicón de colombianismos* (2 vols.; Bogotá, 1983). The interpretive, monographic literature discussing individual authors and specific movements is much too copious to mention, and the reader should consult specialized bibliographies for the subjects of interest. Nevertheless, it is worth pointing out the biographies available in the Twayne World Author series: Donald McGrady, *Jorge Isaacs, 1837-1895* (New York, 1972); Betty T. Osiek, *José Asunción Silva, 1865-1896* (Boston, 1978); Kurt L. Levy, *Tomás Carrasquilla, 1858-1940* (Boston, 1980); and Raymond L. Williams, *Gabriel García Márquez, 1927-* (Boston, 1985). On García Márquez, Colombia's Nobel laureate, see also Stephen Minta, *García Márquez, Writer of Colombia* (New York, 1987), and the bibliographies by Margaret Fau, cited in Section VII of this essay.

There is no comprehensive survey of Colombian philosophy, social and political thought, or theology. Jaime Jaramillo Uribe, *El pensamiento colombiano en el siglo XIX* (Bogotá, 1964), is the most professional overview for any extended period. Three anthologies, however, provide a sampling with brief commentaries. Juan David García Bacca, *Antología del pensamiento filosófico en Colombia, de 1647 a 1761 . . .* (Bogotá, 1955), reproduces texts from the colonial period. Rafael Gómez Hoyos, *La revolución granadina de 1810; Ideario de una generación y de una época, 1781-1821* (2 vols.; Bogotá, 1962), is a collection of primary sources and interpretive essays dealing with the independence period; while Jaime Jaramillo Uribe, *Antología del pensamiento político colombiano* (2 vols.; Bogotá, 1970), encompasses the 19th and 20th centuries.

There is also no very detailed history of Colombian art, but Francisco Gil Tovar, *El arte colombiano* (Bogotá, 1985), is a short introductory survey of goldwork, ceramics, sculpture, painting, and other arts from pre-Columbian times to the present. General studies, such as Leopoldo Castedo, *A History of Latin American Art and Architecture from Pre-Columbian Times to the Present* (trans. and ed. Phyllis Freeman; New York, 1969), and Pál Kelemen, *Baroque and Rococo in Latin America* (New York, 1951), help to provide a general frame of reference in which to interpret Colombian art work; and Diego Angulo Iñíguez et al., *Historia del arte hispanoamericano* (Vol. 3; Barcelona, 1956), has chapters devoted especially to Colombian developments. Luis Alberto Acuña, *Diccionario biográfico de artistas que trabajaron en el Nuevo Reino de Granada* (Bogotá, 1964); Carmen Ortega Ricaurte, *Diccionario de artistas en Colombia . . .* (Bogotá, 1965); and Eugenio Barney Cabrera, *Geografía del arte en Colombia, 1960* (Bogotá, 1963), are useful reference tools. Francisco Gil Tovar and Carlos Arbeláez Camacho, *El arte colonial en Colombia; Arquitectura, escultura, pintura, mobiliario, orfebrería* (Bogotá, 1968), is a recommended survey for the colonial period. The studies of Gabriel Giraldo Jaramillo, *La miniatura en Colombia* (Mexico, D.F., Mexico, 1948), and *El grabado en Colombia* (Bogotá, 1959), are essential for their respective fields of art. Luis Alberto Acuña, *Las artes en Colombia,* Volume 3, *La escultura* (Bogotá, 1967), and Carlos Arbeláez Camacho and Santiago Sebastián López, *Las artes en Colombia,* Volume 4, *La arquitectura colonial* (Bogotá, 1967), are the first installments of a promising attempt to synthesize the history of the arts in Colombia. See also the commentary by Gabriel Giraldo Jaramillo, *Notas y documentos sobre el arte en Colombia* (Bogotá, 1954); and Germán Rubiano Caballero, *Escultura colombiana del siglo XX* (Bogotá, 1983). Pierre Restany, *Botero* (New York, 1983); Cynthia Jaffee McCabe, *Fernando Botero* (Washington, D.C., 1959); and Klaus Gallwitz, *Botero* (New York, 1976), offer comments on one of Colombia's most widely known contemporary painter-sculptors. *Alejandro Obregón: A Loan Exhibition of Paintings from 1952 to the Present, April 30 to June 14, 1970, Art Gallery, Center for Inter-American Relations* (New York, 1970); and *Alejandro Obregón, Recent Paintings/ Obras Recientes* (Bogotá, 1982), reflect the work of Colombia's most influential 20th-century painter. Pedro Nel Gómez, *Pedro Nel Gómez* (Bogotá, 1981), is a lavish picture book depicting the painter's own work; and Manuel Hernández Benavides, *Cuatro artistas no-figurativas de Colombia* (Bogotá, 1982), is a discussion of the work of four abstract artists.

The history of music in Colombia is more accessible. In Spanish, there are at least two standard surveys: José Ignacio Perdomo

Escobar, *Historia de la música en Colombia* (Bogotá, 1963); and
Andrés Pardo Tovar, *Las artes en Colombia,* Volume 6, *La cultura
musical en Colombia* (Bogotá, 1966). A brief introduction in English
can be found in Joseph L. Arbena, Henry Schmidt, and David
Vassberg, *Regionalism and the Musical Heritage of Latin America*
(Austin, Tex., 1980). In addition to these general works, see also
Jorge Añéz, *Canciones y recuerdos: Conceptos acerca del orígen del
bambuco y de nuestros instrumentos típicos y sobre la evolución de la
canción a través de sus más afortunados compositores e intérpretes*
(Bogotá, 1951). The Pan American Union, Music Section, *Compositores de América, datos biográficos y catálogos de sus obras* (Washington,
D.C., Vol. 1-, 1955-); and Heriberto Zapata Cuenca, *Compositores
colombianos* (Medellín, 1962), serve as biographical reference
works. Javier Ocampo López, *Música y folklore en Colombia* (Bogotá,
1980), is a brief survey of popular music; and Harry C. Davidson,
Diccionario folklórico de Colombia . . . (Bogotá, 1970), is a three-
volume source for musical instruments and dances. With a more
contemporary focus, in English, see Delia Zapata Olivella, "An
Introduction to the Folk Dances of Colombia," *Ethnomusicology,*
11:1 (Jan. 1967), 91-96; George List, "The Folk Music of the
Atlantic Littoral of Colombia: An Introduction," *Boletín Interamericana de Música,* 68 (Nov. 1968), 1-6; and List, *Music and Poetry in a
Colombian Village: A Tri-Cultural Heritage* (Bloomington, Ind.,
1983). Joaquín Piñeros Corpas, *Introducción al cancionero noble de
Colombia,* is a three-record anthology with a brief bilingual commentary on the history of Colombian music.

All of Colombia's artists and authors were influenced by the
nation's educational institutions. Luis Antonio Bohórques Casallas,
La evolución educativa en Colombia (Bogotá, 1956); and Rodolfo
Low-Maus, *Compendium of the Colombian Educational System* (Bogotá, 1971), offer the most balanced surveys of educational development. Renán José Silva Olarte, ed., *Historia de la práctica pedagógica
durante la colonia* (Bogotá, 1980); Alejandro Bernal Escobar et al.,
La educación en Colombia (Louvain, 1965); and Orlando Fals-Borda,
La educación en Colombia: Bases para su interpretación sociológica
(Bogotá, 1962), comment on education from historical, legal, and
philosophical viewpoints, probably emphasizing secondary and
higher education. Antonio Pérez Aguirre, "La educación popular,"
Revista de América (Bogotá), 23:74 (Dec. 1951), 623-636, deals with
primary education. From a historical viewpoint, Guillermo Hernández de Alba, "Fuentes para la historia de la cultura en Colombia.
Proyecto del fiscal Moreno y Escandón para la erección de la
universidad pública en el Virreinato de la Nueva Granada, con sede
en la cuidad de Santa Fé de Bogotá, año de 1768," *Thesaurus*

(Bogotá), 16:3 (Sept.-Dec. 1961), 471-493, is an assessment of general educational development at the close of the colonial period. John L. Young, "University Reform in New Granada, 1820-1850," Columbia University, 1970; and Jane M. Loy, "Modernization and Educational Reform in Colombia, 1863-1886," University of Wisconsin, 1969, analyze movements in the 19th century. Sister Teresa de la Inmaculada, *Quién ha educado la mujer colombiana?* (Bogotá, 1960), is a study of the education of women in Colombia; and Miguel Aguilera, *La enseñanza de la historia en Colombia* (Mexico, D.F., Mexico, 1951), is a commentary on the teaching of history. For contemporary reference purposes, see Colombia–United States Workshop on Science and Technology, Fusagasugá, Colombia, 1968, *Institutions of Higher Education, Research, and Planning in Colombia* (Washington, D.C., 1968). The works of George Psacharopoulos and Antoni Zabalza, *The Destination and Early Career Performance of Secondary School Graduates in Colombia: Findings from the 1978 Cohort* (Washington, D.C., 1984); Wava G. Haney, *Educational and Occupational Attainment of Migrants and Nonmigrants from a Colombian Highland Community* (Madison, Wis., 1975); Stanley Wellington, *Colombia: A Study of the Educational System of Colombia and a Guide to the Academic Placement of Students from Colombia in Educational Institutions of the United States* (Washington, D.C., 1984); Bertil Duner, *Cultural Dependence in Latin America: The Case of Colombian Advanced Education* (rev. ed.; Uppsala, 1977); Ana Sofía Moreno de Sharef, *International Technical Assistance to Vocational Training of Middle Level Manpower in the Colombian Industrial Sector* (Düsseldorf, 1975); and André Benoit, *Changing the Educational System: A Colombian Case-Study* (1970-1975), offer evaluative looks at the modern educational structure. For the history of various disciplines, see Salvador Camacho Roldán, et al., *Cien años de la sociología en Colombia, 1882-1982* (Bogotá, 1982); Clara R. Mateus Cárdenas, *Evolución histórica de la geografía moderna en Colombia* (Tunja, 1982); Ramiro Osorio O., *Historia de la química en Colombia* (Bogotá, 1982); Jaime Arocha, et al., *Un siglo de investigación social: antropología en Colombia* (Bogotá, 1984); and Richard Krzys, *A History of Education for Librarianship in Colombia* (Metuchen, N.J., 1969). For a nontraditional educational program, see Farzam Arbab, "University for Rural Development: An Alternative Approach to Colombia," *Journal of Developing Areas,* 16:4 (July 1982), 511-522.

Several authors have treated the economic history of Colombia. Enrique Caballero, *Historia económica de Colombia* (Bogotá, 1981); and Alvaro Tirado Mejía, *Introducción a la historia económica de Colombia* (Bogotá, 1985), are among the most comprehensive interpretations, though not necessarily the most adequately documented. Among the best of Colombia's economic studies are those of Luis Ospina Vásquez, *Industria y protección en Colombia, 1810-1930* (Medellín, 1955), and *Perspectiva histórica de la economía colombiana* (Medellín, 1960). Luis Eduardo Nieto Arteta, *Economía y cultura en la historia de Colombia* (Bogotá, 1962), emphasizes the relationship between cultural patterns and economic development; Abel Cruz Santos, *Economía y hacienda pública* (2 vols.; Bogotá, 1965-1966), is an extensive survey from an institutional-governmental approach. Two works in English—the older one, J. Fred Rippy, *The Capitalists and Colombia* (New York, 1931), and the more recent one, William P. McGreevey, *An Economic History of Colombia, 1845-1930* (Cambridge, U.K., 1971)—tend to stress external factors in the growth of the Colombian economy. Miguel Urrutia Montoya, *The Development of the Colombian Labor Movement* (New Haven, Conn., 1969), is a more specialized survey, though still useful for a broad understanding of Colombian economic history. Edgar Caicedo, *Historia de las luchas sindicales en Colombia* (Bogotá, 1971), is a Marxist account of the development of organized labor in Colombia. See also Ricardo Sánchez, *Historia política de la clase obrera en Colombia* (Bogotá, 1982). René de la Pedraja Tomán, "Colombia," in *Latin American Labor Organizations,* Gerald M. Greenfield and Sheldon L. Maram, eds. (New York, 1987), contains brief encyclopedic entries on Colombia's major labor unions.

On the diplomatic front, the most useful one-volume survey is Raimundo Rivas, *Historia diplomática de Colombia, 1810-1934* (Bogotá, 1961), although it offers nothing on recent history. José Joaquín Caicedo Castilla, *Historia diplomática* (2 tomos; Vol. XVII, *Historia Extensa de Colombia*; Bogotá, 1974), is a more modern survey with extensive attention to recent issues, especially in tomo 2. Germán Cavelier, *La política internacional de Colombia* (4 vols.; Bogotá, 1959-1960), has been termed indispensable; and E. Taylor Parks, *Colombia and the United States, 1765-1934* (Durham, N.C., 1935), remains the standard overview of Colombian-U.S. relations up to the 1930s. Julio Londoño, *Integración del territorio colombiano* (Bogotá, 1967); and Francisco Andrade S., *Demarcación de las fronteras de Colombia* (Bogotá, 1965), deal specifically with the growth of Colombia's national territory and boundary problems. The *Historia de la Cancillería de San Carlos* (Bogotá, 1983-) is an official history of the Ministry of Foreign Relations, and Germán Ramírez Bulla, *Tratados vigentes en Colombia: lista comentada* (Bogotá, 1985), is a useful index and commentary on currently valid international treaties.

John Lloyd Mecham, *Church and State in Latin America: A History of Political-Ecclesiastical Relations* (Chapel Hill, N.C., 1966), and the older, more extended Colombian interpretation of Juan Pablo Restrepo, *La iglesia y el estado en Colombia* (London, 1885), are useful historical introductions to the problem of Church-State relations. Juan Botero Restrepo, *Breve historia de la iglesia colombiana* (Medellín, 1983), is an overall survey of ecclesiastical development in Colombia; while Carlos E. Mesa, *La Iglesia y Antioquia: derrotero histórico y panorama actual* (Medellín, 1983), focuses on one department. Gustavo Pérez and Isaac Wust, *La iglesia en Colombia, Estructuras eclesiásticas* (Fribourg, Switz., and Bogotá, 1961), is a modern sociological analysis of the Church structure in Colombia; and *La Iglesia en Colombia* (Bogotá, 1986) is a general ecclesiastical directory published by the Catholic Church. Eduardo Ospina, *The Protestant Christians in Colombia: A Historical Sketch with a Particular Study of the So-Called "Religious Persecution"* (Bogotá, 1954); and James E. Goff, *The Persecution of Protestant Christians in Colombia, 1948-1958, with an Investigation of Its Background and Causes* (Cuernavaca, Mex., 1968), offer contrasting views on the subject of Protestant-Catholic relations. Daniel H. Levine, *Religion and Politics in Latin America: The Catholic Church in Venezuela and Colombia* (Princeton, N.J., 1981); Cornelia B. Flora, *Pentecostalism in Colombia: Baptism by Fire and Spirit* (Rutherford, N.J., 1976); Lewis Morley, *Now It Can Be Told: The Unforgettable Story of Pentecostalism in Colombia* (Hazelwood, Mo., 1983); and Andrés Küng, *Bruce Olson: Missionary or Colonizer?* (Chappaqua, N.Y., 1977), all deal with contemporary religious movements. José Restrepo Posada, *Arquidiócesis de Bogotá, datos biográficos de sus prelados, 1564-1891, y cabildo eclesiástico* (4 vols.; Bogotá, 1961-1971), is an indispensable reference work.

Joaquín Ospina, *Diccionario biográfico y bibliográfico de Colombia* (3 vols.; Bogotá, 1927-1939), despite its many errors and omissions, is still the best general, all-purpose biographical dictionary. For executive officials, the works of Ignacio Arismendi Posada, *Gobernantes colombianos, 1819-1983: De Bolívar a Belisario* (Bogotá, 1983); and Enrique Carrizosa Argáez, *Linajes y bibliografías de nuestros gobernantes, 1830-1982* (Bogotá, 1983), may be consulted. Other standard biographical or genealogical works include Sergio Elías Oritz, *Franceses en la independencia de la Gran Colombia* (2nd ed.; Bogotá, 1971); M. Leonidas Scarpetta y Saturnino Vergara, *Diccionario biográfico de los campeones de la libertad de Nueva Granada, Venezuela, Ecuador i Perú; Que comprende sus servicios, hazañas y virtudes* (Bogotá, 1879); José María Samper, *Galería nacional de hombres ilustres e notables, o sea colección de bocetos bi-*

ográficos (Bogotá, 1879); José María Baraya, *Biografías militares; o Historia militar del país en medio siglo* (Bogotá, 1874); Gustavo Arboleda, *Diccionario biográfico y genealógico del antiguo departamento del Cauca* (Bogotá, 1962); José María Restrepo Sáenz, *Gobernadores y próceres de Neiva* (Bogotá, 1941), *Gobernadores de Antioquia* (2 vols.; Bogotá, 1944-1970), and "La provincia del Socorro y sus gobernantes," *Boletín de Historia y Antigüedades* (Bogotá), 41:476 (June 1954), 321-378; Gustavo Otero Muñoz, *Hombres y cuidades: Antología del paisaje, de las letras y de hombres de Colombia* (Bogotá, 1948); Juan Botero Restrepo, *Gentes de Sonsón* (Medellín, 1980); Juan Flórez de Ocáriz, *Libro primero y segundo de las genealogías del Nuevo Reino de Granada* (2 vols.; Madrid, 1674-1676 reprint, Bogotá, 1990); José María Restrepo Sáenz and Raimundo Rivas, *Genealogías de Santa Fé de Bogotá* (Bogotá, 1928); Gabriel Arango Mejía, *Genealogías de Antioquia y Caldas* (2 vols.; Medellín, 1942); and Francisco de Paula Plazas Sánchez, *Genealogías de la provincia de Neiva* (Neiva, 1967). For more contemporary figures, consult Ronald R. Hilton, ed., *Who's Who in Latin America: A Biographical Dictionary of Notable Living Men and Women of Latin America* (2 vols.; 1945 ed. reprinted Detroit, 1971); and *Quién es quién en Venezuela, Panamá, Ecuador, Colombia, con datos recopilados hasta el 30 de Junio de 1952* (Bogotá, 1952). Flor Romero de Nohra and Gloria Pachón Castro, *Mujeres en Colombia* (Bogotá, 1961), deals specifically with women in Colombia. For authors, see Sánchez López, *Diccionario de escritores colombianos,* previously cited.

In a miscellaneous category, the student of history may find useful the works of Alfredo D. Bateman, *El observatorio astrónomico de Bogotá: monografía histórica con ocasión del 150 aniversario de su fundación, 1803-Agosto 20-1953* (Bogotá, 1954), and A. M. Barriga Villalba, *Historia de la Casa de Moneda* (3 vols.; Bogotá, 1969), both of which deal with rather unique institutions in Colombian history. Eduardo Serrano, *Historia de la fotografía en Colombia* (Bogotá, 1983); José María Reventos R., *1880-1980, un siglo de publicidad gráfica en Colombia* (Bogotá, 1984); Humberto Salcedo Silva, *Crónicas del cine colombiano, 1870-1950* (Bogotá, 1981); Carlos Alvarez, *Una década de cortometraje colombiano, 1970-1980* (n.p., 1982-1984?); J. León Helguera, "Notes on a Century of Political Cartooning, 1830-1930," *Studies in Latin American Popular Culture,* 6 (1987), 259-280; and Germán Arciniegas, *El Zancudo. La caricatura política en Colombia (Sigo XIX)* (Bogotá, 1975), all deal with an aspect of the graphic arts. Reynaldo Pareja, *Historia de la radio en Colombia, 1929-1980* (Bogotá, 1984), deals with public broadcasting. Luis Duque Gómez, *Colombia: Monumentos históricos y arqueológicos* (2 vols.; Mexico, D.F., Mexico, 1955), is a guide to national monuments, archeological sites, and colonial art treasures; and the two works by Enrique Ortega Ricaurte, *Heráldica colombiana* (Bogotá, 1952), and *Heráldica nacional; Estudio documental* (Bogotá, 1954), explain the evolution of national symbols. Of a topical nature, Andrés Soriano Lleras, *La medicina en el Nuevo Reino de Granada durante la conquista y la colonia* (Bogotá, 1966); Rafael Martínez Briceño and Guillermo Hernández de Alba, *De Hipócrates a Pasteur; Historia de la medicina colombiana* (Bogotá, 1966); Pedro María Ibáñez, *Memorias para la historia de la medicina en Santa Fé* (Bogotá, 1968); Augusto Gast Gálvis, *Historia de la fiebre amarilla en Colombia* (Bogotá, 1982); and Jorge Bejarano, *Nuevos capítulos sobre el cocaísmo en Colombia; Una visión histórico-social del problema* (Bogotá, 1952), serve as introductions to Colombian medical history. Alfredo D. Bateman, *Páginas para la historia de la ingeniería colombiana: Galería de ingenieros colombianos* (Bogotá, 1972), offers background on the profession and institutions of engineering. And Julio Hoenigsberg, *Cien años de historia masónica de la Resp.: Log.: "El Siglo XIX, no. 24-1"* (Barranquilla, 1964), is a commentary on a Masonic Lodge in Colombia. Ildefonso Gutiérrez Azopardo, *Historia del negro en Colombia: sumisión o rebeldía?* (Bogotá, 1980); Itic Croitoru Rotbaum, *De sefarad al neosefardismo; Contribución a la historia de Colombia* (2 vols.; Bogotá, 1967-1971); J. X. Cohen, *Jewish Life in South America: A Study for the American Jewish Congress* (New York, 1941); and Simón Guberek, *Crónicas testimonales colombianos* (Bogotá, 1982), deal with the contributions of specific cultural traditions.

III. AMERINDIAN CULTURES

Seeking information on Colombia's Indian populations is frequently a frustrating task, especially for the English reader. Armand J. Labbe, *Colombia Before Columbus: The People, Culture, and Ceramic Art of Prehispanic Colombia* (New York, 1986); and Gerardo Reichel-Dolmatoff, *Colombia* (New York, 1965), are the only accessible introductory surveys, although various kinds of less cohesively organized data are readily available in the older work edited by Julian Steward, *Handbook of South American Indians* (7 vols.; Washington D.C., 1946-1959); and in the newer but more peripheral *Handbook of Middle American Indians*, by Robert Wauchope et al. (Austin, Tex., Vol. 1-, 1964-). Segundo Bernal Villa, *Guía bibliográfica de Colombia de interés para el antropólogo* (Bogotá, 1969), is a useful point of departure for both English and

Spanish works. For the Spanish reader, one of the most extensive recent scholarly descriptions is the three-part *Prehistoria* of the *Historia extensa de Colombia*. Parts 1 and 2 of this set are entitled *Etno-historia y arqueología* (Bogotá, 1965), and *Tribus indígenas y sitios arqueológicos* (Bogotá, 1967), both by Luis Duque Gómez, and part 3 by Sergio Elías Ortiz, is called *Lenguas y dialectos indígenas de Colombia* (Bogotá, 1965). Each part, in addition to being a useful modern survey, provides a good beginning bibliography for further reading. On a less extensive but perhaps more usable scale, the most up-to-date single-volume work is probably Lucía Rojas de Perdomo, *Manual de arqueología colombiana* (Bogotá, 1985). The works of Jesús Arango Cano, *Revaluación de las antiguas culturas aborígenes de Colombia* (Bogotá, 1981); and Teresa Arango Bueno, *Precolombia; Introducción al estudio de los aborígenes* (Bogotá, 1963), are also helpful introductions; and Estanislao Stasys Gostautas, *Arte colombiano: Arte aborígen; Compendio arqueológico y etnológico de Colombia* (Bogotá, 1960), and Blanca Ochoa de Molina, *Colombia prehispánica: arte e imaginería* (Bogotá, 1983), are also recommended.

The most widely known, and perhaps most complex, of all Colombia's pre-conquest Indian cultures was that of the Chibcha, or Muisca, in the Bogotá-Tunja area. José Pérez de Barradas, *Los muiscas antes de la conquista* (2 vols.; Madrid, 1950-1951), is the most detailed account of this group; although Miguel Triana, *La civilización chibcha* (Bogotá, 1970), and Louis V. Ghisletti, *Los muiskas: Una gran civilización precolombiana* (2 vols.; Bogotá, 1954), also furnish useful overviews. Interpretive comments on the Chibcha are found in Cottie A. Burland, "Chibcha Aesthetics," *American Antiquities,* 27:2 (Oct. 1951), 145-147; Emil W. Haury, "Some Thoughts on Chibcha Culture in the High Plains of Colombia," *ibid.,* 29:1 (July 1953), 76-78; Robert C. Eidt, "Aboriginal Chibcha Settlement in Colombia," *Annals of the Association of American Geographers,* 49:4 (Dec. 1959), 374-392; Sylvia M. Broadbent, *Los Chibchas: Organización socio-política* (Bogotá, 1964); Martin Glassner, "The Chibchas: A History and a Re-evaluation," *The Americas,* 26:3 (Jan. 1970), 302-327; and José Rozo Gauta, *Los muiscas: cultura material y organización socio-política* (Bogotá, 1984). At least four works should be consulted by anyone interested in Chibcha mythology: Jesús Arango Cano, *Mitos, leyendas y dioses chibchas* (Bogotá, 1985); Antonio Núñez Jiménez, "Facatativá, santuario de la rana, Andes Orientales de Colombia," *Islas* (Santa Clara, Cuba), 1:3 (May-Aug. 1959), 665-757; Eliécer Silva Celis, *Arqueología y prehistoria de Colombia; Bochica o Nemquetaba* (Tunja, 1968); and Lilia Montaña de Silva Celis, *Mitos, leyendas, tradiciones y folclor del Lago de Tota* (Tunja, 1970). Ignacio Ramírez Sánchez, *Arqueología e historia precolombina de Facatativá* (Bogotá, 1983), is a brief synthesis of materials on one of the sites important to the Zipa and the old Chibcha capital. Of course, the most unique of Colombia's Indian legends was that of *Eldorado*. For this and the inspirational effect it had on the Spanish conquistadors, see Victor W. von Hagen, *The Golden Man* (Glasgow, Scot., 1974).

The Taironas of the Caribbean Coast were the other well-developed Indian civilization flourishing at the time of the Spanish conquest, although until recently much less was written about them. Bernardo Valderrama Andrade, *Taironaca* (Bogotá, 1984), is a personal memoir of archeological fieldwork in Tairona sites; and Valderrama Andrade along with Jairo Valderrama Barco and Mauricio Valderrama Barco are the authors of *Ciudad Perdida, Sierra Nevada de Santa Marta: Ecological Guide* (Bogotá, n.d.), an informative tourist guide to the Tairona archeological park.

The most famous archeological site in Colombia is San Agustín in the department of Huila. Gerardo Reichel-Dolmatoff, *San Agustín: A Culture of Colombia* (New York, 1972), is the most up-to-date summary by a well-known authority, although Luis Duque Gómez, *Exploraciones arqueológicos en San Agustín* (Bogotá, 1966), is only slightly older and much more technically detailed. Carlos Cuervo Márquez, *Estudios arqueológicos y etnográficos* (2 vols.; Madrid, 1920), is a late-19th-century view of San Agustín and nearby Tierradentro. Alvaro Chaves and Mauricio Puerta, *Tierradentro* (Bogotá, 1985), is a recent synthesis of known materials on the latter site.

Studies of other pre-conquest Indian groups are less well developed, but there are some standard works. For the Quimbayas of the Cauca Valley, for instance, see Luis Duque Gómez, *Los Quimbayas: Reseña etno-histórica y arqueológica* (Bogotá, 1970); and Juan Friede, *Los Quimbayas bajo la dominación española, estudio documental, 1539-1810* (Bogotá, 1963). Enrique Otero D'Costa, *Los Pijaos* (Manizales, 1920); and Enrique Ortega Ricaurte and Carlota Bustos Losada, *Los inconquistables; La guerra de los Pijaos, 1602-1603* (Bogotá, 1949), are basic accounts of the fierce Indians of the Tolima region. Jaime Errázuriz, *Tumaco-Tolita: Una cultura desconocida; An Unknown Precolumbian Culture* (Bogotá, 1980), deals with a southern Colombian culture. For the Caribbean Coast, see Gerardo Reichel-Dolmatoff, *Datos histórico-culturales sobre tribus de la antigua gobernación de Santa Marta* (Santa Marta, 1951), and the same author's "Preliminary Study of Space and Time Perspective in Northern Colombia," *American Antiquities*, 19:4 (Apr. 1954), 352-366; and Gerardo Reichel-Dolmatoff and Alicia Reichel-Dolmatoff, "Investigaciones arqueológicas en el depto. del

Magdalena, Colombia, 1946-1950," *Boletín de Arqueología* (Bogotá), 3:1-6 (1951).

The most detailed coverage of pre-conquest goldwork among the Indians is found in the various volumes of José Pérez de Barradas, *Orfebrería prehispánica de Colombia: Estilo Calima* . . . (Madrid, 1954); . . . *Estilos Tolima y Muisca* . . . (2 vols.; Madrid, 1958); and . . . *Estilos Quimbaya y otros* . . . (2 vols.; Madrid, 1965-1966). However, the Museo del Oro, *El Dorado, the Gold of Ancient Colombia* . . ., by Julie Jones and Warwick Bray (New York, 1974); Bray, *Gold of El Dorado: From the Exhibition "Gold of El Dorado, Heritage of Colombia"* (New York, 1979); and Peter Furst, *Sweat of the Sun, Tears of the Moon: Gold and Emerald Treasures of Colombia* (Los Angeles, 1981), all provide more modern introductions for the English reader. Shorter commentaries can be found in Enzo Carli, *Preconquest Goldsmiths' Work of Colombia in the Museo del Oro, Bogotá* (London, 1957); and in the essays "Anthropomorphic Figurines from Colombia, Their Magic and Art," by Gerardo Reichel-Dolmatoff, and "Pre-Columbian Metalwork of Colombia and Its Neighbors," by William C. Root, in the volume edited by Samuel K. Lothrop, *Essays in Pre-Columbian Art and Archaeology* (Cambridge, Mass., 1961).

S. Henry Wassén, "Algunos datos del comercio pre-colombiano en Colombia," *Revista Colombiana de Antropología* (Bogotá), 4 (1955), 89-109; and Néstor Uscátegui Mendoza, "El tabaco entre las tribus indígenas de Colombia," *ibid.*, 5 (1956), 11-52, are worth consulting for an overview, as are many of the articles generally published in the *Boletín de Arqueología* (Bogotá, Vol. 1-, 1945-), the *Revista Colombiana de Antropología* (Bogotá, Vol. 1-, 1953-), and the *Revista Colombiana de Folclor*, 2nd series (Bogotá, Vol. 1-, 1952-). See also James J. Parsons and William A. Bowen, "Ancient Ridged Fields of the San Jorge River Floodplain, Colombia," *Geographical Review*, 46:3 (July 1966), 317-343. Robert C. Eidt, *Advances in Abandoned Settlement Analysis: Application to Prehistoric Anthrosols in Colombia, South America* (Milwaukee, 1984), is a study in archeological technique.

For a more modern view of the Indian's status in Colombia, see Gerardo Reichel-Dolmatoff, "Indígenas de Colombia," *América Indígena* (Lima), 19:4 (Oct. 1959), 245-253; Hugo Burgos Guevara and Gonzálo Pesántez Reinoso, "Plan nacional indigenista de Colombia: 1966-1969," *ibid.*, 27:4 (Oct. 1967), 751-781; and Alicia Dussan de Reichel, *Problemas y necesidades de la investigación etnológica en Colombia* (Bogotá, 1965). The last work, particularly, has a good bibliography. Julián Narváez Hernández, *Colombia indígena/Colombia's Native Peoples* (trans. Alvaro Wheeler; Bogotá,

1982); and Lyman S. Tyler, ed., *The Indian Cause in the Laws of Colombia* (Salt Lake City, 1982), are comments on the current position of Indians in Colombian society on a national scale. For the problems of Indians coping with the modernization and development processes, see Staffan Burgland, *The New Indianism: A Threat Against Imperialism and Underdevelopment* ... (Umea, Swed., 1979), and Burgland, *Resisting Poverty: Perspectives on Participation and Social Development* (Umea, Swed., 1982), both of which deal with the Cauca region; and Deborah P. Hernández, *Resource Development and Indigenous People: The El Cerrejón Coal Project in Guajira, Colombia* (Cambridge, Mass., 1984).

Among the more recent ethnological studies, the Tukano Indians have received considerable attention. See, for example, the works of Gerardo Reichel-Dolmatoff, *Beyond the Milky Way: Hallucinatory Imagery of the Tukano Indians* (Los Angeles, 1978); Linda L. Glenboski, *The Ethnobotany of the Tukano Indians, Amazonas, Colombia* (Bogotá, 1983); and Jean E. Jackson, *The Fish People: Linguistic Exogamy and Tukano Identity in Northwest Amazonia* (Cambridge, U.K., 1983). Other recent descriptions or studies might include Stephen Hugh-Jones, *The Palm and the Pleiades: Initiation and Cosmology in Northwest Amazon* (Cambridge, Mass., 1979); Juan Bautista Sánchez and Judy Branks, *The Dream of Life: A Study of Life Cycle Customs Among the Guambiano, Colombia, South America* (Dallas, 1978); Robert Reed, *Amazon Dream: Escape to the Unknown* (London, 1977); Gerardo Reichel-Dolmatoff, *The Shaman and the Jaguar: A Study of Narcotic Drugs Among the Indians of Colombia* (Philadelphia, 1975); and Kaj Arhem, *Makuna Social Organization: A Study in Descent, Alliance, and the Formation of Corporate Groups in the Northwest Amazon* (Uppsala, Swed., 1981).

For the experience of missionaries among different Indian groups, see Elof Anderson and Isabel Anderson, *Hacaritama* ... (Wheaton, Ill., 1977-1979?); Robert S. Royster, *Unquiet Pilgrimage: The Journal of Robert Stewart Royster* (Louisville, Ky., 1979); Jean Dye Johnson, *God at the Controls* (Sanford, Fla., 1986); and Andrés Kung, *Bruce Olson, Missionary or Colonizer?*, previously cited.

IV.   CONQUEST AND COLONIAL PERIODS, 1492-1810

There is a plethora of works dealing with the conquest and colonial period, although, strictly speaking, there are few modern scholarly syntheses. Both English and Spanish readers must turn to earlier authors, and chronicles and primary accounts are frequently more plentiful than serious studies.

Aside from works dealing with Columbus and Amerigo Vespucci, both of whom touched briefly on parts of what would become colonial New Granada, the English reader has a number of works to consult. Clements R. Markham, *The Conquest of New Granada* (New York, 1912), is an introduction for the general reader. R. B. Cunninghame Graham, *The Conquest of New Granada, Being the Life of Gonzalo Jiménez de Quesada* (Boston, 1922; reprinted Boston, 1978); and Germán Arciniegas, *The Knight of El Dorado: The Tale of Don Gonzalo Jiménez de Quesada and His Conquest of New Granada, Now Called Colombia* (New York, 1942), tell the story of the conquest by focusing on the major figure in early Colombian history, although the latter work must be used with caution. Juan Rodríguez Freile, *The Conquest of New Granada* (trans. William C. Atkinson; London, 1961), in spite of being the most recently published, is a 16th-century account more widely known in Spanish as *El carnero*.

For the early history of the Isthmus, there is the primary account of Pascual Andagoya, *Narrative of the Proceedings of Pedrarias Dávila in the Provinces of Tierra Firme or Castilla de Oro . . .* (ed. C. R. Markham; London, 1865); and Kathleen Romoli, *Balboa of Darién, Discoverer of the Pacific* (New York, 1953). Clements R. Markham, *Expeditions into the Valley of the Amazons, 1539-1540, 1639* (London, 1859); Pedro Simón, *The Expedition of Pedro de Ursúa and Lope de Aguirre in Search of El Dorado and Omagua in 1560-1* (trans. William Bollaert; London, 1861); and Harry C. Heaton, ed., *The Discovery of the Amazon According to the Account of Friar Gaspar de Carvajal . . .* (trans. B. T. Lee; New York, 1934), all recount explorations in the Colombian interior.

These can all be amplified with more voluminous and extensive Spanish readings. Joaquín Acosta's *Compendio histórico del descubrimiento y colonización de la Nueva Granada en el siglo décimo sexto* (Paris, 1848), available in at least three editions, is still an informative synthesis. José Antonio de Plaza, *Memoriales para la historia de la Nueva Granada desde su descubrimiento hasta el 20 de Julio de 1810* (Bogotá, 1850), has never been reprinted, probably because of its assertively anti-clerical tone. Juan Friede's recent *Descubrimiento y conquista del Nuevo Reino de Granada; Introducción* (Bogotá, 1965), is more appropriately characterized as an analysis of the institutional background rather than a description of the conquest. Groot's *Historia eclesiástica y civil . . .*, previously cited, devotes two of the five volumes to the conquest and colonial periods. In a similar fashion, the Academia Colombiana de Historia's six-volume

Curso superior de historia de Colombia, 1492-1830 (Bogotá, 1950-1951), includes more than three volumes on the period before 1810, but the reader must be prepared for a series of essays by a number of authors rather than a unified narrative.

For the more important chronicles, personal accounts, and early histories, see Pedro de Aguado, *Recopilación historial* (4 vols.; notes and intro. Juan Friede; Bogotá, 1956-1957); Juan de Castellanos, *Obras* (including "Elegías de varones ilustres de Indias"; "Historia de Cartagena"; "Historia de Popayán"; "Historia de la gobernación de Antioquia y de la del Chocó"; "Discurso del Capitán Francisco Draque . . . "; and "Historia del Nuevo Reino de Granada") (4 vols.; prologue by Miguel Antonio Caro; Bogotá, 1955); Gonzalo Jiménez de Quesada, *El antijovio* (ed. Rafael Torres Quintero; intro. Manuel Ballesteros Gaibrois; Bogotá, 1952); Lucas Fernández de Piedrahita, *Historia general de las conquistas del Nuevo Reino de Granada . . .* (Bogotá, 1881); Juan Flórez de Ocáriz, *Libro primero y segundo de las genealogías del Nuevo Reino de Granada . . .* (2 vols; Madrid, 1674-1676; Reprinted, Bogotá, 1990); Antonio Herrera y Tordesillas, *Historia general de las Indias occidentales . . .* (also called *Las Décadas*) (4 vols.; Madrid, 1601-1615); Pedro Simón, *Noticias historiales de las conquistas de tierra firme en las indias occidentales* (5 vols.; Bogotá, 1882-1892); Alonso de Zamora, *Historia de la provincia de San Antonino del Nuevo Reino de Granada . . .* (4 vols.; Bogotá, 1945); Pedro de Mercado, 1620-1701, *Historia de la provincia del Nuevo Reino y Quito de la Compañía de Jesús* (4 vols.; Bogotá, 1957); José Cassani, *Historia de la provincia de la Compañía de Jesús del Neuvo Reino de Granada en la América . . .* (Madrid, 1741); Felipe Salvador Gilij, *Ensayo de historia americana; o sea historia natural, civil y sacra de los reinos y de las provincias de tierra firme en la América, Provincia de Santa Marta . . .* (Bogotá, 1951); Juan de Santa Gertrudis Serra, *Maravillas de la naturaleza* [1756-1767] (Bogotá, 1966); and Francisco Silvestre, 1734-1801, *Descripción del Reyno de Santa Fé de Bogotá . . .* (Bogotá, 1950). These and similar less prominent accounts are cited with annotations in Mario Germán Romero, Guillermo Hernández de Alba, and Sergio Elías Ortiz, *Papeletas bibliográficas para el estudio de la historia de Colombia* (Bogotá, 1961), to which the reader is referred for more detailed descriptions.

In addition to the biographies of Jiménez de Quesada noted above, those by Luis Galvis Madero, *El adelantado* (Madrid, 1957); Nicolás García Samudio, *Crónica del muy magnífico Capitán Don Gonzalo Suárez Rendón* (Bogotá, 1939); Emilio Robledo, *Vida del Mariscal Jorge Robledo . . .* (Bogotá, 1945); Juan Friede, *Vida y viajes de Nicolás Féderman, conquistador, poblador y co-fundador de Bogotá, 1506-1542* (Bogotá, 1960); and Jacinto Jijón y Caamaño, *Sebastián de Benalcázar* (3 vols.; Quito, 1936-1938), focus on the conquest through the lives of major figures.

For the post-conquest period of Colombian colonial history, the most recent surveys are those of Manuel Lucena Salmoral and Sergio Elías Ortiz. As portions of a larger work entitled *Nuevo Reino de Granada; Real audiencia y presidentes,* the books by Lucena Salmoral, *Presidentes de Capa y Espada, 1605-1628* (Bogotá, 1965), and ... *1628-1654* (Bogotá, 1967), and Ortiz, *Presidentes de Capa y Espada, 1654-1710* (Bogotá, 1966), present a chronological narrative of events centering around the chief administrators of the colony. Ortiz's two-volume *Nuevo Reino de Granada, El virreynato, 1719-1810* (Bogotá, 1970), carries the story to the eve of the wars for independence. Besides these works, which have a centralized or administrative view of colonial history, see those of Hernández B., *Urabá heróica;* Restrepo Tirado, *Historia ... de Santa Marta;* Porras Troconis, *Cartagena hispánica;* and Arboleda, *Historia de Cali,* all previously cited; as well as Jaime Arroyo, *Historia de la gobernación de Popayán seguida de la cronología de los gobernadores durante la dominación española* (2 vols.; Bogotá, 1954); Héctor Llanos Vargas and Roberto Pineda Camacho, *Etnohistoria del Gran Caquetá (Siglos XVI-XIX)* (Bogotá, 1982); and Germán Colmenares, *La Provincia de Tunja en el Nuevo Reino de Granada: ensayo de historia social, 1539-1800* (Tunja, 1984). All of these later works have a distinctly regional emphasis, in contrast to the works of Lucena Salmoral and Ortiz.

José María Ots Capdequí, *Instituciones de gobierno del Nuevo Reino de Granada durante el siglo XVIII* (Bogotá, 1950), and *Las instituciones del Nuevo Reino de Granada al tiempo de la independencia* (Madrid, 1958), give an overview of the sociopolitical structure of the empire in colonial Colombia. María Teresa Garrido Conde, *La primera creación del virreinato de Nueva Granada, 1717-1723* (Sevilla, 1965), describes the early period of the viceroyalty. Enrique Sánchez Pedrote, "La idea del poder en dos virreyes neogranadinos," *Estudios Americanos* (Sevilla), 11:56 (May 1956), 405-416; Daniel Samper Ortega, *Don José Solís, virrey del Nuevo Reino de Granada* (Bogotá, 1953); and José Manuel Pérez Ayala, *Antonio Caballero y Góngora, virrey y arzobispo de Santa Fe, 1723-1796* (Bogotá, 1951), comment on the ideas and actions of selected viceroys. The reports of these royal officials are available as *Relaciones de mando de los virreyes de la Nueva Granada* (ed. Gabriel Giraldo Jaramillo; Bogotá, 1954). For other administrative aspects, see Robert S. Smith, "The Consulado in Santa Fe de Bogotá," *HAHR,* 45:3 (Aug. 1965), 442-451; and Peter G. Marzahl, *Town in the Empire: Government, Politics and Society in Seventeenth-Century*

Popayán (Austin, Tex., 1978), and the same author's earlier work, "The Cabildo of Popayán in the Seventeenth Century: The Emergence of a Creole Elite," University of Wisconsin, 1970, and "Creoles and Government: The Cabildo of Popayán," *HAHR*, 54:4 (Nov. 1974), 636-656. George A. Brubaker, "Santa Fe de Bogotá: A Study of Municipal Development in Eighteenth-Century Spanish America," University of Texas, 1960; and James N. Goodsell, "Cartagena de Indias: Entrepôt for a New World, 1533-1597," Harvard University, 1966, analyze developments in the capital city and the principal seaport, respectively.

Magnus Mörner, "Las comunidades de indígenas y la legislación segregacionista en el Nuevo Reino de Granada," *Anuario Colombiano de Historia Social y de la Cultura* (Bogotá), 1:1 (1963), 63-88; Orlando Fals-Borda, "Indian Congregation in the New Kingdom of Granada: Land Tenure Aspects, 1595-1850," *The Americas*, 13:4 (Apr. 1957), 331-351; and José María Ots Capdequí, "El Indio en el Nuevo Reino de Granada durante la etapa histórica final de la dominación española," *Revista de Indias* (Madrid), 17:67 (Jan.-Mar. 1957), 11-57, provide commentary on the Spanish governmental policy toward the Indians. Germán Colmenares, *Encomienda y población en la provincia de Pamplona, 1549-1650* (Bogotá, 1969); Juan Friede, "Demographic Changes in the Mining Community of Muzo After the Plague of 1629," *HAHR*, 47:3 (Aug. 1967), 338-343; and Sherbourne F. Cook and Woodrow Borah, "The Historical Demography of Interior Tribes of Colombia in the Studies of Juan Friede and Germán Colmenares," in the same authors' *Essays in Population History: Mexico and the Caribbean, Vol. I* (Berkeley, Calif., 1971), are indicative of recent studies of the distribution and decline of the Indian population after the conquest. Friede's *Los Quimbayas* . . . and Ortega Ricaurte's *Los inconquistables* . . . *los Pijaos* deal with the fate of specific Indian communities, as does Ulíses Rojas, *El cacique de Turmequé y su época* (Tunja, 1965), which narrates the unfortunate career of a 16th-century mestizo *encomienda* holder. See also Hermes Tovar, *Documentos sobre tributación y dominación en la sociedad chibcha* (Bogotá, 1970); and Allan J. Kuethe, "The Pacification Campaign on the Riohacha Frontier, 1772-1779," *HAHR*, 50:3 (Aug. 1970), 467-481.

The social relationships of Indians, the European conquerors, and Negro slaves are analyzed by Jaime Jaramillo Uribe in his *Ensayos sobre historia social colombiana* (Bogotá, 1968); Julián B. Ruiz Rivera, *Encomienda y mita en Nueva Granada en el siglo XVII* (Sevilla, 1975); and Juan A. Villamarín, "Encomenderos and Indians in the Formation of Colonial Society in the Sabana de Bogotá,

Colombia, 1537 to 1740," Brandeis University, 1972. Alberto E. Ariza S., *Fray Bartolomé de Las Casas y el Nuevo Reino de Granada* . . . (Bogotá, 1974), describes activities of the Protector of the Indians in Colombia. Black slavery is specifically described in James F. King, "Negro Slavery in New Granada," University of California, Berkeley, 1939; Norman A. Meiklejohn, "The Observance of Negro Slave Legislation in Colonial Nueva Granada," Columbia University, 1968; and William F. Sharp, *Slavery on the Spanish Frontier: The Colombia Chocó, 1680-1810* (Norman, Okla., 1976), and the same author's related but shorter essay, "The Profitability of Slavery in the Colombian Chocó, 1680-1810," *HAHR,* 55:3 (Aug. 1975), 468-495. See also David L. Chandler, *Health and Slavery in Colonial Colombia* (New York, 1981); María del Carmen Borrego Plá, *Palenques de negros de Cartagena de Indias a fines del siglo XVII* (Sevilla, 1973); Jorge Palacios Preciado, *La trata de negros por Cartagena de Indias* (Tunja, 1973); Nicolás del Castillo Mathieu, *La llave de las Indias* (Bogotá, 1981); and Allan J. Kuethe, "The Status of the Free Pardo in the Disciplined Militia of New Granada," *Journal of Negro History,* 56:2 (Apr. 1971), 105-117.

For emphasis on the role of the Church in the colonial period, see Juan Manuel Pacheco, *Historia eclesiástica* . . . *la evangelización del Nuevo Reino, siglo XVI* (Bogotá, 1971), and . . . *la consolidación de la iglesia, siglo XVII* (Bogotá, 1975); Mario Germán Romero, *Fray Juan de los Barrios y la evangelización del Nuevo Reino de Granada* (Bogotá, 1960), a study of the career of the first archbishop of the New Kingdom; and Angel Valtierra, *Peter Claver, Saint of the Slaves* (trans. Janet H. Perry and L. J. Woodward; Westminster, Md., 1960), a biographical sketch of Colombia's most famous saint. All of these works emphasize the early colonial period. For more comprehensive works, there are Gregorio Arcila Robledo, "Origin of the Franciscan Order in Colombia," *The Americas,* 5:4 (Apr. 1949), 394-410, and *Las misiones franciscanas en Colombia: estudio documental* (Bogotá, 1950); Luis Carlos Mantilla R., *Los franciscanos en Colombia* (Bogotá, 1984); Juan Manuel Pacheco, *Los Jesuítas en Colombia, 1567-1696* (2 vols.; Bogotá, 1959-1962); Antonio de Alcocer, *Las misiones capuchinas en el Nuevo Reino de Granada, hoy Colombia* (Puente del Común-Bogotá, 1959); Benjamín Agudelo, *Los hijos de San Juan de Dios en Nueva Granada/Colombia* (Cali?, 1983); Eleuterio Nebreda, *Los claretianos en Colombia* (Medellín, 1981); and Roderick Wheeler, "Letter of Fray Francisco Alonso de Jesús, O.F.M., Florida Missionary to the King, Concerning the Conversion of the Indians of Popayán," *The Americas,* 6:2 (Oct. 1949), 235-242, which recount the missionary activity of the clergy in later colonial periods as well. Gary W. Graff, "Cofradías in the

New Kingdom of Granada: Lay Fraternities in a Spanish-American Frontier Society, 1600-1755," University of Wisconsin, 1974, covers an important social dimension of the Church in colonial society. Specifically on the Inquisition, see José Toribio Medina, *La imprenta en Bogotá y la Inquisición en Cartagena de Indias* (Bogotá, 1952); Manuel Tejado Fernández, *Aspectos de la vida social en Cartagena de Indias durante el seiscientos* (Sevilla, 1954); and Carlos Felice Cardot, "El impacto de la 'Inquisición' en Venezuela y en la Gran Colombia, 1811-1830," *Boletín de la Academia Nacional de Historia* (Caracas), 49:196 (Oct.-Dec. 1966), 478-492. For additional materials on the Church, see Restrepo Posada, *Arquidiócesis de Bogotá* . . . , and Pérez Ayala, *Antonio Caballero y Góngora* . . . , cited above.

A number of descriptive accounts exist for the later colonial period. Lionel Wafer, *A New Voyage and Description of the Isthmus of America* (1698) . . . (L. E. Elliott Joyce, ed.; Oxford, 1934); Jorge Juan y Santacilia and Antonio Ulloa, *A Voyage to South America, Describing at Large the Spanish Cities, Towns, Provinces, etc., on That Extensive Continent* . . . (London, 1772; abr. ed., New York, 1964); and Alexander von Humboldt, *Personal Narrative of Travels to the Equinoctial Regions of the New Continent During the Years 1799-1804* (trans. Helen M. Williams, 7 vols.; London, 1814-1829), are among the most famous English works. Vicente de Oviedo y Baños, *Cualidades y riquezas del Nuevo Reino de Granada, manuscrito del siglo XVIII* . . . (Bogotá, 1930); Joseph Palacios de la Vega, *Diario de viaje entre los indios y negros de la provincia de Cartagena en el Nuevo Reino de Granada, 1787-1788* (Gerardo Reichel-Dolmatoff, ed.; Bogotá, 1955); and Pedro Fermín de Vargas, 1741-1830, *Pensamientos políticos y memoria sobre la población del Nuevo Reino de Granada* (Bogotá, 1944), provide complementary materials for the Spanish reader. Gabriel Porras Troconis, *Historia de la cultura en el Nuevo Reino de Granada* (Sevilla, 1952), although a survey of the entire colonial period, concentrates heavily on the 18th century, describing the development of educational, scientific, and religious institutions in the colony. On the artistic life of the new kingdom, see Gil Tovar and Arbeláez Camacho, *El arte colonial* . . . ; Arbeláez Camacho and Sebastián López, . . . *La arquitectura colonial,* both cited previously; Robert Stevenson, "Colonial Music in Colombia," *The Americas,* 19:2 (Oct. 1962), 121-136; and the essays of Santiago Sebastián, such as *Guía artística de Popayán colonial* (Cali, 1964), "Valoración del tesoro artístico colombiano: tres nuevos museos en Boyacá," *Boletín Histórico* (Caracas), 24 (Sept. 1970), 285-302, and "La imaginería colonial en Popayán y Valle del Cauca," *ibid.,* 33 (Sept. 1973), 363-374.

The most thorough of all attempts to describe the resources of New Granada was the Royal Botanical Expedition of the late 18th and early 19th centuries. The literature on this subject is profuse, but according to Guillermo Hernández de Alba, "La Real Expedición Botánica del Nuevo Reino de Granada y su época," in Romero et al., *Papeletas bibliográficas para el estudio de la historia de Colombia,* cited above, the single most comprehensive work is by Miguel Colmeiro, *La botánica y los botánicos de la península hispano-lusitana; Estudios bibliográficos y biográficos* . . . (Madrid, 1858). José Antonio Amaya, *Bibliografía de la Real Expedición Botánica del Nuevo Reyno de Granada* (Bogotá, 1983), is a more recent bibliography. For the major figures Mutis and Caldas, the single most useful volumes are Apolinar Federico Gredilla y Gauna, *Biografía de José Celestino Mutis con la relación de su viaje y estudios practicados en el Nuevo Reino de Granada* . . . (Madrid, 1911); and Alfredo D. Bateman, *Francisco José de Caldas, el hombre y el sabio* . . . (Manizales, 1954). For Mutis, see also Polidoro Pinto Escobar and Santiago Díaz Piedrahita, *José Celestino Mutis, 1732-1982* (Bogotá, 1983). For many related themes, see the aforementioned essays by Hernández de Alba.

Emilio Robledo, *Bosquejo biográfico del señor oidor Juan Antonio Mon y Velarde, visitador de Antioquia, 1785-1788* (2 vols.; Bogotá, 1954); and Arthur P. Whitaker, "The Elhuyar Mining Mission and the Enlightenment," *HAHR,* 31:4 (Nov. 1951), 558-585, deal with another attempt to apply scientific principles to New Granada's resources. For background on the mining industry, see the classic study by Vicente Restrepo, *Estudio sobre las minas de oro y plata de Colombia* (Bogotá, 1952); and Robert C. West, *Colonial Placer Mining in Colombia* (Baton Rouge, La., 1952). For other aspects of education and culture, see Renán Silva, *Saber, cultura y sociedad en el Nuevo Reino de Granada, siglos XVII y XVIII* (Bogotá, 1984); and Juan Manuel Pacheco, *Ciencia, filosofía y educación en Colombia (siglo XVIII)* (Bogotá, 1984).

For the colonial economy as a whole, see Ann Twinan, *Miners, Merchants, and Farmers in Colonial Colombia* (Austin, Tex., 1982). Maurice P. Brungardt, "Tithe Production and Patterns of Economic Change in Central Colombia, 1764-1833," University of Texas, 1974, is a well-documented study of colonial agricultural production. Comments on economic conditions in the Antioquia region can be found in Ann Twinan, "Enterprise and Elites in Eighteenth-Century Medellín," *HAHR,* 59:3 (Aug. 1979), 444-475; and two works by Gabriel Poveda Ramos: *Historia económica de Antioquia* (Medellín, 1988), and *Minas y mineros de Antioquia* (Bogotá, 1984). Germán Colmenares, *Cali, terratenientes, mineros y comerciantes, siglo XVIII* (Bogotá, 1983); and Raymond L. Grahn, "Contraband,

Commerce, and Society in New Granada, 1713-1763," Duke University, 1985, focus on the economies of Cali and Cartagena, respectively.

Richard Pares, *War and Trade in the West Indies, 1739-1763* (Oxford, 1936), offers a frame of reference for the specific Colombian events described by James A. Robertson, "The English Attack on Cartagena in 1741, and Plans for an Attack on Panama," *HAHR*, 2:1 (Feb. 1919), 62-71; James F. King, "Admiral Vernon at Portobelo, 1739," *ibid.*, 23:2 (May 1943), 258-282; Juan Manuel Zapatero, "La heróica defensa de Cartagena de Indias ante el almirante inglés Vernon, en 1741, " *Revista de Historica Militar* (Madrid), 1:1 (1957), 115-152; Charles E. Nowell, "The Defense of Cartagena," *HAHR*, 42:4 (Nov. 1962), 477-501; and Russell W. Ramsey, "The Defeat of Admiral Vernon at Cartagena in 1741," *Southern Quarterly*, 1:4 (July 1963), 332-335. One might also consult the older, romanticized work of Soledad Acosta de Samper, *Los piratas en Cartagena; Crónicas histórico-novelescas* (Bogotá, 1886); and Lucia Burk Kinnaird, "Creassy's Plan for Seizing Panama, with an Introductory Account of British Designs on Panama," *HAHR*, 13:1 (Feb. 1933), 46-78; and Martin E. Thomas, "Creassy's Plan for Seizing Panama," *ibid.*, 22:1 (Feb. 1942), 82-103. For a somewhat earlier threat of foreign occupation, see Francis R. Hart, *The Disaster of Darien: The Story of the Scots Settlement and the Causes of Its Failure, 1699-1701* (Boston, 1929); and John Prebble, *The Darien Disaster: A Scots Colony in the New World, 1698-1700* (New York, 1968).

Germán Colmenares, *Las haciendas de los Jesuítas en el Nuevo Reino de Granada; Siglo XVIII* (Bogotá, 1969), is an interesting account of the economic position of the Jesuits at the time of their expulsion from New Granada. José Yarza, "La expulsión de los Jesuítas del Nuevo Reino de Granada en 1767," *Revista Javeriana* (Bogotá), 38:188 (Sept. 1952), 170-183; Juan Manuel Pacheco, "La expulsión de los Jesuítas del Nuevo Reino de Granada," *Revista de Indias* (Madrid), 28:113/114 (July-Dec. 1968), 351-381; and Charles J. Fleener, "The Expulsion of the Jesuits from the Viceroyalty of New Granada, 1767," University of Florida, 1969, describe the impact of Charles III's decision to terminate Jesuit activities in his realms.

Allan J. Kuethe, *Military Reform and Society in New Granada, 1773-1808* (Gainesville, Fla., 1978), analyzes another of the reform efforts under Charles III. The works of John L. Phelan, *The People and the King: The Comunero Revolution in Colombia, 1781* (Madison, Wis., 1976); Jane M. Loy, "Forgotten Comuneros: The 1781 Revolt in the Llanos of Cansanare," *HAHR*, 61:2 (May 1981), 235-257; David P. Leonard, "The Comunero Rebellion of New Granada in

1781: A Chapter in the Spanish Quest for Social Justice," University of Michigan, 1951; and Pablo E. Cárdenas Acosta, *Del vasallaje a la insurrección de los comuneros; La provincia de Tunja en el virreinato* (Tunja, 1947), and *El movimiento comunal de 1781 en el Nuevo Reino de Granada; Reivindicaciones históricas* (2 vols.; Bogotá, 1960), provide recent interpretations of the Commoners' Revolt, provoked at least in part by Bourbon tax reforms. This and other manifestations of discontent with royal policies between 1770 and 1810 are the subject of Roberto María Tisnés, *Movimientos preindependientes grancolombianos* (Bogotá, 1962); Enrique Caballero, *Incienso y pólvora: comuneros y precursores* (Bogotá, 1980); and Anthony McFarlane's "Civil Disorders and Popular Protests in Late Colonial New Granada," *HAHR*, 64:1 (Feb. 1984), 17-54.

V. INDEPENDENCE PERIOD AND THE REPUBLIC OF GRAN COLOMBIA, 1810-1830

The independence period in Colombian history has been treated often but uncritically by most Colombian historians. See, for example, *Homenaje a los próceres; Discursos pronunciados en la celebración del sesquicentenario de la independencia nacional, 1810-1960* (Bogotá, 1961), and *El congreso grancolombiano de historia, 1821-1971* (Bogotá, 1972), both published by the Colombian Academy of History. The serious student, however, is confronted by a vast array of books and articles, many of which lack coherence, documentation, and objectivity. The reader should approach this literature with caution. For detailed study, the student would do well to begin with Javier Ocampo López, *Historiografía y bibliografía de la emancipación del Nuevo Reino de Granada* (Tunja, 1969), a partially annotated guide to more than 2,000 published works with some archival references as well.

The single most unified work on the the wars of independence is still probably José Manuel Restrepo, *Historia de la revolución de la República de Colombia* . . . (1825, revised 1848), an early-19th-century account by one of Colombia's first modern historians, who was himself a participant in many of the events—factors that reveal both the strengths and the weaknesses of the work. First published in 1827, it is available in several editions, but the most usable is the four-volume one, Besanzon, 1858. John Lynch, *The Spanish-American Revolutions, 1808-1826* . . . (New York, 1973); Jay Kinsbruner, *The Spanish-American Independence Movement* (Hinsdale, Ill., 1973); and Richard Graham, *Independence in Latin*

America: A Comparative Approach (New York, 1972), provide an international setting for specifically Colombian events. Within the context of Colombian history itself, Tisnés, *Movimientos pre-independientes* . . . ; Restrepo, *Historia de la revolución* . . . ; and Jaramillo Uribe, *El pensamiento* . . . , all give some background for the revolutionary events.

Rafael Gómez Hoyos, *La revolución granadina de 1810* . . . ; and Javier Ocampo López, *El proceso ideológico de la emancipación: las ideas de génesis, independencia, futuro e integración de los orígenes de Colombia* (Bogotá, 1982), are useful for understanding the ideological currents of the time; and Sergio Elías Ortiz, *Génesis de la revolución del 20 de Julio de 1810* (Bogotá, 1960), narrates the specific events that precipitated the declaration of independence. Manuel José Forero, *La primera república* (Bogotá, 1966); Peter Paul Guzzo, "The Independence Movement and the Failure of the First Republic of Cartagena de Indias," Catholic University of America, 1972; and Roberto María Tisnés, *Historia eclesiástica . . . el clero y la independencia en Santafé, 1810-1815* (Bogotá, 1971), focus on events in the early stages of the wars for independence. A diary account of this period by José María Caballero is given in *La patria boba* (ed. Eduardo Posada; Bogotá, 1902). The works of Oswaldo Díaz Díaz, *La reconquista española* (2 vols.; Bogotá, 1964-1967), and *Los Almeydas: Episodios de la resistencia patriota contra el ejército pacificador de Tierra Firma* (Bogotá, 1962); and Brian Hamnett, "The Counter-Revolution of Morrillo and the Insurgent Clerics of New Granada, 1815-1820," *The Americas*, 32:4 (Apr. 1976), 597-617, concentrate on the era of Spanish resurgence after 1815. Several authors provide surveys of the Republic of Gran Colombia. In English, the standard is David A. Bushnell, *The Santander Regime in Gran Colombia* (Newark, Del., 1954). From a Colombian viewpoint, see the older work by Joaquín Tamayo, *Nuestro siglo XIX, La Gran Colombia* (Bogotá, 1941); or the more recent one by Luis Galvis Madero, *La Gran Colombia: 1819-1830* (Bogotá, 1970). Three of the volumes of the previously cited *Curso superior de historia de Colombia, 1492-1830,* cover the period 1781-1830. José M. Ots Capdequí, "The Impact of the Wars of Independence on the Institutional Life of the New Kingdom of Granada," *The Americas,* 17:2 (Oct. 1960), 111-198, is an effort to analyze the effect of the revolutionary movements on the day-to-day functions of society.

The literature relating to the exploits of individual *próceres,* or heroes of the independence period, cannot be dealt with here in any thorough manner. It is simply too profuse. Of the major figures, however, Simón Bolívar, the Liberator, clearly predominates. Francis L. Petre, *Simón Bolívar "El Libertador"* (London, 1910); Salvador de Madariaga, *Bolívar* (London, 1952); Gerhard Masur, *Simon Bolivar* (Albuquerque, N.M., 1969); and Augusto Mijares, *El Libertador* (Caracas, 1964), are representative biographical studies. Jules Mancini, *Bolívar y la emancipación de las colonias españolas desde los orígenes hasta 1815* . . . (trans. Carlos Docteur, 2 vols.; Bogotá, 1944); J. B. Trend, *Bolívar and the Independence of Spanish America* (London, 1946); and Francisco Antonio Encina, *Bolívar y la independencia de la América española* (8 vols.; Santiago de Chile, 1954-1965), emphasize his role as an international figure. Caracciolo Parra Pérez, *Bolívar: A Contribution to the Study of His Political Ideas* (trans. Andrew N. Cleven; Paris, 1928); and Víctor A. Belaúnde, *Bolívar and the Political Thought of the Spanish American Revolution* (Baltimore, 1938), help to explain his philosophy. For his military career, see Francisco Rivas Vicuña, *Las guerras de Bolívar* (4 vols.; Bogotá, 1934-1939); Vicente Lecuna, *Crónica razonada de las guerras de Bolívar* . . . (3 vols.; New York, 1950); and Carlos Cortés Vargas, "Military Operations of Bolívar in New Granada: A Commentary on Lecuna, Crónica razonada de las guerras de Bolívar," *HAHR*, 32:4 (Nov. 1952), 615-633. Alfredo Boulton, *Los retratos de Bolívar* (Caracas, 1955); and Enrique Uribe White, *Iconografía del Libertador* (Bogotá, 1967), are both useful pictorial guides to the Liberator's career. John J. Johnson and Doris M. Ladd, *Simón Bolívar and Spanish American Independence, 1783-1830* (Princeton, N.J., 1968); and David A. Bushnell, *The Liberator Simón Bolívar: Man and Image* (New York, 1970), are useful interpretive introductions for the English reader. Indications of the controversy surrounding the meeting between Bolívar and San Martín can be found in William S. Robertson, "The So-called Apocryphal Letters of Colombres Mármol on the Interview of Guayaquil," *HAHR*, 23:1 (Feb. 1943), 154-158; W. H. Gray, "Bolívar's Conquest of Guayaquil," *ibid.*, 27:4 (Nov. 1947), 603-622; Gerhard Masur, "The Conference of Guayaquil," *ibid.*, 31:2 (May 1951), 189-229; and Vicente Lecuna, "Bolívar and San Martín at Guayaquil," *ibid.*, 31:3 (Aug. 1951), 369-393. The controversies surrounding this and other actions of Bolívar are suggested in Vicente Lecuna, *Catálogo de errores y calumnias en la historia de Bolívar* (3 vols.; New York, 1956-1958). The February 1983 issue of the *Hispanic American Historical Review*, 63:1, contains a series of recent interpretations: John Lynch, "Bolívar and the Caudillos," 3-36; Simon Collier, "Nationality, Nationalism, and Supranationalism in the Writings of Bolívar," 37-64; David Bushnell, "The Last Dictatorship: Betrayal or Consummation?" 65-106; and Germán Carrera Damas, "Simón Bolívar, El Culto Heróico y la Nación,"

107-146. For a description of the published documents relating to the Liberator's life, see Manuel Pérez Vila, comp., *Cartas del Libertador, Tomo XII, 1802-1830* (Caracas, 1959), x-xxi; and for archival material, see the guides of Vicente Lecuna et al., *La Casa Natal del Libertador* . . . (Caracas, 1954); and Pedro Grases, *Archivo del Libertador, Casa Natal-Caracas, indice* (Caracas, 1961).

From the Colombian viewpoint, an equally important (perhaps even more important) liberator was Francisco de Paula Santander, 1792-1840, for whom there is no biography in English. Neither does the volume of work available on Santander rival that of Bolívar. Báltazar Isaza Calderón and Carlos Alberto Mendoza, *Santander, padre de la democracia en Colombia* (Panama, 1983), is a relatively brief biographical introduction; but Pilar Moreno de Angel, *Santander* (Bogotá, 1989), is the most recent and ambitious study. The most extensive work is probably still that by Julio Hoenigsberg, *Santander ante la historia: Ensayo histórico-biográfico* (3 vols.; Barranquilla, 1969-1970). Among the other most oft mentioned biographical studies are Manuel José Forero, *Santander en sus escritos* (Bogotá, 1944); Max Grillo, *El hombre de las leyes: Estudio histórico y crítico de los hechos del General Francisco de Paula Santander en la guerra de la independencia y en la creación de la república* (Bogotá, 1940); and Laureano García Ortiz, *Algunos estudios sobre el General Santander* (Bogotá, 1946). The Academia Colombiana de Historia, *1840: Muerte de Santander* (Bogotá, 1940), is a commemorative album. The politically polemical *El mito de Santander,* by Laureano Gómez (2 vols.; Bogotá, 1966), is indicative of the controversy that surrounds the interpretation of Santander's actions. Alirio Gómez Picón, *Bolívar y Santander; Historia de una amistad* (Bogotá, 1971), is a curious effort to analyze the relations between these men, the first two important presidents of republican Colombia. Although Santander has not received adequate biographical treatment, he did leave some autobiographical works: *Memorias sobre el orígen, causas y progreso de las desavenencias entre el presidente de la República de Colombia, y el vicepresidente de la misma, Francisco de P. Santander, escritas por un colombiano en 1829* (Bogotá, 1909); *Diario del General Francisco de Paula Santander en Europa y los EE. UU., 1829-1832* (ed. Rafael Martínez Briceño; Bogotá, 1963); and *Apuntes para las memorias sobre Colombia y la Nueva Granada* (Bogotá, 1837). Bushnell, *The Santander Regime* . . . ; Eduardo Acevedo Latorre, *Colaboradores de Santander en la organización de la república* (Bogotá, 1944); Rodolfo Oswaldo Rivera, "Francisco de Paula Santander: His Role in the Making of Colombia," Duke University, 1932; and Theodora McKennan, "Santander and the Vogue of Benthamism in Colombia and New

Granada," Loyola University, 1968, all concentrate on his role as chief executive, either as Vice President of Gran Colombia or President of New Granada. For documentary materials, see Roberto Cortázar, ed., *Cartas y mensajes de Santander* (10 vols.; Bogotá, 1953-1956); Cortázar, ed., *Correspondencia dirigida al General Francisco de Paula Santander* (14 vols.; Bogotá, 1965-1970); and Ernesto Restrepo Tirado et al., *Archivo Santander* (24 vols.; Bogotá, 1913-1932).

Like the careers of Bolívar and Santander, that of Antonio Nariño, 1765-1823, spans most of the revolutionary period, and his actions are no less disputed than theirs. Jorge Ricardo Vejarano, *Nariño; Su vida, sus infortunios, su talla histórica* (Bogotá, 1938); and Camilo Riaño, *El teniente general don Antonio Nariño* (Bogotá, 1973), are perhaps the most carefully reasoned treatments. Eduardo Posada and Pedro Ibáñez, *El Precursor; Documentos sobre la vida pública y privada del General Antonio Nariño* (Bogotá, 1903), is an older documentary collection. Raimundo Rivas, *El andante caballero: Don Antonio Nariño . . .* (Bogotá, 1936); and Guillermo Hernández de Alba, *Proceso contra don Antonio Nariño, por la publicación clandestina de la Declaración de los Derechos del Hombre y del Ciudadano* (Bogotá, 1980), deal with his early career and prison experiences. Carlos Restrepo Canal, *Nariño, periodista* (Bogotá, 1960), emphasizes his career as a political essayist; and works such as Arturo Abello, *"Don Dinero" en la independencia* (Bogotá, 1966), represent a critical, revisionist viewpoint. Thomas Blossom, *Nariño: Hero of Colombian Independence* (Tucson, Ariz., 1967), is an uncritical but readable introduction in English. See also Blossom, "The Library of a Revolutionary Leader, Antonio Nariño, Precursor of Colombian Independence," *Proceedings of the Arkansas Academy of Science,* 11 (1958), 44-57.

A reference should also be made in passing to Camilo Torres, author of the *Memorial de agravios . . .* (fac. ed.; Bogotá, 1960), November 20, 1809, which gave formal expression to the grievances that led many *granadinos* to consider independence from Spain. See Manuel José Forero, *Camilo Torres . . .* (Bogotá, 1960). Juan Botero Restrepo, *El prócer historiador, José Manuel Restrepo (1781-1863)* (Medellín, 1982); Nelson Leyva Medina, *General Josef de Leyva, fundador de la primera escuela militar de la Nueva Granada . . .* (Bogotá, 1982); Emilio Díaz del Castillo Z., *Agualongo, caudillo pastuso y prócer colombiano* (Bogotá, 1983); and Roberto María Tisnés, *Los mártires de la patria, 1810-1822* (Medellín, 1967), are representative of the widely varying approaches to the independence period from biographical perspectives. For other major leaders, see the bibliographies of Ocampo López, cited above, and the briefer annotations of Sergio Elías Ortiz, in Romero et al., *Papeletas bibliográficas para el estudio de la historia de Colombia* . . . Camilo Riaño, *Historia militar* . . . *la independencia, 1810-1815* (Bogotá, 1971); Guillermo Plazas Olarte, *Historia militar* . . . *la independencia, 1819-1828* (Bogotá, 1971); Rivas Vicuña, *Las guerras de Bolívar;* and Lecuna, *Crónica razonada* . . . , provide an overview of the military history of the wars of independence. Francisco J. Vergara y Velasco, *1818; Guerra de independencia* (Bogotá, 1960), analyzes the successes and failures of the campaign of 1818; and Camilo Riaño, *La campaña libertadora de 1819* (Bogotá, 1969), is a much more technically detailed account of the decisive battles of 1819. For specific engagements, the reader may find useful such works as Cayo Leónidas Peñuela, *Album de Boyacá* (2 vols.; Tunja, 1969-1970); and the works of Roberto Ibáñez Sánchez, *Presencia granadina en Carabobo* (2 vols.; Bogotá, 1971), and *Campaña del sur, 1822: Bomboná-Pichincha* (Bogotá, 1972). The older *Participación de Colombia en la libertad del Perú, 1824-1924* (3 vols.; Bogotá, 1945-1947), by Carlos Cortés Vargas, has both military and diplomatic import. William A. Morgan, "Sea Power in the Gulf of Mexico and the Caribbean Sea During the Mexican and Colombian Wars of Independnece, 1815-1830," University of Southern California, 1969, deals with naval operations. Eduardo Pérez O., *La guerra irregular en la independencia de la Nueva Granada y Venezuela, 1810-1830* (Tunja, 1982), deals with guerrilla tactics in the wars for independence; and Zamira Díaz de Zuluága, *Guerra y economía en las haciendas, Popayán, 1780-1830* (Bogotá, 1983), treats the economic impact in the southern region.

General descriptions of the diplomatic history of the era can be found in Rivas, *Historia diplomática* . . . ; Londoño, *Integración del territorio* . . . ; Andrade S., *Demarcación de las fronteras* . . . ; Parks, *Colombia and the United States;* and Caicedo Castilla, *Historia diplomática,* cited above; and in Arthur P. Whitaker, *The United States and the Independence of Latin America, 1800-1830* (New York, 1962); and D.A.G. Waddell, *Gran Bretaña y la independencia de Venezuela y Colombia* (Caracas, 1983). Eugene R. Huck, "Colombian–United States Commercial Relations, 1821-1850," University of Alabama, 1963, emphasizes economic problems. More specialized aspects are available for the English reader in W. S. Robertson, "The Beginnings of Spanish American Diplomacy," in the collection *Essays in American History Dedicated to Frederick Jackson Turner* (New York, 1910); William R. Shepherd, "Bolívar and the United States," *HAHR,* 1:3 (Aug. 1918), 270-298; J. Fred Rippy, "Bolívar as Viewed by Contemporary Diplomats of the United States," *ibid.,* 15:3 (Aug. 1935), 287-297; Lewis Hanke, "Baptis Irvine's Reports on Simón Bolívar," *ibid.*, 16:3 (Aug. 1936), 360-373; Hanke, "Simón Bolívar and Neutral Rights," *ibid.*, 21:2 (May 1941), 258-291; Charles H. Bowman, "The Activities of Manuel Torres as Purchasing Agent, 1820-1821," *ibid.*, 48:2 (May 1968), 234-245; Bowman, "Manuel Torres in Philadelphia and the Recognition of Colombian Independence, 1821-1822," *Records of the American Catholic Historical Society of Philadelphia*, 80:1 (Mar. 1969), 17-38; and Wilkins E. Winn, "The Issue of Religious Liberty in the United States Commercial Treaty with Colombia, 1824," *The Americas*, 26:3 (Jan. 1970), 291-301. Luis Cuervo Márquez, *Independencia de las colonias hispano-americanas; Participación de la Gran Bretaña y de los Estados Unidos; Legión Británica* (2 vols.; Bogotá, 1938); Pedro Ignacio Cadena, *Anales diplomáticos de Colombia* (Bogotá, 1878); Nicolás García Samudio, *Capítulos de historia diplomática* (Bogotá, 1925); Francisco José Urrutia, *Páginas de historia diplomática; Los Estados Unidos de América y las repúblicas hispano-americanas de 1810 a 1830* (Bogotá, 1917), and *Política internacional de la Gran Colombia* (Bogotá, 1941); and Pedro A. Zubieta, *Apuntaciones sobre las primeras misiones diplomáticas de Colombia . . . 1809-1830* (Bogotá, 1924), and *Congresos de Panamá y Tacubaya . . .* (Bogotá, 1912), should be consulted for Colombian viewpoints. Edgar Vaughan, "Fracaso de una misión: La historia de Alejandro Cockburn, primer enviado extraordinario y ministro plenipotenciario británico en Colombia, 1826-1827," *Boletín de Historia y Antigüedades* (Bogotá), 52:609/611 (July-Sept. 1956), 529-566, deals with the period of Gran Colombian diplomacy.

Robert L. Gilmore, "The Imperial Crisis, Rebellion and the Viceroy: Nueva Granada in 1809," *HAHR*, 40:1 (Feb. 1960), 1-24; and Héctor Conte Bermúdez, "Los virreyes en Panamá: Don Benito Pérez," *Lotería* (Panamá, Rep. of Panama; 2nd series), 6:71 (Oct. 1961), 54-74, cover the reactions of the later viceroys to the independence movements. Russ T. Davidson, "Salvador Jiménez de Enciso y Cobos Padilla: Royalist Bishop in Republican New Granada, 1818-1827," Vanderbilt University, 1972; and John D. Roney, "The Political Career of Archbishop Fernando Caycedo y Flórez, 1810-1832," Vanderbilt University, 1974, comment on two members of the clerical hierarchy and their political stances. Sergio Elías Ortiz, *Agustín Agualongo y su tiempo* (southern Colombia) (Bogotá, 1958); Alfonso Zawadzky C., *Las ciudades confederadas del Valle del Cauca en 1811 . . .* (Cali, 1943); Horacio Rodríguez Plata, *La antigua provincia del Socorro y la independencia* (Bogotá, 1963); and Gabriel Porras Troconis, *La magna epopeya de Cartagena; El sitio del año 1815* (Bogotá, 1965), all offer a regional emphasis for the struggles. Alfred Hasbrouck, *Foreign Legionaries in the Liberation of Spanish*

South America (New York, 1928); Sergio Elías Ortiz, *Franceses en la independencia de la Gran Colombia* (Bogotá, 1971); and Enrique Naranjo, "Alexander Macaulay, an Unknown Hero: His Family and Early Life," *HAHR*, 25:4 (Nov. 1945), 528-535, focus on foreign participation in the wars. Américo Carnicelli, *La masonería en la independencia de America, 1810-1830* (2 vols.; Bogotá, 1970), studies the role of freemasonry in the independence period; and José D. Monsalve, *Mujeres de la independencia* (Bogotá, 1926); and Horacio Rodríguez Plata, *Antonia Santos Plata, genealogía y biografía* (Bogotá, 1969), treat the role of women.

For the decade of the 1820s, in addition to works previously cited, Jaime Duarte French, *Poder y política: Colombia, 1810-1827* (Bogotá, 1980), is a study in political leadership. David Bushnell, "The Development of the Press in Great Colombia," *HAHR*, 30:4 (Nov. 1950), 432-452; and Rodrigo Miró, "La imprenta y el periodismo en Panamá durante el período de la Gran Colombia, 1821-1831," *Lotería* (Panama; 2nd series), 8:87 (Feb. 1963), 40-69, discuss the development of printing and political journalism. Church-State relationships are the subject of David Bushnell, "The Religious Question in the Congress of Gran Colombia," *The Americas*, 31:1 (July 1974), 1-17. Harold A. Bierck, "The Struggle for Abolition in Gran Colombia," *HAHR*, 33:3 (Aug. 1953), 365-386, deals with the attempts to abolish slavery. Zamira Díaz de Zuluaga, "Haciendas of the Gobernación of Popayán: Socio-Economic Changes Brought by the Independence Wars," Vanderbilt, 1983, is a self-explanatory regional study. Roberto Cortázar, Luis Augusto Cuervo, and José Joaquín Guerra have published documentary collections for most of the major congresses between Angostura in 1819 and Ocaña in 1829. The works of Roberto Botero Saldarriaga, *El Libertador-Presidente; El intruso;* and *República de la Nueva Granada . . .* (Bogotá, 1969); Aldolfo Romero Luengo, *Presencia vital de Urdaneta en la emancipación y en el gobierno de Colombia la Grande . . .* (Caracas, 1981); *General José María Córdoba, 1799-1829* (Bogotá, 1970); and Jane M. Rausch, "The Taming of a Colombian Caudillo," *The Americas*, 42:3 (Jan. 1986), 275-288, serve to delineate the details of the collapse of Gran Colombia, as does the first volume of Arboleda, *Historia contemporánea . . .* , cited below. For a useful, first-hand account of these events, see José Manuel Restrepo, *Diario político y militar: Memorias sobre los sucesos importantes de la época para servir a la historia de la revolución de Colombia y de la Nueva Granada desde 1819 para adelante* (5 vols.; Bogotá, 1954-1957).

There are a number of descriptive travel accounts for the decade of the 1820s, particularly for the English reader. See [Alexander

Walker], *Colombia: Being a Geographical, Statistical, Agricultural, Commercial, and Political Account of That Country State* . . . (London, 1824); William Duane, *A Visit to Colombia, in the Years 1822 and 1823* . . . (Philadelphia, 1826); Charles Stuart Cochrane, *Journal of a Residence and Travels in Colombia During the Years 1823 and 1824* (2 vols.; New York, 1971); E. Taylor Parks and Alfred Tischendorf, "Cartagena to Bogotá, 1825-1826: The Diary of Richard Clough Anderson, Jr.," *HAHR*, 42:2 (May 1962), 217-231; anonymous, *The Present State of Colombia* . . . *by an Officer Late in the Colombian Service* (London, 1827); John P. Hamilton, *Travels Through the Interior Provinces of Colombia* (2 vols.; London, 1827); and Sergio Elías Ortiz, "Informe de Henri Ternaux Compans sobre la Gran Colombia en 1829: Notas de viaje por Panamá, Quito, y Provincia de Popayán," *Boletín de Historia y Antigüedades* (Bogotá), 56:651/653 (Jan.-Mar. 1969), 59-73.

VI. REPUBLICAN PERIOD, 1830-1990

Gustavo Arboleda, *Historia contemporánea de Colombia, desde la disolución de la antigua república de ese nombre hasta la época presente* (6 vols.; Bogotá, Popayán, and Cali, 1918-1935), is the most comprehensive survey of the era of New Granada, 1830-1860, although José Manuel Restrepo's *Historia de la Nueva Granada, 1832-1854* (2 vols.; Bogotá, 1952-1963), and the same author's *Diario político y militar* . . . , are useful contemporary accounts of the same period. Carlos Restrepo Canal, *La Nueva Granada, 1831-1840* (Bogotá, 1971), deals specifically with the presidencies of Santander and José Ignacio de Márquez.

Antonio Pérez Aguirre, *25 años de historia colombiana, 1853 a 1878, del centralismo a la federación* (Bogotá, 1959); and Estanislao Gómez Barrientos, *Páginas de historia; 25 años a través del estado de Antioquia* . . . (Medellín, 1918), cover the latter part of New Granada and the early portion of the Liberal ascendancy. Important overviews are given by Eduardo Rodríguez Piñeres, *El olimpo radical* (Bogotá, 1950); James W. Park, *Rafael Núñez and the Politics of Colombian Regionalism, 1863-1886* (Baton Rouge, La., 1985); Helen Delpar, *Red Against Blue: The Liberal Party in Colombian Politics, 1863-1899* (University, Ala., 1981); *Diez años de política liberal, 1892-1902* (Bogotá, 1945); and Charles W. Bergquist, *Coffee and Conflict in Colombia, 1886-1910* (Durham, N.C., 1978). Julio Holguín Arboleda, *21 años de vida colombiana: Historia, política y literatura* (Bogotá, 1967), is a much more personal account of the 1863-1885 period. For the later 19th and early 20th centuries, see Luis Martínez Delgado, *República de Colombia, 1885-1910* (2 vols.; Bogotá, 1970). Antonio Alvarez Restrepo, *Los golpes de estado en Colombia* (Bogotá, 1982), comments on coups d'état in Colombian history. David Lee Sowell, "The Early Latin American Labor Movement: Artisans and Politics in Bogotá, Colombia, 1832-1919," University of Florida, 1986, is a survey of 19th-century political developments from a popular or lower-class point of view.

There is a gap in the survey literature for the early 20th century. Martínez Delgado carries his account to 1910. Darío Mesa, "La vida política después de Panama," in Volume III of the *Manual de Historia* (ed. Jaime Jaramillo Uribe), 83-176, traces events from the turn of the 20th century to the early 1920s; as do Jorge Villegas and José Yunis, *Sucesos colombianos, 1900-1924* (Medellín, 1976). José Fernando Ocampo, *Colombia Siglo XX . . . ,* Vol. I, *1886-1934* (Bogotá, 1980), emphasizes foreign influences in Colombian history; and Vernon Lee Fluharty, *Dance of the Millions: Military Rule and Social Revolution in Colombia, 1930-1956* (Pittsburgh, 1957), picks up the narrative following the Great Depression. But overall, for the period 1910-1930, works are scarce. For recent history, see John D. Martz, *Colombia: A Contemporary Political Survey* (Chapel Hill, N.C., 1962); Robert H. Dix, *Colombia: The Political Dimensions of Change* (New Haven, Conn., 1967); and Dix, *The Politics of Colombia* (New York, 1987); James L. Payne, *Patterns of Conflict in Colombia* (New Haven, Conn., 1968); and A. Curtis Wilgus, ed., *The Caribbean: Contemporary Colombia* (Gainesville, Fla., 1962), a symposium by 21 authorities, including several from Colombia, who present selective views of history and national problems in the early 1960s.

Edwin G. Corr, *The Political Process in Colombia* (Denver, 1972); Reza Rezazadeh and Joseph MacKenzie, *Political Parties in Colombia: Continuity in Political Style* (Ann Arbor, Mich., 1978); and Rodrigo Lara Bonilla et al., *Los partidos políticos colombianos: presente y futuro* (Bogotá, 1983), are comments on the evolution and future of the two major political parties. In addition to Delpar's *Red Against Blue,* see Milton Puentes, *Historia del partido liberal colombiano* (Bogotá, 1961), for a survey of the Liberal Party. Medófilo Medina, *Historia del Partido Comunista de Colombia* (Bogotá, 1980); and the Communist Party of Colombia, *Treinta años de lucha del Partido Comunista de Colombia . . .* (Bogotá, 1960), are accounts sympathetic to the political group in question. Although strictly speaking not a history, *Los programas conservadores de 1849 a 1949* (Bogotá, 1952), by the Directorio Nacional Conservador, provides commentary on the Conservative Party's position. Robert L. Gilmore, "Federalism in Colombia, 1810-1858," University of California, Berkeley, 1949; and José de la Vega, *La federación en Colombia, 1810-1912* (Bogotá, 1952), are interpretive analyses of the principal points of contention between parties in the 19th century. A large part of the accessible data for the last 150 years of Colombia's history is to be found in the diaries, memoirs, and biographies of the leading figures in the nation's history. These works must be used with caution and constant attention to their partisan orientation, but they are almost indispensable sources. No guide could attempt to list all of the available titles, but an effort to suggest their richness and variety might include any of the following:

José Manuel Restrepo, *Diario político y militar* . . . , and the studies of Santander are good starting points for New Granada. Carlos Cuervo Márquez, *Vida del Doctor José Ignacio de Márquez* (2 vols.; Bogotá, 1917); Eduardo Posada and Pedro María Ibañez, *Vida de Herrán* (Bogotá, 1903); Francisco A. Zuluaga, "The Emergence of a Colombian Regional Caudillo: José María Obando, 1795-1832," Vanderbilt University, 1983; and Antonio J. Lemos Guzmán, *Obando, de Cruzverde a Cruzverde, 1795-1861* (Popayán, 1959), are biographies of presidents. Raimundo Rivas, *Mosquera y otros estudios* (Bogotá, 1936); Joaquín Tamayo, *Don Tomás Cipriano de Mosquera* (Bogotá, 1936); Antonio García, *El General Tomás Cipriano de Mosquera* (San José, C.R., 1939); Joaquín Estrada Monslave, *Mosquera, su grandeza y su comedia* (Bogotá, 1945); J. León Helguera, "Tomás Cipriano de Mosquera as President," *South Eastern Latin Americanist*, 25:1 (June 1981), 1-14; and J. León Helguera and Robert H. Davis, *Archivo epistolar del General Mosquera* . . . (Bogotá, Vol. 1-, 1966-), interpret the life and times of General Mosquera, head of the Colombian state on four occasions. José María Arboleda Llorente, *Vida del Illmo. Señor Manuel José Mosquera, Arzobispo de Santa Fe de Bogotá* (2 vols.; Bogotá, 1956); and Terrence B. Horgan, "Manuel José Mosquera, Archbishop of Bogotá, 1835-1853," Vanderbilt University, 1973, comment on the life of a major ecclesiastical figure. Estanislao Gómez Barrientos, *Don Mariano Ospina y su época; Páginas de historia neogranadina* (2 vols.; Medellín, 1913-1915); Angel Cuervo and Rufino J. Cuervo, *Vida de Rufino Cuervo [1801-1853] y noticias de su época* (2 vols.; Bogotá, 1946); and Joaquín Tamayo, *Don José María Plata y su época [1811-1861]* (Bogotá, 1933), have more than biographical import. Ricardo J. Alfaro, *Vida del General Tomás Herrera* (Barcelona, 1909); Gabriel Henao Mejía, *Juan de Dios Aranzazu [1798-1845]* (Bogotá, 1953); Gustavo Humberto Rodríguez, *Ezequiel Rojas y la Primera República Liberal* (Bogotá, 1984); Eduardo Lemaitre, *El General Juan José Nieto y su época* (Bogotá, 1983); and Jaime Duarte French, *Florentino González; Razón y sinrazón de una lucha política* (Bogotá, 1971), are biographies of secondary but nonetheless influential political figures. Darío Ortiz Vidales, *José María Melo: la razón de un rebelde* (Ibagué, 1980), is a biography of the man who led the 1854 coup d'état. Joaquín Posada Gutiérrez [1797-1881], *Memorias histórico-políticas* . . . (4 vols.; Bogotá, 1929); José María Samper [1828-1888], *Historia de una Alma* . . . (2 vols.; Bogotá, 1946-1948); Salvador Camacho Roldán [1827-1900], *Memorias* (Bogotá, 1923); and Aníbal Galindo [1834-1901], *Recuerdos históricos, 1840-1895* (Bogotá, 1900), are autobiographical accounts. Glenn T. Curry, "Nicolás Tanco Armero: A Mid–Nineteenth Century New Granadan's View of China," Vanderbilt University, 1972, is an unusual description of New Granada's perspective on Asia. See Jo Ann Rayfield, "Daniel Florencio O'Leary: From Bolivarian General to British Diplomat, 1834-1854," Vanderbilt University, 1969; and Robert F. McNerney, "Daniel Florence O'Leary, Soldier, Diplomat, and Historian," *The Americas,* 22:3 (Jan. 1966), 292-312, for aspects of the career of Bolívar's most famous aide and biographer.

In the latter part of the 19th century, two figures are preeminent: Rafael Núñez (1825-1894) and Miguel Antonio Caro (1843-1909). On Núñez, see Joaquín Tamayo, *Núñez* (Bogotá, 1939); Indalecio Liévano Aguirre, *Rafael Núñez* (Bogotá, 1944); and Joaquín Estrada Monsalve, *Núñez, el político y el hombre* (Bogotá, 1946). Gustavo Otero Muñoz, *La vida azarosa de Rafael Núñez; Un hombre y una época* (Bogotá, 1951), is not only a biography, but a narrative national history, 1859-1893. In contrast to the literature on Núñez, there is only one biography of Caro: Guillermo Torres García, *Miguel Antonio Caro; Su personalidad y política* (Madrid, 1956). For biographical fragments, see Margarita Holguín y Caro, *Los Caros en Colombia; Su fe, su patriotismo, su amor* (Bogotá, 1953).

Other biographies useful for the period are Enrique Pérez, *Vida de Felipe Pérez* [1836-1891] (Bogotá, 1911); Eduardo Rodríguez Piñeres, *Selección de escritos y discursos de Santiago Pérez* (Bogotá, 1950); José Dolores Moscote and Enrique J. Arce, *La vida ejemplar de Justo Arosemena* [1817-1896] (Panama, Panamá, 1956); Gustavo Otero Muñoz, [Marco Aurelio] *Wilches y su época* [1854-1893] (Bucaramanga, 1936); Luis Martínez Delgado, *A propósito del Dr. Carlos Martínez Silva* [1847-1903] Bogotá, 1926; and Guillermo Vargas Paúl, *Los Paúl en América; Remembranzas de familia* (Bogotá, 1945).

The autobiographical accounts of José María Quijano Wallis, b. 1847, *Memorias autobiográficas, histórico-políticas y de carácter* social . . . (Grottaferrata, [near Rome, Italy] 1919); and Aquileo Parra, *Memorias de Aquileo Parra, presidente de Colombia de 1876 a 1878, comprenden de 1825 a 1876* (Bogotá, 1912), give a broad personal view. José María Quijano Otero, *Diario de la guerra civil de 1860 y otros sucesos políticos* (Bogotá, 1982), covers the events of the 1860s, while Constancio Franco Vargas, *Apuntamientos para la historia de la guerra de 1876 i 1877* (2 vols.; Bogotá, 1877); Manuel Briceño, *La revolución, 1876-1877; Recuerdos para la historia* (Bogotá, 1947); and *Episodios de la Campaña de Occidente en 1876 i 1877; Tomados del "Diario Histórico" de aquel ejército* (Bogotá, 1877), describe the rebellion of the 1870s. Foción Soto, *Memorias sobre el movimiento de resistencia a la dictadura de Rafael Núñez, 1884-1885* (2 vols.; Bogotá, 1913); and E. Guillermo Martín, *Campaña del Ejército del Norte en 1885 . . .* (Bogotá, 1887), interpret the civil strife of the 1880s.

For the late 1800s and early 20th century, see Alvaro Holguín y Caro, *Al servicio de la república: Vida de Carlos Holguín, Presidente de Colombia* (2 vols.; Bogotá, 1981); Julio H. Palacio, b. 1875, *Historia de mi vida* (Bogotá, 1942); José Manuel Marroquín, *Don José Manuel Marroquín íntimo* (Bogotá, 1915); Luis Martínez Delgado, *Jorge Holguín, o El Político* (Bogotá, 1980); Jorge Sánchez Camacho, *El General [Pedro Nel] Ospina; Biografía* (Bogotá, 1960); Eduardo Lemaitre Román, *Rafael Reyes; Biografía de un gran-colombiano* (Bogotá, 1981); Fernando Galvis Salazar, *[Rafael] Uribe Uribe* (Bogotá, 1962); Jorge Sánchez Camacho, *Marco Fidel Suárez* (Bucaramanga, 1955); José A. Osorio Lizarazo, *[Jorge Eliécer] Gaitán, vida, muerte y permanente presencia* (Buenos Aires, 1952); and Richard Sharpless, *Gaitán of Colombia: A Political Biography* (Pittsburgh, 1978).

For more monographic approaches to the political history of New Granada and Colombia, see J. Fred Rippy, "The Dictators of Colombia," in A. Curtis Wilgus, *South American Dictators During the First Century of Independence* (Washington, D.C., 1937), which superficially discusses Mosquera, Núñez, and Reyes. Alvaro Tirado Mejía, *El estado y la política en el siglo XIX* (Bogotá, 1981), is an interpretation of 19th-century politics. Thomas F. McGann, "The Assassination of Sucre and Its Significance in Colombian History, 1828-1848," *HAHR*, 30:3 (Aug. 1950), 269-289, deals with one of the controversial events of the early republican period. J. León Helguera, "The First Mosquera Administration in New Granada, 1845-1849," University of North Carolina, 1958, is a detailed view of one presidential period. Robert H. Davis, "Acosta, Caro, and Lleras: Three Essayists and Their Views of New Granada's National Problems, 1832-1853," Vanderbilt University, 1969; and Harold E. Hinds, "José María Samper: An Introduction to His Character and Aspects of His Writing During the Period 1828-1865," Vanderbilt University, 1967, deal with philosophical currents in New Granada. Robert L. Gilmore, "Nueva Granada's Socialist Mirage," *HAHR*, 36:2 (May 1956), 190-210; and David Bushnell, "Voter Participation in the Colombian Election of 1856," *ibid.*, 51:2 (May 1971), 237-249, treat political issues and popular responses in the 1850s. Anthony P. Maingot, "Social Structure, Social Status, and Civil-Military Conflict in Urban Colombia, 1810-1858," in Stephen Thornstrom and Richard Sennet, *Nineteenth-Century Cities* (New Haven, Conn., 1969); J. León Helguera, "The Problem of Liberalism Versus Conservatism in Colombia: 1849-1889," in Frederick B. Pike, *Latin American History: Select Problems—Identity, Integration, and Nationhood* (New York, 1969); and Frank Safford, "Social Aspects of Politics in Nineteenth-Century Spanish America: New Granada, 1825-1850," *Journal of Social History*, 5:3 (Spring 1972), 344-370, interpret events from a social viewpoint. David M. Lassiter, "Views of Some United States Observers During the Colombian Federal War of 1860," Vanderbilt University, 1971, comments on the war that brought the collapse of New Granada. Two interesting regional studies focusing on Antioquia are Roger J. Brew, "Aspects of Politics in Antioquia, 1850 to 1865," St. Antony's College, Oxford, 1971; and Luis H. Fajardo, *The Protestant Ethic of the Antioqueños: Social Structure and Personality* (Cali, 1966?). Land changes are studied for the Bogotá environs in Glenn T. Curry, "The Disappearance of the *Resguardos Indígenas* of Cundinamarca, Colombia, 1800-1853," Vanderbilt University, 1981; and labor tensions on the frontier are treated by Catherine LeGrand, "Labor Acquisition and Social Conflict on the Colombian Frontier, 1850-1936," *Journal of Latin American Studies* (Cambridge, U.K.), 16:1 (May 1984), 27-49.

Pablo E. Cárdenas Acosta, *La restauración constitucional de 1867: Historia de un contragolpe de estado* (Tunja, 1966), explains the removal of President Mosquera for misconduct in office. Helen Delpar, "Aspects of Liberal Factionalism in Colombia, 1875-1885," *HAHR*, 51:2 (May 1971), 250-274; James Park, "Regionalism as a Factor in Colombia's 1875 Election," *The Americas*, 42:4 (Apr. 1986), 453-472; Gonzalo España, *La guerra civil de 1885: Núñez y la derrota del radicalismo* (Bogotá, 1985); and Luis Martínez Delgado, *Historia de un cambio de gobierno: Estudio crítico-histórico de la caída del gobierno del Doctor Manuel Antonio Sanclemente* (Bogotá, 1958), comment on political factionalism in the late 1800s. Martha C. Child, "Politics, Revolution, and Reform: The Liberal Challenger to the Colombian Status Quo: Rafael Uribe Uribe, 1859-1914," Vanderbilt University, 1969; and Charles W. Berquist, "The Politi-

cal Economy of the Colombian Presidential Election of 1897,"
HAHR, 56:1 (Feb. 1978), 1-30, cover aspects of the civil war at the
turn of the century. For the work of cartoonists commenting on the
political events, see the article by J. León Helguera, "Notes on a
Century of Colombian Political Cartooning: 1830-1930," *Studies in
Latin American Popular Culture*, 6 (1987), 259-280.
Terrence B. Horgan, "The Liberals Come to Power in Colombia,
por Debajo de la Ruana: A Study of the Enrique Olaya Herrera
Administration, 1930-1934," Vanderbilt University, 1983; and
Richard Stoller, "Alfonso López and Liberal Radicalism in 1930's
Colombia," Duke University, 1986, are theses on the decade of the
1930s. Alvaro Tirado Mejía, *La reforma constitucional de 1936*
(Quito, 1982); Tirado Mejía, *Aspectos políticos del primer gobierno de
Alfonso López Pumarejo, 1934-1938* (Bogotá, 1981); and Hernán
Jaramillo Ocampo, *1946-1950, de la unidad nacional a la hegemonía
conservador* (Bogotá, 1980), cover much of the 1930s and 1940s.
See also Alexander Wilde, "Conversations Among Gentleman:
Oligarchical Democracy in Colombia," in Juan Linz and Alfred
Stepan, eds., *The Breakdown of Democratic Regimes* (Baltimore,
1978). James D. Henderson, *Conservative Thought in Twentieth
Century Latin America: The Ideas of Laureano Gómez* (Athens, Ohio,
1988); and Christopher Abel, "Conservative Politics in Twentieth-
Century Antioquia (1910-1953)," St. Antony's College, Oxford,
1973, provide a national and a regional focus on Conservative
viewpoints. The issue of land reform is treated by Francine B.
Cronshaw, "Landowners and Politics in Colombia, 1923-1948,"
University of New Mexico, 1986); Gloria Gaitán, *La lucha por la
tierra en la década del 30* (Bogotá, 1976); Darío Fajardo M.,
Haciendas, campesinos y políticas agrarias, 1930-1980 (Quito, 1983);
Carlos Lleras Restrepo, *La cuestión agraria, 1933-1971* (Bogotá,
1982); Albert Hirschman, "Land Reform and Land Use in Colombia," in his *Journeys Towards Progress* (New York, 1963); and
Santiago Perry, *La crisis agraria en Colombia, 1950-1980* (Bogotá,
1983).
   La Violencia, the sociopolitical turmoil that dominated Colombian history between the late 1940s and the mid-1960s, has a body
of literature all its own, and the reader might be well advised to
begin with Russell W. Ramsey's two works, "Critical Bibliography
on La Violencia in Colombia," *Latin American Research Review*, 8:1
(Spring 1973), 3-44, and *Sources and Bibliography of La Violencia in
Colombia* (Gainesville, Fla., 1974); or Gonzalo Sánchez, "La Violencia in Colombia: New Research, New Questions," *HAHR*, 65:4
(Nov. 1985), 789-807. A good beginning survey insofar as it goes
is Paul Oquist, *Violence, Conflict, and Politics in Colombia* (New

York, 1980). Jay Cordell Robinson, "Jorge Eliécer Gaitán and His Socio-Political Movement in Colombia, 1930-1948," Indiana University, 1971; Abelardo Patiño, "The Political Ideas of the Liberal and Conservative Parties in Colombia During the 1946-1953 Crisis," American University, 1955; James D. Henderson, "Origins of 'The Violence' in Colombia, 1946-1965," University of Florida, 1970, are dissertations with emphasis on the causes and the development of the turbulence. Herbert Braun, *The Assassination of Gaitán: Public Life and Urban Violence in Colombia* (Madison, Wis., 1985); James D. Henderson, *When Colombia Bled: Politics and Violence in Colombia* (University, Ala., 1985); Peter Schmid, "Saints, Sinners, and Civil War," *American Mercury,* 75:3 (Sept. 1952), 23-31; Richard S. Weinert, "Violence in Pre-Modern Societies: Rural Colombia," *American Political Science Review,* 60:2 (June 1966), 340-347; Norman A. Bailey, "La Violencia in Colombia," *Journal of Inter-American Studies,* 9:4 (Oct. 1967), 561-575; Robert C. Williamson, "Toward a Theory of Political Violence: The Case of Rural Colombia," *Western Political Quarterly,* 18:1 (Mar. 1965), 35-44; Steffen W. Schmidt, "La Violencia Revisited: The Clientelist Bases of Political Violence in Colombia," *Journal of Latin American Studies* (Cambridge, U.K.), 6:1 (May 1974), 97-111; and John Walton, *Reluctant Rebels* (New York, 1984), 72-102, are books, chapters, and journal articles with a similar focus.

Roberto Pineda Giraldo, *El impacto de la violencia en el Tolima; El caso de El Líbano* (Bogotá, 1960); Aaron Lipman and A. Eugene Havens, "The Colombian Violencia: An Ex Post Facto Experiment," *Social Forces,* 44:2 (Dec. 1965), 238-245; Charles W. Anderson et al., *Issues of Political Development* (Englewood Cliffs, N.J., 1967), chapter 7; and John J. Finan's essay in Doris M. Condit et al., *Challenge and Response in Internal Conflict,* Vol. 3, *The Experience in Africa and Latin America* (Washington, D.C., 1968), tend to interpret consequences of *La Violencia.* For a related influence in foreign affairs, see Graeme S. Mount, "The Colombian Press and the Cold War, 1945-1968," *North-South Canadian Journal of Latin American Studies,* 8:16 (1983), 21-41.

For later periods and post-Violence politics, see Robert H. Dix, *The Developmental Significance of the Rise of Populism in Colombia* (Houston, 1975); John Bailey, "Pluralist and Corporatist Dimensions of Interest Representation in Colombia," and Robert Kaufman, "Corporatism, Clientelism, and Partisan Conflict," both in James Malloy, ed., *Authoritarianism and Corporatism in Latin America* (Pittsburgh, 1977); Albert Berry, Ronald Hellman, and Mauricio Solaún, *Politics of Compromise: Coalition Government in Colombia* (New Brunswick, N.J., 1980); and Javier A. Torres,

"Military Government: Political Crisis and Exceptional State: The Armed Forces of Colombia and the National Front, 1954-1974," State University of New York at Buffalo, 1985, provide interpretive overviews. See also Dix, *The Politics of Colombia*. Luis E. Agudelo Ramírez and Rafael Montoya y Montoya, *Los guerrilleros intelectuales: Cartas, documentos, e informaciones que prohibió la censura* (Medellín, 1957); and Gustavo Rojas Pinilla, *Rojas Pinilla ante el senado: El gobierno militar ante la historia* (Bogotá, 1959), offer conflicting views on the dictatorship, 1953-1957.

Jonathan Hartlyn, "Military Governments and the Transition to Civilian Rule: The Colombian Experience of 1957-1958," in Abraham Lowenthal and J. Samuel Fitch, eds., *Armies and Politics in Latin America* (rev. ed., New York, 1986), 415-436; Robert Dix, "Consociational Democracy: The Case of Colombia," *Comparative Politics*, 12:3 (Apr. 1980), 303-321; and Jonathan Hartlyn, *Consociational Politics in Colombia: Confrontation and Accommodation in Comparative Perspective* (New Haven, Conn., Yale, 1981), all emphasize transitional experiences. Kenneth F. Johnson, "Political Radicalism in Colombia: Electoral Dynamics of 1962 and 1964," *Journal of Inter-American Studies*, 7:1 (Jan. 1965), 15-26; and Thomas G. Sanders, *Colombian Politics in 1982* (Hanover, N.H., 1982), comment on specific elections. See also Bruce Bagley, "National Front and Economic Development," in Robert Wesson, *Politics, Policies and Economic Development in Latin America* (Stanford, Calif., 1984), 124-160; John Peeler, "Colombian Politics and Political Development," *Journal of Inter-American Studies and World Affairs*, 18:2 (May 1976), 203-204; and the works of Jonathan Hartlyn— "The Impact of Patterns of Industrialization and of Popular Regime Type: A Case Study of Colombia," *Studies in Comparative International Development*, 19:1 (Spring 1984), 29-60, and "Producer Associations, the Political Regime, and Policy Processes in Contemporary Colombia," *Latin American Research Review*, 20:3 (1985), 111-138. For the 1980s, see the articles by Gary Hoskin, "Colombia Under Stress"; Ricardo Santamaría and Gabriel Silva, "Colombia in the Eighties"; and Bernard Diederich, "Betancur's Battles," in *Caribbean Review*, 15:1 (Winter 1986), 6-15; and Bruce Bagley, "Colombian Politics: Crisis or Continuity," *Current History*, 86:516 (Jan. 1987), 21-24.

Walter J. Broderick, *Camilo Torres: A Biography of the Priest-guerrillero* (New York, 1975); and *Camilo Torres, His Life and Message* (John Alvarez García and Christián Restrepo Calle, eds.; Virginia M. O'Grady, trans.; Springfield, Ill., 1968), describe Colombia's rebel priest. Richard Maullin, *Soldiers, Guerrillas, and Politics in Colombia* (Lexington, Mass., 1973), is useful for the origins of various guerrilla movements. Olga Behar, *Las guerras de la paz* (Bogotá, 1985); and Arturo Alape, *La paz, la violencia: testigos de excepción* (Bogotá, 1985), are attempts at chronological records of *La Violencia* through personal accounts of those who have experienced it. Carlos Arango Z., *FARC, veinte años: de Marquetalia a La Uribe* (Bogotá, 1984), is an account of one of the oldest guerrilla movements in modern Colombia; and Patricia Lara, *Siembra vientos y recogerás tempestades* (Bogotá, 1982), is a collection of interviews with members of the Movimiento Diecinueve de Abril (M-19). Arturo Alape, *Un día de septiembre* (Bogotá, 1980); Richard L. Maullin, *The Fall of Dumar Aljure: A Colombian Guerrilla and Bandit* (Santa Monica, Calif.; 1969); and Evelio Buitrago Salazar, *Zarpazo the Bandit: Memoirs of an Undercover Agent for the Colombian Army* (University, Ala., 1977); Steve Estes, *Called to Die: The Story of American Linguist Chet Bitterman, Slain by Terrorists* (Grand Rapids, Mich., 1986); Virgilio Lovera, *Tiempo de guerrilleros: prisioneros en Bogotá* (Bogotá, 1981); Russell Stendal, *Rescue the Captors* (Burnsville, Minn., 1984); and Diego Asencio and Nancy Asencio, with Ron Tobias, *Our Man Is Inside* (Boston, 1983), all treat aspects of terrorism in Colombia.

Other aspects of post-Violence politics can be found in Andrew H. Whiteford, "Aristocracy, Oligarchy, and Cultural Change in Colombia," in Arthur J. Field, ed., *City and Country in the Third World: Issues in the Modernization of Latin America* (Cambridge, Mass., 1970); David W. Dent, "Oligarchy and Power Structure in Urban Colombia: The Case of Cali," *Journal of Latin American Studies* (Cambridge, U.K.), 6:1 (May 1974), 113-133; and A. Eugene Havens and William L. Flinn, *Internal Colonialism and Structural Change in Colombia* (New York, 1970).

In the realm of international politics, Gordon Ireland, *Boundaries, Possessions, and Conflicts in South America* (Cambridge, Mass., 1938); Antonio José Uribe, *Colombia y el Perú: Las cuestiones de límites y de libre navegación fluvial* (Bogotá, 1931); Arthur P. Whitaker, *The United States and South America: The Northern Republics* (Cambridge, Mass., 1948); and Robert N. Burr, "Colombia and International Cooperation," University of Pennsylvania, 1948, treat the problems of hemispheric diplomacy in broad overviews. For the 19th-century U.S.-Colombian relations, see John W. Kitchens, "Colombian-Chilean Relations, 1817-1845: A Diplomatic Struggle for Pacific Coast Hegemony," Vanderbilt University, 1969; and Rob Roy MacGregor, "The Treaty of 1846: Seventeen Years of American-Colombian Relations, 1830-1846," Clark University, 1928. For the first half of the 20th century, see Richard L. Lael, *Arrogant Diplomacy: U.S. Policy Toward Colombia,*

1903-1922 (Wilmington, Del., 1987); Stephen J. Randall, *The Diplomacy of Modernization: Colombian-American Relations, 1920-1940* (Toronto, 1977); and David A. Bushnell, *Eduardo Santos and the Good Neighbor, 1938-1942* (Gainesville, Fla., 1967). Diplomatic issues relating to the Isthmus of Panama are covered by J. B. Lockey, "A Neglected Aspect of Isthmian Diplomacy," *American Historical Review,* 41:2 (Jan. 1936), 295-305; Richard S. Patterson, "The New Granadan Draft of a Convention for the Settlement of the Panama Riot Claims," *HAHR,* 28:1 (Feb. 1947), 87-91; John H. Kemble, *The Panama Route, 1848-1869* (Berkley, Calif., 1943); Paul J. Scheips, "Gabriel Lafond and Ambrose W. Thompson: Neglected Isthmian Promoters," *HAHR,* 36:2 (May 1956), 211-228; Dwight C. Miner, *The Fight for the Panama Route: The Story of the Spooner Act and the Hay-Herrán Treaty* (New York, 1940); Thomas R. Favell, "The Antecedents of Panama's Separation from Colombia: A Study in Colombian Politics," Tufts University–Fletcher School of Law and Diplomacy, 1950; Eduardo Lemaitre Ramón, *Panamá y su separación de Colombia; Una historia que parece novela* (Bogotá, 1972); Ernesto J. Castillero R., *Historia de la comunicación interoceánica y de su influencia en la formación y en el desarrollo de la entidad nacional panameña* (Panamá, 1935); Mary C. Mullen, "Diplomatic Relations Between the United States and Colombia About the Panama Canal," Fordham University, 1935; and the works of Joseph L. Arbena, "The Panama Problem in Colombian History," University of Virginia, 1970; "The Image of an American Imperialist: Colombian Views of Theodore Roosevelt," *Studies in the Social Sciences (West Georgia College),* 6:1 (June 1967), 3-20; and "Colombian Interpretations of the Role of the United States in the Independence of Panama," *North Dakota Quarterly,* 41:2 (Spring 1973), 29-42.

Other aspects of Colombian foreign relations are dealt with by William S. Robertson, "An Early Threat of Intervention by Force in South America," *HAHR,* 23:4 (Nov. 1943), 611-631; John W. Kitchens, "General Mosquera's Mission to Chile and Peru: A Turning Point in New Granadan Diplomacy," *The Americas,* 29:2 (Oct. 1972), 151-172; Robert N. Burr, *The Stillborn Panama Congress: Power Politics and Chilean-Colombian Relations During the War of the Pacific* (Berkeley, Calif., 1962); L. F. Senasabaugh, "The Attitude of the United States Toward the Colombia–Costa Rica Arbitral Proceedings," *HAHR,* 19:1 (Feb. 1939), 16-30; Paolo E. Coletta, "William Jennings Bryan and the United States–Colombian Impasse, 1903-1921," *ibid.,* 47:4 (Nov. 1967), 486-501; Peter Calvert, "The Murray Contract: An Episode in International Finance and Diplomacy," *Pacific Historical Review,* 35:2 (May

1966), 203-224; Irving F. Gellman, "Prelude to Reciprocity: The Abortive United States–Colombian Treaty of 1933," *The Historian*, 32:1 (Nov. 1969), 52-68; and Suzanne M. C. Dailey, "United States Reactions to the Persecution of Protestants in Colombia During the 1950's," Saint Louis Universtiy, 1971. Bruce M. Bagley, Roberto Alvarez, and Katherine J. Hagedorn, eds., *Contadora and the Central American Peace Process* . . . (Boulder, Colo., 1985); and U.S. Congress, House of Representatives, Committee on Foreign Affairs, *Legislation Concerning Latin America: Colombia, the Contadora Process, and El Salvador* (Washington, D.C., 1984), help to clarify somewhat the Colombian role in recent Central American events. The Colombian Ministerio de Relaciones Exteriores issues periodic volumes on selected subjects in the series *Anales diplomáticos y consulares de Colombia* (Bogotá, Vol. 1-, 1900-). Pablo Ojer, *El golfo de Venezuela: una síntesis histórica* (Caracas, 1983); and Leandro Area and Elke Nieschulz de Stockhausen, eds., *El Golfo de Venezuela: documentación y cronología* (Caracas, 1984), attempt to provide background on a territorial issue. For other recent events see Gerhard Drekonja-Kornat, "Colombia: Learning the Foreign Policy Process," *Journal of Inter-American Studies and World Affairs*, 25:2 (May 1983), 229-250; Bruce Bagley and Juan Totkatlian, "Colombian Foreign Policy in the 1980s: The Search for Leverage," *ibid.*, 27:3 (Fall 1985), 27-62; and Malcolm Deas, "Colombian Peacemaking," *Third World Quarterly*, 8:2 (Apr. 1986), 639-657.

A number of works provide surveys of recent economic history. José Antonio Ocampo, *Colombia y la economía mundial, 1830-1910* (Mexico City, 1984), emphasizes Colombia's 19th-century exports in general. Robert C. Beyer, "The Colombian Coffee Industry: Origins and Major Trends, 1740-1940," University of Minnesota, 1947; Marco Palacios, *Coffee in Colombia, 1850-1970: An Economic, Social, and Political History* (Cambridge, U.K., 1980); Francie R. Chassen, *Café y capitalismo: el proceso de transición en Colombia, 1880-1930* (Toluca, Mex., 1982); and Mariano Arango, *El café en Colombia, 1930-1958: producción circulación y política* (Bogotá, 1982), all focus on the coffee industry. José María Rojas Garrido, *Empresarios y tecnología en la formación del sector azucuarero en Colombia, 1860-1980* (Bogotá, 1983); and Yezid Soler and Fabio Prieto, *Bonanza y crisis del oro blanco, 1960-1980* (Bogotá, 1982), cover sugar and cotton production. Germán Mejía et al., *El Banco de Bogotá: 114 años en la historia de Colombia* (Bogota, 1984), discusses the history of Colombia's oldest functioning bank. Rafael Gama Quijano, *El Banco de la República, o, la banca central de Colombia, 1923-1983* (Bogotá, 1983); and Fabio Gómez Arrubla, *Historia del Banco de la República: 60 años* (Bogotá, 1983), describe Colombia's central banking institution; and

Diego Castrillón Arboleda, *Historia del Banco de Estado y la moneda rodando como propiedad privada* (Bogotá, 1983), treats banking with an emphasis on Popayán. Malcolm Deas, "The Fiscal Problems of Nineteenth Century Colombia," *Journal of Latin American Studies,* 14:2 (May 1982), 287-328, is a theoretical overview, and Catherine Legrand, *Frontier Expansion and Peasant Protest in Colombia: 1850-1936* (Albuquerque, N.M., 1986), is a survey of specifically rural issues. Charles Bergquist, *Labor in Latin America . . .* (Stanford, Calif., 1986), compares developments in Argentina, Chile, Colombia, and Venezuela.

For the 19th century, other economic studies (arranged more or less chronologically by the time period covered) would include Eugene R. Huck, "Economic Experimentation in a Newly Independent Nation: Colombia Under Francisco de Paula Santander, 1821-1840," *The Americas,* 29:1 (July 1972), 17-29; Frank Safford, "Commerce and Enterprise in Central Colombia, 1821-1870," Columbia University, 1965; and Safford, "Foreign and National Enterprise in Nineteenth-Century Colombia," *Business History Review,* 39:4 (Winter 1965), 503-526; Robert Charles, *Underdevelopment and the Development of Corporations and Corporation Law in Nineteenth-Century Colombia* (Chapel Hill, N.C., 1980); Everett E. Hagen, *On the Theory of Social Change: How Economic Growth Begins* (London, 1964); and Hagen, "The Entrepreneur as Rebel Against Traditional Society," *Human Organization,* 19:4 (Winter 1960/1961), 185-187; John P. Harrison, "The Colombian Tobacco Industry from Government Monopoly to Free Trade, 1778-1876," University of California, Berkeley, 1952, and "The Evolution of the Colombian Tobacco Trade to 1875," *HAHR,* 32:2 (May 1952), 163-174; Luis F. Sierra, *El tabaco en la economía colombiana del siglo XIX* (Bogotá, 1971); Jane Alice Stuntz, "The Salt Monopoly in Colombia, 1845-1853," Vanderbilt University, 1955; Richard P. Hyland, "A Fragile Prosperity: Credit and Agrarian Structure in the Cauca Valley, Colombia, 1851-87," *HAHR,* 62:3 (Aug. 1982), 369-406; David A. Bushnell, "Two Stages in Colombian Tariff Policy: The Radical Era and the Return to Protection, 1861-1885," *Inter-American Economic Affairs,* 9:4 (Spring 1956), 3-23; and Malcolm Deas, "A Colombian Coffee Estate: Santa Bárbara, Cundinamarca, 1870-1912," in Kenneth Duncan and Ian Rutledge, eds., *Land and Labour in Latin America . . .* (Cambridge and New York, 1977), 269-298.

Twentieth-century economic topics are treated in Samuel Crowther, *The Romance and Rise of the American Tropics* (New York, 1976, reprint of 1929 work); Maurice P. Brungardt, "The United Fruit Company in Colombia," in Henry C. Dethloff and C. Joseph

Pusateri, *American Business History: Case Studies* (Arlington Heights, Ill., 1987), 235-256; J. Fred Rippy, "The Development of Public Utilities in Colombia," *HAHR*, 25:1 (Feb. 1945), 132-137; George H. Faust, "Economic Relations of the United States and Colombia, 1920-1940," University of Chicago, 1946; Alfonso Patiño Rosselli, *La prosperidad a debe y la gran crisis, 1925-1935* (Bogotá, 1981); David S. C. Chu, *The Great Depression and Industrialization in Colombia* (Santa Monica, Calif., 1977); José Eduardo Padrón, "Economic Development in Colombia Since World War II," University of Florida, 1970; Calvin P. Blair, "Fluctuations in the United States Imports from Brazil, Colombia, Chile, and Mexico, 1919-1954," University of Texas, 1957; Jorge García García, *The Effects of Exchange Rates and Commercial Policy on Agricultural Incentives in Colombia, 1953-1978* (Washington, D.C., 1981); Ernest A. Duff, "Agrarian Reform in Colombia, Problems of Social Reform," *Journal of Inter-American Studies*, (Jan. 1966), 75-88; Jan Peter Wogart, *Industrialization in Colombia: Policies, Patterns, Perspectives* (Tübingen, 1978); François J. Lombard, *The Foreign Investment Screening Process in LDCs: The Case of Colombia, 1967-1975* (Boulder, Colo., 1979); David R. Decker and Ignacio Duran, *The Political, Economic, and Labor Climate in Colombia* (Philadelphia, 1982); Miguel Urrutia, *Winners and Losers in Colombia's Economic Growth of the 1970s* (New York, 1985); and David Morawetz, *Why the Emperor's New Clothes Are Not Made in Colombia: A Case Study in Latin American and East Asian Manufactured Exports* (Washington, D.C., 1981). Luis J. Garay, *El Pacto Andino, creación de un mercado para Colombia?* (Bogotá, 1981); and Gabriel Poveda Ramos, *ANDI y la industria en Colombia, 1944-1984* (Medellín, 1984), are concerned with associations aimed at promoting industrial development in Colombia.

For the development of various kinds of transportation-communication facilities, see Theodore E. Nichols, "The Caribbean Gateway to Colombia: Cartagena, Santa Marta, and Barranquilla and Their Connections with the Interior, 1820-1840," University of California, Berkeley, 1951; Nichols, "The Rise of Barranquilla," *HAHR*, 34:2 (May 1954), 158-174; Robert L. Gilmore and John P. Harrison, "Juan Bernardo Elbers and the Introduction of Steam Navigation on the Magdalena River," *ibid.*, 28:3 (Aug. 1948), 335-359, deal with the early 19th century. J. Fred Rippy, "Dawn of the Railway Era in Colombia," *ibid.*, 23:4 (Nov. 1943), 650-663; Theodore H. Hoffman, "A History of Railway Concessions and Railway Development Policy in Colombia to 1943," American University, 1947; Hernán Horna, "Francisco Javier Cisneros: A Pioneer in Transportation and Economic Development in Colombia," Vanderbilt Universtiy, 1970; and Alfonso Orduz Duarte, *Pasado, presente y futuro de los Ferrocarriles Nacionales de Colombia* (Bogotá, 1980), cover aspects of railroad development in Colombia. For highways and overland transportation in general, see James H. Neal, "The Pacific Age Comes to Colombia: The Construction of the Cali-Buenaventura Route, 1856-1882," Vanderbilt University, 1971; Robert C. Beyer, "Transportation and the Coffee Industry in Colombia," *Inter-American Economic Affairs*, 2:3 (Winter 1948), 17-30; Donald S. Barnhart, "Colombian Transportation Problems and Policies, 1923-1948," University of Chicago, 1953; and Barnhart, "Colombian Transport and the Reforms of 1931: An Evaluation," *HAHR*, 38:1 (Feb. 1958), 1-24. On the history of aviation, see Guillermo Echavarría M., *De la mula al avión: Compañía Colombiana de Navegación Aérea* (Medellín, 1982); Herbert Boy, *Una historia con alas* (Madrid, 1955); José Ignacio Forero F., *Historia de la aviación en Colombia* (Bogotá, 1964); and James S. Randall, "Colombia, the United States, and Interamerican Aviation Rivalry, 1927-1940," *Journal of Inter-American Studies and World Affairs*, 14:3 (Aug. 1972), 197-324.

Alvaro Concha, *La concesión Barco: síntesis histórica de la explotación petrolífera del Catatumbo* (Bogotá, 1981); Jorge Villegas, *Petróleo, oligarquía e imperio*, previously mentioned; and Gustavo Almario Salazar, *Historia de los trabajadores petroleros* (Bogotá, 1984), are samples of works appearing on the history of oil production in Colombia.

For Church history in the 19th century, see Carey Shaw, "Church and State in Colombia as Observed by American Diplomats, 1834-1906," *HAHR*, 21:4 (Nov. 1941), 577-613; Robert J. Knowlton, "Expropriation of Church Property in Nineteenth-Century Mexico and Colombia: A Comparison," *The Americas*, 25:4 (Apr. 1969), 387-401; and José Restrepo Posada, *La iglesia en dos momentos difíciles de la historia patria* (Bogotá, 1971). Overviews of 20th-century developments are given in Daniel H. Levine, *Religion and Politics in Latin America: The Catholic Church in Venezuela and Colombia* (Princeton, N.J., 1981); and Kenneth Medhurst, *The Church and Labour in Colombia* (Manchester, U.K., and Dover, N.H., 1984). For pre-Violence social protest, see Gonzalo Castillo-Cárdenas, *Liberation Theology from Below: The Life and Thought of Manuel Quintín Lame* (Maryknoll, N.Y., 1987). For contemporary social problems, see also *Social Activist Priest: Colombia, Argentina*, LADOC Keyhole Series (Washington, D.C., 1970-1976), as well as the biographies of Camilo Torres Restrepo cited above. The missionary memoir or biography provides a partisan but often informative view of some aspects of recent church history. See, for example, Víctor Landero, Bob Owen, and David M. Howard, *The Victor: The Víctor Landero Story* (Old Tappan, N.J., 1979); Wilma Ross Westphal, *Heretics at Large* (Washington, D.C., 1976); David M. Howard, *The Costly Harvest: Hammered as Gold* (Wheaton, Ill., 1975); and Lewis Morely, *Now It Can Be Told: An Unforgettable Story of Pentecostalism in Colombia* (Hazelwood, Mo., 1983); in addition to Estes, *Born to Die;* Turnage's *Island Heritage;* and the work of Cornelia B. Flora, previously cited.

Gonzalo Bermúdez Rossi, *El poder militar en Colombia: de la colonia al frente nacional* (Bogotá, 1982); Gustavo Gallón Giraldo, *La república de las armas: relaciones entre fuerzas armadas y estado en Colombia, 1960-1980* (Bogotá, 1983); and Daniel L. Premio, "The Colombian Armed Forces in Search of a Mission," in Robert Wesson, *New Military Politics in Latin America* (New York, 1982), 151-153, discuss the overall question of the role of the military in government. More selective, but nonetheless related, comments on various aspects of military history are found in J. Mark Ruhl, *Colombia: Armed Forces and Society* (Syracuse, N.Y., 1980); Anthony P. Maingot, "Colombia: Civil-Military Relations in a Political Culture of Conflict," University of Florida, 1967; J. León Helguera, "The Changing Role of the Military in Colombia," *Journal of Inter-American Studies*, 3:3 (July 1961), 351-358; Russell W. Ramsey, "Colombian Battalion in Korea and Suez," *ibid.*, 9:4 (Oct. 1967), 541-560; and Jorge A. Sánchez Ramírez, "The Colombian Marine Corps," *Marine Corps Gazette*, 50:1 (Nov. 1966), 33-36.

The development of the Colombian educational system is studied in W. E. Browning, "Joseph Lancaster, James Thomson, and the Lancasterian System of Mutual Instruction, with Special Reference to Hispanic America," *HAHR*, 4:1 (Feb. 1921), 49-98; Robert H. Davis, "Education in New Granada: Lorenzo María Lleras and the Colegio del Espíritu Santo, 1846-1853," *The Americas*, 33:3 (Jan. 1977), 490-503; Jane M. Loy, "Primary Education During the Colombian Federation: The School Reform of 1870," *HAHR*, 51:2 (May 1971), 275-294; and Horacio Rodríguez Plata, "Orígenes de la Universidad Nacional de Colombia," *Boletín de Historia y Antigüedades* (Bogotá), 53:624/625 (Oct.-Nov. 1966), 609-622, cover the middle of the 19th century. For the latter part of the century, see the Safford-Bergquist interchange: Frank Safford, "In Search of the Practical: Colombian Students in Foreign Lands, 1845-1890," *HAHR*, 52:2 (May 1972), 230-249, and *The Ideal of the Practical: Colombia's Struggle to Form a Technical Elite* (Austin, Tex., 1975); Charles Bergquist, "On Paradigms and the Pursuit of the Practical," and Frank Safford, "Reply," *Latin American Research Review*, 13:2 (1978), 247-260.

Eduardo Posada and Carlos Restrepo Canal, *La esclavitud en Colombia; Leyes de manumisión* (Bogotá, 1933); Carlos Restrepo Canal, *La libertad de los esclavos en Colombia esclavitud en Popayán, 1832-1852* (Cali, 1980), narrate the events surrounding the abolition of slavery in New Granada. Gabriel Murillo Castaño, *Migrant Workers in the Americas* . . . (La Jolla, Calif., 1984), treats migrant laborers in Colombia, Mexico, the United States, and Venezuela. Steffen Schmidt, "Women in Colombia," in Lynne Iglitzin and Ruth Ross, eds., *Women in the World, 1975-1985: The Women's Decade* (2nd ed., rev., Santa Barbara, Calif., 1986), 273-324, summarizes the recent developments in women's rights.

Medófilo Medina, *La protesta urbana en Colombia en el siglo XX* (Bogotá, 1984); and Jaime Carrillo Bedoya, *Los paros cívicos en Colombia* (Bogotá, 1981), deal with mass movements in Colombia; and Edgar Vásquez Benítez, *Historia del desarrollo urbano en Cali* (Cali, 1982), focuses on urbanization in Cali.

Because of the importance of the Magdalena River and the capital city, Bogotá, in Colombian history, the reader may also find useful such works as Aníbal Noguera Mendoza, *Crónica grande del Río de la Magdalena* (Bogotá, 1980); Antonio Ybot León, *La arteria histórica del Nuevo Reino de Granada, Cartagena–Santa Fé, 1538-1798* . . . (Bogotá, 1952); Enrique Pérez Arbeláez, *Hiléa magdalenesa; Prospección económica del valle tropical del Río Magdalena* (Bogotá, 1949); María Angeles Eugenia Martínez, "El puerto y camino de Carare en Nueva Granada," *Anuario de Estudios Americanos* (Sevilla), 30 (1973), 263-294; Janet Townsend, "Magdalena, River of Colombia," *Scottish Geographical Magazine,* 97:1 (1981), 37-49; Pedro María Ibañez, *Crónicas de Bogotá* (4 vols.; Bogotá, 1913-1923); Daniel Ortega Ricaurte, *Cosas de Santafé de Bogotá* (Bogotá, 1959); Moisés de la Rosa, *Calles de Santafé de Bogotá* (Bogotá, 1938); and Camilo Pardo Umaña, *Haciendas de la Sabana; Su historia, sus leyendas y tradiciones* (Bogotá, 1948). Andrés Mesanza, *Nuestra Señora de Chiquinquirá y monografía histórica de esta villa* (Bogotá, 1913), is a history of the nation's principal religious shrine.

Material on the recent development of the narcotics traffic is somewhat sparse and uneven. Paul Eddy, Hugo Sabogal, and Sara Walden, *The Cocaine Wars* (New York, 1988), attempts to document the Florida-Caribbean-Colombian connections. Rensselaer W. Lee, *The White Labyrinth: Cocaine and Political Power* (New Brunswick, N.J., and London, 1989), is a useful overview of the drug trade in Colombia, Peru, and Bolivia; as is Scott B. MacDonald, *Dancing on a Volcano: The Latin American Drug Trade* (New York, 1988), although the latter is somewhat less reliable. Charles Nicholl, *The Fruit Palace* (New York, 1985), gives a detailed personal account of experiences with the scene in Colombia. Other available publications include Bruce Bagley, "The Colombian Connection: The Impact of Drug Traffic in Colombia," in Deborah Pacini and Christine Franquemont, eds., *Coca and Cocaine: Effects on People and Policy in Latin America* (Cambridge, Mass., 1986); Richard B. Craig, "Domestic Implications of Illicit Colombian Drug Production and Trafficking," *Journal of Inter-American Studies and World Affairs,* 25:3 (Aug. 1983), 325-350; U.S. Congress, House of Representatives, Select Committee on Narcotics Abuse and Control, Ninety-sixth Congress, First Session, *Factfinding Mission to Colombia and Puerto Rico . . .* (Washington, D.C., 1979); and U.S. Congress, House of Representatives, Committee on Foreign Affairs, *Recent Developments in Colombian Narcotics Control . . .* (Washington, D.C., 1984); and the Cuban American National Foundation, *Castro and the Narcotics Connection: Special Report* (Washington, D.C., 1983). In Spanish, see *Libro necio sobre Colombia* (Caracas, 1985); and Alvaro Camacho Guizado, *Droga, corrupción y poder: marihuana y cocaina en la sociedad colombiana* (Cali, 1981).

The literature on contemporary economic development and current social change is too profuse to list in any definitive way. For general overviews, however, see James A. Hanson, "Growth and Distribution in Colombia: Some Recent Analysis," *Latin American Research Review,* 22:1 (1987), 255-264; Carlos Díaz-Alejandro, *Colombia* (New York, 1976); Antonio García, *A dónde va Colombia?: de la república señorial a la crisis del capitalismo dependiente* (Bogotá, 1981); John Sheahan, *Aspects of Planning and Development in Colombia* (Austin, Tex., 1977); International Bank for Reconstruction and Development, *Colombia: Economic Development and Policy Under Changing Conditions* (Washington, D.C., 1984); Michael Hopkins, *Alternatives to Unemployment and Underemployment: The Case of Colombia* (Boulder, Colo., 1985); and A. Kruiderink, *Colombia: Current Development Strategies and Current Government Practices—A Review of Inconsistencies* (Utrecht, 1983). For more specialized phases of planning and development, see Bruce Bagley, "Political Power, Public Policy and the State in Colombia," University of Southern California, 1979; Robin Ruth Marsh, *Development Strategies in Rural Colombia: The Case of Caquetá* (Los Angeles, 1983); Alberto Carrizosa et al., *Communications Policies in Colombia* (Paris, 1977); Richard E. Hartwig, *Roads to Reason: Transportation, Administration, and Rationality in Colombia* (Pittsburgh, 1983); Harvey F. Kline, *Energy Policy and the Colombian Elite: A Synthesis and Interpretation* (Washington, D.C., 1982); Thomas G. Sanders, *Food Policy Decision-Making in Colombia* (Hanover, N.H., 1980); R. Albert Berry and Ronald Soligo, eds., *Economic Policy and Income Distribu-*

tion in Colombia (Boulder, Colo., 1980); and Edgar Reveiz and María José Pérez, "Colombia: Moderate Economic Growth, Political Stability, and Social Welfare," in *Latin American Political Economy* (Boulder, Colo., and London, 1986), 265-291. A sampling of other studies of current social conditions might include Camilo Alfonso Sabogal Otálora, *Historia del control de precios en Colombia* (Bogotá, 1980); James E. Boyce and François J. Lombard, *Colombia's Treatment of Foreign Banks: A Precedent Setting Case?* (Washington, D.C., 1976); R. Albert Berry and Miguel Urrutia, *Income Distribution in Colombia* (New Haven, Conn., 1976); Charles H. Savage and George F. Lombard, *Sons of the Machine: Case Studies of Social Change In the Working Place* (Cambridge, Mass., 1986); Carmen Diana Deere and Magdalena León de Leal, *Women in Andean Agriculture: Peasant Production and Rural Wage Employment in Colombia and Peru* (Geneva, 1982); Gloria Carvallo and Fernando Ramírez, *The Improvement of the Situation of Women and Its Impact on the Welfare of Children . . . Cartagena . . .* (New York, 1980); John P. Walter and William H. Leahy, *Deprived Urban Youth: An Economic Cross-Cultural Analysis of the United States, Colombia, and Peru* (New York, 1975); Howard Handelman, *High Rises and Shanty Towns: Housing the Poor in Bogotá and Caracas* (Hanover, N.H., 1979); and Michael B. Whiteford, *The Forgotten Ones: Colombian Countrymen in an Urban Setting* (Gainesville, Fla., 1976).

Finally, for visual materials to supplement the textual histories of New Granada and Colombia, the student should consult Daniel Ortega Ricaurte, *Album del Sesquicentenario* [1810] (Bogotá, 1960); Eduardo [Edward Walhouse] Mark, *Acuarelas de Mark; Un testimonio pictórico de la Nueva Granada* [1843-1856] (ed. Eduardo Arias Robledo and Joaquín Piñeros Corpas; Bogotá, 1963); Julio Londoño, ed., *Album de la Comisión Corográfica* [1850-1858] (Bogotá, 1953); Ramón Torres Méndez, *Cuadros de costumbres* [1851] (Bogotá, ca. 1965); *Papel Periódico Ilustrado 1881-1887 . . .* (Bogotá, 1968); *Bogotá, IV Centenario, 1538-1938* (Bogotá, 1938); Benjamín de la Calle, *El comercio en Medellín, 1900-1930* (Medellín, 1982); and Edward Popko, *Transitions: A Photographic Documentary of Squatter Settlements* (Stroudsburg, Pa., 1978).

VII. BIBLIOGRAPHIES AND GUIDES TO FURTHER STUDY

Bibliographical aids to the study of Colombian history vary widely in form and content. Among the most useful, one-volume, all-purpose guides to Colombian subjects are Robert H. Davis, *Colombia* (Oxford, U.K., 1990); and Gayle Hudgens Watson, *Colombia, Ecuador and Venezuela: An Annotated Guide to Reference Materials in the Humanities and Social Sciences* (Metuchen, N.J., 1971). Arthur Gropp, *A Bibliography of Latin American Bibliographies* (Metuchen, N.J., 1968), and Supplements published in 1971, 1979, 1982, and 1993 offer a much broader context; while Gabriel Giraldo Jaramillo, *Bibliografías de bibliografías colombianas* (rev. Rubén Pérez Ortiz; Bogotá, 1960), has a specifically Colombian orientation. Undoubtedly the most consistently published, up-to-date guide to both bibliographical and monographic materials is the *Handbook of Latin American Studies,* published annually since 1935. Jorge Eliécer Ruiz and Valentina Marulanda, *Cultural Policy in Colombia* (Paris, 1977), is a description of government practices regarding cultural materials in general.

For a general introduction to Colombian topics, see Charles C. Griffin and J. Benedict Warren, eds., *Latin America: A Guide to the Historical Literature* (Austin, Tex., 1971); and for diplomatic history, David F. Trask, Michael C. Meyer, and Roger Trask, eds., *A Bibliography of United States–Latin American Relations Since 1810: A Selected List of Eleven Thousand Published References* (Lincoln, Neb., 1968). Kent E. Miller and Gilberto V. Fort, *Major Latin American Collections in Libraries of the United States* (Washington, D.C., 1970); Steven M. Charno, comp., *Latin American Newspapers in United States Libraries: A Union List . . .* (Austin, Tex., 1969); and Rosa Quintero Mesa, *Colombia: Latin American Serial Documents,* Vol. I (Ann Arbor, Mich., 1968), all may be helpful in locating specific materials.

Publicaciones periódicas en Colombia, 1965 (Bogotá, 1967), by the Departamento Administrativo Nacional de Estadística, División de Información, Publicaciones y Biblioteca, is a guide to departmental and municipal publications. Sara de Mundo Lo and Beverly Phillips, *Colombian Serial Publications in the University of Illinois Library at Urbana-Champaign* (Austin, Tex., 1978), lists works in a specific collection. For law and legal literature, see Alberto Villalón-Galdames, *Bibliografía Jurídica: Latin American Legal Bibliography, 1810-1965,* Volume II: *Brazil, Colombia, Costa Rica, Cuba* (Boston, 1984). James B. Childs, *Colombian Government Publications* (Washington, D.C., 1941); and Richard C. Backus and Phanor J. Eder, *A Guide to the Law and Legal Literature of Colombia* (Washington, D.C., 1943), should be consulted for older references.

For specialized areas, see Sturgis E. Leavitt and Carlos García Prada, *A Tentative Bibliography of Colombian Literature* (Cambridge, Mass., 1934); Gabriel Giraldo Jaramillo, "Contribución a la bibliografía filosófica de Colombia," *Anuario Colombiano de Historia*

Social y de la Cultura (Bogotá), l:l (1963), 107-129; Manuel Lucena Salmoral, "Mil doscientos títulos de antropología colombiana," *Boletín Cultural y Bibliográfico*, (Bogotá) 12:9 (Sept. 1969), 16-61; Segundo Bernal Villa, *Guía bibliográfica de Colombia de interés para el antropólogo* (Bogotá, 1969); Jesús E. Ramírez, *Bibliografía de la biblioteca del Instituto Geofísico de los Andes Colombianos sobre geología y geofísica de Colombia* (Bogotá, 1957); Gabriel Giraldo Jaramillo, *Bibliografía colombiana de viajes* (Bogotá, 1957); Giraldo Jaramillo, *Bibliografía selecta del arte en Colombia* (Bogotá, 1955); Vicenta Cortés Alonso, *Catálogo de mapas de Colombia* (Madrid, 1967); and Richard Hartwig, *Transportation Policy and Administrative Responsibility in Colombian Government: A Selected Bibliography* (Monticello, Ill., 1980). Therrin C. Dahlin, Gary P. Gillum, and Mark L. Grover, *The Catholic Left in Latin America: A Comprehensive Bibliography* (Boston, Mass., 1981), lists 243 references on current Church and theological issues.

For biographical references, see Sara de Mundo Lo, comp., *Index to Spanish American Collective Biography*, Volume 3: *The Andean Countries* (Boston, Mass., 1981). Margaret E. Fau, *Gabriel García Márquez: An Annotated Bibliography, 1947-1979* (Westport, Conn., and London, 1980), and its supplement, *Bibliographic Guide to Gabriel García Márquez, 1979-1985*, by Fau and Nelly Sfeir de González (Westport, Conn., 1986), are indispensable for studying the work of Colombia's Nobel prize winner. Mary Alvarez Restrepo, *Bibliografía de autores antioqueños* (Antioquia, 1966); Rafael Romero Castañeda, *Autores magdalenses* (Bogotá, 1968); Gerardo Reichel-Dolmatoff, "Bibliografía de la Sierra Nevada de Santa Marta," *Revista de la Academia Colombiana de Ciencias Exactas, Físicas y Naturales* (Bogotá), II:44 (Dec. 1962), 367-374; Reichel-Dolmatoff, "Bibliografía de la Guajira," *ibid.*, 12:45 (Nov. 1963), 47-56; Luis Eduardo Acosta Hoyos, *Bibliografía anotada del Departamento de Nariño* (Pasto, 1966); and María Teresa Cobos, "Guía bibliográfica para los llanos orientales de Colombia," *Boletín Cultural y Bibliográfico* (Bogotá), 8:12 (1965), 1888-1935, have regional emphases in their listings. Lino G. Canedo, "Fuentes para la historia del Nuevo Reino de Granada," *Museo Histórico* (Quito), II:33 (Apr. 1959), 170-195; Germán Colmenares et al., *Fuentes coloniales para la historia del trabajo en Colombia* (Bogotá, 1968); and Pedro Grases and Manuel Pérez Vila, "Gran Colombia: Referencias relativas a la bibliografía sobre el período emancipador en los países grancolombianos, desde 1949," *Historiografía y Bibliografía Americanista* (Sevilla), 10 (1964), 151-159, speak to more specific historical subjects, as does Ocampo López's bibliography of the independence period.

Archival guides to Colombian collections are few and incomplete. Roscoe R. Hill, *The National Archives of Latin America* . . . (Cambridge, Mass., 1945), is a brief introduction to major depositories in the Latin nations. John P. Harrison, *Guide to Materials on Latin America in the National Archives* (Washington, D.C., 1961-), discusses materials available in the United States. For the Colombian National Archives, see Francisco J. Vergara y Velasco, *Archivos nacionales: Indice analítico, metódico y descriptivo* (Bogotá, 1913); and Archivo Nacional, *Indice del Archivo Colonial* (4 vols.; Bogotá, 1935-1946); Vicenta Cortés Alonso, "La sección de la colonia del Archivo Nacional de Colombia," *Studium* (Bogotá), 2:6 (Oct.-Dec. 1958), 183-218; and Cortés Alonso, "La colección de mapas y planos del Archivo Nacional de Colombia," *Revista de Archivos, Bibliotecas y Museos* (Madrid), 67:1 (Jan.-June 1959), 21-34. Alberto Lee López, ed., "Indices de la sección de archivos y microfilmes de la Academia Colombiana de Historia," *Archivos* (Bogotá), 1:1 (Jan.-June 1967); and the Archivo Central del Cauca (Popayán), *Catálogo general detallado* . . . (Popayán, 1969-[title page has 1944-in error]), are works in progress on the collections of the Colombian Academy of History and the Central Archive of the Cauca, respectively. Vicenta Cortés Alonso, "El Archivo de San Agustín de Santa Fé de Bogotá," *Revista de Archivos, Bibliotecas y Museos* (Madrid), 69:1 (Jan.-June 1961), 19-40, is a guide to an extensive institutional archive. For the student of the 19th century, the Biblioteca Nacional de Colombia (Bogotá), *Catálogo del "Fondo Anselmo Pineda"* . . . (2 vols.; Bogotá, 1935); and *Catálogo de Materias del fondo Vergara de la Biblioteca Nacional de Colombia* (Amherst, Mass., 1975), are very helpful for periodicals, pamphlets, and handbills in the collection of the national library.

Works relating to Colombian history are frequently to be found in more generalized bibliographies, such as Robert A. Humphreys, *Latin American History: A Guide to the Literature in English* (London, 1958); John A. Sinclair, *Protestantism in Latin America: A Bibliographical Guide* (Austin, Tex., 1967); S. A. Bayitch, *Latin America and the Caribbean: A Bibliographical Guide to Works in English* (Coral Gables, Fla., 1967); Martin H. Sable, *Latin American Urbanization: A Guide to the Literature, Organizations, and Personnel* (Metuchen, N.J., 1971); and A. Curtis Wilgus, *The Historiography of Latin America: A Guide to Historical Writing, 1500-1800* (Metuchen, N.J., 1975), which includes the lives and works of writers who published accounts about the areas included in New Granada. Of course, one should never overlook the bibliographical references to be found in many of the individual works cited elsewhere in this guide.

ABOUT THE AUTHOR

ROBERT H. DAVIS, Professor of History, has studied and taught a variety of subjects dealing with world affairs since joining the Luther College History Department in 1966. He holds academic degrees (B.A., Illinois College; M.A. and Ph.D., Vanderbilt University) in history and Latin American studies. He has been director of both Luther College's International Studies Program and its academic center in Nottingham, England. He has traveled and lived in several Latin American countries including Colombia, where he was elected a foreign corresponding member of the Academia Colombiana de Historia in Bogotá. Over the years Dr. Davis has been a member of the American Historical Society and the Conference on Latin American History. He is a past president of the North Central Council of Latin Americanists. Previous publications include *Colombia* (1990), which describes more than 600 works on various aspects of Colombian society.